Illustrated
HISTORY of EUROPE

© Hachette, 1992
79, boulevard Saint Germain
75006 Paris
France

First published in France in 1992
by Hachette under the title *Histoire de l'Europe*

Editor: Hachette Classiques, Barthélemy de Lesseps
Design concept: Patrick Fébié, Horizon Graphique
Layout and captions: Annie Herschlikowitz
Maps: Hachette Classiques, Noël Meunier, Latitude

English translation © Richard Mayne 1993

First published in Great Britain in 1993 by
George Weidenfeld and Nicolson Ltd
Orion House
5 Upper St Martin's Lane
London WC2H 9EA

A catalogue record for this book is available from
the British Library

English-language edition typography by Tim Higgins
House editor: Lucas Dietrich
Phototypeset by Deltatype Ltd, Ellesmere Port, Cheshire
Printed and bound in Italy

ILLUSTRATED HISTORY OF
EUROPE

A UNIQUE PORTRAIT OF EUROPE'S COMMON HISTORY

FRÉDÉRIC DELOUCHE GENERAL EDITOR

JACQUES ALDEBERT
Honorary Professor of Upper Grades at Louis-le-Grand
Secondary School, Paris, France

JOHAN BENDER
History Teacher at the Aarhus Secondary School, Aarhus, Denmark

JIRI GRUSA
Historian, Ambassador of the Czech Republic to Germany

SCIPIONE GUARRACCINO
Secondary School Teacher in Italy

IGNACE MASSON
Secondary School Teacher in Bruges, Belgium

DR KENNETH MILNE
Honorary Director, Church of Ireland College of Education,
Dublin, Ireland

FOULA PISPIRINGOU
Doctor of History and Secondary School Teacher in Athens, Greece

DR JUAN ANTONIO SANCHEZ Y GARCIA SAÙCO
University Professor, Spain

ANTONIO SIMOES RODRIGUES
Professor of History Teaching, Coïmbra University, Portugal

BEN W. M. SMULDERS
Professor of Education, Tilburg University, The Netherlands

DIETER TIEMANN
Professor, Dortmund University, Germany

DR ROBERT UNWIN
Lecturer in Education, Leeds University, United Kingdom

Translated from the French by Richard Mayne

WEIDENFELD AND NICOLSON London

Contents

PREFACE

by Frédéric Delouche

What does Europe mean today – and tomorrow? Paradoxically, only history can provide answers. Hence this history of Europe, not written by one author but by twelve Europeans of different nationalities. They believe, as I do, that in addition to focusing on national history – which is indispensable – we need a broader view of Europe's historical adventure. By good fortune, I have British, French and Norwegian nationality. It is therefore understandable perhaps that I came to initiate the present work. Not belonging wholly to any one nation often made me seem suspect in the eyes of my British and French schoolfellows. Which side should I have backed in the Hundred Years' War, the War of Spanish Succession or the Napoleonic Wars?

Fortunately, that atmosphere has changed. But there are still sporadic outbursts of nationalism, sometimes used for anti-democratic ends, or fear of foreign meddling, or even domination, aroused by the very idea of limiting national sovereignty. As Europe gropes towards the future, something intangible seems to be holding Europeans back from mutual rapprochement. In varying degrees, they are hindered by economic interests, by language, by cultural traditions and often by irrational prejudice. Such prejudice is deep-rooted, sometimes barely consciously, and very tenacious; it tends to be passed on from generation to generation not only within families, but also by the history we read.

The history we learned at school usually began with national history, the heart and heritage of the nation. But national ideology is only a few centuries old. And seen against the broader span of time, the nation-state looks artificial and precarious. Education has often been exploited to establish (and sometimes pervert) nationalist emotion. Could it not help us now to raise our eyes across national frontiers and see Europe – and the world – as a whole? It is a delicate discipline, but utterly absorbing. It helps us to understand where we came from, what tensions we have inherited from the past and why they still haunt parts of Europe today. It helps us to recognize what Europeans have in common, but also that the past cannot be dismissed. Most Europeans of today's nation-states are not fully and freely prepared for the European union to which their governments are more or less committed. Many ask why Europe needs to become more than a vast free trade area. Is there, or indeed should there be, more to Europe than trade?

Not everyone sees that this question is vital. We hope that this book may encourage parents, teachers, pupils, educationalists and even politicians to consider taking a wider view than that obtained from a primarily national standpoint.

It has taken four years' unceasing effort to bring this book to birth. Its twelve parts, each written by an author of a different nationality, reflect different approaches and styles – a diversity that negates artificial uniformity. To cover the history of Europe, from the mists of antiquity to the present day into 380 pages has not been easy; it has involved hard decisions about which subjects to tackle; and reaching agreement on those decisions was the most rewarding aspect of our joint work. Published in more than sixteen languages, this book will be read in all the countries of Europe, and beyond.

It is a book for the family and the general reader, but we hope that it will be a practical and stimulating adjunct to the education of a coming generation that will be ever more concerned with Europe. It is not a work of propaganda in praise of Europe or the 'European idea'. Its only aim is to understand and explain. Democracies must educate their citizens and their citizens must educate themselves. As a nineteenth-century author wrote, 'God, although He is omnipotent, cannot change the past. So He created historians'. We should all of us, however modestly, become historians if we are to understand our turbulent past so as to work for a peaceful future without wars and suffering.

It is a great pleasure to see an idea become reality, and I owe a profound debt of gratitude to all those who have brought it about. We should never have been able to begin without the enthusiasm and team spirit of our twelve authors, and without the commitment of Marc Moingeon, Christian Travers, Jacques Montaville, Françoise Laurent, Corinne Jouanin, and all the staff of Hachette Education in Paris. We launched something new but once launched the ship had to be fitted and sailed, so I wish to thank all those publishers in Europe, the United States and East Asia who have been joined in the venture. In particular I wish to thank Anthony Cheetham and Emma Way at Weidenfeld & Nicolson, who have risen to the challenge of publishing an English edition and Richard Mayne who, as a European and a historian, has translated the text and the spirit of this work into English. I thank the Directorate of Books at the Ministry of Culture in Paris for their important contribution to the considerable cost of translating the book into the many European languages. I wish to thank the Haniel Stiftung of Duisburg, Germany, for their great support in promoting, and contributing to, publication in Eastern Europe, as well as contributing to translation costs.

Finally, and above all, I thank my wife, Diana, for her unflinching support through thick and thin.

① EUROPE IN HARMONY

The Effects of Good Government. Part of a fresco by Ambrogio Lorenzetti in the Town Hall (Palazzo Pubblico), Siena, Italy

This fresco was painted from 1337 to 1339. The prosperity of the city can be seen within its walls, in the square where work and trade are being carried out. It is also evident in the country, where people's dwellings are surrounded by well-kept vineyards and well-tilled fields. The balance between them slightly favours the town, but not overmuch: while the walls symbolize urban dignity, they seem to offer no great barrier to townspeople, country-dwellers, or strangers. The winged figure above them is a symbol of Security, 'Securitas'.

This landscape is in many ways similar to that of Tuscany today; its like can be found in many parts of Europe. Its sense of balance, its adroit use of space, can be said to have characterized Europe for centuries: in the countryside, mastering nature without desecrating it; in the cities, creating an environment for people with harmonious buildings, squares and fountains. Today this harmony is threatened by the growth of giant cities and sprawling suburbs, often inhuman, which face major problems in feeding themselves and disposing of their waste. This is the challenge for contemporary Europe. But Europe has responded to challenges before.

② EUROPE'S GEOGRAPHY

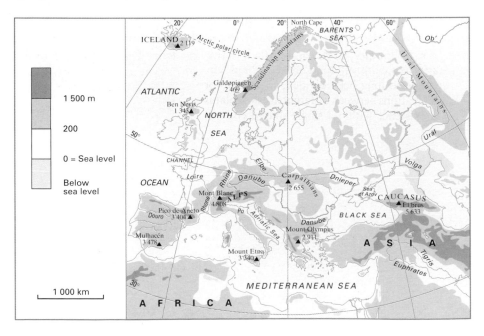

THE IDENTITY OF EUROPE

In Greek mythology, Europa was the daughter of the King of Tyre, now in Lebanon. She was snatched from the shores of Phoenicia and carried away to Crete by Zeus in the guise of a bull. He gave her a son who became King Minos. Can this story be a mythical account of the way that culture and literacy, already highly developed in the Middle East, were brought to the less polished world of Greece?

The name 'Europe' first appears in a text by Hesiod, the 8th-century BC Greek poet. There is no scientific explanation of why the continent bears this name. Even Herodotus, the Greek historian of the 5th century BC, known as the father of history-writing, could not explain it. The reason is probably accidental, just as the American continent derived its name from Amerigo Vespucci.

Ignorance of its derivation has never prevented anyone using the word 'Europe'; but it has meant different things at different times. Hence the need to analyze its meanings and try to define Europe's nature and extent.

Geographically, Europe is marked by natural frontiers, gradually modified as they have been more fully explored. Fragmented as it is in a mosaic of contrasting regions, it has seen the birth and development, over the centuries, of different languages and cultures. But if these explain why Europe has so long been divided, the scope for communications between different areas explains their coexistence within a single shared civilization.

Politically, too, Europe has evolved over time, veering between relative unity and relative fragmentation as ideas and attitudes have changed. But since when – if at all – has the notion of 'a European' existed? It must be relatively recent: the growth of cross-frontier transport, ever more frequent and rapid, has made it ever easier for people to meet and merchandise to be traded. So, in varying degrees among different groups, habits and ways of life have tended to converge. This has both encouraged and been intensified by recent efforts to unite Europe.

3 THE MYTH OF EUROPA
Fresco from Pompei in the National Archaeological Museum, Naples
The beauty of Europa captivated Zeus. To win her, he changed himself into a bull and carried her off to Crete. There he made her his queen and the mother of the Minoan kings. For historians, this poetic legend may represent the westward movement, from the Semitic Near East to the 'nameless' continent, of colonizing peoples who brought with them some elements of the civilization of Western Asia.

1 Europe's Geography

❶ EUROPE, A PROMONTORY OF ASIA

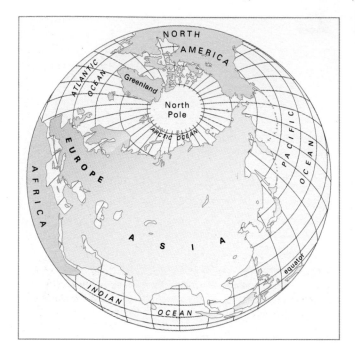

❷ EUROPE'S LANDS

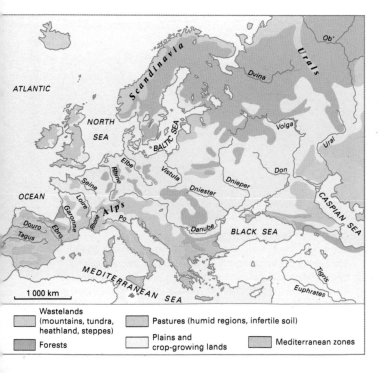

1 000 km

Wastelands
(mountains, tundra,
heathland, steppes)

Forests

Pastures (humid regions, infertile soil)

Plains and
crop-growing lands

Mediterranean zones

A *peninsula of Eurasia*

Seen from Asia, Europe looks like a western peninsula of that old continent, or more precisely of Eurasia. Traditionally, it extends from the Atlantic in the west to the Urals in the east. Its northern extremity is the North Cape: its southernmost outpost is Crete. Until the 17th century, Russia was not regarded as part of Europe. It was Peter the Great who established an outlet on the Baltic at the expense of Sweden and made his capital St Petersburg on the tip of the Gulf of Finland, thereby anchoring Russia to Europe at the same time as he expanded eastwards beyond the Urals. In fact, the inclusion of Russia in Europe was a matter of politics as much as geography. Beyond the Urals, indeed, Europe virtually melts into the immensity of the steppes and the Siberian forests that stretch for thousands of miles as far as Mongolia, China and the Pacific Ocean.

Not only Europe's eastern frontiers are ill-defined. Others, which look definite, are less so than the accidents of geography make them seem. The Straits of Gibraltar, for example, like the Bosphorus, lie between land-masses which are very similar on either side.

Great diversity in a small space

More than any other continent, Europe's regions are on a small scale. It has an infinite variety of different landscapes, with none of the monotony of the great American plains or the African, Asian or Australian deserts. With the exception of the far North and the Russian steppes, it also has the great advantage of lying within a temperate climatic zone. The variety of its landscapes extends from areas of the Netherlands that are below sea-level – inspiring the epigram 'God made the world, but Man made the Netherlands' – to the Alpine mountain-tops, the Spanish sierras or the glaciers of Iceland.

These geographical differences have helped to shape peoples whose physique, mentality and culture are very diverse.

A *land of immigrants*

Europe's mountains, whether as barriers or passes, have likewise determined the course of its trade routes – used by invaders as well as merchants. Invasion has especially affected

Europe's eastern regions, repeatedly overrun by waves of invaders mostly from Asia. Among them were the Celts, Indo-Europeans from the second millennium BC, traces of whose language still remain in a number of European languages today. Beginning in the 4th century AD, the Germans crossed the Rhine and in the fifth century crossed Gaul as far as Spain. The Huns, the Bulgars, the Avars, the Magyars and the Mongols all entered Europe across the broad Eastern plains. Some of these invaders settled and mixed with the local population; others returned to the East. But all these great waves of immigration, and the resultant intermingling of peoples, were essential factors in forming Europe's cultural mosaic.

A *land of migrations*

Such shifts of population, migrations and invasions, were also caused by internal pressure, which at various times impelled people to leave their own lands. In the 8th century BC, Greeks began to colonize the west, Anatolia and the Middle East. At the time of the Vikings, Norwegians invaded Scotland and Ireland; in about the year 1000 AD, they reached America via Greenland. The Danes set their sights on England, then set out for Normandy, Portugal, Provence and Tuscany. The Swedes, with more openings towards the east, crossed the Baltic and drove into western Russia. From there, following the course of the rivers and practising haulage and portage, they reached the Black Sea. The Italians, heirs to Rome's *Mare Nostrum*, concentrated on the Mediterranean basin. In the 14th century, Spain and Portugal exploited their position on the Atlantic coast by sending their explorers to the West coast of Africa, the East Indies and indeed America. From the 16th century onwards, Great Britain developed her maritime power and her sailors travelled all over the world. France, with her central position in Europe, enjoyed the double advantage of a coastline and of long land frontiers: she therefore turned towards Europe as well as towards the rest of the world. Germany looked mainly towards Baltic and continental Europe.

In these ways, the different geographical circumstances of various European countries helped to form, in the course of history, societies whose political, economic and even cultural interests were very diverse.

No river or mountain range acts as a barrier to language. Most parts of Europe are easily accessible and distances between them are relatively small. The result has been a constant intermingling of people and ideas, making Europe a permanent ethnic and cultural melting-pot.

❸ THE TIME OF THE GREAT MIGRATIONS

Ornament from a shield-plate.
Historical Museum, Berne

The Roman Empire broke up owing to more and more frequent attacks by the barbarians: the Germans, the Goths, the Vandals and the Burgundians, themselves driven on by Asiatic peoples (Alans and Huns). The horseman illustrated is undoubtedly similar to the 4th- and 5th-century invaders of Rome.

❹ EUROPEAN LANGUAGES IN THE WORLD

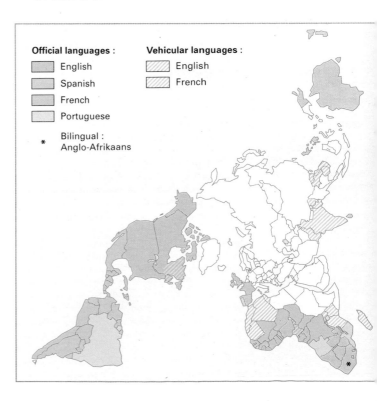

Official languages :
- English
- Spanish
- French
- Portuguese

* Bilingual : Anglo-Afrikaans

Vehicular languages :
- English
- French

-2 Do Languages Divide Europe?

A *common origin*: Sanskrit?

Even if most European languages have Greek, Latin or Germanic roots, they are nonetheless very different. At various times in European history, one language has been dominant as the chief means of communication among cultivated élites: Greek through the Roman Empire, Latin in the Middle Ages, French in the 18th century and, in our day, probably English.

It is now an established fact that writing came to Europe from the Middle East: the alphabet was introduced by the Phoenicians in the 14th century BC. But the exact roots of the European languages remain rather uncertain. It would seem that these languages have links with classical Sanskrit, an Indian language used by the Brahmins which has many similarities with Greek and Latin. Experts agree that these languages, stemming from a common root, evolved differently in different regions of Europe: hence Europe's linguistic diversity.

Forty-three languages

In varying degrees, Europeans speak some 43 languages. They use three alphabets, all with the same origin and all based on consonantal, not ideographic systems. These alphabets are: Greek, derived from Phoenician writing; Latin; and Cyrillic – both of the latter derived from Greek. Another unifying factor is that many technical or conceptual terms are based on ancient Greek or Latin. Without these shared roots, scientists of different nationalities would find it very hard to communicate, for their technical terms refer to very precise concepts and could probably not be expressed accurately in any other way.

Yet language has also exacerbated differences among Europeans. At the Protestant Reformation, translations of the Bible into vernacular languages helped to stimulate national culture, as did the Kralitz Bible in Bohemia, 'the German translation made by Martin Luther, the Authorized Version in English or the translation ordered by the Dutch in the 16th century. These encouraged the spread of literacy and heralded the emergence of new national identities, expressed in languages which more people understood. Cultural nationalism also arose in the Catholic countries, but it did so through the medium of lay culture, as embodied in Italian writers or in France's 16th-century poets.

---

❶ The word 'mother' in various European languages

Sanskrit *matar*	**Gallic** *matres, matrebo*
Greek μήτηρ	**German** *Mutter*
Latin *mater*	**French** *mère*
Armenian *magr*	**Italian** *madre*
Irish *moder*	**Spanish** *madre*
Tocharian *macar, madhar*	

---

❷ EUROPEAN ALPHABETS

1 000 km

□ Latin   ■ Cyrillic   ■ Greek   □ Arabic   *1 Serbia*   *2 Montenegro*

Language and national unity

The use of a common language also serves, in varying degrees, as a means of unification used by central authorities or conquering powers. Thus English was imposed on the Celtic nations of Wales, Scotland and Ireland. French gradually spread throughout the Kingdom of France and then the Republic. Castilian was imposed in Spain and Dutch in Friesland. In the Habsburg Empire, German was imposed on the civil service and the imperial army, in Bohemia, Moravia, Slovakia, Slovenia and Croatia. Poland, after being several times partitioned, suffered an even worse fate when its language was banned and only German and Russian were allowed. Any such imposition of an alien culture helped to exacerbate nationalist feelings, generally centred on the revival of national languages.

In practice, however, Europeans seem largely to have surmounted the divisive effects of their linguistic diversity. And another point needs to be made. Although the diversity of language acts as a brake on communication, most Europeans see it as a rich cultural asset.

3 THE SCHOOL

Illustration by Rosalie Koch, 1874

Only educated people can be masters of their own fate and aspire to lead the nation. Until the 19th century there were many forms of education, most of them limited to the wealthy. Free schooling brought education within the reach of all young people in Europe and literacy became general. Today language is still a factor serving national unity, but the unification of Europe puts a premium on the study of foreign languages.

4 LANGUAGES IN EUROPE

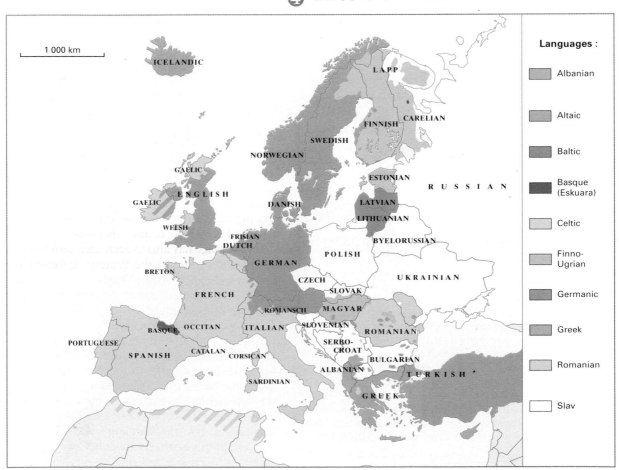

1 000 km

ICELANDIC

LAPP

CARELIAN

FINNISH

SWEDISH

NORWEGIAN

GAELIC

ESTONIAN

RUSSIAN

GAELIC

ENGLISH

DANISH

LATVIAN

LITHUANIAN

WELSH

FRISIAN
DUTCH

BYELORUSSIAN

BRETON

GERMAN

POLISH

CZECH

UKRAINIAN

FRENCH

SLOVAK

ROMANSCH

MAGYAR

BASQUE

OCCITAN

ITALIAN

SLOVENIAN

ROMANIAN

PORTUGUESE

SERBO-
CROAT

SPANISH

CATALAN

CORSICAN

BULGARIAN

ALBANIAN

TURKISH

SARDINIAN

GREEK

Languages :

- Albanian
- Altaic
- Baltic
- Basque (Eskuara)
- Celtic
- Finno-Ugrian
- Germanic
- Greek
- Romanian
- Slav

3 Are There Such Things as European Civilization and Culture?

❶ A CIVILIZATION DEDICATED TO THE GLORY OF THE GODS

The Temple of Hera (misnamed Tempio di Nettuno), 5th century BC, at Poseidonia, now Paestum, Southern Italy

Greek civilization is immortalized in a number of buildings, relatively modest in Greece but of gigantic splendour elsewhere, as in Southern Italy and Sicily. This Temple of Hera, sometimes known as the Temple of Poseidon, embodies colossal ambitions, exaggerated by the extreme simplicity of its Doric style.

---

❷ Christianity and Individual Freedom

A certain nobleman went into a far country to receive for himself a kingdom, and to return. And he called his ten servants, and delivered them ten pounds, and said unto them, Occupy till I come . . .

But his citizens hated him, and sent a message after him, saying, We will not have this man to reign over us. And it came to pass, that when he was returned . . . he commanded these servants to be called unto him . . . . Then came the first, saying, Lord, thy pound hath gained ten pounds. And he said unto him, Well, thou good servant: because thou hast been faithful in a very little, have thou authority over ten cities. . . .

And another came, saying, Lord, behold, here is thy pound, which I have kept laid up in a napkin: For I feared thee, because thou art an austere man: thou takest up that thou layedst not down, and reapest that thou didst not sow. And he saith unto him, Out of thine own mouth will I judge thee, thou wicked servant . . . . Wherefore then gavest not thou my money into the bank, that at my coming I might have required mine own with usury? And he said unto him that stood by, Take from him the pound, and give it to him that hath ten pounds.

For I say unto you, That unto every one which hath shall be given; and from him that hath not, even that he hath shall be taken away from him. But those mine enemies, which would not that I should reign over them . . . and slay them before me.

The Gospel according to St Luke, 19, 12–24, Authorized Version.

Before trying to find out whether there is a European civilization and one or more European cultural traditions, it is essential to define the terms that apply to so complex a subject.

In any given geographical area, itself usually ill-defined, a civilization is the sum total of political, social, economic, religious and cultural phenomena that can be observed in a society.

Culture is a more subjective matter. Traditionally, it is defined as all the knowledge that a person should acquire so as to enrich the spirit through art, literature and science. The means of doing so are supplied, essentially, by education and the media.

It is important to remember, however, that through such means of communication culture can be controlled by a centralizing, authoritarian power, which can pervert it to its own ends. Sometimes, such imposed culture can even clash with the values of that civilization which it claims to express. History offers plenty of examples, of which Nazi Germany and the Communist countries are only the most recent.

The work of 20th-century anthropologists has extended the notion of culture to all those practices that are regularly characteristic of a particular group. Thus, one can speak of Scottish culture, Lapp culture, Sardinian culture and so on.

European values

The democratic ideal, which is based on the conviction that collective well-being depends on each citizen taking an active part in civic life, is an inheritance from the ancient Greeks. True, in their day such ideals applied only to part of the population, but over more than two thousand years they have gradually been extended to all citizens. The democratic ideal also derives from the assemblies of 'free men' held by the Germanic peoples to counterbalance the powers of the leader in time of peace.

In 1762, in *Du contrat social*, the philosopher Jean-Jacques Rousseau argued that people, as a political entity, enjoyed absolute, indivisible and inalienable sovereignty. In the West, democracy has come to be expressed through parliamentary representation, guaranteed by free elections.

In the ancient world, while Greek democracy was taking root, the fledgling society of Rome was establishing what would become its contribution to Europe and then to the world as a whole: the ideal of law and written statutes. By codifying relations between the various public authorities, Rome added a further basic element to European values. The idea of the *res publica*, together with the political traditions of Northern Europe, gave birth to constitutional thought; and in the 17th and 18th centuries John Locke from England and the Baron de Montesquieu from France added the modern concept of the separation of powers – legislative, executive and judiciary.

Statute law gradually spread to cover all the acts of life, whether civil or public. The notion of written contracts replaced custom, affording protection against arbitrary actions. From Rome, the ideal of law gradually extended throughout Europe and then the world.

To the democratic ideal and to that of the rule of law, Europe added another – individual liberty. Christianity, by linking humanity to God and proclaiming 'Jesus as God made Man', had already added a personal dimension to everyone's destiny. Salvation, seen as supreme happiness, was not a collective affair, but individual. The Christian spirit, which refused to link human success with birth, wealth, rank or glory, taught that happiness was to be found in a tranquil conscience. By doing so, it established a new ideal for Europeans to serve.

At the Renaissance in the 15th century, with the rediscovery of the ancient world, humanist intellectuals achieved a synthesis of the Greco-Roman heritage and Christian thought. They saw themselves as Europeans for the first time. So four ideals came together: democracy, equity under the rule of law, human equality and personal happiness based on individual freedom. These essential values were elaborated in their modern forms by the philosophers of the 18th-century Enlightenment, English and French. In 1774 Denis Diderot declared: 'I want society to be happy, but I want to be happy too'. A few years later, Jeremy Bentham preached: 'The greatest happiness of the greatest number'.

In Europe the conviction slowly grew that society should guarantee basic freedoms; and the State took the initiative in condemning torture and slavery. The eventual upshot was the 1948 Declaration of Human Rights adopted by the United Nations. Communist regimes that neglected them, as for example in Eastern Europe, were unable to establish that their political system could make people safe and happy.

Many other peoples have come to share these values – so much so that European civilization is now dissolving into what may be called Western civilization, shared by peoples of European origin in places as far away as Australia and America.

❸ A CIVILIZATION DEDICATED TO THE GLORY OF CHRIST
Paray-le-Monial, Basilica of the Sacred Heart
Christian fervour is embodied in masterpieces of stone. A perfect example is Paray-le-Monial, built without interruption between 1090 and 1110 on the orders of St Hugh, the great Abbot of Cluny. It is a jewel of the Burgundian Romanesque style with a raised Eastern apse dominated by an elegant octagonal bell-tower, at the centre of the transept, whose spire rises 56 metres above the ground.

---

❹ Montesquieu: On the Constitution of England

There are in every State three sorts of power: the legislative power, the executive power over things that depend on the law of nations and the executive power over those that depend on the common law.

For the first, the Prince or the ruler makes laws for a time or for ever, and corrects or abrogates those that exist. For the second, he makes peace or war, sends or receives embassies, ensures security and prevents invasion. For the third, he punishes crimes or gives judgment in private disputes. This last may be called the power to judge, and the other simply the executive power of the State.

All would be lost if the same man, or the same body of leaders, or of nobles or of the people, exercised all three powers: that of making laws, that of carrying out public decisions and that of judging crimes or private disputes,

De l'esprit des lois (1748)

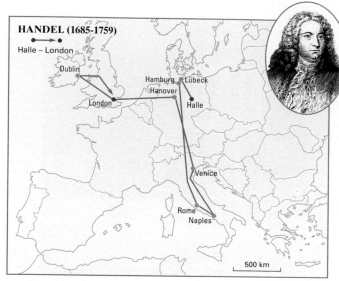

HANDEL (1685-1759)

Halle – London

①Born in Halle, Germany, Georg Friedrich Handel went to Hamburg in 1703 to present his first Italian operas. Their success secured him the protection of Giovanni Gaston de'Medici who took him to Italy. His playing at the organ and the harpsichord won him fame and the title of Kapellmeister in Hanover (1710). He stayed there only a short time, being tempted away by the intellectual élite of London. Thereafter, except for short trips to the continent, he never left England and he took British nationality in 1726.

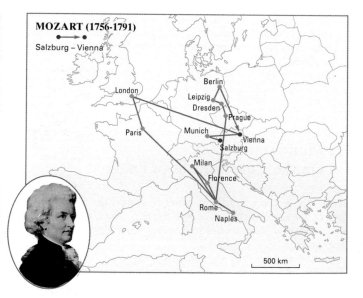

MOZART (1756-1791)

Salzburg – Vienna

②Wolfgang Amadeus Mozart left Salzburg at the age of 6 for his first concert tour in Germany, Austria, France, England and the Netherlands. In London the infant prodigy took lessons with Johann Christian Bach and in Paris with the harpsichordist Johann Schobert. He returned to Salzburg to study with Joseph Haydn before leaving for Italy, which he visited three times between 1769 and 1773. He returned to Salzburg and took his mother on a tour of Munich, Augsburg, Mannheim and Paris. In 1779 he resumed his role of Kapellmeister. Relations with the Bishop becoming intolerable, he then left for Vienna, for good.

The European citizen

In ancient Greece education meant studying the work of philosophers, writers and artists. At the time of Alexander the Great, the Greeks also studied Eastern culture. In Rome any cultivated person was heir to all this. The language and culture of Greece were part of the Latin heritage and were taught throughout the Empire.

In the Middle Ages, among the Christian peoples subject to the authority of the Pope in Rome, an educated person had to learn Latin; Western European culture was both Latin and Christian. The universities taught in it; and professors and students could change universities to complete their studies. From the 16th to the 18th century, despite the emergence of national identities and the gradual replacement of Latin by national languages, a cultivated person remained essentially a citizen of Europe.

The upsurge of nationalism in the 19th century lessened the weight of this common heritage. All past history began to be regarded as national, if it had occurred within national frontiers. This led to disputes. Charlemagne was claimed by the Germans, but also by the French; Joan of Arc and Napoleon became symbols of the struggle between France and Britain; Italy boasted of its artists but played down the internecine strife among its myriad rival city-states. There are countless examples of a nation's history being rewritten to exalt glorious events or characters to the detriment of those who seem too alien to much-vaunted national unity.

After the Second World War, with Western Europe forming the European Community and Eastern Europe being integrated along Soviet lines, culture became more international, although its ends and means were obviously different on either side of the 'Iron Curtain'.

Would anyone still deny that the works of Dante in Italy, Spinoza in the Netherlands, Cervantes in Spain, Shakespeare in England, Descartes in France, Goethe in Germany, Dostoyevsky in Russia, James Joyce in Ireland, Ibsen in Norway, Camoës in Portugal – and many others – are part of the intellectual inheritance of all educated people in Europe?

From the 16th century onwards, through the discovery of foreign lands and the formation of colonial empires, European culture spread well beyond Europe. At the same time it acquired new riches from elsewhere. Europe exported its beliefs, its languages, its way of living; but it received lessons in other life-styles and artistic forms. Europeans may thus feel themselves to be above all citizens of the world – a feeling they may well share with the Americans. Is not the European citizen already a citizen of the West?

The diversity of cultures in Europe

If the definition of 'culture' includes all the habits and ways of life of a particular group, the diversity of the cultures to be found in Europe is truly astonishing. It all depends on the area.

In view of their history since the break-up of the Roman Empire in the 5th century, three great cultural zones co-exist in Europe. In the southeast there is the Balkan zone, heir to the Byzantine Empire, under which it flourished before coming under Moslem influence from the 15th to the 19th century. In the east is the Slav zone, largely open to Asian, Byzantine, Moslem and Western influence. In the west is the occidental zone, with its intimate blend of Nordic or Anglo-Saxon cultures with the legacy of Greece and Rome. For some sixteen centuries these three zones have regularly influenced each other.

At the level of the city, at the other extreme, cultural characteristics are very much alive. Parisians have their own culture, which distinguishes them from inhabitants of Prague, Florence or Berlin. The Corsicans, the Welsh, the Catalans, the Bavarians, the Savoyards – all insist on their own culture, which distinguishes them from their neighbours. The Italians, the Germans, the British, the Danes, heirs of states that have become nations, are vividly aware of their national identities, often jealously preserved.

It is certainly at regional and national levels that cultural differences are most passionately upheld – sometimes against each other. The identity of the Catalans and the Basques is asserted on both sides of the Pyrenees. The identity of French-speaking peoples extends beyond France: a famous example was the late Jacques Brel, from Belgium. Northern Ireland lives out the tragic drama of its double identity, Irish and British. Switzerland and Luxembourg, by contrast, are countries in which contrasting linguistic cultures live happily side by side. Here too there are many other examples of cultural similarities and contrasts within Europe.

Europe's cultural diversity dates back to the Bronze Age, if not earlier still. Geography and history have brought together many groups in Europe, each seeking to preserve its own characteristics. Is this a feature of Europe that should be encouraged? European integration, begun in the West with the formation of the European Community, has often been attacked by champions of national identity. Is this a handicap? Or is it a diversity to be cherished? Will Europeans ever have the degree of cohesion that exists in North America or China? Should they?

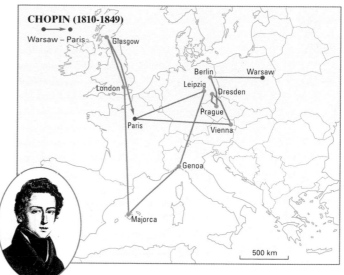

③ Frédéric Chopin was still a pupil at the Warsaw Conservatoire when he had his first successes. After a period in Berlin and then in Vienna (1829), he left his native Poland to settle in Paris (1830). Despite initial difficulties, he became a piano teacher much sought after in Parisian society. His meeting with the writer George Sand plucked him from this undemanding existence and engendered ten intensely creative years. The couple separated in 1847. After an exhausting journey to London and Glasgow in the following year, Chopin returned to Paris, where he died on 17 October 1849.

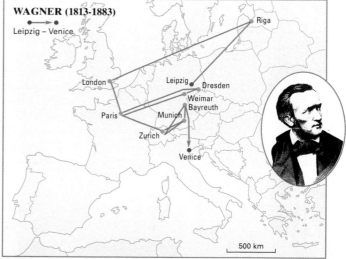

④ Richard Wagner was born in Leipzig, where he completed his higher education. His discovery of Carl Maria von Weber and Ludwig van Beethoven in 1827 encouraged him to become a composer. From 1837 to 1839 he was a conductor in Riga, but left hurriedly on account of debts. He headed for London and Paris, but met only indifference. He then went to Dresden, where, espousing Socialist ideals, he was threatened with arrest and fled to Weimar, then Paris, then Zurich (1849). Then his luck changed. Despite his gloom at failing in Paris, he undertook a tour of Europe. Ludwig II of Bavaria saved him from despair, inviting him to Munich, where he produced Tannhäuser, The Flying Dutchman and Tristan (1864). The scandal of his liaison with Cosima von Bülow made him leave Munich for Switzerland, where in six years he composed his greatest works. In Bayreuth (1872) he decided to build the theatre required for his Ring Cycle. He died in Venice at the age of 70.

4 Society and Economics

Unbridled economic power

The Greeks ran an organized economy. They established colonies in the Mediterranean partly to control trade in the goods they needed. The Romans also organized their Empire for economic as well as political ends.

But the wealth produced in Greece and Rome benefited only the powerful. The slave was wholly subject to the master, the poor to the rich, and there was no enforced redistribution of resources. Such largesse as there was depended only on the goodwill of the rich or, at times of rebellion, on the fear of massacre.

The rise of the monasteries

Christianity brought revolutionary change. By valuing human beings, regardless of their rank or wealth, under a single God, protector of the poor, it rooted the idea of equality. After the fall of the Roman Empire, monasticism gave practical expression to the links between religion, economics and society. The monastery, based on the *Rule* written by St Benedict in the early 6th century AD, lived on the proceeds of its own production, gave each member a fair share and organized the care of the needy. Until the 19th century, all over Europe, the Church used part of its revenue to spread wealth more evenly. The redistribution was limited by comparison with what is done by nation-states today: but it worked.

Capitalism arose in the 15th century, beginning with banks in Florence and Augsburg and developing through the stock markets of Antwerp and Amsterdam. It very soon threw off the close supervision of the Church. Whether Protestantism provided an ethic for capitalism remains debatable. The growing power of the nation-states rapidly attracted leading bankers to the courts of Europe, where they became influential advisers. But until the 19th century state intervention in the economy was hardly ever motivated by social concerns.

The birth of Socialism

Beginning in Britain, the Industrial Revolution spread to continental Europe towards the end of the 18th century and above all in the 19th. It completely reorganized methods of production and brought about unprecedented social change.

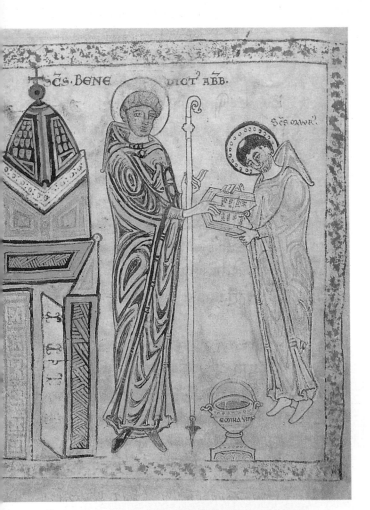

① THE RULE OF ST BENEDICT OF NURSIA
Book of Martyrs of the Abbey of the Holy Sepulchre, Cambrai
Having founded the monastery of Monte Cassino in about AD 529, St Benedict drew up in about 540 a Rule that was taken up by Benedict of Aniane. Widely adopted in Carolingian times and still the fundamental law of the Benedictines, it imposes poverty, chastity and obedience, but also manual and intellectual labour. Here, Benedict's disciple St Maurus receives the Rule from the hands of his master, henceforth celebrated as the Father of European monasticism.

Wealth was concentrated in the hands of a few leading families and many people left the countryside to become rootless, cooped up in towns or coal-mining areas. This raised once more, often dramatically, the problem of redistribution.

Utopian Socialists, like Robert Owen in Britain or the Comte de Saint-Simon in France, tried at the beginning of the 19th century to establish 'lay monasteries'. They failed. But others worked out means of action that proved effective. Trade unionism, born in Britain, harnessed forces strong enough to stand up against the interests of the wealthy and obliged governments to pay attention. Soon, social movement turned to politics. Karl Marx, analyzing the actions of society in terms of the class struggle, put forward a new vision that spread from Europe throughout the world. True, the Russian government, under the Soviets, perverted Marx's doctrine into a form of imperialism. But political intervention in the redistribution of wealth became a means of achieving better social justice, whatever its faults.

The Welfare State

The roots of the present system of redistribution can be traced back to the philanthropic movements of the 19th century and to measures taken to counter the great depression of the 1870s. In 1878 Bismarck set up a system of workers' insurance that was unique in Europe. From 1933 onwards Franklin Roosevelt in the United States, like the governments of Western European democracies, established aid for the unemployed and the aged. But these measures had their limits.

It was after 1945 that the present system of social security really began. With Europe in ruins, there was clearly need for the state to undertake and coordinate reconstruction.

Between the 1950s and the 1980s European society developed a real protective organization based on social solidarity and designed to supply the vital needs of almost all its members. The proportion of everyone's revenue claimed in taxation continued to grow. At present, on average, it is more than 40 per cent of Europe's Gross Domestic Product.

The size of the redistributive system raises a number of problems. There is some uncertainty about the financing of retirement for new generations of contributors; and the high level of income tax encourages evasion.

But never before has social security offered so much protection to the weak, the poor, the young, the old or the infirm. It may well be that this, rather than sheer wealth, explains the attraction that Europe now exerts on people in the rest of the world.

❷ The Manifesto of the Communist Party

The scale of working-class poverty led to a general denunciation of the capitalist system. A German journalist, Karl Marx, undertook a 'scientific' analysis of history and economics. With Friedrich Engels in 1848 he drew up The Manifesto of the Communist Party. *It denounced capitalism, encouraged the class struggle, called for the overthrow of the existing social order and preached the union of the proletariat to change the world. People hailed Marx's ideas, parties were formed around them and a part of the world (the USSR) took him as its teacher.*

In the earlier epochs of history we find almost everywhere a complicated arrangement of society into various orders, a manifold gradation of social rank. In ancient Rome we have patricians, knights, plebeians, slaves; in the Middle Ages, feudal lords, vassals, guild-masters, journeymen, apprentices, serfs . . . . The modern bourgeois society that has sprouted from the ruins of feudal society has not done away with class antagonisms. It has but established new classes, new conditions of oppression . . . in place of the old ones. Our epoch, the epoch of the bourgeoisie, possesses, however, this distinctive feature: it has simplified the class antagonisms. Society as a whole is more and more splitting up into two great hostile camps, into two great classes directly facing each other: Bourgeoisie and Proletariat. The Communists everywhere support every revolutionary movement against the existing social and political order of things. In all these movements they bring to the front, as the leading question in each, the property question, no matter what its degree of development at the time. Finally, they labour everywhere for the union and agreement of the democratic parties of all countries. The Communists disdain to conceal their views and aims. They openly declare that their ends can be attained only by the forcible overthrow of all existing social conditions. Let the ruling classes tremble at a Communistic revolution. The proletarians have nothing to lose but their chains. They have a world to win.

WORKING PEOPLE OF ALL COUNTRIES, UNITE!

Karl Marx and Friedrich Engels, translated by Samuel Moore, 1888

❸ Total of compulsory taxation

	1970[1]	1975	1980	1985	1988
FRANCE	35.1	36.9	41.7	44.5	44.3
ITALY	26.1	26.2	30.2	34.4	37.1
GERMANY (FR)	32.9	35.7	38	38	37.4
UK	37	35	35.3	37.8	37.7
EC[2]	30.8	33.4	36.4	39.4	40.61

1. In percentage of GDP.
2. Non-weighted average.
SOURCE: OECD: Statistics of public receipts of OECD Member Countries (1965–88), 1989 in *Economic Studies of OECD*, France, 1990.

'THE UNIVERSAL, DEMOCRATIC, AND SOCIAL REPUBLIC'

There are two levels in this picture, a popular representation of the
lyrical illusion underlying the so-called 'People's Springtime' – the
revolutionary movements that broke out in the early months of 1848.

*In the heavens, Christ raises His hand in blessing, haloed by the
Sun of Fraternity, while two winged spirits bear cornucopia –
promising future prosperity – surrounded by the martyrs of
liberty, moustachioed and bearded angels holding the victor's
palm.*

*On earth, in the foreground, lies the debris of the past:
shattered crowns, broken cupboards . . . . The various people are
now united, as symbolized by the long ribbon that links their
procession, although they still uphold national flags: of France,
Germany, Austria, the Two Sicilies, Lombardy, Romagna –
German and Italian unity being as yet unachieved – Poland,
Britain . . . Switzerland . . . . This is the Europe of the Nations*
*under the aegis of the Rights of Man and in the shadow of the
Tree of Liberty. The procession is hailed by representatives of
traditional economic activities – a ploughman and a shepherd –
and of new developments – the railway and a steamship.*

*This universal harmony seems to echo the following lines
printed in Le Moniteur on 13 April 1848: 'May the word
"hate" be banished from now on from the French language. Love,
which is the prime basis of fraternity, is also the basis of the
world: may it unite us and weld us together in common feelings.'*

*It took only a few months before this dream of a Europe of the
Nations built in peace and concord was banished by the cruel
light of day.*

UNANSWERED QUESTIONS IN EUROPE'S HISTORY

A history of Europe might take each of the strands we have isolated so far as permanent features and trace their development over several millennia.

That is not the intention of the authors of this book. A thematic study of that kind, interesting as it might be, would soon end up by juxtaposing a number of parallel histories of Europe, without being able to investigate their interaction over the centuries.

That interaction, positive and negative, is the stuff of history; and it is on this that we have concentrated our collective gaze. It has led us to identify a number of broad chronological epochs, often comparable to those of world history, itself greatly influenced by that of Europe.

These chronological epochs are not simply tracts of time. Each has a *leitmotiv*. Some, for example, are periods of withdrawal, others of expansion, including exploration of the wider world.

To give this division into periods its full significance, this section of the book asks a number of questions, both about the history of Europe and about Europe in history.

Since their arrival in Europe, people have not ceased to influence, oppose and unite with each other. The history of Europe is above all the history of the Europeans.

1 THE HEADQUARTERS OF THE COUNCIL OF EUROPE, STRASBOURG

The Council of Europe was established on 5 May 1949 and is based in Strasbourg, like the European Parliament. Its original purpose was to achieve political, economic, cultural and social unity among the countries of Europe. The 26 member states retain full national sovereignty. In the non-political field, the council's main achievement has been to draw up a European Charter of Human Rights.

2 The Council of Europe in 1991

AUSTRIA	HUNGARY	POLAND
BELGIUM	ICELAND	PORTUGAL
CYPRUS	IRELAND	SAN MARINO
CZECHOSLOVAKIA	ITALY	SPAIN
DENMARK	LIECHTENSTEIN	SWEDEN
FINLAND	LUXEMBOURG	SWITZERLAND
FRANCE	MALTA	TURKEY
GERMANY	NETHERLANDS	UNITED KINGDOM
GREECE	NORWAY	

THE TAUTAVEL MAN

Originating in Africa, homo erectus *spread to other parts of the world, dominating the temperate zones between 1.5 million and 650,000 years ago. On 22 July 1971, at Tautavel in the eastern Pyrenees, prehistoric human remains including the skull of a 20-year-old man were found, making it possible to reconstruct the* homo erectus *above, known as 'the Tautavel man'. His bones are very like those of modern man, but more robust; they show that he was perfectly capable of standing and walking erect.*

CRO-MAGNON MAN

Homo sapiens sapiens appeared during the last glacial period, some 35,000 to 40,000 years ago. He was tall (about 1.65 metres to 1.8 metres) with a vertical forehead, a flat face and a well-developed chin, characteristics resembling those of present-day Europeans. Cro-Magnon habitats, in the open air or in the entrances of caves, attest to a family-based life. Cro-Magnon people made weapons of flint, bone and wood for hunting.

A *single stock*?

The first hominids, of the species *homo erectus*, seem to have come from Africa and occupied Southern Europe some 1.5 million years ago. Then, from about 100,000 years ago, a number of remains bear witness to the presence of Neanderthal Man (*homo sapiens*). Finally, some 40,000 years ago, Cro-Magnon Man (*homo sapiens sapiens* – our own species) spread throughout Europe.

At the time Europe's geography was not what it is today. For long periods glaciers covered northern Europe as far south as present-day Belgium. The British Isles were connected to the continent and the sea level was much lower than at present.

The melting of the glaciers, between 15,000 and 10,000 BC, gave Europe its present shape and brought it – save for the far north – into the temperate zone. Europeans, who had previously lived by fishing, hunting and gathering, became farmers and stockbreeders. Were these changes, which some call 'revolutions', gradually brought into Europe from the Mesopotamian area? Or was there a specific civilization, or neolithic culture, indigenous to Europe itself?

Around 3500 BC, when writing was being invented in the Middle East and the first pyramids were being built in Egypt, Europe was still populated by farmers working with tools made of stone.

Bronze metalworking, invented in Egypt in about 3000 BC, spread to the Aegean and the valley of the Indus, but took nearly 2000 years to reach the whole of Europe and fitfully at that. After Anatolia and Greece, it spread to Spain, then Bohemia, the Rhine valley, Italy and finally the Nordic countries and the British Isles. The slowness of this process may well have isolated even more the regional cultures in Europe that were already quite distinct.

Celts, Greeks and Persians

Metalworking in iron, already practised in Anatolia and the Caucasus in about 1500 BC, spread more rapidly towards Western Europe than towards the Asian East. It became, indeed, a European speciality. But it was not the mark of a single civilization. The Greeks, who took to it early, in about 1200 BC, developed on either side of the Aegean a civilization of their own whose basis was more philosophical than technological.

At the same time, i.e. between 1000 and 500 BC, the Celts gradually came to dominate Western and central Europe. From what is now southern Germany they spread towards Great Britain, Ireland, Bohemia, Gaul, the Iberian Peninsula, Italy and the Balkans. The area covered by this

Celtic culture had no political unity and was not an empire. Its peoples remained disparate, acting according to local circumstances.

For the Greeks, divided as they were among rival city-states, the threat came from the East. The Persians had recently conquered the kingdoms of Anatolia and the great empires of Mesopotamia: did they now seek to conquer Greece? What significance was there in their defeats at Marathon (490 BC) and Salamis (480 BC)? Was it the confrontation of two value-systems, the Greeks claiming that theirs was superior to that of the East? Was this a frontier between Europe and Asia?

Did Europe stretch as far as the Indus? As far as the Sahara?

The Macedonian Alexander the Great (356–23 BC) did not treat the Indus as a frontier. Arriving there in 325 BC, he did his best to amalgamate Greek and Persian traditions – resulting after his death in the so-called 'Hellenistic' civilization.

Nor did the Romans halt their expansion on the shores of the Aegean. They settled in Greece, then in Asia Minor, as early as the 2nd century BC. In AD 20 Augustus set the eastern frontier of the Empire on the Euphrates.

Colonized by the Phoenicians at the end of the second millennium BC, the African shore of the Mediterranean became Roman after the final defeat of Carthage in 146 BC and the conquest of Egypt in 30 BC. The Empire expanded to include African provinces.

After the short-lived Kingdom of the Vandals in the 5th century AD and the reconquest of the Emperor Justinian in the 6th century, the Romans' African territory passed to Islam and the Mediterranean became Europe's southern frontier, as it is today. In the 19th and 20th centuries, however, French, British and Italian colonization of North Africa temporarily linked the Mediterranean's northern and southern shores.

Was Europe confined to between the Rhine and the Danube?

Concerned to control the Mediterranean basin and imbued with Hellenistic culture, the Romans did not conquer the north until about the mid-1st century BC). The Rhine and the Danube, travel and trade routes for millennia, became the Empire's frontiers. Caesar conquered much of England, and Hadrian protected it with the wall that bears his name. However, in AD 101 Trajan led his legions beyond the Danube, conquered Dacia (roughly, present-day Romania) and turned it into a Roman province.

---

❸ Marathon, Salamis and Plataea

The Persians, by Aeschylus, was shown in Athens in the spring of 472 BC, barely eight years after the Persian defeat at Salamis. The action of the play takes place at Susa in the Palace of Xerxes, where the King's mother, widow of Darius, hears the news of the Persians' disaster. The words of the chorus, composed of the Great King's Counsellors, reveal the significance of the event: it was a victory won by free men.

line 241	THE QUEEN	*And what chief acts as leader and master of the army [of Athens]?*
242	CORYPHAEUS	*They are neither slaves nor subjects.*
585	CHORUS	*And for a long time in the land of Asia the law of the Persians will cease to be obeyed; tribute will no longer be levied at the imperial command; there will be*
590		*no more kneeling to receive orders: the power of the Great King is at an end!*

Aeschylus, *The Persians*

---

❹ ALEXANDER'S EMPIRE

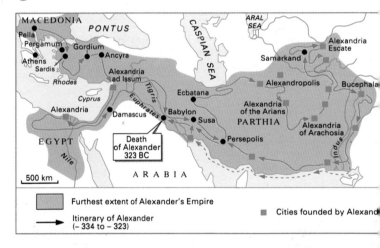

Furthest extent of Alexander's Empire

→ Itinerary of Alexander (– 334 to – 323)

■ Cities founded by Alexander

❺ EUROPE AS FAR SOUTH AS THE ALGERIAN DESERT

Trajan's Triumphal Arch, third century, Timgad, Algeria

Timgad was built around AD 100 under Emperor Trajan, on the frontier of the Roman Empire, and based on a chequerboard pattern. Its famous library made it an embryo of Roman civilization.

① TRAJAN'S COLUMN

Marble. Height: 39.81 m. Diameter: 3.83 m. AD 107–17. Rome, Forum

This column recounts the epic conquest of Dacia, a land rich in gold and silver on the left bank of the Danube, by the Emperor Trajan (53–117). It shows the embarkation of troops, the trenches, the sieges, skirmishes and battles, in very realistic fashion, with a cast of 2,500 people. It might be called one of the first historical strip cartoons on one of Rome's last conquering generals.

In the northern part of the Empire, the conquered peoples acquired Latin culture. Beyond the northern frontier lived the peoples that the Romans called *Germani*, Germans. If the military frontier was impregnable, the cultural frontier was not: many Germans became Latinized. But in the West the barrier crumbled in the 5th century under the waves of invasion. Germanic kingdoms were established from the shores of the North Sea to the African Atlas Mountains.

A *frontier between Latin and Greek*?

In fact, Greco-Roman unity, not much assisted by Christian unity, then still in its infancy, came to an end shortly before the great invasions. In 395, on the death of the Emperor Theodosius, the Empire was divided between his two sons along a linguistic frontier: Latin in the west and Greek in the east. For Greek, even in the heyday of Rome, had never ceased to be the language spoken by the peoples in the eastern part of the Empire. While the élite spoke both languages, the people spoke Latin in the west and Greek in the east. Until the 19th century the cleavage dating from 395 continued to distance Greece from the west. In effect, the Roman Empire in the west came to an end in 476. After Justinian's short-lived western reconquests in the 6th century, the Eastern Empire, by then Byzantium, flourished in the eastern Mediterranean. Then the unity of Christendom was broken by the schism of 1054: the Catholic Church obeyed the Pope in Rome, the Orthodox Church the Patriarch in Constantinople. The Ottoman conquest and the capture of Constantinople in 1453 accentuated the division by imposing Moslem influence on the Balkans. At the beginning of the 19th century, the Ottoman Empire grew weaker; and Greece, with the help of Britain, France and Russia, recovered her long-lost independence (1830). The Greeks accepted as their ruler first a Bavarian and then a Danish prince, thereby showing their attachment to Europe. The Romanians, Bulgarians and (for a time) Albanians had similar European allegiances.

Was Charlemagne the Father of Europe?

Germanic kingdoms emerged on the ruins of the Western Roman Empire – and soon quarrelled. Did they share a common culture? Did Latin influence disappear in the economic recession that struck the West? Did conversion to Christianity save that cultural heritage?

In the 8th century, when the Arabs conquered Spain and threatened the Franks, the plight of Western Europe seemed dramatic. Frankish

② THEODOSIUS THE GREAT (346–95)

In the Imperial Tribune of the Hippodrome, Theodosius the Great, flanked by his two sons Arcadius and Honorius, prepares to bestow the silver crown upon the winning charioteer. This place is a political institution. Theodosius was crowned here; he paraded prisoners and chariots filled with booty after victorious campaigns; he summoned the people here when he re-established and imposed religious unity. At his death in 395 he left the Roman Empire to his under-age sons, who were soon dominated by the court and the bureaucracy.

princes, Lombards and Anglo-Saxons were, in their respective regions, battling amongst themselves. The fresh impulse came from a Frankish family, the Carolingians. One of them, Charles Martel, halted an Arab/Islamic onslaught at Poitiers in 732 – an important victory for the West in Europe. In 751 the victory also gave the Carolingians access to the Frankish throne, which henceforth supported the Pope.

Charlemagne restored imperial authority, the memory of which was still very much alive. Reorganizing the Empire, he gave his reign the appearance of a Renaissance. It seemed all the more brilliant in retrospect, because it was followed by a further break-up of the Christian West. The Carolingians respected the Germanic law that obliged a father to divide his legacy among his sons. In 843, at Verdun, Charlemagne's three grandsons split the Empire into three kingdoms; from these slowly emerged the German, French and Italian nations. But if Charlemagne achieved unity for Roman, Germanic and Christian values, does this make him, as some would claim, the Father of Europe?

Feudalism faces the Church

Even before the division of the Empire, it was attacked in the north by Viking raids and in the east by Hungarian horsemen. In the south, Arab raids on the Mediterranean coastline forced the terrified inhabitants to take to the hills. Feudalism then took root in the former Carolingian Empire. At the top, Charlemagne's descendants retained royal power. In 962 Otto I founded the future Germanic Holy Roman Empire and in 987 Hugh Capet was elected King of France.

But since every lord owed allegiance to a more powerful superior in exchange for land (the fief), the monarch's contact with the lesser nobility became very distant. The system overstretched the cohesion of the state, but the castle (the seigneury) protected the people in each fief.

Much weakened by the feudal system, the Roman Church gradually came to terms with it, turning feudal practices into ritual and trying to modify its worst excesses. Helped by the spiritual revival associated with the rise of the Cluniac Order in Europe, the Papacy under Gregory VII (1073–85) began a reform that freed it from the tutelage of the Emperor. From now on, it regarded itself as a spiritual and temporal power superior to lay rulers. It was the Papacy, with the Cluniac Order, that backed the idea of a Crusade to liberate Spain and the Holy Places of Palestine from Islam. From the 11th to the 14th century the Church remained the undisputed point of reference for the Western world.

③ CHARLEMAGNE (742–814)
Albrecht Dürer, Germanisches Museum, Nuremberg
The idea of Europe became more definite and began to replace that of the West. On attaining power, Charlemagne conquered Lombardy and added the title of King of Italy to those of Neustria (between North Sea, the Meuse and the Scheldt). He mounted more than sixty military expeditions before being crowned Emperor in the year 800 and ruling over the first Christian Empire, dominated by the Franks.

Was Byzantium European?

As heir of the Eastern Roman Empire, the Byzantine Empire – beginning with Justinian in the 6th century – dreamed of recovering the West from the Germans. But at the beginning of the 7th century it faced a dangerous threat from the Arabs in the eastern Mediterranean. The failure of their siege of Constantinople in 677 halted their northward expansion and saved Christian civilizations as the victory at Poitiers did in 732.

From then onwards the Byzantine Empire looked to the East and Constantinople remained until the 18th century one of the richest and most brilliant cities in the world. Relations with the West worsened, but did not cease. The religious schism of 1054 separated the two Churches and Byzantium suffered from the transit of successive waves of Crusaders. The growth of Turkish power involved it in incessant warfare. Its repeated appeals to the West fell on deaf ears and in 1453 Constantinople fell to the Ottoman Sultan. Yet for nine centuries Byzantium had helped to protect Christendom from Arab expansion in the south and repeated invaders from Asia in the east.

The conversion of the Slavs

The integration of the Slavs into the Christian world began mainly from Byzantium. Around the middle of the first millennium BC the Slavs were living in tribes beyond the Carpathians. Having little contact with Greco-Latin civilization, they found themselves subject to the Germans. In the 5th century, as the latter moved westwards, the Slavs advanced towards the Danube and settled as far as the Adriatic. There were many of them and they covered a vast area. At that time they formed three distinct groups: the eastern Slavs occupied the Russian plain; the western Slavs, except for the Poles, did not remain autonomous for long; and the southern Slavs, in the 15th century, fell under Ottoman domination. Relations between the Germans and the Slavs were often stormy and they left their mark on central Europe. Between the two, the Baltic peoples (Estonians, Latvians and Lithuanians) had to resist German pressure, but for a long time cast ambitious eyes on Slav territory.

In the 9th century the eastern Slavs and the majority of the southern Slavs (Serbs and Bulgarians) preferred Byzantium to the Germans as a source of Christian conversion. Cyril and Methodius, summoned by the rulers of Moravia around 863, fashioned an alphabet for them inspired by Greek and the ancestor of present-day Cyrillic. But the western Slavs (Poles, Czechs and Slovaks) and some of the southern Slavs (Croats, Slovenes) were converted by Frankish or Germanic monks, a lasting divisive factor into the Slav world.

The formation of the first eastern Slav state was undertaken by Scandinavian warriors and merchants who traded between the Baltic and the Black Sea. Their first kingdom was set up in Kiev in 882 and became Christian a century later following the conversion of Vladimir I. In the 13th century the successors of Genghis Khan set out to conquer the Russian plain, and Kiev fell in 1240. The Russian Slavs were henceforth cut off from the Western world. This episode in their history may explain their early conquest of northern Asia. The conversion of the Mongols to Islam brought them under Moslem influence, but the Greek Orthodox religion was not persecuted. The Russian reconquest began from the north and it was Peter the Great, at the end of the 17th century, who once again made Russia part of Western history.

Nationalism versus cosmopolitanism?

In the West a number of political, economic, cultural and religious factors destroyed the balance of medieval feudalism. The Hundred Years' War in France (1346–1453) ravaged both the country and the authority of the king. Appalling epidemics, including the Black Death of the 14th century, decimated whole regions. The Holy Roman Empire gradually abandoned its imperial universalism. Finally, the Church was torn apart by the Great Schism, between the Papacies of Avignon and Rome, paving the way for the great clashes of the 16th century.

In the face of these crises people gradually felt the desire to rally more closely round a particular ruler. Thus the Italian city-states asserted their identity; Bohemia rallied to Wenceslas and Hungary to Matthias Corvinus; France united against the English, who had long been united already. In Spain, Castile and Aragon were unified in 1479. Switzerland came into being in 1499 when a few Alpine cantons obtained political independence from the Holy Roman Emperor. But these manifestations of nationalism led some rulers to do some previously unthinkable things. In England, when the Pope refused to annul Henry VIII's first marriage, the king in 1534 detached the Anglican Church from Rome and declared himself its head. In 1536, Francis I of France appeared to break with Western values in seeking an alliance with the Ottoman Sultan in order to rid himself of Charles V's grip. Throughout Europe, national languages developed at the expense of Latin: the Bible was translated into 'vulgar languages', and in 1539 Francis I made French the official language of the Kingdom of France.

③ JAROSLAV MARRIES OFF HIS CHILDREN

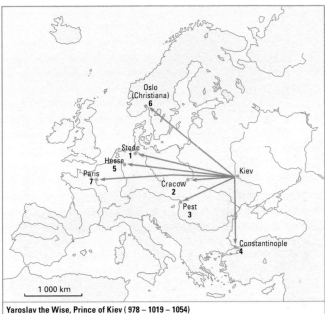

Yaroslav the Wise, Prince of Kiev (978 – 1019 – 1054)

1 Vladimir, Prince of Novgorod, marries Oda of Stade, c. 1043
2 Izyaslav I, Prince of Kiev, marries Gertrude of Poland, c. 1043
3 Anastasia marries Andrew, King of Hungary, c. 1046
4 Vsevolod I, Prince of Kiev, marries the daughter of Constantine Monomachos, Emperor of Byzantium from 1042 to 1055
5 Svyatoslav II marries the daughter of Count Etheler of Hesse
6 Elisabeth marries Harald, King of Norway, in 1044
7 Anne marries Henry I, King of France, in 1051

When one is Prince of Novgorod and Grand Prince of Kiev (1019–54), how can one peacefully extend the influence of an Empire that already stretches as far as the Baltic? By marrying off one's children to European rulers. This system of alliances made Kiev one of the most powerful states in Europe. Russia's first law-giver, the Grand Prince of Kiev, was also a great lover of art: he embellished his city to such a degree that it rivalled Constantinople.

④ The Villers-Cotterêts Ordinance (1539)

ARTICLE 51: *Registers shall be compiled as proof of baptism, in which shall be stated the time and date of the birth and, from an extract from the said register, it shall be possible to prove the date of attaining majority.*

ARTICLE 111: *We desire that henceforth all orders, registers, inquiries, commissions, testaments and other acts shall be pronounced, registered and delivered to the parties concerned in the French mother tongue and not otherwise.*

1 THE SPLENDOUR OF GERMAN BAROQUE
The Wieskirche near Steingaden in the Bavarian Oberland
Politically weakened, Germany turned its immense energies to artistic and musical creation. Catholic society, to affirm its strength against Protestantism, encouraged the development of religious art. Monasteries, churches and sanctuaries began to abound in gilded stucco, multicoloured statues, frescoes in pink, green and gold. The Baroque and Rococo styles exploded with exuberance. The pilgrimage church shown here, the Wieskirche in Bavaria, built between 1749 and 1756 by Dominikus Zimmermann, is one of the European masterpieces of its kind.

2 FREDERICK II OF PRUSSIA, PHILOSOPHER KING
The round table at Sans Souci, with Voltaire. By Adolf Menzel, Berlin
Voltaire and the 'philosophical menagerie' of Sans Souci helped to give Frederick the Great of Prussia his reputation as 'the Solomon of the North'. Dazzled by Louis XIV, he did everything in his power to make Prussia powerful and intellectually pre-eminent.

The power of independent states continued to grow until the two dramatic European wars which became the two World Wars.

But the states were far from being watertight compartments. The reigning dynasties continued the policies of intermarriage that made Europe look like a great aristocratic family whose quarrels did not destroy its cohesion, while intellectuals and artists gave all of Europe the international character of a 'Republic of Letters'. From the 15th to the 18th century there was a high degree of cultural cosmopolitanism: it even spread across the Atlantic. Humanism, making man the measure of all things, created the atmosphere from which emerged, for example, the works of Erasmus, Thomas More, Calvin, Loyola, Descartes, Locke, Montesquieu and Voltaire. The Renaissance, beginning in Italy, reached northern Europe, and in particular France, Flanders and Britain. In the 17th century it was succeeded by the classicism of Versailles, which affected all of Europe in the century that followed. At the same time, in Rome, the Catholic Counter-Reformation encouraged Baroque, which spread to Europe and its colonial possessions. During these four centuries, in fact, artists, writers and scientists formed a working community throughout Europe. Books were translated, works were exhibited, music was performed, trade and exchange took place.

Is the nation-state a model society?

Paradoxically, the cosmopolitanism of the Enlightenment may well have been a victim of the ideas that it helped to spread. It may seem surprising that the revolutionary movements that were inspired by its ideology, whether in the United States, Europe or Latin America, produced national, even nationalistic self-assertion.

Of course, the philosophy of the 18th century saw itself as universalist, but it touched only the aristocracy and the 'enlightened' bourgeoisie. It was wholly alien to the masses, and especially the peasantry.

To ensure the survival of the French Revolution, attacked by the combined strength of the old regime in the rest of Europe, those in charge of France's future had to rely on national feeling, hitherto latent among the people but given new vigour by revolutionary enthusiasm and external threats. From then onwards the conflict among states became battles among peoples.

Gradually, too, arose the idea that the sovereignty of states should be exercised over geographically homogeneous territory. Foreign enclaves within more powerful states therefore became prey to annexation.

The desire to organize homogeneous states led 19th-century Europe to assert the nationality principle, that is 'the right of self-determination'. On this principle, the Spaniards fought against the rule of Napoleon, the German and Italian nations were formed, and the Ottoman and Austro-Hungarian Empires broke up. In the 20th century the same principle led to the disappearance of the great European colonial empires. But Adolf Hitler carried it to excess and criminality, systematically enslaving, deporting, interning and exterminating people he judged to be inferior to the supposed 'Aryan purity' of the Germans – the tragic illusion of a 'homogeneous' people.

A *new Europe*?

The Second World War, born of nationalist madness, left Europe destroyed, divided and dominated by two giant powers, the United States and the Soviet Union.

In the West, the revival of Europe was due to three essential political choices: democracy, guaranteed by free elections; a market economy, assisted from 1947 to the 1960s by American aid; and reconciliation among Europeans, in particular between the French and the Germans. It was on these bases that Benelux was formed in 1946, the EEC in 1951 and 1957 by the European Community, whose growth and enlargement has not been without crises and tensions.

In the East, the USSR saw itself as the model on which all the countries liberated by the Red Army should align themselves. Their integration was achieved under Soviet control through the intermediary of their national Communist parties, dependent on Moscow. Democratic uprisings were crushed in East Berlin (1953), Hungary (1956), Czechoslovakia (1968) and Poland (1956, 1970, 1981). In the face of economic and social difficulties, the new Secretary-General of the Soviet Communist Party, Mikhail Gorbachev, opted in 1985 for liberalization. The countries of Eastern Europe won their freedom, within the frontiers established when the continent was divided in 1945. When Communism collapsed in the Soviet Union itself, in the summer of 1991, did it not call into question the whole balance of affairs in Europe? Did Western Europe not seem like an over-protected bastion of peace and prosperity?

Such unanswered questions about Europe's identity and history are the subject of this book. It will try to provide some answers. Not all questions have answers: history is also a debate. New questions will arise; and it is as much on the future as on the past that the present study of Europe's history hopes to stimulate reflection.

③ PRAGUE, 21 NOVEMBER 1989
In front of the national museum and the statue of their patron saint Wenceslas, Czechoslovaks contemplate their candle-lit national flag. Their revolution began on 17 November; on the 20th the leadership of the Communist Party resigned. The writer Vaclav Havel, a lifetime opponent of the totalitarian regime and symbol of the democratic ideal, was soon elected president of the new republic. The 'other Europe' was changing course.

④ THE SPECTRE OF NATIONALISM
Cartoon by Auth in *The Philadelphia Enquirer*, February 1991
Mikhail Gorbachev, having dug the grave of Soviet totalitarianism, is at once attacked by the resurgent ghost of nationalism.

FROM THE TUNDRA TO THE TEMPLE

BC	
1,500,000	The first men in Europe (?)
150,000	Neanderthal Man
35,000	Cro-Magnon Man: revolution in the use of tools, cave paintings
30,000	Knossos at its height
12,000	Melting of glaciers in Northern Europe
4000	The first farmers: the building of megaliths
2000	Minoan Crete: the Bronze Age
1250	Heyday of Mycenean cities
1100	Destruction of Troy; beginning of the Iron Age
1050	Beginning of Dorian migration
776	First Olympic Games
800–300	Etruscans in Italy; Celts in central Europe
750–600	Greek colonization in the Mediterranean
700	Lydians create coinage
594	Solon's reforms in Athens
560–27	Pisistratus, Tyrant of Athens
490–80	Persian Wars: Marathon, Salamis
495–29	Pericles
431–04	Peloponnesian War
338	Philip of Macedon ruler of Greece
356–23	Alexander the Great
146	Greece becomes a Roman province

❶ THE WILLENDORF VENUS
Natural History Museum, Vienna, Austria
The Willendorf Venus, approximately 25 cm tall, dates from 25,000 BC. It may be evidence of a matriarchal society, but it is more likely a fertility goddess and patroness of the hunt. Many of these statuettes have been found between the Atlantic and the Urals, the vast hunting-ground of the first Europeans.

❷ THE VENUS OF MILO
Height: 1.98 meters. Louvre Museum, Paris
The 'Venus' of Milo was found in 1820 on the island of Milos. It is in fact a marble statue of Aphrodite, the Greek goddess of Beauty and Love, amalgamated with the Romans' own goddess of Fecundity, Venus. Though of uncertain date, it signals the onset of Hellenistic Baroque.

CHAPTER *I*

FROM THE TUNDRA TO THE TEMPLE

PREHISTORY TO THE 4TH CENTURY BC

This chapter covers several hundred thousand years in the history of Europe, from the first primitive caves to the highly developed communities of the ancient Greek city-states in the centuries before the birth of Christ. This long transition was from a brute state of nature to a mature culture – from the tundra to the temple.

For several thousand years our European ancestors lived in caves, constantly at war with wild beasts and án environment resembling the cold dry expanse of present-day Siberia. They were hunters and nomads, moving from place to place in a Europe where vast stretches of land were for a long time covered in ice.

The final melting of the glaciers, which in northern Europe took place around 12,000 BC, made possible a quite different civilization. During the millennia that followed farmers replaced the hunter-gatherers of the Ice Ages. Trade among the various parts of Europe gradually developed common characteristics, as in the case of the Celtic culture, which spread from the Black Sea to the Atlantic.

The shores of the Mediterranean offered ideal conditions for intensive trade and fostered links with the ancient cultural centres of the East. Greece was the first country in Europe to develop a mature culture of its own. Temples and theatres were built there; schools were founded; assemblies were elected by the people in order to make laws. Later European democracies took the city (the *polis*) as their model.

Greece and its flourishing communities aroused the avarice of oriental despots; but the Greeks fought off the first attack on Europe at the beginning of the 5th century BC. Their civilization was then at its height.

❸ TUNDRA LANDSCAPE
A vast cold space, scoured by the wind, the tundra and its meagre vegetation could support only nomadic peoples moving on in search of more hospitable land.

❹ A TEMPLE IN ATHENS
Although known as the Theseion, this is the Temple of Hephaistos, God of Fire and Metal. The first great monument built after the Persian Wars, in 450 BC, it is a fine example of Doric architecture.

1 The First People in Europe

❶ THE GREAT GLACIATION

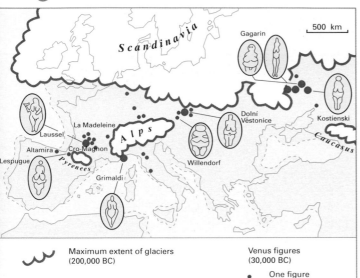

∿∿ Maximum extent of glaciers (200,000 BC)	Venus figures (30,000 BC)
	• One figure
--- Approximate coastline	⬤ Several figures

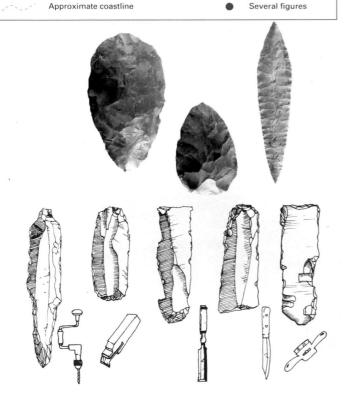

❷ BIFACIAL STONE TOOLS

The oldest known tool is the flattish pebble chopper, made by chipping a flint stone. This was virtually a prolongation of the hand. It was being used in Africa some 1.4 million years ago. In Europe, in about 40,000 BC, it was replaced by 'improved' flake tools, as shown in the illustration comparing them with their present-day counterparts.

The Neanderthals

Human beings have certainly lived in Europe for millions of years; but our knowledge of those distant times remains uncertain. In the 1980s excavation in France and Italy uncovered stone tools (axes), which make it likely that Europe had been inhabited from very early times. It is possible that these first tribes came from Africa, where archaeologists have found traces of people who lived some three-and-a-half million years ago.

Until about 12,000 BC northern Europe and much of central Europe were covered by glaciers, although not continuously. Three times, in the intervals between the glaciations, intervals lasting tens of thousands of years, the atmosphere became warmer and the ice melted. Even then, however, the climate remained harsh and the land barren, as in the Siberian tundra. It was inhabited by the cave bear, the mammoth, the woolly rhinoceros, the reindeer and the wild horse. When the glaciers retreated northwards, the animals followed them and so did the first Europeans.

Remains of skeletons from the third inter-glacial period (100,000 to 150,000 years long) show that the people who lived in Europe before the last glaciation had apelike features, with receding foreheads, large orbital arches, powerful jaws and a strong, hardy constitution. The name given to this early ancestor is Neanderthal, derived from the place where the most important discoveries were made. These people were human: they were able to walk upright and hence to use their hands freely to make and use tools. The manufacture and use of tools presuppose a capacity for observation and abstract thought. They were able to communicate with each other and they were familiar with fire.

Archaeologists have also discovered dwelling-places, which show that Neanderthal people lived in small tribes and helped each other. They hunted large wild animals, which they killed with their sharp stone weapons. To shelter from the cold and from bad weather they took refuge in deep caves. There, perhaps, they invented the first legends about the dangerous forces of nature. In their primitive graves, they carefully laid their dead in positions of rest, surrounded by flint offerings. This funeral custom reveals that the people of the Ice Ages looked death in the face and were concerned with more than just the search for food and shelter.

The Cro-Magnons

During the last ice age, some 40,000 years ago, Neanderthals seems to have disappeared, perhaps overcome by natural forces, perhaps driven out by a new type of human being which appeared at the end of this period. It is also possible that the appearance and habits of Neanderthals may have changed – a slow cultural evolution that may have been helped by the arrival of a new race.

However that may be, archaeologists and ethnologists can identify at this time a type of human being the size and shape of whose skull and the bone-structure of whose body resemble those of people today. *Homo sapiens sapiens*, the intelligent human being, had appeared in Europe.

Most prehistoric dwelling-places have been discovered in northern Spain, in France and in Germany. There, the peoples concerned were at some distance from the glaciers that covered northern Europe; they had easy access to caves; and the forests and rivers abounded in animals and fish. The most interesting and revealing excavations have been in the caves of Altamira in northern Spain and in the Cro-Magnon caves of southern France. That is why the Ice-Age people of this period in Europe's history are often collectively known as the Cro-Magnons.

These dwelling-places have yielded not only tools, bones and skeletal remains, but also a number of astonishingly skilful paintings on the walls of the caves. This cave art was not purely decorative in aim and was not merely a pastime: it almost certainly had religious or magic significance. At the end of the Ice Ages, hunting became more and more organized and systematic; and it may be that before the chase began the hunters met in front of the paintings of animals for some kind of magic or religious ceremony. A successful hunt may also have been followed by a feast in the same place, attended by all the tribe.

While cave art was at its height in this ice age, 35,000 years ago, there was at the same time a revolution in the manufacture and use of tools. Traditional stone tools were improved and new tools were invented. This was accompanied by greater security in living conditions, greater cooperation within the tribes and perhaps also between tribes.

The hunting peoples no longer lived from hand to mouth as perpetual nomads. They began to form stable communities, better organized. These beginnings of more halcyon days in the Ice Ages marked the emergence of a Europe in some respects more 'modern'.

③ THE PROPELLANT
This 15,000-year-old propellant was found at Bruniquel in the Tarn-et-Garonne Département of France. Carved from reindeer horn and artistically decorated with a leaping horse, this implement proves that Cro-Magnons did not work only in stone and bone.

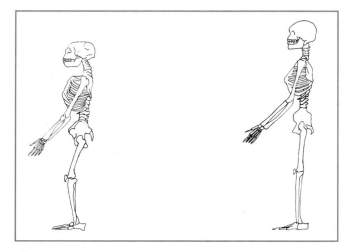

④ OUR ANCESTORS
Skeletons of a Neanderthal (left) and a Cro-Magnon (right). The latter was taller and had a bigger brain.

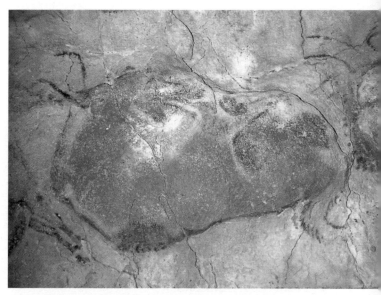

⑤ CAVE PAINTINGS AT ALTAMIRA, SPAIN
On the walls of their caves the people of this period painted life-sized animals, well observed but distorted by stylization, with small heads, big bellies and short legs, and their horns and hoofs seen from an oblique angle. The illustration is from the Magdalenian period (15,000 BC), the time of cave paintings like this at Altamira.

Europe's First Farmers

❶ THE LIFE OF THE VILLAGE
Illustration by P. Joubert from *La Vie privée des Hommes aux temps préhistoriques*, Hachette, 1990
Forest-dwellers captured young wild boars, which were reared in pens with domestic pigs. The dog, tamed from about 17,000 BC, guarded the flock and protected the village from wolves.

❷ THE FIRST FARMERS
Illustration by P. Joubert (see above)
To plant wheat, large planks were dragged on to the threshing-floor. These tribula were studded with flint chips which split the husk and freed the grain. In the illustration a man is repairing the tribulum by hammering in a flint chip.

Agrarian civilization

Europe witnessed changes still more profound than the small technological revolution brought about by the Stone-Age hunters at the end of the Ice Ages. When the glaciers melted and freed northern Europe, from 10,000 BC onwards, the first agrarian communities were developing in the Middle East; and from there, during the millennia that followed, this farming civilization spread through Europe. It reached Scandinavia and the British Isles in the fourth millennium BC.

The independent but precarious existence of the Stone-Age hunter-gatherers was gradually replaced by a way of life that was both less hazardous and less free. Such was agrarian society. Not until the Industrial Revolution of the 19th century or the technological society of the atomic age after 1945 was there again so profound a mutation in the history of Europe.

Historians used to believe that this agrarian revolution had been accepted by people simply because it brought them such great intrinsic advantages. But in the light of present debate among experts, scholars have concluded more and more that the hunter-gatherers were much closer to nature than were the agrarian communities. They have also noted the hard and constant labour involved in cultivating the land and raising cattle, by contrast with the life of the hunter-gatherers. They have therefore wondered what it was that induced the hunters to become farmers.

One answer, undoubtedly, was the rise in population that was an indirect result of the improvement of weaponry at the end of the Stone Age. As the population grew, the stock of game was depleted; and human inventiveness was now such that it shaped the new structure of society. Free nomadic hunters were replaced by settled farmers and stockbreeders.

This explanation challenges the theories that have been current since the 1960s, according to which agriculture was brought to Europe by tribes from the East who gradually supplanted or interbred with the hunting tribes. If that was not what happened, agriculture either developed in Europe under Eastern influence or it was an autonomous evolution without any input from outside. Alternatively, all these elements may have had a combined effect.

From chipped to polished stone

Whatever the reason for the agrarian revolution in the fifth and fourth millennia BC, one precondition for it was the change of climate that had taken place several millennia earlier with the melting of the glaciers in northern Europe. From that time onwards farmers began to till the soil and sow seeds which probably came from Southern Europe. For this they needed more effective axes than those used by the Stone-Age hunters.

The clear improvement in tool-making that accompanied the arrival of agrarian civilization was the polishing of stone axes. With these the farmers could clear large tracts of forest and turn them into fields. The innovation was so important that it is seen as one factor in the transition from the palaeolithic period to the neolithic, or from chipped to polished stone. As soon as one unearths a polished flint one can be sure that it comes from a neolithic agricultural site.

A more clement climate, and the clearing of the forest with new tools, enabled the inhabitants of Europe to leave their caves and settle in the plains, where farmers began to build real houses in fixed sites, which became Europe's first villages. Nomadic life gave way to the first organized settled societies; and, whereas the average life expectancy for a hunter-gatherer, as shown by skeletal remains, was between 20 and 30 years, that for a farmer was considerably longer.

Rather than depending wholly on the hazards of nature, people now began to master it and, within limits, adapt it to their own ends. They cut down trees and burned them, using the ashes as fertilizer; they tilled the soil with a new implement, the swing-plough, a stave pulled by draught animals; they reaped grain with a sickle, threshed it with a flail and stored it for later use. They improved pottery-making techniques to produce large vases with thin walls. They also used the wheel and the waggon; and they raised stock. The palaeolithic hunters had tracked and killed wild animals: neolithic farmers captured them and tamed them. Cattle became a living store.

Storage, indeed, made agrarian society more independent of nature and this led to labour-saving and specialization. Farmers could exchange their surpluses for the products of other craftsmen, such as stone-cutters, potters and weavers.

Specialization and the division of labour, together with increased production and storage, gradually resulted in a difference between the rich and the poor. Those who owned land, cattle, a loom or a potter's wheel had greater economic scope and more influence than those who had only their own ability to offer. Gradually, a class society began to emerge, with the appearance of a

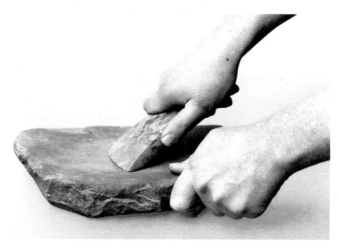

❸CUTTING A STONE AXE
The art lay in the cutting process, handed down from father to son. It needed flint of very high quality and endless practice to chip and polish the stone so that, as legend had it, the sun was reflected at every angle in it.

❹THE SWING-PLOUGH
Wall engraving at Bohuslan, Sweden
Once established in the plains, our ancestors became farmers. The swing-plough, which had no wheels, was carved from bone or reindeer horn. Fixed to a long wooden handle, it was hauled by reindeer or domesticated oxen.

❺CORDED POTTERY
National Museum, Copenhagen
Pottery replaced stone vessels. Made by hand, it suffered only from accidents. It could be used to cook food, unlike leather containers. A simple rope was often used to impress decoration on the wet clay.

1 TRANSPORTING A MEGALITH
This re-enactment shows how these massive stones were manoeuvred and that it was perfectly possible 4000 years ago. In this case a menhir of 4 metres is being dragged on wooden rollers, with ropes and human muscle-power as in pre-historic times.

2 NEW GRANGE TUMULUS, IRELAND
The upper chamber contains the funeral chamber and the corridor leading to it, which is 70 metres across and 14 metres in height. Originally, it was surrounded by 35 carved standing stones, some of which can be seen in the foreground.

3 PLAN OF NEW GRANGE
The chamber has an internal height of 6.5 metres and the access corridor is 18 metres long.

concept such as the right of ownership; little by little, some families came to possess more land and greater means of production than others. This was a novelty. In the world of hunter-gatherers, all the members of the clan worked as a team of equals.

The great Stone-Age tombs and the megaliths

These changes in the conditions of production left more time free, which probably encouraged people to elaborate more coherent views of life and death, of human destiny and the influence of the gods. As time went on, something like a clergy may have emerged.

The monumental tombs of this agrarian society bear more obvious witness to it than the ephemeral graves of the hunter-gatherers. By studying their contents, ethnologists can form some idea of the religious customs that inspired them.

One practice that was common to all these farming civilizations of the Stone Age in most of Western Europe was the transport and erection of huge blocks of stone. These took the form of menhirs (single pillars) and of dolmens or cromlechs (groups of stones in slabs or circles), which sheltered the dead and acted as temples or holy places for the tribe. The whole tribe must have joined in the construction of these imposing tombs. They remain as a visible mark of its social and religious cohesion, as well as of its limits.

Most of the dolmens consist of four or so blocks of stone on top of one another, bearing in their turn one or more flat stones that may weigh more than 20 tons.

In places, the burial chambers were surrounded by a circle of standing stones that protect the sacred site. When covered by a mound, these chambers are known as *tumuli*. Denmark alone has more than 3000 megalithic tombs; France has 5000 chambers with dolmens; the British Isles have 2000. For several generations the chambers were used as family sepulchres. In some of the tumulus tombs the passages and funeral chambers may be up to 10 metres long: they are reached by an even longer covered walk.

The most impressive constructions of the Stone Age consist of these megalithic monuments in England, Ireland, France and Malta: the word 'megalith', from the ancient Greek *megas* and *lithos*, means 'great stone'. Although these monuments vary from one country to another, they have so many characteristics in common that experts see them as a possible link in a single

European civilization covering the coastal regions of Western Europe. At one time it was thought that this megalithic tradition could be traced back to ancient oriental cultures and that it was inspired by the pyramids of Egypt. The theory was that it had been transmitted by migration along west European coasts.

According to more recent speculation, the tradition was spread not by migration but by frequent contacts between the different regions of Western Europe, from which inland areas were remote. In this view, it was not people but ideas, technical knowledge and religious concepts that travelled from place to place, creating as early as the Stone Age a common European civilization.

④ MEGALITHIC SITES IN WESTERN EUROPE

⑤ STONEHENGE, ENGLAND

Both a holy place and an observatory, Stonehenge (north of Salisbury, Wiltshire) is the largest known megalithic site. A nucleus of 100 stones, 42 of them standing, forms two horseshoes, ending in an altar stone. The whole is oriented towards the point where the sun rises at the summer solstice on 21 June. Carbon 14 dating shows that the site was built c. 1850 BC.

3 The Age of Metal and Mediterranean Trade

① TRADE IN THE MEDITERRANEAN
(2000–1450 BC)

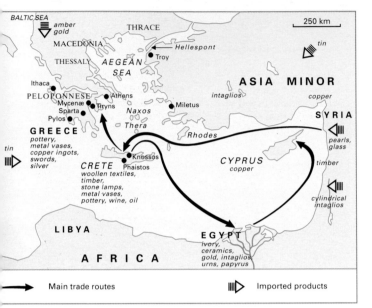

Main trade routes →   Imported products ▷

② FRESCO OF THERA (SANTORINI)
Wall painting in a house on Thera, 1500 BC. Its height is 40 cm

Thera is built on the side of a cliff, on several levels, and can be reached by a winding path from the sea. The earth is red, because the town is on the inner wall of a volcano which exploded in 1500 BC. Lying as it did on the sea route from Syria and Egypt, it was sought after for its wine, its pumice-stone and its clay.

The Bronze Age in Europe

During the second millennium BC a new revolutionary technique reached Europe: metalworking.

The making of bronze had developed in the East in the third millennium BC. Most regions of Europe depended on imports for tin or copper or both and, since bronze was an alloy of these two metals, the Bronze Age produced a great increase in trade. The Mediterranean became the new centre of economic activity.

The meeting-place of the Mediterranean trade routes was Crete, where the Palace of Knossos was the centre of a carefully organized bureaucratic society led by a powerful chieftain. This now became the first genuine European state. In some respects, Crete was a Greek bridgehead for the Middle East and it established Europe's first contacts with the civilizations of Mesopotamia and Egypt.

The Cretans went to Cyprus to obtain copper, which they mixed with tin from Spain or Britain. From Egypt came wheat, gold, ivory and papyrus, and with them the powerful influence that a more ancient and mature culture always exerts on a younger. Crete's art, its cult of animals and its religion were all influenced by Egypt. The Cretans adopted a pictorial, hieroglyphic writing of the Egyptian type: it evolved towards a syllabic system known as 'Linear A', quite unlike Greek. It is possible that a Norwegian, Kjell Aartun, has recently deciphered it, but his discovery has yet to be confirmed. If he has, it will be possible to read the numerous clay tablets found on Crete, giving a better idea of life there at the time, which now is known only through archaeological finds.

Crete was an island rich in wine and olives, and it produced wool and woven stuffs. Its artisans and artists played an important role, as witness the large number of vases, frescoes, statuettes and jewels that have been found there.

The intense economic and cultural activity on the island between about 2000 and 1450 BC is known as the Minoan civilization, after King Minos, mentioned in numerous legends by the Greeks. Some of these stories may be fanciful; but excavation has shown that they have a basis of truth. One such is the legend of Europa and the Bull; another is that of the Minotaur in the Labyrinth, which sought to devour the brave Prince Theseus. He was finally saved by the Princess Ariadne.

The first writing in Europe

Knossos was destroyed in about 1450 BC. The reasons for its fate remain uncertain. One theory suggests that it was the result of a natural catastrophe: the eruption of the Thera volcano to the north of Crete. That the volcano erupted is agreed by experts: it caused a tidal wave and covered Crete with ashes. Another theory, however, argues that Knossos was crushed by invaders from mainland Greece.

This theory may find some support in the fact that, during the Minoan period, a powerful and prosperous Greek civilization developed in the Peloponnese, with fortified cities like Pylos on the west coast, Tiryns and above all Mycenae. The ramparts of these towns were built with enormous blocks of stone, which the Greek poet Homer, some centuries later, called 'Cyclopean': only the Cyclops or giants, he thought, could have moved blocks that weighed up to 15 tons. Excavation undertaken in the 19th century by the German archaeologist Heinrich Schliemann confirmed Homer's description.

These powerful and prosperous cities were inhabited by warlike people headed by strong leaders and with a dominant caste that ruled over a peasant population living outside the walls and tilling the soil for its masters. Such are the kings described by Homer when recounting the Trojan War in the *Iliad*.

Mycenaean art, although inspired by the organic, sinuous lines of Minoan art, developed in its warrior society towards more and more rigid, schematic and monotonous forms.

The Greeks also adopted Minoan writing, the so-called 'Linear A', which they developed into 'Linear B', based on the Greek tongue and deciphered in 1952 by the British scholar Michael Ventris. The introduction of writing was crucial for both the society and the historian. It marks the transition, in fact, from 'Prehistory' to 'History'.

Starting from the Peloponnese, the early Greeks plied the sea. They traded with Crete, Cyprus and Egypt. The Trojan War was one episode in their efforts to reach the Black Sea. They were also in contact with the peoples living on the banks of the Danube, the Oder and the Elbe, and even as far as Scandinavia. At Mycenae and Pylos, archaeologists have found as many as 1500 pieces of amber from the Baltic – a proof of how far Greek traders had gone.

The flourishing Bronze Age civilization of Mycenae, between 1600 and 1100 BC, influenced the tribes of central Europe. The wealth of its ruling class was clear from the funerary offerings found in the tombs, many of them imported from other Mediterranean regions.

③ MYCENAEAN WRITING-TABLETS
Height: 15 cm. Heraklion Museum
Linear A, from 1550 BC, may represent a dialect close to Hittite. It spread in the Greek islands. With the arrival of the Achaean Greeks in Crete, it was replaced by Linear B (above, right), which dates from 1450 BC and was a transcription of archaic Greek.

④ MINOAN STELE
Height: 1.35 cm. National Museum, Athens
A funerary stela for a warrior of the Minoan period (1500 BC). At that time a warrior owning a chariot belonged to a veritable order of 'knights'.

⑤ THE LIONS OF MYCENAE
(1600–1200 BC)
It was Heinrich Schliemann who excavated the acropolis of Mycenae, in 1874. The Lion Gate is surrounded by gigantic walls that Herodotus and Euripides thought had been built by the Cyclops. They protected a real treasure: nearly 20,000 objects of copper, bronze and above all gold, in five separate tombs.

① THE 'WARRIORS' MIXING-BOWL
National Archaeological Museum, Athens
This vase represents the Mycenaean art of the 13th century BC. It is made from very fine clay and was produced on a potter's wheel. After the first bake the potter traced on it a series of foot-soldiers, demonstrating a new form of military strategy.

② GEOMETRIC AMPHORA
National Archaeological Museum, Athens
An amphora with geometrical decoration which was the product of national art not as yet inspired by Eastern influence. The geometrical drawings are traced with great care. The lying-in-state shown between the handles is stylized and primitive. This amphora comes from the Kerameikos cemetery outside the gates of ancient Athens.

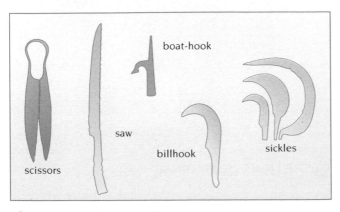

③ CELTIC IRON TOOLS
Tools like these were used everywhere in the Hallstatt civilization, after 800 BC. Compare them with those shown on page 32.

The Iron Age and the Greek 'Middle Ages': 1100–750 BC

In the 12th century BC the rich Mycenaean Bronze-Age civilization suffered a fatal blow. Archaeologists have concluded that Mycenae, Tiryns and other cities were destroyed; from then onwards the objects found there are rare and insignificant. The population shrank: there remain few tombs and none of the monumental funeral chambers filled with offerings that marked the Mycenaean age. In times of poverty, cremation prevailed. The production of gold and bronze jewels, of pottery and domestic objects, practically ceased; so did trade. Large-scale commerce was replaced by self-sufficiency and barter.

Economic and political decadence made the art of writing superfluous. Linear script disappeared and illiteracy became general again for a time. The decoration on vases from this period was poor and simple, mainly abstract and geometrical. Later, stylized figures reappeared, but they were very different from the luxuriant style of Crete and the grandiose style of Mycenae.

The period between 1100 and about 750 BC is often called the Greek 'Middle Ages', by analogy with medieval Europe.

The works of art from this period belong to what is called the 'geometric style'. It was during this austere time that the use of iron spread through Europe and the splendour of the Bronze-Age civilization gave way to the bleakness of the Iron Age.

At the same time people emigrated from mainland Greece to the Aegean islands and the western coast of Asia Minor, Ionia, which became an important part of the Greek world.

In the past historians used to explain the destruction of Mycenaean civilization and the emigration to Asia Minor in terms of what they called 'the migration of the Dorians'. The Dorians were the last of the Greek tribes that invaded the peninsula at the end of the second millennium BC; they were a warrior people equipped with horses, fighting chariots and iron weapons. They destroyed Mycenae and disrupted trade routes, driving out the creative and artistic Ionian tribes. But for a long time they were incapable of building a new civilization. At the same time Troy was destroyed by the Achaeans.

The most recent archaeological discoveries seem to support a rival theory: that a period of drought and bad harvests led to famine. It may well be that this, rather than the migration of the Dorians, was the main reason for the crisis — together with internal strife among the cities of the Peloponnese and the revolt of their peoples against the kings.

A European civilization as early as the first millennium BC

Whether or not there was a Dorian invasion, experts agree that the decline of the Mycenaean cities ushered in a gloomy period, a 'Middle Ages' that lasted for centuries before the renaissance that produced classical Greek culture, which in turn, via the Roman Empire, became the basis of European civilization.

It was in Greece that new cultural influences appeared, giving to that country its fundamental role in the history of Europe.

The rest of Europe followed much the same evolution, but two centuries later. Throughout central Europe, in Spain, in the British Isles and in northern Europe, weapons made of bronze, then iron, tools, pottery, decoration, funeral customs and dwelling-places all had common features, similar to those that had preceded them in Greece. Such cultural similarities imply that there was much communication among different peoples. We cannot assume that there was an ethnic or political link, but there was a common way of life.

From the Danube to the Atlantic, Europe was made up of ill-organized Celtic tribes led by warrior chieftains. They had numerous mutual contacts, which made it possible for goods and ideas to be exchanged, but which also led to conflicts, as is shown by the great variety of weapons that have been unearthed.

Already in the 19th century archaeologists had been struck by these signs of European unity in the first millennium BC. The period, and the whole region, have been given the name of the 'Hallstatt civilization', after the site in the Tyrol where more than 20,000 objects have been found, in a very large number of tombs.

The funeral offerings, and the richly decorated tombs, show that this was a prosperous civilization, led by a warrior caste whose symbols of authority included finely wrought weapons, votive cups in hammered bronze, jewels and decorated vases – showing that they were in contact with Greece.

In the first millennium BC the practice of cremation spread beyond Greece, as witness the many urns found throughout most of Europe.

The use of iron also spread from Asia Minor through Greece to reach Europe. The Celts, identified for the first time in the 6th century BC in the upper valley of the Danube, developed from 500 BC onwards a virtually uniform style of iron weapons and tools. Metallurgical technique promoted common practices and a similar way of life throughout central Europe.

④ THE HALLSTATT CULTURE
(800–400 BC)

Area covered by the Hallstatt Culture

⑤ A RITUAL CHARIOT
Height: 49 cm. Landesmuseum Joanneum, Graz, Austria
Small threatening figures on a ritual chariot made of iron, found in the necropolis of Hallstatt in the Austrian Alps. This site, unearthed in 1824, was an important mining centre and a trading-post for commerce between central Europe and the Mediterranean.

4 Greek Expansion in the Mediterranean

① LOADING GOODS ON TO A SHIP

Bibliothèque Nationale, Paris: Cabinet des Médailles, c.560 BC

This picture was copied on to a fabric or rug, then painted on a cup of 29 cm diameter. The freight, suspended in a net, certainly came from the colony of Cyrene, in Africa. The king, who is supervising the loading, sits in the shelter of a tent. The characters in the picture are identified by name, written in archaic Greek letters which are those of the Corinthian alphabet.

② Homer's *Odyssey*: Ulysses and the Invocation to the Muse

The hero of the tale which I beg the Muse to help me tell is that resourceful man who roamed the wide world after he had sacked the holy citadel of Troy. He saw the cities of many peoples and he learnt their ways. He suffered many hardships on the high seas in his struggles to preserve his life and bring his comrades home. But he failed to save those comrades, in spite of all his efforts. It was their own sin that brought them to their doom, for in their folly they devoured the oxen of Hyperion the Sun and the god saw to it that they should never return. This is the tale I pray the divine Muse to unfold to us. Begin it, goddess, at whatever point you will.

All the survivors of the war had reached their homes by now and so put the perils of battle and the sea behind them. Odysseus alone was prevented from returning to the home and wife he longed for by that powerful goddess, the Nymph Calypso, who wished him to marry her and kept him in her vaulted cave.

Homer, *The Odyssey*, I, 1–21, translated by E. V. Rieu

Activity in the Mediterranean after 750 BC

The Greek 'Middle Ages' ended in the 8th century BC. In the 400 years that followed Greece grew into an economic power and a cultural center: it established political institutions and cultural traditions that influenced all of Europe.

There is reason to believe that the population grew very rapidly after centuries of poverty. Archaeologists have discovered a larger number of 8th-century tombs; they have noted the appearance of new cities in Attica and have found more wells in the *Agora* of Athens. Similar signs of progress can be found in other parts of Greece. Similarly, Greek potteries spread around the coast of the Mediterranean. The growth in the population was so great that it could not be absorbed by Greece alone.

Written sources confirm that during the centuries that followed there was much emigration to other parts, where the Greeks founded new cities. They founded their first colonies in eastern Sicily, southern Italy and north Africa. In these regions the Greeks found themselves competing with the Etruscans and the Phoenicians. The Phoenicians were sailors and traders who, from the coast of present-day Lebanon, had formed a trading network throughout the Mediterranean, including the Iberian Peninsula, where they had founded Cadiz. Carthage was their most important base; and it was on their account that the Greeks were unable to have greater influence in the western Mediterranean countries, although they founded the colony of Massalia in the south of France and made some progress up the Rhône Valley.

The second stage of the Greek advance was towards the Black Sea. Byzantium became an important trading centre and controlled the Bosporus. The Greeks also established colonies in Macedonia and Thrace.

The first of them were agricultural colonies, whose purpose was to feed the capital city. Many then became trading colonies, host to a body of craftsmen able to exchange their products with the interior and with the cities of Greece. The colonists built new cities on the model of those they came from. The colonies were independent and autonomous – so much so that the words 'colony' and 'colonist' are not really appropriate if they are taken to mean what they did in Europe's imperialist period.

The reasons for colonization

The basic reason why people emigrated from their cities was a general crisis due mainly to the aforementioned growth of the population. There was a lack of arable land, because the best of it was in the hands of the nobles, while many 'free' men were obliged to work as agricultural labourers on the great estates. The growth of the population made the shortage of land acute, triggering off an economic crisis and social upheavals, which caused political tension between the landowning nobility and the rest of the population.

As Aristotle wrote in *The Constitution of Athens*, there were long periods of internecine strife between the nobility and the people, because the poor and their families were in a state of servitude and had no political rights.

These tensions in Greek society drove a large part of the population to quit the cities and establish communities overseas. But it should be realized that this pressure stirred more than a passive response: it was natural for this adventurous sea-going people to throw itself into adventures like those of the hero Ulysses in Homer's

---

❸ Aristotle: *The Constitution of Athens*

In his Politics, Aristotle (384–22 BC) analyzed some 150 known constitutions. This extract from The Constitution of Athens *is the beginning of the historical section of the work, probably written in 330 BC.*

After the abortive attempt by Kylon[1] to establish a tyranny, the nobles[2] and the people were for a long time at odds. In all respects, in fact, the political regime was an oligarchy;[3] and in particular the poor, their women and their children were the slaves of the rich. They were called 'clients' or 'sextarians', because they received only a sixth of the harvest in return for working on the lands of the rich. Land in general was in a small number of hands; and, if the peasants failed to pay their rent, they and their children could be taken into slavery, since until Solon, the first leader of the Popular Party, all loans were secured on the person of the debtor.

1. In 630 BC the Athenian noble Kylon tried to proclaim himself Tyrant of Athens, but his attempt failed.
2. The nobles, administrators of the state, were the largest landowners.
3. Oligarchy: a political regime under which the state is ruled by a small number of people (*oligoi* in Greek).

Aristotle, *The Constitution of Athens*, II

---

❹ GREEK AND PHOENICIAN COLONIZATION IN THE MEDITERRANEAN

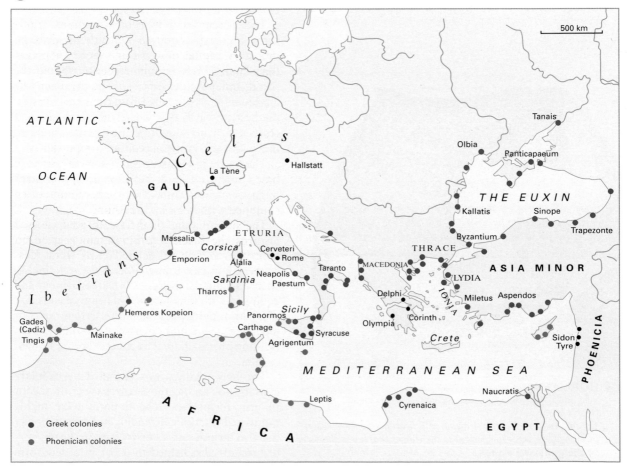

- ● Greek colonies
- ● Phoenician colonies

❶ GOLD AND SILVER COINS
National Museum, Copenhagen
The first coins date from c. 6th century BC. Here: a Lydian gold coin with lions and bulls on the reverse; a silver coin from Aegina with a tortoise; an Athenian silver coin with Athena and an owl.

❷ HOPLITES
Villa Giulia, Rome. 660 BC: made in Corinth, found in Etruria.
Height: 26 cm
The growing use of a new strategy, with heavily armed footsoldiers, called hoplites, was so important to the citizens that it was illustrated on a large number of vases.

stories. The *Odyssey* reflects the conditions of life in the period of colonization and provides a portrait of the first 'European' man – inquisitive, enterprising, determined and persistent, pushing back the frontiers of the unknown and able to improvise solutions in the face of any challenge.

The large-scale trade undertaken by the Greeks brought them into contact with other Mediterranean peoples: Phoenicians, Egyptians, Etruscans, Italians and Gauls from north-west Europe. The Mediterranean became the first great common market.

The first currency and the great expansion

During the colonial period an 'international' division of labour began: each region specialized in what it produced best. A hitherto closed economy began to be more open.

In the past archaic and restricted barter had hindered trade. In about 700 BC a monetary system appeared for the first time in the history of the world. It was in Lydia (Asia Minor) that the first coins began to circulate; but it was the Greek cities of Ionia that used currency beyond their own locality and made it a medium of international trade. From there the practice spread among all European peoples.

The advent of a monetary economy transformed social conditions in urban societies: monetary capital now became more important than land. This economic evolution shifted the social and political centre of gravity from the landowning aristocracy (from the Greek *aristoi*, the best) towards new classes of merchants and craftsmen, who sought political power more in line with their growing economic importance.

The power of the aristocracy, however, was not based solely on land, but also on the military might of an army with solid bronze armour, often equipped with horses and chariots.

The new middle class tried to protect itself against this mounted army by taking up arms. Shortly after 700 BC painted vases show footsoldiers, hoplites (from the Greek *hoplon*, shield), wearing lighter and less costly leather armour and equipped with long lances and heavy shields. On the field of battle they fought in serried ranks or phalanxes. This more democratic military organization proved more than a match for the nobles' cavalry.

The new infantry was recruited by ordinary conscription among those citizens with the means to arm themselves. The hoplites were highly motivated warriors, defending not only their city but also the interests of their class. So the phalanx of hoplites also helped to usher in a new form of democratic government, that of the *polis* (city-state).

Slavery

At the same time as a new and influential middle class emerged from the process of colonization, the peasantry faced serious difficulties. When the Greek cities began to import grain from overseas, prices at home collapsed and it became difficult to sell locally produced wheat. The nobility reacted to this competition by a change of agriculture, replacing cheap wheat with vines and olives.

This required capital, which the poorer peasants lacked. Not only did vines and olive trees need more attention: they also took a generation to become productive. Anyone who chose not to emigrate had therefore either to borrow, mortgaging his land to the owners of large estates, or to give it up and become a share-cropper. Many were unable to honour their obligations and by reason of their debts became slaves, automatically excluded from the community of the *polis*.

The peasants, together with the new middle class, sought to change the system of government. Town-dwellers wanted to share in political power; country-dwellers wanted fair and tolerable living conditions. The result, in many towns, was a series of violent clashes. Sometimes the losers left to found colonies elsewhere.

The outcome of these economic and political changes was a new category of people: immigrant slaves. Increased production created the demand; the overseas colonies met it. As well as domestic slaves, there were now craftsmen slaves and industrial slaves, most of whom worked in the Attic silver mines. They were not usually recruited from among the town-dwellers, but from among barbarians and enemies from far-off countries. Altogether, these slaves made up between a quarter and a half of the population in the larger towns.

As social tensions grew during the colonial period, the aristocracy had to admit that it could not retain its political and economic privileges without risking endless civil war. In a number of cities one noble became a dictator, called by the Greeks a Tyrant. Several of these Tyrants were competent leaders who reformed the government, enabling more and more citizens to have a say. This avoided either further civil strife or the dissolution of the state.

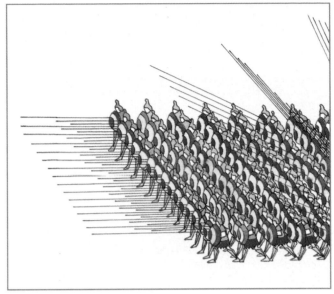

❸ THE PHALANX

'It was magnificent and awe-inspiring to see them march in step to the sound of the clarion, without breaking ranks and with no fear in their hearts.' Plutarch, *Life of Lycurgus*, XIII, 4–5

❹ SLAVERY IN ATHENS

The slave was a worker who depended on his master for food and lodging. He had a civic status, but no civic rights. He could not offer his services as he chose. While he received no wages, he could have rewards and gratuities, and so accumulate savings. But his private life was not his own: his marriage, for example, had no legal validity.

❶ Solon, poet and reformer
(594 BC)

Solon (c.640–c.558 BC) was not only a statesman: he was also a poet. The original texts of his poems have not survived, but they are quoted by Aristotle in particular.

I have given enough power to the people, without curbing or increasing their rights. I have ensured that those who had power, and imposed their will by means of their wealth, have suffered no indignity. I have remained upright, covering both parties with my solid shield, and I have let neither succeed unjustly.

Then, once more demonstrating how the people should be treated, he went on:

The people will best follow their leaders if they are neither brutalized nor given too much of their own way. Surfeit leads to excess when a great fortune comes to those with insufficient wisdom.

Aristotle, *The Constitution of Athens*, XII

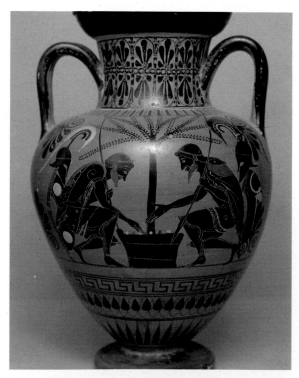

❷ ARCHAIC BLACK-FIGURE VASE
c.450 BC, Villa Giulia, Rome
For some two centuries the art of pottery was characterized by painting in black. The style was archaic: stiff figures, almost always seen in profile, with angular gestures and identical expressionless faces. The subjects were often mythological. Here, Ajax and Achilles are playing with dice. Against the colour of the clay, silhouettes were filled in with black pigment and the details and contours drawn with a stylus, revealing the red.

Written laws and the encouragement of art

In some cities, the aristocracy entrusted the task of reforming the law and removing the worst injustices to a highly respected citizen. Solon of Athens was one. In 594 BC he was elected head of the administration (*Archon*). His laws favoured greater democracy in Athens. The situation of the peasants improved, mortgages on land were cancelled and the harshest laws on indebtedness were modified. All free citizens had the right to vote in the People's Assembly, but only the well-to-do could be elected to positions of authority.

Solon's reforms did not put an end to class rivalry, but they opened the way to popular participation in public affairs. In a number of cities the middle class had the laws codified, whereas in the past they had relied on custom.

Pisistratus was Tyrant of Athens from 560 to 527 BC. He energetically continued Solon's law reforms and redistributed part of the nobles' land among the poorer peasants. But above all he did a great deal for the economic life of the cities, where pottery in particular began to prosper. Under Pisistratus a new firing technique was developed and vases with red figures replaced those with simpler black figures.

The first philosophers in Europe

The great economic and social changes associated with colonization – large-scale trade, agricultural reform, slavery and a monetary system – inevitably produced new artistic ideas and tendencies.

In art as in philosophy a more confident and enquiring approach to humanity emerged. The first philosophers appeared, trying by human reason to find a logical explanation for phenomena that primitive civilizations had attributed to religious powers. They sought to explain the unknown in terms of the known, instead of relating it to another unknown, for example the gods. Nature (*physis* in Greek) was the concrete starting-point for their ideas. They set forth the first fundamental natural laws and thereby founded the scientific principles to which research in Europe has referred ever since.

The first scientists came from Ionia, to the west of Asia Minor, the frontier between young Europe and the old oriental civilizations. This is why they are known as the Ionian nature philosophers. There is no doubt that the rapid social changes they witnessed had a great influence on their thought and their conception of life.

Their thinking must also have been stimulated by the new monetary system, with its abstract signs allotting values to a large number of totally different things.

The ambition they shared was to find a single form of matter from which all the elements derived and which must therefore have contained within it the origin of the universe. They sought for one idea or one principle (in Greek, *archē* or origin) that would provide a universal explanation for everything.

Thales of Miletus, for example, believed that water was the source of everything, whereas Heraclitus showed that it was change. Everything, he pointed out, was born and died. 'Everything passes' (*panta rei* in Greek) was one of his favourite phrases, confirmed by all the great changes that took place in his lifetime. Heraclitus also believed that change was brought about and guided by contradictions – an observation that underlies his remark that 'Combat is the father of all things'. In Greek the word for war is *polemos*, a term which covers other kinds of confrontation, for instance of opinions or of opposite sexes. To illustrate his thought, Heraclitus used the image of the bow and the lyre: tension producing strength in the one and harmony in the other.

❸ Heraclitus

Most of the writings of the Greek philosopher Heraclitus (c.550–c.480 BC) have survived through the intermediary of other authors. His philosophy is based on the notion of flux. The difficulty of grasping a work written in brief fragments has led him to be nicknamed 'Heraclitus the Obscure'. The following quotations from him give some idea of the field of interests covered by the Ionian nature philosophers.

You do not understand how what is disparate is in accord with itself – an artefact in tension[1] like the yoke of a lyre.

Invisible harmony is more powerful than visible harmony.

War is our father and our king. It gives some the appearance of gods and others that of human beings. It makes some people slaves and others free men.

This world, the cosmos,[2] is the same for everyone and has produced neither gods nor men. It has always existed and will exist for ever – a fire eternally smouldering that burns brightly in some places and in others is snuffed out.

Everything can change into fire and fire can change into anything, like goods that can be changed into money and money into goods.

Everything passes.

1. In Greek, 'a harmony pulled backwards' (originally, harmony meant union).
2. In Greek, cosmos meant the world, beauty, harmony.

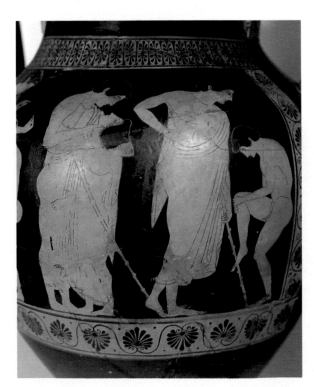

 THE HEYDAY OF CERAMICS
*c.*500 BC. Attributed to the painter Dikaios.
Louvre Museum, Paris

Vases in the Attic style marked the highest point of Greek ceramics. Recognizable from their black glaze, their myrtle garlands, the grace of their characters' expressions and the delicacy of their painting, they often portray everyday scenes, domestic or romantic, as with the ephebes above.

New Centres of Power in Europe

❶ ETRUSCAN EARTHENWARE SARCOPHAGUS

Cerveteri, c.515 BC. Louvre Museum, Paris

The Etruscans excelled in polychrome clay sculpture. The lid of this sarcophagus shows a couple, life-size, reclining for a banquet, symbol of a contented life. The custom that allowed men and women to converse intimately in public was purely Etruscan.

❷ THE CERVETERI NECROPOLIS

The burial-ground at Cerveteri, like all Etruscan cemeteries, covered several hundred acres. Varying in size, the tumuli could be as large as 40 or 50 metres. The burial-chambers, carved out of the rock, were modelled on the homes of the living. Some had windows and were furnished with benches and beds, as well as being ornamented with bas-reliefs depicting daily life.

The Etruscans

The Etruscans, whose homeland was Etruria in present-day Tuscany, developed in the 8th century BC an advanced form of civilization which endured for 400 or 500 years before being crushed by the Celts in the north and the Romans in the south, who finally overwhelmed it.

The heartland of Etruria consisted of twelve fortified cities linked in a federation. To begin with, each city had a king; but gradually the rich nobility gained more influence. For several centuries the Etruscans dominated Italy from the Po valley as far as the Greek possessions in the south. Until 500 BC Etruscan kings reigned in Rome.

The power of the Etruscans lay in their access to minerals, and especially iron ore, mined on the island of Elba. This was why the Greeks were interested in making contact with them. Greek craftsmen came to Etruria: in Veii, Tarquinia, Cerveteri and other Etruscan towns large numbers of Greek vases have been found.

The Etruscans also adopted the Greek alphabet, of which Latin letters were a derivative. It is therefore easy to read their inscriptions, but hard to interpret them, for the language is not Latin or Greek or Celtic. It has, in fact, disappeared.

The Etruscans were great engineers and builders, who invented the semi-circular arch, whose strength increases, paradoxically, the more weight it bears. The Romans adopted this technique and used it to build aqueducts, city walls and doorways. They also learned from the Etruscans the art of temple building and a number of religious practices.

The Celts: a pan-European people

Etrusco-Greek civilization was in contact with northern Europe; and, as soon as the Celtic tribes living north of the Alps acquired the new technology of iron-working and the other craft specialities learned from the Etruscans and the Greeks, they became dominant in northern Europe owing to the large numbers of metal-ore mines between the Atlantic and the Balkans that were easy to access. During the centuries that followed a Celtic civilization developed in these regions. It was a society built on the basis of the tribes, headed by a dynasty of leaders and a warrior aristocracy of knights.

At times Celtic political influence extended beyond the Alps and in 387 BC it even threatened Rome, the great up-and-coming power. This marked the end of Etruscan greatness. The Celts became dominant in central and Western Europe until the Romans pushed their Empire to the west and north of the Alps.

It was the Celts who built, in the parts of Europe they conquered, the first real towns. These were concentrated around strong fortresses which gave military protection both to specialized craftsmen and to active trade, between towns and with the Mediterranean countries, especially when the Celts began to use money.

At La Tène, in present-day Switzerland, large numbers of weapons, jewels and tools of many kinds dating from the Celtic Iron Age have been found: they include sickles, scythes, scissors, axes, wedges, saws, etc. The objects in question were probably offerings to the Celtic gods, but they are identical to those found in all Celtic regions. The new technique of iron-working made possible a number of inventions that had not been feasible in either the Bronze Age or the Stone Age.

The weapons discovered show that Celtic blacksmiths made handy and effective arms of a standard type, suitable not only for a restricted warrior caste but also for real 'people's armies'. This certainly explains how the Celts spread from the Black Sea to the Atlantic and down into Italy and Greece.

Theirs was, however, a definitely aristocratic society with kings reigning over vassals, as witness the richly decorated tombs. The typical grave of a leading chieftain might contain chariots made of wood with bronze fittings.

The Druids were another important group within the population. Posterity thinks of them as magicians: they were in fact the educated class of wise men and priests, in charge of tribal rites and interpreting legal customs. Their great influence was based on their knowledge of Celtic script, more or less inspired by the Greek alphabet, which they kept as a secret and their own monopoly. For this reason the Celts in general may be said to have lacked a written language until the beginning of the Christian era.

Celtic art was partly influenced by Greece, but it developed stylized forms that make the Celts a major civilization in a European context.

Even if the Celtic people formed neither a national nor an ethnic unit, they were nevertheless very different from the Germans in the north and the Slavs in the east. Celtic civilization was one of the high points of early European history. The Celts formed in central Europe the first European cultural entity.

❸ CELTIC BEAUTY
National Museum, Prague
This Celtic hero, a valiant warrior, represents a people that occupied a vast tract of land between the Atlantic and the Black Sea. Gradually mixing with the peoples of Greco-Roman antiquity, the Celts remained autonomous only in Ireland.

❹ THE GUNDESTRUP CAULDRON
National Museum, Copenhagen, Denmark
The cauldron measures 69 cm in diameter and is 42 cm tall: the seven exterior scenes depict gods and goddesses; the five interior scenes show wars and sacrifices.

Classical Civilization at its Height

❶ THE POSEIDON OF CAPE ARTEMISION

More than life-sized bronze statue found in the sea off the promontory of the Artemision on the island of Euboea. National Museum, Athens

The god of Artemision, probably Poseidon, in severe style, c.460 BC. It may have been a thank-offering for the victory over the Persians. With his trident (now lost) in his right hand, Poseidon was certainly oriented against the enemy coming from the East.

❷ THE PERSIAN WARS

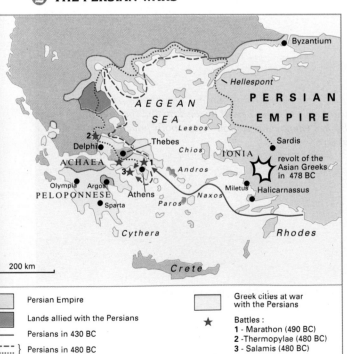

200 km

Persian Empire	Greek cities at war with the Persians
Lands allied with the Persians	★ Battles :
—— Persians in 430 BC	1 - Marathon (490 BC)
┈┈} Persians in 480 BC	2 -Thermopylae (480 BC)
	3 - Salamis (480 BC)

The Persian threat

While the Greeks were increasing their contacts with the Etruscans and Celts in the West, a great Persian Empire was developing in the East. The formation of such an empire, like the alliances among Greek city-states that were being forged during the Iron Age, was connected with the development of metal-working techniques: there was a quest for raw materials and new markets.

Whereas the Greeks were active partners with the Etruscans and the Celts, their Eastern neighbours, the Persians, were an ever-growing danger. During the centuries before 500 BC their armies of knights and archers, led by powerful kings, had conquered an immense empire stretching from India to the Greek towns of western Asia Minor, which became subject to the Persian king. He installed tyrants, imposed taxes and aided their commercial rivals, the Phoenicians.

Tension between the Greeks and the Persians was due to several factors. There were fundamental differences between their forms of government and their views of life (political and ideological antagonism). There was competition for trade routes, markets and raw materials (economic rivalry). There was the strategic factor of the Persians' desire to extend their empire to Greece and other parts of Europe. One reason for Persian aggression, according to the Persian general Mardonios, quoted by Herodotus, the Greek historian of the period, was 'that Europe is a fair land, where trees of all sorts are grown, with a very fertile soil, and that of all mortals the king [of the Persians] is worthy to possess it'.

Herodotus was the first historian to use the name 'Europe' – unsurprisingly, since this was a time when Europeans confronted non-European peoples. As both sides expanded, war between them became inevitable.

The Persian Wars involved three phases. The first took place in Asia Minor, where the Greek town of Miletus tried to throw off the Persian yoke in 494 BC. The revolt was crushed, the town destroyed and the population massacred or deported to Babylon.

The Athenians sent a fleet to help Miletus and this sparked off a second war, this time against Athens itself. In 490 BC the Persian king sent a fleet carrying ten to fifteen thousand crack troops. On the Plain of Marathon, 42 kilometres north-east of Athens, the Persian archers were mown down by the lances of the hoplites, counter-attacking in their phalanx formation. It was a great psychological victory for the Athenians. The Persians had been halted in their expansionist policy and the first assault on Europe had been repulsed. But the danger remained. There was the threat of a third war.

The Persians spent ten years preparing a large-scale attack on Greece as a whole. But under the leadership of the far-seeing Themistocles the Athenians built a fleet and modernized the port of Piraeus. In 480 BC Xerxes, King of the Persians, led a huge army across the Hellespont into Europe and swooped on the Greek peninsula. Herodotus estimated the army to comprise several million men, but modern historians believe that a figure of 100,000 to 300,000 is more likely. The northern Greek states surrendered and followed the Persian advance; but Athens and Sparta decided to fight rather than accept the same fate as Miletus. They made an alliance between them, under which Sparta led the land battle and Athens the war at sea.

While Leonidas, King of Sparta, used 300 hoplites to halt the Persian army in the narrow pass of Thermopylae, the Greeks prepared for the final assault. The inhabitants of Athens were evacuated to the Peloponnese and to the island of Salamis, where Themistocles assembled the Greek fleet. Xerxes would have to destroy it, if he were to feed his enormous army. Although the Persian fleet comprised 1200 ships, three times as many as that of the Greeks, it was destroyed in the strait of Salamis in 480 BC. From then on, the die was cast: in the following year, 479 BC, the Persian land forces were destroyed at Plataea. The freedom of the Greeks had been saved and Europe had been protected, for the time being, from Asian domination.

Reconstruction and fresh progress

Herodotus, who was born during the Persian Wars, saw them as a struggle between despotism and democracy, tyranny and liberty. He considered that East–West antagonism, by strengthening solidarity among the Greeks, was the driving force in their history. He knew that Athens had played a vital role in the victory over the Persians.

However, to explain how a few small Greek city-states had been able to defeat the greatest military power on earth, he invoked the gods. This religious attitude was characteristic of the generation of the Persian Wars and can be seen in its drama, its temples and its art. The archaic smile vanished from sculpture and the severe or classical style became dominant in all forms of art until the middle of the 4th century BC.

❸ Herodotus and the Persian Wars

The Greek historian Herodotus (c.484–c.420 BC) was born five years after the Battle of Marathon and five years before that of Salamis. For this reason the wars fought by the Greeks were the most important problem in his life. He tried to understand how the Greeks had managed to win the Persian Wars. In the extract below, immediately before the attack on Greece by King Xerxes of the Persians, he recounts the king's conversation with Demaratus, who had been banished from Sparta and had taken refuge with the Persians.

Having sailed from one end to the other of the line of anchored ships, Xerxes went ashore again and sent for Demaratus, the son of Ariston, who was accompanying him in the march to Greece. 'Demaratus', he said, 'it would give me pleasure at this point to put to you a few questions. You are a Greek and a native, moreover, of by no means the meanest or weakest city in that country – as I learn not only from yourself but from the other Greeks I have spoken with. Tell me, then – will the Greeks dare to lift a hand against me? My own belief is that all the Greeks and all the other Western peoples gathered together would be insufficient to withstand the attack of my army – and still more so if they are not united. But it is your opinion upon this subject that I should like to hear.'

'My Lord', Demaratus replied, 'is it a true answer you would like, or merely an agreeable one?'

'Tell me the truth', said the king; 'and I promise that you will not suffer by it.' Encouraged by this, Demaratus continued: 'My lord, you bid me speak nothing but the truth, to say nothing which might later be proved a lie. Very well then; this is my answer: poverty is my country's inheritance from of old, but valour she won for herself by wisdom and the strength of law. By her valour Greece now keeps both poverty and bondage at bay.

'I think highly of all Greeks of Dorian descent, but what I am about to say will apply not to all Dorians, but to the Spartans only. First then, they will not under any circumstances accept terms from you which would mean slavery for Greece; secondly, they will fight you even if the rest of Greece submits. Moreover, there is no use in asking if their numbers are adequate to enable them to do this; suppose a thousand of them take the field – then that thousand will fight you; and so will any number, greater than this or less.'

Herodotus, *The Histories*, Book VII. Translated by Aubrey de Selincourt, Penguin Books, 1954, pp. 447–8.

❶ PERSIAN ARCHERS
Louvre Museum, Paris
Glazed bas-relief depicting the Royal Guard at the Palace of the Persian Emperor Darius I, at Susa. It was his son Xerxes who led these charismatic and invincible warriors with empty quivers to their defeat at the battle of Plataea in 479 BC.

Aeschylus wrote his tragedies with the experience of the Persian Wars still haunting him, body and soul. He had taken part in the fighting and in *The Persians*, produced seven years after the battle of Salamis, he describes how the lance defeated the bow. In his view the outcome of the war had been in the hands of the gods: the Greeks were simply the means whereby the gods punished the pride or *hubris* of the Persians.

A historian today would more probably ascribe the Greeks' victory to a number of factors. They were determined; they were fighting for survival; they were good soldiers and sailors; they knew the terrain and the coastal waters; and the barbarian threat created solidarity between different city-states, which was hard to achieve in normal times. Battles are not decided by arms alone. The Persians had more weapons than the Greeks; but morale played a decisive role, as it has done since. The battles of Marathon and Salamis can perhaps be regarded as the first in the history of Europe.

To commemorate their victory and to thank the gods, the Greek cities agreed to restore the Temple at Olympia, the site of the Pan-Hellenic Games. At some time after 470 BC they built in the same place a great temple to Zeus and a huge statue of him.

The Athenians decided to leave the smoke-stained ruins on the Acropolis as witness to the sack of their city by the Persians.

❷ THE ACROPOLIS OF PERICLES
Agora Museum, Athens
A model of the Acropolis hill. The rays of the setting sun shone through the Propylaea, the doorway of the Acropolis in the foreground, on to the ivory statue of Athena. In the background is the Parthenon, whose apparent symmetry is misleading: the building contains no right angles. It was inaugurated in 432 BC, three years before Pericles's death.

Pericles and the height of classicism

After Salamis a number of Greek city-states banded together against the continuing Persian menace in the Delian League, headed by Athens. They had either to supply their own troops or pay a contribution to the federal exchequer, based on the island of Delos. Most of the cities chose the simpler method of paying their levy and letting Athens arm and direct the fleet. In this way, they became dependent on Athens, which soon led to conflicts among the Greek city-states.

Once a peace treaty had put an end to the Persian Wars, in 449 BC, Pericles worked energetically to rebuild Athens and turn it into a leading commercial centre. To secure both its defence and its supplies, he had a double wall constructed linking the city with its port of Piraeus, which became the defensive base of Athenian imperialism. Economically, Piraeus came to be a centre of transit for all trade in the Mediterranean. As memories of the war faded, the naval levies accumulated by the Delian League were used more and more for the reconstruction of Athens.

Pericles commissioned the sculptor Phidias to transform the Acropolis into a site reserved for the city's protecting deities. A number of temples were built. The most celebrated was the Temple of the Parthenon, used as a treasury for the funds of the Delian League. It also housed a 12-metre gold and ivory statue of Pallas Athena, the goddess of Athens. Phidias made another statue of her, so large that the tip of her lance was used as a mark by sailors when they had passed Cape Sounion in the south of Attica. The Greek historian Plutarch described Pericles and the role that the rebuilding of Athens played in his policy as a whole.

When Pericles secured the assent of the People's Assembly to the buildings on the Acropolis, it was not primarily to respond to the religious needs of the Athenians. He belonged to the young postwar generation, whose thinking was more political and rationalistic. For him such public works would create jobs, make for progress in the construction industry and attract all sorts of foreign workers. This would benefit the middle class of craftsmen, merchants and shippers – thereby strengthening Pericles's supporters, the democrats, against the conservative oligarchs, whose partisans were recruited from among the peasants of Attica. Pericles thus obtained recognition for his imperialist policy, which made Athens predominant among her allies, attracted wealth and laid the foundations for what is regarded as the heyday of Greek classical culture.

③ PERICLES
Height: 59 cm. Roman copy in the British Museum, London
Born to a noble family, the great-nephew of Cleisthenes and creator of democracy, Pericles ruled Athens from 462 to 429 BC. Under him Athens became the richest state in Greece. It was said of this 'best of Athenians' that he practised democracy at home and imperialism abroad. A friend of the sculptor Phidias, the architect Callicrates and the philosopher Anaxagoras, he made Athens the finest and best-educated city in Greece.

---

④ Pericles and the Athenian Constitution

The Greek historian Thucydides (460–406 BC) recounted the story of the Peloponnesian War, during which Pericles pronounced the funeral oration for the Athenian soldiers who fell during the first winter of the war, in 430 BC.

Our system of government does not copy the institutions of our neighbours. It is more the case of our being a model to others, than of our imitating anyone else. Our constitution is called a democracy because power is in the hands not of a minority but of the whole people. When it is a question of settling private disputes, everyone is equal before the law; when it is a question of putting one person before another in positions of public responsibility, what counts is not membership of a particular class, but the actual ability that the man possesses. No one, so long as he has it in him to be of service to the state, is kept in political obscurity because of poverty . . . .

It is for you to try to be like them. Make up your minds that happiness depends on being free and freedom depends on being courageous. Let there be no relaxation in face of the perils of the war.

Thucydides, *The Peloponnesian War*, Book II. Translated by Rex Warner, Penguin Books, 1954, pp. 117, 121.

❶ATTIC RED-FIGURE CUP DEPICTING A SCENE AT SCHOOL
Found at Cerveteri, Etruria; 480 BC. Diameter: 29 cm
Collection of Antiquities, Berlin
There were no state schools in Athens. Teachers of literature and music taught the cithara, initiated their pupils into the elementary laws of rhythm and had them play and sing the best-known works of the lyric poets. Education was not specialized, but opened the way to almost all lines of thought.

❷OSTRACISM·
Agora Museum, Athens, 5th century BC
Fragments of pottery (ostraka) bearing the names of politicians who had been ostracized – exiled for ten years – after a popular vote. The name of Pericles has also been found, although he was never ostracized.

Greek democracy

The evolution from monarchical government to democratic government, via an aristocratic regime, began in the colonial period and reached its culminating point under Pericles, at the end of the 5th century BC.

The economic progress made in the colonial period conferred influence on broader groups in the population. Under the reign of the Tyrants in the 6th century, these groups played a greater part in public affairs, even if the ranks of senior officials were still reserved for the rich.

During the Persian Wars the whole population was united in doing its duty, irrespective of rank: even the slaves took part in the defence. This feeling of community and equality continued after the war and affected political life: all free men now had the right to take part in government.

Pericles held that poverty, in a democracy, should not prevent a citizen from playing his part in public affairs. To ensure that everyone could do so on an equal footing, Pericles introduced monetary compensation and the drawing of lots for public office. Office-holders were appointed for one year only so that many people could have their chance.

Greek democracy was the response to oriental despotism and an attempt to ensure that all citizens should be equal before the law. Nevertheless, it cannot be likened completely to modern democracies in the West. In Athens all the citizens of the city could present themselves in person and vote: that was direct democracy, as against representative democracy in our countries today. Furthermore, a large number of the inhabitants were debarred from citizenship: slaves, women and immigrant workers. It was they who did the work, while the citizens made the policy. In Periclean Athens there were some 150,000 free citizens (including families), 125,000 slaves and 40,000 immigrant workers.

The Greeks saw nothing abnormal or shocking in this discrimination. Societies in the classical world were slave societies based on the right of private property. Those who had only their muscles to offer had no time to participate actively in public affairs and were not counted as active citizens (in Greek, *politēs*) but as private persons (in Greek, *idiotēs*).

For Aristotle a human being was simply someone who played a part in the affairs of the community; and women, slaves and immigrant workers did not. The Greeks saw no injustice or discrimination in this state of affairs.

Democratic institutions

The People's Assembly (the *ecclēsia*) was the soul and the voice of democracy. In Athens it normally met every nine days and it took all the decisions. Every male citizen over 18 could attend, speak and vote. Not all took part in every session: the peasants, in particular, who had work to do in Attica, were often absent. But it was not exceptional for there to be five or six thousand people present. So large an assembly required a certain discipline. So all the matters to be discussed were prepared beforehand by the Council, which acted as intermediary between the Assembly and the executive authorities.

The Council (the *boulē*) was made up of 500 men chosen annually by drawing lots, 50 from each of the ten tribes (*phylai*) of Athens which were administrative sub-divisions of the *polis*. The 50 representatives of each tribe exercised the executive functions of the Council for one-tenth of the year, during which time they bore the title of *prytaneis*. Together with their officials, they presided over the government of the city in the *agora*, the main square.

After a year in office the officials gave up their posts or were allotted others. The oldest and most experienced entered the Tribunal of the Areopagus, on the hill of that name. As democracy developed under Pericles, this court lost influence. Judicial power passed into the hands of a tribunal of jurors elected by the people, the *hēliaia*; in large trials, it could consist of up to 501 citizen-judges. The law was the supreme authority, the collective will of the *polis*, and was binding on the citizens. The tribunals supervised it. To protect democracy against tyranny, the Assembly could exile any politician who became too popular and therefore dangerous.

As it had in Athens, democracy gained ground in other city-states. Craftsmen and merchants liked this form of government, but it also had its enemies, especially among the landed proprietors in the agricultural districts of the *polis*. These oligarchs opposed all the expansionist activities of the Delian League, the intensive rebuilding of Athens and the imperialist policy. They looked rather towards conservative Sparta, which favoured the cities' oligarchical circles.

So long as the Persians posed a threat to both Athens and Sparta, the two city-states were at one; but, when the Persian danger diminished, disputes arose. Sparta's highly disciplined army was used by a few very influential families to maintain their grip on subject regions. Her citizens existed only to serve the state. Other city-states with the same form of oligarchy united to form the Peloponnesian League.

③ CLEPSYDRA FROM A COURT OF JUSTICE

Agora Museum, Athens

The clepsydra was a water-clock. The water ran out through a hole in the upper receptacle. It was used in assemblies to give every speaker a fair share of the time: six minutes or five litres.

④ ATHENS AT THE TIME OF PERICLES

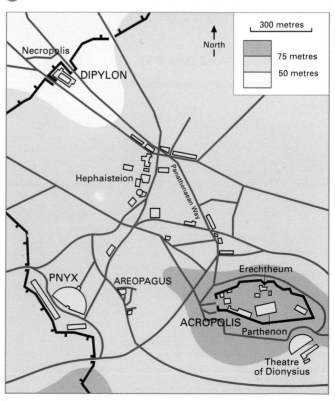

300 metres	
	75 metres
	50 metres

North

Necropolis
DIPYLON
Hephaisteion
Panathenaean Way
PNYX
AREOPAGUS
Erechtheum
ACROPOLIS
Parthenon
Theatre of Dionysius

7 Unity or Division?

❶ THE SALAMIS WARRIORS

Height: 181 cm.
Piraeus Museum

A funeral stele or slab found on the island of Salamis, erected to the memory of two young warriors killed in the Peloponnesian War (420 BC).

The Peloponnesian War: 431–404 BC

Although the two allies in the Persian Wars tried as long as possible to avoid an open conflict between them, their basic disagreements were too great. War between Athens and Sparta broke out in 431 BC. The powerful Athenian fleet pillaged the Peloponnesian coast, while Sparta's élite army pillaged Attica every summer, forcing its inhabitants to take refuge behind the 'long walls' of Athens. During the second summer of the war, the plague struck the overcrowded city, decimating its population. Pericles himself died of it.

In the long run, the Peloponnesian League, together with Sparta's strict military discipline, faced the rigours of war more successfully than did Athens, where democracy showed its weaknesses. The peasants of Attica wanted peace while the inhabitants of the cities sought to continue the struggle. At the same time, several of Athens's allies took this opportunity to free themselves from her policy of economic imperialism.

The turning-point in the war came when the Spartans built a fleet financed by the King of the Persians. This enabled Sparta to establish a blockade from the Black Sea to the Hellespont and to defeat Athens in a number of decisive naval battles. In 404 BC the Athenians capitulated and had to accept a peace treaty.

Under it Athens agreed to hand over its fleet, dissolve the Delian League and demolish the long walls that had protected the city's supplies. It was also forced to allow a 30-man commission to apply an oligarchical constitution, while a Spartan garrison occupied the Acropolis.

Much of our knowledge of the Peloponnesian War comes from the *History* of it written by Thucydides. As a historian he was very different from Herodotus, the so-called 'father' of written history, who had recounted the past in such a way as to confirm his religious conception of life. Thucydides sought to describe reality and undertook an objective analysis of his source. He has been called 'the founding father of historical research'. He was a product of the generation after the Persian War; like Pericles, he was guided by reason rather than religion. This, however, did not prevent Thucydides judging events by moral criteria. He was well aware of how destructive war could be for a community where everyone pursued his own interests rather than doing his duty to the state.

❷ THE PELOPONNESIAN WAR

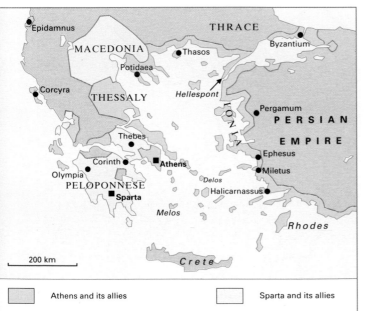

Epidamnus
THRACE
MACEDONIA
Thasos
Byzantium
Potidaea
Corcyra
THESSALY
Hellespont
IONIA
Pergamum
PERSIAN
Thebes
EMPIRE
Corinth
Athens
Ephesus
Olympia
Delos
Miletus
PELOPONNESE
Halicarnassus
Sparta
Melos
Rhodes
Crete

200 km

Athens and its allies   Sparta and its allies

The Sophists and Socrates

The decline of old religious beliefs had already begun before the Peloponnesian War, partly under the influence of the Sophists.

Their name came from the Greek word *sophia*, wisdom. They continued the tradition of the 6th-century BC Ionian nature philosophers, but were more interested in the problems of society. They established a number of subjects that have since been pursued in schools in Europe. In their own eyes, Logic and Rhetoric were the most important. Their pupils had to learn to think clearly and to speak convincingly: this was the path to political and social success.

For the Sophists, it was neither the community nor the gods, but the individual that counted as the focus of philosophical investigation. As one of them put it: 'Man is the measure of all things'. This idea implies that the world is as we perceive it and that there is no such thing as a universal Truth to which everyone is subject. Any point of view could be defended if only rhetoric were mastered.

There were two sides to Sophism. On the one hand, its principle of free thought was a good basis for democratic debates; but, on the other, if pushed to the limit, it could lead to subjectivism and the abandonment of collective ethics.

By the end of the 5th century BC, many Athenians had the feeling that the Sophists were undermining the ideological foundations of the state. And, when they were assailed by the misfortunes of the Peloponnesian War, the Athenians looked for someone to blame. They picked on an eccentric citizen of Athens who in some respects resembled the Sophists. It was the philosopher Socrates. Like the Sophists, he was surrounded by a group of disciples whom he provoked with pitiless questioning, in search of the truth. He was accused of blasphemy and of debauching the young, because of his manner of thinking, which was held to be Sophism.

The accusation was unjust. All his life, Socrates attacked the demoralizing relativism of the Sophists; he believed in absolute values independent of anyone's opinion: justice, truth, God. He held that the destiny of mankind and the purpose of human life were to deepen knowledge of these ideas and to live in conformity with them.

Education, teaching and dialogue were in his view the means to that end. At his trial, Socrates was unable to convince the jury of his innocence. He had stirred up too much passion. He was condemned to death, unjustly, in 399 BC.

③ SOCRATES
Height: 27 cm. Archaeological Museum, Naples
*c.*330 BC
This bust is a Roman marble copy of a Greek statue made for the Athenians after Socrates's death.

④ PLATO
Capitol Museum, Rome
*c.*350 BC
Plato was one of Socrates's pupils. This is a Roman marble copy of a Greek statue in bronze.

⑤ The Sophists and the Truth

SOCRATES   *What you seem to be saying is that knowledge is not objective. That is what Protagoras said himself. He defined it as you do, but in different terms. He said in fact, didn't he, that man is the measure of all things – of the existence of things that exist and the non-existence of those that do not. You have read that, I suppose?*

THEAETETUS   *Yes, more than once.*

SOCRATES   *Does it not mean roughly this? That a thing is for me what it appears to me to be and for you what it appears to you to be? For you and I are men.*

THEAETETUS   *Yes, that is exactly what it means.*

SOCRATES   *We can take it that a wise man does not just talk in the air. So let's see where that leads. Does it not sometimes happen that, if two people face the same wind, one feels cold and the other not; or one feels it lightly and the other finds it more blustery?*

THEAETETUS   *Certainly.*

SOCRATES   *So it appears like that to each of them?*

THEAETETUS   *Yes.*

SOCRATES   *But to appear means to be felt?*

THEAETETUS   *It does.*

SOCRATES   *So appearance and feeling are the same things, as regards heat and all such phenomena: for the way that each person feels them is the way that they seem for that person.*

THEAETETUS   *Very likely.*

Plato, *Theaetetus*, 151d–152b

❶ ALEXANDER THE GREAT
Portrait based on a statue sculpted during his lifetime.
c.150 BC, from Pergamum. Archaeological Museum, Istanbul
The King of Macedonia, Alexander III (356–23 BC) led the expansion of Greece into the Orient. He destroyed Thebes in Asia Minor, seized Babylon and Susa, burned Persepolis and reached the Indus. His army, exhausted by too much fighting, forced him to halt there. In 324 BC, seeking to unite the heritage of Greece with that of the Orient, he arranged for 10,000 of his soldiers to be married to Persian girls. He died at the age of 33.

❷ ALEXANDER IN BATTLE
Height: 70 cm. 4th century BC. Archaeological Museum, Istanbul
The finest sarcophagus to which the name of Alexander is linked was found at Sidon in Lebanon. Alexander is shown on the far right, mounted on a horse about to leap over a Persian.

The Crisis in Greece– Unification under Alexander the Great

After the Peloponnesian War the Greek world seemed to change. Whereas the 5th century BC had been highly civilized, the centuries that followed were marked by crises and decadence.

In 387 BC a pupil of Socrates, Plato, opened his *Academia*, which remained for more than a thousand years the focal point of ancient Greece's cultural heritage. Plato was worried by the decadent tendencies of his day. He bent every effort to build a philosophy that might save society from the Sophists' relativism and from that implied by philosophies of hedonism.

Plato believed that behind external phenomena (from the Greek *phainomenon*, that which appears), which indeed were only apparent, there was an eternal and imperishable idea, of which the phenomena were the reflection and towards which human beings should aspire in order to live a just life. In *The Republic*, Plato shows Socrates and his companions debating the ideas which should lead to the ideal state.

The Greek city-states risked losing their freedom if, at a time when new empires were emerging, their democracy became decadent owing to internal quarrels.

In the East, the Persian Empire was already a multinational state dominated by an all-powerful sovereign. In the Mediterranean, the Phoenicians were forming a great empire centred on Carthage. In the West, Rome had begun to expand; and the Celts had extended their influence in the north.

A greater threat to the freedom of the Greek cities, however, was Macedonia, a Greek kingdom in the north. Its King Philip conquered southern Greece in 338 BC, but died two years later. His son Alexander conquered the whole of the Persian Empire as far as the frontier of India: hence his name, Alexander the Great.

The aim of his conquest was to eliminate the Persian threat and open the East to enterprising Greek merchants. Alexander gave orders for the coffer of Persian treasure to be opened, then turned the gold and silver into coins, which he put in circulation. This stimulated production and trade; a number of new towns appeared in the Empire, several bearing the name Alexandria.

Thus was established a common market and a shared culture, Hellenism, dominated by the Greek language, Greek art and Greek science, but with Persian adjuncts. Yet, although Greek culture spread in this way, political and economic power was ebbing away from Greece. The up-and-coming power was Rome. The Romans greatly admired Greek culture; but this did not stop them conquering Greece in 146 BC.

The legacy of Greece

Although Greece never formed a unitary state, Greek culture was so original and so striking that it became the basis of Western culture as a whole. The Greeks learned from Oriental civilizations, from which they adopted the alphabet, mathematics and astronomy; but in a large number of fields the Greeks were themselves the creators.

Greece was the first country in the world where citizens could take part in public affairs. The preconditions for such democracy were liberty and equality, including freedom of expression, which made possible criticism of existing situations and the emergence of new forms of thought. The gift of withdrawing from the real world and proposing utopias is characteristic of Greek civilization.

Greek thought freed itself from old mythological explanations in order to explore the unknown and explain it by the known and by logical reasoning. The Greeks were thus the originators of experimental science, which the West later developed.

Education had an important role in the city, for without it there could be no way to take part in political life. The concept of the school is of Greek origin: at first it meant free time, then studies and educational establishments. The Greeks espoused a number of scholarly subjects: mathematics, natural sciences, grammar, logic, rhetoric and the social sciences. Their curriculum underlies many later educational systems in Europe.

For the Greeks opposition was very important as a challenge and an incentive, in the stadia as on the battlefield. In the People's Assemblies dialogue was also an essential element if the city was to maintain the interests of its citizens – just as debate was vital for philosophers and scientists seeking knowledge. Even dramatists took part in an annual competition for a first prize awarded to the best play.

Theatre, with its double aspect of tragedy and comedy, was a Greek invention. It was not merely for entertainment: it also had a religious purpose, venerating the gods, and a political function, exposing problems and involving the people in the affairs of the city.

In literature, too, the Greeks were innovators. It is significant that the words *epic*, *drama*, *tragedy* and *lyric* are much the same in different European languages and they all derive from Greek. Greek architecture, as exemplified in theatres, temples and stadia, has also become a model, not only for the Romans but also, through the Renaissance, for architects down to the present day.

❸ ART AND SCIENCE IN GREECE

Hockey was already played by the Persians.

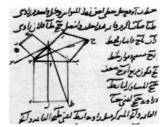

Part of an Arab manuscript from 1284. Bibliothèque Nationale, Paris
A *summary of the* Elements *of Euclid of Alexandria, founder of plane geometry. Here, Pythagoras's Theorem.*

Archaeological Museum, Naples
Actors appeared with their faces covered by masks which acted as megaphones. Usually made of linen and equipped with a wig, the mask was predetermined for the particular role. 40 comic masks have been identified, against 25 tragic.

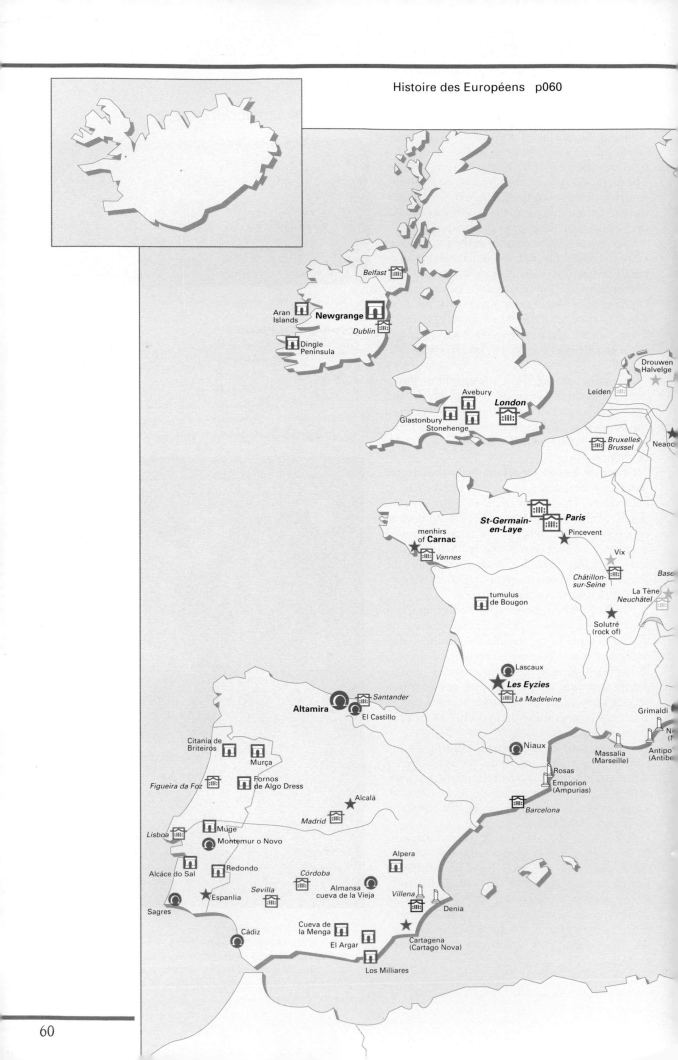

Belfast

Aran
Islands   **Newgrange**

Dublin

Dingle
Peninsula

Drouwen
Halvelge

Leiden

Avebury

Glastonbury   **London**
Stonehenge

Bruxelles
Brussel

Neano

menhirs
of **Carnac**

Vannes

**St-Germain-
en-Laye**   **Paris**

Pincevent

Vix

Châtillon-
sur-Seine

Base

La Tène
Neuchâtel

tumulus
de Bougon

Solutré
(rock of)

Lascaux

Les Eyzies

La Madeleine

Grimaldi

N
(I

Altamira   Santander

El Castillo

Niaux

Massalia
(Marseille)

Antipo
(Antibe

Citania de
Briteiros

Murça

Figueira da Foz   Fornos
de Algo Dress

Rosas

Emporion
(Ampurias)

Barcelona

Alcalá

Madrid

Lisboa   Muge

Montemur o Novo

Alpera

Alcáce do Sal   Redondo

Córdoba

Almansa
cueva de la Vieja

Villena

Denia

Sevilla

Espanlia

Sagres

Cádiz

Cueva de
la Menga

El Argar

Cartagena
(Cartago Nova)

Los Milliares

The Past in the Present Day
FROM THE TUNDRA TO THE TEMPLE

	Prehistory	The Ancient World	Celts	Etruscan	
cave					
site					
monument					
town that was important in antiquity but has little to tell the tourist about that time					
Greek colony					
museum, treasury or library whose collections cover the epoch above					

frontiers of 20th-century states

500 km

København

Berlin

Zavist

Würzburg

München   Willendorf

uneburg   Hallein   Wien

Hallstatt

Olbia

Jassy

Théodosia

Tyras

Chersonèse

Istros

Tomi (Constanta)

Bucuresti

Callatis

Lepenski Vir

Odessos (Varna)

Beograd

Mésembria

Sofija

Apollonia

Sésamos

Tios

Héakléa

Firenze

Arezzo

Volterra   Cortona

Chiusi

Byzance

Tarquinia   Caere (Cerveteri)

lalia (Aleria)

Roma

Kyme (Cuma)

Neapolis (Napoli)

Epidamnos (Durrës)

Amphipolis

Thessaloniki

Pella

Ilion (Truva)

Apollonia

Pergamon (Bergama)

Taranto

Posidonia (Paestum)

Buthroton (Butrint)

Aigai (Vergina)

Smyrna (Izmir)

Dodoni

Orchomenos

Kercyra (Corfu)

Chalkis

Crotone

Delfi

Athinai

Ephessos (Selçuk)

Thivé

Dílos

Miletos (Milet)

Kórintos

Sunion

Halikarnassos (Bodrum)

Aspendos

Segesta

Olympia   Mykinai

Epidavros

Kos

Xanthos

Locri

Sparti

Rhegion (Reggio di Calabria)

Pylos

Milos

Rodos

Selinus (Selinunte)

Filakopis

Acragas (Agrigento)

Siracusa

Iráklio   Knossós

Mália

Festós   Kriti

1 AUGUSTUS (1st century AD)
Vatican Museum, Rome
The founder of the Empire, dressed for battle, addresses his troops. The decoration of his breastplate commemorates his victories. At his feet, Cupid, the son of Venus, recalls the divine affiliation of his family.

BC 753	Rome founded		**312–37**	Constantine
509	Fall of the Tarquins. The Republic		**313**	Christianity legalized
219–201	Second Punic War		**330**	Constantinople, 'the second Rome'
81–79	Dictatorship of Sulla		**364**	Goths begin to invade the Empire
44	Assassination of Julius Caesar		**395**	Death of Theodosius: Empire divided in two
31	Octavius defeats Mark Antony at Actium		**397**	Death of St Martin
27	Octavius named Augustus Caesar by the Senate: the Empire		**410**	Alaric takes and sacks Rome
AD 14	Death of Augustus		**449–52**	Attila and the Huns in the West
98–117	Reign of Trajan		**461**	St Patrick converts Ireland
235–284	Military anarchy		**476**	End of the Roman Empire in the West
284–305	Diocletian: the tetrarchy		**498**	Baptism of Clovis, King of the Franks
			493–526	Theodoric King in Italy

CHAPTER II

ROME

FROM THE 6TH CENTURY BC TO THE 5TH CENTURY AD

2 ROME AND THE MEDITERRANEAN WORLD AT THE DEATH OF ALEXANDER (323 BC)

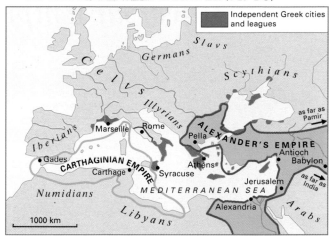

Independent Greek cities and leagues

3 THE ROMAN EMPIRE AT THE DEATH OF TRAJAN (117 AD)

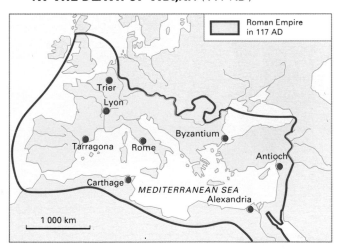

Roman Empire in 117 AD

4 THE BARBARIAN KINGDOMS (c. 500 AD)

Frontiers of the Eastern Empire
Frontiers of the Barbarian Kingdoms

More than a thousand years elapsed between the founding of Rome (traditionally dated 753 BC) and the fall of the Roman Empire of the West in AD 476. This was the Roman millennium. It can be looked at in three stages.

To begin with, at a time when Greek civilization was still flourishing, there came into being, at the cost of efforts and setbacks, the first of the universal empires to affect the greater part of Europe: the Roman Empire. How was it that a small group of villages in Latium could create the metropolis of a world that was centred on the Mediterranean but reached from Scotland to Mesopotamia and from the Sahara to the Carpathians?

We should look, secondly, at the Empire in its heyday, at the beginning of the 2nd century AD in the reigns of Trajan and Hadrian, to study the content of Roman civilization. As a unifying force it left its mark on Europe, more in some regions than in others, but most often indelibly.

Finally, the Empire slowly and insidiously disintegrated as the Germanic kingdoms emerged. Their rise was linked to the fitful weakening of Rome's dynamism and especially of its ability to absorb foreign peoples on either side of its frontiers. Contacts with these nomadic tribes was often peaceful; but some violent episodes in many areas justified the term 'Great Invasions'. Yet the memory of Rome's imperial greatness lingered on, partly sustained by the survival of the (Byzantine) Roman Empire in the East. The continuing prestige was what made possible the Empire's revival in the West by Charlemagne and Otto the Great.

1 From the Seven Hills to Universal Empire

① AENEAS AND ANCHISES

Villa Giulia Museum, Rome. Terracotta from the 5th century BC found at Veii, near Rome

On the terrible night when the Greeks burned Troy, Aeneas obeyed his mother Venus and fled, carrying his sick father on his shoulders. Thus began the incredible voyage described by Virgil in the Aeneid (1st century BC). After seven years of wandering in the Mediterranean, Aeneas reached the Italian coast at the mouth of the Tiber. He brought there the Trojan gods, gave his people the name of Latins and left it to his son to found Rome. The date and origin of this work show how old was the tradition that the Latins were descendants of the Trojans.

② THE ROMAN SHE-WOLF

Roman coin, Bibliothèque Nationale, Paris, Cabinet des Médailles

According to legend, it was on the site of Rome that the she-wolf, sent by the god Mars, suckled Romulus and Remus.

A marsh surrounded by hills – traditionally seven, but actually more; a river, the Tiber, faster flowing than now and with easily watched crossing-points: such was the site of Rome. Strategically, it was well placed; but that alone cannot account for the Eternal City's exceptional role.

An Etruscan city

For many reasons, the origins of Rome remain obscure. Those who first described its creation were already writing several centuries later. No Roman histories earlier than the 1st century BC have survived, and the earliest date from the time when Augustus was establishing the Empire, a political system that was in fact new, but which he wanted to present as the 'restoration' of Rome's glorious past. Thus, the *Aeneid*, the epic poem by Virgil (70–19 BC) in honour of Rome, develops the myth that the Latins were descended from the Trojans – giving the city's founder Romulus both heroic and divine ancestry. The *History of Rome* by Livy (54 BC to AD 19) is similarly biased in its praise of the Romans' extraordinary qualities.

This blend of history and legend, long accepted at face value, was totally rejected by the systematic criticism of late 19th-century historians. Today's experts are more guarded in their approach. Archaeological research on the oldest parts of Rome – in the Forum, on the Palatine and on sites further afield – has shown after nearly a century that these stories, although more or less mythical, reflected historical realities. While defective on the details of events, they none the less revealed their deeper meaning.

Archaeologists, for example, date the earliest remains of habitats found on the Palatine no earlier than the mid-8th century BC, thereby confirming the traditional date of 753 for the foundation of Rome. But at that time it was not a town: there were simply villages of a few huts, whose shallow foundations have been found dug into the ground.

In Book I of his *History of Rome* (9–13), Livy tells the well-known story of the rape of the Sabine women by the Romans, anxious for heirs, followed by the war between the Sabines and Rome, and then their reconciliation – the Sabine women having interceded between their fathers and their husbands – and finally the fusion of the two peoples. The passage shows the place occupied by women in Rome, admittedly inferior in law, but wholly responsible as guarantors of the agreement that ended the struggle. The text also bears witness to the fact that very diverse peoples met here – the Latins from the coastal plain, the Sabines from the surrounding mountains.

Other passages show the still greater importance of the Etruscans. For them control of Rome's strategic position was essential to safeguard their communications with Campania, which they had conquered. It is certain, in fact, that Rome was ruled by Etruscan kings at the end of the 7th century BC or during the 6th. It was they who turned its league of villages into a town. They surrounded it with ramparts (attributed to King Servius Tullius); they replaced the mud and thatch huts with stone houses; they drained the original marsh by means of a sewer, the *Cloaca Maxima* and they established in its place the Forum, a public square which became the political and economic centre of the city and later that of the ancient world as a whole.

Still clearer was the mark the Etruscans left on Roman religion. The faithful must seek the favour of the omnipresent gods by trying to understand the signs that were sent them – observing the flight of birds or the entrails of sacrificial victims.

No less decisive a legacy was writing. The Latin alphabet is derived from the Etruscan. The importance of this can be seen from the fact that Roman letters have since been adopted in most of Europe and a large part of the world.

The Roman Republic

Halted in the south by Greek resistance and threatened in the north by the Celtic invasion of the Po valley – then known as Cisalpine Gaul, Etruria declined. Rome seized the opportunity to throw off Etruscan domination, incarnated by the royal family of the Tarquins. The establishment of the Republic in 509 was a turning-point in the history of Rome: henceforth the idea of monarchy had no place in Roman political thought. But the word 'Republic' should not be misunderstood. Like the Tyrannies of the earlier Greek city-states, the monarchy enjoyed popular backing: the establishment of the Republic was a victory for the aristocracy.

Contrary to the view expressed by the Roman annalists, social strife between patricians and plebeians did not date from the foundation of Rome. It was at the end of the 6th century that the most prominent families, the *gentes*, who claimed to be really or metaphorically descended from the highest in the land, rallied around them a large clientele and succeeded in distancing themselves from those whose origins were obscure and who had only numbers on their side: i.e., the *plebs*.

❸ The founding of Rome

When founding Rome, Romulus followed the 'Etruscan ritual', tracing its boundary but cutting a furrow with a ploughshare, thereby fixing the Pomerium or forbidden zone which ensured the city the protection of the gods.

. . . This done, the founder of the city taketh a plough, to which he fastened a culter or ploughshare of brass and, so yoked in the plough an ox and a cow, he himself holding the plough did make round about the compass of the city a deep furrow. Those which followed him, had the charge to throw the turfs of earth inward into the city, which the ploughshare had raised up, and not to leave any of them turned outward. The furrow thus cast up was the whole compass of their wall, which they call in Latin Pomerium, by shortening of the syllables, for post murum: to wit, after wall. But in the place where they determined to make a gate, they did take off the ploughshare, and draw the plough, with leaving a certain space of earth unbroken up: whereupon the Romans think all the compass of their walls holy and sacred, except their gates. For if their gates had been hallowed and sanctified, they would have had a conscience through them to have brought in, or carried out of the city, any things necessary for the life of man, that had not been pure and clean.

Plutarch, *Life of Romulus*, translated by Sir Thomas North, 1579; J. M. Dent, London, 1898, Vol. I, pp. 105–6

❹ ROME WHEN THE REPUBLIC BEGAN

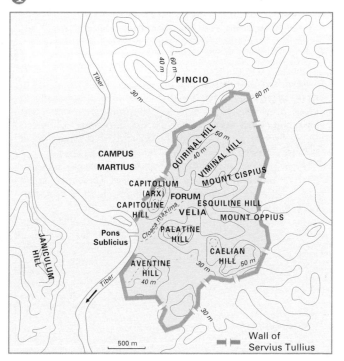

❶ THE VOTING BRIDGE

Bibliothèque Nationale,
Paris. Cabinet des Médailles

In the 2nd century BC *Rome adopted the secret written ballot. To avoid pressure from petitioners, every citizen in turn crossed a bridge into the* septum, *where he was given a wooden token on which he scratched the sign indicating yes or no before dropping it into the ballot-box.*

❷ The Roman Constitution

Polybius (c.200–c.125/120 BC) was the first Greek historian to have centred his historical writings on Rome, where he lived for sixteen years, at first as a detainee but later as an admirer. His description of the Roman constitution remains a model of its kind.

. . . Three systems, aristocracy, monarchy and democracy, coexisted in the Roman Republic, each given so exactly equal a share and all working so well for the administration, that no one could say with certainty, even in Rome itself, whether the Republic was an aristocracy, a monarchy or a democracy. How could they? The power of the consuls made it look like a monarchy; that of the Senate suggested an aristocracy; while the power of the people made it seem like a democratic State . . . .

The consuls, when they were not commanding the army but were working in Rome, were masters of all public affairs. The other public officials were their obedient subordinates, with the exception of the tribunes. As regards preparing and waging war, their power was virtually absolute.

The main task of the Senate was to administer public finance. It supervised both income and expenditure. If a mission had to be sent to settle a quarrel, to request or command something, to accept a surrender or declare war, only the Senate was competent to act. When foreign ambassadors came to Rome, it also had the task of deciding how to act with them and what response to make.

The people . . . were the masters when it came to passing or rejecting laws and declaring war or peace. They alone could judge alliances, truces and treaties, confirming them or declaring them null and void.

Polybius, *Histories*, VI

Such was the identity of the patriciate, the élite of the *gentes*, which monopolized power.

The *plebs* defended itself against the pretensions of this caste and even went so far as to secede on the Aventine Hill in 494 BC, setting up a plebeian city alongside the patrician city.

Little by little, however, matters evolved. The patriciate allowed the *plebs* a limited role in the city's political life. In the middle of the 5th century BC the Law of the Twelve Tables – a kind of legal code, no doubt inscribed on bronze tablets erected in the Forum – revealed a new frame of mind. Even if what remains of its content seems largely to favour the aristocrats, the fact that there was now a corpus of written law, 'the source of all public and private law' as Livy called it (*History of Rome*, III, 34, 6), marked considerable progress. Roman law was immensely influential: its principles are still applied in Europe and the world today.

The institutions of the Roman Republic were based on a relative separation of powers and on mutual control by the different organs of government. The *Comitia* or People's Assembly elected the public officials and voted laws, sometimes involving plebiscites; but, although it appeared democratic, it was dominated by the rich.

The public officials wielded executive power. To prevent a disguised return to monarchy, they were appointed for one year only, not renewable and they had to act as a collegiate body. Gradually there came to be a system of seniority, the *cursus honorum*: to make a career, one had first to be a *quaestor* (handling the budget), then *aedile* (municipal administrator), then *praetor* (judge), then *consul* in charge of general policy and in command of the armies.

Alongside this *cursus* the Tribunes of the Plebs, established in 494 BC and limited to plebeian members, enjoyed an inviolable right of veto on decisions by other public officials.

The *Senate*, composed of former officials, remained aristocratic. It was a key body in the government of Rome.

A hereditary aristocracy, the rising power of money, 'outsiders' seeking a role: these three competing forces in European history were already present in the Roman Republic. The balance between them did not survive the results of Rome's conquests.

Rome's conquests: Rome and Italy (5th and 4th centuries BC)

It was by no means obvious that Rome would become a great power. Until the mid-4th century BC the Senate, which was in charge of foreign policy, had shown great caution and rejected any idea of foreign adventures. Indeed, it had had to face immediate danger, owing to the presence of rival Latin or Etruscan cities like Veii, 17 kilometres to the north, as well as the pressure from mountain-dwellers descending on the coastal plains. While this was the traditional rivalry between shepherds and settled farmers, there was also, from 390 to 386 BC, a raid on Rome by Gauls from northern Italy, who captured all of the city except for the Capitol.

When Rome sent its legions against the Samnites towards the end of the 4th century BC, it seemed a distant expedition, although Samnium was little more than 200 kilometres from Rome. This marked the beginning of some hard-fought wars – the three Samnite Wars (343–290 BC), in which Rome suffered several resounding defeats, but was finally victorious.

In this way, by the beginning of the 3rd century BC, Rome was master of the whole peninsula save for the Greek cities in the south. Within ten years they had also fallen to Rome: the last to succumb was Taranto, in 272. Would the installation of a garrison at Rhegium, across the straits from Messina, the key to Sicily, lead to a conflict with Carthage, already settled in the west of the island which it saw as its private preserve? The risk was all the greater in that Rome was seeking to become a sea power, as suggested by its building the port of Ostia in about 355 BC.

Rome's conquests: Rome and the Mediterranean (3rd–1st centuries BC)

The conflict with Carthage, known as the Punic Wars, revealed how Rome's political horizons had broadened. The timidity it had shown in the first centuries of its history now gave way to imperialism, often highly aggressive. It took only two-and-a-half centuries to dominate almost the whole of the Mediterranean world.

During the first Punic War (264–241 BC) the fighting was still confined to Sicily, which Rome's victory made a Roman province. Then, while Carthage was building a new empire in Spain, the Romans extended their rule to Cisalpine Gaul and the edge of the Adriatic. The second Punic War (219–202 BC) was fought in Spain, Italy, North Africa and the Greek world. The brilliant Carthaginian commander Hannibal inflicted some memorable defeats on the Roman legions, as at Lake Trasimene in 217 BC and Cannae in 216 BC. But Rome did not weaken: in 202, having crossed to Africa, Scipio obliged Carthage to surrender after winning the battle of Zama. Sixty years later the third Punic War (149–146 BC) ended in the destruction of Carthage and the creation of the Roman province of Africa.

③ ROME AND THE CONQUEST OF ITALY
(5th–2nd century BC)

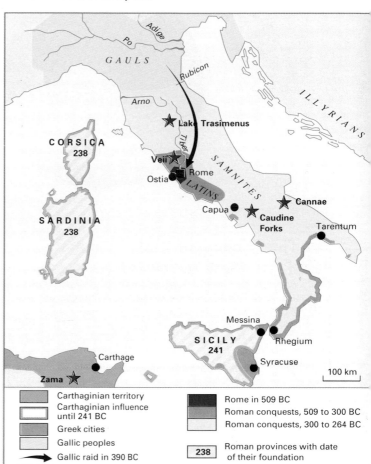

- Carthaginian territory
- Carthaginian influence until 241 BC
- Greek cities
- Gallic peoples
- → Gallic raid in 390 BC
- Rome in 509 BC
- Roman conquests, 509 to 300 BC
- Roman conquests, 300 to 264 BC
- 238 Roman provinces with date of their foundation

---

④ Victory over Carthage

The Roman historian Florus (1st and 2nd centuries AD) saw this as the decisive turning-point in the history of Rome.

. . . *For the Roman Empire there was no greater day[1] than that on which the two greatest generals of all time both before and since that war – one the conqueror of Italy, the other of Spain – led their armies to battle against each other. But the leaders themselves met to discuss the peace terms. They remained motionless for a long time, paralysed by the esteem in which each held the other. When no peace agreement was reached, the trumpets sounded. Both confessed that the lines of battle could not have been better organized and that no one could have fought with greater spirit: Scipio said so of Hannibal's army and Hannibal of Scipio's. Yet Hannibal yielded. Africa was the reward of victory and, straightaway afterward, the world.*

1. The day of the battle of Zama (202 BC).

Florus, *Epitome of the Wars of the Roman People*, I, 22

❶ A NEW MILITARY RESOURCE: THE ELEPHANT

Decorated plate, 3rd century BC

Before its use by Hannibal, the elephant was first employed against Rome by Pyrrhus, fighting on behalf of Taranto.

---

❷ The Triumph of Paulus Aemilius

... Next unto them, he came himself in his charret triumphing, which was passing sumptuously set forth and adorned. It was a noble sight to behold: and yet the person of himself only was worth the looking on, without all that great pomp and magnificence. For he was apparelled in a purple gown branched with gold, and carried in his right hand a laurel bough, as all his army did besides: the which being divided by bands and companies, followed the triumphing charret of their captain, some of the soldiers singing songs of victory, which the Romans use to sing in like triumphs, mingling them with merry pleasant toys, rejoicing at their captain.

Plutarch, *Life of Paulus Aemilius*, translated by Sir Thomas North, 1579; J. M. Dent, London, 1898, Vol. III, pp. 125–6

In the eastern Mediterranean there were still the Hellenistic kingdoms, heirs of Alexander's Empire and bitter mutual rivals. Rome had not as yet any settled policy towards them: it was well aware that they were well-organized states with an economy and a civilization that inspired respect – unlike the situation in the West.

Two Roman attacks on Philip V of Macedon forced him to abandon his possessions in Southern Greece. Then the Seleucid Antiochus III, King of Syria, was driven out of the Aegean, Asia Minor and the Hellespont.

By establishing new provinces – e.g. the province of Gallia Narbonensis in southern Gaul or the province of Asia, the former Kingdom of Pergamum bequeathed by its king to the Roman people – Rome had come to dominate almost the entire Mediterranean world by the end of the 2nd century BC. In the 1st century BC Caesar added 'Long-haired Gaul' (*Gallia Comata*), and Octavius added Egypt. The Roman Empire (including Cleopatra's Egypt) was European, but also African and Asian: it was now universal; and the Mediterranean had become 'our sea' – '*Mare Nostrum*'.

The ends and means of conquest

Such expansion would not have been possible without the exceptional quality of the Roman legions. They were a citizen's army, whereas the other powers at that time, Carthage or the Hellenistic Kingdoms, had to rely on mercenaries.

But the conquerors faced long and powerful resistance: from the Nervii and then the Eburones under Ambiorix in Gallia Belgica; from Vercing-

---

❸ THE CONQUEST OF THE MEDITERRANEAN

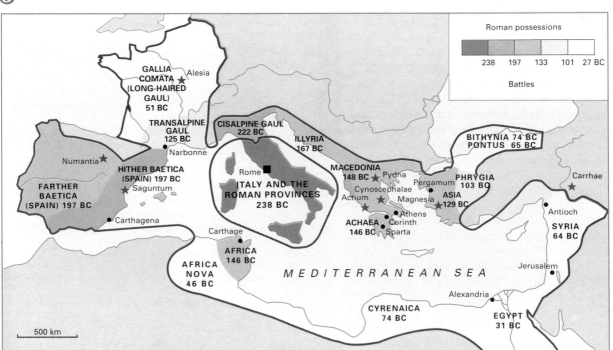

etorix, who for a time managed to raise almost all of Gaul against Caesar; and from Boudicca, the Queen of the Iceni, in what is now Norfolk, England. In AD 9, Arminius, a Cheruscan prince, defeated the Roman general Varus in the Teutoburg forest and thereby limited Rome's grip on the borders of Germany. Earlier, north-east of Old Castile, there had been the dramatic siege of Numantia in 133 BC, in which the Numantians had preferred to burn their city and commit mass suicide than surrender. This heroic gesture, which acquired symbolic status, eclipsed for ever the victory of Scipio Aemilianus.

The spoils of conquest were of benefit only to the Romans – in the narrow sense of the inhabitants of the city – whether it was the booty collected by the soldiers, the tribute exacted by Roman governors like the famous Verres in Sicily or the gifts given to the people of Rome, who from 167 BC onwards no longer paid direct taxes.

In the conquered regions the Senate followed the policy of divide and rule: hence the great diversity of jurisdictions. Some cities became subject to Rome, directly by the fact of surrender; at the other extreme were the colonies, made up of Roman citizens who had left the capital to found new Romes, overseeing the surrounding areas and beginning to Romanize them. Between these two extremes there was a variety of allied towns and *municipia* which kept their original institutions, but some or all of whose citizens enjoyed the same rights (civil in the case of colonies or *municipia* under Latin law, political if under Roman law) as the inhabitants of Rome.

In Italy these distinctions tended to disappear at the beginning of the 1st century BC, as a result of the paradoxical 'Social War', in which the allies made war on Rome in the hope of becoming Roman citizens, were defeated by the Roman armies, but then were granted their wishes by the Senate. Only from that time onwards was it legitimate to speak of a Roman Italy.

Outside Italy, however, the provinces were shamelessly exploited; and, if the Empire had not changed its policy, the Europe of the 20th century would no doubt lack any sense that its civilization owed much to Rome.

The death-throes of the Republic (2nd and 1st centuries BC)

The rapid growth of the empire led to more than a century of crises, out of which arose the Imperial regime in Rome. The institutions of the old Republic proved ill-adapted to virtual world domination: the economy, society and people's mentality all changed.

④ LEGIONARIES OF THE REPUBLICAN PERIOD
Louvre Museum, Paris
Wearing a helmet and breastplate, the legionary carried an oval, convex wooden shield. Here, his short sword cannot be seen, nor his sharp iron javelin with its wooden shaft.

⑤ ROME AS A NAVAL POWER
A cast made from Trajan's Column: embarking at Brindisi in AD 105. Bucharest, Historical Museum of the Romanian Socialist Republic; Rome, Vatican Museum
The struggle against Carthage obliged the Romans to build a fleet and they went on developing it to safeguard their lines of communication in the Mediterranean and the Channel. Naval technology barely changed from the Republic to the Empire.

❶ The exploitation of the provinces

Cicero, a lawyer and statesman in the Republican tradition, made famous the misdeeds of Verres in Sicily

... There is not a single property, inherited from a father or grandfather, that he has not adjudged confiscated by reason of his sovereign power. Incalculable sums of money have been levied from the possessions of arable farmers by means of criminal additions to the laws; the most faithful allies have been counted as enemies and treated as such; Roman citizens have been tortured and put to death as if they were slaves ....

Cicero, *First prosecution of Verres*, V

❷ THE MONARCHICAL TEMPTATION

The decline of the Republican institutions as Rome's possessions expanded led victorious generals to try their luck with experiments bordering on monarchy, in the teeth of the traditionalism of the senatorial aristocracy.

SULLA

(138–78 BC)
Louvre Museum, Paris
Having defeated Mithridates in Asia, Sulla seized Rome by force in 83 BC and ruled it as a dictatorship for several years before 'abdicating' in 79 BC.

JULIUS CAESAR

(?100–44 BC)
Barraco Museum, Rome
After conquering the Gauls, Caesar took Rome by force, but his monarchical style of government led to his assassination by the senatorial party.

Rural smallholdings declined and the great estates (*latifundia*) grew. Being called up for war every year the peasants could not look after their fields or restore them if, as too often happened, they had to be abandoned. Even when they were successful, they were undercut by low-price wheat imported from the provinces. So they left the land and swelled the urban proletariat, where they became the clients of their former military leaders and had to serve their political interests. Plebeian status now was no longer a matter of birth but of poverty.

The *nobilitas*, on the other hand, i.e. senators who had made their fortunes in politics, seized the *ager publicus* – the land taken from defeated enemies. The estates that they thus accumulated were devoted to stockbreeding and run by slaves.

At the same time there developed a class of merchants and financiers whose wealth was not locked up in land. They profited from the development of trade and taxation. These 'knights' had political ambitions and relied for support at some times on the senatorial aristocracy and at others on the *plebs*.

There was also a psychological change. True, the people remained superstitiously attached to old beliefs and past rituals. But the best educated in society were attracted by Greece and later by the East. Roman religion became imbued with mythology that had sprung from the imaginative spirit of the Greeks, but alien to Rome. Thus the austere Jupiter of the Romans and Etruscans came to be credited with the same adventures among mortals as his Greek predecessor Zeus – with whom he was soon amalgamated.

Stoic philosophy, also from Greece, acquired a number of followers. Its praise of moderation and self-control corresponded to the moral ideal of *gravitas* upheld by Roman tradition. The education of a young man of good family now had to include a long stay in Greece. This produced the Greco-Roman civilization of which Europe is the heir: it combined the down-to-earth practicality of Romulus's descendants with the intellectual and artistic sophistication of those of Pericles.

The politicians of this period were most often attached to their immediate personal interests or those of their class: they were sometimes unaware that these changes in material reality called for similar reform of the institutions. Even when they could imagine reforms, they rejected them. This was the time of Rome's 'civil wars'.

Tiberius, and then Caius Gracchus, tried to restore peasant smallholdings at the expense of the senatorial aristocracy. But they were only feebly supported by the potential beneficiaries and were later assassinated – at a ten years' interval – by the henchmen of the *nobilitas*. They thereby won the reputation of revolutionaries – whereas the spirit of their policy was rather that of restoring the past. The time of reformers gave way to that of the conquerors.

Marius, a knight, enrolled in his army a number of plebeians, who had hitherto been excluded. They became devoted to him body and soul, and backed his ambition to become head of state. But he was a better general than a politician and he failed to carry through his reform. The same fate dogged Sulla, who seized power by force of arms, liquidated his enemies by a series of lethal proscriptions and exercised a sort of permanent dictatorship, in fact a disguised monarchy. In 79 BC he abdicated, for reasons that remain obscure.

Both Pompey and Caesar also owed their political success to their armies, which were more loyal to their leaders than to the Republic and its discredited institutions. Their military campaigns, by Pompey in the East and Caesar in Gaul, were dictated less by the interests of Rome than by their need to win glory and gold to promote and finance their careers. Factional struggles led to the assassination of first one and then the other, without, however, securing the impossible – the restoration of the former Republic.

It was Octavius, the nephew and adopted son of Julius Caesar, who succeeded where his predecessors had failed. Abandoning the violence that he and Mark Antony had used on those responsible for Caesar's assassination, Octavius incarnated Roman virtues, by contrast with his former ally, who in the arms of Cleopatra had succumbed to the seductions of the Orient.

Octavius's institutional 'reforms were discreet and gradual, so much so that historians cannot clearly date the moment when the Republic came to an end. Theoretically, the Senate retained all its prerogatives and Octavius was only its *Princeps*, the first among others who were equal to him, or *primus inter pares*. It was on this account that his regime has been called a principate. The traditional offices of state remained and year by year he filled one or other of them, jointly with other citizens, thus seeming to respect both annual rotation and collective rule.

But he took among his *praenomina* that of *Imperator* – whence the words emperor and empire – the title by which the victorious general was hailed at the ceremony of his triumph, meaning that victory was a function of his inborn virtues. The Senate proclaimed him Augustus, a religious title which gave him a sacred character and became the *praenomen* of all his successors. So behind its republican façade, the Roman Empire was in fact an adaptation of the Hellenistic type of monarchy.

❸ OCTAVIUS

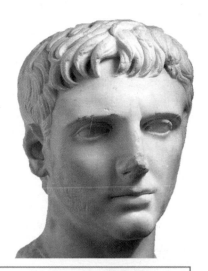

(63 BC–AD 14)
Arles, Musée lapidaire d'art païen
Octavius was 19 when the dictator died. For this reason the Senate thought he was inoffensive, and backed him against Mark Antony, who headed the Caesarian party.

❹ The establishment of monarchical power

40 BC Octavius takes the *praenomen* of Imperator[1]
30 BC Octavius receives the power of a tribune[2]
27 BC Octavius receives the *praenomen* of Augustus[3]
19 BC Augustus becomes *Praefectus morum*, supervisor of public behaviour[4]
12 BC Augustus becomes *Pontifex maximus*, chief of the high priests[5]

1. *Title given to a victorious general at his ceremonial triumph; by becoming Octavius's praenomen, it both implied an innate link between him and victory, and gave him* imperium – absolute military power – over the provinces.
2. *As a patrician, Octavius could not be a tribune. But he was given the corresponding privileges of inviolability and the right of veto.*
3. *This title implied a religious 'authority', a novelty in Roman institutions.*
4. *Like the Censor, the Praefectus morum appointed new Senators.*
5. *This title made Augustus the head of the national religion.*

❺ The restoration of a republican façade

. . . In my sixth and seventh consulates (28–27 BC), after I had put an end to the civil wars, being invested with absolute power by universal consent, I divested myself of the powers I exerted and put them in the hands of the Senate and People of Rome. In return, I was given by decree of the Senate the praenomen of Augustus.[1] . . . From that moment, I enjoyed authority over all [auctoritas]; but I never had greater legal power [potestas] than any of the other officials who were my colleagues . . . .

1. The name Augustus (from the verb *augere*, to increase), hitherto reserved for places and objects consecrated to the gods, gave him religious authority (*auctoritas*).

Res Gestae Divi Augusti, 34, 1

Roman Europe

① HADRIAN'S WALL
The wall stretched 118 kilometres from the North Sea to the Irish Sea. On the inner side were roads and garrisons; on the outer there were fortified outposts.

② THE EMPIRE IN THE 2ND CENTURY AD
Italy and the provinces

Although centred on the Mediterranean, the Roman Empire extended well beyond it, especially in Europe. Here, it spread Greco-Roman civilization, bringing with it a limited but real degree of unity.

The 'Pax Romana'

A peaceful foreign policy? With the establishment of the Empire, Rome's conquests were not complete. Augustus and his immediate successors had to give up their hope of conquering Germany as far as the Elbe and limited themselves, very largely, to the Rhine and the Danube. Great Britain was occupied as far as the Scottish border. Trajan conquered a large part of present-day Romania. But after his death, in AD 117, Hadrian was content simply to maintain and defend the Empire as it was.

Henceforth, the frontiers were protected by the fairly complex system of the *limes*: permanent encampments of legionaries like those of *Mogontiacum* (Mainz), *Argentorate* (Strasbourg), or *Aquincum* (Budapest). Behind the *limes*, consisting of ditches and palisades, were smaller garrisons, with small forts in the front line, linked by an elaborate system of roads. Such fortifications

represented an essentially defensive strategy.

Furthermore, the number of legions was reduced and many provinces became *inermes* (literally, unarmed), i.e. without military garrisons. The army was growing unpopular as a career for Italians: increasingly, it was made up of provincials. By comparison with the expansionist policy of earlier centuries and the Germanic raids that began at the end of the 2nd century BC, there now seems to have been relative peace.

Peace within the Empire? Here too, the convulsion of civil war was a thing of the past. True, contemporary histories might suggest otherwise. Names like Caligula, Nero or Domitian have sinister connotations. But these historians, however outstanding, were neither impartial nor comprehensive, because men like Suetonius and above all Tacitus, who came from a Senatorial background, were nostalgic for the Republic and excessively critical of the imperial regime and its incumbents. And they failed to be comprehensive because the events they described were confined to the Imperial Palace, or at best to the city of Rome, not the whole of the Empire.

Gradually, the ambiguity of the Imperial regime began to fade: the traditional offices of state became more formal than real, while real power was wielded by the prefects, officials appointed by the Emperor, mainly from the equestrian order: this was the triumph of the knights.

The volume and variety of matters with which the Emperor had to deal led to the development of a bureaucracy, dominated by freed men of Greek origin, who had a real sense of the state. The Imperial chancellery was a centralizing administrative institution prefiguring those of modern states, although hampered by the slowness and difficulty of communications at that time.

During the 2nd century AD the Senate was gradually supplanted by the Council of the Prince, which assembled round the Emperor the senior officials and heads of office of the Imperial chancellery. This regime did not become wholly monarchical, because the Emperors could not or dared not establish a permanent system of hereditary succession. Under the Antonines, when the Empire was at its height, they practised adoption – 'entrusting the Empire to the most worthy'. But the problem was never finally solved.

Roman society remained stratified, but there was at times a certain class mobility. No one dreamed of abolishing slavery – both the cause and the effect of technological stagnation. But the *Pax Romana* helped to reduce the number of slaves put on the market and their conditions appreciably improved. The number of freed men constantly increased and some of them played an important economic and political role.

❸ The promotion of knights and freed men under Claudius (AD 41–54)

Justice, traditionally administered by the Praetors, came more and more to be the province of Procurators, chosen by the Emperor from among the equestrian order. The last sentence in the following extract shows Tacitus's critical view of this practice.

In the same year the Prince was often heard to remark that the judgements given by his Procurators should have the same validity as his personal decisions. And, lest it be thought that this statement had been made only by chance, a decree of the Senate repeated it more precisely and comprehensively than ever before. In fact, the divine Augustus had given legal competence to the Roman knights who governed Egypt and had laid down that their decisions should be just as valid as if they had been made by officials in Rome. Then, in other provinces and even in Rome itself, the right to know what had previously been confined to the Praetors was extended to the knights . . . . After that, it would be pointless to recall Matius, Vedius and other Roman knights, famous for their power, when Claudius applied to himself the same laws as the freed men that he had put in charge of his domestic affairs.

Tacitus, Annals, XII, 60

❹ Improving the lot of the slaves

Gaius was a jurist in the 2nd century AD. His Institutes, written in about AD 161, were a methodical summary of the principles of Roman law and were largely copied by those who worked for Justinian.

Thus slaves are under the potestas *of their masters. This* potestas, *in fact, is part of the law of nations: for we may observe that in general, in all peoples, masters have the power of life or death over their slaves; and anything acquired by the slave is acquired by the master.*

But in our day neither Roman citizens nor any other of those who are under the rule of the Roman people are allowed to treat their slaves unduly harshly and without good reason. For, under an order of the Emperor Antoninus, anyone who kills his own slave without reason is no less responsible than someone who kills the slave of another. Even excessive strictness on the part of masters was forbidden by a decree of the same Prince. Consulted by certain provincial governors on the subject of slaves who sought asylum in the temples of the gods or at the statues of the princes, he decreed that if the masters' severity was intolerable they should be obliged to sell their slaves. And he was right in both cases: for we should not misuse our rights; and that is also the reason why the spendthrift is deprived of the right to dispose of his property.

Gaius, Institutes, I. 52–3

➊ 'INSULAE' AT OSTIA

These tenements were of three or four storeys, the ground floors often being used as shops while the roof was a flat terrace. The sanitary arrangements were rudimentary.

➋ THE IMPERIAL FORUMS

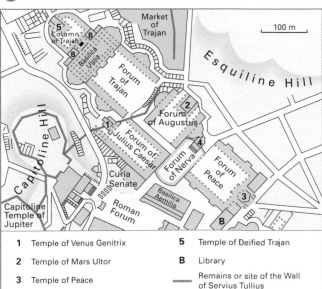

1	Temple of Venus Genitrix	5	Temple of Deified Trajan
2	Temple of Mars Ultor	B	Library
3	Temple of Peace	—	Remains or site of the Wall of Servius Tullius
4	Temple of Minerva		

Rome's attitude towards the indigenous population also changed. More and more natives of the provinces were individually or collectively given citizenship under Latin or Roman law. This process led to the Edict of Caracalla, in AD 212, under which all free men living in the Empire were henceforth Roman citizens. This integration into the Roman system was much more a function of belonging to a common civilization than a matter of race. Racial discrimination was in any case outflanked in advance, since it was common for Romans and non-Romans to marry.

This was no doubt linked with the Roman idea of the family, which was concerned less with perpetuating the race than with perpetuating the family name. If there were no male heirs, an heir was adopted. This very common practice made possible a range of choice that natural inheritance did not. It may just possibly be that this was one of the reasons for Rome's falling birth-rate.

At all events, early in the 1st century AD the situation of the Roman woman began to improve. The traditional form of marriage, which had made her a perpetual minor, passing from the tutelage (*manus*) of her father to that of her husband, gave place gradually to marriage *sine manu*, or without tutelage. While the husband still retained the dowry, the wife could acquire personal possessions and deal with them as she wished. As customs evolved, moreover, women began to enjoy greater personal freedom, so much so that some fathers hesitated to marry off their daughters without their consent. This was not far from marriage by mutual agreement.

Rome and the provinces

The *Pax Romana* made possible the harmonious development of the provinces, but their Romanization went deeper in some places than in others. It was greater in the regions that had been longest in the Roman domain, such as Gallia Narbonensis as compared with the rest of Gaul. It was also very intense in frontier zones, along the Rhine or the Danube, where the permanent installation of the legions more effectively introduced both the material appurtenances of Roman civilization and its cultural effects.

Everywhere, the model was Rome itself, whose population in Trajan's time was probably more than half a million. Such a metropolis, enormous for its day, could not live without supplies from the entire Roman world. This, inevitably, was why the port of Ostia was developed. Henceforth Rome was inseparable from the sea.

The poorest members of the population lived in collective buildings of several storeys, grouped in islands (*insulae*). The traditional Roman villas, with their *atria* open to the sky and their cloisters enclosing a garden, were built only on the surrounding hills.

The heart of the city was made up of public monuments and their attendant public works. Roman town-planning, inspired by Greek models, combined a rigour that had its own beauty with a utilitarian aim: the object was to serve the citizens' welfare.

The imperial *fora*, of which there were many, responded to the needs of urban growth, but also embodied their creators' desire to leave a permanent mark of their glory. More regular in shape than their Greek models, they were esplanades surrounded by porticos, with temples, basilicas and libraries. Those in the provinces followed a similar pattern.

Rome was full of temples, altars, permanent markets, theatres, amphitheatres for gladiatorial combat and circuses for chariot races. The Roman baths – rather like the hammams of the East – portray better than any other monument the style of life of the Romans, with their rooms of different temperatures, hot and cold swimming pools, massage rooms and gymnasia. They required an abundant supply of water, which meant building aqueducts on lines carefully calculated by trained hydraulic engineers.

Rome left its mark on the provinces by the development and creation of towns, linked by a network of roads. Every town, imitating Rome as much as its means allowed, was centred on its forum, the meeting-place of the two perpendicular axes of its town plan, the *cardo* and the *decumanus*. Many aqueducts survive to this day, as at Segovia in Spain or the Pont du Gard near Nîmes in France. Those that served Lyon even included siphons. Theatres and amphitheatres were built, as at Arles, and triumphal arches, as at Orange, whose theatre is one of the few to retain its rear wall, which Louis XIV called 'the finest wall in the realm'. There are countless Roman baths: those at Trier in Germany and Bath in England are particularly rich.

An essential feature of every town was the temple or altar dedicated to Rome and Augustus, *Romae et Augusti*. By linking his own prestige to that of Rome, the Emperor made popular veneration of him a little more abstract but rather more immune from the ravages of time.

The imperial cult embodied the loyalty of the city to the Empire and to Roman civilization. It was a little cold, for it involved the official authorities far more than the spontaneous reaction of individual people.

Rome was also the model as regards institutions. Every city had its officials, appointed annually and acting in concert: the names might

❸ TOWN MONUMENTS IN THE PROVINCES
From the top downwards: the theatre and amphitheatre in Arles (France); the aqueduct at Segovia (Spain); the Roman baths at Trier (Germany); the temple of Evora (Portugal).

① A LARGE RURAL VILLA: VILLIERS-SUR-AILLY

Somme, France

Aerial photography, in the right weather conditions, can reveal traces that are invisible on the ground. Where there were puddled-clay or cob-mortar walls, deep digging brought to the surface clay soil, whose outlines show the plan of the villa.

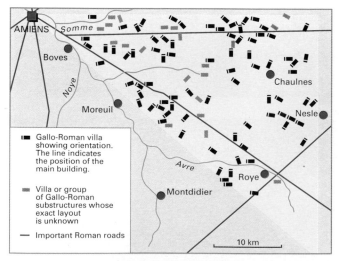

Gallo-Roman villa showing orientation. The line indicates the position of the main building.

Villa or group of Gallo-Roman substructures whose exact layout is unknown

— Important Roman roads

10 km

② RURAL SETTLEMENT IN PICARDY

A systematic study to the south-east of Amiens, in ancient times Samarobriva, has revealed 103 villas in a triangular area of just over 500 square kilometres. They were scattered homesteads, contrasting with today's villages and bearing witness to the sense of security resulting from the Pax Romana or Roman Peace.

differ from those in Rome, but not the functions. The main role was that of the local senate, made up of one hundred decurions chosen from among former officials or the richest citizens. Some of these decurions went to the Senate in Rome.

In any case, as in Rome, it was the wealthiest who governed the cities, which gained from their 'euergetism' – from a Greek word meaning benefactor.

Was the countryside untouched by this process of Romanization? This was long believed to be the case, owing to the scarcity of documentation on the subject. But the progress of archaeology has modified modern historians' views. Aerial archaeology has made it possible to draw a real map of rural occupation in the great grain-growing plains of northern France, especially in Picardy.

Studies of the same kind elsewhere in France but also in Britain may even help to quantify, in some sectors at least, the degree to which the land was used in Roman times. What emerges is a picture of an already advanced agricultural economy, in which the landowners were rich and the farmers, who tilled the soil, were quite the reverse. This was no doubt one of the keys of 'euergetism': through it, the city lived by exploiting the countryside.

But it was not entirely neglected. Recent discoveries have identified rural civic centres in the open countryside, with no town or villa nearby – which shows that they were independent. Near to a temple or some sacred place more or less Romanized, there can be found baths and – more significantly – a theatre/amphitheatre for gladiatorial fights.

Some fifteen or so such places have been found in Gaul. They must have made it easier to gather from time to time the country-dwellers who were normally dispersed and bring them some of the benefits and distractions of the town.

The economic unity of Roman Europe

At its height the Roman Empire covered nearly 3½ million square kilometres, with 10,000 kilometres of frontier and an estimated population of 70 million people.

With territory in Africa, from Tingitanus (the area round *Tingi*, now Tangier) to Egypt, in Asia Minor, Syria and Palestine, the Empire was more than European; and its non-European provinces played a vital role in the imperial economy.

It was also less than European, because its legions stopped at the Rhine and the Danube, leaving outside its frontiers the greater part of the Germanic, Scandinavian and Slav worlds, as well as Ireland, which for this reason became a kind of

Celtic reservation. That did not prevent these places having many contacts with the Roman Empire and therefore being influenced by it.

But the centre of gravity of the Roman Empire was the Mediterranean, which became a virtual Roman Lake. It was in fact the fundamental unifying factor in the economy of the ancient world, even if sea trade practically ceased from mid-November until the beginning of March, owing to bad weather. This was the period of the *mare clausum*, the shut-down sea. Port installations were improved: Claudius built a lighthouse at Ostia and Trajan added jetties and a mole. All over the Mediterranean, ship-chandlers opened agencies and depots. The lighthouse at *Gesoriacum* (Boulogne-sur-Mer, France), built under Caligula to facilitate links with Britain, continued to be used until the 17th century. Ship-building, on the other hand, made little progress and sailors still faced considerable risks, as underwater archaeology has confirmed. Divers have found many sunken Roman ships, which have revealed the size and nature of typical cargoes – rarely more than a thousand tons – as well as how the ships were made.

Alongside the development of sea trade there was much use of the rivers. The port of Arles, for example, began to overtake the older port of Narbonne, since goods from there could be carried up the Rhône and the Saône to reach the armies of the Rhine.

❸ The importance of the *annona*

The administrators of the annona were responsible for supplying Rome with food. The Emperor Claudius was unjustly ridiculed at the time for contravening the custom of the mare clausum at a time of scarcity. A later text by Gaius laid down the conditions for enjoying the advantages described below by Suetonius: the ships must be available for the annona for six years, and they must have a capacity of 10,000 modii, that is 31 casks of 2.8 cubic metres each.

He always had the very greatest concern for the city and for the annona . . . . Since during one serious reduction in the annona, owing to continually bad harvests, he had been detained in the middle of the Forum by a crowd that booed him and threw crumbs of bread – to the point that he had great difficulty in reaching the safety of his house on the Palatine and even then had to use a service entrance – he decided to organize the arrival of supplies even in the depths of winter. To that end, he promised guaranteed profits to the wholesalers, taking responsibility himself for any losses they might incur owing to bad weather. He also offered a large number of advantages to those willing to build merchant ships, each according to his social situation . . . .

Suetonius, *Lives of the Twelve Caesars*, Claudius, 18–19

❹ THE ECONOMY OF THE ROMAN EMPIRE IN THE 2ND CENTURY AD

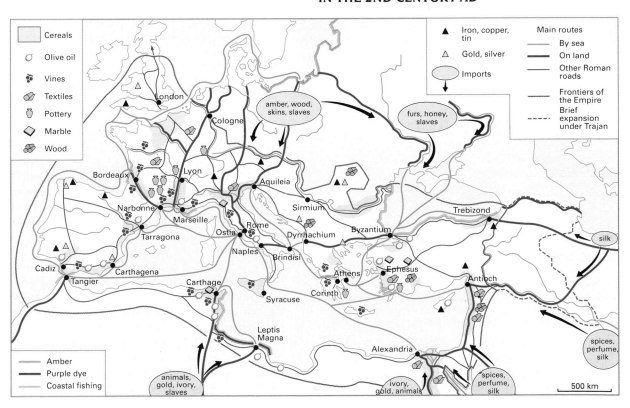

① MERCHANT SHIP IN THE PORT OF OSTIA
Torlonia Collection, Rome

The ship, with her steering oar at the side, is passing in front of the lighthouse, where a lamp is burning. Her sails bear the likeness of Romulus and Remus with the she-wolf. She is greeted on the left by a guardian spirit and the Roman eagle, and on the lower right by Neptune, with Bonus Eventus, the god of happy endings, above him.

② THE REAPING-MACHINE OF TRIER
Gaumais Museum, Virton, Belgium

Discovered in the ramparts of Montaubon-Buzenol, in the south-east corner of Belgium, associated with Trier in ancient times, this bas-relief depicts the front of a reaping-machine, pushed by a mule. In his Natural History, Pliny the Elder described such machines:

... great reaping-machines are pushed across the wheat-fields. The side is covered with teeth, mounted on two wheels, to which a draught animal is harnessed, back to front: the ears of grain thus torn off fall into the reaping-machine.

Important as river traffic was, it did not prevent the Romans building a network of roads, whose aims were both political and military, although trade benefited too. They often followed the route of earlier roads; but they were notable for being so straight, marching from one town to another regardless of the countryside, rather like motorways today.

The imperial postal system set up by Augustus established posting-houses spaced out at intervals depending on the difficulty of the intervening journeys. There were stables with the necessary harness, coach-houses for vehicles, warehouses for goods and inns or hostelries for travellers. They were somewhat reminiscent of the caravanserais of the East and often turned into markets or even actual towns. This is recalled in the name of Saverne in France (north-west of Strasbourg), which is derived from *tabernae*, shops.

Good communications enabled the economy to be universal – within the Empire, that is – and not only regional or local. This was further encouraged by the fact that the whole Empire used one currency.

Despite the persistence of local customs, the common use of Roman law, especially with regard to trade and property, had a similar effect.

It would obviously be anachronistic to speak of a Roman 'common market'; but on certain points – law and currency – it is the 20th century that lags behind.

Agriculture was the key sector of the economy at that time. Landowning was set out in a register: aerial photography has revealed its broad outlines in the Po valley and the valley of the Rhône. Some fragments of the Orange register have been found carved on stone. Large properties dominated the scene, but they were more and more often divided up into smallholdings.

Agricultural productivity was not high and biennial crop rotation was by far the most frequent. Tilling by wooden swing-plough was more common than the use of the wheeled plough, invented in Gaul because better adapted to the heavier, richer soil in some of its regions. The main product of the soil was grain, especially wheat, followed by wine, whose production spread further and further north. Olive-growing developed in Spain and Gallia Narbonensis.

Fishing led to a particularly prosperous industry in Spain, that of *garum*, a highly spiced and very nutritious sauce made of small fish, especially the scomber, and comparable to the *nuoc-mâm* of Vietnam.

Industrial activity rarely went beyond the artisan level. The state had a monopoly of the mines, highly developed in Spain, and of quarries, which were very important for an empire of builders.

Textiles were worked by the family or on the estate. Some regions, however, rich in wool or in murex (a mussel-like gastropod yielding purple dye), built up a real textile industry. Padua was renowned for drapery, Spain for woollen coats and *Mediolanum Santonum* (Saintes in south-west France) for the Gallic cowl, a coat with a hood. The greatest textile centres, nevertheless, were in the East.

Pottery was by far the most active industry. Grain, wine and oil could not be transported or preserved except in earthenware vessels, usually amphorae. The wooden cask, invented by the Gauls, remained a local speciality. The earthenware manufacturers of *Arretium* (Arezzo) and *Puteoli* (Puzzuoli), then the greatest industrial centres in Italy, faced vigorous competition from Gaul.

Every potter left his mark on his products – thereby greatly helping, without knowing it, the historians and archaeologists of today. To find in Egypt, for example, among the countless shards unearthed at a dig, the mark of a Gallic potter is to discover that the amphora made in Gaul must at least once have carried all that way some commodity which can sometimes be identified. A statistical analysis of these potsherds can reveal the broad outlines of the trade patterns both within and beyond the Roman world.

There was more activity in the Eastern than in the Western part of the Empire: but two regions were almost solely importers. One was Rome, where the authorities in charge of the *annona* bought wheat from the provinces, mainly Egypt and Africa, and also oil and wine. This trade made the fortune of Ostia; and the debris of amphorae near the Tiber, downstream from the centre of Rome, even became a hill, the *Monte Testaccio*, or Shard Hill. The other pole of attraction was the *limes* with its garrisons. Arles served those of the Rhine, via the Rhône-Saône route; Aquileia, at the far north of the Adriatic, served those of the Danube via the eastern Alpine passes and the provinces of Noricum and Pannonia.

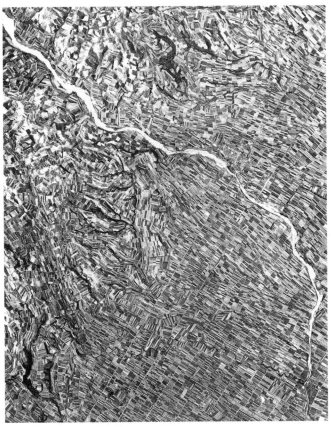

3 **A SURVIVAL FROM ROMAN LAND OWNERSHIP**
Military Geographical Institute, Rome
This high-altitude aerial photograph was taken above Imola, watered by a tributary of the Reno in the Bologna province. It shows very clearly the chequered pattern of Roman fields, all alike, rectangular and aligned north to south. Emola was founded by Sulla in the 1st century BC.

4 **THE LABOURS OF THE MONTHS**
Mosaic from Saint-Roman-en-Gal near Vienne, France, now in the Museum of National Antiquities, Saint-Germain-en-Laye
This mosaic dates from the first half of the 3rd century AD. It is one of forty elements in a rustic calendar. The scene portrays one of the activities of autumn, no doubt the picking of olives. Rome encouraged the growing of olives in Roman Provence, but the climate did not allow olive trees to grow in the Vienne area. This picture is therefore probably symbolic.

② The cult of Isis

*Metamorphoses or The Golden Ass, a Latin novel by Apuleius, dates
from the 2nd century AD. It tells the story of a young Greek who wanted to
imitate a magician who could turn himself into a bird. Unfortunately, he
succeeded only in turning himself into an ass: hence the book's alternative title.
The Egyptian goddess Isis put an end to his torments. The goddess of fecundity
and salvation, she had put together the scattered fragments of her husband
Osiris and brought him back to life.*

*The tone of the following prayer is profoundly mystical, which explains the
success of the cult throughout the Empire. It foreshadowed that of Christianity.*

*... O Holy One, who watches tirelessly over the safety of the
human race ... you show to the unfortunate the tenderness of a
mother. No day or night or moment passes, but you mark it with
your bounty, protecting people on land and sea, driving away
from them the storms of life and stretching forth the helping
hand that frees them from the toils of Fate ....*

*The gods of Heaven pay homage to you; the gods of Hell
respect you. You move the earth on its axis, you light the fires of
the Sun, you govern the universe, you trample Tartarus down.
At your gesture the winds blow, the clouds swell, the seeds
spring up, the plants grow.*

Apuleius, *The Golden Ass*, XI, 25

The cultural diversity of Roman Europe

There was limited but real unity in the economic
field. Was the same true of cultural affairs? A
superficial glance might suggest that there was.
Latin was the language of the whole Empire.
Towns were built on similar lines from one end of
the Mediterranean to the other. The gods of the
Greco-Roman pantheon were worshipped everywhere. All that is true; but more detailed analysis
shows that differences persisted.

Was Latin the Empire's only language? Certainly not, because in the East Greek was used as
an administrative language alongside Latin. In
any case, the administrative language, like the
literary language, could not then – as now – claim
to be the same as the spoken language, which was
much closer to indigenous idioms.

There was most probably a degree of bilingual-
ism, closer to Latin in the towns, but in the
countryside closer to Celtic and Iberian.

Gradually, in Gaul and the Iberian Peninsula,
but much less in Britain and the lands of the Rhine
and the Danube, the local language died out, but
left its traces in vocabulary and grammatical
forms. It may well be then that there were
different kinds of Latin in Gaul and in Spain – and
perhaps even several in each of these large areas.
These ways of speaking were certainly the origins
of the Romance languages, still called 'neo-Latin',
but it is hard to know when they really differentiated themselves from Latin. At the earliest, it was
during the 3rd-century crisis in the less Romanized regions; elsewhere, it was very much later.

Religion in the Empire also provides surprises.
Undoubtedly there are inscribed slabs in all the
provinces dedicated to the gods of the Greco-
Roman pantheon. But the Roman name is often
accompanied by an indigenous nickname.

For example, in a small site at the foot of the
central Pyrenees near to *Lugdunum Convenar-
um*, now Saint-Bertrand-de-Comminges, some
twenty inscribed slabs were discovered in the
19th century. They were fairly primitive. Some
were dedicated to the god Mars, others to Mars
Leherenn and others still to Leherenn alone. Such
dedications have been found only in this one site.
It seems clear that Leherenn was a god – no doubt
a local god – worshipped by the faithful and that
for them the name of Mars was additional. Gaul
alone had tens of other names for the god Mars.

As for images of the gods, here too, alongside
traditional stereotypes there continued to be very
particular gods such as Cernunnos, shown with a
head bearing a stag's antlers, or Tarvos Trigaranus, a bull with three cranes on its back.

Religious sites also differ. In the countryside
there was often a building, the *fanum*, very

different from the traditional temple. Usually small, quadrangular, polygonal or circular, it always centred on a *cella* facing the rising sun.

A final element in the Empire's religious diversity was the fashion for Oriental cults, whose 'missionaries' seem to have been merchants and above all soldiers. Neither the imperial cult nor the rigid tradition of Roman religion could meet the spiritual and mystical needs of a large part of the Empire's population.

Among the most widespread of these cults was that of Cybele, the Great Mother of Mount Ida near Troy, and her companion Attis. It offered immortality to those who practised the rite of *taurobolium* – the sacrifice of a bull. The faithful entered a kind of ditch with a ceiling that had holes in it: through the holes they were sprayed with the blood of a bull whose throat was slit over their heads.

Later came the cult of Mithras, of Persian origin. As god of the Sun, Mithras favoured vital energy and moral discipline. Its initiates were recruited mainly in the army. In every part of the Empire archaeologists have found *mithraea*, small vaulted rooms with benches along the walls and at one end a picture of the god sacrificing a bull, whose spilt blood was the symbol of creative energy.

Judaism and Christianity were different from other religions by virtue of their belief in one God. The many Jewish communities in the Empire fitted into it well. They enjoyed a status that exempted them from practices contrary to their religion. Nor should antisemitism be blamed for the destruction of the Temple in Jerusalem by Titus in AD 70 or for the expulsion of Jews from that city, ordered by Hadrian in AD 132. These actions were in response to nationalist revolts, and were not followed by any measures against Judaism as such.

This was not the case with Christianity, which spread among the devotees of pagan cults and thereby in the long term seemed to threaten the Roman Empire's spiritual cohesion.

Unity without uniformity: that seems the best description of the Roman Empire in its heyday. The Empire was a sort of federation of cities, under the aegis of Rome and the Emperor, leaving to each of them real autonomy, so that they could enjoy the benefits of the Pax Romana without being under too heavy a form of tutelage. In this way the conqueror won over his former enemies with such success that he offered them Roman citizenship. Hence the solidity of the Empire, which enabled it to survive the ordeals to which it was subject from the end of the 2nd century onwards. Hence the place that it rightly occupies in Europe's collective memory.

❸ A GALLIC GOD: TARVOS TRIGARANUS
The mariners' pillar, Cluny Museum, Paris
Offered by the mariners – the boatmen – of Lutetia (Paris), this pillar dedicated to Jupiter was decorated with reliefs showing both Roman and local deities. Among them was Tarvos Trigaranus, a bull crowned with foliage carrying three large cranes on its back. This scene is echoed in an Irish legend in which the hero chases a bull god who is warned of his danger by three cranes.

❹ THE CULT OF MITHRAS
Wall painting at Marino, near Rome. End of the 2nd century AD
Dressed in Persian robes, the god slits the throat of the bull in the presence of the sun and the moon. The dog and the serpent, beneficent animals, drink the life-giving blood of the victim.

3 Invasions and Changes: A New Europe Emerges

In the last third of the 2nd century AD, the Pax Romana was disturbed by a long period of internal and external disorder. Until the 10th century the whole of Eurasia was in turmoil owing to complex movements of peoples, in which the Germans and the Slavs migrated, sometimes of their own accord, but more often under pressure from the peoples of the steppes, the best known of which were the Huns. These 'Great Invasions' were one reason for the fall of the Roman Empire in the West and with it – at least in appearance – the disappearance of the unity that it had managed to build in Europe.

One of the reasons – but not the only reason – was that its very size had multiplied its problems without supplying the means to solve them. The crises in succession to the imperial throne, the growing burden of taxation, economic and social difficulties: all these sapped the Empire from within and contributed to its fall.

Another change, which had begun before the crisis and which was to become very important, affected Europe's creeds and culture. That was the spread of Christianity. Although the Empire had persecuted them, missionaries had found it a useful stamping-ground in which to preach the gospel. Paradoxically, the fall of the Empire made the Christian Church, and in particular its bishops, the heir of Greco-Roman civilization. In this way a Europe emerged that was very different from the Europe of the ancient world, but which also claimed to be its descendant.

Germanic invasions and enduring Roman traditions

In the year AD 166, in the reign of the Emperor Marcus Aurelius, Germanic tribes – Quadi, Marcomanni and Lombards – broke through the defences of the *limes*, crossed the Danube and after some vicissitudes reached the great port of Aquileia on the Adriatic in AD 170. So began the 'Great Invasions' which for more than three centuries regularly overran the Roman Empire.

Yet for a long time Rome had had peaceful relations with its German neighbours. True, it regarded them as barbarians because they lived outside its cultural realm. But it knew that the tribes living near the *limes* were Romanized enough for its generals to have recruited some of them for its defence; in this way, paradoxically, the Roman army was being 'barbarized'.

The Germanic tribes were very diverse and often fought each other. All they had in common were religion and a few customs and techniques. Being peasants and stockbreeders only now becoming settled rather than nomadic, they had no knowledge of urban civilization, nor the conception of the state so central to the Romans.

Their society was based on the existence of free men – warriors – bound to each other and to their leader in a kind of comradeship sealed by an oath. In war they owed absolute obedience to their leader; but in time of peace these free men met in assemblies which wielded such political power as there was more effectively than the king. Could these be seen as the distant ancestors of parliaments and an early affirmation of individual liberties – even if, as in Athens in a different institutional context, only a small number of people was involved?

Attacked from without by Germanic invasions and sapped within by the instability of imperial power that was known as military anarchy, the 3rd-century Roman Empire seemed destined for an early death. The Emperor Valerian was captured and executed by the Persians (AD 260). Aurelian abandoned Dacia in 271 and surrounded Rome with a further defensive wall. It was Diocletian (284–305) who restored the Empire and, to defend it more effectively, divided it into the Eastern Empire and the Western. Constantine continued Diocletian's work, but in the second half of the 4th century came a new wave of internal disorder. At the same time there were further barbarian incursions, like that of 31 December 406, when the Vandals, the Suevi and the Alans crossed the frozen Rhine and spread throughout Gaul.

Finding themselves unable to contain this pressure, the Emperors allowed the Germans to settle as *foederati* (from the Latin *foedus*, a treaty) within the Empire, keeping their own laws, their customs and their leaders, although under the fiction of Roman sovereignty. The fiction came to an end in 476 when Odoacer, King of the Herulians, deposed the last western Emperor, the child Romulus Augustulus, and sent the Imperial insignia to Constantinople.

The Germanic kingdoms that gradually took the place of the Western Empire had fluctuating frontiers, but these seem to have been stabilized in the last quarter of the 5th century – a good point at which to try to assess the profound changes wrought in Europe by the confrontation between two different civilizations.

The newcomers were much fewer than the Romans and those who had long been Romanized. That may be one reason for the persistence of Roman civilization in the greater part of the

3 ROME: AURELIAN'S WALL
The barbarian threat forced the cities to enclose themselves inside fortifications. Under Aurelian (270–75) Rome surrounded itself with solidly built walls. In the provinces the town fortifications often incorporated existing monuments like baths or amphitheatres and were buried in the mass of fragmented monuments destroyed by the barbarians.

4 'FIBULA' IN THE FORM OF AN EAGLE
German National Museum, Nuremberg
This fibula – a large clasp intended to hold the folds of a garment on the shoulder – dates from about AD 500. Discovered in Italy, it was made by Ostrogoth goldsmiths, influenced by the Scythian art of the Black Sea, as seen in the use of cloisonné gold and garnets. But the stylization is typically Germanic. This piece shows what masters the Germans were in the art of metalwork.

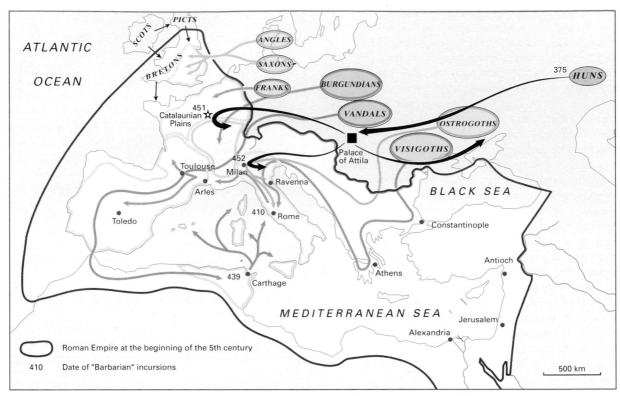

① THE GREAT INVASIONS OF THE 5th CENTURY

Roman Empire at the beginning of the 5th century

410   Date of "Barbarian" incursions

500 km

② RAVENNA, THEODORIC'S CAPITAL

Theodoric's Palace. Mosaic on the south wall of the nave of the Basilica of Sant' Apollinare Nuovo, Ravenna (beginning of the 6th century)

Honorius, the Western Emperor, had made Ravenna his capital in 404. It was also that of Odoacer and then of Theodoric, before it became the centre of Byzantine power in Italy after Justinian's reconquest. This political role explains why Ravenna has so many monuments with mosaics from the 5th and 6th centuries.

former Western Empire; but there were other reasons.

The German rulers saw themselves as the heirs of Rome; in 450, indeed, the Romans and the Visigoths united to fight Attila's Huns and drive them out of Gaul. Settling in Aquitaine and then in Spain, the Visigoths founded the kingdom of Toledo and won the full allegiance of the Latin population when King Reccared (586–601) renounced Arianism, a Christian heresy espoused by many Germanic peoples. Spain's Visigothic past is still remembered as part of its heritage.

More significant still was the case of Theodoric the Great, King of the Ostrogoths (493–526). Sent at the age of seven as a hostage to the court of the Emperor Zeno at Constantinople, he spoke Latin and Greek and was in a position to weigh up the Empire's strengths and weaknesses. With the Eastern Emperor's agreement, he set out with his people to drive Odoacer out of Italy. He succeeded and set up his capital in Ravenna, which he enriched with remarkable monuments. In his view, the Goths and the Romans had different but complementary roles. The Goths – the soldiers – had to provide the Empire's material strength: only the Romans were able to govern it. But the relationship between the Ostrogoths and Constantinople remained ambiguous: hence the reconquest of Italy by the Emperor Justinian.

Curiously, the kingdom that lasted longest, in the end, was that of the Franks, fairly late arrivals in history and as obscure as their king Clovis had been until his coming to power in 481. He gave up paganism in favour of Christianity and was thus the first of the Germanic kings to share the faith of the Gallo-Romans, among whom he settled when he made Paris his capital. He was more successful than Theodoric in blending Frankish and Roman traditions. From the Eastern Emperor Anastasius he received the titles of Consul and Patrician in 508 – a proof of Eastern benevolence towards the West. The importance of Clovis's role for the future kingdom of France is shown by the number of times that his name – which evolved into the forename 'Louis' – recurs among the kings that followed him.

Further proof that Roman traditions survived can be seen in the matter of language. Most parts of the Roman West in mainland Europe continued to use Romance dialects and it was here that the neo-Latin languages arose: Spanish, Portuguese, Italian and French. They have few borrowings from Germanic roots, mostly to do with the army and with war.

Barely 12 per cent of the Roman West on the mainland adopted Germanic languages: Flanders, the Rhineland, Rhaetia, Noricum (between the Danube and the Alps). The linguistic frontier extended to the west of the Rhine and even more to the south of the Danube; but it did not coincide with today's line of division between Germanic and Romance. Toponomy – the study of place-names – suggests that Germanic later advanced in the Alps and partly retreated in French Flanders, Lorraine and Alsace. The present language frontier, especially where it divides present-day Belgium, reflects no geographical reality, nor – so far as is known – any political drawing of boundaries. The origin of what seems an arbitrary division may have been a greater concentration of Germanic colonies after or perhaps before the Roman conquest: but this is only conjecture.

The case of Britain is quite different. Roman civilization there almost wholly disappeared under successive waves of invasion by sea – from the east in the case of the Frisians, Jutes, Angles and Saxons, from Ireland in the case of the Scots. Britain was not colonized by being surrounded by Germanic tribes, as on the continent, but by being re-peopled. It took over the Anglo-Saxon linguistic heritage, together with Latin, but leaving no islands of purely Roman tradition and few Celtic survivals. From Breton English borrowed fewer than a score of words.

Only Britain's western peninsulas, in Scotland, Wales and Cornwall, escaped Germanic influence, while some refugees escaped to Armorica (which took the name of Brittany) or to Spanish Galicia. Outside Ireland, Celtic culture survived only in such *fines terrae*, the ends of the earth.

❸ The conversion of Clovis

Letter from Avitus, Bishop of Vienne, to King Clovis

Here, Avitus is replying to Clovis, who had invited him and all the other bishops of France to come to his baptism. The political importance of Clovis's conversion can be seen from this letter, given the fact that bishops in their diocese had more than a religious role. By comparing Clovis to the Emperor of the East, Avitus is bestowing on the Frankish Kingdom a unique position among the barbarian kingdoms. This was confirmed three centuries later when Charlemagne was crowned Emperor of the West.

Divine Providence has found . . . an arbiter for our age! By your choice you have become the judge of the whole world: your faith is your victory!

Most men, when exhorted by their priests or advised by their friends to give up their errors, do not seek healthy belief: they are content to oppose the custom of their nation and the rites of their ancestors . . . . Henceforth, no such excuses can be accepted. Of all your ancient ancestry you have wished to retain only your nobility and you have wanted your descendants to thank you alone for all the glories of a noble birth. Among your forefathers there were those who performed good works; you have wished to do better still. You have paid the debts of your ancestors who reigned on earth and at the same time you have ensured that your descendants may reign in heaven.

The East may rejoice at having elected an Emperor who shares our faith; henceforth it will not be alone in this good fortune. The West, thanks to you, will also shine with its own brightness and can see one of its own sovereigns resplendent in the light of old.

In P. Riché and G. Tate, *Textes et documents du Moyen Âge, V^e–Xe siècles*, SEDES, Paris

❹ THE EMERGENCE OF LANGUAGE BARRIERS

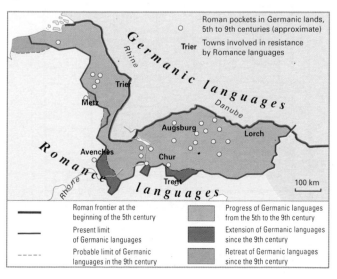

1 CONSTANTINE
Bibliothèque Nationale,
Paris. Cabinet des médailles
*Gold coin found in
Syria. It was minted in
AD 336 or 337. The
inscription reads:*
CONSTANTINUS
MAX|IMUS| AUG|USTUS|

2 DIOCLETIAN'S PALACE AT SPLIT
Built from AD 295 onwards, the palace, whose ground-plan is
shown below, was laid out on the model of the Roman camp.
It covered some 30,000 square metres. Being well fortified, it
became the headquarters of the town during the invasions.
(The name Split or in Italian Spalato is derived from palatium,
the Latin word for palace.) Additions outside its walls are no
older than the 18th century.

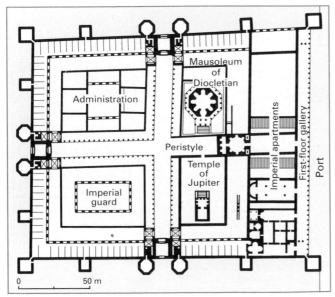

3 PLAN OF DIOCLETIAN'S PALACE

Internal changes

While the map of Europe's peoples was being
redrawn, the Roman Empire was undergoing a
very serious internal crisis, from which it emerged
profoundly changed.

The struggle against the Germans, and in the
East against the Parthian Empire, gave the armies
and their leaders ever greater political weight.
The legions made and unmade Emperors. Diocletian, proclaimed Emperor by his soldiers in AD
284, as his predecessors had been, put an end to
this 'military anarchy', and for more than a
century there was relative stability again.

The fundamental problem was to adapt the
Empire's structure to the needs of defence. It led
Diocletian to review the political and administrative organization of the state and also to intervene
more and more in the economic life of the Roman
world, and even in its social make-up.

He established the Tetrarchy, whereby the
Roman world was divided into four parts, at the
head of which were two Caesars and two Augus-
tuses – the former seen as natural successors to
the latter, when the time was right.

Defence considerations dictated the choice of
headquarters by these four rulers: Trier, Milan,
Sirmium (today known as Sremska Mitrovica,
west of Belgrade) and Nicomedia in Asia Minor,
100 kilometres east of Constantinople. For the
first time Rome was no longer the true capital.

When the tetrarchical system became more or
less unworkable, the Emperor Constantine re-
established unity in the Empire and settled his
capital in Byzantium, which became Constantinople. This 'new Rome' – which was how Constantine saw it – was better placed than its
predecessor to face the danger from the barbarians and the Sassanids. The changeover confirmed the East's superiority over the West. In
fact, the East had always been superior, economically and culturally, enriched as it was by the
immediate heritage of Hellenistic civilization and
the influence of cities like Athens, Pergamum,
Antioch and especially Alexandria. Thus were
laid the foundations of the Byzantine Empire. But
with Theodosius – who incidentally made the
Roman Empire a Christian Empire – the Empire
was once more divided in two. In 395 Theodosius
assigned the Eastern Empire to his elder son
Arcadius and the Western Empire to his younger
son Honorius. Unity was now a thing of the past.

The reforms affected also the various levels of
the administration. The provinces, now made
smaller so that their governors might be closer to
the cities they governed, rose in number from
about forty to about one hundred. Italy lost its
privileges and was partitioned in the same way.

The provinces were grouped into dioceses, each ruled by a *vicarius* or deputy. This system was completed by three and later four Praetorian Prefects, directly dependent on the Emperor.

The aim of these reforms was to strengthen central control of the Empire and make possible better liaison between the head of the state and the base. Paradoxically, they resulted in the development of local loyalties, based on smaller and more human subdivisions – no doubt owing to the frequent gaps in the succession at the top.

Defence was costly, so taxes had to be raised. This was felt the more sharply in that trade was stagnating and the currency depreciating. The establishment of a new tax, known as capitation tax, in principle a poll tax but seemingly based also on goods, required use of a census, which was often resented.

For convenience of tax-gathering – in money or in kind – the state fixed by decree the prices of goods and services, not always successfully. In order to ensure that land produced the same yield in taxes, the state insisted that those who tilled it should remain on it. Such 'settlers' – *coloni* – were still theoretically free; but, bound as they were to the land, they more and more resembled slaves.

This hesitant intervention by the state, in a society officially made static to their disadvantage, led the poor to react at times by flight and brigandage. In Gaul and Spain the Bagaudae revolted under Diocletian and it took long and bloody military operations to crush them.

With the first waves of invasion, the city withdrew behind a fortified wall, often built with the debris of monuments destroyed in the barbarian attack. For more than a millennium, the city came to be defined by the wall surrounding it. But, despite a widely held notion, the city did not disappear, but became a kind of storehouse of Greco-Roman culture.

Even so, the richest citizens, the Senatorial aristocracy and their descendants, did desert the city to settle on their rural estates, where there were craftsmen as well as farmworkers. They drew to them a whole clientele of *coloni*, or of country people hitherto free. In this way the *villa* gave birth to the village, which still bears that name. The *villa*'s owner protected his people against the insecurity of the time, but above all against the tax collectors. These, the *curiales*, officials from the town whose own fortune depended on their meeting tax quotas, were then faced with either ruin or flight.

This 'ruralization' of society and the economy weakened the authority of the town officials and state itself. Soon, they could operate on the estates only with the owner's consent. This may be one of the older roots of feudalism.

④ ROME IN THE WEST (after the administrative reforms of the 3rd century AD)

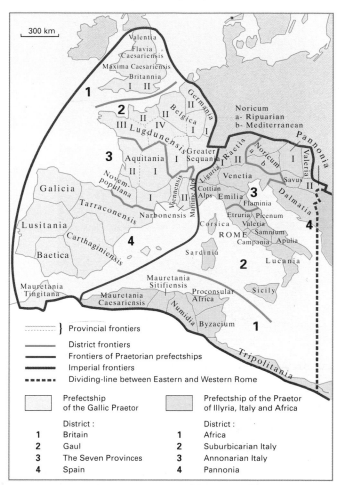

The new geographical organization of the Empire was an attempt to bring government closer to the governed. In the East the administrative divisions were similar to those in the West.

⑤ The weight of taxes in the 5th century

After having been a hermit in a valley of the Pyrenees, Orens (c.370–439) became Bishop of Auch, in Aquitaine. His remarks were repeated by Salvianus (390–484), whose career, first as a layman then as an ecclesiastic, led him from Trier to Marseille. In other words, they had more than local significance.

Who could be eloquent enough to speak of the following brigandage and crime? The Roman State, already dead or at least breathing its last in this land where it still seems alive, is being strangled to death by the bonds of taxation as if by the hands of brigands. There are many rich people whose taxes are paid by the poor.

Orens, quoted by Salvianus

❶ AN ARISTOCRAT ON HIS ESTATE
3rd-century tomb. Landesmuseum, Trier
The cities declined, to the advantage of the great estates, where the rich landowners made their own law. They liked noble pursuits such as hunting (above), but they preferred above all to receive the levies owed them by the peasants who worked on their estates (below).

❷ THE VILLA OF MONTMAURIN
This villa in south-west Gaul dates from the 4th century. It replaced a villa rustica of the 1st century, which grouped the farm buildings around the master's residence. There is no such rustic arrangement here: this villa urbana offers its inhabitants every comfort: hot-air central heating, porticos, gardens, private baths (on the left). The farm buildings are scattered over the 7000 hectares of the estate.

At all events, the Roman idea of the state grew weaker in the West. It was surely paradoxical that within the Empire itself there were established Germanic kingdoms which had their own customs and their own rulers. The fall of the Roman Empire in 476 clearly confirmed a situation that already existed. From now on there coexisted a number of peoples whose customs, institutions and attitudes were different if not contradictory. Thus arose the idea of the law of a particular people, under which everyone had the right to be judged by his own people's law, whereas Rome regarded law as linked to the territory over which it exercised its sovereignty.

But this differentiation between Romans and non-Romans was probably less total than has hitherto been thought. In the Code of Euric, King of the Visigoths, or the Lex Burgundiorum, are many borrowings from Roman Law. Indeed, the fact of writing down a code of laws corresponds more to Roman than to Germanic custom.

So long in the service of an empire which they finally destroyed without ceasing to admire, the Germanic kings continued the slow process of blending the Roman and Germanic worlds to give Europe a new physiognomy.

Christian Europe

The development of Christianity also changed the face of Europe. From the moment it separated itself from Judaism, it became subject to attack by the crowd, because its devotees refused to sacrifice to pagan gods.

But the persecution of Christians was rarely systematic and never universal. The many stories of Christian martyrdom are due in part to the eager exaggeration of hagiographers, and should not blind us to the overall progress of Christianity, more rapid in the East than in the West.

The 4th century marked the decisive turning-point. Diocletian's persecution of the Christians in 303, which was the religious aspect of his policy of restoring the Empire, was one of the most violent attacks on them but also virtually the last. In 313 the two Emperors, Constantine and Licinius, met together in Milan and recognized Christianity as one of the religions of the Empire, signalling its definitive victory. Constantine was baptized before he died. Between 381 and 392 Theodosius banned pagan practices: temples were destroyed or turned into churches and in 393 the Olympic Games were ended. The Roman Empire had become a Christian empire.

This situation was not altered by the establishment of the Germanic kingdoms in the West. Except for the Franks, these peoples had been converted to Christianity, in its heretical Arian version (see below), before they had been incorporated in the Empire.

The Christian religion spread first through the towns. The fact that the Latin word *paganus*, peasant, also meant pagan is significant. It was only in the 5th and 6th centuries that rural parishes began to be numerous, but it was not until Pope Gregory I (the Great, 590–604) that missionary work became really effective.

Every Christian community organized itself within the city. At its head was a bishop, *episcopos* – i.e. supervisor – elected by the faithful and the city's leading person, well beyond his religious authority. As the number of churches grew, there were soon bishops only in the important centres, while other cities had presbyters – from the Greek *presbuteroi*, elders – from which derives the word priest. The Bishop of Rome had more moral authority because he was 'successor to the Apostle Peter'; it was not until the end of the 6th century that he acquired the title of Pope (from the Greek *papas*, father) and the right to govern the Church.

However, in so far as the Empire had become Christian, the Emperor fully intended to intervene in Church affairs, in particular in appointing bishops. This was the origin of the conflicts that were to dominate relations between spiritual and temporal power. It was also at Constantine's bidding that the first Nicene Council was held in 325: it drew up the creed against the Arian heresy.

In fact, the Church was involved in doctrinal labours which were not without currents of dissent. Almost spontaneously agreement was reached on the authenticity of the texts making up the New Testament. But their interpretation was another matter, especially on one of the most delicate points of Christian thinking: how to reconcile the uniqueness of God with the existence of the other members of the Trinity, the Son and the Holy Spirit. Arianism, the doctrine preached by Arius, a priest from Alexandria, essentially denied the divinity of Christ and was condemned by the Council of Nicea. These theological disputes were more lively in the East than in the West, although in the 2nd century Irenaeus, Bishop of Lyon, played an active part.

Although born of Judaism, Christianity differentiated itself more and more from it, especially when Theodosius adopted it for the Empire. There then appeared the first instances of purely religious anti-semitism: to the Christians, the Jewish people was responsible for the death of Christ. Persecution of the Jews initially was sporadic and did not aim to destroy them: but it sought to exclude them. They were banned from honorific employment and forbidden to have Christian slaves.

❸ THE BEGINNINGS OF CHRISTIAN ART
The praying woman (mid-3rd century). Rome, catacomb of Priscilla
The praying woman (from the Latin orare, *to pray) – in this case, the dead – stands with her palms turned towards heaven. Kneeling became the practice only very much later. This fresco adorns one of the Roman catacombs, subterranean cemeteries cut from the rock on several levels. With Christianity cremation was replaced by burial.*

❹ THE FIRST CHURCHES
Santa Sabina, Rome, 5th century
Designed to hold a fairly large congregation, the church is rectangular, on a ground plan like that of a Roman civil basilica (hall). It has a timber ceiling; the altar is in an apse. The pillars are of marble, as are the flagstones of the floor and the lower parts of the walls. Paintings or mosaics show scenes from the Gospels.

1 RAVENNA, BAPTISTERY OF THE ORTHODOX
This baptistery dates from the first quarter of the 5th century. At that time baptism was performed outside the church, by total immersion: hence the size of the font in the foreground. From the 13th century onwards the West performed baptism by affusion (pouring water on the head); but the baptismal fonts, true to tradition, were still placed at the entrance of the churches.

2 CHRISTIAN SYMBOLS
Length: 26 cm, width: 19 cm, height: 15 cm. From the Benedictine Abbey of Sainte-Croix near Poitiers
This wooden desk, which belonged to St Radegund (587) is rich in symbols: the lamb, recalling the sacrifice of Christ, as do the crosses; the doves, representing the Holy Spirit; at the top, the letters chi (x) and rho (p), the first two in the Greek name Christos; in the corners, the symbols of the Evangelists – the eagle of St John, the man for St Matthew, the lion of St Mark and the bull for St Luke.

A similar attitude influenced the way the Christian worship developed. This distinguished itself from Jewish practices, as for instance in making the Sunday the sabbath rather than Saturday. Communal prayer, the reading of Biblical texts, the singing of psalms and preaching: these were practised throughout Christendom. One could join the church only by baptism, given in baptisteries adjoining the churches. This concerned adults rather than children, because congregations grew by conversion rather than birth. The basic service of the Christian Church was the Eucharist: at first celebrated as a communal meal, the *agapē*, intended to recall and renew the Last Supper, this gradually came to include only the essential symbols, the bread and the wine. Thus there arose the Mass in various Catholic liturgies.

Places of worship evolved as the new religion developed. Private houses were replaced by churches, modelled on the cruciform Roman basilica, with the altar in place of the tribune. This model remained that of the great majority of Christian religious buildings until the present day. The building of churches saw the birth of Christian figurative art, often full of symbolism, such as is found also on the walls of the underground burial-places around the cities, the catacombs, of which those of Rome are the most famous.

The changeover from the Christian community as a minority of the faithful, prepared to face martyrdom, to a triumphant and even dominating church led to a cooling of faith. Some Christians failed to practise Christ's teaching in their daily lives. In this climate arose, in Egypt in the late 3rd century, the hermit movement, whose devotees were repelled by such negligence.

Withdrawing to the desert alone – *monos* in Greek, whence the word monk – the hermit led an ascetic life of prayer and meditation, sometimes disturbed by visits from those attracted by his reputation for wisdom and sanctity.

The first monasteries, which brought monks together under the same rule, spread eastwards with Basil, towards Rome with John Cassian and towards Tours with Bishop Martin. In the 5th century, Ireland was so moved by the preaching of St Patrick that in the next century it became an outstanding centre of monasticism and missionary work, despite its location on the edge of Christendom. On a similar basis, Benedict of Nursia at the monastery of Monte Cassino, in the Italian Campania, drew up the rule that so many monasteries later adopted for themselves.

St Benedict's Rule called for monks to remain in one place, to take vows of poverty, chastity and obedience to the abbot, and to share in the work. The monastery owed duties of hospitality, charity to the poor and education. Everywhere the monasteries became centres of peaceful pursuits, where the monks wrote and copied history and undertook farming and stock-breeding.

The changes that Europe underwent in so many fields also affected culture and education. Greco-Roman culture survived, but it lost part of its hold as Greek studies declined and with them the study of philosophy and science. In oratory and poetry, sophisticated forms could not wholly disguise somewhat conventional content.

Even so, classical culture continued to dominate barbarian culture, rather as Greek culture had dominated that of Rome in the 3rd and 2nd centuries BC. Contact with Rome in particular caused the Germanic world gradually to move from oral to written practices. But this left Europe with two problems. First, traditional Roman education had been intended to train citizens for the political jousting in the Forum: but was it still useful in the new Germanic kingdoms? Secondly, classical culture was fundamentally pagan: was this not a threat to Christianity?

For young Roman aristocrats, traditional education led only to subordinate posts; and, if they were now living in country villas, such education was harder to acquire. So their training became 'barbarized', stressing physical ability and the handling of weapons.

The Church continued for a long time in its attachment to what might be called classical Christian culture, combining the intellectual content of the new faith with that of Roman traditions. The paganism that inspired them seemed harmless, a matter of poetry and myth. But zealots denounced this easy-going eclecticism: they believed that a choice had to be made between paganism and Christianity, especially in preaching. The Gospel, they said, must be 'taught to sinners, not rhetoricians'. This attitude was particularly widespread in the monasteries, which gradually worked out a new type of education based almost exclusively on Scripture. In this way, Christianity took over from the Greco-Roman tradition in the education of Europe.

At the beginning of the 6th century Islam had not yet conquered the African part of Christendom and much of its Asian outpost; Europe was beginning to be identified with Christendom.

⑤ IRISH CHRISTENDOM

The 5th century saw a great development of monasteries in Ireland. In the Dingle peninsula in south-west Ireland, oratories (small places reserved for prayer) were built with fragments of limestone like those in the windbreaks that cover the countryside. Ireland's 5th-century monasteries gave it unique intellectual prestige in Europe.

❸ The end of classical culture

Cassiodorus (c.480–c.575) was a Roman statesman in the service first of Odoacer and then of Theodoric. He sought to reconcile Christianity with classical culture.

What is the point of so many people hiding the fact that they have had a literary education? Their children want to go to secondary school and could soon become worthy to appear in the Forum. But as soon as they return to their country villas they begin to know nothing. They make progress at school, only to forget what they have learned; they are taught, but think no more of it. Devoted to the love of their fields, they lose all self-respect . . . . It is altogether scandalous that a nobleman should educate his children in the wilderness.

Cassiodorus, *Variae Epistulae*, VIII, 31

❹ Towards a Christian culture

After having been a monk at Lérins (on what is now known as the Côte d'Azur), one of the earliest centres of Western monasticism, Caesarius became Bishop of Arles.

. . . I humbly ask that the ears of the educated be content to hear without complaint expressions that seem to them rustic so that the Lord's whole flock may receive its celestial nourishment in simple and down-to-earth language. Because the ignorant and the uninstructed cannot rise to the level of the lettered, may the latter deign to lower themselves to their humble state. Educated people can understand what has been said to simple people, whereas simple people are unable to profit from what might have been said to scholars.

Caesarius of Arles, *Sermon LXXXVI*

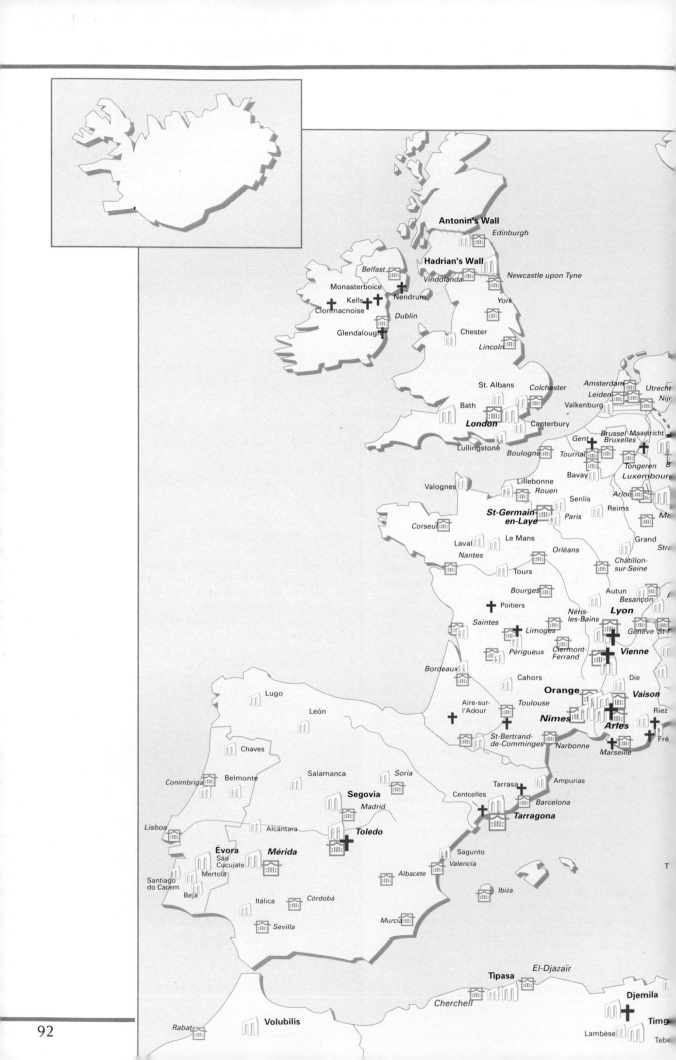

Antonin's Wall

Edinburgh

Hadrian's Wall

Belfast

Vindolanda

Newcastle upon Tyne

Monasterboice

Nendrum

York

Kells

Clonmacnoise

Dublin

Chester

Glendalough

Lincoln

St. Albans

Colchester

Amsterdam

Leiden

Utrecht

Nijr

Valkenburg

Bath

London

Canterbury

Brussel
Bruxelles

Maastricht

Lullingstone

Boulogne

Gent

Tournai

Tongeren

Bavay

Luxembourg

Lillebonne

Valognes

Rouen

Arlon

Senlis

Reims

Me

Valognes

St-Germain-
en-Laye

Paris

Grand

Stra

Corseul

Le Mans

Laval

Orléans

Châtillon-
sur-Seine

Nantes

Tours

Autun

Besançon

Bourges

Lyon

A

Poitiers

Néris-
les-Bains

Saintes

Limoges

Genève

St-F

Périgueux

Clermont-
Ferrand

Vienne

Bordeaux

Cahors

Orange

Die

Vaison

Lugo

Aire-sur-
l'Adour

Toulouse

Nîmes

Arles

Riez

León

St-Bertrand-
de-Comminges

Narbonne

Fré

Chaves

Marseille

Salamanca

Soria

Ampurias

Conimbriga

Belmonte

Tarrasa

Centcelles

Barcelona

Segovia

Madrid

Lisboa

Alcántara

Toledo

Tarragona

Évora

Mérida

São
Cucujate

Sagunto

Santiago
do Cacem

Mertola

Valencia

Albacete

Beja

Itálica

Córdobá

Murcia

Ibiza

Sevilla

Tipasa

El-Djazaïr

Djemila

Cherchell

Rabat

Volubilis

Lambèse

Timg

Tebe

92

The Past in the Present Day
ROME

Legend:

- ruin or monument from the Roman epoch (8th century BC to 4th century AD)
- Christian ruin or monument (2nd to 6th century)
- *museum, treasury or library whose collections cover the epochs above*
- maximum extent of the Roman Empire
- frontiers of 20th-century states

500 km

1 THE EMPEROR JUSTINIAN

Detail from mosaic in the Church of San Vitale, Ravenna, 6th century

A sincere Christian, ardent jurist and a builder of great monuments, Justinian I was Emperor from AD 527 to 565. Backed by his wife Theodora and his Generals Narses and Belisarius, he did his best to revive the former Roman world. He left to posterity the Code of Civil Laws that bears his name (529). It greatly influenced medieval Christendom, which was also enriched by the Byzantine art of Justinian's time.

482	Birth of Justinian		**842**	Strasbourg Oaths
527–65	Reign of Justinian		**843**	Treaty of Verdun: Charlemagne's Empire partitioned
528–9	Code of Civil Laws		**843**	End of Iconoclast dispute
532	Nika insurrection		**863**	Slavs converted to Christianity
622	The Hegira: flight of Mohammed from Mecca to Medina		**863**	Photian Schism
626	First confrontation between Arabs and Byzantines		**936–73**	Reign of Otto I the Great
			955	Battle of the Lech
681	Bulgarians settled in Lower Moesia		**972**	Foundation of the Great Laura monastery on Mount Athos
717–18	Siege of Constantinople by the Arabs		**989**	Russians converted to Christianity
732	Victory of Charles Martel over the Arabs at Poitiers		**1018**	Destruction of the Bulgar State
			1042–66	Reign of Edward the Confessor
751	Creation of the Papal State		**1054**	Schism between Eastern and Western Churches
768–814	Reign of Charlemagne			

CHAPTER *III*

BYZANTIUM AND THE WEST

FROM THE 6TH TO 11TH CENTURY AD

In the 6th century, under the Emperor Justinian, the Roman Empire in the East began to change in several ways. The period that followed was marked by contradictions: on the one hand, precarious reconquests; on the other, remarkable intellectual achievements. The territorial changes that transformed the Byzantine Empire had one crucial result: it turned its back on the past – i.e. on the Roman world.

Byzantium now had a homogeneous population and a predominantly Hellenic way of life. This change was later reinforced by decentralization, economic progress, 'Christian conversion, the religious crisis and the feudalization of the state. It was completed in the 10th and 11th centuries, while frontiers were altered and new institutions set in place.

The face of Europe changed too, as new states emerged on the scene. For rulers' efforts to establish and maintain a universal authority proved impermanent in the West as in the East. That ideal no longer suited the times, as history was to show.

Yet, despite its divisions, Europe managed in the centuries that followed to play a leading role in the history of the world. Gradually, in fact, the achievements of people transcended the confines of the isolated communities in which they lived. Cumulatively, and together, they built up a priceless heritage that offered a broader future to the generations that followed.

② POWER DERIVES FROM GOD
Mosaic of the Triclinium of the Scala Santa, Lateran Palace, Rome
St Peter is handing to Leo III, on the left, the pallium, the band of white linen with black crosses that the Pope wore over his pontifical robes. Charlemagne, on the right, is receiving the papal standard.

1 Justinian and the Byzantine Empire in the 6th and 7th Centuries

① THE FIGURE OF THE EMPEROR
The Barberini diptych, in ivory, 5th century AD, Louvre Museum, Paris
The Emperor, chosen by God, was master of the universe and the symbol of religious and political unity.

② JUSTINIAN'S EMPIRE (527–65)

While profound changes shook the West, the Roman Empire in the East continued. But it had been centred on Constantinople since the 4th century and now it too changed, as witness the name of 'Byzantine Empire' by which it was henceforth known.

'One state, one religion'

In some ways, the 6th century was the continuation of its predecessors. But it was also new, the result of both a period of gestation (527–533) and a time of great difficulty (540–565).

Justinian (527–565) and his successors sought to make their Empire a geographical unit to govern it better. Through religion they tried to establish social and ethnic unity. 'One state, one religion' was their doctrine. The Church agreed to serve the political authorities and a single dogma was imposed on a single state. The extremist policy of the Emperor provoked political and social conflicts: it included constraints on conquered Christian peoples and the Monophysites (adherents of an ephemeral 7th-century heresy denying the divine nature of Christ) and the suppression of the Platonic Academy in Athens in 529. It was impossible, in fact, for the notion of the Church's subordination to the temporal power, which clashed with deeply held convictions, to be upheld without serious conflict.

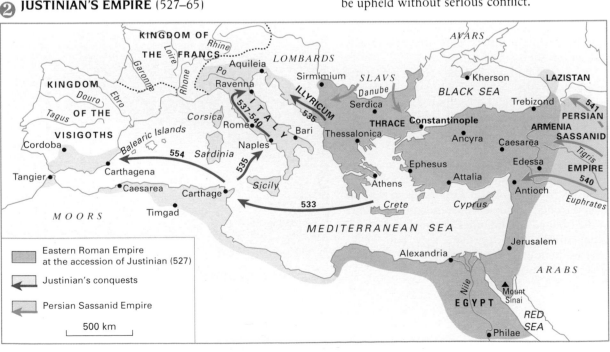

Eastern Roman Empire at the accession of Justinian (527)

Justinian's conquests

Persian Sassanid Empire

500 km

Administrative reforms and economic measures

Justinian's domestic policy included administrative reform, economic measures and the reduction of landed property. His decrees were aimed at the great landowners, whose growing power often gave them political superiority – challenging the authority of the state. Although there were no radical reforms, supervision of the public services and tax changes to protect smallholders curbed the great landowners' greed.

The Emperor's economic measures were designed to increase trade. Because the economic stagnation of the cities in the West prevented their engaging in large-scale commerce, the Byzantine State turned eastwards, to obtain luxury goods from China and India. But the land and sea trade-routes were controlled by the Persians, with whom it was therefore necessary to maintain good relations. This was not always possible: indeed, Byzantium had to pay them tribute-money even in time of peace. Attempts were made to establish new routes to China via Kherson in the Crimea, the Cimmerian Bosporus and from Lazistan to the Caucasus; and access to the Indian Ocean was achieved through the Red Sea. But the Persians continued to regulate this trade until the Byzantines began producing silk in their larger towns (Constantinople, Antioch, Thebes), thanks to the ruse whereby two monks had brought back silkworm eggs concealed in their staffs. In these cities, commercial and craft activities went on developing until the 12th century.

Constantinople and Thessalonica were the two great trading centres of the Byzantine State. At that time, indeed, Constantinople was the commercial capital of the known world. The *mesē* or central street with its large shops was a place for buying and selling every kind of merchandise. True, the Byzantine economy was based essentially on agriculture, but the merchant fleet also contributed to the growth of trade, making it possible to export local products such as jewels, utensils, woollens, linen and leather.

The state based its firm authority both on Christianity and on Hellenism: power was bestowed by and upon the Emperor. The Hippodrome, for sporting spectacles, was the only place where the people could come into contact with the central authorities. It was there that the various associations – known by the name of *demes* – expressed their opinions on government policy, often using great force. This was the case at the famous Nika insurrection in 532 (*Nika* – victory – being the password of the rebels). Justinian repressed it to avoid the danger of civil war; but the *demes* made common cause and

❸ The 'Novels' (*Novellae*) of Justinian

This Novel of Justinian (no 17, chapter 13), issued in 535, was aimed at the powerful landowners and regional rulers.

. . . At all costs put an end to the illegal protection that we find is practised in our provinces. Allow no one to exploit the life of others, to appropriate land that does not belong to him, to promise protection to those who are liable for damages or to use his own power to neutralize that of the State. Pay no attention to the power of those who act thus. The law and the approval of the sovereign should above all be enough for you to exercise your power.

❹ THE HIPPODROME AT CONSTANTINOPLE
Fragment of an ivory diptych portraying a *quadriga*, or chariot race with four horses drawing each chariot. Christian Museum, Brescia
The Hippodrome was where the demes *held their athletic contests, made their political demands and clashed with the authorities, as in the Nika insurrection of 532.*

❶ Preface to Justinian's *Institutes*

... In order that the State may be equally well governed in time of peace and in time of war, His Imperial Majesty needs the support of both weapons and laws.

With much care and trouble, and with the all-powerful help of God, we have accepted this double task. The barbarian nations, subdued by force of arms, know our military might; Africa and so many other provinces, so long under Roman domination and now recovered by the success that divine providence has accorded our armies, are the resounding proof....

In these Institutes we have briefly expounded what was in force in past times; what was once obscured by disuse has been brought to light again by our imperial care.

These Institutes ... have been presented to us by three jurisconsults.... We have read them, studied them, and given them the full force of our law.

Receive them then with devotion and alacrity; and show your zeal by hoping that, once your legal studies are completed, you will be able to take part in the government of the State in those places that are assigned to you.

Institutes de l'empereur Justinien, Editions M. Blondeau, Vol. I, pp 6–8, Paris, 1889.

❷ THE CISTERNS OF CONSTANTINOPLE

Water was no problem for the inhabitants of Constantinople. Thanks to Justinian, aqueducts brought water to underground cisterns or reservoirs all over the city. Above is the 'Sunken Palace' cistern, or Cistern Basilica (Yerebatan Saray in Turkish). Its 336 columns, eight metres tall in twelve rows, cover an area of 140 by 70 metres. The cistern supplied the Imperial Palace and its gardens.

threatened his authority. At the instigation of the Empress Theodora, Justinian ordered the crowd to be massacred. The *demes*, the only vehicle for the expression of public opinion, ceased to exist and despotism triumphed.

Legislation

Justinian's most important and lasting achievement was to codify Roman Law. To remedy the legislative anarchy of the time, he set up a commission headed by the jurist Tribonianus. It very quickly produced a great work, the *Corpus Juris Civilis*. This comprised:

- THE JUSTINIAN CODE (*Codex Justinianus*, 528–29), a compilation of all the imperial laws issued since Hadrian in the 2nd century. It was based on the Theodosian (5th century), Gregorian (6th century) and Hermogenian codes
- THE PANDECTS (*Digesta*, 533), extracts from works and legal opinions by Roman jurists
- THE INSTITUTES (*Institutiones*), a practical textbook for the use of law students
- THE NOVELS (*Novellae Constitutiones Post Codicem*, 514–565), a collection of 168 decrees on social and private life

The Code, the Pandects and the Institutes were published in Latin; but most of the Novels were written in Greek so that the decrees could be understood and used by the administration and the citizens. The *Corpus Juris Civilis* was not simply copied from old Roman Law. The jurists modified it, adapting its decrees to the needs of a new society based on Christian ethics, customary law and a new mentality different from that of the old Roman Empire. The juridical and political concepts that derived from the *Corpus Juris Civilis* show how great an impact it made both on Byzantium and on the West.

Even if the Byzantine State could not survive as a geographical unit, the work of Justinian endured: it became the basis of Western legislation for centuries. Among other things, it inspired Napoleon's Civil Code and its imitations.

Public works and works of art

The frontiers of the Empire in Europe and Asia were partly protected by a large number of fortresses, especially along the Danube. While the public works completed in Justinian's reign did not match those of the Roman Emperors, they were nevertheless very impressive. The Emperor gave orders for the construction of walls, public buildings, charitable institutions and grandiose churches like Sancta Sophia, archetype of the domed basilica. Architecture, painting and sculp-

③ SANCTA SOPHIA

Founded by Constantine in 325 on the main hill in Constantinople, Sancta Sophia is a three-naved, domed basilica with atrium, narthex and exonarthex. The crown, 55 metres above the ground, gives the building immense lightness. The daylight enters through the windows commemorating the 40 martyrs, bathes the marble of the capitals and plays on the figures in the magnificent Byzantine mosaics in the upper galleries. The black hanging tablets are later Islamic additions.

① SANT'APOLLINARE IN CLASSE, RAVENNA

Basilica begun in 543 at Classe, the port of Ravenna, by the architect known as Julian the Silversmith, to receive the relics of the Saint. The semi-cupola shows the transfiguration of Apollinarius: its style is the purest Byzantine.

② The prestige of the Byzantine Empire

Throughout Byzantine history, foreign ambassadors expressed their astonishment at the ceremonial of Imperial audiences. One such was Liutprand, Bishop of Cremona, sent to Constantinople by Berengar, King of Italy.

In front of the Emperor's throne stood a tree of gilded bronze, whose branches were filled with birds of various kinds, also in gilded bronze, singing their own characteristic songs. The imperial throne, which is immense, is fashioned with such skill that in an instant it rises from the ground into the air, where it remains suspended. One wonders whether it is made of wood or of brass. Lions covered in gold act as guards, beating the ground with their tails, their jaws open and their tongues moving as they roar. I was brought there before the Emperor, born on the shoulders of two eunuchs. When, at my entrance, the lions began to roar and the birds to sing, I felt neither fright nor surprise, for I had been forewarned by those who knew the ceremony. Having bowed three times in respect for the Emperor, I raised my head. I had just seen him seated at some height from the ground; now he was among the panels of the ceiling and wearing a different robe. I could not imagine what had happened or how, unless he had been raised by the device whereby a wine-press is lifted. Unable to speak a word in the uncomfortable position he was in, he inquired through an official about the state of Berengar's health. I replied fittingly and then, at a sign from the interpreter, I went to the residence that had been assigned me.

Liutprand of Cremona, quoted in André Guillou, *La Civilisation byzantine*, Collection *Les Grandes Civilisations*, Paris, Arthaud, 1974

ture obeyed the new conception of religion, which aimed at imposing Christianity on all forms of art. Classicism lost favour: statuary, associated with idolatry and opposed to the ideology that dominated Byzantine religious art, fell into disrepute. Mosaics and paintings expressed the new orthodoxy. In the centuries that followed, the figure of the Emperor remained dominant as both a political and a religious leader.

The defence of the frontiers

In his effort to rebuild the former *imperium*, Justinian was inspired by 'universalism'. His Generals, Belisarius and Narses, set out to fulfil what proved an ephemeral dream.

They succeeded in destroying the kingdoms of the Vandals (533–4) and the Ostrogoths (555), and they managed to weaken that of the Visigoths (554). But if this showed how vulnerable such states had been, it also enmeshed Byzantium in problems. Likewise, although the Mediterranean and the Black Sea once more became 'lakes' within the Empire, their reconquest imposed a price: a drain on the public purse, an increase in taxation and a growth of popular discontent. During this time, moreover, Byzantium could no longer resist Slav invasions on the Danube frontier, as well as demands by the Persians. The Balkans were therefore transformed by the arrival of new peoples.

Justinian's successors tried desperately to protect the reconquered territory – by making continual concessions to the Persians. At the same time new enemies, the Avars, appeared in the north. They finally spread through the Balkan peninsula and settled there for good.

The efforts to retain reconquered territory led to the establishment of an administrative union of the Exarchates (Ravenna and Carthage in particular). From this there grew up a new administrative system, later applied on a larger scale. The impoverishment of the people owing to the high taxes raised for military ends, the weakening of the army and the ill-starred attempts to repulse the Persians, the Slavs and the Avars, created a general sense of insecurity. Conflicts arose between different social classes, and between the people and the central authorities. The Empire could not cope with this situation, which spread as far as the eastern provinces.

It continued, in fact, until the Exarch of Carthage, Heraclius (610–41), came to the imperial throne. The fatherland and religion then became the basis of a theocratic state. Greek was made the official language. To be able better to face the enemy, Heraclius re-established internal order and established the 'Themes', new administrative districts. This reform strengthened small-holders, made it possible to get rid of foreign mercenaries and at the same time stimulated the economy. The new governors were required to make their own arrangements to provide for the equipment and subsistence of their 'Themes'. This reform of administration in the provinces was accompanied by a reform of the central government, establishing new offices of state with more extensive powers.

After these reforms, in 622, the Byzantines attacked the Persian 'infidels' – a term which for the Byzantines was synonymous with 'barbarian', i.e. non-Christian. This was a war of religion: it might conceivably be seen as a forerunner of the Crusades. Six years later the Persians were forced to return Armenia, Syria, Palestine, Egypt and Mesopotamia to the Empire.

In 626 the Avars tried to besiege Constantinople, but failed. This finally broke their hegemony, encouraging the Slav tribes to shake off their yoke and to claim rights of sovereignty in the Balkans.

But the real danger came from the Arabs, who began to organize from the time of the Hegira or 'flight' in 622. The Hegira, starting-point of Moslem chronology, marked also the beginning of Islamic expansion. The Prophet Mohammed laid the foundations of Moslem society, putting an end to the Arabs' rudimentary tribal organization and their lack of political unity. Their economic and social development, however, was as varied as the nature of their territory.

❸ OMAR'S MOSQUE, JERUSALEM
19th-century lithograph
This rock is doubly sacred. For the Jews, it is where the patriarch Abraham bound his son Isaac to sacrifice him; for the Moslems, it is from here that the Prophet Mohammed began his ascent to the throne of Allah.

❹ THE ISLAMIC-ARAB ATTACKS ON EUROPE (7th–8th CENTURIES)

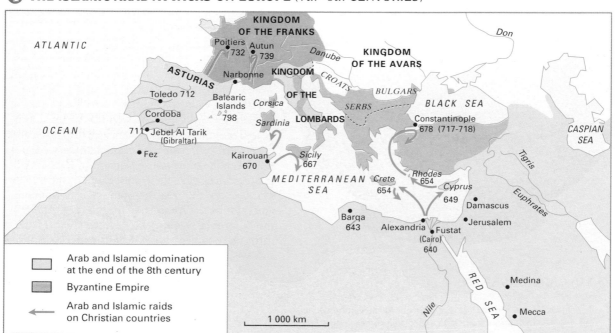

❶ The Arabs and Greek culture

The Abbassid Caliph Mamoun was the son of Haroun al-Rashid (786–833)

The Caliph Mamoun completed the work commanded by his grandfather Mansour .... He entered into relations with the Emperors of Byzantium, gave them rich presents and asked them to give him the books of philosophy that they possessed. The Emperors sent him those works of Plato, Aristotle, Hippocrates, Galen, Euclid and Ptolemy that they had. Mamoun then chose outstanding translators and bade them make the finest translations of these works that they could .... The wise vied with each other to study, for they saw their master, full of regard for men who cultivated the sciences, admit scholars into his intimate circle.

Sa'id, *Tabaqat al-Umam*

Their gains at the expense of Byzantium and Persia began after the death of Mohammed. They advanced at lightning speed, seizing Syria, Mesopotamia and Egypt. The Empire was exhausted by war: the Arabs were united by religion. People living in the land they conquered looked on them as liberators from Byzantine oppression. A little later, the Arab war fleet, which had begun to be built in 649, threatened to dominate Byzantine shipping in the eastern Mediterranean.

Arabia's favourable geographical position determined the type of trade it undertook. In fact, since they enjoyed commercial links with Europe, Africa and Asia, the Arabs became an important link in the network of world trade. They bought and resold spices, rare woods, textiles, ivory and even slaves; but from now on they also controlled access to the Indian Ocean.

The Arab world also helped enrich literature and the arts (in mathematics, translations of Aristotle and Hippocrates, architecture and decoration). But the Caliphate, whose authority was both religious and political, was a prey to bitter rivalry. The Omayyads of Damascus were violently ousted in 750 by the Abbasid Caliphs of Baghdad. But these crises did not prevent the Arabs from remaining a threat to the Byzantines.

In 626 there appeared the Bulgars from central Asia. Led by Kubrat, they broke the hold of the Avars and established their kingdom between the River Kuban and the Sea of Azov. In 679 the Hazaras Turks (Khazars) conquered part of the Bulgar people. The rest, under the orders of Asparukh, emigrated and settled in 681 in Lower Moesia, between the Danube and the Balkans. This new Bulgar kingdom was in the territory of the Byzantine Empire, of which it was administratively a dependency.

In the 7th century there was greater religious and dogmatic unity in the Byzantine Empire because it had finally lost its oriental provinces, which had been the seedbed of various heresies.

Power was now held by two Emperors in association and the succession was orderly. Public and economic services were well organized and the government took care of smallholders. Migration in the region (the settlement of the Serbs in the provinces near the Danube and of the Croats in Dalmatia; the creation of the Bulgar kingdom; and raids by the Avars) had the effect of confining the Empire to strongly Hellenized areas. Henceforth, the peoples of Asia Minor under Byzantine rule were wholly Hellenized and Christian.

❷ BULGAR HORSEMEN

Vase from the Nagyszemtmiklos Treasure, Budapest Museum

The figure on this 9th-century gold vase shows the determination of the new people to settle in the region they had chosen.

New peoples and new states

In the West, the Germanic kingdoms that began to replace the Roman Empire, even before its final collapse in 476, evolved differently. Their frontiers were as insecure as their leaders.

The kingdom of the Ostrogoths, founded in Italy by Theodoric the Great with the consent of the Eastern Emperor, was the first to disappear. Justinian, in fact, undertook the reconquest of the West in order to restore the integrity of the Empire. The Byzantine generals Belisarius and Narses intervened in the kingdom's dynastic conflicts, but faced resistance from the Ostrogoths: it took eight years before the Byzantines conquered Italy. Ravenna, the capital, was not captured until 540. The Ostrogoths vanished, leaving barely a trace in the Italian people and language.

At the same time the Visigoths had to confine their rule to the Iberian peninsula, for their defeat by Clovis and the Franks at Vouillé in 507 lost them Aquitaine. The reconquest begun by Justinian was limited to the former Roman province of Baetica and then only for some fifty years. Despite official recognition by Constantinople and despite giving up Arianism for the doctrine of the Trinity, the Visigoth kings in the 7th century lost their authority in the face of the nobility and the often intolerant Church. Their weakness gave an opportunity to the invading 'Arabs' (in reality mostly Islamicized Berbers), who between 711 and 713 seized all but the north of the peninsula, remaining there for almost eight centuries.

In 568 the Lombards came on the scene. They were a Germanic people, who had earlier migrated from the mouths of the Elbe to Pannonia. Now they crossed the Alps and in four years made themselves masters of the Po valley. Their king, Alboin, made his capital in Pavia. Other Lombard leaders in the rest of the country carved out for themselves practically independent duchies or counties. Byzantine Italy was reduced to its southern portion, to the Exarchate of Ravenna, which slanted across the peninsula as far as Rome, and to a number of coastal regions. Although in the mid-7th century the Lombards were converted to Christianity, which brought them closer to the original inhabitants, they continued to be weakened by their lack of a genuine state.

The Frankish kingdom, which in a century had managed to dominate much of central and Western Europe, did not lose its dynamism with the death of Clovis in 511, although it was partitioned among his four sons. In 532 it absorbed the kingdom of Burgundy, which however retained its own language for a long time. By 555 the

❸ THE CHURCH OF SANT'APOLLINARE NUOVO, RAVENNA
This church was built by Theodoric (454–526) for the devotees of Arianism, at a time when Goths and Latins freely followed that faith.

❹ SMALL VISIGOTHIC CHAPEL
Santa Comba de Bande, in the province of Orense, Spain
The Visigoths were not great innovators in architecture. They mainly adapted and transformed existing Greco-Latin buildings.

1 THE BAPTISM OF CLOVIS, 25 DECEMBER 496
Clovis had promised to embrace Christianity if the 'God of Clothilde', his wife, gave him victory. Bishop Remigius baptized him with 3000 of his soldiers.

2 THE CONQUESTS OF THE FRANKS

- Frankish Kingdom, end of the 5th century
- Clovis's conquests
- Conquests by Clovis's sons and grandsons

3 A bishop in Merovingian Gaul

Fortunatus was one of the last Latin poets. Born in Italy in about 530, he settled in Gaul, where he died in about AD 600. As Bishop of Poitiers, he here praises, rather emphatically, the work of Felix, Bishop of Nantes from 549 to 582, in both the civil and the religious field.

Of Felix when he changed the course of the river

Let the poets of old renounce their tales of a few great deeds. The exploits of yore are outshone by those of today. If Homer had seen rivers blocked, he would have filled his fine work with that achievement; and all would have chosen Felix and not Achilles to glorify their art. O Thou, inventive spirit, by changing their sinuous course, hast made ancient rivers obey a new law. By diverting them from their course to the abyss by means of a dyke, thou hast obliged them to take a direction that nature refused them . . . . Where once passed the prows of ships there now pass chariots. . . .

Fortunatus, *Carmina*, III, 7 and 10, *Monumenta Germaniae Historica, Auctores Antiquissimi*, Berlin, IV

Franks had extended their rule in Germany, from Alsace to Bavaria; and for the first time Gaul and Germany formed part of the same political grouping.

The harmony was broken at the end of the 6th century by conflicts among the kings of Neustria (north-west Gaul), Austrasia (eastern Gaul and Germany) and Burgundy. From 610 onwards Clothaire II and then Dagobert restored unity.

But at the end of the 7th century the Merovingians (the dynasty of Merovaeus or Mervig, ancestor of Clovis) came to be dominated by the aristocracy, whose most powerful leaders assumed the functions of Mayors of the Palace. The Mayors' responsibilities had originally been domestic: now they began to include political and military affairs. Predominant among them was Pepin of Herstal, near Liège, who was Mayor of Austrasia. In 687 he became Mayor of all three Frankish kingdoms.

His son Charles Martel, who succeeded him in 714, reconquered Neustria and fought the Saxons and the Alemanni. His victory over the Arab and Islamic invaders at Poitiers in 732 put an end to Arab expansion in the West and won him great prestige. He was thus able, shortly before his death in 741, to divide the succession between his two sons, Carloman and Pepin 'the Short'. It was a truly regal partition.

At the end of the 6th century the Saxon kingdoms in England enjoyed relative peace. Before the 6th century was over Pope Gregory I the Great sent a monk, Augustine, to England. He converted the King of Kent in 597 and founded the bishopric of Canterbury. The Irish monk Columba did similar missionary work in Scotland and the north of England. This caused difficulties, because Irish liturgy at the time differed from the practice at Rome. The problem was solved at the Synod of Whitby in 664 and a Greek monk, Theodore, was appointed Bishop of Canterbury by the Pope in 669.

Great Britain and Ireland became intellectual centres, one of whose most notable luminaries was the Venerable Bede, who was born in about 675 and died in 735 or 736. Bede was a scholar: he wrote an *Ecclesiastical History*, beginning with Caesar's arrival in Gaul and ending in 731. Both Britain and Ireland sent missionaries to the Germanic countries: Columba, Willibrord, Boniface, Fiacre and Gall (who gave his name to the town of Saint-Gall in Switzerland). As in the other parts of the West, the Rule written by St Benedict of Nursia in about 540 became generally accepted. Monastic copyists played a crucial role in passing on Latin culture and illuminators, especially in Ireland, made a vital contribution to Christian art.

④ THE BOOK OF KELLS
Trinity College Library, Dublin

A page of the Gospels known as the Book of Kells. It probably dates from the early 8th century, when the first masterpieces of manuscript illumination in British and Irish abbeys were produced. Before that, missionaries left the monasteries to spread the Gospel in the pagan parts of the Frankish world, preparing the way for the efflorescence of medieval civilization.

Byzantium and the New European States, 8th and 9th Centuries

① SCENES FROM COUNTRY LIFE
11th-century miniature. *The Homilies of St Gregory of Nazianzus*
These miniatures show the various tasks of Byzantine peasants, watching their flocks, pruning vines, fishing and so on. Whatever their occupation, their taxation was fixed according to the output of the soil and the quality of the products.

The Byzantine Empire was predominantly Hellenic, united in religion and politically stable. The regions inhabited by foreign peoples conquered by the Arabs and the Slavs, and hence removed from the Empire, strengthened this unity. The Greek language predominated and the orthodox 'titulary' ('Emperor Caesar Augustus, King faithful to Christ') imposed his authority. The administration, finally, was centralized in the capital but enjoyed a certain autonomy in the provinces, owing to the danger from without. This autonomy took the form of administrative units known as 'Themes'.

Economics, administration and law

The Byzantine economy became more agricultural. The Arabs now controlled the main trade routes and the establishment of 'Themes' in the Empire obliged each of them to become economically independent.

As in the West, the role of the countryside was strengthened and towns became more isolated. This transformed society. Social class was now determined by the ownership of land. Differences thus arose between the great landowners (which included the vast monastic estates), smallholders and simple peasants.

The publication of collections of laws shed light on economic policy and on relations within the rural world. Meanwhile, the state became military. The 'Themes', created to meet the needs of defence, faithfully reflected this new situation: the same person was invested with both political and military power. Finally, legislation – the *Collection of Laws* (726) and the *Kakoseis* (811) – supported the new policy: henceforth, defence depended on the provincial administrators, and the economy relied on agricultural taxpayers.

Foreign policy: old and new enemies

In the 8th and 9th centuries the Byzantine State faced new enemies as well as old. In 717 and 718 the Arabs besieged Constantinople by land and sea. But their attack, and their attempt to break into Europe, failed. A sharp winter, Greek fire, famine in the Arab camps, a counter-attack by the Bulgars and the support of the Hazaras Turks – all enabled the Byzantines to resist the attack. In 740 the Arabs resumed their incursions into Asia Minor, where they faced the Emperor Leo III. A few years later internal dissension in the Arab world forced them to be less belligerent vis-à-vis their neighbours. In 750 the Omayyads family was massacred by the Abbasids in Damascus, with the exception of Abd-er-Rahman I, who founded an independent emirate at Córdoba in Spain, which became a Caliphate in 929. The Abbasids then made their capital Baghdad. In the Mediterranean war soon gave way to piracy on the part of the Saracens, who captured Crete and made it one of the bases for their operations against Byzantium and the West from 827 to 961.

At the same time the northern frontier of Byzantium was threatened by the Bulgars, who had assimilated with the Slavs to form a state. During the first conflicts (755−75) neither side long had the upper hand. The Bulgars were defeated in 762 at Anchialus in the Gulf of Burgas, but then were victorious at Fort Markellai in 792. At the same time the destruction of the Avar State by Charlemagne encouraged the Bulgars to expand northwards. The raids, which were particularly violent, were followed by the defeat of the Byzantines in 811. In 813 the Bulgars threatened Constantinople, but withdrew and signed a treaty of peace.

In the mid-9th century there were changes both inside and outside Byzantium. This period of transition, which brought the Empire to the height of its development, covered the reign of Michael III (842−67). In 863 the Emperor favoured the Christian conversion of the Slavs in Greater Moravia by the missionary brothers Cyril and Methodius. They translated the Holy Scriptures into Slavonic, using the Glagolitic alphabet (replaced in the 10th century by Cyrillic, based on the Greek alphabet), and preached in the same language. In 864, still following the same policy, the Byzantines undertook the Christian conversion of the Bulgars. Linked by both language and religion, the Bulgars and the Slavs developed Slav writing and established a cultural identity.

It was also thanks to Michael III that the University of Magnaura (so called because it occupied part of the Magnaura Palace) was founded in Constantinople in 863. But this attempt at renovation did not affect the arts. Painting was still marked by the results of the iconoclastic dispute (see below); sculpture was virtually non-existent. As for the mosaics and frescoes, they were destroyed and replaced by hippodrome scenes and animal motifs. Even so, artists still found ways to express themselves by illuminating manuscripts, mostly in the workshops of monasteries.

② GREEK FIRE

In this 14th-century miniature the Byzantines are shown using Greek fire, a mixture of gunpowder, pitch and saltpetre which had the property of burning on water. This new defensive technique enabled them to resist the invasion of Constantinople by sea.

③ ARAB AND BULGAR INVASIONS
(9th–10th CENTURIES)

FRANKISH EMPIRE
(divided from 843 onwards)

BULGARS

Genoa 934
La Garde Freinet 889
Barcelona
Corsica 809
Rome 876
Sardinia 750
Naples 837
Bari 841
924
915
919
915 Thessalonica
Constantinople
Taranto 840
Brindisi 856
Tunis
Sicily 827
Taormina 902
Syracuse 878
Kairouan
Malta 824
904
IFRIKIJA
Crete 823-28
Alexandria
Damascus

500 km

Arab and Islamic states		Arab (Saracen) raids and invasion routes
Byzantine Empire		Bulgar invasions
Frankish Empire		Areas of the Byzantine Empire controlled by the Bulgars in the mid-10th century

① A BULGAR BAPTISM
Manuscript of the Chronicle of Constantine Manasses.
Vatican Library, Rome

This miniature portrays the baptism of a convert in the presence of the Emperor Michael III and the Empress Theodora. The presence of Byzantine legates at the ceremony and the name Michael (that of the Byzantine Emperor) given to the Khan show how important both peoples believed that conversion to Christianity was.

② The Carolingians in power

1. The race of the Merovingians, from which the Franks were accustomed to choose their kings, is reckoned as lasting to King Hilderich, who, by the order of Stephen, the Roman Pontiff, was deposed, tonsured and sent into a monastery. But this race, though it may be regarded as finishing with him, had long since lost all power and no longer possessed anything of importance except the empty royal title. For the wealth and power of the kingdom was in the hands of the Praefects of the Court, who were called Mayors of the Palace, and exercised entire sovereignty . . . .

2. When Hilderich was deposed Pippin, the father of King Charles, was performing the duties of Mayor of the Palace as if by hereditary right. For his father, Charles, who put down the tyrants . . . had nobly administered the same office . . . and Pippin, after he was made King instead of Mayor of the Palace by the authority of the Roman Pontiff, exercised sole rule over the Franks . . . .

Eginhard, *The Life of Charlemagne*, edited by Professor A. J. Grant in *Early Lives of Charlemagne*, London, 1905, pp. 8–11

The new states in the West

In the 8th and 9th centuries there were already signs of the future dominance of the Frankish kingdom and of Germanic power.

The King of the Lombards, Liutprand (712–44), and his successors sought to impose their authority on the whole of Italy: they took Ravenna in 752. But this expansion worried the Pope. Knowing that the Byzantines in Italy had become weak, he asked for help from the Franks in 754. Pepin the Short intervened and restored to the Pope the lands that the Franks had taken from the Lombards. These were to be the Papal States ('the Donation of Pepin').

As the price of this alliance the Pope recognized Pepin as King of the Franks, at the expense of the last of the Merovingians, who was deposed. Pepin had himself anointed, first by Boniface, Bishop of Mainz, then a second time by the Pope himself. From now on the King of the Franks was a personage chosen by God as well as by his people: the Carolingian dynasty had begun.

Byzantium watched passively the birth of the Papal States (Rome, Ravenna and the Pentapolis – along the Adriatic from Rimini to Ancona). But they were to contribute to the loss of Byzantine possessions in Italy, to the strengthening of the Roman Church and to the establishment of the Carolingian State.

Charlemagne

The frontiers of the states remained relatively stable; and it was within the Carolingian State that linguistic differences foreshadowed the future division into the German and French nations. Shortly before his death in 768, Pepin the Short reconquered Septimania – Languedoc – from the Arabs and imposed his authority on Aquitaine. His two sons shared the kingdom, but the death of Carloman made Charles his only successor. A warrior and reformer, Charles was also responsible for a cultural revival.

In 774 he annexed the Lombard kingdom. It took a number of murderous campaigns to subdue the Saxons; and by doing so he accentuated the Germanic character of the Empire, which now reached as far as the Slav world, where it clashed with the interests of Byzantium. The defeat of the Arabs in northern Spain cost Charles (according to legend) the death of his nephew Roland in the valley of Roncevaux in the Pyrenees. This was the origin of one of the most beautiful medieval epics, the *Song of Roland*. Having also conquered the Avars in Pannonia (present-day Hungary), Charles established the greatest Frankish State of the Middle Ages, justifying his title of Charlemagne, *Carolus Magnus*, or Charles the Great.

The Frankish State was reorganized, the law was applied to all its subjects and legislation respected the customs of the conquered countries – the aim being to adapt the laws to all the peoples of the Empire. In all its regions Charles appointed governors, Counts (from *comes*, a companion), who depended directly on the Emperor. *Missi dominici* (royal inspectors) travelled through the new Empire to supervise the local authorities. Charlemagne made all the important people in the Empire swear oaths of fidelity at annual assemblies in Aachen. Those who attended were principally officials, bishops and the very rich. In this way, certain sections of the population took part in the administration.

What was more, Charlemagne attracted the most learned men of the day, contributing to the education of the people. The English scholar Alcuin set up a famous school for copying the Latin manuscripts; he founded religious and elementary schools, and he drew up textbooks. Alcuin was also responsible for the celebrated Palace Academy, where it is said the Emperor himself attended courses.

Eginhard, by writing a biography of Charlemagne, also contributed to what is known as the Carolingian Renaissance. The Lombard Paul the Deacon, the Goth Theodulf and Angilbert the Frank made up the Emperor's Council and promoted his cultural initiatives. Carolingian

③ THE IRON CROWN OF LOMBARDY
Monza Cathedral, Italy
According to legend, this crown was manufactured for Theodalinda, widow of the Lombard king Authari. It consists of six gold plaques linked by an iron hoop, on which are set flowers made of enamel and precious stones. In 774 Charlemagne wore the iron crown when he proclaimed himself King of the Lombards. Other kings also wore it, as did Napoleon Bonaparte in 1805.

④ THE CAROLINGIAN EMPIRE

	Kingdom in 751		Area of Carolingian influence, 814
	Conquests of Pepin the Short		Frontiers of the Carolingian Empire at the Partition of Verdun, 843
	Charlemagne's conquests		Arab possessions
	Charlemagne's dependent territories		Byzantine possessions

❶ THE PARTITION OF VERDUN (843)

Kingdom of Charles the Bald (Francia occidentalis)

Kingdom of Lothair (Francia media)

Kingdom of Lewis the German (Francia orientalis)

Byzantine Empire

❷ THE LAST INVASIONS OF THE 9th CENTURY

The Christian world before the invasions

Scandinavian settlements

Vikings

Varangians

Moslems

architecture threw off Byzantine influence and founded the style that later became Romanesque.

Charlemagne's ability was such that he imposed his authority on the Church of Rome. This led to his coronation there at Christmas 800. Was the Roman Empire being reborn in the West? The objections raised by Byzantium were diplomatically brushed aside and good relations were re-established. This reconciliation returned Venice and Istria to Byzantium, which in turn recognized the Frankish Empire; and free trade was restored. But the new Roman Empire, despite its name, remained a Germanic state.

Charlemagne's successors, and in particular Louis I the Pious and his sons, were unable to preserve his heritage. United against their elder brother Lothaire, Lewis the German and Charles the Bald swore allegiance to each other in front of their armies, in the Strasbourg Oaths of 842. These are the oldest texts written in both Romance and Teutonic languages, ancestors of French and German. Of all the partitions then worked out, that of Verdun in 843 had the most lasting results. It divided the Empire into three entities, which became Italy, France and Germany. Italy retained its Latin identity, while France and Germany developed along different lines.

To this one must add the inability to stave off the attacks of the Normans in France, the Saracens in Italy and the Magyars in Germany. Only local units were effectively able to defend themselves: hence the subdivision of political power and the establishment of those personal links that later developed under feudalism.

Danes, Norwegians and Swedes

The 9th century saw the entry on the European scene of the Scandinavian countries and Great Britain. The Scandinavians, whose origins were Germanic, consisted of three peoples: the Danes, the Norwegians and the Swedes.

The Swedes headed in the general direction of the Gulf of Finland and up the Russian rivers as far as the Black Sea. They fortified all their operational bases; and these, thanks to new colonists, the Varangians, became small states, notably at Kiev (840) and Novgorod (850). At first, the Swedes had only trade relations with the Byzantines. Later, in the 10th century, they threatened the Byzantine State with their fleet and so obtained a favourable trade agreement.

Unlike the Swedes, the Norwegians and the Danes headed south and west and laid waste the territory in their path. For two centuries they were a threat to the West. These fearsome invaders, who advanced as far as Ireland, Great Britain, Germany, Holland, France and even the

Mediterranean, where they reached Greek territory, were called 'Norsemen' (men of the north). They were the Vikings, the kings of the sea, who took advantage of the general anarchy to impose themselves – if only temporarily – on Western Europe. Their ships were very fast and strong, enabling them to sail the sea as they did on shallow rivers. The Scandinavian forests supplied the wood they needed to build their fleets. They were also traders, founding towns and ports like Grimsby and Waterford and bringing prosperity and political weight to northern Europe.

In 875, having invaded Ireland and founded kingdoms there, the Norwegians turned towards the coasts of Iceland, where in 930 was held the Althing, believed to be Europe's earliest parliament. From there they set out to discover new lands. We know today that Norwegian voyagers reached the coast of America six centuries before Christopher Columbus. But the great distance to be covered and the meagre resources of the time prevented them from settling there.

The main invaders of the West, the true 'Norsemen', were the Danes. They infiltrated various countries up the river valleys. This was how, in 834, they reached what are now the Netherlands and Germany, and a little later landed in Ireland. They settled in these countries, which became the bases for their further operations. They also ravaged England, and settled a large part of northern and eastern areas – the 'Danelaw'. In 885 the Saxon Alfred the Great reconquered London and its surrounding regions, giving England some unity, and laying the foundations of the Saxon kingdom in England.

The Danes also attacked the coast of France. In 896, after a series of well-organized expeditions, they reached Paris (whose siege was described by the monk Abbo) and they continued their piratical exploits until the end of the century. They settled definitively on French territory. In 911 the Carolingian King Charles the Simple signed a treaty with Rollo or Rolf, the leader of the Danish settlers, recognizing him as Duke of Normandy. The Viking period put the Nordic peoples in touch with Christianity. In 826 the missionary Ainsgar founded a church on the Danish-German border and in the next century the Viking King Harald 'Blue-tooth' was baptized.

The Scandinavian offensives had very important results. The Norsemen settled in France, then England, southern Italy and Sicily. There was a loss of confidence in the Frankish kings. And there was a feeling of insecurity among the people. This insecurity led to the building of castles; and they were one aspect of feudalism.

③ SWEDISH STELA OR INSCRIBED UPRIGHT SLAB
9th century. Historical Museum, Stockholm
Inscribed stele from Gotland, an important crossroads of trade and haunt of brigands. It was with ships like those portrayed here that the Swedes later threatened the Byzantines, who were obliged to make trade concessions to put an end to the invasions.

---

④ The Danish siege of Paris

Abbo, a monk of Saint-Germain-des-Prés, was present at the siege. He left an account of it in verse.

While the sun shone from a copper-coloured sky, the Danes followed the banks of the Seine in the region belonging to the Blessed Denis [the plain between the Seine and Saint-Denis] and they worked to establish, not far from Saint-Germain-le-Rond [today Saint-Germain l'Auxerrois opposite the Louvre] a camp whose fortifications included stakes, earth and piles of stones. Then these savages, some on foot and some on horseback, went through hills and fields, forests, plains and villages. Children of all ages, young people, white-haired old people, fathers and sons and mothers, they killed them all . . . . But in the midst of terrible carnage, Paris stood upright, fearless, mocking the bolts aimed at her.

Abbo, *The Siege of Paris by the Danes,* 9th-century poem

3 Byzantium at its Height in the 10th and 11th Centuries

❶ THE DANGER FROM THE NORTH
This miniature shows a naval battle between the Byzantines and the Russians. It was no doubt during one of the attacks on Constantinople made in the 10th century by the Russian state of Kiev. That danger was not as great as the Bulgar threat. Emperor Basil II (976–1025), known as 'the Bulgar-Slayer', waged ceaseless war against them and in 1018 western Bulgaria became a Byzantine province.

❷ THE SUBMISSION OF ARMENIA
Miniature by Ioannis Skilitzes (11th century). National Library, Madrid
The Armenian sovereign surrenders the keys of his capital Ani to the Emperor Constantine IX, known as 'the Gladiator', in 1045.

The apogee of the Byzantine world coincided with the foundation of the Macedonian dynasty (867–1081). The Empire was almost as extensive as in the time of Justinian and its ability to stave off its enemies impressed other peoples. The administration was efficient, the economy stable and the frontiers secure. This made possible a cultural renaissance. Later, however, external pressure and the incompetence of certain Emperors combined to hasten the Empire's decay.

The age of the great offensives

The most remarkable period of the 'heyday of Byzantium' (963–1025) saw brilliant exploits by distinguished Emperors: Nicephorus II Phocas, John I Tzimisces and Basil II. Thanks to them, who led their armies to recover their lost lands, Byzantium was great again.

Their first attack was against the Arabs, now weakened. At the beginning of the 10th century the Arab war fleet had fought the Byzantines, capturing even Sicily and Crete. The Mediterranean thus became the scene of wars. The Arab capture of Thessalonica (modern Salonica) and the massacre of its inhabitants, in 904, left a permanent mark. But from 961 onwards, when Byzantium recaptured Crete, the Aegean was freed from pirates. The Arabs beat a retreat, losing Cilicia, Syria and part of Mesopotamia and Palestine. At the beginning of the 11th century, the imperial troops reached Jerusalem and in

1036 the protection of the Holy Land was guaranteed by treaty. Finally, Byzantium extended its influence into Armenia and, further north, into Caucasian Georgia.

The long period of peaceful coexistence with the Bulgars ended when the Bulgar kings Simeon I and Samuel came to the throne. In their reign the bonds of shared Christianity that had linked Bulgars and Byzantines no longer held and a period of conflict began. In 917 the Bulgars were victorious at Anchialus. But in 997 Samuel was defeated at Sperchios, although he founded a powerful state around Prespa and Ochrid. Again, in 1014, the Byzantines won the battle of Strymon. The total surrender of the Bulgars took place in 1018: their country was annexed by Byzantium and divided into two 'Themes'. The Bulgar Patriarchate was abolished and the autonomous archbishopric of Ochrid was established. It was another 150 years before Bulgaria recovered its independence.

The Arab threat of previous centuries reappeared in Italy and the Adriatic, where Byzantium was trying to re-establish its weakened prestige. But the foundation of the Holy Roman Empire in 962 by the German King Otto I led to further difficulties. Otto was trying to recreate the Roman Empire of the West and relations between the two governments grew tense. A remedy was in intermarriage between the respective families; but the situation remained critical until the beginning of the 11th century, owing to the Norman threat. They had begun as the paid mercenaries of Byzantium: but they later became the conquerors of southern Italy and Sicily.

❸ Basil II, the conquering Emperor

Michael Psellus (1018–78), a brilliant philosopher and admirer of Plato and Aristotle, was the secretary of the Emperor Constantine IX. He wrote the Chronography, *a history of the years 976–1078, the latter part based on personal observation of the Emperors he knew. The period of Byzantium's cultural renaissance was recorded by his lively personality.*

Basil had advanced ahead of his troops and he stood upright, sword in hand. In the other hand he held tight the icon of our Saviour's Mother, using it as the most solid rampart against the irresistible onrush of the enemy . . . .

He did not undertake his expeditions against the barbarians as most of the emperors were accustomed to do, taking the field in the middle of spring and returning at the end of summer. For him, the only signal to return was the attainment of the aim for which he had set out. He could endure both bitter cold and the burning heat of summer; and when he was thirsty he did not go at once to a spring. Truly, in the face of every necessity, he was by nature as strong and resistant as steel . . . .

He knew the various procedures for the useful deployment of troops. Some he had learned from books; others he invented himself by natural intuition, under the pressure of events.

Michael Psellus, *Chronography*, XVI, XXXII, XXXIII

BYZANTIUM (10TH AND 11TH CENTURIES)

❹

Legend:
- Byzantine Empire before the reign of Basil II
- Conquests of Basil II
- Extent of Basil II's Empire
- THRACE Names of army groups
- Frontiers of army groups
- Areas acquired after the death of Basil II in 1025

① THE CONVERSION OF VLADIMIR OF KIEV

In 989 Vladimir, the founder and ruler of the empire of Kiev, was converted to Christianity by the Byzantines. The Church of Russia was placed under the jurisdiction of the Patriarchate of Constantinople, which strengthened the latter's religious influence.

② BYZANTINE GOLDSMITH'S WORK

Binding of a Gospel-book belonging to the Treasury of San Marco, Venice

In the 11th century Abbot Didier sent a monk to Constantinople to make ten icons, sculpted on plates of silver, for his monastery. This cover of a Gospel-book reproduces one of them. The central figure of St Michael is in gold and enamel. In the surrounding enamel medallions there are busts of the saints.

At the same time the Varangians, who were Russians of Scandinavian origin, began to pose a threat to Byzantium, even though they were trading with it. However, once they had been converted to Christianity in 989 there was a rapprochement. The Russian Church was now a dependency of the Patriarchate of Constantinople and the first Metropolitan was sent to Kiev shortly afterwards.

Between 1025 and 1055 the first signs of decadence appeared under the successors of Basil II. They were unable effectively to oppose the feudal forces and external dangers that threatened the Empire. The Seljuk Turks settled in Asia Minor after their victory at Manzikert in 1071; and in the same year the Normans under Robert Guiscard seized Bari.

The policy in Byzantium's heyday was reflected not only in expansionist wars, but also in a set of laws known as the *Epanagoge*. This maintained that 'prestige was the reward of the just'. Any 'just' war, therefore, and any attempt at reconciliation must seek to preserve the authority of the state. Military and diplomatic activities were intended to consolidate power. This policy was followed by the scholar-emperors, Leo VI the Wise and Constantine VII Porphyrogenitus, as well as by the military Emperors Phocas, Tzimisces and 'the Bulgar-Slayer', all of whom were backed by the Church despite any disagreements.

The spiritual achievements and influence of Byzantium

The context was favourable for a cultural renaissance. Security was assured both within and without. The Iconoclast crisis may also have contributed to the appearance of clear thinkers, in the 10th and 11th centuries, in science and art.

Scholars were educated at the reorganized university of Constantinople. So the rich heritage of classical antiquity was at the service of the state, which imposed the new way of thinking and encouraged other social classes to adopt it too. The intellectual élite also contributed to more general education by compiling a *Historical Encyclopaedia*. Photius, later appointed Patriarch, was the leader of this intellectual movement. He published the *Myriobiblion*, summarizing, quoting and commenting on ancient Greek works. A century later Michael Psellus, the main reformer in the Platonic tradition, developed another and more philosophical line of thought. Other important publications included histories, chronicles and lives of the saints, as well as the *Lexicon of Suidas*, on the meanings of words, and on biography and many other works. The social classes that such works did not reach were more interested in

③ THE CHURCH OF THE VIRGIN OF THE BRAZIERS, THESSALONICA

This church, built in 1028, is typical of its time, with its ground-plan a Greek cross inside a square building. All the churches in Constantinople were built on this same model. The use of bricks, apart from their acoustic qualities, made it possible to ornament the façade with geometrical patterns.

the *Epic of Digenes Akrites* (about rulers and heroes of the frontiers), which survives in several versions: they and other Akritic ballads describe the extermination of enemies, giving legendary dimensions to feats of arms.

The new spirit was evident also in art. Architecture, painting, mosaics and craftsmanship all sprang into vigorous life. Churches built on the ground-plan of a Greek cross, surmounted by a cupola, expressed a concern for external appearance, exactitude and perfection. Painting became symbolic and abstract in style, portraying the ideals of asceticism. The technique of illustration obeyed precise rules. These influences affected all of Greece, Italy and Russia. Illuminated manuscripts, superb multicoloured mosaics inspired by painting and using enamel (an Arabic influence), all revealed the Byzantine artists' creativity. Their fame spread beyond the Empire's frontiers, arousing admiration and envy.

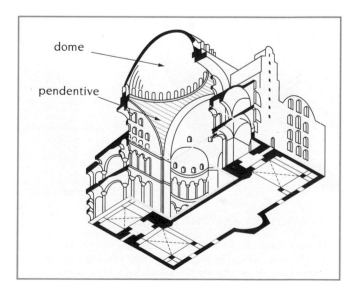

dome

pendentive

④ BYZANTINE ARCHITECTURAL FEATURES

❶ THE NOTARY AND THE BLACKSMITH

Miniature from a 9th-century manuscript of Ioannis Damaskinos
(St John Damascene), Bibliothèque Nationale, Paris

In Byzantium, these two very different crafts were organized in
corporations, whose field of action was limited to certain domains.
Their internal rules were strict: they determined the price of
products, the quantity of production, the profit and the entry
of new members.

Legislation

Legislation was one of the great achievements of
the time. The Macedonian dynasty sought to use
the law to consolidate its own position and to
support the various groups in society. From the
beginning of the 9th century onwards a number
of decrees envisaged a return to Roman Law. As
well as the *Procheiros Nomos*, a legal textbook
published between 870 and 879, and the *Epanagoge* of 879, which laid down the powers of the
Patriarch and the Emperor, the most important
legal compilation of this period, modifying Justinian's laws, was the *Basilica*. This used for the
first time Greek adaptations of Latin originals,
together with 6th and 7th-century Greek com-
mentaries. Clearly, only Greek could be understood, not only by ordinary citizens, but also by
experts. But it was the *Novels* that were most
characteristic of the age.

Administration, the economy and society

The power of the Emperor was defined by law;
and this introduced bureaucracy into the administration of economic and social life. A senior
official, the eparch, who supervised the economy
of the capital, established the relationships between the public bodies and laid down the rules
they must obey. The Emperors tried to limit by
decree the power of the nobility. In 928 one such
edict set forth the procedure whereby farmers
ruined by drought, famine or danger could sell
their land. The aim was to curb the greed of the
great landowners, always eager to buy at low
prices from the victims of unexpected misfortune.
The *Allelengyon* of Basil II similarly obliged
over-mighty subjects to contribute their share to
taxation. This had a double advantage for the
state, since the larger contribution of the rich was
now added to that of the poor.

But Byzantine society was far from egalitarian,
either in the distribution of wealth or in the
sharing of rights and duties. Taxation weighed
heavily on the less well off, while the senior clergy
and the great landowners enjoyed a number of
privileges. On the one hand, the Emperors' edicts
were not always adequate to defend the poor; on
the other, the rich were emboldened by their
economic and political position to demand more
power. The rural population, meanwhile, was
oppressed by the landed proprietors; and the
great estates were in the hands of the military
aristocracy and the Church, which exploited to
their own advantage every slightest weakening of
the central power. Thus, in 1057, Isaac Com-
nenus seized the imperial throne.

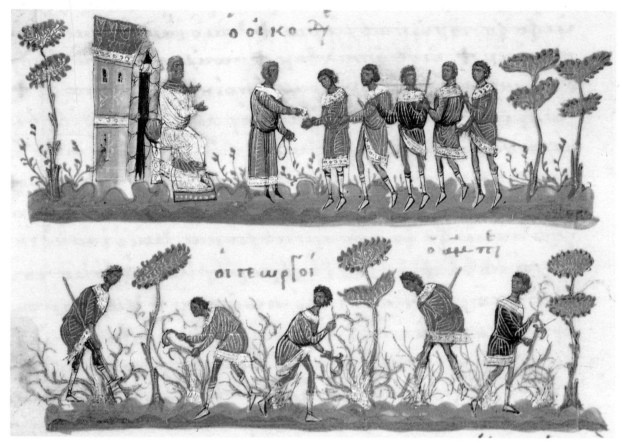

② DISTRIBUTING MONEY AND PRUNING VINES
Miniature from a Greek Gospel of the 11th century, Bibliothèque Nationale, Paris

The Emperors that followed the Macedonian dynasty were more interested in palace intrigues than in problems of state. This situation grew worse as laxity in the provincial administration, together with the weakening of the army, now prevented Byzantium from resisting the Turks and the Normans. But the Emperors were blind to the gravity of their plight. They even abolished the *Allelengyon* and gave privileges to the rich, who in exchange for their services to the state received land whose income they could keep for themselves. To begin with this was an annual arrangement; but over time it became a hereditary right.

The institutions of the Empire grew weaker and the role of the people was limited. Soldier-farmers paid to be exempt from military service and became mere taxpayers – a practice that was fatal for the Emperor's prestige. The state's defences weakened and the 11th century presaged the catastrophe to come. Byzantium relied more and more on foreign mercenaries; the currency (*solidus*) was devalued; the economy became unstable.

③ THE BYZANTINE SOLIDUS
Justinian II (705–11). Weight: 4.5 grams. Solidus from the workshops of Constantinople. Bibliothèque Nationale, Paris
The solidus, the Byzantine gold coin, was a symbol of economic stability. Its devaluation mirrored the Empire's decline.

① THE WEDDING OF OTTO II AND THEOPHANO

10th-century ivory book cover, Cluny Museum, Paris

On 14 April 972 in Rome Otto II, heir to the German throne (973–83), married the princess Theophano, niece of the Byzantine Emperor John Tzimisces. The young princess deeply influenced the German court, and introduced Greek literature to her adopted country.

② THE EMPIRE OF OTTO THE GREAT

Kingdom of Otto I	Byzantine Empire
Expansion under Conrad II in 1032	Frontiers of the Empire at the death of Otto I
Regions dependent on the Empire	Slav and Hungarian raids

Otto the Great

The last of the invasions, the creation of new states from the mid-9th to the 11th century and the growth of new institutions – all helped to transform Western Europe. After the fragmentation of the Carolingian Empire, the duchies on the right bank of the Rhine elected their own kings. One of them, the Saxon Otto I (936–73) eliminated rival claimants to the throne, consolidated his own power and went to Rome to be crowned like a new Charlemagne in 962.

Otto I imposed his authority on the Church. He decided personally on the consecration of bishops and the distribution of titles and land. At the same time, to consolidate his power further, he sought to be recognized by Constantinople. Byzantine agreement was all the more easy to obtain because the Empire was suffering under the wars against the Bulgars and the Russians. The result was a compromise: Otto II, Otto's son, was married to the princess Theophano of Byzantium in 972. The marriage led to German interest in Greek literature and Byzantine art and so had an impact on intellectual life.

The new physiognomy of Europe

At the time of Otto I the Hungarians were threatening Europe. Having settled in the Caucasus, they fled under pressure from other peoples and took refuge near the mouth of the Don.

Driven from there by the Turks, in 895 they crossed the Carpathians and found a home between the Danube and Tisza rivers. Later, they marauded as far as Venice in 899 and Germany in 905. From 955 onwards, however, after being defeated by Otto I at Lechfeld, they settled for good in the plains of present-day Hungary. They were converted to Christianity by the Byzantines, but in 1001 the Hungarian Church acknowledged the authority of Rome.

Otto I undertook the Christian conversion of the Czechs, the Danes and the Poles. At the same time, he reorganized the nascent feudal system and established assemblies which later became Diets (*Reichstag*). Some historians see these changes made by Otto I as harming Germanic unity. In the 11th century the Saxon dynasty was replaced by the Franconian dynasty when Conrad II (1024–39) came to the throne.

The feudal system was emerging in Italy and France. Important fiefs, like the duchies of Burgundy, Aquitaine, Normandy and Brittany, enjoyed *de facto* autonomy: they had their own authorities, their own systems of taxation and justice, and their own commercial centres. Their lords, fighting to maintain their power, hindered the unity of the state.

Setting aside the last Carolingian, Hugh Capet was elected King of the Franks by the kingdom's feudal vassals in 987 – precisely because he seemed weak. But his descendants, the Capetians, ruled France for more than 800 years. His initial authority was limited to the royal domain, from Senlis to Orléans. But gradually the Capetians extended their power. The fact that there were male heirs for three centuries precluded crises of succession and the monarchy which had originally been elective eventually became hereditary.

In England the Saxon King Alfred the Great (871–99) defeated the Danes and brought order to the Kingdom of Wessex. Under the reign of Aethelstan (924–41), England established a single administrative and legislative system; it could then have shared in the life of continental Europe. But the Danes prevented this, first by imposing a tribute, Danegeld. Another raid, led by Canute the Great (1014–35), led to the subjugation of the country. After many battles Canute made his headquarters in London and proclaimed himself king. A great conqueror, he united lands from the Baltic to the coast of Greenland. But rivalry among his successors prompted the people to choose an Anglo-Saxon to re-establish the dynasty.

Edward the Confessor was proclaimed King (1042–66). But his power was limited by that of the lords. He nevertheless divided the kingdom into counties. The council of the Anglo-Saxon kings was the Witan, which included royal household officials, great landowners and top churchmen. Edward's death, without an heir, led to the conflict that is illustrated in the over seventy scenes of Bayeux tapestry: Duke William of Normandy conquered England from Harold, Earl of Wessex, who had been elected by the Witan. Harold was killed at the Battle of Hastings (October 1066) and the victor became King of England under the name of William I, known as the Conqueror.

William protected the English Church and reorganized it with the help of Lanfranc, a religious scholar whom he brought from Normandy and made Archbishop of Canterbury. William refused to submit to the power of the Pope and he opposed the intervention of Papal legates in the English Church's affairs. Gradually, however, the Roman Church and the English Crown were linked while monasteries were set up as teaching establishments and libraries, where Greek and Latin literature was introduced.

③ CANUTE THE GREAT, KING OF DENMARK AND THEN ENGLAND
Winchester New Minster Register, 1020–30, British Library
Canute the Great (1016–35) and his first wife Aelfgyfu place a cross on an altar. Converted to Christianity, he had received the Greek title of Basileus (king). His dynasty reigned until 1042.

④ THE SEAL OF EDWARD THE CONFESSOR
Both sides of the seal bear the same inscription: Sigillum Edwardi Anglorum Basilei. This title was also accorded to his predecessors Aethelstan (946–55) and Edgar (925–40), both Anglo-Saxon.

Religious Life in the East and West, 6th to the 11th Century

❶ SIMEON STYLITES

Stylites appeared very early in Byzantine history and continued until its final days. They devoted themselves to prayer, fasting and wakefulness and spent much of their lives on pillars. Simeon Stylites, the first of them, spent 37 years on his.

❷ THE VATOPEDI MONASTERY ON MOUNT ATHOS

In the 7th century, fleeing from the Arabs, monks took refuge on the peninsula of Mount Athos, where a score of monasteries was established, making it the most important centre of the Orthodox Church. The holy peninsula is the last monastic republic of our day.

Monasticism

Asceticism and monasticism developed in the Byzantine Empire in ways that were virtually inseparable from the evolution of the state itself. At least until the 9th century, in fact, the state and the Church were regarded as practically identical.

Monasticism involved the renunciation of property, life in common, obedience to superiors and compulsory labour. In the 9th century the rules of 'cenobitism' (life as a community as distinct from 'eremitism' or solitary life) were made even stricter by the iconoclast monk Theodore of Stoudion. It was at this time that other tasks, like the copying of ancient manuscripts, became obligatory. Monasteries owned great estates that were exempt from taxes, giving rise to conflicts with the political authorities.

The creation and the protection of monasteries were matters for the Emperor and the Patriarch. While they were not always on good terms, the imperial authorities and the Church were mutually dependent and mutually helpful. Monasteries often served the aims of foreign policy.

Monasteries in regions where the presence of foreign peoples posed problems for the Empire were characteristic of Byzantine policy. A number of religious figures (Methodius, Cyril, Photius, Athanasius, Leo the Mathematician) put themselves at the disposal of the Empire, which sought to transform the Hellenic territory of the Balkans into a base for religious and political expansion. Mount Athos became its greatest cultural centre and its influence extended beyond the Empire. From the 10th century Iberians (from Georgia), Amalfitans and Christian Slavs settled there.

In the late 10th century and the early 11th, Varangians (Russians) and Bulgars appeared. They also founded monasteries, which became great economic centres. Arid regions were brought into cultivation and the monastic establishments became landowners. Economic growth was rapid and the monasteries were linked with the towns. Influenced by this spiritual and economic development, the Balkans later played an important part in the evolution of the West.

The peoples of the West, although divided politically, were united by their faith and their recognition of a supreme spiritual authority, based in Rome, whose title was no longer challenged after the 10th century. The Church of Rome asserted its power everywhere.

Monasticism, originating in the East, spread

northwards from the Mediterranean from the end of the 4th century onwards. Kings founded monasteries, such as those of Clovis in Paris (Saints-Apôtres, Sainte-Geneviève) and that of the King of the Burgundians, Chilperic. At first the monks adopted the internal regulations applied in the Eastern monasteries; then this Rule was adapted by the Italian Benedict of Nursia (540) and by the Irish monasteries with their own traditions. Supported by the kings, the monks acquired greater autonomy and extended their activities. From the 7th century, however, the bishops took the initiative in monastic foundation.

The principles of monastic life were strict. The monks studied sacred and philosophical texts, founded schools and sought to impose great rigour on the whole Church. They supported the power of the Pope and tried to strengthen it throughout the West. Even if their convictions were not universally shared, their influence spread and some monasteries like Cluny in Burgundy (founded in 910) ended by being directly dependent on the Pope. Over time, however, many monks became more interested in worldly affairs.

With different monastic rules the monks in the East were less in contact with the outside world than those in the West. But both contributed to the spread of Christianity and encouraged the life of the mind. Sometimes, however, obedience to authority clashed with independent thought. Pagan festivals were Christianized: in 353 Christmas, for example, replaced the feast of *Natale Solis Invicti* – the birth of the unconquered sun.

Relations between Rome and Constantinople

In Constantinople relations between church and state had changed from the time of Justinian in the 6th century to that of the Macedonian dynasty in the 11th; and their repercussions had been felt both inside and outside the Empire.

Justinian had tried to achieve unity by converting his subjects to Christianity. But by trying to impose 'the true faith' he had brought about a resurgence of paganism and heresy. All his decisions had been intended to place all of Christendom under his own authority so that the Church – in Rome and in Constantinople – would be directed by the Emperor. He penalized the recalcitrant by confiscating their property, banning them from public office and abolishing the Platonic Academy. This drove some scholars to take refuge at the Persian court, where they introduced Hellenic culture.

The 8th and 9th centuries witnessed a serious

❸ The foundation of Cluny, 909

I, William [Duke of Aquitaine], by the grace of God Count and Duke, after deep reflection and desirous of providing for my salvation, deliver to the Holy Apostles Peter and Paul, wholly and completely, the domain of Cluny which belongs to me . . . .

I make this donation under the following particular conditions: that there be built at Cluny, in honour of the Holy Apostles Peter and Paul, a regular monastery; that the monks live there in common according to the Rule of St Benedict and that they possess this property, hold it, keep it and govern it for ever. That they neglect not to fill this venerable house of prayer with their praise and supplications; that they devote all their concern and ardour to inquiry . . . . We desire also that here be accomplished every day the work of mercy towards the poor, the needy, strangers and pilgrims.

A. Bernard and Bruel, *Recueil des Chartes de l'abbaye de Cluny*, Paris, 1876

❹ MONASTIC LIFE
Miniature

Writing was an important task in a monk's life. Translators, illuminators and copyists ensured that ancient texts were passed on to posterity. The monk shown above could represent St Luke, the mildest and most modest of the Apostles and, according to tradition, the author of the third Gospel and of the Acts of the Apostles.

① CONSTANTINE V HAS ICONS BURNED

Constantine V (741–75) condemned sacred images, dispersed the monks and confiscated monastic property. He even wrote pamphlets against image-worship. An Imperial Council confirmed his stand and in 754, with the backing of the people, he ordered all icons to be destroyed.

② The Pope justifies the cult of icons

Letter from Pope Gregory II (715–31) to the Byzantine Emperor.

But you, since you seized the Empire, have in no way upheld the decisions of the Fathers. On the contrary, having found the holy churches resplendent in gold, you have stripped them and left them bare. For what are our churches? They are not stone, wood, thatch and clay fashioned by the hand of man. No: they have been embellished with the help of paintings, portraying the miracles and sufferings of the Lord and of his holy and glorious Mother, as well as the Holy Apostles. It is for these representatives and these portraits that many spend their fortunes. Men and women, holding in their arms the little children that have just been baptized, and those who are young in age and those who come from among the Gentiles, they point at these pictures: it is thus that they are edified and that they raise to God their spirit and their heart . . . .

In your view, we bow down before stones, walls and planks of wood. It is not so, O Emperor. We find there a reminder, an inspiration, which lifts toward Heaven our dull and heavy spirit. That is the reason for their names and titles to be written there and for their distinctive features: but we do not treat them as gods, as you claim. May that never happen! For it is not in them that we place our hopes; and if it be an image of the Lord we say: 'Lord Jesus Christ, Son of God, help us and save us.' If it be an image of the Holy Mother we say: 'Thou Who hast carried God, Holy Mother of the Lord, intercede with Thy Son, our true God, for the salvation of our souls.'

Quoted by Hugo Rahner, L'Eglise et l'Etat dans le christianisme primitif, Paris, Editions du Cerf, 1964

and fateful dispute: the Iconoclast crisis. In fact, iconolatry – the worship of images – led to a conflict both religious and ideological, pitting the people against the central power.

For the Byzantines reverence for icons was a profound expression of respect and something to which the Hellenic regions, in particular, were deeply attached. The more eastern provinces of the Empire, by contrast, were attracted by iconoclasm, the destruction of images. In those regions, the monophysites – 7th-century heretics who minimized the human aspect of the Incarnation – were still numerous and the Moslem world, which was hostile to all forms of imagery, was very influential and very close.

So two forces confronted each other: the power of the state and the will of the people, supported by the monks. Their conflict went through two phases, from 726 to 787 and from 815 to 843. The first began with the imperial decree of Leo III calling for icons to be abolished – which sparked off popular uprisings. The Emperor's interference in the ecclesiastical affairs of Christendom also poisoned relations between East and West. When Pope Gregory III protested, the Emperor reacted by withdrawing from his authority the churches in Calabria, Sicily and Illyria. The Pope then turned towards the Franks. This first phase of the dispute ended with the seventh Ecumenical Council of 787, which once more authorized the cult of icons in both East and West.

In the year 800, in the reign of Charlemagne, Rome called for the abrogation of all measures taken during the Iconoclast crisis. In reality, the Church wanted to bring Illyria, southern Italy and Sicily once more under its jurisdiction.

The same crisis – in effect an imperial reaction against the monks' growing power – was revived in the time of the Emperor Theophilus (829–42) and the icon-worshipping monk Theodore of Stoudion. Monasteries still enjoyed certain privileges: monks were exempt from the military and the monastic estates were exempt from taxes. In 843 the cult of images was finally re-established: the Church had triumphed over the Emperor. But the crisis had changed the relationship between Constantinople and Rome: from now on there was a growing gap between the Byzantine East and the Latin West.

In 863 a new crisis broke out between the two churches as represented by the Byzantine theologian Photius and Pope Nicholas I. When the Emperor appointed Photius as Patriarch, Pope Nicholas angrily demanded his dismissal, as Photius was opposed to a number of Roman 'innovations', such as fasting on Saturday, priestly celibacy and, above all, the affirmation that the Holy Spirit proceeded from the Father and from the Son. Photius deposed Nicholas I in 867; but a palace intrigue drove the Patriarch from power. A complete break had been avoided, but the divergences had deepened.

A definitive split between Rome and Constantinople was now only a matter of time. The myth that they shared a common religion and a common spiritual life was dying, for the context that had maintained the idea of religious ecumenism in a Christian world already divided politically and culturally had changed out of all recognition.

Two men confronted each other in the last dispute, in the 11th century: the Patriarch Michael Cerularius (Kerularios) and Cardinal Humbert, the legate of Pope Leo IX. Both were bold, determined and intransigent; and they disagreed, once more, about various liturgical practices in the Roman Church, none of them major. On 16 July 1054 the Papal legates placed a Bull deposing Michael Cerularius on the High Altar in Sancta Sophia. The Patriarch, with the consent of the Emperor, responded by excommunicating the legates. The Christian world watched the conflict passively, believing it to be one more episode in an already long-standing dispute. No one foresaw that it would prove to be a definitive break, revealing above all the depth of the division that had gradually come about between the Christian worlds of East and West.

Romanesque art

In the second half of the 10th century the West built many new churches of varying size and importance, from great abbeys to simple country chapels. The reason was the growth of population that resulted from the cessation of Norman, Saracen and Hungarian raids.

Romanesque art united in one style the architecture, the sculpted decoration and the religious images. That did not exclude the great degree of regional diversity, depending on the nature of the buildings, the local economy and the materials to hand.

This variety resulted also from the different solutions that were sought to the problem of the vault, given that wood was too ready a prey to fire. The thrust exerted by a stone arch made it necessary to strengthen the walls, at the expense of the opening and hence of the light within the church. The Gothic pointed arch was the later solution to the problems tackled by the Romanesque architects.

The basilica of St Ambrose (940) in Milan, Saint-Etienne in Caen (1068), and Santiago de Compostela (1075) in Spain are, among many others, masterpieces of the art that flourished in the 11th and 12th centuries.

③ MICHAEL CERULARIUS
Miniature from an 11th-century manuscript, Madrid Library
1054 was a crucial year for the Eastern and Western Churches. The schism finally separated the two worlds. This miniature probably portrays the Patriarch of Constantinople with representatives from the Greek and Roman clergy. Violently hostile to the latter as he was, Michael Cerularius would not rest until he had divided the two Churches.

④ SAINT-ETIENNE OF NEVERS

This ancient priory, which dates from the 11th century, is a fine example of Romanesque architecture in free-stone. To uphold the span of the vaults and arches, Romanesque builders invented pillasters joined to the main piers to support the vaulting arches. The lighting came from semi-circular arches.

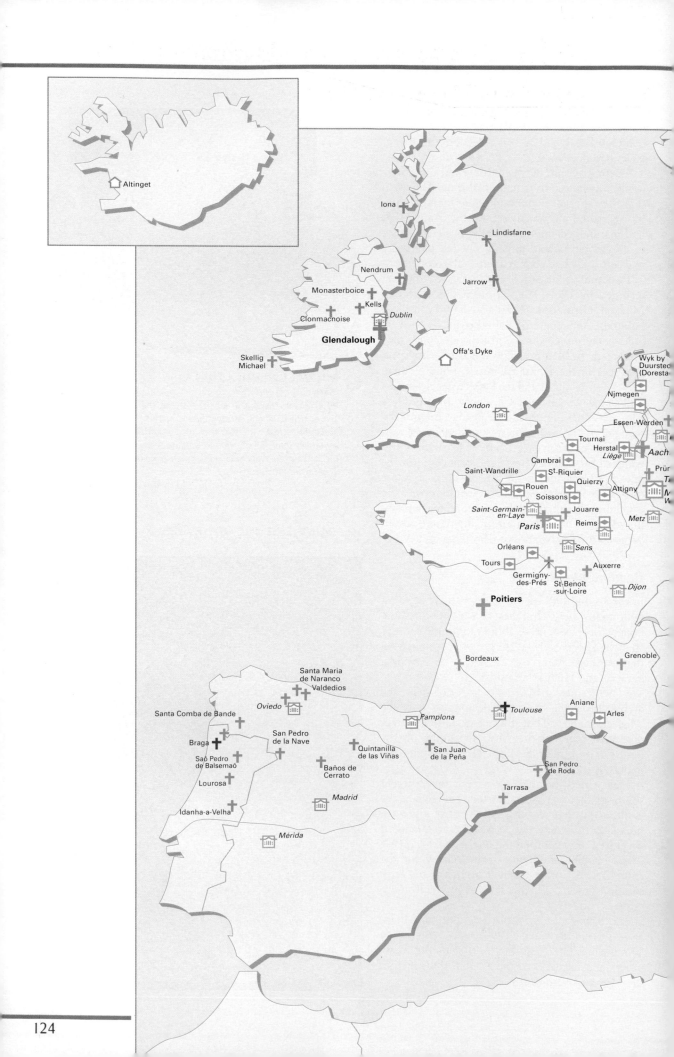

Altinget

Iona

Lindisfarne

Jarrow

Nendrum

Monasterboice

Kells

Clonmacnoise

Dublin

Glendalough

Offa's Dyke

Skellig
Michael

London

Wyk by
Duursted
(Doresta

Njmegen

Essen-Werden

Tournai

Herstal

Liège

Aach

Cambrai

Prür

Saint-Wandrille

St-Riquier

Quierzy

Attigny

T

M
W

Rouen

Soissons

Saint-Germain-
en-Laye

Jouarre

Reims

Metz

Paris

Orléans

Sens

Tours

Germigny-
des-Prés

St-Benoît
-sur-Loire

Auxerre

Dijon

Poitiers

Bordeaux

Grenoble

Santa Maria
de Naranco
Valdedios

Aniane

Arles

Oviedo

Toulouse

Santa Comba de Bande

Pamplona

Braga

San Pedro
de la Nave

Quintanilla
de las Viñas

San Juan
de la Peña

San Pedro
de Roda

Saó Pedro
de Balsemaó

Baños de
Cerrato

Lourosa

Tarrasa

Idanha-a-Velha

Madrid

Mérida

The Past in the Present Day
BYZANTIUM AND THE WEST

Celts   **Visigoths**   **Franks**   **Byzantium**

place that was important at the time but with no surviving remains

civil monument

religious monument

museum

frontiers of 20th-century states

500 km

Birka

Gotland

Fyrkat

Roskilde   Lund

Trelleborg

Ladby

Hamburg

Berlin

Hildesheim

ey

Fulda

Nürnberg

Regensburg

Wien

Reichenau   *Salzburg*

allen

Mustair   Spittal

Malles

eprio nza

Cividale

Milano   *Aquileia*

Verona

Venezia   *Porec*

Zadar

Ravenna

Firenze

Trogir

Roma

Montecassino   Bari

Napoli   Brindisi

Benevento   Taranto

Crotone

Dubrovnik

Durrës

Ohrid

Stobi

Beograd

Sofija (Sofia)

Preslav

Adrianoupolis (Edirne)

Filippi

Thessaloniki

Athos

Nikopolis

Orchomenos

Korinthos

Athinai

Chios

Kiyev

Constanza

Varna

Samsun (Tzanik)

Constantinoupolis (Istanbul)

Nikomidia (Izmit)

Nikaia (Iznik)

Proussa (Bursa)

Pergamon (Bergama)

Smyrna (Izmir)

Sardis (Sardes)

Ikonio (Konya)

Ephessos (Selgouk)

Pammukale (Ierapolis)

Rodos

Antalya

Siracusa

Iraklio

Kriti

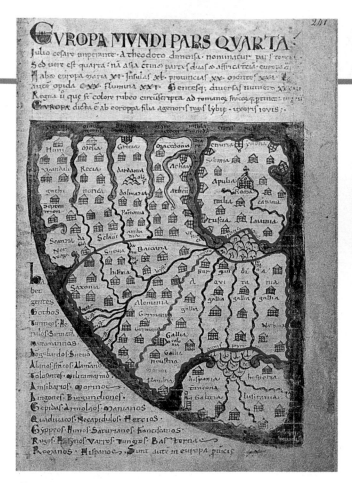

EVROPA MVNDI PARS QVARTA

① EUROPE IN THE 12TH CENTURY

The *Liber Floribus* of Lambert of Ardres (*c*.1120),
in the Central Library, Ghent

*This map is one of the first medieval attempts to represent the world.
Its author believed that Europe made up one quarter of the world
and Africa another: Asia occupied the other half. Charts intended to
give precise information about distances and directions appeared in
the 13th century, as navigational aids.*

962	The Empire re-established by Otto I the Great
987	Hugh Capet elected King of France
1016–35	Canute I rules the Anglo-Danish Empire
1054	Religious schism between Rome and Constantinople
1059	Decree of Pope Nicholas II conferring on cardinals the right to elect Pope
1075	Pope Gregory VII's Decree on Investitures
1077	Emperor Henry IV at Canossa
1085	Christian forces recapture Toledo from the Moslems
1095–99	The First Crusade – Crusaders capture Jerusalem
1152–90	Reign of Emperor Frederick I Barbarossa
1154–89	Henry II Plantagenet King of England
1180–1223	Philip II Augustus King of France
1187	Fall of Jerusalem, recaptured by the Sultan Saladin
1189–99	Richard I the Lionheart King of England
1198–1216	Pontificate of Innocent III
1204	The Fourth Crusade – Crusaders capture Constantinople
1209	Foundation of the Friars Minor by St Francis of Assisi
1214	Battle of Bouvines
1215	John, King of England, grants the Magna Carta to his subjects
1220–50	Reign of the Emperor Frederick II of Hohenstaufen
1261	The Byzantines recapture Constantinople from the 'Latins'
1226–70	Louis IX (St Louis) King of France

② THE THREE ORDERS

The dream of Henry I, three details from *The Worcester
Chronicle*, *c*.1130–40, Corpus Christi College, Oxford

*The medieval doctrine of the Orders took account of three
basic social activities: prayer, combat and working the land.
The royal dream depicted here shows that the Orders were
regarded as the instruments of monarchical power.*

CHAPTER

MEDIEVAL CHRIST-IANITY

IN THE WEST

FROM THE 11TH TO THE 13TH CENTURY

European civilization in the Middle Ages was based on three essential elements: the Holy Roman Empire, Christianity and the Germanic influence.

But the Empire and the classical cultural tradition were also Mediterranean phenomena, affecting the Near East and North Africa as well as Europe. The concept of Christian universality, likewise, was influenced by the administrative geography of the Empire.

The emergence of medieval Europe in the West connoted a certain number of breaks with the past: the end of unity in the Mediterranean, the exposure of north-west and continental Europe to a common fate on account of the great invasions and the gradual separation of the Greek and Roman Churches.

Whereas the Edict of Constantine (313) reconciled Rome and Christianity within Mediterranean civilization, this was by no means true of a second great symbolic event: the coronation of Charlemagne.

With that act the Germanic king established a new geopolitical entity, stretching from the North Sea to central Italy, and from the Pyrenees to the river Elbe. The Bishop and people of Rome – a city now geographically peripheral but symbolically central – offered him the crown of an Empire which claimed to be heir to the Roman Empire but which in fact was something completely new.

Can it be said that this was the birth of Europe? Events soon showed that political and religious ideas were well in advance of reality: the Carolingian Empire came to an end before the 9th century was over. A new Europe did not begin to emerge until after the year 1000.

❸ THE GROWTH OF TOWNS
The Effects of Good Government, by Ambrogio Lorenzetti (1338–40), fresco in the Town Hall (Palazzo Pubblico), Siena, Italy
This is only part of the allegorical fresco on Good and Bad Government. It shows masons at work in the midst of close-packed buildings – signs of rapid expansion in a town eager to be greater, more secure and better organized.

❹ EUROPE IN THE YEAR 1000

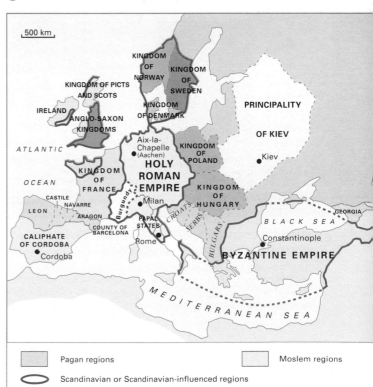

Pagan regions   Moslem regions
Scandinavian or Scandinavian-influenced regions

1 Europe and Christendom in the Middle Ages

① DOORWAY OF THE CHURCH OF SAINT-MICHEL D'AIGUILHE AT PUY-EN-VELAY

The Arab and Byzantine influence evident here is due to the influence of the Crusaders returning from Constantinople and of pilgrims to Santiago de Compostela, for whom Le Puy was an important stage on their journey.

The Mediterranean and the civilization of the ancient world

In the Middle Ages, as in the ancient world, the idea of Europe was mainly geographical. 'Europe' was contrasted with 'Asia' and with the area long known as 'Scythia' – that land of nomadic horsemen and stock-breeders beyond the middle and lower Danube and north of the Black Sea.

But belonging to a common civilization can scarcely be determined by purely geographical criteria. The Romans, like the Greeks, believed that they belonged to 'the civilized world' by contrast with the 'barbarians'; and in so far as the Romans, more than the Greeks, believed that peoples could be redeemed from barbarism, the frontiers of their civilization were not geographical but cultural. Their civilization ended wherever their way of life ceased: where there were no more villas, no Roman roads, no imperial officials, no Roman law, no settled agriculture.

Geographically, however, the Roman Empire was centred round the Mediterranean and it was from there that it succeeded in annexing large areas of the continent. Within the Roman world there remained many differences arising from the varied history of its constituent parts, but its internal unity was real. From Spain to Sicily and to the provinces of North Africa it embodied the same civilization. In the Rhineland, in Rhaetia and in Noricum (Switzerland, Austria and part of present-day Bavaria), the 'barbarian' world began.

From the Mediterranean to Europe

The great invasions that followed one another in the 4th, 5th and 6th centuries scarcely changed this situation. As proof one need only analyze changes in languages, which bear witness to the ways in which Roman civilization evolved.

In fact, leaving aside Britain, only the Flemish areas, the Rhineland, Rhaetia and Noricum were influenced by Germanic dialects. Throughout the rest of Western Europe later generations spoke Italian, French, Spanish or Portuguese. Germanic idioms barely affected the transition from Latin to Romance or neo-Latin languages; only a few hundred words were borrowed from them.

Furthermore, in areas where the Germanic invaders were in the majority or were an important ethnic group, they in no way challenged the existing life of the towns. Even where notable changes took place, the Roman town network survived the transition from late antiquity to the Middle Ages.

By contrast, the changes in Balkan towns (especially after the Slav invasions) were revolutionary, as was the incorporation of North Africa into Islamic civilization.

A decisive stage in the transition from Mediterranean to what was to become European civilization took place between the end of the 7th century and the middle of the 10th. It involved four factors.

The first was the expansion of the Islamic world. In the 8th century all of the eastern Mediterranean fell under Arab domination, while at the same time relations between Byzantium and the West gradually weakened, until the Adriatic remained their only major area of contact.

The second was the growing autonomy of the Western Church vis-à-vis the Byzantine Emperors. They, in fact, had no role in the preaching missions carried out in Anglo-Saxon Britain or in the more thoroughgoing conversion of the continent during the 8th century. It was English monks like Boniface (680–755) who preached the Gospel to the Germanic peoples beyond the Rhine, but in doing so they were simply obeying the directives of the Bishop of Rome.

The establishment of the Carolingian Empire was the third decisive factor. With a Germanic ruling class and a continental geographical base, it claimed double universality: as the heir of Rome and of Christendom.

The fourth factor, finally, was invasion – by Vikings, Saracens and Hungarians – in the 9th and 10th centuries. In the centuries that followed, invasions from central Asia did not deeply affect the entity that had emerged in the meantime: Europe, if seen geographically, and Christendom, in terms of values and civilization.

A new contrast and confrontation, between Christians and 'infidels', replaced the old distinction between Romans and barbarians. The idea of 'Christendom' now became so precise, in fact, as to exclude other Christians and 'Romans' – i.e. the Byzantines.

The frontiers of Christendom after the year 1000

The Romano-Christian Empire was reborn in 962 with the coronation of Otto I. The Duchy of the Saxons, forcibly integrated into Christendom under Charlemagne, became the base of a new Empire which was much more German than Carolingian.

❷ THE IRISH SCRIPTURE CROSS

Cross from Clonmacnois, 10th century, Ireland

The great period of the Irish Church began in the 5th century with the preaching of St Patrick. From the 6th century onwards the monasteries became centres of spiritual life and their influence spread throughout Europe. This Calvary is one of the 50 that survive of the 800 that Ireland once had. Christ can be seen at the intersection, with the serpent under His feet and the dove of the Holy Spirit on His head. In His left hand He holds the Cross of sacrifice, in His right the palm of resurrection. On His right, an angel blows a trumpet; on His left, a devil turns his back.

❸ How Boniface converted the Germanic pagans

The English monk Winfred (who took the name of Boniface in 719) was for nearly 30 years the grand master of the German Church and he made it his personal task to convert the Germanic peoples beyond the Rhine. The following episode, which occurred in 723, is described by his biographer Willibald.

Boniface set about to cut down a magnificently large oak tree, called by ancient pagan tradition the Oak of Job, near Geismar. With him were the servants of God. And when, sustained by constancy of spirit, he cut the oak down (in the presence of a crowd of pagans, all silently cursing the enemy of their gods), no sooner was it struck than its immense mass, shaken from on high by a divine gust, its top torn, and as if by a superior will, it crashed to the ground and split into four equal parts. From that immense mass there sprang four trunks of equal size, without any of the brothers present having to intervene.

At the sight of that, the pagans, who had at first been hostile, ceased their cursing, became believers, and gave homage to the Lord. With that, the steward of His supreme sanctity, after consulting the brothers, built with the wood of this tree an oratory which he dedicated to the honour of the Apostle St Peter. Having done these things with the will and aid of the Lord, he left at once for Thuringia.

Vitae Sancti Bonifatii Archiepiscopi Maguntini, edited by W. Levison, Hanover, 1905

❶ Merchants of Venice and Amalfi

In 968 the Emperor Otto I sent Liutprand, Bishop of Cremona, on a mission to the Byzantine Emperor Nicephorus Phocas. The stories he included in his report, Mission to Constantinople, give very valuable details about the role that merchants from Venice and Amalfi then played in trade between Italy and the Eastern Empire.

'*Because we believe that on the orders of Otto I you have acquired a number of* pallia, *we command that they be brought into our presence: that those worthy of you be marked with a lead seal and returned to you; but that those which are* koluomena, *i.e. forbidden to all nations save to us Romans, be taken from you against reimbursement of their price.*'

This they did and they took from me five precious pallia, *in their belief that you and all the Italic, Saxon, French, Bavarian, Swiss and other nations were unworthy to wear such vestments. For it is an offense and an insult that soft, effeminate men, with long sleeves, tiaras and feminine robes – liars, hermaphrodites and cowards – should wear the purple instead of heroes, strong men, experienced in war, full of faith and charity, obedient to God and above reproach!*

But what then had become of the word of the Emperor and his Imperial promise? When I had greeted him, I had begged him to allow me to buy pallia *to decorate the Church, at no matter what price. And he had said: 'Which do you want and for how much?' – speaking of* poiotēta *and* posotēta, *i.e. quantity and quality; and he had made no mention of differences and had not said 'Except for these or those'.*

'*. . . This garment cannot be so extraordinary,*' *I said, 'because where we come from it is used by the cheapest prostitutes and mountebank magicians.' 'Who do you get them from?' 'From Venetian and Amalfi merchants,' I said, 'who import them and receive our products in exchange.'*

Liutprand of Cremona, in *Italia e Bizanzio alla soglie dell'anno Mille*, Europa, Novara, 1987, pp. 244–5

❷ THE CID (EL CAMPEADOR) (1043–99)

14th-century manuscript, Academy of Sciences, Lisbon
Rodrigo Diaz de Vivar, known as the Cid, was a great figure in the Reconquista. He resolved the dispute between his own country of Castile and Navarre by defeating Jimeno Garcès, from Navarre, in single combat.

What was more, the new Empire of Otto's Saxon dynasty no longer fitted within the frontiers of Christendom established by the Carolingians. The end of the 10th century and the beginning of the 11th saw a marked retreat of the 'pagan' world to the north and east of Europe. Thus enlarged, Christendom was by no means a homogeneous civilization.

The lands in the north and east, sparsely inhabited, still had more or less Christian populations. True, the episcopal see of Hamburg had been established in 943 very close to the Slav world; but Christianity and town life did not really begin to take root in Poland and Bohemia until the two archbishoprics of Magdeburg and Prague were founded shortly after 970, on the joint initiative of Otto I and the Pope.

After Otto's army had defeated the Hungarians in 955, they ceased their incursions into Italian and German territory. In the year 1000 their Duke was converted to Christianity and crowned king with the blessing of the Holy See. Twenty-five years later it was the turn of the Polish monarchy to be legitimized by the Roman Church.

Finally, between 1010 and 1030, after the conversion of the dukes of Normandy, the kings of Norway, Sweden and Denmark entered the Christian Church.

In the far south of the continent, in Mediterranean Europe, the heritage of ancient Rome was very definite and city life was more developed. This region had forged close bonds with the great Arab and Byzantine civilizations, in whose eyes the Christian West was still only a world of barbarians.

In the 10th century trade between Europe and the East very much resembled that which in the present day links the industrialized with the developing countries. The East exported luxury goods (e.g. silks) and costly exotic products (e.g. spices); the West sold slaves and raw materials (e.g. wood and metal). The Venetians already played a predominant part in this trade with Byzantium; and there was also trade with the Islamic states, although it was officially banned. In the 10th century and at the beginning of the 11th Italian merchants from Amalfi were very active at Alexandria; but there is also reason to believe that other merchants from the Campania, as well as Pisans, were also present at the same time in Egypt, Tunisia and Sicily.

It was during the second half of the 10th century that the Spanish Caliphate of Córdoba reached its heyday, threatening the small Christian kingdoms of León and Castile. The Saracen military bases in Provence and Gaeta had been destroyed in 915 and 972; but there had subsequently been fresh incursions into southern Italy, launched from Arab Sicily and from Tunisia. On the eve of the year 1000, while Europe's northern and western frontiers were no longer threatened, that of southern Italy was in turmoil. The Byzantines seemed on the point of reaffirming their power there and they were incessantly at war – often reversing alliances – with the Lombard Duchies of the south, with the armies of the Saracens and with the small Duchies of the Campania such as Amalfi and Naples, which were theoretically dependent on Byzantium.

In the middle of the 11th century a number of events radically altered the situation on this southern frontier of Europe. From 1040 onwards both the Caliphate of Baghdad and the Byzantine Empire had to face invasion by the Seljuk Turks. And, at the very moment when Byzantium had to deal with such serious problems, its domination of the Italian south could hardly survive the attacks of the Norman hordes (1040–75), whose mercenaries had been there since the beginning of the century. Meanwhile, relations between the Roman and Greek Churches were growing more and more tense, leading up, in 1054, to a schism which unlike its predecessors proved to be final.

Christian Western Europe, having secured its frontiers against invasion (and against Byzantine influence), was now able to prepare a first counter-offensive against Islam. From the middle of the century onwards, with the help of Frankish knights, the Christian kingdoms of northern Spain began a war of 'reconquest'. The capture of Toledo in 1085 showed that the relative strength of Islam and Christianity, at least in Europe, had completely changed. Five years later, Arab domination of Sicily came to an end: the island fell to the Normans and became the centre of the kingdom of the Altavilla, which extended to most of the Italian south.

Paradoxically, the result of these annexations was that Byzantine and Arab culture began to exert great influence on the Christian West. The Bishopric of Toledo, which from 1130 onwards established a veritable school of translators, was a perfect illustration of the point. Christian, Arab and Hebrew scholars, who had been welcomed at the time of the Córdoba Caliphate, were thus able to supply Europe with Latin translations of Arabic scientific and philosophical works, and then of those of Aristotle, which were received in the universities of Europe.

③ THE RECONQUISTA

In the 11th century Moslem Spain was divided into independent kingdoms. This fragmentation assisted the reconquest then beginning: it was Christian Spain's Crusade. The reconquest consolidated religious unity, but not political unity. It was accompanied by systematic efforts to repopulate and restore devastated areas and attracted, especially just south of the Pyrenees, an appreciable number of peasants from the south of France.

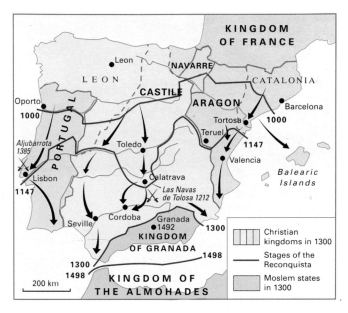

④ AMALFI CATHEDRAL (1066)

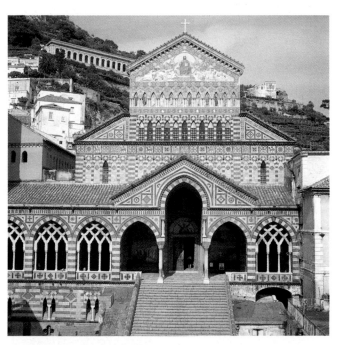

The Duomo Sant'Andrea was built at Amalfi in the 11th century. By that time, this town in southern Italy had been a flourishing republic for two centuries, a rival of Genoa and Pisa.

2 Feudal Europe

At the Battle of Hastings the Normans were recognized as the most professional and best armed warriors in Europe. All their horses were equipped with stirrups, making it harder to unseat their riders. The knights, in helmets and chain mail, used a new weapon, the lance, which became their distinguishing mark.

---

② The *Commendatio*

The Commendatio – the recognition of the authority of a powerful personage in exchange for fealty and service – was a social relationship very widespread in Carolingian times. The text below is an extract from a legal formulary written between 725 and 750.

For those who would commit themselves to the power of another. To the kind lord Such-and-such of – , I Such-and-such of –. It being well known to all that I have nothing wherewith to feed or clothe myself, I have implored your pity and you have allowed me in your great goodness to confide and commit myself to your mundio *(protection); and this I have done; and so you must help and support me, for food and clothing, in proportion to my service and my merit; and as long as I live I must lend you service and obedience as much as a man of free estate may do, and I must not withdraw from your might and* mundio, *but for all the days of my life must remain under your power and protection. It is agreed that if one or the other of us seeks to withdraw from this agreement, he will pay so much (a sum to be decided) to the other and this agreement will retain its full validity.*

Formulae Merowingici et Karolini aevi, in Monumenta Germaniae Historica, Legum sectio V, edited by K. Zeumer, Hahn, Hanover, 1886

Feudal institutions

At the beginning of the Middle Ages (in the 8th and 9th centuries) the relations between lord and vassal were one of the possible forms of relationship between one person and another.

Since the Roman State had long since disintegrated, personal links between people had become the cement of society, whether in public or in private life.

Hierarchical and one-sided, these links were generally formed by the protection that a powerful person accorded to another free citizen in exchange for devotion and fidelity: slaves, although still very numerous, were excluded. The 'man of another man' was called a 'vassal' or 'antrustion' – two Germanic terms that meant the same thing.

Within this complex network of ties which replaced the impersonal power of the state, now at an end, the military service undertaken by men-at-arms soon became especially important. One feature of the Germanic tribes' warrior democracies had always been the right and duty of free armed men to take part in military campaigns.

From the 7th century onwards, however, this system was weakened by two developments, both irreversible and both interdependent. One was specialization in the arts of war, particularly as the image of the warrior and that of the knight came more and more to coincide. The second was the ever-growing cost of training and equipment for war. This process of change, with all its consequences for society, technology, the economy and prestige, reached its climax only in the 10th and 11th centuries; but it was already discernible under the Carolingian dynasty.

To become military vassal to a lord, the vassal had to receive from him a 'benefice' (the Germanic term 'fief' later replaced the Latin-derived word). The fief was a larger or smaller collection of land and serfs, enabling the holder to devote himself exclusively to the military service of his lord.

In the feudal investiture ceremonies codified at the end of the 8th century, 'homage' and the 'fealty oath' were sworn by the vassal before the benefice was bestowed. Later, homage was sworn in order to obtain a fief.

The feudal relationship first emerged in northwestern Gaul (France in the strict sense of the term), where the Franks were in a majority. Later it spread from the Loire to the Rhine and to much of Europe. Charlemagne's knights imposed it in northern and central Italy from the 9th century onwards; the Normans brought it to England and Sicily, neither of which had known it before. It was in the decades that followed the Norman Conquest in 1066 that England entered the feudal world. Sicily did so during the long war to conquer the Italian south, which began in about 1040 and ended fifty years later, marking the cessation of Arab rule on the island.

The development of feudalism was slower in the south of France and in Spain, where the Frankish knights who took part in the 'Reconquista' played a fundamental role. In the various German Duchies feudalism took nearly two centuries to become established, from the beginning of the 10th century to the end of the 11th.

Lordships and castles

The existence of military fiefs, vassals and a monopoly of arms by the heavy cavalry, using the lance as an assault weapon (but not as a projectile) – all these were only one aspect of what historians commonly call 'feudalism'.

Feudalism was generally linked to a profound crisis in public authority and its anarchic parcelling out among local lords. The adjective 'feudal', like the concept of 'feudalism', is often used quite improperly and even in error. Feudal institutions – vassalage – already played an important role at the time of Charlemagne; but it would be inaccurate to call the Carolingian Empire 'feudal'.

It would be equally wrong to apply that adjective to the reigns that followed the Empire's dissolution. Despite the wars which divided the successors of Louis the Pious and which went on for decades in France and Italy, public authority (military, administrative and judicial) was retained by the counts and marquesses. This was all the more so in Germany, where the power of the dukes, who elected the king, was never compromised by feudal anarchy.

Nevertheless, from the end of the 9th century, and increasingly in the 10th, all over the Carolingian Empire fortifications began to be built around small towns and a large number of castles began to spring up at strategic points on natural or artificial vantage-points (feudal mounds).

The growing numbers of fortresses in the countryside were very striking. Church authorities and local lords were generally the initiators in this spontaneous development, whose aim was to organize an effective defence against Viking, Saracen and Hungarian invasions. But castles went on being built well after the first half of the 10th century, when the threat of enemy incursions was on the wane. In France, as in northern

❸ FIGHTING WITH LANCES
Scenes inspired by the *Song of Roland* (1125–35). Lintel of the central doorway of Angoulême cathedral

In battle or in tournaments the lance was used mainly as a frontal assault weapon, to unseat the enemy knights. Those exceptionally strong used it as a formidable projectile. Victories were counted according to the number of lances broken.

---

❹ A ceremony of homage

In 1127 vassals swore an oath of fealty to William, the new Count of Flanders, who gave them fiefs in return.

On Thursday the seventh of April further homage was sworn to the Count. To begin with, it was done thus. The Count asked if (the person facing him) wished to become wholly his man and the latter replied: I wish it. And with his hands together, pressed between those of the Count, he and the Count sealed their alliance with a kiss. Afterwards, he who had given homage swore fealty to the Count in these terms: 'I swear upon my faith that from this moment onwards I shall be loyal to Count William and against all, I shall wholly respect my homage [hominium], in good faith and without fraud.' In the third stage, the same person swore upon the relics of the saints. Then, with the rod that he held in his hand, the Count gave the investiture to all those who, by this pact, had sworn him fealty and given him homage and together had pledged their oath.

① THE MEDIEVAL CASTLE
Detail from the picture of General Guido Riccio da Foligno by
Simone Martini, Palazzo Pubblico, Siena, Italy

*The castle became a characteristic feature in the rural landscape
of northern Europe from the 10th century onwards. Henceforth,
even in Italy at the height of the city-state, castles continued to be
the basis on which the territory was organized. In this fresco, the
towers and the surrounding wall clearly show that the prime role
of the castle was to defend the countryside: in case of danger,
country-dwellers took refuge in it.*

**② Capitulary of 864 against
private castles**

*Until the end of the 9th century castles and fortifications had embodied royal
power in the land. Thereafter they more and more came to represent the power
of the lords, misused and contrary to the express prohibition of the sovereign.
The capitulary issued on 25 June 864 at Pitre (a village near Rouen) by King
Charles the Bald explains the matter clearly.*

*May all without exception come to the defence of the country.
May the counts watch over the fortresses; and may these
fortresses one and all be built, zealously and without delay. . . .
We further desire and expressly command that all those who
recently have built castles, fortifications and stockades without
our permission should destroy them before 1 August: for their
neighbours and those who live nearby are suffering from much
pillaging and other trouble on their account.*

Monumenta Germaniae Historica, Capitularia regnum francorum,
Vol. II, edited by A. Boretius, Hahn, Hanover, 1883

---

and central Italy, the emergence of lordships
reflected the irreversible loss of power by the
kings and the counts. (No such development
occurred, however, in Germany.) The establishment of local power centres with rather limited
geographical scope, replacing those of the king or
the count, was in some respects society's response
to the prevailing insecurity. But, while the
lordships took an active part in the general
violence that marked the 10th century, they were
in fact a reaction to anarchy rather than its cause.
Since public authority had vanished, a new political and social system had to be put in its place.
So the rise of the lordships should not be seen
merely in a negative light – the eclipse of the state
and of all central authority. It had its positive
side: rebuilding from the base upwards by local
authorities wholly lacking in legitimacy owing to
the absence of any central power.

Villages, castles and 'bannal' lordships

Castles, which went on being built long after the
end of the 10th century, were the basis on which a
new rural and territorial society was organized. It
was around castles, in fact, that inhabitants of the
countryside now gathered. Not until the 11th
century did they acquire the stone walls and
towers that are so familiar: but they were on the
increase, very often being built around a village,
and in any case forming the hub of much rural
life.

The former local authorities of the Carolingian
Empire – the counts and viscounts – substantially
contributed to this change. Their role in it was in
some ways equal and opposite to that of the
ecclesiastical authorities and warlords. The latter
seized political power and denied the counts any
authority over the territory dependent on their
castles; the counts and viscounts privatized the
public revenues they had received and turned
them into hereditary family wealth.

The landowning lords, whose families had
supplied numerous knights, had for a long time
(and certainly since before the 7th century) enjoyed full power over their serfs. But they also
wielded considerable authority over those who
had sworn fealty to them and over other free men.
Once they had superimposed 'bannal' lordship (a
term derived from the old German word *Bann*, a
command, territory or jurisdiction) on the former
system of lordship based on land, the lords seized
judiciary power, which they exercised over all the
inhabitants of the lordship. Furthermore, they
imposed taxes and required services (forced
labour to maintain the castle or the duty of
hospitality owed to knights on campaign). These
'bannal' duties also included the obligation to use

(and pay for) the facilities provided by the lord for milling grain or baking bread.

It would be a mistake to believe that 'feudalism' of this kind appeared simultaneously all over Europe. The authority of the dukes of Normandy was in no way weakened by the lords' usurpation of powers. The same was true of England, although it was the Normans themselves who had introduced feudal-vassal relationships there, as well as in those parts of Ireland that they conquered. Attempts by knights and local lords to usurp power were also thwarted in the Kingdom of Sicily under Norman rule. In Germany, feudalism emerged later, in the 12th and above all the 13th century; while in France it took root shortly before the end of the 10th century. The last Carolingian kings, indeed, saw their power shrink inexorably and the inauguration of a new dynasty with the coronation of Hugh Capet in 987 scarcely altered the situation. It was under Hugh Capet's son Robert the Pious (996–1031) that the French monarchy was most seriously threatened and the fragmentation of public authority was most pronounced.

In northern and central Italy, this process of feudal erosion of central power was less marked at the beginning of the 11th century. Alongside the great hereditary aristocratic families of counts and dukes, a very powerful ecclesiastical feudal authority arose. Many bishops had obtained from the ruling authorities (kings in the 10th century, then Saxon emperors) the title of count and the privileges that went with it; but many more wielded the same power without having won the title. In 1037 the *Constitutio de feudis* issued by the Emperor Conrad II guaranteed to 'vavasours' (military vassals of the great lay and Church lords) hereditary possession of the benefices they had received from bishops and counts. This gave such local authorities genuine legitimacy and marked considerable progress for the feudal system. It should be stressed that the situation in Italy was then somewhat different from that in the rest of Europe, because most of the Italian 'vavasours' tended to settle in the towns, leaving the castle unoccupied. Feudalism arose in northern and central Italy, in fact, just when a new and autonomous element was coming to the fore: the town.

The Church and knighthood

One of the last changes to occur, in France and Italy in particular, between 980 and 1030 has led certain historians to attribute to this half-century a 'feudal revolution'.

The knights, who were chiefly responsible for the emergence of lordships and the usurpation of

③ THE FORTIFIED CITY
Fra Angelico, detail of Jerusalem; in the Convent of San Marco, Florence, 1387–1455
Jerusalem, like all medieval towns, was a vast castle built on a hill — in this case the Hill of Judea. It thus offered protection to the surrounding territory.

---

④ Conrad II affirms that minor fiefs are to be hereditary

In 1035–6 the minor vassals of Milan rebelled against the Archbishop and formed an alliance with the townspeople. The Emperor Conrad II (1024–39) intervened and besieged the town. He soon realized that the danger came from another quarter – from the immense power that the Archbishop had acquired. The Emperor then changed his mind and on 28 May 1037 he issued a Constitution. This affirmed that minor fiefs were hereditary: it applied throughout the Germanic Empire.

We command and decide:

That no military vassal of a Bishop or Abbot or Abbess or Marquess or Count or any other person who holds a benefice from our public purse or from the property of the Church, or who has held such benefice – even if now he has unjustly lost it – whether he be one of our major vassals or vassal of our vassals, shall lose his benefice unless he have committed a certain and proven fault, on the basis of our predecessors' Constitutions and after judgment by his peers . . . .

We command furthermore that when a military vassal, major or minor, departs this earthly life, his son shall inherit the benefice. If on the contrary the vassal have no son, but leave a son by his son, that grandson shall have the same right to the benefice.

Constitutiones et acta publica Imperatorum et regnum, *in* Monumenta Germaniae Historica, *Vol. I, pp. 90–1*

1 DUBBING A KNIGHT

Giving a young knight his arms had originally been a wholly lay rite, an initiation ceremony marking the passage from adolescence to adulthood. Gradually, it became something like a sacrament. At the age of 18, the young man spent a night in prayer, alone or with other future knights. On the next day his lord gave him the sword and spurs. The new knight promised to be loyal and to protect widows, orphans and servants of God.

2 The religious ritual of dubbing a knight

The intervention of churchmen in the ceremony of dubbing a knight came some time later than the institution of the 'Peace of God'. The latter dates from between 980 and 1030, whereas the oldest document mentioning a religious dubbing is from the end of the 11th century. It describes a ritual used at the church of Cambrai in about 1093.

First, the Bishop blesses the knight's standard in this way: 'Let us pray. Omnipotent and eternal God . . . sanctify we pray this standard prepared for war with Thy heavenly benediction that it may be strong against all adversary and rebellious nations and that, fortified by Thy protection, it may be terrible against the enemies of the Christian people . . . .'

Then he brings together the lance and the standard and the Bishop sprinkles them with holy water while the knight holds them in his hand.

Then the Bishop blesses the sword in this way . . . : 'Be pleased to bless this sword wherewith thy servant will be girt that he may protect and defend the Church, widows, orphans and all servants of God, against the ferocity of their adversaries and that it may inspire fear, fright and terror among all those who set traps . . . .'

public authority, long appeared as agents of disorder, violence and injustice.

By about the year 1030 it had become clear that the kings could no longer curb the powers accumulated by the counts or usurped by the lords. It was only then that the Church raised the question of legitimizing the role of the knights.

Many bishops contented themselves with condemning the present situation and lamenting the disappearance of a time when the king had been the guarantor of justice and peace. But still more bishops and abbots (following the example of Cluny Abbey) firmly decided to lead a large-scale campaign to neutralize the violence of the warlords.

Lords and vassals were brought together and obliged to swear, on pain of excommunication, solemnly to respect the 'peace of God'. Later (not before the end of the 11th century, according to the surviving documents), the Church tried to go beyond mere prohibitions and to give the profession of arms a deeply Christian meaning.

Knighthood then became a kind of corporation, to which new members were admitted after a ritual requiring the presence of a churchman and the blessing of their weapons. What was more, it became the knight's duty to defend the Church and the weak or poor.

It is hard to ascertain what concrete results these measures achieved in their early years. The violence of the knights was partly channelled into the Reconquista in Spain and the Crusades in the Holy Land; but it still represented a major threat to those without means of defence. In the middle of the 12th century knighthood was still characterized by the play on words *'non militia sed malitia'* – 'not courage but cunning'.

It has to be recognized, however, that the 'peace of God' and the consecration of the knight's role did in the long run transform the image of knighthood. By the end of the 12th century it was no longer seen in terms of sheer violence, but had become an ethical and religious ideal: chivalry.

The Europe of villages

As we have seen, the emergence of feudal powers was accompanied by a radical reorganization of the countryside and its people. From 950 onwards, moreover, the population of Europe as a whole began to grow and continued for a long time. Before that, the situation had been different.

In the last days of the ancient world the population had been decimated by widespread epidemics of bubonic plague. These had affected all of the Mediterranean basin as well as Gaul between 542 and the end of the 7th century. They continued in the eastern Mediterranean for two or three generations more, but apparently spared the Western world with the exception of southern Italy, which was still in contact with the Byzantine Empire.

During those three centuries, from 650 to 950, the growth of the population was slow and irregular, bringing the total back, with a few exceptions, to the 5th-century level. At the same time, in the 8th century certain regions appear to have been relatively overcrowded. In the 9th century European agriculture seems still to have been based on the resources of the forest (hunting, gathering and the raising of free-range pigs) rather than on the settled growing of grain.

The forest was so important for daily survival that people hesitated to cut it down. The data available show clearly that the large estates of the 9th and 10th centuries consisted essentially of woods and wasteland. They also show that the rural population, which as a whole was sparse, was often densely concentrated in these regions. In these conditions (huge estates cultivated extensively rather than intensively and an economy based on the forest rather than on grain-growing), man's relationship with nature was such as to prevent the population's rising beyond the levels attained at the beginning of the 9th century. In the Carolingian period the Europe of tilled fields and evenly scattered villages had not yet come into existence and clusters of people were separated by large tracts of uninhabited land.

Already, however, Europe had the knowledge and the tools needed to change from a civilization based on the forest to one based on agriculture, especially on the mainland. The Ancient world had left in the Mediterranean basin a model of urban and rural civilization and an agriculture combining grain-growing, market-gardening, vine-growing and olive-growing, all of which needed simply to be revived. The mainland regions of Europe, however, had to find completely new solutions, using relatively novel and largely untried techniques. Three such elements may be singled out. One was iron-working, which made it possible to produce basic tools and accessories such as metal parts for ploughs, horseshoes, nails and forestry equipment. A second was the heavy plough with a coulter and mould-board, capable of turning over low-lying land which was more fertile but harder to plough. The third was three-year crop rotation, which reduced fallow land from 50 per cent to 30 per cent of the total and made it possible to grow spring crops such as oats. All three techniques had been known for some time: they simply had to be applied to the new land brought into production during the

③ PIG-BREEDING
November in the Book of Hours of the Duchess of Burgundy, Musée Condé, Chantilly
Very rapidly the countryside began to be studded with village communities, whose institutions were designed to protect crops and animals from marauders and thieves. The pig, a highly profitable beast, was reared in free-range conditions, but under close supervision.

④ REAPING WITH A SICKLE
Harvesting technique long remained primitive. During the 14th century the scythe began to be more widely used, but the commonest reaping tool was still the sickle. It forced the user to adopt an uncomfortable position, but it enabled the grain to be cut at the ear, so that the straw could be kept for the animals.

① REGIONS OF DIFFERENT FARMING METHODS

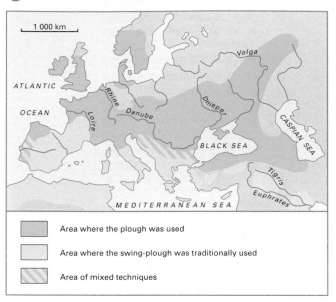

1 000 km

ATLANTIC OCEAN

Volga

Rhine

Loire

Danube

Dnieper

CASPIAN SEA

BLACK SEA

Tigris

Euphrates

MEDITERRANEAN SEA

Area where the plough was used

Area where the swing-plough was traditionally used

Area of mixed techniques

② MONKS CLEARING THE FOREST

Cîteaux manuscript of 1115, in the Municipal Library, Dijon

At this time the monasteries were in the countryside. In the ideal of monastic life, work on the land was an important and holy element, for idleness was the enemy of the soul. With the emergence of towns, agricultural production had to be increased. It was therefore necessary to clear the forests to make room for extensive agriculture. Many monks introduced the peasants to this skilled task.

10th century to meet the needs of a growing population. The 'revolutionary' change from the Europe of the forests to the Europe of the fields was in fact not merely technological, but also social and cultural: it took place over three centuries, from 950 to 1250.

The growth of population and the development of agriculture

During that time Europe's population continued to grow, rising from 38 million in the 10th century to more than 75 million at the beginning of the 14th. Agriculture developed, making decisive inroads into forests, marshes and wastelands; the technological power of the continent grew apace.

All three factors were closely linked. More people meant more hands for deforestation, itself assisted by better tools. More land under cultivation, with greater productivity owing to new methods, could in turn support more people.

Other technical innovations supplemented those already mentioned (iron-working, ploughing and rotation of the crops). Horse-breeding, made possible by the growing of oats, allowed much heavier and stronger ploughs to be used. The invention of water-mills and then windmills freed a considerable labour force: the 5624 mills in existence in England in 1086 are estimated to have saved 7.5 million hours of work per year. The 'open-field' system, likewise, spread throughout almost all of northern and central Europe. It was based on three-year crop rotation and use of the heavy plough; individual properties were long strips in the large grain fields where rotation was applied. After the harvest, following a strict agricultural calendar, the stubble area became a vast 'open field' used to pasture the community's animals. This practice, which strengthened the cohesion of the village, became a characteristic feature of agricultural civilization in continental Europe and in Britain.

This new organization of the countryside was a real agricultural revolution, affecting eating habits (grain slowly replacing the products of the forests) and also people's attitudes. But it did not yet make possible large-scale cattle-breeding, which would have produced a great amount of manure; so the growing of grain continued to be extensive rather than intensive.

This was no real problem because, while agriculture gained ground from forests and marshes, external frontiers were pushed back too. Many peasants emigrated at this time, from Germany and the Low Countries towards lands beyond the Elbe, sparsely populated and inhabited in the north by Baltic tribes and in the south by Slav peoples, only a minority of whom were subject to the Polish kings.

In Western Europe various communities obtained statutes and franchise charters from their lords; but they were unable effectively to stem the gradual but rapid reduction of the peasants to the status of serfs.

In the east, by contrast, in the newly deforested regions (Brandenburg, Mecklenburg, Pomerania and Prussia), the bishops, abbots and secular lords who favoured colonization had to make more important concessions. Eastern Europe was therefore free of serfdom.

In the Scandinavian countries it had never existed. In the Low Countries it came to an end earlier than elsewhere. In the Iberian Peninsula the demands of the *Reconquista* made it necessary for serfs to be freed. At the same time, moreover, the possibility of acquiring slaves by war or by commerce made serfdom superfluous.

To the east of the Elbe, in general, there was personal freedom, villages were autonomous and rents were low by comparison with the west, where the peasants had to perform forced labour and where their serfdom affected many aspects of family law and private property.

During the 12th century the situation worsened still more. The old meaning of the word now being forgotten, *servus* came to mean someone who could not marry outside the lordship without asking permission from his lord and master, could not inherit from his parents without paying 'mainmorte' dues and who had to pay an annual sum as a sign of submission.

❸ The Villis Capitulary on forest clearance

At the beginning of the 9th century the clearing of forests was strictly limited by law. After the year 1000 these restrictions tended to disappear, since the growth of the population required more land to be tilled.

May our woods and forests be well supervised; and where there is an area to be cleared may our stewards have it cleared and not allow the fields to gain on the woods; and where there should be trees let them not allow them to be cut too much or damaged, and may they safeguard our game in the forests; and may they also concern themselves with the goshawks and sparrow-hawks for our service; may they collect with care the taxes that are due to us. And may the stewards, if they have sent their pigs to pasture in our forests, may our mayors and their men be the first to pay the tithe to give a good example so that in consequence other men may pay their tithe in full.

Ch. M De La Roncière, R. Delort, M. Rouche, *L'Europe au Moyen Age*, I, A. Colin, Paris, 1969, p. 225

❹ GERMAN EXPANSION (970–1175)

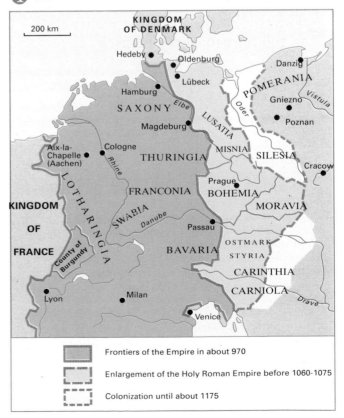

Frontiers of the Empire in about 970

Enlargement of the Holy Roman Empire before 1060-1075

Colonization until about 1175

3 The Empire and the Papacy

① OTTO THE GREAT (912–73)
13th-century miniature, Bibliothèque Nationale, Paris

After becoming German King in 936, he imposed his authority on Lotharingia and Italy and defeated the Hungarians and the Slavs, among whom he sent monks in the hope of securing conversions. Crowned Emperor in Rome in February 962, he clashed with the Papacy over the nomination of bishops and abbots. This was the beginning of the Investiture Dispute.

---

② The role of the Emperor Henry III in the reform of the Church

In *his* short Liber gratissimus, *written in about 1050, Peter Damian (1007–72) celebrated the intervention of Emperor Henry III (1039–56) in the battle against simony.*

Everyone knows that until the reign of the very merciful Emperor Henry and the papacy of the excellent Clement [II, 1046–7], followed by the very saintly Leo [IX, 1049–54] [both German Popes, directly appointed by Henry III], by whom the Holy Church is grateful to be governed, the pestilential evil of the simoniac heresy proliferated in all the kingdoms of the West . . . .

It can be said that it is to him, after God, that we owe our delivery from the jaws of the dragon of simoniac heresy, for it is he who beheaded that hydra with his sword . . . . And because he refused to conduct himself as his predecessors had done, but sought on the contrary to respect the precepts of the eternal King, God conferred upon him as a reward what he had refused to the great majority of the Emperors before him: that the Holy Church of Rome emerge from disorder under his banner and that henceforth no one be elected bishop at the apostolic see without his agreement.

Monumenta Germaniae Historica, Libelli de lite, *Hahn, Hanover, 1891, Vol. I, pp. 53, 71*

Carolingian political doctrine and the reform of the Church

In the Carolingian period the argument that imperial authority derived directly from God was universally recognized. Moreover, no one contested the fact that the Emperor had to give his consent for the election of bishops, who under canon law had to be freely chosen by the diocesan clergy. The Emperor's right and duty was to prevent bad priests becoming bishops. At the same time, according to the political theory worked out under the Carolingian Empire, bishops were also called upon to play a direct part in the secular government.

The renaissance of the Germanic part of the Empire under Otto I of Saxony in 962 saw a powerful revival of this political doctrine. In Germany, and to a lesser extent in Italy, bishops generally received the title of count; and they wielded secular power because bishoprics involved benefices with land and buildings, as a result of concessions made by the Emperors. So the sovereign began appointing the bishop and investing him with the powers of his office by handing him the symbolic ring and crook.

Relations between the German Emperor and the Pope were more complex. The Emperor had to receive his crown from the Pope's hands. He was therefore obliged not only to remove the election of the Pope from the influence of the Roman aristocracy, but also to intervene in the election itself, approving or appointing the person most worthy of the role. Thus, for example, in 963 Otto I had him deposed by a Roman Council. This *privilegium Othonis* was a precedent that gave the Emperor the lasting right to supervise the conduct of Papal elections.

The movement to reform the Church, which gathered speed in the years 1030 to 1040, won valuable support from the Emperor Henry III of Franconia (1039–56). His role, however, was based on elements that were mutually contradictory. It was the monks, and especially those of Cluny, who spearheaded the movement for reform. They – in particular the members of the hermit orders founded in 1012 and 1030 in Camaldoli and Vallombrosa in Tuscany – expressed deep mistrust of the traditional clergy and accused the bishops of having compromised themselves with the secular power. The accusation of 'nicolaism' – breaking the rule of celibacy

– applied to many priests, who often lived with women. But that of simony – selling the sacraments and, by extension, selling benefices to those who administered them – was easily applicable to all those Popes who thought it a matter of course to collaborate with the lay rulers to whom they owed their investiture. Paradoxically, it was in line with the Church reformers' aims, though strictly against their doctrine, that Henry III had unworthy Popes deposed and so at first won the reformers' approval. In 1046, in equally authoritarian fashion, he settled a Roman dispute in which three candidates (including the infamous Benedict IX) were vying for the Holy See. And between 1046 and 1057 the Emperor personally nominated three German Popes and greatly influenced the choice of a fourth.

The Investiture Dispute

On the death of Henry III traditional political doctrine and practice were brutally contested. In 1057 the Milanese rose up against their bishop, who had been appointed by the Emperor. In 1068, a great popular movement arose against the Bishop of Florence, accusing him of simony. In 1059, a Council convoked in Rome by Pope Nicholas II laid down that the Pope should be elected by a College of Cardinals, made up of the seven bishops of the Rome diocese and the clergy of the four largest churches in the city.

The struggle between the reformers, most of whose leaders came from the monasteries, and the bishops, appointed by the Emperor, grew more intense. Milan, for example, had two bishops in violent disagreement with each other, which came to a head when the monk Hildebrand of Soana became Pope in 1073, taking the name of Gregory VII. A decisive battle took place between him and the Emperor Henry IV from 1075 onwards; it included such famous episodes as the Emperor's theatrical submission to the Pope at Canossa and the violent civil war that Gregory fomented against Henry in Germany.

After such dramatic events the only outcome could be a compromise; but it was not reached until 1122. In fact, the Emperor's claims were closely linked with the public authority and wealth of the bishops.

Two important points, however, were established. On the one hand, the secular authorities now had no hand in the investiture of bishops, who were subject to growing Papal power. On the other, the reform movement lost its popular character, which had empowered the reforming Popes, and the clergy became very hierarchical. The result was disillusion and the emergence of heretical groups, especially in the towns.

③ THE HUMILIATION OF EMPEROR HENRY IV AT CANOSSA (1077)
Illumination from the manuscript *Vita Mathildis* by the monk Denis in 1114. Vatican Library, Rome

The German King Henry IV, excommunicated by Pope Gregory VII and abandoned by his followers, was obliged to don penitent's robes and in the depths of winter to beseech absolution from his adversary, who had taken refuge at Canossa in the castle of Countess Matilda of Tuscany. She had interceded for the king. Once back in Germany, Henry hastened to depose Gregory VII and to have the Antipope Clement III elected in his stead.

④ The supreme power of the Pope

This text, known as the Dictatus papae, was written in the form of personal notes by Gregory VII (1073–85) in about 1075, shortly before his dispute with Henry IV. The Dictatus summarizes in twenty-seven points Gregory's definition of the role of the Pope in the Church. These are some of them.

1. *The Roman Church was founded by God alone.*
2. *Only the Sovereign Roman Pontiff can rightly be called 'universal'.*
3. *He alone may appoint or depose bishops . . . .*
6. *It is forbidden to be in relations with, or to be in the same house as, any person excommunicated by him . . . .*
8. *He alone may use the insignia of the Empire.*
9. *Princes should kiss the feet of no one save the Pope . . . .*
11. *His title is unique in the world.*
12. *He has the power to depose the Emperor . . . .*
19. *No one may judge him . . . .*
22. *The Church of Rome has never been mistaken, nor will it ever be, as is written in the Holy Scriptures.*
23. *The Sovereign Pontiff, ordained after election by the Council, is invested with the powers of St Peter . . . .*

In *Chiesa e stato attraverso i secoli*, edited by S. Z. Ehler and S. B. Morrall, Vita e Pensiero, Milan, 1958

Towns and Trade Routes

❶ EUROPEAN TEXTILE CENTRES (13th CENTURY)

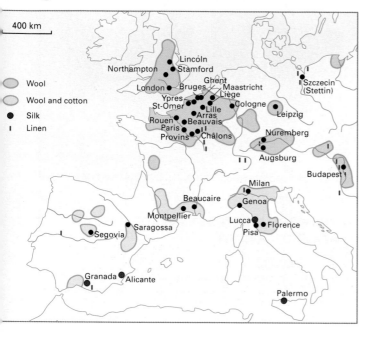

400 km

Wool
Wool and cotton
Silk
Linen

Lincóln
Northampton • Stamford
London • Ghent • Szczecin
Bruges • Maastricht (Stettin)
Ypres • Liège
St-Omer • Cologne
Arras • Lille
Rouen • Beauvais Leipzig
Paris • Nuremberg
Provins • Châlons
Augsburg
Budapest
Milan
Beaucaire • Genoa
Montpellier Lucca • Florence
Saragossa Pisa
Segovia
Granada • Alicante
Palermo

❷ SIENA: THE BIRTH OF A NEW TOWN

The Piazza del Campo with the Palazzo Pubblico and the Torre del Mangia (1297–1310)

Located at a crossroads of the routes to Rome from France and Venice, Siena became from the 10th century onwards an important banking and commercial centre, in direct competition with Florence. At the end of the 13th century it acquired a university, as well as magnificent brick churches and palaces in the Gothic style.

The birth – or the renaissance? – of towns

During what past historians in the past rather dismissively called the 'Dark Ages', European towns were comparatively small (covering about 75 acres and with some 5000 inhabitants).

They very nearly disappeared, because other institutions fulfilled their role. A society organized around great estates and monasteries, with limited movements of goods or money, can in fact very easily do without towns. If the *civitates* of the ancient Roman world managed to survive the general ruralization of the time, it was because bishops continued to live in them, maintaining an urban pattern of life.

The notion of the 'Dark Ages' was usually linked with that of a 'renaissance after the year 1000'. The growth of towns which began at that time was seen as equal and opposite to their earlier decline.

For a long time now, however, historians have given more credit to the 'dark' 10th century's inventiveness. In that light medieval Europe looks more like a new departure than a continuation of the distant past in the 5th or 6th centuries. A closer look at medieval towns offers proof of that. In the ancient world towns fell into two groups: in the east they were usually great trading centres like Alexandria or Antioch; in the west they were *civitates*, places where the landed aristocracy lived, with a number of characteristic buildings such as the forum, the baths, the arena and the theatre. The development of western towns in the Mediterranean basin was never determined by commercial or industrial activities.

From the second half of the 10th century in Europe two phenomena need to be noted. On the one hand, within the frontiers of the old Roman Empire wholly new urban centres appeared. On the other, even where there was some continuity between Roman and medieval cities, their order of importance radically changed. While Milan and Lyon, for instance, had already been major centres in Roman times, Siena and Florence had then been only of moderate size.

Towns in the Middle Ages

To understand how and why towns grew in the Middle Ages, it is simplest to divide them into three categories.

The first consists of those towns in southern Italy, first among them Amalfi, which from the 10th century onwards played a key role in trade between Europe on the one hand and Byzantium and the Islamic countries on the other.

The Turkish invasions had a direct impact on life in the Mediterranean basin. The great trade routes to the East avoided the Persian Gulf and went through Egypt and the Red Sea, in the long term giving the Italians a greater role. At the same time the Italians flocked to Constantinople, since it was still linked to the Far East by the land routes through central Asia.

However, during the 10th and 11th centuries there began to be greater demand for exotic and luxury products to supply what might be called the feudal aristocracy and the strategic centres of Italian trade shifted northwards. Venice, Pisa and Genoa took the place of Amalfi.

If this first category of towns reflected the 'renaissance' of the Mediterranean basin, the second was very much newer. It comprised industrial centres that sprang up to serve an inchoate but very extensive European market. Flemish towns like Ghent, Bruges or Ypres, which mainly produced woollen textiles, had no tradition behind them. The same was true of Lucca, with its silk production, the Lombard textile towns and later – at the end of the 13th century – Florence.

Europe's industrial centres had their counterparts in trading and financial cities: each needed the other. Once again Italy enjoyed pride of place, with not only the three seaports already mentioned, but also Florence and Milan on the one hand and Piacenza and Asti on the other.

However, as the Germans expanded beyond the Elbe, a new Nordic 'Mediterranean basin' emerged around the Baltic. New trading cities grew up: Hamburg, Lübeck and, further east, Danzig and Riga. From the mid-13th century onwards they joined together in trading leagues or Hansas, which later included some places in the Rhineland such as Cologne and eventually, a century later, led to the formation of a single Germanic Hanseatic League.

❸ PLAN OF FLORENCE

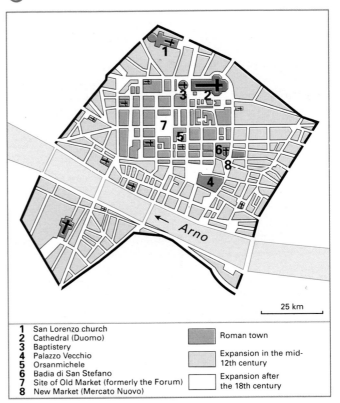

25 km

1 San Lorenzo church
2 Cathedral (Duomo)
3 Baptistery
4 Palazzo Vecchio
5 Orsanmichele
6 Badia di San Stefano
7 Site of Old Market (formerly the Forum)
8 New Market (Mercato Nuovo)

Roman town

Expansion in the mid-12th century

Expansion after the 18th century

❹ Economic and social life in Florence

In Chapter 94 of Book XI in his Chronicles, *Giovanni Villani (1276–1348) described economic and social life in Florence in genuinely statistical terms.*

Florence at that time had about 25,000 male inhabitants of an age to bear arms, i.e. between the ages of 15 and 70, all of them citizens, including 1500 noble and mighty individuals. . . . It was estimated that Florence had some 900,000 mouths to feed, counting men, women and children, calculated on the amount of bread the town needed each day. On average, there were 1500 foreigners, travellers and soldiers staying in Florence, not counting the religious orders of monks and nuns in the monasteries and convents. Boys and girls of reading age numbered between 8000 and 10,000, and the children learning the abacus and arithmatic, in six schools, between 1000 and 2000. Those studying grammar and logic, in four large schools, numbered 550 to 600. There were 110 churches in Florence and its environs, including abbeys and monastic churches . . . . There were 200 or more workshops for woollen manufactures and they made between 70,000 and 80,000 pieces of cloth, valued at 1,200,000 gold florins. Of this sum, more than a third remains in the ground for the work [was paid in wages], not counting the profits; and more than 30,000 people gained their livelihood from wool.

❶ ROADS TO ROME IN THE 13TH CENTURY

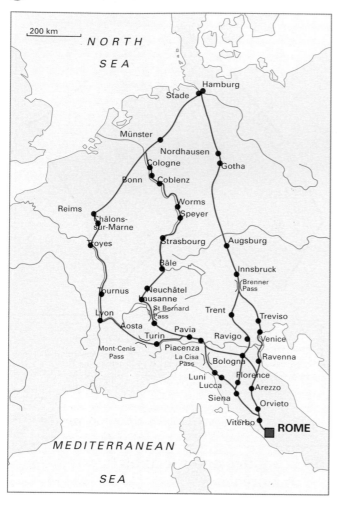

❷ The Lombard communes as seen by Otto of Freising

Extract from the Gesta Frederici, a biography of Frederick Barbarossa written by Bishop Otto of Freising (who was his uncle).

The Lombards are attached to their liberty and, to avoid the insolence of governors, they prefer to be ruled by consuls rather than by princes. And since they are divided into three estates, the captains, the vavasours [major and minor vassals] and the plebs, to avoid overweening pride these consuls are chosen not by one estate but by all three. So that they may not covet power, they are replaced every year. For this reason the land is divided into cities which oblige their citizens to live within their walls; and it would be hard to find a man noble or powerful enough to be able to ignore the laws of his city . . .

Otto of Freising, *Gesta Frederici*, II, 13

Towns and communes in Italy

There was, however, a third type of town, created by the nobility: it was found in northern and central Italy. Examples were Milan and the most important centres in the Po valley, such as Verona, Padua and Bologna. These in particular, which were absolutely not industrial nor commercial centres of any importance, none the less had 40,000 or 50,000 inhabitants by the beginning of the 14th century. The nobility also played a fundamental role in the development of towns like Genoa and Pisa.

In the 11th and 12th centuries Italian cities evolved differently from other European towns. This was because of their ruling class and what was called 'the communal movement'. Almost everywhere in Europe towns acquired what autonomy they had under the strict supervision of the local authorities – dukes, viscounts, kings. In Italy, by contrast, the communal institutions took advantage of the German Emperors' long absence to acquire real sovereignty, not only over their own territory but also over neighbouring lands. Frederick I of Swabia, nicknamed Barbarossa by the Italians, tried from 1162 to 1183 to destroy the communes; but in the end he had to give in and accept a compromise. After his death in 1190 the communes again began to extend the area subject to their authority.

In the 13th century they were racked by violent civil wars, in which the aristocracy fought 'the people' (in reality the commercial and industrial middle class). But these conflicts scarcely affected the way in which the main cities, and especially Milan and Florence, were centralizing their control over the surrounding territory.

The communal movement had far-reaching results, whether it was dominated by consuls representing the urban aristocracy or by 'corporations' of merchants. It deeply affected relations between country and town.

The towns of mainland Europe remained 'bourgeois' in the original sense of the word, enclosed by fortifications and ruled by laws quite different from those of the countryside. Those of Italy were quick to purchase new territory and they violently rebelled against the seignorial power, of the lords, destroying the latter's hold on the peasants. In northern and central Italy serfdom and forced labour were abolished as a result of the many collective amnesties decreed by the communes in the 13th century. Agrarian contracts for renting land or share-cropping replaced lifetime commitments and the power over individuals that they implied. The tightening of ties between the town and the countryside turned land into an investment rather than a symbol of power.

Pilgrim routes

In about the year 1000 Europe could only roughly be defined by two contrasting criteria: its material geography and its spiritual attachment to Christianity. It had no official frontiers and both the Church and the Empire were theoretically universal. Yet all of Europe was divided into thousands of local lordships, all isolated from each other. Only a few merchants, churchmen or statesmen had any overall grasp of its extent.

During the 11th century, however, the network of links that formed the basis for unity in Europe began to diversify and develop. Pilgrimages played a large part in this growing cohesion.

Two main pilgrim routes are worth closer attention: the road to Rome and that to Santiago de Compostela.

The first, which ran from France to Rome, emerged gradually in the 8th and 9th centuries. It was a medieval road, bearing no relation to Gallo-Roman routes: it originated at the time when the Lombards and the Byzantines were fighting over central Italy. To link the Po valley with Tuscany, the Lombards made a road through the Cisa pass, forming a new itinerary between Piacenza and Lucca. The next stage on the road, from Lucca to Siena and then to Lake Bolsena, was open when the Franks descended on Rome. Further north, on a level with Pavia, this route offered two alternatives: one via Mont-Cenis and from Lyon to Champagne, the other via the St Bernard pass to Lausanne and then to Champagne or to the Rhineland towns. After the long battles for the reform of the Church and the Papacy, more and more pilgrims went to Rome and their path became the busiest in Europe in the 11th and 12th centuries.

The second great pilgrim route led to Santiago de Compostela in Galicia in north-west Spain, where the relics of the apostle St James the Greater were said to have been brought by miraculous means. A first basilica was built there at the beginning of the 9th century to receive the faithful in a region recently freed from domination by the Arabs. It was destroyed by the Arabs shortly before the year 1000, but rebuilt in about 1020 and many pilgrims came there from all over Europe. They included in particular Frankish knights, who came to Galicia to do penance and to purge themselves of their sins of violence. These same knights, with the blessing of the monks of Cluny, played a decisive part in the Reconquista between 1060 and 1085, which ended in triumph with the taking of Toledo. From France four routes converged on Puente-la-Reina near Pamplona in Navarre: two of them came from Champagne and the Loire; the third, taken

❸ SANTIAGO DE COMPOSTELA
The body of St James in Galicia. Prado Museum, Madrid

The patron saint of Spain and brother of St John the Evangelist, St James the Greater almost certainly did not preach in Spain. His supposed mission there is not mentioned in Spanish texts until the 7th century and popular belief in the fact did not spread until a century later, after a star had miraculously revealed the site of the tomb said to be his, in a place called campus stella, *the field of the star. From the 10th century onwards this became one of the most famous pilgrim centres in Christendom.*

---

❹ Pilgrims and people miraculously healed at Santiago de Compostela

In about 1140 an anonymous work entitled The Pilgrim's Guide *explained in detail the route that every pilgrim ought to take.*

The church was begun in the year 1078 . . . and from that year, when the first foundation stone was laid, until the last was added, forty years elapsed.

Since the day when the church began to be built, until today, it has never ceased to glow with the light of the miracles of the apostle James. Within its walls, in fact, the sick find health, the blind recover their sight, the mute can speak, the deaf can hear, the lame can walk, the possessed are freed; and what is much more, the prayers of the faithful are heard, their wishes are granted, their sins are lifted from them, the heavens are opened to those who invoke them and consolation is offered to all the afflicted. All people from foreign lands and from all the climes of the world flock there to give glory to the Lord . . . .

The Pilgrim's Guide to Santiago de Compostela

❶ PILGRIM ROUTES TO SANTIAGO DE COMPOSTELA

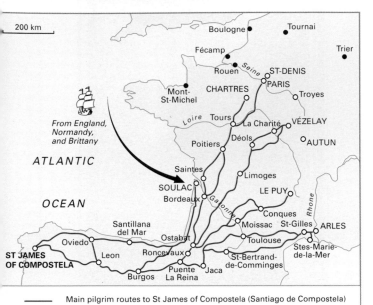

200 km

Boulogne
Tournai
Fécamp
Trier
Rouen
Seine
ST-DENIS
Mont-St-Michel
CHARTRES
PARIS
Troyes
Loire
Tours
La Charité
VÉZELAY
Poitiers
Déols
AUTUN

ATLANTIC
Saintes
Limoges
SOULAC
Bordeaux
Garonne
LE PUY
Rhône

OCEAN
Santillana del Mar
Ostabat
Conques
Moissac
St-Gilles
ARLES
Oviedo
Roncevaux
Toulouse
Stes-Marie-de-la-Mer
ST JAMES OF COMPOSTELA
Leon
St-Bertrand-de-Comminges
Puente La Reina
Jaca
Burgos

From England, Normandy, and Brittany

——— Main pilgrim routes to St James of Compostela (Santiago de Compostela)

❷ THE WEST RETURNS TO GOLD CURRENCY

Both sides of a florin. National Museum, Florence

The gold coins minted in the great Italian trading towns kept their weight and purity for a very long time. They were one of the media of Italian trade in Europe and in the East. The florin shown here, minted in Florence in 1252, weighs about 3½ grams. The two designs used are the lily, symbol of the city, and St John the Baptist, the Tuscan capital's patron saint.

---

by German pilgrims, began in Burgundy; the fourth, starting in Arles, was used above all by Italians.

In England, a very busy pilgrim route led from London to Canterbury, to the tomb of St Thomas Becket, murdered in the Cathedral in 1170 by knights of King Henry II.

Trade routes

In the 12th century the road to Rome also became a trade route. The first Italian merchants to use it regularly on the way to Mont-Cenis were probably from Lucca. The Lombards had already chosen Lucca as the capital for the Duchy of Tuscany and the town took advantage of its position as an obligatory staging-post. This same route made the fortunes of Piacenza and Asti in the north and Siena to the south: a number of bankers and money-changers made their headquarters there.

As has been seen, the people of Lucca specialized very early in silk-weaving, using raw material imported from the East. At least as early as 1153 they took part in the Champagne fairs. These six great annual events, in Troyes, Provins, Bar-sur-Aube and Lagny, were spread throughout the year in the county of Champagne: during the 12th century they became the main meeting-places of Mediterranean and Nordic Europe. It was there that Italian merchants bought the woollen textiles made in the Flemish towns and sold their silks and the spices they had imported from the East.

In the 12th century the needs of trade rather than pilgrimage led to a growth in the means of communication. Around the year 1000 a route through the St Gothard pass was added to those via Mont-Cenis and the Great St Bernard; it was used in particular by Venetian merchants and linked the Po valley to the upper Rhineland and to Swiss and German towns. At the end of the century the Milanese made a road through the Simplon pass, which became the route for carrying Lombard textiles to the upper Rhône valley and then to Switzerland, Germany and France. At the end of the 13th century the Venetians turned the Brenner route – which led to Innsbruck, Augsburg, Nuremberg and Frankfurt – into a road suitable for vehicles throughout its length. It was by that route and, further east, via the Tarvis pass (leading to Vienna, Budapest and Prague, the most important trading towns in central Europe) that the Venetians pursued their trade in pepper, spices, sugar and cotton, crossing en route metals coming south from Germany as well as meat from the Hungarian plains.

During the second half of the 14th century Flanders lost its monopoly on the European market for woollen textiles. The centre of gravity of international trade shifted southwards as fairs in Geneva and Lyon complemented those of Champagne.

In about 1300 a still more important development had occurred: in 1291 the Genoese, soon followed by the Venetians, opened a new sea route from the Mediterranean to the North Sea via the Straits of Gibraltar. This hastened the decline of the Champagne fairs. It also included Seville and Lisbon, and ended at Bruges. In this way the centre of Europe's trading system was displaced and its network embraced both mainland Europe and the Mediterranean. The new sea route also made trade more rapid and effective, partly as a result of two technological innovations. One was the compass, which made it possible to sail direct, out of sight of land; the other was the Genoese invention of heavy merchant ships. These could carry not only the light luxury goods that had previously been shipped on such long voyages, but also heavy, bulky products such as salt, alum, oil, wine, fish, wool, wood and metal.

❸ THE JUNE FAIR (LENDIT) NEAR PARIS

Register of the ceremonies, 14th century. Bibliothèque Nationale, Paris

The Lendit Fair was held in June between the feast of St Barnabas and that of St John in the Saint-Denis plain. It began with the blessing of trade. The stalls and shops were solidly built and the waggons bore corporate insignia. As can be seen above, the innkeeper's stall was one of the first to open.

❹ TRADE ROUTES AND COMMERCIAL CENTRES AT THE END OF THE 13TH CENTURY

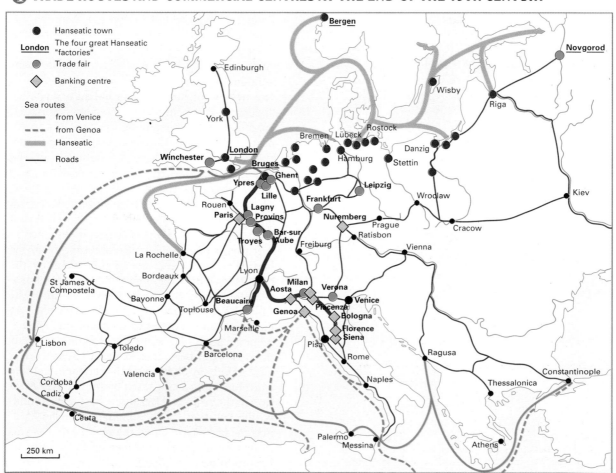

5 Europe Beyond Europe

❶ The Crusades

1095	Pope Urban II calls upon the knights to go on a Crusade against the 'infidels'
1099	Capture of Jerusalem
1147–49	After the fall of Edessa, the second Crusade fails following the siege of Damascus
1187	Saladin recaptures Jerusalem
1189–91	The third Crusade, led by Frederick I, fails after the death of the Emperor
1202–4	Led by the Venetians, the fourth Crusade seizes Constantinople and puts an end, temporarily, to the Byzantine Empire
1217–21	Fifth Crusade, in Egypt
1228–9	Sixth Crusade, led by Frederick II, temporarily restores Jerusalem to the Christians
1249–54	Seventh and eighth Crusades, led by the King of France, Louis IX, in Egypt and Tunisia

❷ THE CRUSADER STATES

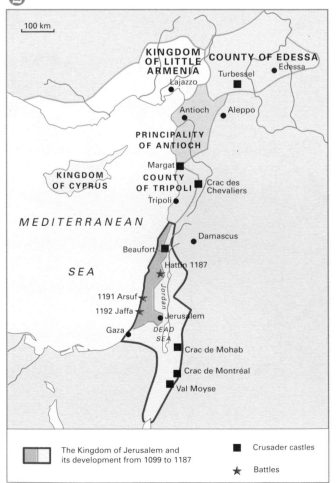

The Kingdom of Jerusalem and its development from 1099 to 1187

■ Crusader castles

★ Battles

The Crusades

After the capture of Toledo in 1085, the war of the Spanish *Reconquista* broke off for nearly a century, following the invasion of the Iberian peninsula by Berber tribes from Morocco. From 1096 onwards, moreover, Christian knights (and especially the Franks) continued their battle against Islam further afield. Generally speaking, the Arab domination of Jerusalem had not been intolerant or fanatical; in the 11th century Christian churches continued to exist throughout Syria. But, when the Turks arrived in Syria and Palestine, this situation seemed bound to change. At all events, the liberation of the Holy Land was the official objective of the first Crusade.

The 12,000-strong 'People's Crusade' led by Peter the Hermit was annihilated by the Turks. That of the Barons, numbering some 30,000 knights and infantry, eventually seized Jerusalem in 1099. The Crusaders established a Latin kingdom based on the feudal model of Western Europe and founded new orders of religious knights (the Hospitallers and the Templars) to defend it. The Crusades led to a deep worsening of relations between Christendom and 'alien' civilizations. When the first Crusade was announced, the Rhineland was subjected to a violent wave of anti-semitism and the first ghettos appeared. The Crusaders, moreover, committed appalling massacres among the civilian population of the towns they conquered in the Holy Land. Finally, they showed little loyalty to the Byzantine Empire: the fourth Crusade made a detour to Constantinople and captured it in 1204. The Crusades helped to create a more Christian image of the knight; but it was also closely linked to something that contradicted it: intolerance.

It used to be thought that the capture of the Holy Land's Mediterranean ports marked the beginning of Italy's domination of the Mediterranean, heralding the urban trading world of the Middle Ages. In fact, the Crusading spirit had no tacit economic motives to set against its explicit religious goals. To assess the economic interests that may have been at stake in the Crusades, it is vital to bear in mind two other factors: first, the enormous upheaval caused by the Turkish invasion of the Arab and Byzantine East and, secondly, the fact that Italy's domination of the Mediterranean long predated the year 1099 – as was shown by its purely commercial links with the Egypto-Syrian Caliphate.

The Latin Crusader states in the Middle East began to crumble under the onslaught of the Turks from 1135 onwards; and in 1187 Jerusalem was once more in the hands of the Sultan of Egypt, renowned for his tolerance. The second and third Crusades, led (unlike the first) by great European rulers, proved fruitless. To the fourth (1202–4) we have referred already: the Venetians diverted the more ambitious of the small feudal lords towards Constantinople and secured for themselves the strategic trading position held by the Byzantine Empire.

Europe and the East in the 13th century

From 1240 onwards the lower Danube region was threatened more and more by nomadic peoples from the steppes of Asia. What was happening was an event unprecedented since the time of the Huns: the Eurasian continent was being shaken by the birth of the Mongol nation. In all Christendom, only Russia was the victim of two centuries of Mongol invasion. But after the panic of the year 1242, when the Mongol forces defeated the Poles, the Germans and the Hungarians at the Battle of Liegnitz, the Mongols suddenly withdrew into Asia, and Europe subsequently found only benefit in the new Mongol Empire. It made possible the reopening of the central Asian trade route. Repaired and pacified, this led from China to Samarkand and then from the lower Volga to the Sea of Azov and the Crimea. For a short time the Christians were tempted by the idea of converting the khans; and even before the merchants (of whom Marco Polo was the most famous) it was Franciscan missionaries who set out for the khans' encampments in Mongolia.

Christendom had learnt virtually nothing about Islam, despite the fact that in Syria it had for a long time been in contact with Arab civilization. But it was very inquisitive about far-off central Asia, China and even India, forming an essentially positive image of these mythical places – rich, magical and undoubtedly 'civilized'.

Nor, finally, did the loss of the Holy Land, followed by the restoration of Byzantine Empire, really harm the Venetian and Genoese merchants. The former resumed their links (officially banned) with the sultans of Egypt; the latter went off to explore the wealth of the Orient beyond Constantinople, also founding colonies on the banks of the Black Sea. The most important of these, Kaffa in the Crimea, became in the 14th century a multi-ethnic city where Genoese rubbed shoulders with Hebrews, Tartars, Turks, Bulgars, Hungarians and Poles.

❸ An account of the capture of Jerusalem

The first Crusade culminated on 15 July 1099 with the capture of Jerusalem. This account of the event was written by a Christian historian, Raimondo d'Aguilers.

Scarcely had our men occupied the walls and towers of the city than they saw terrible things. Some, and it was their good fortune, were beheaded; others fell from the walls, pierced by arrows; many others burned in the flames. In the streets and squares there were piles of severed heads, hands and feet; men and horses ran among the corpses. But that was nothing: what of the Temple of Solomon, where the Saracens had held their religious ceremonies? If we told the truth about what had happened there, we should not be believed. Let us say only that in the Temple and in the porch of Solomon one had to wade in blood up to the knees and bits of horses. And it was by the just judgment of God that this place, which had so long borne insults against God, should receive the blood of His enemies. After the town was captured, it was wonderful to see the devotions of the pilgrims before the Sepulcre of Our Lord and to hear how they showed their joy as they sang a new hymn to God. And their hearts offered to victorious and triumphant God such praises as could not be expressed in words.

❹ THE CAPTURE OF ANTIOCH (1097)
During the first Crusade the siege of Antioch lasted two years. One Crusader in seven died beneath its walls, as much from illness and the plague as from the fighting. When famine in the city reached catastrophic proportions, its inhabitants surrendered. Despite the Crusaders' losses, enough of them were left to sack the city – a fate that, after Antioch, was suffered by all the towns they conquered.

6 Cultural Unity and Political Fragmentation

THE ❶ SMILING ANGEL
Most of the Gothic cathedral of Rheims was built between 1211 and 1228. On the left-hand portico, the smiling angel was sculpted between 1236 and 1245.

❷ St Bernard of Clairvaux condemns luxury in churches

In the 12th century St Bernard of Clairvaux was the advocate of the Cistercian movement's ascetic and austere ideal. Here he inveighs against the link established between ascetic and religious or spiritual values – a link clearly illustrated in the basilica of Saint-Denis.

. . . O vanity of vanities, but yet more folly than vanity! The church glitters on every side, but the poor are hungry! The church walls are covered with gold: the children of the church are naked. . . . Tell me, then, poor monks – if poor ye be – what is gold doing in this holy place? To speak clearly, it is cupidity that wreaks evil – cupidity, enslavement to idols . . . for the sight of sumptuous and surprising vanities leads people to give rather than to pray. Thus wealth attracts wealth; money attracts money. For what reason I know not, the more that wealth is displayed, the more willingly people give. They dazzle the eye by offering gold covers for relics and the cash-boxes open; they make fine sculptures of saints both male and female, all the more worthy of veneration because they are more brightly coloured.

Letter to Abbot William of St Thierry

The culture of Gothic art

For many centuries the clergy had a monopoly of written culture (which was identified with Latin). For that reason rulers were usually obliged to resort to churchmen for advisers, for administrators able to draft decrees and diplomas, and for writers to produce biographies of kings and histories of dynasties. Thus, in the 12th century, it was the monks of the abbey of Saint-Denis (where the kings of France had been buried since Merovingian times) who were given the task of drawing up their sovereigns' official chronicles.

For nearly thirty years this sanctuary of the French monarchy was headed by Abbot Suger. He was adviser to two kings and it was he who in 1144 gave the monks their role as official historians. The same year saw the completion of the church of Saint-Denis, begun and supervised by Suger since 1129 and generally regarded as the first example of Gothic architecture.

Suger was an ardent advocate of light, colour and scintillating splendour in religious buildings. His assistants worked out architectural techniques to enable windows to replace stone walls, and spires and arches to defy the laws of gravity. At the same time, however, St Bernard of Clairvaux proposed returning to austere church architecture, bare and full of shadows: he condemned the monstrous and imaginative sculptures of Romanesque churches and the excessive luxury of Cluny, in the name of a quite different idea of religious art.

But it was finally Gothic art that spread from the Paris region to every country in Western Christendom, offering the faithful flock living pictures of the people and great events in sacred history. This art also accurately reflected 12th and 13th-century society. At Beauvais in 1270 the builders achieved the impossible, completing a vault 48 metres tall (compared with 37 metres at Bourges cathedral); but in 1284 the chancel collapsed. This event has been interpreted, not without cause, as marking the end of the expansion of the society of the high Middle Ages. The optimism of the 13th century is well illustrated by the smiling angel on the portico of Rheims cathedral, contrasting as it does with the suicide of Judas Iscariot, surrounded by grimacing demons, portrayed in the Romanesque cathedral of Autun.

The culture of chivalry

Outside the sphere of the Church there was a second form of culture, long lacking written expression: that of feudal vassals and soldiers. It was based on values like courage and 'prowess', fidelity and loyalty – which had an unfortunate tendency to turn into their opposites: blind violence against those without weapons, treason and 'felony'. It was in this unfavourable light that chivalric values tended to appear in documents written in about the year 1000.

At that time the 'Peace of God' movement led by the clergy was trying to combat these excesses. The Peace of God was the first step in a process. Others included the introduction of Christian elements into the 'dubbing' of knights; the war against the infidel; and the creation of a *nova militia* (preached by St Bernard of Clairvaux in 1115) with the founding of the Knights Hospitaller and Knights Templar. The process, in the 11th and 12th centuries, led to the supervision and partial sublimation of knightly violence. The Order of the Templars was founded in 1119; that of the Hospitallers of St John of Jerusalem was officially inaugurated some years later.

Somewhat earlier, almost as if with foresight, a literary work had given this religious significance to the profession of arms. This was the *Song of Roland*, written between 1050 and 1080. It has to be admitted, however, that throughout the first half of the 12th century the culture of chivalry still found its main expression in lays vaunting purely feudal values (fidelity and honour) and condemning their opposites (treason and vengeance). Examples include the lay dedicated to Raoul of Cambrai, or those recording the exploits of William of Aquitaine, liegeman and 'cousin' of Charlemagne. In the same period pride figured in the forefront of the mortal sins, the origin of all evils. Not until the end of the 12th century did knights and churchmen agree in seeing trade and money as the source of a new evil: avarice.

So the culture of chivalry was gradually 'civilized' and markedly so at the end of the 12th century. By then it had come to display two separate characteristics: courtly love and knightly faith. Both are found in the verse romances written by Chrétien de Troyes between 1160 and 1190: the first in *Lancelot* and the second in *Perceval*, his last romance and one that signals the beginning of a whole cycle describing the quest for the Holy Grail. This was a more or less mythical relic – the cup supposedly used by Christ at the Last Supper and in which Joseph of Arimathaea is said to have collected the blood flowing from the crucified Saviour's side, pierced by the lance of a centurion.

③ NOTRE-DAME DE LA BELLE VERRIÈRE (CHARTRES)

173 stained-glass windows of the 12th and 13th centuries, covering more than 2000 square metres, make up a kind of illuminated manuscript recording biblical events. This 12th-century window, miraculously saved from a fire, shows the Virgin carrying the Child in majesty before her. The light makes the blues and the reds glow. The intense and brilliant 'flax blue', sometimes called Chartres blue, is the dominant colour.

---

④ Suger replies to his opponents

To the religion of bare, dark churches proposed by St Bernard, the Abbot of Saint-Denis preferred one synonymous with light, beauty and splendour.

Let everyone follow his own opinion. For myself, I declare that it has always seemed to me just that all that is most precious should serve above all to celebrate the Holy Eucharist. If gold cups, gold phials and little gold mortars are used, according to the word of God and the order of the prophet, to collect the blood of goats or calves or of a red heifer, how much more, to receive the blood of Jesus Christ, should one have at one's disposal gold vases, precious stones and all that is held most valuable in creation.

J. Gimpel, *Les Bâtisseurs des cathédrales*, Éditions du Seuil, Paris, 1975, p. 20

① THE CASTLE OF MONTSÉGUR

The castle stands at a height of 1215 metres, dominating the plain of Languedoc on the French slopes of the Pyrenees. It was a closed fortress, whose ramparts had no towers and were deemed to be impregnable. It was one of the last refuges of the Cathars. Here, on 16 March 1244, 215 of them, men and women, decided to die rather than abjure their faith.

② The Albigensian heresy

Extract from an anonymous text dating from the years 1208–13.

The group of heretics that inhabit our region, that is the dioceses of Narbonne, Béziers, Carcassonne, Toulouse, Albi, Cahors, Agen and Périgueux, believe and have the audacity to declare that there are two divinities: one a good God and the other a strange God . . . . They believe that the world and all its visible contents were created and made by the evil God. They speak insultingly of carnal marriage, for Christ said 'Whosoever regardeth a woman', etc. They reject the baptism of children, who have no faith, and they cite the Scripture, saying that those without faith shall be condemned. They do not believe in the resurrection of the earthly body, citing St Paul, who said 'Flesh and blood cannot possess the kingdom of God'. They describe all the rites observed in the Catholic Church as vain and absurd, for its doctrine is a human thing and without any foundation . . . .

Heresies of the High Middle Ages, edited by W. L. Wakefield and A. P. Evans

The culture of cities

Also outside the ecclesiastical world a second form of lay culture developed. At first, it was limited to legal documents drawn up by notaries and in the 10th century it was confined to Italy. Subsequently (in the mid-12th century) the archives of the notary Giovanni Scriba of Genoa supplied documentation that was unique in Europe. It was at this time that cities like Genoa and Pisa were renowned for their authors of urban 'annals'. Later, in the 13th and 14th centuries, a more specifically 'bourgeois' culture emerged in Italy. It produced two types of writing: the 'memoranda' of merchants, in which they noted both family and business events and those concerning the political life of the city; and the 'trade manuals' written to facilitate economic activity, which gave information on trade routes, currencies, units of measurement and the goods that could be found in more or less distant countries.

Towards the end of the 12th century heretical doctrines became widespread in the cities of central and northern Italy and southern France, areas which culturally and socially were ahead of their time.

There were two main types of heresy. The first, which was the heir to the urban popular movements that had backed Gregory VII's 11th-century reform of the Church, called for a return to the sources of Christianity. It involved polemics about the status of the clergy, the right of lay people to preach the Gospel and the demands of the poor. A typical example was the Waldensian heresy. The second, very different, type of heresy was that of the Cathars, known in Languedoc as Albigensians. With its Manichean doctrine (good and evil being regarded as two divine principles), its ethical practices, its own organization and proselytizing methods, it was in effect laying the foundations of a religion that had little in common with traditional Christianity.

These heresies were very firmly crushed. But they had an indirect effect on the Church, notably by inducing it to recognize the specific social and cultural nature of the towns. The orders of Friars Minor (Franciscans) and teaching Friars (Dominicans) tried in various ways to canalize the wave of protest, adopting on their own account two of the heretics' main demands: for a communal life based on poverty and for the Gospel to be preached in the vernacular.

The towns were also the birthplace of something fundamental to Europe's shared culture: the universities. After the first corporations of masters and pupils had been set up in Salerno and Bologna, universities continued to proliferate throughout the 12th century, from Paris to Oxford and Cambridge, and including Palencia, Salamanca and Padua. The existence of a university which taught law, medicine, theology and philosophy became a considerable advantage for the city that harboured it. This was especially so in Bologna and, to a lesser degree, Paris.

The universities were corporations which defended their autonomy against the political authorities. They had serious problems when they began to teach the philosophy of Aristotle, which had been brought to the West through Moorish Spain, via translations from Arabic into Latin. Aristotle was doubly suspect, both as a pagan Greek and as a philosopher translated and admired by the infidels; and he was the indirect cause of the first crisis in the universities' battle to retain their autonomy. In 1270 and 1277 the Bishop of Paris, Étienne Tempier, condemned Aristotelianism and put an end to the freedom of teaching that had reigned in Paris since the days of the theologian Abélard two centuries earlier (although the Sorbonne had been founded only in 1257). Some years later, paradoxically, the Dominican St Thomas Aquinas's interpretation of Aristotelian philosophy became the official doctrine of the Church.

Christendom and the Europe of kings

In the Middle Ages the great majority of European people lived without leaving their village or going further than the market of their nearest town. Only a few churchmen, pilgrims, knights, scholars and merchants had broader horizons. They pushed back the frontiers as far as the great places of pilgrimage, the university cities, the ports, the fairs and (in the case of merchants) the Genoese colonies on the Black Sea.

Those who lived 'in the shadow of the church tower and the castle' were never the less linked by certain symbols to the Universal Church and to Jerusalem. The jubilee proclaimed by Pope Boniface VIII in 1300 had a real European impact: that year nearly two million pilgrims went to the City of the Apostles. But this was the last manifestation of a united and powerful Christendom, for shortly after the jubilee the Papacy was violently challenged. In 1250 the death of Frederick II of Hohenstaufen, who had been more interested in Italy (where he had lost his battle against the communes) than in the Carolingian heritage, had left the Empire vacant. Falling under German domination, it lost all authority.

Between the immense horizons of Christendom and the geopolitical fragmentation experienced in daily life, it was not until the end of the 14th century that there appeared the first signs of

③ THE UNIVERSITIES (12th–14th CENTURIES)

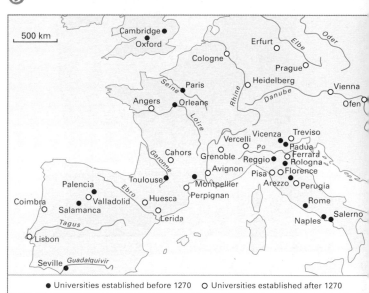

● Universities established before 1270   ○ Universities established after 1270

④ The Bishop of Paris attacks philosophical error

The Bishop of Paris, Étienne Tempier, concerned by the disputes that raged in the University of Paris after the rediscovery of Aristotle's works, intervened to condemn 210 statements which he believed to be contrary to religious orthodoxy. From this condemnation, issued in 1277, we quote below part of the Preamble and the three theses on 'the errors concerning the nature of philosophy'.

. . . Certain students of the arts in Paris, going beyond the bounds of their own Faculty, have the audacity to expound and discuss in the schools certain manifest and execrable errors and, more than errors, ravings and crazy follies, as if they were simply subjects for academic discussion. . . . They assert, in fact, that these things are true in the domain of philosophy but false as regards the Catholic faith, as if there could be two mutually contradictory truths, one for pagan philosophers and one, opposing it, being that of Holy Scripture. . . . Therefore, lest imprudent chatter lead simple men into error, after having heard the opinion of masters of theology and other wise men, we absolutely forbid such discussion, we condemn en bloc these errors, and we excommunicate all those who have taught them, in whole or in part . . . .
[They are that:]

Only philosophers possess the wisdom of the world.

We should believe nothing that is not known in itself or cannot be explained by known principles.

Man should not be content with authority alone as a means of acquiring certainty about a given question.

Étienne Tempier in *Aristotelianism and Scholasticism,* 1277

① RAMON BERENGUER THE ELDER (1115–62)
13th-century Catalan manuscript, Barcelona

*Count of Barcelona and Prince of Aragon, he ruled Provence as
Regent for his nephew. He brought Catalan influence into the
Languedoc and had prepared* The Usages of Barcelona, *Europe's first feudal code. He is shown here, beside his wife, having
drawn up a list of his acquisitions north of the Pyrenees.*

② FRANCE AND BRITAIN (11th and 12th CENTURIES)

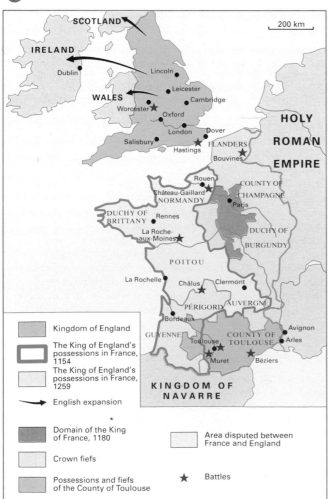

200 km

SCOTLAND
IRELAND
Dublin
Lincoln
Leicester
Cambridge
WALES
Worcester
Oxford
London
Dover
Salisbury
Hastings
FLANDERS
Bouvines
HOLY ROMAN EMPIRE
Rouen
Château-Gaillard
NORMANDY
COUNTY OF CHAMPAGNE
Paris
DUCHY OF BRITTANY
Rennes
La Roche-aux-Moines
DUCHY OF BURGUNDY
POITOU
La Rochelle
Châlus
Clermont
PÉRIGORD
AUVERGNE
Bordeaux
GUYENNE
Toulouse
COUNTY OF TOULOUSE
Avignon
Arles
Muret
Béziers
KINGDOM OF NAVARRE

Kingdom of England

The King of England's
possessions in France,
1154

The King of England's
possessions in France,
1259

English expansion

Domain of the King
of France, 1180

Crown fiefs

Possessions and fiefs
of the County of Toulouse

Area disputed between
France and England

★ Battles

territories anything like the nation-states of today. It would be quite wrong to imagine that the
frontiers with which we are familiar today were
already present in the inextricable medieval
mosaic of powers and lordships.

Take the case of the dukes of Normandy. For
their duchy, they were vassals of the King of
France: but at the same time they were kings of
England. During the reign of the Plantagenet
Henry II (1154–89) the frontiers of France
became very different from those of the country
today. A large part of Atlantic France, from
Brittany to Aquitaine, was subject to the King of
England by vassalage; a huge region east of the
Rhône (including Lyon and the Dauphiné) was
part of the Germanic Holy Roman Empire, under
the name of 'the Kingdom of Burgundy'; and the
southern regions of present-day France had no
link at all with the Capetian dynasty. Provence
was under the domination of the counts of
Barcelona and Catalonia (who were also kings of
Aragon), while the county of Toulouse was
totally independent, with a culture and traditions
that made it closer to Catalonia than to the
'France' north of the Loire.

The Iberian peninsula was divided into a
number of kingdoms. Although the dynasties that
ruled them were interrelated, they in no case
formed a single bloc. Portugal had been independent since 1139; but León and Castile did not
unite for good until 1230, while Aragon and
Catalonia remained two separate entities.
Throughout the 12th century, moreover, the
south of the peninsula remained in the hands of
the Moslems and seemed likely even to unite as a
single country with Morocco.

During the first decades of the 13th century the
political framework of Europe radically changed.
After the famous Battle of Bouvines the English
lost almost all their fiefs on French soil, retaining
only the Bordeaux area. This defeat also had
repercussions in England itself. King John 'Lack-
land', defeated by Philip Augustus of France
(1180–1223) and forced to proclaim himself the
vassal of Pope Innocent III, had further to face a
revolt by his barons and to grant them, in 1215,
the *Magna Carta*. This celebrated constitutional
document laid the foundations for parliamentary
sovereignty in fiscal matters and proclaimed that
no free man could be arrested except after
judgment 'by his peers'. In 1283 Edward I
annexed Wales and in 1301 his son, the future
Edward II, received the title of Prince of Wales.

Three years before *Magna Carta*, in 1212,
under the leadership of Navarre, Aragon and
Castile, volunteers from all over Christendom,
answering an appeal by Pope Innocent III, won
the Battle of Las Navas de Tolosa. This opened

the way to the conquest of Andalusia. A number of lands were then annexed by Castile and León and, to a lesser extent, Catalonia and Aragon. Portugal succeeded in driving the Moors from the Algarve; and in 1252 it became the first country to establish its present-day frontiers. For a long time, indeed, it was the only one.

For the Capetian dynasty of France the Battle of Bouvines was the culmination of a long effort, begun in the 1130s, to re-establish royal authority over the greatest fiefs in the kingdom. The feudal principle, which had led to the dismantling of royal power in the 11th century, when the king's authority was confined to the area between Paris and Orléans, was now used by the kings of France to remind the barons of their duties to the crown. Philip Augustus completed his predecessors' work by recovering the English fiefs of Normandy, Anjou and Aquitaine, and reclaiming the counties of Champagne and Flanders.

In 1208 the King of France began a 'Crusade' against the count of Toulouse, whom he accused of protecting the Albigensian heretics. The Frankish knights (rather different from their image in the romances) attacked a world more civilized than their own with a violence no less ferocious than that employed against the Moslems of Syria and Palestine. The King of Aragon tried to intervene, but failed: this cut the links between the Languedoc and Catalonia. For decades careful preparations were made for Toulouse to become part of the kingdom of France. It finally did so in 1271. Meanwhile, however, Provence fell under the domination of the Angevin dynasty, founded by Charles I, the brother of St Louis; it was not annexed by France until two hundred years later. None of these events, moreover, could be considered to have settled matters until the middle of the 15th century.

The kingdom of Naples and Sicily showed greater stability; but between the 11th and the 14th centuries three different dynasties ruled it – Norman, Swabian and Angevin. In 1302 Sicily fell to a fourth, that of the kings of Aragon. Northern and central Italy remained a case apart, free from monarchical authority, even on paper, and consisting of dozens of large or middle-sized cities already a prey to numerous crises.

One notable new event occurred in Germany in the second half of the 13th century. The power of the monarchy, theoretically attached to the Imperial Crown, was replaced by an increasingly confusing myriad of regional and local authorities, lay and ecclesiastic. This contradiction between real fragmentation and theoretical universality left a deep mark on German experience and was not without influence on Germany's future.

---

❸ Louis VI (Louis the Fat) against feudal anarchy

In about the year 1144 Abbot Suger of Paris (1081–1151) wrote the biography of King Louis VI (1108–37). The episode described here dates from about 1104–5, when Louis was still prince. By marrying his son to the daughter of the Lord of Montlhéry, the king believed that he had managed to make the castle subordinate to the crown.

When as a result of his marriage the young Philip had received in trust the castle of Montlhéry, for the King and his son it was a great joy, as if a splinter had been removed from their eyes or they had been let out of prison. The King bore witness to this when in our presence he reminded his son Louis of the great worries that castle had caused him. 'Louis, my son, take great care to see that this fortress be retained; the troubles it has caused me have kept me awake at night; deceit and malevolent disloyalty have never let me enjoy peace or rest.'

Such lack of good faith made the faithful infidels and the infidels more faithless still; it was a hotbed of perfidy from far and near; and in all the kingdom there was no evil that was not authorized or supported by the masters of that castle.

Suger, *Life of Louis the Fat*, edited by H. Waquet, Champion, Paris, 1929, pp. 36–42

❹ THE CORONATION OF ROGER II OF SICILY
12th-century mosaic in the church of Santa Maria del Ammiraglio, Palermo

King Roger II of Sicily, shown here being crowned by Christ, took control of all southern Italy in 1130, a period when the area's borders were redefined. The stability of the kingdom was maintained despite the diverse traditions and religions of its disparate population.

Reykjavik
Thjoominjasfind

Stavanger

Saint-Andrews

Devenish Island
Carrickfergus
Boyle
Carlingford
Monasterboice
Mellifont
Trim
Dublin
Jerpoint Abbey
Holycross Abbey
Rock of Cashel
Cahir

Durham
Rievaulx Abbey
Fountains Abbey
York
Conway
Lincoln

Utrecht

Tintern Abbey
Gloucester
Malmesbury
Colchester
Norwich

Wells
Salisbury
Romsey
London
Rochester
Canterbury
Hastings
Gent
Ieper (Ypres)
Tournai
Brussel Bruxelles
Maastricht
Liège
Maria Laach
Manderscheid
St
Amiens
Coucy
Rouen
Pierrefonds
Laon
Soissons
Reims
Echternach
Mont-Saint-Michel
Bayeux
Caen
Château-Gaillard
Senlis
Paris
Houdan
Strasbou
Fougères
Chartres
Sens
Orléans
Freiburg Breis
Angers
Saint-Benoît-sur-Loire
Fontenay
Bas
Fontevrault
Bourges
Vézelay
Dijon
Citeaux
Poitiers
Saint-Savin
Nevers
Autun
Romain
Aulnay
Cluny
Tournus
Lau
Tournoël
Paray
Genève
Périgueux
Clermont-Ferrand
Saint-Nectaire
Le Puy
La Grande Chartreuse
Bordeaux
Souillac
Conques
Cahors
Sénanque
Santiago de Compostela
Moissac
Albi
Arles
Le Tho
León
Carcassonne
Saint-Gilles
Silvacane
Braga
Guimarães
Zamora
Burgos
Pamplona
Leyre
Toulouse
Peyrepertuse
Quéribus
Marseille
Porto
Bragança
Fromista
Jaca
Montségur
Saint-Michel de Cuxa
Montemor o Velho
Coimbra
Santo Domingo de Silos
Tudela
Loarre
Tahull
Ripoll
Saint-Martin du Canigou
Sant-Pere de Roda
Pombal
Leiria
Segovia
Avila
Santa Maria de Huerta
Cardona
Girona
Obidos
Toman
Avila
Madrid
Lleida
Tarrasa
Lisboa
Tarragona
Barcelona
Évora
Alcacer do Sal
Beja
Silves

The Past in the Present Day
MEDIEVAL CHRISTIANITY IN THE WEST

Legend:
- castle or fortifications
- religious monument
- secular monument
- museum
- frontiers of 20th-century states
- 500 km

Visby
borg
Århus
København
Roskilde
Lund
Hedeby
Danneyirke
Hamburg
Hildesheim
Magdeburg
Naumburg
Schulpforta
Dornburg
Coburg
Bamberg
Nürnberg
Praha
Regensburg
Wien
München
Salzburg
enau
Seckau
Gniezno
Kraków
L'vov
Esztergom
Budapest
Pécs
Alba Iulia
Milano
Verona
Cremona
Parma
Nonaviola
dena
Pistoia
Bologna
Arezzo
Firenze
nano
Siena
ano
Sant'Antimo
Assisi
Castel Sant'Elia
Roma
Casamari
Casauria
Fossanova
Troia
Ravello
Salerno
Castel del
Monte
Palermo
Monreale
Cefalù
Zadar
Trogir
Studenica
Beograd
Trani
Bari
Constantinopolis
(Istanbul)
Nikaia (Iznik)
Thessaloniki
Athos
Athinai
Mystras
Rodos
Kriti

① THE ANGERS APOCALYPSE

Tapestry, Château of Angers, end of the 14th century

This tapestry was made by Jean Blondol between 1375 and 1380 in the workshop of Nicolas Bataille. It comprised seven great sections (144 metres long by 5 metres tall), with 90 scenes, 71 of which have survived. The simplicity of the design and the careful contrasts of form and colours make it one of the most remarkable illustrations of the Apocalypse that the Middle Ages have handed down to us.

c.1300	*Sea link between northern and southern Europe. Decline of the fairs*
1309–76	*Avignon Popes*
1316	*Famine in Europe. Beginning of the agrarian crisis*
1337– 1453	*Hundred Years' War*
1347–74	*Black Death in Europe. Population declines*
1351	*Boccaccio completes the* Decameron
1356	*The Golden Bull organizes imperial elections. Ottoman invasion of Europe*
1356– 1450	*Age of the Hanseatic League*
c.1360	*Philip the Bold receives the Duchy of Burgundy in apanage: beginning of Burgundian power*
1378–82	*Insurrections throughout Europe*
1378	*The Great Schism divides the Church*

1397	*Union of Kalmar brings together Denmark, Norway and Sweden*
c.1400	*Beginning of the Italian Renaissance: the Quattrocento. Flemish primitives in the Low Countries*
1410	*Victory of Poland over the Teutonic Knights*
1417–19	*Brunelleschi designs the dome of Florence Cathedral (the Duomo)*
1414–18	*Council of Constance: end of the Schism. John Hus condemned as a heretic*
1452– 1519	*Leonardo da Vinci*
1453	*Fall of Constantinople to the Turks*
1461–83	*Louis XI founds the modern state in France*
1469	*Marriage between Ferdinand of Aragon and Isabella of Castile: pledge of the unification of Spain*
1492	*Fall of Granada. End of Moorish rule in Spain.*

CHAPTER  V

CRISES AND RENAISS-ANCE

14TH AND 15TH CENTURIES

At the beginning of the 14th century Europe entered a period marked by calamities of every kind.

Over and over again, famines weakened the people, making them more vulnerable to the many epidemics, such as the Black Death, in which very large numbers died. Repeated wars were equally catastrophic, resulting in bad administration, heavy taxes and pillage by soldiers.

At the same time, economic growth petered out and it was country-dwellers who were hardest hit. Hoping to make their fortune in the towns, they found only poverty and hardship there, all of which led to growing social unrest.

Far from being limited to a single region, variants of these phenomena affected the whole continent. Politically, however, the 13th-century unity of Europe had come to an end: both the Empire and the Church were threatened by dissension.

But it would be a mistake to see this period only as one of destruction and decline. Over two centuries, feudal fragmentation was replaced by sovereign states, slowly developing a new form of administration. Prosperity returned and both trade and industry revived. The Church recovered the unity it had temporarily lost in the Great Schism of 1378 and other manifestations of the religious life developed. A new period of dazzling cultural achievement began with the Flemish primitives and the Italian Renaissance.

Thus, within two centuries, Europe underwent a remarkable change.

➋ THE GOLDEN BULL: THE ELECTION OF THE EMPEROR

National archives, Vienna

There were several Golden Bulls. The most famous was issued by the German Emperor Charles IV (1316–78). Promulgated at the Diets of Nuremberg and Metz, this Bull, dated 1356, collected a series of decrees, laying down the procedure for the election of the Emperor. Also King of Bohemia, Charles IV set up his court and the university in Prague, where he was born and he died.

➌ EUROPE, EARLY 14TH CENTURY

_1_ Economic Life

① TRADE BY SEA IN THE 14TH CENTURY
Bas-relief from the house of Jacques Cœur, Bourges
In the 14th century trade by sea displaced the mainland fairs. Big ships – three-masted carracks – were commissioned by bold businessmen like Jacques Cœur, who engaged in profitable trade with Italy, Spain and Normandy.

② Means of Transport

The figures below compare two means of transport between Lübeck and Danzig.

	By sea	By land
Means of transport	ship	carriage
Length of time en route	4 days	14 days
Cargo	120 tonnes	2 tonnes
Crew	25 sailors	1 driver + guards

From the year 1000 onwards Europe's population had never stopped increasing. This was the main reason for the growth of trade and of new towns. In about 1100 more and more ships began to ply the Mediterranean. By land, several trade routes were once more heavily frequented; one such was the road linking northern Europe to southern Europe via Champagne, whose fairs were still rapidly expanding. It was not uncommon to find there merchants from all over Europe, come to trade their goods.

Around 1300, however, this expansion came to an end. Between 1316, the year of the great famine, and the second half of the 15th century, Europe underwent a series of setbacks and crises. In many places the economy stagnated and even shrank.

It would be over-hasty, however, to speak of a general decline. While one sector of the economy was declining, another might well be growing; and what was happening in one region was not always happening all over Europe at the same time. In France, it is true, economic disaster seems to have been almost total, owing not only to such ills as epidemics and famines, but also to the constant state of war. In other areas, by contrast, such as Brabant and Flanders, the economy flourished. Progress and decline actually alternated and changed places, as a few examples may show. When the textile industry in Flanders shrank, that in Brabant expanded; and when the Champagne fairs lost their pivotal role in international trade, their place was taken first by Geneva and a number of German towns, and then by Leipzig. The growing prosperity of the Mediterranean, Burgundian and Rhineland vineyards largely made up for the decline of those around Bordeaux; Danish butter made up for Normandy butter whose production was reduced by wars; and salt from Setubal in Portugal likewise replaced that from the Bay of Bourgneuf in France.

Altogether, the word 'mutation' seems more appropriate as a description of this period than the word 'decline'. It certainly showed symptoms of crisis: but there was dynamism too.

Trade

One of the major changes affecting international trade was the evolution of means of transport. Trade by land was losing its supremacy to trade

③ EUROPEAN TRADE AT THE END OF THE MIDDLE AGES

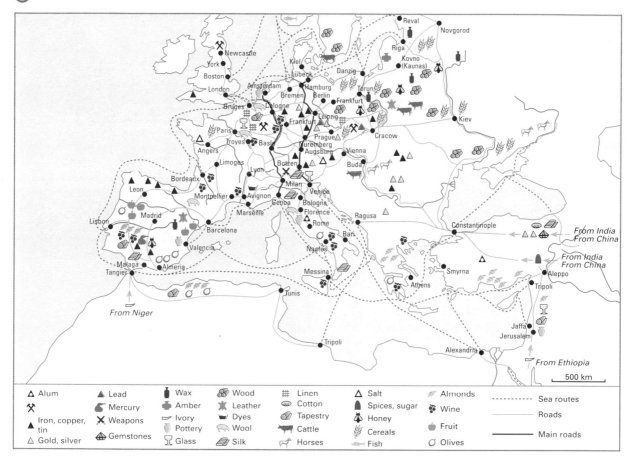

△ Alum	▲ Lead	🍾 Wax	🪵 Wood	⊞ Linen	△ Salt	🌿 Almonds	---------- Sea routes
⚒ Iron, copper, tin	🐚 Mercury	🏺 Amber	✶ Leather	◯ Cotton	🐚 Spices, sugar	🐝 Wine	——— Roads
▲ Iron, copper, tin	✕ Weapons	✎ Ivory	🐗 Dyes	◔ Tapestry	🌾 Honey	🍐 Fruit	▬▬▬ Main roads
△ Gold, silver	🐚 Gemstones	🏺 Pottery	🐖 Wool	🐄 Cattle	📦 Cereals	◯ Olives	
		🍷 Glass	📚 Silk	🐎 Horses	🐟 Fish		

by sea. There were several reasons for this. Road transport relied on four-wheeled waggons drawn by oxen or horses, on badly maintained and unsafe roads. True, it was sometimes supplemented by river transport. One boat could replace several dozen waggons. This explains the large number of towns built on the banks of rivers. Even so, in certain places on the rivers and on the roads, travellers had to pay tolls. Now something new overthrew old habits.

In about 1300 a direct sea route was established via the Mediterranean, the Straits of Gibraltar and the Atlantic coast, linking the towns of Italy (Genoa and Venice) with the North Sea. It was first used by the Italians, then by the Hanseatic League and the British. With that, the long and dangerous land route fell out of favour, with the result that the Champagne fairs were ignored.

Although the ships of the time were not very large, they had increased their carrying capacity. Mooring and unloading charges in the ports, moreover, were lower than road and river tolls. So ships became the cheapest and safest means of transport.

④ AN APOTHECARY'S SHOP
Detail from a fresco in the castle of Issogne, Val d'Aosta, end of the 15th century

From the 13th century onwards more and more guilds were established. Their stalls were grouped by streets, making it easy to keep an eye on the competition. Buying and selling were strictly controlled, especially in the apothecaries' district. For, even if the shop seemed 'honest', people were suspicious of a guild that traded in substances whose nature and cost were a mystery to the layman.

1 BRUGES: A GREAT COMMERCIAL CENTRE

Engraving by Sanderus, Communal Library, Bruges

For nearly two centuries Bruges was a great European trading centre. The Van de Beurze family gave its name to the square on which stood its town house, which became the premises of the Venetian merchants. Gradually, Italian dealers got into the habit of meeting in the square, buying and selling and exchanging news. It was the birth of La Bourse (the Stock Exchange).

2 AN ITALIAN BANK

In this Italian bank the documents are account books and letters which are very likely bills of exchange, a monetary device very much used by merchants buying abroad. Convenient and very safe, they quickly became popular with the general public, encouraged by the bankers, who saw them as a very good form of credit.

At the same time new techniques were generally adopted, such as the stern-rudder, the compass and charts showing sandbanks and tides. With their invaluable help it was no longer necessary to follow the coastline: ships could take the shortest and fastest routes.

Many towns sprang up along the sea route between southern and northern Europe: Mallorca (now Palma de Mallorca), Seville, Lisbon, Bordeaux, La Rochelle. Bruges became the nerve centre of north–south trade.

Another important change was that merchants now tended to settle in one place. Originally, they had travelled with their merchandise, often accompanied by armed escorts. Now, they not only ceased travelling, but also grouped into associations to limit the risks inherent in trade. To begin with, they might cooperate for a single voyage; but gradually, especially in Italy, they set up more lasting trading companies like that of the Peruzzi in Florence (1275–1343), which had a large number of subsidiaries in London, Pisa, Naples, Avignon, Bruges, Cyprus and elsewhere.

The Hanses provided another means of co-operation by traders. They were associations of merchants acting together to protect their commercial interests, acquire privileges in the cities and protect the transport of their goods. The Hanses developed in a number of countries and had their warehouses in many of the great trading towns such as Novgorod, Bergen, London and Bruges.

Sometimes an association of towns was better able to defend commercial interests than a hanse of merchants. One such was the German Hanseatic League. This made its appearance in 1356, when the city of Lübeck organized for the first time a meeting among the Hanseatic towns. For about a century the League dominated trade in north-eastern and central Europe. It included more than 60 towns in the Low Countries and northern Germany. From Novgorod, goods such as cereals, beeswax and Baltic amber were brought via Danzig to Lübeck, then by land to Hamburg and after that by sea or river as far as Kampen or Bruges. From these towns a great flow of merchandise, especially textiles and salt, was despatched to other destinations. But from the middle of the 15th century onwards the Hanses slowly declined.

The chief means of payment was still ready money. Europe at that time had a great variety of currencies in gold and silver, which circulated irrespective of where they had been minted. Some were reputable: others were discounted. In these circumstances the profession of money-changer became important, since it exerted some supervision of the coins in circulation. Not only that, but for reasons of security travelling merchants often left their money on deposit with a money-changer. In return, they were given a receipt certifying how much they had handed over. So, gradually, the profession of money-changer began to evolve into that of banker.

During the 14th century a new method of payment was developed. This was the bill of exchange, a letter whereby one person instructed another to pay a certain sum of money, in a certain place, to a third person specified in the letter. The bill of exchange also specified the currency to be used. Thus, if a Bruges merchant wanted to buy goods in Venice, he paid the necessary sum to the office in Bruges representing his Venetian supplier. In return, he received a bill of exchange which he sent to Venice with his order. The vendor endorsed the bill of exchange as a means of payment and was given the corresponding sum of money. So no funds had to travel: the money remained in Bruges where it could be used to pay for the purchase of goods by a Venetian merchant. Given the length of time

❸ TOWNS OF HANSEATIC TRADE (1374–1435)

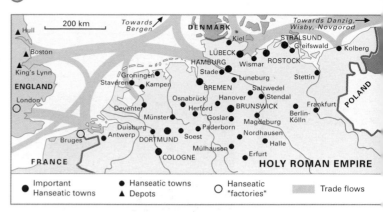

● Important Hanseatic towns	● Hanseatic towns	○ Hanseatic "factories"		Trade flows
	▲ Depots			

Originally an association of merchants, the Hanse rapidly became a league of German and north European towns, closely linked but without political unity. Its political influence was nevertheless great. It intervened, for example, in the question of succession to the Danish throne. But new states such as Poland and Lithuania, and competition from Dutch and British towns, led to a decline which was completed when the Hundred Years' War halted Baltic trade.

❹ A HANSEATIC PORT

Miniature from the end of the 15th century, National Archives, Hamburg
Three carracks have just arrived. Smaller boats transfer the goods and are unloaded with the help of a crane under the watchful eye of the ship-owners. On the left, the harbour-master gives orders. On the right, the merchants, richly dressed and wearing fur hats, discuss future purchases. The same scene was repeated throughout the 14th and 15th centuries in all the ports of Europe.

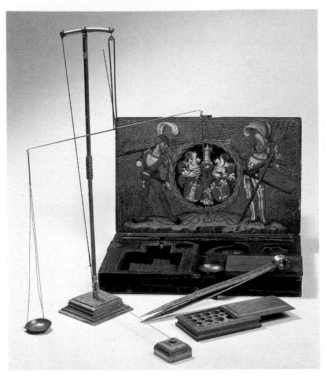

① A MERCHANT'S SCALES

National Museum, Nuremberg

A trader's main implement was a pair of scales. The balance shown above, with its small pans, fragile supports and delicate tongs, must have belonged to a jeweller.

② DYEING CLOTH

In the 14th century dress became more important. Cottons and silks were more and more elaborately worked, while linen and hemp came into fashion. Long before tailors, dyers set up shop. Each day they used a different colour. The customer had only to bring his cloth on the right day to be able to take away a piece of material in the latest hue.

that sometimes elapsed between the drawing up of the bill of exchange and the payment of the money, interest was often charged on the original sum.

Bankers furthermore organized a trade in bills of exchange, which rapidly became an appreciable source of revenue. Florence, Bologna, Milan, Venice and Rome were some of the financial centres where this lucrative business was carried on; and Barcelona, Valencia, Paris, Avignon, Geneva and London were not slow to follow suit. As for Bruges, it was regarded as northern Europe's chief banking centre.

The rich banking families gradually came to wield considerable political influence in their cities, and later at the royal and Papal courts. In some places they also acted as artistic patrons, winning thereby great prestige. Notable examples included the Medici and Strozzi in Italy, the Fuggers and Welsers in the Holy Roman Empire and Jacques Cœur in France.

Industry

In the 13th century cloth manufacture was already an important export industry and an essential factor in the prosperity of those involved in it. The main textile workshops were in Flanders (Ghent, Ypres and Bruges) and the north of France (Paris, Beauvais and Provins). As a result of social tensions and disputes in the Flemish centres, the industry moved, either to new regions or to the surrounding countryside. So it was that around 1320 Brabant (Malines, Brussels and Louvain) became a serious rival to Flemish clothmaking.

Brabantine scarlet was then very much in fashion at royal courts. Even so the Brabant textile centres in their turn suffered a decline. This was due partly to a change in tastes, with a vogue for Norman or English cloth, but also to the fact that England was limiting its wool exports so as to help its own growing textile industry. From then on no single centre dominated the cloth trade. As wool became scarcer, Brussels followed Paris and Tournai in manufacturing tapestries, and Flanders looked northwards to profit from the growth of the German Hanseatic League.

The decline of the large-scale cloth industry was largely balanced by the growth of manufactures in luxury and quality goods. They included various items: tapestry, cabinet-making, enamelling, leather and metal work, dressmaking, munitions and building.

As well as wool, the textile industry used linen, hemp and cotton. The demand for cotton increased as more and more people wore shirts. And the use of cotton led to the growth of another industrial sector, that of paper made from rags. In the 13th century, not without difficulty, paper gradually replaced parchment as material for writing on.

The 14th century saw a change in European diet. Previously, cereals had formed the basis of meals, eaten as bread, porridge, or girdle-cakes. Now, people ate more vegetables and meat. This increased the demand for salt, which was needed in large quantities to preserve both meat and fish. So it became a major commodity in international trade.

Meanwhile, the mining industry was also developing. As mining techniques improved, the number of workings increased. As well as tin, copper and silver, mining now produced iron. Until the beginning of the 14th century objects made of iron had been relatively rare; but the gradual adoption of hydraulic bellows simplified the work of the forge. The ironworks of Styria and Liège were important suppliers.

Agriculture

Between 1150 and 1300 Europe's population had grown rapidly. The result was increased demand for grain, which in turn raised its price. To meet the demand less suitable land had been put under crops. In the Low Countries, peat marshes were exploited; in France, Germany and England trees were cut down; to the east of the Elbe, vast areas were cultivated; in the Alpine valleys, peasants tried to farm the uplands. As was to be expected, poorer soil gave smaller crops.

While total production increased, therefore, agricultural productivity fell; and the population went on growing. Sometimes, reserves of food were barely adequate: a hard winter or a meagre harvest spelt catastrophe.

As a result, many peasants left the land to settle in the cities. But these offered little solution: already, too many unskilled people were looking for work. With more hands than jobs on offer, wages fell drastically.

In 1316 all Europe suffered from famine. It was the beginning of an agrarian crisis that lasted more than a century and a half. Whereas in the 13th century people had been fairly well fed, the 14th century witnessed not only short-term regional scarcity, but also widespread famine.

This had many results: fewer marriages and a falling birthrate; many more epidemic diseases; and social unrest. The population declined, so there were now farm surpluses, leading to falling prices; and this made the rural crisis worse.

Everywhere in Europe great areas of land were left fallow. In Germany, whole villages were abandoned (*Wüstungen*). In England, many ar-

❸ Cloth-making in Brussels

1 *No one shall scour the cloth or pieces of cloth to wash or to dye them . . . without having had them inspected to see that they are good and intact . . . on pain of a 10-sous fine.*

4 *No wool-comber may use his comb unless it has from now on 21 teeth . . . on pain of a 20-sous fine and confiscation of the comb.*

5 *No female wool-comber may comb outside Brussels on pain of a 20-sous fine and confiscation of the comb; that shall go to the benefit of the workmate who denounced her.*

8 *A weaver who has work and who goes drinking during the day shall pay 4 livres.*

11 *No one shall fold or stow the cloth marked by the inspectors without having shown them to the guild for checking.*

For fulling a piece of broad white . . . 56 livres shall be paid; the two workers shall receive 40 livres, the master 12 livres and for the fuller's earth 4 livres.

Every apprentice fuller who wishes to learn the craft shall pay to the guild one old écu.

Extract from Brussels cloth-making rules, 14th century

❹ AN IRON MINE
Kutna Hora in central Bohemia, in a minstrel's miniature from the end of the 15th century. National Library, Vienna

The urge for military superiority and the development of mechanization made work for miners. At the bottom, the face-workers, dressed in white because of the darkness, attack the rock with hammers and crowbars. Coming up from work, the miners are searched, on the left. Above ground, the iron ore is broken with mallets, put in sloping bowls and drenched in water. Then it is sorted and checked by the foremen.

❶ SHEEP-SHEARING

Miniature by the Limburg brothers: Poitiers castle.
Les Très Riches Heures du duc de Berry, Musée Condé, Chantilly
The book of hours here shows the work done in July. In the foreground, sheep-shearing; in the background, reaping with sickles. Sheep-breeding grew because wool fetched a good price: the cloth industry had to meet increasing demand. There was new diversity in clothing, which began to reflect social rank.

❷ MILKING COWS

Diet was also changing. Meat and vegetables gradually replaced game and grains. Milk, consumed on the farm, was already used by monks to make cheese.

able fields were turned into pasture for sheep; and there too whole villages were deserted.

Grain production fell unremittingly. This may have been due to a series of hard winters and even a climatic change. But there may also be an economic explanation. Every peasant, naturally, tried to get the best income from his land; and now stockbreeding and cash crops for the wealthy began to be more profitable than growing grain, especially in view of changing food habits. A peasant who followed the new fashion could save enough money to buy the grain he needed from large-scale producers elsewhere in Europe. So trade in grain became a lucrative business, notably for Genoa, which handled large quantities of grain from the Black Sea, Sicily, Crete and Sardinia. In northern Europe the Hanseatic League imported grain, chiefly Polish and Prussian rye.

Stockbreeding flourished. There were many more sheep, owing to the great demand for wool. England, the main supplier of wool to the cloth industry in France and Flanders, increased its own production by breeding more sheep, but limited its export quotas to assist its own cloth-making industry. Flemish and Italian wool merchants therefore sought new sources of supply. They found them in Spain, which already in Roman times had produced wool from its native sheep. In about 1340 these began to be replaced by merino sheep from north Africa, whose wool was of better quality. From the beginning of the 14th century, indeed, rich Iberian landowners had been turning a vast amount of their arable land into pasture. And Spain had to import grain, which in the past it had produced in abundance.

The number of sheep also increased in other European countries, where they were often kept on fallow land. Cattle production also grew rapidly, notably in the French Auvergne, thereby ensuring supplies of beef.

Changing food habits further led to a fall in the demand for land and a growing taste for butter. This influenced dairy production in Norway, Sweden, Denmark, the Netherlands and Normandy. Elsewhere, as in Friesland, the Camargue and the Romagna, horse-breeding increased. In France, large ponds were prepared for freshwater fish-farming. This was all the more useful in so far as fasting on Fridays and in Lent was a universal practice.

To meet the great demand for fruit and vegetables, orchards were planted in Italy and Portugal to grow oranges, lemons, figs and grapes for the export market.

Among cash crops wine production profited from the stability of wine prices at this time. Greek and Spanish wines, and those from Cyprus and Rhodes, found ready markets in Western Europe; and on the banks of the Rhine, in Alsace and in Burgundy, vineyards were flourishing. Industry, too, encouraged specialized crops such as flax, hemp and dye-plants (saffron, woad, etc.) for textiles.

The growth of stockbreeding, market-gardening and cash crops coincided with the decline of grain production. This was not a catastrophe; but it was one element in the process of change affecting the farming world.

❸ THE GRAPE HARVEST

Pierre de Crescens, 15th century. Bibliothèque de l'Arsenal, Paris

The grape harvest was one of the occasions for merriment and feasting. Every estate had its vineyard; the grapes were pressed and the wine put in casks at the château. Day-labourers looked for work on the grape harvest when there was no work in the towns.

❹ TILLING THE FIELDS

Pierre de Crescens, 15th century. British Library, London

The conditions of rural life varied from one region to another; so did the use of the land. But usually a lay or ecclesiastical lord was in charge and there was strict division of labour. Different crafts were often recognizable by their clothing. Even when home-made, this also differed from one community to another.

2 Society

❶ THE BLACK DEATH

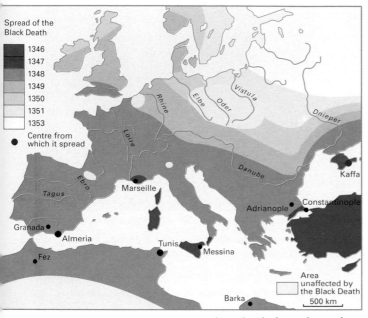

Spread of the Black Death

- 1346
- 1347
- 1348
- 1349
- 1350
- 1351
- 1353
- ● Centre from which it spread

Rhine · Elbe · Oder · Vistula · Dnieper · Loire · Danube · Kaffa · Tagus · Ebro · Marseille · Adrianople · Constantinople · Granada · Almeria · Tunis · Messina · Fez · Barka

Area unaffected by the Black Death
500 km

Brought from the East in Genoese ships, the Black Death spread to Britain and Scandinavia in only a few years. Its triple form – bubonic, pulmonary and intestinal – made it catastrophic. Its massive death toll explains the ensuing economic depression, which lasted a long time, and the consequent movements of population. These changes so reduced the demographic pressure on Europe that the spectre of overpopulation vanished for four hundred years.

❷ The Great Plague

In the year of Our Lord 1348 almost the whole surface of the globe suffered from such mortality as has rarely been seen. The living were barely sufficient to bury the dead, or were so horrified as to avoid the task. So great a terror seized nearly everyone that no sooner had an ulcer or a swelling appeared on someone, usually in the groin or the armpit, than the victim was deprived of all help and even abandoned by his family . . . . And so, many people died owing to lack of care . . . . Many more . . . who were thought bound . . . to die . . . were transported . . . to the grave to be buried: in this way a large number were buried alive . . . . And this plague continued . . . for two years in succession.

Vitae Paparum Avenionensium: Clementis VI Prima vita

Death from the Plague

The teeming Europe of the 13th century was followed by the 'empty' Europe of the 14th. Between 1150 and 1300, the population had risen from 50 million to 73 million. By 1350, it had fallen to 51 million and by 1400 to 45 million. Why? The main reason was the Black Death (1347–51).

A number of factors combined to bring about catastrophe: famines, illness (smallpox, influenza) and war. The grain crisis in the 14th century affected the poorest people in Europe. The plague, when it came, hit an underfed and hence vulnerable population. The coastal regions of the Low Countries, where more fish than grain was eaten, saw far fewer deaths.

For four years, from 1347 to 1351, the plague ravaged Europe. It took two forms: bubonic, with 80 per cent mortality, and pulmonary, with 100 per cent. It reached Europe from Asia and the Orient, where it was a frequent occurrence, on board a Genoese ship. The Genoese had had warehouses on the shores of the Black Sea since the 11th century; and in 1346 one of them, Kaffa, was besieged by the Mongols. They were decimated by an epidemic of plague and got rid of the corpses by catapulting them into the besieged city. Its panic-stricken inhabitants fled in galleys to Sicily, bringing the disease with them. It spread like wildfire. By the end of 1347 it had reached northern Italy and Provence, and from there went up the Rhône Valley to Paris. In 1348 it was raging in Portugal and Britain, and the following year in Flanders and Germany. It then reached Scandinavia and entered Russia from the north. Europe was united, as it were, by disease.

Panic among the people became frenzied when bubonic plague turned into pulmonary plague. In bubonic plague the rat's bite was visible; but pulmonary plague was spread by invisible microbes. The Black Death was one of the greatest tragedies in the history of Europe. In a few months it killed a third of the population.

It returned several times, in 1360, 1369 and 1374. The social and demographic results were striking. While the number of marriages and births increased, the average expectation of life fell sharply. In England in 1348 it had been 25 years; by 1376 it was only 17. Not until the end of the 16th century did Europe's population return to its 1316 level.

❸ THE PLAGUE IN TOURNAI, 1349
Gilles de Muisit: *Annales de la peste de Tournai*, Royal Library, Brussels
The plague came from Asia to Europe in 1347. It killed an estimated 25 million Europeans.

Confronting a mysterious evil, people looked for scapegoats. Some blamed it on the Jews, whom many accused of having poisoned the wells and springs. To escape from pogroms, many Jews took refuge in the county of Avignon, under the protection of the Pope, or in Poland and Lithuania, which were more hospitable.

Social unrest

The first decades of the 14th century were marked by revolts. In themselves, these were not new: similar unrest had occurred in the 13th century. Then, it had mainly been confined to the towns; but this time it affected both town and country-side. What was more, the revolts took place almost simultaneously all over Europe, as if it were 'united by revolution'.

The rapid growth of towns and the crisis in the countryside explain the general outburst. When country-dwellers flocked to the towns they caused problems: rents rose and the labour market was flooded. Despite the combined efforts of the local authorities and the guilds, there was no remedy. Prices, except for bread and other wheat products, rose everywhere, faster than wages. Medieval society began to be pauperized.

❹ THE PERSECUTION OF THE JEWS
Nuremberg Chronicles, 1493
In times of crisis, people like to find scapegoats. The Jews were often assigned this rôle. During the Black Death, on 14 February 1493, the Jews of Saint-Veltin were accused of having poisoned the wells. Those who agreed to be baptized escaped with their lives. Two thousand were burned alive.

① PILLAGING A TOWN
Jean Froissart, *Chroniques de France*, 15th century. Bibliothèque Nationale, Paris
For centuries pillage was one of the normal aspects of war. The booty was sometimes very substantial, making up for the irregularity with which mercenaries were paid. It is easy to see why for some of them war became an end in itself.

② The status of women

In the Middle Ages Woman was sometimes idealized as a divine being, but for most of the time, owing to Eve's original sin, she was considered a worthless object. Here are some medieval verdicts.

Woman was created to help man, but only in the act of procreation, because for all other tasks he can find a far better support elsewhere . . . (St Thomas Aquinas).

Sometimes, when a woman wants to be taken as intelligent, she finally just looks twice as foolish . . . . (Erasmus).

The protection of women's legal status matched these views:

A man has the right to beat his wife, to stab her, to break her from head to foot, to warm his feet in her blood and then to sew the remains together so that she stays alive. . . . (The Aardenburg Charter)

But some voices were raised in women's defence:

Women are naturally good. . . . (Naerlant)

If women were not good and their advice was useless, God would never have made them men's helpmeets but rather made them the cause of evil . . . . (Chaucer)

From R. Linekens, *Wat'n leven* (*What a life*)

The gap in wealth between the rich and poor worsened the tension. By making advantageous marriages, rich patricians and merchants joined the distressed nobility. In imitation of aristocratic fashion they wore luxury clothes and bought recherché objects such as precious stones, alabaster or tapestries. Amidst appalling poverty the sharp contrast aroused widespread hatred.

At the same time, within the guilds, the solidarity that had been their raison d'être began to weaken. In each craft, the masters now formed a caste apart and opposed the entry of new members. The stricter conditions that they imposed on recruitment reduced the number of apprentices; while the obligation on aspirants to produce a 'masterpiece', an expensive proof of their skill, acted for many as an insurmountable barrier. By the end of the 15th century social mobility was less marked than it had been in the 12th and 13th.

The situation was little better in the countryside. War and the grain crisis forced many peasants to become beggars, if not criminals. Yet it was not they who rebelled, but those who were better off and had more to lose than those who had nothing. Driven less by poverty than by the threat to their privileges, they rebelled against the disorder of royal finances, an untimely tax, the depreciation of the currency, the greed of the nobility and the misdeeds of the clergy. However, these *jacqueries* – so called after the nickname 'Jacques' given to French peasants – did not seek to overturn hierarchical society or to overthrow the sovereign; they were protests against unfair taxes or perverted justice. Nor was it the poorest people, in the towns as in the countryside, who were responsible for the riots.

Sometimes, the towns helped the countryside. In 1323, for example, a revolt in the coastal regions of Flanders was supported by the towns of Ypres and Bruges. In France, taking advantage of the fact that the King, John the Good, was a captive in England, much of the area round Beauvais rose up in rebellion, while Paris rebelled against the behaviour of the merchants' provost, Etienne Marcel (1357–59).

Between 1378 and 1382 similar movements spread throughout Europe. In Florence the textile workers seized the city government. Copying the weavers of Ghent, Flanders revolted again. Taking as their motto 'Long Live Ghent!', Rouen, Béziers and Montpellier rebelled. In the Languedoc the 'Tuchins' ravaged the province, together with gangs of looters. In Catalonia, the peasants rose up against the nobility. In England, led by Wat Tyler, discontented peasants marched on London. In the Holy Roman Empire, unrest was mainly confined to the towns, with the countryside remaining on the fringes of such riots until 1525. At the beginning of the 15th century, a new wave of rebellion affected France, Catalonia and Bohemia.

Many motives – religious, economic and social – lay behind these uprisings. People were fighting for a better and fairer society. Broadly speaking, the problem was continued insecurity owing to the profound changes that were taking place.

❸ THE JACQUERIES IN MEAUX, 1357
Jean Froissart, *Chroniques de France*, 15th century.
Bibliothèque Nationale, Paris
Crushed by taxation, the peasants rebelled against the nobles, who derided the rebels by calling them the 'Jacques', from the nickname for a peasant, 'Jacques Bonhomme'. The desperate peasants pillaged and burned down castles, massacring all their inhabitants irrespective of class. To put an end to the murderous madness, Gaston de Foix organized its bloodthirsty repression.

❹ On the fringe of society

The lower classes included serving women, day labourers, workmen, many women and illegitimate children. The blind, the lepers and the paralysed, as well as many poor people, were rejected by society.

The lower classes in certain cities
(in percentages)

1380	Lübeck	42 (of c.22,000 inhabitants)
1428	Frankfurt	70 (of c.10,000 inhabitants)
1440	Strasbourg	29 (of c.18,000 inhabitants)
1444	Basel	27 (of c.10,000 inhabitants)
1475	Augsburg	66 (of c.18,000 inhabitants)

❺ BEGGING
Jean Froissart, *Chroniques de France*, Bibliothèque Nationale, Paris
Many survivors of the plague, war and famine had to resort to begging at the doors of palaces and churches.

Politics and Government

① THE EMPEROR CHARLES IV (1316–78)
Bibliothèque royale, Brussels

The Holy Roman Emperor, surrounded by the seven members of the Electoral College: on the left, three ecclesiastical Electors, the Archbishops of Mainz, Cologne and Trier; on the right, four lay Electors, the King of Bohemia, the Count Palatine of the Rhine, the Duke of Saxony and the Margrave of Brandenburg.

② THE HOLY ROMAN EMPIRE (15th CENTURY)

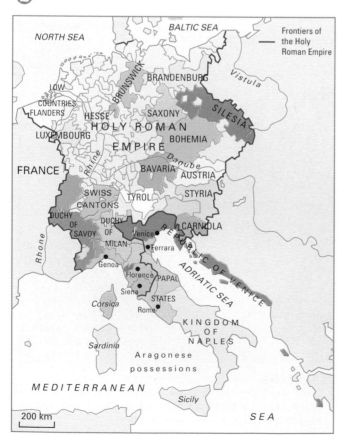

At the beginning of the 14th century the idea of a universal authority, inherited from the Roman Empire through that of Charlemagne, was still embodied in the German Holy Roman Empire founded in 962 by Otto the Great. It enjoyed privileges associated with its imperial dignity, some of which gave it powers extending well beyond its own frontiers.

The Pope, successor of St Peter, had been strengthened by the Gregorian reform (1073) and limited in power by the schism between East and West (1054). He was the leader of Western Christendom, but saw himself as the champion of the universal and triumphant Church.

During the 14th century, however, these universal ideals were overshadowed by national realities. The Holy Roman Empire lost its universal significance in the face of Britain and France, the only great Christian kingdoms in the West that could dispute its supremacy. As they grew, the two kingdoms fought each other. Meanwhile, the Burgundian states emerged; and in Italy, alongside the Kingdom of Naples, and Sicily, and the Papal states, there was a whole series of cities and small states, often locked in mutual combat. In the south-west of Europe, three kingdoms shared the Iberian peninsula: Aragon, Castile and Portugal. In northern and Eastern Europe, principalities were established in Lithuania, Poland, Hungary, Moscow and Scandinavia.

Europe's territorial evolution

At the end of the Middle Ages various political entities in Europe were evolving in different ways. In the Holy Roman Empire the maintenance of imperial prerogatives was losing ground to the claims of the German principalities of which the Empire was made up. There were two reasons for this. The first was that the Empire was such a mosaic of small lay or clerical states and free cities; the second was that it was not hereditary but elective. Since the 'Golden Bull' of 1356, in fact, the Emperor had been elected by a college of seven Electors, chosen permanently from among the great lay and ecclesiastical princes. Such a system sapped the Emperor's authority.

Northern Italy was part of the Holy Roman Empire; but the Emperor's power there was purely formal, real power being in the hands of the city officials. But the cities did not unite, at least on a permanent basis: Venice, Genoa,

Florence and Milan either would not or could not, owing to their sharp competition for trade. In the 14th and 15th centuries they were ruled by a few great families. In Venice the chief administrator, the Doge, was not an autocrat: once elected, he depended on the Great Council, where only noble families could sit. In Genoa, a small élite governed the city. In Milan the lords, led by the Visconti, made up the magistrature. In Florence, the Medici family ran the administration.

The Iberian peninsula, by contrast, was moving toward unity. Aragon was already a federation of three states: the County of Barcelona and the Kingdoms of Valencia and Aragon. Linked by blood to the Kingdom of Sicily, Aragon's rulers extended their influence to Sardinia and Corsica, and in 1442 to the Kingdom of Naples. Aragon thus became a great sea power, dominating all of the western Mediterranean.

Further west, the Kingdom of Castile was looking for sea outlets at the expense of Portugal. It first tried, unsuccessfully, uniting the two crowns; then it resorted to force of arms. Portugal resisted: the *Cortes* of Coimbra and the victory of Aljubarrota in 1385 enabled it to retain its independence. Castile made up for its reverses in the West by successes in the East.

The struggle against the Moors had given Castile and Aragon mutual solidarity. This was the basis for Spanish unification, in which the marriage of Isabella of Castile and Ferdinand of Aragon in 1469 was an essential step. It was the prelude to the completion of the Reconquista by the capture of Granada in 1492. The entire Iberian peninsula was now Christian.

An important element in the development of nation states in Western Europe at this time was the relationship between France and England. Their political and economic life was very much dominated by the Hundred Years' War (1337–1453), in fact a succession of short battles punctuated by long periods of truce. It was also the first conflict on a European scale: as well as France and England, it involved Aragon, Castile, Anjou, Burgundy and Scotland. Its origin was a purely feudal problem. The Kings of England, successors to William the Conqueror, Duke of Normandy, remained vassals of the King of France. Since 1066, moreover, through a policy of matrimonial alliances, they had increased their possessions on French soil, in Anjou and Guienne; and they did all they could to avoid paying the homage they owed to the King of France. When King Philip VI of France (1328–50) occupied Guienne, hostilities began. Towards the end of the Hundred Years' War, in 1430, French national feeling was crystallized in the figure of Joan of Arc.

Between the Rhine and the Rhône a new

❸ The power of Ferdinand of Aragon

From the beginning of his reign he attacked the Kingdom of Granada and this expedition became the basis of his power. It gave him a way to absorb the ambitions of the great [lords] of Castile, who were entirely occupied with this war; while he acquired over them, through his fame, an ascendancy that they failed to notice. What was more, the money supplied him by the Church and levied by him from the people enabled him to maintain armies which, trained by this long series of wars, made him so much respected later.

After this enterprise, and still covering himself with the mantle of religion . . . he set about with pious cruelty persecuting the Moors and driving them out of his kingdom. Finally he attacked Africa, came in arms to Italy and last of all made war on France.

Machiavelli, *The Prince*, 1513

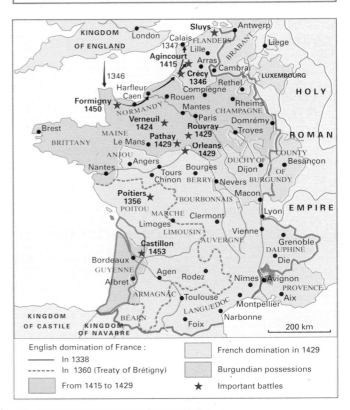

English domination of France :
— In 1338
---- In 1360 (Treaty of Brétigny)
▨ From 1415 to 1429
▢ French domination in 1429
▢ Burgundian possessions
★ Important battles

❹ THE HUNDRED YEARS' WAR

The French did not recognize royal succession through the female line, so the English King Edward III, as the son of Isabelle of France, would have no right to the Capetian throne. The French were disastrously defeated in the first battles, in Flanders, Crécy and Calais. In 1360 the combatants came to terms: all south-west France passed to the English, as did Calais. The peace lasted 35 years. But civil war between the Armagnacs and the Burgundians led to renewed hostilities. The French defeat at Agincourt (1415), the madness of the King of France and the Queen's betrayal led in 1420 to the Treaty of Troyes, which delivered France to the English. The triumphs of Joan of Arc (1429–31) returned confidence to the Dauphin's armies. The end of the civil war enabled Charles VII to raise a new army which from 1429 to 1453 drove the English out of France.

❶ France during the Hundred Years' War

The inhabitants of the countryside and the outskirts of the cities preferred to take refuge in walled towns or to flee like animals to the heart of the woods with their wives, their children and all their possessions, rather than risk meeting the king's men (the collectors of taxes), whom they feared more than the enemy himself. They soon learned to their cost, in fact, that there was no difference between these people and the English, or rather that the king's men held them to ransom and robbed them even more, and carried out intolerable acts of brigandage. They extorted by violence gold, silver and all their most precious possessions. Their cruelty inspired so much fear that churchmen took from the churches, and hid in safe places, the jewels consecrated to God and the saints, because these thieves seized everything that they could find outside fortified towns and carried it off without scruple.

Chronicle of Saint-Denis, 1415

❷ EASTERN EUROPE, END OF 16TH CENTURY

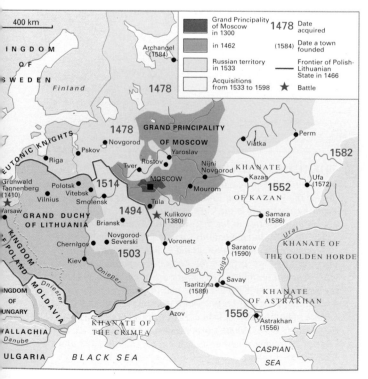

political entity was emerging: Burgundy. King John the Good of France (1350–64) gave the Duchy of Burgundy in apanage to his younger son Philip the Bold. John's elder son and successor Charles V (1364–80), anxious to subdue Flanders while the war against England was raging, organized a marriage between his brother Philip the Good and the heir to Flanders, Marguerite de Male. This union laid the basis for the future Grand Duchy of Burgundy. By about 1400 the Duke of Burgundy possessed numerous lands obtained by marriage or inheritance or in other cases bought. To these assets he wanted to add the episcopal sees of Liège, Cambrai and Utrecht. But the ambition of Philip the Good's grandson, Charles the Bold, and the determination of King Louis XI of France to block it, met head-on at the siege of Nancy, where Charles died in 1477. The dream was at an end.

In northern Europe, the Union of Kalmar (1397) placed the three Scandinavian crowns of Denmark, Norway and Sweden under the authority of the Norwegian Queen Margaret, leading to a new balance of power.

In Eastern Europe, from the 12th and 13th centuries Germanic peoples had been moving into Slav lands and clearing them for crops, which turned rapidly into economic and cultural domination, which the Slavs did their best to oppose. Answering the call of the Emperor Frederick II in 1226, the Order of Teutonic Knights had conquered Prussia. The knights were a serious threat to any emancipation of the Slavs – a threat felt all the more keenly in 1240, when there came a Mongol danger from the East. These two threats drove the people of Eastern Europe to a common cause.

In 1241 the Mongols sacked Hungary so savagely that they almost destroyed the country. King Bela IV appealed for colonists from Italy, the Germanic countries and from Western Europe. When they came, they revived agriculture and developed the towns. They also built historic links with the West, which grew stronger when first Angevin and then German princes were elected to the Hungarian throne. But a fresh threat, from the Ottomans, prompted the Hungarian Jan Hunyadi to lead a revolt which in 1458 secured the throne for his son Matthias Corvinus.

The Czechs and the Poles also founded independent states. Bohemia, subject to strong German influence, feared that it might lose its identity. A revolt by the University of Prague was encouraged, from 1402 onwards, by the preaching of Jan Hus, who mingled attacks on the clergy's misdeeds with calls for a free Bohemia. This first wave of national feeling found an echo in the countryside, where the Hussite movement, after Hus's execution in 1415, played a major role in the development of the Czech State.

Poland also wanted political and cultural freedom from the Holy Roman Empire, because the Teutonic Knights were turning aside from the struggle against Islam to convert the pagan lands of Lithuania – and conversion looked very much like conquest. In 1386 King Jagello of Lithuania married the Polish Princess Hedwig, became a Christian and assumed the Polish crown. The two countries were united by the Treaty of Kosice. In 1410 Jagello defeated the Teutonic Knights at Tannenberg; and the Polish nation was born.

Russia, in the 13th century, became a tributary of the Mongol state (the Golden Horde) and by the beginning of the 14th was no longer autonomous. The Russian leaders were locked in fierce rivalry: those of Moscow and Kiev vied for the title of Grand Prince, allowed by his Mongol masters to collect taxes – the so-called 'Jarlick' privilege. In 1327 Ivan of Moscow secured the title and moved the capital of Russia from Kiev to Moscow. Backed by the Russian Church, his successors did their best to bring the Russian principalities under their control. In 1380 the Grand Prince Dmitri defeated the Golden Horde and Mongol power began to wane.

Further south, the Byzantine Empire in the 13th century was no more than a mosaic of small states divided among the descendants of former imperial families. The Palaeologus dynasty was the last to rule the former Empire itself, which by the early 14th century had shrunk to Constantinople and was only a minor power, fought over by the Italian trading republics. The commercial privileges won by the Genoese made what was left of the Empire a mere dependency.

In the East, the military power of the Turks was a far more serious threat, as they carved out an Empire known as 'Ottoman' in honour of Osman I, the head of their tribe. In 1356 they crossed the Dardanelles and added to their Asian conquests. As an outpost of Christian Europe, Byzantium was reinforced by an army of Crusaders from Hungary; but it was defeated near Nicopolis in 1396. Although Tamerlane threatened Ottoman power in Asia and revived European hopes by saving Byzantium once, the Turkish Sultan Murad I soon relaunched Moslem expansion. The Turks' military resources included the Janissaries – an élite corps recruited from Christian children systematically abducted from their parents and trained as warriors for Islam.

In 1453 Byzantium received the *coup de grâce*. The Sultan Mehmet II used enormous cannons to destroy its defences. A thousand years after the fall of the Roman Empire in the West, the Eastern Empire also came to an end.

③ MARIENBURG: THE RESIDENCE OF THE GRAND MASTER OF THE TEUTONIC KNIGHTS

Marienburg, founded in 1280, became the residence of the Grand Master of the Order in 1309. At once a castle and a monastery, it stands on the Nogat, a tributary of the Vistula.

④ THE SIEGE OF CONSTANTINOPLE

Miniature by Jean Mielot in *Advis pour le passage d'Outremer*, 1455. Bibliothèque Nationale, Paris

The first major military exploit of Mehmet II (1451–81), known as 'the Conqueror', was the capture of Constantinople on 29 May 1453. He made his capital there. The picture shows the site of the fortified city between the Bosporus and the Golden Horn. On the left are slides on which the besieging forces conveyed their ships.

❶ Bertrand du Guesclin

And then Sir Bertrand excused himself once more, saying: 'Dear lord and noble King, I am a poor man and of low degree. And the office of Constable is so great and noble that he who would fulfil it well must most powerfully command, and this more over the great than over the humble. And here be my lords your brothers, your nephews and your cousins, who will have charge of men-at-arms in the armies and in the cavalcades. How should I dare to command them? And so I pray you most earnestly to deliver me from this office and to grant it to another who will take it more willingly than I and acquit himself of it better.'

Jean Froissart, *Chroniques*, Vol. VIII, edited by S. Luce, G. Raynaud and L. & A. Mirot, 15 volumes, Paris, 1869–1975

❷ THE DUCHY OF BURGUNDY

▬▬▬	Frontier between France & the Empire
▨	Possessions of Philip the Bold (1364-1404)
▨	Acquisitions of Philip the Good (1419-1467)
▨	States under Burgundian influence
▨	Conquests of Charles the Bold (1467-1477)
⇗	Attacks by Charles the Bold

From the feudal to the modern state

So the 14th and 15th centuries saw an immense transformation of Europe's political geography. Territorial change was accompanied by a change in the way states were governed. The institutions born of feudalism in the 12th and 13th centuries made way for a new form of rule.

Of course there were overlaps between the old and the new, making it difficult to give precise dates for the change. The administration was based on feudal custom and on a maze of feudal loyalties, exclusive links between one man and another. Vassalship and lordship formed a pyramid at whose summit was the king. The state's institutional system was thus a network of small powers, all interlinked. But this structure was beginning to evolve; and the interests of the sovereign were no longer so closely identified with those of the nobility alone. They now began to extend to the welfare of the whole nation.

The notion of 'the public good', so dear to Roman Law, reappeared and the sovereign became identified with the interests of his subjects. They were no longer assigned to a given place in the feudal hierarchy, but members of a group, a social category then known as an 'estate'.

A new group appeared in this classification by 'estates': the urban middle class. From now on, there were three estates – the clergy, the nobility and the bourgeoisie. They did not include the mass of the people, in either countryside or town.

The meetings of representatives of the estates, or assemblies of estates, no longer confined themselves to listening to the sovereign's wishes: they expressed their own, and he asked the estates' authorization to levy taxes. The exercise of power was no longer unilateral: the sovereign shared it with the estates, whose rights were defined in a charter of privileges. The aim of the assemblies of estates was broadly to defend recognized privileges and prevent the sovereign from increasing his powers.

With slight variations from one country to another, this new manner of administration became general in Europe. The shift from personal loyalties to group solidarity in some cases gave rise to what would later be called national feeling.

This national feeling was not based on loyalty to a country's cultural cohesion – with the notable exception of Britain. The inhabitants of the Kingdom of France did not think of themselves as Frenchmen, but as subjects of the King of France. What might appear to be 'nationalism' at this time was simply the feeling of unity on the part of a group that was able to defend itself against attack by another. Men fought in France against the English marauders and in Spain against the infidel Moors. The Slavs of Eastern

Europe resisted the Teutonic Knights and the onslaughts of the Mongols.

At the same time, the formation of politically and geographically defined countries in Europe marked the end of a Christendom united behind the Pope and sometimes the Emperor.

The growth in the role of the state led the sovereign to recruit civil servants who owed direct allegiance to him. They usually came from the minor nobility or the bourgeoisie; and they intervened at all levels. In France, for example, the Bailiff, acting in the king's name, took on public duties such as the administration of justice. The royal court surrounded itself with lawyers and economists holding university degrees.

As the tasks of the state multiplied and were entrusted to civil servants, so the influence of royal governments increased. And the royal civil servants began to regard themselves more as agents of the crown than as servants of the king's person. The establishment of an embryonic permanent army further strengthened the central power. With this in view rich merchants made loans to the king to cover the cost of mercenaries.

During the 14th and 15th centuries the state did not develop at a steady pace. Hard times like the Hundred Years' War acted as a brake. Only in the late 15th century was royal power firmly re-established. In France, Louis XI (1461–83) and his successors managed to create the model of a modern state. In England, Henry VII (1485–1509), the first of the Tudors, bolstered the power of the monarchy after the nobility had been weakened by the Wars of the Roses, in which the York and Lancaster families had fought each other for the throne.

The case of Burgundy was different, although it was subject to the inducements to move from a feudal to a modern state. A federation of autonomous sovereign states under a single ruler, Burgundy had an administrative system that reflected its complex structure. The dukes of Burgundy, anxious to strengthen their own power, entrusted each territory to a representative chosen from among the nobility and had him assisted by a council and by the Assembly of the Estates. To improve the structure of their domains, the dukes also set up a chancellery, the Great Council, an organ of government that acted as supreme court of justice, the chamber of accounts which supervised the administration of finance, and the 'States General' which brought together the representatives of the three estates (nobility, clergy and bourgeoisie).

Although Charles the Bold's defeat by King Louis XI of France in 1477 put an end to Burgundian aspirations, the administrative structure established in Burgundy found imitators.

❸ THE CAPITULARY ASSEMBLY OF THE GOLDEN FLEECE

Guillaume de Fillastre, *Histoire de la Toison d'or* (1470–80), Bibliothèque royale, Brussels

In Bruges, on 10 February 1430, Philip the Good established the Order of the Golden Fleece, to secure allegiance from the nobility of various inherited fiefs. Here, Jean Wauquelin presents to the young Charles the Bold his chronicle of Hainault. He is surrounded by the Chancellor, Nicolas Rolin and by Jean Cheviot, a member of the Great Council. Seven years later, when Maximilian of Austria became Duke of Burgundy, he extended the Order to Austria.

❹ The English Parliament in 1407

. . . The Commons of this present Parliament were asked to come before our Lord the King [the Lancastrian Henry IV] and the said Lords a certain number of the persons of their company, to hear and report to their companions what they should hear on command of our Lord the King aforesaid . . . . That it be licit for the Lords to debate among themselves in this present Parliament, and any other in time to come, in the absence of the King, about the state of the Realm and of the remedy it might need. And in similar manner that it be licit for the Commons, for their part, to debate together of the state and remedy aforesaid. Provided, however, that the Lords for their part, and the Commons for theirs, make no report to our said Lord the King of any Grant by the Commons granted, and by the Lords assented, nor of communications of the said Grant, before the same Lords and Commons be of one assent and one accord in this matter . . . .

Rotuli Parliamentorum, III, 611 (21), in Eleanor C. Lodge and Gladys A. Thornton (eds), *English Constitutional Documents, 1307–1485*, Cambridge, 1935 (translated from old French)

Religion and Spiritual Life

❶ THE PALACE OF THE POPES, AVIGNON

In 1309 Clement V took the Papacy back to Avignon. But it was not until thirty years later that Benedict XII decided to have a palace built on the Doms Rock. It began as an austere fortress: Clement VI added a luxurious palace. Completed in 1362, it harboured a stately court, sheltered all kinds of victims of persecution and attracted every kind of brigand. Bought in 1348 from Jeanne, Queen of Naples and Countess of Provence, Avignon remained the property of the Popes until 1791, when the town and its surrounding county were reunited with France.

❷ The crisis of the Papacy

Given the division that at present exists within the Holy Church, owing to the Popes (for there are three claimants to the Papal throne): one lives in Rome, where he goes by the name of Martin V and is obeyed by all Christian Kings; the second lives . . . in the Kingdom of Valence and goes by the name of Pope Clement VII; few people know where the third lives, except the Cardinal of Saint-Estienne: he goes by the name of Pope Benedict XIV. The first, known as Pope Martin, was elected at Constance by the consent of all Christian nations; he who goes by the name of Clement was elected . . . by three of his Cardinals; the third, who calls himself Benedict XI . . . was elected secretly by the Cardinal of Saint-Estienne. Please pray Our Lord Jesus Christ in His infinite mercy to tell us which of these three is the true Pope and which it please Him we should obey henceforth . . . and in which we should believe.

Letter from a French nobleman, beginning of the 15th century

The Pope and the Church

Since the Gregorian Reform in the 11th century the Church had claimed universal supremacy and hence Papal theocracy, expressed in the theory of the 'two swords' (spiritual and temporal), according to which only the Pope had the right to appoint the Emperor. The privilege of naming and then investing abbots and bishops was the stake in the subsequent struggle between the Emperor and the Pope. If in the 13th century the Pope seemed to have the upper hand, a new threat was in the offing from the King of France.

In 1294 the newly elected Pope was an Abruzzi hermit of great piety but no practicality. The cardinals, who had succumbed to French influence, secured his resignation and elected Cardinal Gaetani under the name of Boniface VIII. He was an ambitious man who wanted to consolidate Papal power. He proclaimed the Pope's *plenitudo potestatis*, or plenitude of power, stressing the Church's direct link with God. According to this theory, secular rulers were tributaries of the Papacy. But when Boniface tried to apply his doctrine, he came into conflict with Philip IV of France (1285–1314). In September 1303, at Anagni, Philip defeated and humiliated Boniface, who soon died. His successor Clement V, the former Archbishop of Bordeaux, took office in 1309, but in Avignon, not Rome. Although at that time Avignon belonged to the Kingdom of Naples, the Pope was now in the orbit of France. In Rome, this period of the Avignon Papacy was known as the 'Babylonian Captivity'.

It ended in 1377, when Pope Gregory XI returned to the Eternal City on the prompting of the mystic Catherine of Siena. When he died in 1378, the Romans demanded a Roman Pope. Under their pressure, the cardinals elected the Bishop of Bari, an Italian who had lived for a long time in Avignon. Taking the name of Urban VI, he expressed his attachment to the city, the *urbs*. But his authoritarian behaviour led the cardinals to depose him. He refused to go; and the cardinals then elected a new French Pope, Clement VII, who returned the Papacy to Avignon.

Thus began the Great Schism in the west. For forty years, from 1378 to 1417, it divided European Christendom. Each Pope, in Rome and in Avignon, appointed a college of cardinals entitled to elect a successor – thereby deepening the schism. The Avignon Pope was backed by Spain, Portugal, France, the Kingdom of Naples and

Scotland; the other countries supported the Pope in Rome.

The Church of Rome was undergoing the most serious crisis in its history. For thirty years none of the parties to the dispute could secure unanimous support, despite the efforts of many distinguished people. The doctors of theology of the University of Paris proposed either joint resignation or arbitration by an independent tribunal or a general council. Ever since the conflict between Boniface VIII and Philip the Fair, a theory had been developing according to which the supreme power in the Church should be vested in a council of Bishops, as representatives of the Church and of all believers. This was a new conception of the council and one that could be compared to the assemblies of estates or States-General.

In 1409 the Ecumenical Council of Pisa put this theory into practice. It deposed the two Popes as heretics and elected a new one. But Rome and Avignon would not give in. There were now three Popes. Yet, although this attempt had failed, everyone remained certain that only a council could solve the problem, so long as the three Popes agreed to recognize it. From 1414 to 1418 the Council of Constance met, under the aegis of the Emperor Sigismund, and decided in principle to set itself above the Pope. It was made up of 'nations' — Italian, German, French, English and Spanish. Each nation could examine the major questions on its own. In the face of the council's determination the Popes of Rome and Pisa resigned; the Avignon Pope was deposed. The newly elected Pope, Martin V, was universally recognized. His successors tried to restore their supremacy over the councils and those held in Basle and Florence (1431–49) did for a time confirm it.

Heresies

The Council of Constance also undertook to settle Hussite agitation in Bohemia. Jan Hus, a theologian at the University of Prague, drew inspiration from the Englishman, John Wyclif (1324–84), who held that the Bible alone expressed the true faith and that all later texts were to be rejected. Holy Scripture was the supreme power, in matters temporal and spiritual. Wyclif condemned the wealth of the clergy and the monasteries as robbing the poor, and he questioned the Pope's right to raise taxes. His followers renounced worldly goods and travelled the country to preach. At Wyclif's death they were hunted down and took refuge in Bohemia.

At the University of Prague the Czechs clashed with the Germans, whose growing cultural influence they saw as a threat. The new rector, Jan Hus, who preached in the vernacular, enjoyed

❸ THE ROSE-WINDOW OF ANGERS CATHEDRAL
In the Middle Ages the art of stained-glass windows reached perfection. The master glaziers added colour to the molten glass, blew it to the desired thickness and baked it in the oven. When it had cooled, they cut it, engraved the details, added enamel and baked it again. They then assembled the coloured pieces of glass with lead strips and fixed them with metallic bars.

❹ JAN HUS BEING LED TO HIS DEATH
Ulrich von Richental: from the *Chronicle of the Council of Constance* (5 November 1414 to 22 April 1418). National Museum, Vienna
Jan Hus (1371–1415), preached the ideas of Wyclif and the reform of the Church. Excommunicated and summoned to the Council of Constance, he was condemned and burned alive on 6 July 1415.

THE ANNUNCIATION

Les Heures de François de Guise, 14th century. Musée Condé, Chantilly
The art of illuminating manuscripts evolved. Ornamental capitals were designed in a new style, Gothic or uncial. They took the form of interlaced foliated scrolls, with figures inside their loops, showing great decorative skill. The initial letters and ornaments invaded the margins and all the free spaces on the page. Gouache outlines replaced simple water-colour drawings, giving the whole picture greater realism.

② The internal voice

I will hearken what the Lord God will speak in me. [Psalm 85: 8]
Blessed is the soul which heareth the Lord speaking within her [I Sam, 2: 9] and receiveth from His mouth the word of consolation.
Blessed are the ears that gladly receive the pulses of the Divine whisper [Matt, 13: 16, 17] and give no heed to the many whisperings of this world.
Blessed indeed are those ears which listen not after the voice which is sounding without, but for the Truth teaching inwardly.
Blessed are the eyes which are shut to outward things, but intent on things eternal.
Blessed are they that enter far into things internal and endeavour to prepare themselves more and more, by daily exercises, for the receiving of heavenly secrets.
Blessed are they who are glad to have time to spare for God and shake off all worldly impediments.
Consider these things, O my soul, and shut up the door of thy sensual desires that thou mayest hear what the Lord thy God shall speak in thee. [Psalm 85: 8]

Thomas à Kempis, *The Imitation of Christ*, 15th century, Book III, Chapter 1

great notoriety. He adopted the ideas of Wyclif and, with massive support from the people, called for the reform of the clergy. When he tried to justify himself after he had been summoned to appear before the Council of Constance, the Conciliar fathers threw him into prison; and a safe conduct promised by the Emperor could not save him from the stake (1415). The result was a violent popular uprising in Bohemia, led by a radical group, the 'taborites'. Together with a more moderate Hussite group, the 'calixtans', they fought off a crusade against them. In the 16th century the Hussites were close to the Lutherans.

Mysticism

The spiritual life of the time often took the form of mysticism: it was no doubt encouraged by the rigours of existence, including sickness and famine. It implied a deepening of religious perceptions, in which feelings counted more than reason. By meditating and detaching themselves from the world, people could communicate with the transcendental from which they came. They had to lead a virtuous life and resist sin.

Mystical ideas had been current among theologians for centuries. In the 14th and 15th centuries they were preached in the vernacular and they spread from a number of centres in Europe.

In Germany, the main representatives of the mystical school included the Dominicans Eckhart, Tauler and Suzo. In Belgium, the mystic of the greatest importance was Jan van Ruysbroeck. At first the vicar of Saint-Goedele near Brussels and then Prior of the Groenendaal monastery, he wrote a number of works in Brabant dialect, of which the best known is *Spiritual Marriage*. In England, mysticism was mainly practised by hermits, such as the anonymous author of *The Cloud of Unknowing*. Catherine of Siena is the great exemplar of Italian mysticism. It was she who persuaded Pope Gregory XI to end the 'Babylonian Captivity'. Her writings are among the masterpieces of Italian literature. In the Netherlands, there arose at the end of the 14th century a religious movement close to mysticism, the *devotio moderna* founded by Geert Groote. After studying and leading a comfortable life in Paris, he turned to preaching and to renouncing worldly goods. Although they risked being accused of heresy, his followers, 'the brothers and sisters of communal life', formed at his request a number of lay communities in which they led a quasi-monastic life. Thus was established the congregation of Windesheim, based on the precepts of St Augustine.

The *devotio moderna* stressed individual piety

and intimate communion with God. It found expression in the work of Thomas à Kempis, *The Imitation of Christ*, completed in about 1427. It described the meaning for humanity of the love of God and divine grace. Written in the vernacular, mystical works like those of the *devotio moderna* were very influential in individualizing late-medieval religion.

③ GLOUCESTER CATHEDRAL

Gloucester became a cathedral in 1540. Its history began with the foundation of a nunnery in the 7th century which in 1022 passed into the hands of the Benedictines. The original Norman or Romanesque building was begun in 1089 and completed in 1160, then enlarged and reworked in the 12th, 14th and 15th centuries, finally being transformed by the addition of a great extension. The verticals of this Perpendicular Gothic style dominate the Lady Chapel (c.1500).

Cultural Changes

1 THE TRES RICHES HEURES DU DUC DE BERRY
The month of September, Musée Condé, Chantilly
The Limbourg brothers produced a calendar of 12 miniatures between 1413 and 1416. Through the agricultural activities depicted – here, a grape harvest – can be seen the love of precise detail and vivid colours. Those in the foreground were the work of Jean Colombe.

2 STRALSUND AND THE HANSEATIC LEAGUE
Stralsund, after Lübeck, was the most important Hanseatic town on the Baltic. The Town Hall and the Church of St Nicholas, built in brick, are typical of northern European architecture. The church was used both for patricians' tombs and for municipal meetings.

General evolution

In much of Europe medieval culture continued that of the immediate past.

Sculpture was at the service of architecture and devoted essentially to embellishing religious buildings. Sculptures, reliefs and Biblical scenes supplied rich decoration for church doorways and baptismal fonts. Funeral statues, recumbent images of the dead, were sculpted on tombs.

Painting was another form of ornamentation. Religious themes predominated. Biblical scenes appeared in Gothic churches and in their stained-glass windows.

A further form of expression was the art of illumination, as seen in decorated prayer-books like *Les Très Riches Heures* of Jean, Duc de Berry.

Architecture perpetuated the Gothic style. With more exuberant ornamentation, full of curves and counter-curves, like flames, it fully justified the adjective 'flamboyant'. St John's Cathedral at Bois-le-Duc is a fine example.

In England, the Decorated Gothic style of the 14th century was followed by the 'Perpendicular', owing to its emphasis on the vertical. In Germany, hall-churches were built, with the lateral naves as tall as the central nave, as in the Holy Cross Minster at Schwäbisch Gmünd. In the Iberian peninsula, the flamboyant style appeared later. In Portugal, the king brought an architect from Rouen to build cathedrals.

Lay architecture showed more originality. Town halls, hospitals, cloth halls, city gates and houses were often masterpieces of late Gothic. Notable examples include the Bourges house of the French merchant Jacques Cœur, the gates of Freiburg and Lübeck, and the Palazzo Vecchio in Florence. Bruges still has a number of fine patrician houses built at that time.

It was in the midst of a Europe suffering from the Hundred Years' War, from disease and from the grain crisis that two regions enjoyed a veritable 'golden century' of cultural achievement: the cities of northern Italy and of the Low Countries.

Burgundian culture

In the Low Countries, at the end of the 14th century, the court of Philip the Bold and his successors became the centre of a flourishing cultural life. The economic prosperity of the Burgundian towns made the Duke the richest ruler in Western Europe. Only the prosperous

Republic of Venice matched his wealth. Riches, and the appetite for luxury and refinement, created a climate in which culture thrived. Confined hitherto to frescos and miniatures, painting reached new heights, its colours enhanced both by technical improvements and by the use of oils. Now on wooden panels, pictures were portable.

The 'Flemish Primitives' of the Low Countries came midway between late Gothic and the Renaissance. But there was nothing primitive about their art. They showed perfect mastery of oil painting and of the nuances of colour. Detail became very important, often creating an illusion of reality. Symbols were frequently used: the lily stood for the chastity of the Virgin and the rose for charity. Melchior Broederlam worked at the Court of Dijon with Jan van Eyck until Philip the Good (1419–67) settled in Bruges. Van Eyck, the most famous of the Flemish Primitives, and his brother Hubert painted *The Adoration of the Lamb*, now in the Cathedral of St Bavon in Ghent. Mention should also be made of the Master of Flémalle, Dirk Bouts, Rogier van der Weyden, Hans Memling and Hugo van der Goes.

Sculpture, too, flourished at the Burgundian Court. Under Philip the Bold (1364–1404) Claus Sluter distinguished himself. A native of Haarlem, he was responsible for the doorway of the Carthusian monastery at Champmol, on the outskirts of Dijon, where he also carved the famous Well of

❸ THE RELIQUARY OF ST URSULA
Hans Memling, 1489. Museum of the Hospital of St John, Bruges
This is a superb miniature house dating from the end of the Gothic period – a blend of architecture, sculpture and painting as a setting for the relics of the saint. The painted panels are by Memling: like a strip cartoon, they describe her pilgrimage to Rome with 11,000 virgins. The three panels seen above show her embarkation for her return to Basle, then her assassination by Huns outside Cologne.

❹ 'THE ADORATION OF THE LAMB'
Polyptich by the brothers Van Eyck, 1432, lower section. Cathedral of St Bavon, Ghent
On an altar the mystic Lamb dominates the Fountain of Life. Around them are the Knights and the Honest Judges, right, and the Hermits and Pilgrims, left. In the background are the Martyrs and Confessors of the Faith, right, and the Virgins, left.

183

① GRANDIOSE AND REALISTIC SCULPTURES

The tomb of Philip the Bold, 1385–1410. Musée des Beaux Arts, Dijon

Begun in 1404 by Claus Sluter, the master of Burgundian sculpture, the tomb was completed by his nephew Claus de Werwe. While its architectural features were the work of Jean de Marville, the figures were basically by Sluter, who could reveal a state of mind simply by the set of the clothing.

② The Papacy according to Boccaccio

Jeannot de Chauvigny, a rich Parisian merchant, wants a Jewish friend of his to become a Christian convert. His friend seems hesitant.

'Listen, Jeannot. You insist I should become a Christian. Well, I'm prepared to do it; but first I want to go to Rome to look at the person you call God's representative on earth and see how he lives and how his brothers the Cardinals live. If they prove that your religion is better than mine, then I shall keep my promises: if not, I shall remain a Jew, as I have always been.' The Jew left for Rome. He settled there and began to watch how the Pope and his courtiers behaved. He very quickly realized that they gave themselves over to licentiousness with people of both sexes. When he thought that he had seen enough, he decided to return to Paris. Jeannot soon asked him what he thought of the Holy Father and the Cardinals. 'It seems to me that your Lord and his acolytes put all their energy into destroying Christianity and banishing it from the earth. But I observe that your religion grows apace and gains in lustre and magnificence. I think that this can only be the work of the Holy Spirit and that therefore it must be the one true religion. So nothing in the world could now prevent my accepting your religion.' Such was his friend's reply . . . .

Boccaccio, *The Decameron, c.*1350

Moses and Philip the Bold's funeral monument.

Music was another important part of Burgundian culture. Essentially, it was vocal and polyphonic. Its most popular exponent, Guillaume Dufay, had the official title of choirmaster. Religious music was taught in the schools of singing attached to many cathedrals.

The Renaissance and Humanism in Italy

The Renaissance began in Italy – a cultural awakening stimulated by the prosperity of the towns. Its central background was the landscape of Tuscany and the city of Florence: from there, it cast its glow over the whole of Italy: Umbria, Padua, Venice and elsewhere. Florence was in its heyday in the 15th century.

Italy retained many relics of classical antiquity, works by the Greeks and the Romans regarded as the summit of human achievement. Scholars from Byzantium such as Vissarion and Constantine Lascaris taught Greek and in about 1440 founded academies in Florence and Venice.

The word *renaissance*, like the Italian *rinascimento*, means rebirth. But the artists of the Renaissance were not content to imitate the culture of antiquity: for them, it was simply an important source of inspiration. They expressed themselves in all media: architecture, painting, sculpture, literature and music.

The philosophy of the Renaissance was known as Humanism. Whereas the Middle Ages in the West had put God and the transcendental at the centre of their thinking, the Renaissance focused attention on humanity and this world. The change affected scholarship: theology lost its dominant position and there was greater interest in people and nature. The study of classical texts, originally for linguistic reasons, now tacitly shifted to the study of classical values. Individualism began to replace the corporatism of the Middle Ages. Plato supplanted Aristotle. Humanity was held to incarnate the perfect image of God. Human nature took on an importance that was both primordial and optimistic, for mankind was thought to be by nature good. Humanism spread the idea of individual freedom.

The fruitful relationship between humanity and nature was reflected in a keen interest in science in all its forms and in the quest for universal knowledge. Such knowledge was no longer to be the prerogative of a limited circle of intellectuals, but with the help of printing (1455) could now be shared by a wider public.

Humanism arose in northern Italy, the home of Dante (1265–1321). Although he still belonged to the Middle Ages, as the founder of Italian literature Dante heralded a new era. In his *Divine Comedy* he described in the vernacular his travels beyond the grave. They took him successively to hell, to purgatory and to paradise, where he was reunited with Beatrice, his beloved.

Following Dante, Petrarch (1303–74) and Boccaccio (1313–75) stimulated interest in both innovation and classical antiquity. The Italian humanists did not write only in Latin, Europe's common language, but very often in Italian.

Boccaccio wrote his *Decameron* at a time of plague (1347–51). It described how seven young women and three young men fled from the plague that was raging in Florence and took refuge in a villa near Fiesole. There, for ten days they fought off boredom with music, argument, dancing and stories. Love and reason were the central themes of the book, which had immense success. Boccaccio found devoted readers among almost all his contemporaries, despite his book's being condemned by the Church.

From the 14th century onwards and especially in the 15th the princes and rulers of the Italian city-states surrounded themselves with artists and humanists. Following the example of the Medici, they founded schools and academies where great philosophers like Marsilio Ficino and Pico della

❸ THE GUTENBERG BIBLE
Mainz, 1456

A large number of Bibles in the vernacular appeared in the 15th century: 18 in Germany and 16 in Italy, as well as editions in Catalan, Czech and Dutch. The version most sought after was the Vulgate, in Latin, of which there were at least 163 editions, 71 of them in Germany, at accessible prices and with a reliable text. The above, from the presses of Gutenberg, is one of the most famous.

❹ Christian humanism

Let us return to the study of Scripture; it alone contains the teaching of Christ, free from any human taint. But we need preparation: the literature of classical antiquity offers it to us. It nourishes the mind and enables it to understand holy doctrine . . . . As well as the poets and orators, the Christian will study the philosophers and preferably the Platonists, who are closer to the Prophets and the Gospel . . . . He will approach the Bible with respect and veneration, certain of finding there infallible truth . . . . I have not written the Enchiridion *to display knowledge or eloquence, but to wean from their errors those who reduce religion to observances and external practices, and strangely mistake the true nature of piety.*

Erasmus, *Enchiridion*, 1504

① GIOTTO: THE FLIGHT INTO EGYPT

One of the frescos of the lives of the Virgin and Christ in the Scrovegni Chapel, Padua, c.1303–7

This fresco, ordered by the Scrovegni, was painted by Giotto (c.1266–1337) before he became supervisor of Florence Cathedral. Here, he is seeking perfect dramatic and pictorial unity, enhanced by the delicacy of the colours. There is nothing anecdotal. By making the figures in the foreground bigger than those in the background, Giotto uses the play of perspective. He was one of the first painters to be famous in his lifetime: he was praised by Dante, Boccaccio and Petrarch.

② THE DOME OF FLORENCE CATHEDRAL OR THE BIRTH OF MODERN ARCHITECTURE

This dome was a great achievement. It was the first time that an architect, in this case Brunelleschi (1377–1446), had built a dome with a span of 41 metres and 106 metres tall. It is octagonal, with two concentric domes linked by props, curved in such a way as to avoid the need for further reinforcement: it crowns the Cathedral of Santa Maria del Fiore.

Mirandola revived interest in Greek philosophy, spread by the printing press all over Europe.

Humanism and its new understanding of the world also encouraged a new aesthetic, concerned with the reconstruction of space. Architects began to use the elements of classical antiquity, such as the column and dome, as well as symmetrical façades. In Florence, for example, Brunelleschi (1377–1446) built the dome of the Cathedral that gives it the name of *Duomo*, redefining interior space.

Sculpture, which in the Middle Ages had been the handmaiden of architecture, freed itself. Religious themes remained important; but now sculptors borrowed subjects from daily life or mythology. However, the Florentines Ghiberti (1378–1455) and Donatello (c.1386–1466) drew direct inspiration from the work of Brunelleschi.

With Simone Martini and the Lorenzetti brothers from Siena, and the Florentines Cimabue and Giotto, painting threw off Byzantine influence. Masaccio and Piero della Francesca sought to place the human body within a defined space. At the end of the 15th century Florentine painting reached its zenith: Botticelli depicted the movement of the human body rather than anatomical exactness. Leonardo da Vinci was a painter, but also an architect, a sculptor and a mathematician. As a scientist he came close to the ideal of the *homo universalis* or universal man. When he left for France in 1516, it was a sign that the Renaissance had become European.

The 14th and 15th centuries were long considered, not without reason, a sombre period in European history. It seemed a time of uncertainty and confusion, marred by poverty and unhappiness, the grain crises, famine, war, plague and rebellion, as well as religious disputes.

Nevertheless, the period can be seen in a less gloomy light. It was a time of crisis, but also a time of hope. By the late 15th century, the population was increasing and the economy was growing. As modern states emerged, there was a new emphasis on individual experience, in religious life as in humanist philosophy. In the arts, the Quattrocento was the heyday of Italian culture and the harbinger of similar achievements elsewhere. In about 1450 the invention of printing and the use of paper instead of parchment made possible a new and very widespread diffusion of ideas.

These two centuries, then, which some considered autumnal, are now seen by others as a springtime in the gestation of modern Europe.

❸ DONATELLO'S DAVID

Bargello Museum, Florence.
From 1430 to 1440 this bronze statue stood in the centre of the courtyard of the Medici Palace. The delicate modelling, the free treatment of anatomy and the strange hair-style make it very much more than a revival of classical antiquity. It is one of the masterpieces by Donatello (1386–1466), the greatest Italian sculptor of the early Renaissance and an inspiration to Michelangelo.

❹ BOTTICELLI'S 'PRIMAVERA'

Uffizi Museum, Florence (203 × 314 cm). Painted between 1476 and 1480 for the villa of a Florentine prince
Botticelli here depicts eternal Spring in a celestial garden. In the centre, Venus; on the left, the three Graces and Mercury; on the right, Springtime covered with flowers. Everything here is light and delicate.

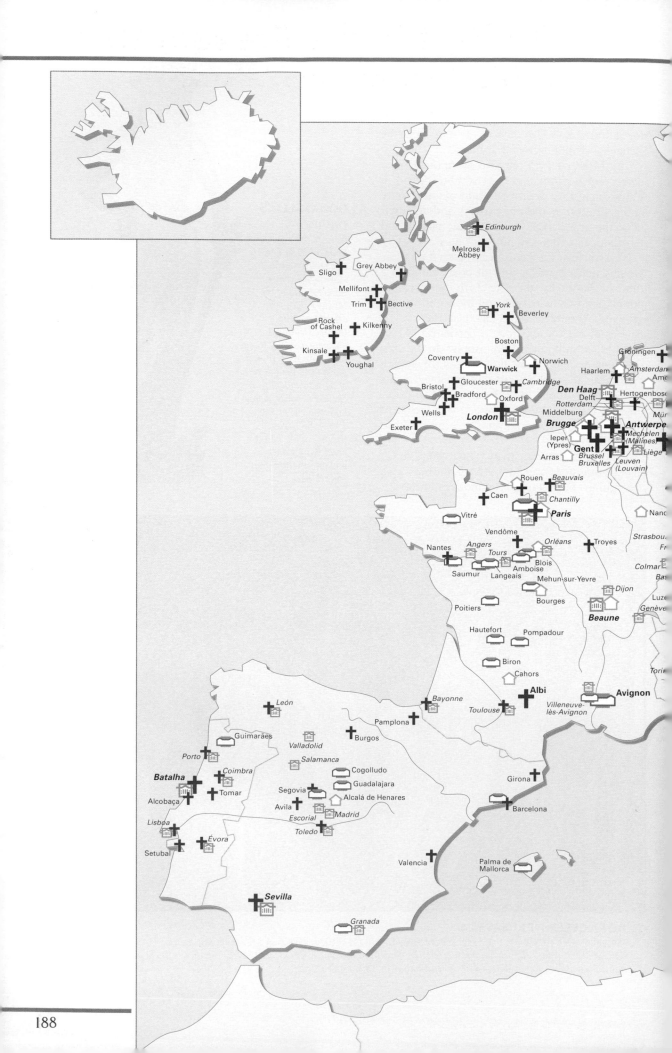

Edinburgh

Melrose
Abbey

Sligo   Grey Abbey

Mellifont

Trim   Bective   York   Beverley

Rock
of Cashel   Kilkenny   Boston

Kinsale   Coventry   Norwich   Groningen

Youghal   Warwick   Haarlem   Amsterdam
Ame

Bristol   Gloucester   Cambridge   Den Haag
Delft   Hertogenbosch

Bradford   Oxford   Rotterdam   Mür
Wells   Middelburg

Exeter   London   Brugge   Antwerpe
Mechelen
(Malines)
Ieper   Liège
(Ypres)   Gent   Brussel
Bruxelles   Leuven
Arras   (Louvain)

Rouen   Beauvais

Caen   Chantilly   Nanc

Vitré   Paris

Vendôme   Orléans   Troyes   Strasbou
Fr

Nantes   Angers   Colmar
Tours   Blois   Bas
Saumur   Amboise
Langeais   Mehun-sur-Yevre   Dijon   Luze
Bourges   Genève

Poitiers   Beaune   Tori

Hautefort   Pompadour

Biron

Cahors

Bayonne   Albi   Avignon

Toulouse   Villeneuve-
lès-Avignon

Pamplona

León   Burgos

Guimarães   Girona

Porto   Valladolid

Batalha   Coimbra   Salamanca   Barcelona

Tomar   Cogolludo
Alcobaça   Guadalajara
Segovia   Alcalá de Henares
Avila   Escorial   Madrid
Lisboa   Toledo
Évora   Valencia   Palma de
Setubal   Mallorca

Sevilla

Granada

188

The Past in the Present Day
CRISES AND RENAISSANCE

Legend:

- castle or palace
- secular monument
- religious monument
- museum, treasury or library whose collections cover this period
- frontiers of 20th-century states

500 km

Place names on map:

Linköping, Riga, Roskilde, København, Vil'njus, Trakai, Gdansk, Malbork, Rostock, Stralsund, Prenzlau, Tangermünde, Berlin, Warszawa, Brandenburg, Poznan, Torun, Halberstadt, Dresden, Wroclaw, Erfurt, Nysa, Tarnów, Annaberg, Bamberg, Praha, Krakow, Rothenburg, Nürnberg, Košice, Maulbronn, Stuttgart, Ulm, Augsburg, Landshut, Zwettl, Krumau, München, Konstanz, Salzburg, Wien, Budapest, Innsbruck, Verona, Vicenza, Bucuresti, Venezia, Mantova, Padova, Bologna, Ferrara, Prato, Faenza, Rimini, Beograd, Casaggiolo, Arezzo, Urbino, Perugia, Montepulciano, Orvieto, Dubrovnik, Dečani, Roma, Thessaloniki, Athos, Napoli, Dečani, Athinai, Rodos, Kriti

① HENRY THE NAVIGATOR

Panel of the Infanta. Polyptych for São Vicente by Nuno Gonçalves. (*c*.1460). National Museum of Ancient Art, Lisbon

This Portuguese Prince (1394–1460) was fully backed by his father, King John I, in encouraging maritime exploration. In particular, he took on a number of navigators to explore the west coast of Africa.

1434	Gil Eanes rounds Cape Bojador
1445	Dinis Dias reaches Cape Verde and Senegal
1469–74	Portuguese navigators explore the region of the Gulf of Guinea
1483	Diogo Cao explores the river Zaïre
1492–93	Christopher Columbus discovers the island of San Salvador off the American continent
1497	John Cabot reaches the coast of North America
1498	Vasco da Gama discovers the sea route to India
1499	Amerigo Vespucci enters the Gulf of Maracaibo
1500	Pedro Alvares Cabral reaches the coast of South America (Brazil)
1519–21	Ferdinand Magellan and Sebastian del Cano first circumnavigate the globe
1534–41	Jacques Cartier's voyages to North America
1577–80	Francis Drake achieves the second circumnavigation of the world
1586	Willem Barents sails in the Arctic Ocean
1608–15	Samuel de Champlain makes several expeditions in North America
1610	Henry Hudson explores the coasts of North America
1616	Dirck Hartog reaches the western coast of Australia
1642–44	Abel Tasman reaches New Zealand
1725–41	Vitus Bering explores the northern coasts of Asia and America
1766–69	Count Louis Antoine de Bougainville achieves the first French circumnavigation of the earth
1769–79	Captain James Cook's three voyages provide knowledge of the Pacific Ocean
1785–88	Pacific expedition by Jean-François Galoup, Comte de la Pérouse

② THE DUTCH EAST INDIA COMPANY'S FLEET

Painting by Albert Cuyp, Dutch School

This Dutch ship-owner is pointing to his caravels, at anchor in Batavia (now Jakarta). Founded in 1619 by the Dutch, the port gave them control of Indonesia by land and by sea until 1799, when the Dutch East India Company was dissolved.

EUROPE AND THE WIDER WORLD

15TH TO 18TH CENTURIES

③ A PORTUGUESE CARAVEL
Model, one-thirtieth life size. Naval Museum, Lisbon
Sailing depends on the characteristics of the ship. The caravel, 30 metres long and 8 metres wide, was particularly prized. On this caravela rotunda, with square rig on the two forward masts and a lateen-rigged mizen, the square-rigged sails gave the ship speed while the lateen made it more manoeuvrable, enabling it to sail to windward and skirt the coast against the current.

The discoveries that led to the overseas expansion of Europe brought about a revolution in the history of humanity. They overthrew traditional ways and opened up a 'world economy' that was a prelude to the industrial development of modern times.

Paradoxically, it was Europe that explored the world, although the Moslems, the Indians and the Chinese, all from the East, had begun to do so earlier. Arab ships had long plied the Indian Ocean; and the powerful fleets of the Chinese Admiral Zheng-He were active in it between 1405 and 1433. Then, for no clear reason, they stopped. The way was open to the Europeans.

As they spread throughout the world, they established great colonial empires, bringing with them European languages and ways of life. Their empires gave them political power and hence produced rivalry and tension.

The same process brought to Europe new plants and species of animal hitherto unknown to Europeans. This helped to eliminate or alleviate Europe's periodic shortages of food.

With Europe's overseas discoveries, capitalism developed and Atlantic trade routes became more important than those in the Mediterranean. There were also drastic price changes and serious social upheavals.

While slavery and the slave trade involved shameful degradation, the contact now established between different peoples in the world also led to the affirmation of humanitarian ideals and eventually to multi-cultural awareness and a new, dynamic view of the world.

④ NEW TECHNOLOGY
Naval Museum, Lisbon
The arbalest and the sword were indispensable to the sea-captain. The former, with an astrolabe, a chart and a timepiece, made up the main navigational instruments. The latter was a reminder that unknown lands could be dangerous. At that time every sea-captain needed both science and courage if he was to survive.

The Expansion of Europe: the Motives and the Means

① THE TRAVELS OF MARCO POLO

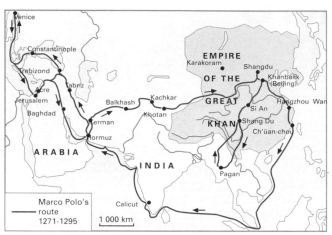

Marco Polo was the son of a Venetian merchant. In 1271 he embarked on a long journey along the Silk Road that led him to China and to the Court of the Mongol Emperor Kubla Khan in Peking (Beijing). Dazzled by the wealth of the region, he described the town of Hangchow (Hangzhou Wan) as 'the noblest and most beautiful city in the world'.

② IMAGES OF DISTANT LANDS
Drawing by Sébastien Munster, *Cosmographie universelle*. Bibliothèque Nationale, Paris

An example of 14th-century imaginings. Fed on such phantasmagoria, people feared meeting monsters when they explored.

The voyages of discovery were Europe's great 'saga'. Seeking new lands, the Europeans transcended their old view of the world, confined to their own continent and the Mediterranean, and lifted their eyes to the oceans. The mastery of new techniques helped them enlarge their horizons, transform their economy and alter their views of other peoples in the world.

The European world-picture

The Orient, despite its distance, was very much part of Europeans' mental picture of the world. Its attraction lay in its fabulous wealth, its jewels and precious metals and above all in its spices.

The taste for the exotic, which at the time was very widespread, stirred Europeans' curiosity about the strange and mysterious peoples they imagined living in distant lands. Medieval literary tradition, embodied in works like the *De situ orbis* by Pomponius Mela or Pliny the Elder's *Natural History*, mixed the real with the fanciful. Stories were told of human beings living near the source of the Ganges, who ate snakes and lived to be 400 years old, while others had only one leg but were exceptionally agile. . . . It was also said, on the basis of an apocryphal letter, that a powerful Christian sovereign, Prester John, lived somewhere in the East and possessed fabulous riches. Missionaries and merchants who had managed to penetrate this mysterious world before the fall of the Mongols in the 14th century brought back descriptions that whetted the appetite for adventure.

The extraordinary adventures of Marco Polo at the Court of the Mongol Emperor Kubla Khan at the end of the 13th century were described by Rustichello da Pisa in a book entitled (in French) *La Description du monde*. Its many different versions in various languages show how very popular it was. Jehan de Mandeville, from France, enjoyed similar success in the 14th century with his *Livre des merveilles*. His extremely fertile imagination evoked trees producing lambs and human beings with a single leg and a dog's head. Later, the chivalric romances picked up similar descriptions of these fabulous worlds, inflaming the imagination. The spirit of adventure was somewhat checked, however, by legends of the Sea of Darkness, where the ocean raged, the winds were terrifying and the waves gigantic.

Geographical 'science'

Was there really science before Galileo and Newton in the 17th century? Is it right to speak of medieval 'science', if that was based on reading authorities, logically analysing phenomena and empirically observing nature – but not conducting experiments?

Medieval geography, influenced by speculation on the part of theorists of the cosmos, maintained that 85 per cent of our planet was land and 15 per cent water.

The 2nd-century Greek astronomer Ptolemy, known in the West from the 15th century onwards, at least considered the problem of the earth's surface mathematically; but his geography suffered from underestimating the circumference of the earth. On his calculations, Asia was as near to Europe by the westward route as by the East and it was impossible to reach India and China by sailing round Africa; he believed, in fact, that the Indian Ocean was an inland sea. The Catalan Atlas of 1375, drawn up in the famous Mallorcan map school by the Jewish cartographer Abraham Cresques, continued to place Jerusalem at the centre of the world; but it offered a more realistic picture, based on Jewish, Moslem and Christian learning, and on information supplied by travellers and coastal guides. It showed Western Europe, the Mediterranean and the Black Sea with a certain degree of realism, but this was not the case for Asia, and southern Africa did

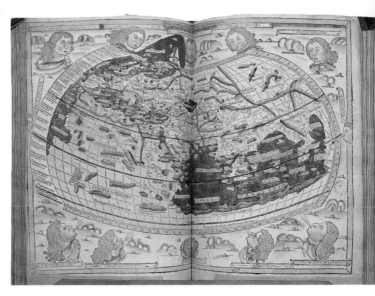

③ MAP OF THE WORLD ACCORDING TO PTOLEMY
Portulan by Gabriel Valseca (1439)
The discovery of the world could not have been made without maps, however rudimentary. The greatest astronomer of classical antiquity, Ptolemy (2nd century AD) came back into fashion. His Geographia *and* Cosmographia *were used to teach map-making.*

④ PORTULAN OF THE MEDITERRANEAN
Gabriel de Valseca. Maritime Museum, Barcelona
A portulan or portolan chart amplified a map for mariners, showing the layout of ports (whence its name). It should not be confused with a portolano, which contained sailing directions.

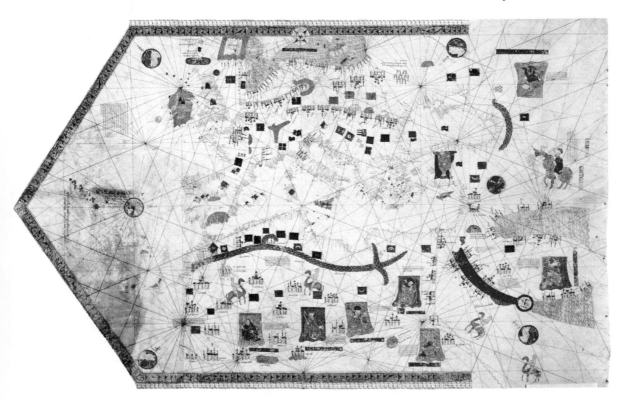

❶ THE ASTROLABE

Astrolabe belonging to Philip II.
Naval Museum, Madrid

Invented by the Arabs as early as the 10th century, the astrolabe was designed to interpret the heavens. It consisted of a round plate on which there revolved a largely cut-out disc, the 'spider'. This was a kind of map of the sky showing the main fixed stars, including the sun. It made it possible to determine the time of sunrise and sunset and the position of the stars.

❷ The Scientific Aspect of the Voyages of Discovery

It is clear that the discovery of coasts, islands and continents has not been made by chance. Our sailors were well trained and knew the rules and instruments of astronomy and geometry, all things of which they had to be informed, as Ptolemy says in the first book of his Geometry. They took with them charts precisely showing the compass points, unlike those used by the Ancients, who knew only twelve winds and navigated without compasses. That is no doubt why they ventured to sail only with a favourable following wind, following the coast as much as they could, as will be seen by attentive reading of Ptolemy's account of the Ancients' voyages on the Indian Sea. Our charts are very different from theirs.

Text extracted from the *Tratado de defensao da carta de marear* (*Treatise in defence of the maritime chart*), by Pedro Nunes

❸ THE COMPASS

Marco Polo, *Book of Marvels*

The compass originated in China. It consisted of a dial in the centre of which was fixed a moveable magnetized needle whose tip pointed north. It was brought west by the Arabs and used in the Mediterranean from the 12th century onwards. It was one of the most valuable instruments used on Christopher Columbus's voyages. It led to the drawing up of precise, scaled charts.

not appear at all. Portulans, or maritime charts, existed already in the 14th and 15th centuries. In Portugal they were known as *roteiros*: they described sea-routes. Portulan maps, already in use in the 13th century, showed the known part of the globe. Their origin – Genoese, Catalan or Portuguese – is still debated by historians.

Modern cartography really began in Portugal. Jaime de Mallorca, who arrived in Portugal at the beginning of the 15th century, was one of the founders of the celebrated map-making school. Until the 17th century, maps were drawn on parchment, with illuminations; but, from the end of the 15th century onwards, they included important innovations such as a scale of latitude, worked out from observation of the sun and the stars. In the 16th century, the number and quality of Portuguese map-makers were unrivalled in Europe. Their influence was such that in Germany, for example, they gave rise to Portuguese–German cartography, while in the Low Countries they inspired the famous Flemish school (1570–1670) of Mercator, Ortelius and Hondius.

Naturally, as maritime discoveries progressed, map-makers were able to show land and sea more realistically. 'State secrecy', practised by governments that refused to divulge certain information and severely punished anyone who did, probably slowed down the development of cartography. Not until the 18th century was the earth mapped more rigorously, owing to more precise measurement of longitude.

Technical resources

Countries and regions with good natural ports, and whose way of life depended partly on sea trade and fishing, were foremost in developing the sciences of the sea.

The Vikings were great sailors. As early as the 10th century, during their raids in the Mediterranean, they had collected geographical and maritime information from Moslems, Jews and Christians. It was to all of them that the Iberian peoples owed the crucial knowledge on which their great voyages of discovery were based.

To sail the Atlantic, however, technical skill was needed far surpassing the practical knowledge that sufficed for inland waters. The ocean stretched almost from pole to pole, with great climatic differences, and violent winds and currents. Here, the techniques of coastal navigation were not enough. To explore the coast of Africa as the Portuguese did, after a series of attempts of which some were fatal, required 'knowledge forged by experience'. On the way back, to avoid sailing against wind and tide in the northern part of the Gulf of Guinea, ships had to stand out to sea and use a system of navigation in which the compass and the portulan or the table of nautical calculations were inadequate. And it was vital to get back, to supply information and to profit from the voyage. So navigators had to understand 'the way the world worked' – i.e. the basic elements of the cosmos – and have some ideas about astronomy, to be able to work out where the ship was each day while out of sight of land.

They steered by observing the sky and reckoning the positions of the stars with instruments such as the astrolabe, the quadrant and the arbalest. This required knowledge of mathematics and astronomy, much of which derived from research that the Moslems had done in Toledo and from work by Jewish astronomers who had settled in Portugal. The instruments in question had probably been made known in Europe by the Moslems. But navigators also used books of sailing directions which gave rules and formulae for checking latitude by observing the skies. One such book, well-known to nautical historians, was the *Regimento da estrela polar*, written by Portuguese astronomers and navigators in the 15th century. It marked the beginning of celestial navigation.

A different type of ship, moreover, was needed to sail the Atlantic. This was the caravel, a revolutionary design which in some degree accounted for the progress made by the Portuguese in the 15th century.

It was easily manoeuvrable, could sail upwind and was intended to travel long distances. It had cabins for the crew and stowage for the food and drink required on a fairly long voyage. It measured some 30 metres in length by eight metres across the beam and it drew three metres. The rudder was fixed on the sternpost. The early *caravela latina* was lateen-rigged; but the ocean-going *caravela rotunda* derived its sail power from square rig on two forward masts, with a lateen-rigged mizen which made it more manoeuvrable and able to beat upwind.

The origins of the caravel are still debated. It may be a descendant of the Arab carrack; but its boat-building technique came from northern Europe and the Mediterranean. Later, nefs and galleons appeared. These were more imposing and better adapted to ocean voyaging, with space for more cargo and bigger crews.

④ CALCULATING LATITUDE
Jacques de Vault, *Les Premières oeuvres*. Bibliothèque Nationale, Paris
All that has to be done is to observe the height of the sun at noon, then use the corrective tables according to the date.

⑤ Life on board ship

Pigafetta, who accompanied Magellan on his circumnavigation, left us these details in his logbook:

Wednesday 28 November 1520: We have come through the straits and into the Pacific Ocean. We have spent three months and 20 days without any kind of fresh food. We were eating biscuits that were no longer biscuits but crumbs full of weevils and stinking of rats' urine. We were drinking yellowish water which had long been putrid. We also ate a few cow hides that covered the top of the main yard to prevent its chafing the rigging: but they had grown so hard, owing to the sun, the rain and the wind that we had to soak them in the sea for four or five days. We then put them on the embers for a time and that was how we managed to eat them. We also often ate sawdust. Rats were sold for half a ducat each (about 1.16 gold escudos), but even at that price they were very hard to find.

⑥ THE GALLEON
Manuel Fernandez, *Treatise on shipbuilding*. Naval Museum, Lisbon
The size of its holds and the power of its sails made it suitable for sending cargoes of Mexican gold to Spain.

Exploration: Spain and Portugal (The 15th and 16th Centuries)

① THE WEALTH OF AFRICA
Alkemi, King of Guinea, anonymous 17th-century engraving.
Bibliothèque Nationale, Paris
*Alkemi was one of the richest and most powerful monarchs in Africa.
He sent a delegation to Louis XIV of France to guarantee him a
special place in his country's trade in gold and slaves.*

② THE WEALTH OF THE NEW WORLD
Théodore de Bry: *Les Grands voyages*, Vol. III.
Bibliothèque Nationale, Paris
*Long before the traders in slaves from Africa, the conquistadors used
natives from the West Indies to work in the gold mines. Since
conquest was costly, there was no question of sailing home without
cargo. Gold, spices and precious stones were the booty sought after.*

What is often called the expansion of Europe, between the 14th and the 18th centuries, transformed the world. It opened new sea routes that brought peoples into contact with each other and put an end to the isolation of the world's different civilizations.

During the first phase, in the 15th century, the most significant voyages of exploration were made by the Spaniards and the Portuguese: Bartolomeu Diaz de Novaes, Christopher Columbus, Vasco da Gama and Ferdinand Magellan.

The beginnings

The expansion of Europe did not result only from the efforts of the Portuguese Prince Henry the Navigator, the audacity of sailors like Christopher Columbus or indeed the ambitions of the whole of Christendom. It originated rather with privileged groups in the towns, notably Lisbon and Seville. Columbus's *Diary* (1492), an authentic document, clearly reflected his motives: greed, certainly, but also a desire to convert non-Christians, inspired by the Franciscan ideal of brotherly love. A certain number of other factors also help to explain how the expansion of Europe began.

Towards the end of the 14th century, Europe began to recover from its economic depression, although it persisted in some regions until the beginning of the 15th century. The further growth of the population, and movement into the towns, created new needs which in turn spurred economic expansion.

The expansion of Europe was a way out of the crisis for the economy of the Iberian peninsula, which was unable to supply enough grain and meat to feed the population. Only a sizeable increase in farm and pasture land, with greater productivity owing to technical progress, could possibly meet the new needs. International trade with the Levant, which had helped the Italian cities to prosper in the 13th and 14th centuries, was in a state of crisis owing to Moslem intolerance. How was paralysis to be avoided? How were Europeans' eating habits to be maintained, now that they could not do without sugar and spices? How was the ever-expanding textile industry to get its raw materials and find new market outlets? How, finally, was money to be found to finance growing trade – and where were precious metals to be found to make it with and give it value?

Gold, which reached the ports of the Maghreb from Sudan and other parts of Africa, stimulating the European economy, was not used only to mint coins, to store in treasuries or to make jewellery: it was also traded for goods from Asia, where it was much in demand for ornamenting the temples, the palaces and even the clothing of the nobility. In about the middle of the 15th century, more silver was produced in central Europe, but it was not enough to meet the demand.

A further cause of the expansion of Europe was overpopulation in the western Mediterranean. Was there a link between this and the expulsion of the Jews, and later the Moors? Or between it and the wars of the 14th and 15th centuries, which weakened the economic power of the nobility?

Religion was also a factor that cannot be ignored. The role of the Church and the intellectual climate of the time ensured that exploration also involved a missionary element and almost the spirit of a crusade. In the early days it was the Franciscans who were in the forefront of this movement.

While these general reasons may explain the expansion of Europe as a whole, one question that remains unanswered is why Portugal pioneered it. Why did such a movement stem from a small country with only a tiny percentage of Europe's total population?

The answer undoubtedly lies in a whole series of circumstances. They include geography, sea-going tradition, mastery of shipbuilding techniques, political stability, the economic advantages to be gained by particular social groups, and religious motives.

The Near Atlantic

In the 13th century the Aragon confederation was already very active in maritime affairs; but it was not until the following century that Mallorca became an important maritime and map-making centre.

Expansion into the Atlantic began in the 14th century with the discovery of the Canary Islands: it is not known by whom. There is every reason to believe that they were reached by many different explorers – Mallorcans, Portuguese, French, Catalans, Genoese, Castilians and English. It is certain that in 1390 an Aragonese ship dropped anchor there and brought back a number of captives.

Later, it was Castile, with ships well suited to the winds and tides, based in its ports on the Bay of Biscay and in Andalusia, that came to dominate the Canaries. They became its major possession in the Atlantic, enabling it to thwart the plans of the Portuguese and the French.

❸ MISSIONARIES
A baptism among the Aztecs. *Codex Azcatitlan.*
Bibliothèque Nationale, Paris
To convert the Indians, the missionaries were obliged to set an example. They lived in total poverty, clad in homespun, going barefoot, sleeping on boards and eating roots. To teach the catechism they used pictures and mime.

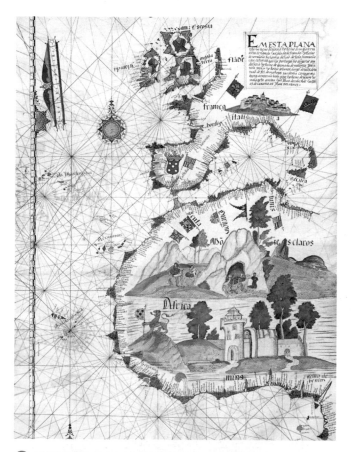

❹ EUROPE AND THE AFRICAN COAST
Atlas by Lazaro Luis, a manuscript of 1563.
Academy of the Sciences, Lisbon
This map shows how much cartography had progressed. Europe is easily recognizable, and though the African interior is vague, all the coastal ports are named, those in red being the major harbours.

① ATLANTIC DISCOVERIES IN THE 15TH CENTURY

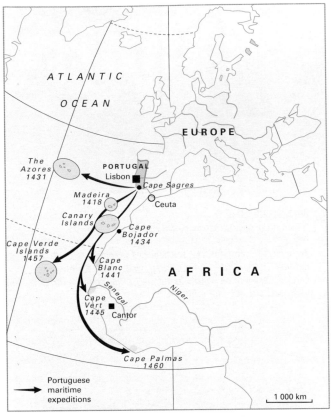

Portuguese
maritime
expeditions

1 000 km

② FRONTISPIECE OF 'AFRICA' BY PIGAFETTA
1624, Municipal Library, Versailles

Under Prince Henry the Navigator (1394–1460), the period of organized and systematic exploration began. This Portuguese Prince, who had a strong will and a great spirit of initiative, gathered round him people with the most diverse background and training, and inspired them with genuine missionary zeal. Jews, Moslems and Christians from different parts of the Mediterranean and North Africa made a combined effort to make a dream come true.

Prince Henry did not strictly speaking found a traditional school at Sagres. What he established there was in fact a 'maritime academy' of a new kind, based on practical navigation, improved shipbuilding and better instruments with which to fix one's position by celestial observation and also to advance the art of map-making.

The great epic began with the occupation of the Madeira archipelago. Between 1418 and 1425 the islands of Madeira and Porto Santo were occupied by Gonçalves Zarco, Tristan Vaz Teixeira and Bartolomeu Perestrelo. They did not discover them. The archipelago had already been recorded on Italian and Catalan charts as well as in a 14th-century manuscript. It is likely, therefore, that before the 15th century ships put in there on the way back from the Canaries.

The discovery of the Azores archipelago is still the subject of dispute among historians. A letter by Valsequa seems to indicate, however, that in 1427 Diogo de Silves reached the islands of Santa Maria and San Miguel. The islands of Flores and Corvo were not discovered until 1452.

The Atlantic islands, previously uninhabited, became colonial outlets for the Portuguese population and a kind of experimental laboratory for the Portuguese Empire. In Madeira, the colonists introduced the growing of grains, vines and sugar canes. Sugar became the island's main source of wealth and one of Portugal's chief exports. In the Azores, the leading activities were cattle-breeding, grain production and fishing. But equally important for the islands' economy was the growth of woad and archil, both used in dyeing and exported to Europe's manufacturing regions.

At the same time, but in a quite different spirit, Portugal began to conquer the towns of Morocco. It started with the capture of Ceuta in 1415. This city occupied a strategic position, dominating the Straits of Gibraltar and hence the sea route from the Mediterranean to the Atlantic. It was also an important crossroads for trade on the Moroccan coast: the caravan routes for Sudanese gold converged on it. It was the centre for a great grain-growing area whose produce could have met Portugal's unfulfilled needs. Unfortunately, however, the conquest of Ceuta and other

Moroccan towns disappointed Portuguese hopes. Not only did Ceuta fail to supply either the gold or the wheat that had been expected: it was soon a human and financial drain on Portugal's resources. All that its conquest secured was control of a strategic area and protection for both the merchant and fishing fleets and the coast of the Algarve, often the target of Moorish pirate raids.

In the 16th century King John III of Portugal decided to abandon these strongholds, isolated as they were in the immensity of the Moslem world. His grandson Sebastian tried to revive the dream of a Christian Empire in North Africa; but his project was defeated, and he himself was killed, at the battle of Alcazarquivir in 1578. This was one of the turning-points that marked the fall of the Portuguese Empire in North Africa.

Along the African coast

To sail down the coast of Africa, it was essential to know the Atlantic wind patterns. To the north, west and south-west, winds were dominant; in the tropical zone just north of the Equator, north-east winds; below the Equator, south-east winds; while in the temperate zones of the Southern Hemisphere there were the 'roaring forties', with very violent winds from the west. As well as the winds, ships had to use the tides when trying to find the most suitable courses to steer.

③ AFRICAN ART
British Museum, London

At the end of the 15th century the Portuguese visited Benin. It supplied more pepper and ivory than slaves. The missionaries encouraged the natives in their bronze casting, which they used to narrate their impressive history.

④ WORLD MAP SHOWING WINDS AND CURRENTS

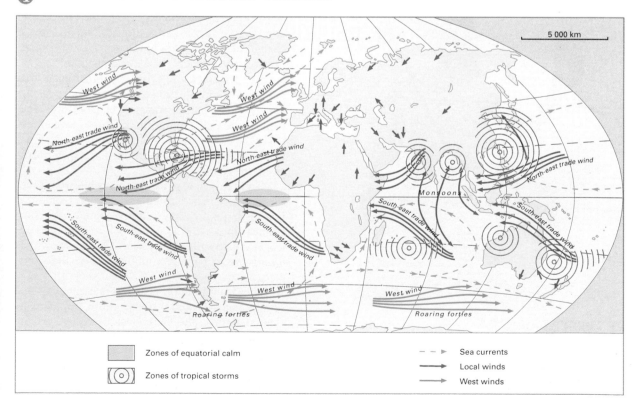

Zones of equatorial calm	Sea currents
Zones of tropical storms	Local winds
	West winds

① THE GREAT 15TH-CENTURY DISCOVERIES

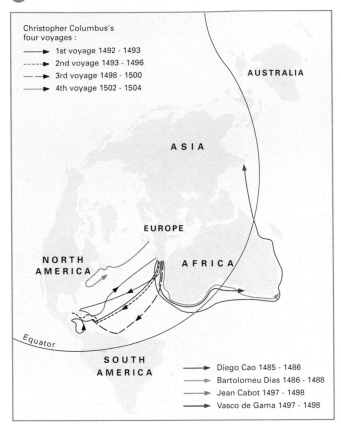

Christopher Columbus's
four voyages :

→ 1st voyage 1492 - 1493
---▶ 2nd voyage 1493 - 1496
→ 3rd voyage 1498 - 1500
→ 4th voyage 1502 - 1504

AUSTRALIA

ASIA

EUROPE

NORTH
AMERICA

AFRICA

Equator

SOUTH
AMERICA

→ Diego Cao 1485 - 1486
→ Bartolomeu Dias 1486 - 1488
→ Jean Cabot 1497 - 1498
→ Vasco de Gama 1497 - 1498

② PRESTER JOHN
Catalan Atlas, 1375. Bibliothèque Nationale, Paris

Prester John, Emperor of Ethiopia, was reputed to be a Christian, so Prince Henry the Navigator wanted to make an alliance with him against the Moors. Cartographers put his kingdom in Africa or Asia.

Navigation advanced by the gradual accumulation of such experience.

In 1434 Gil Eanes sailed a simple, traditional *barca* past Cape Bojador, one of the most difficult obstacles on the African coast, which had previously defeated all European sailors. After that time the Portuguese began to use caravels, which were safer and faster ships. They embarked on many expeditions and in 1445 Dinis Dias reached Cape Verde and Sénégal. The Portuguese thought that they had discovered the gold-bearing regions of Africa and the way leading to Prester John, with whom Prince Henry sought an alliance.

At all events the Portuguese were now on the threshold of a new, populous and wealthy region of Africa. From it they obtained gold, slaves, Malaguetta pepper and ivory, which they exchanged for European products. The 15th-century chronicler Zurara, in his *Chronicle of the Discoveries and the Conquest of Guinea*, pointed out that there were more and more trading expeditions to Guinea. This led to the development of human contacts, with the result that the explorers began to learn native languages and to teach local interpreters Portuguese. Diogo Gomes and the Venetian Alvise da Cadamosto, both in the service of Portugal, established trade relations with Gambia, one of the gold-bearing regions, and they sent some small caravels up the Gambia river. The Portuguese attended the Cantor fairs, where they traded European products for gold.

When Henry the Navigator died in 1460, Portuguese explorers had advanced as far as Sierra Leone. After that came a lull, caused not only by the death of the Prince, but also by a change of policy, switching expansionist efforts towards the conquest of Moroccan cities.

The navigators also faced new horizons in the Southern Hemisphere. To reach this part of the Atlantic, they had to traverse the Doldrums, the windless region around the Equator, with thick mists, heavy showers and tornados, as well as tackling the Benguela Current that flows north along the African coast.

During this time private persons began to take the initiative. The Crown gave Fernao Gomes, a rich Lisbon merchant, exclusive trading rights in Guinea. In return, he undertook to explore 100 leagues of coastline every year. This was how the islands of São Tomé, Annobón and Fernando Póo were discovered.

Under King John II Portugal's maritime expansion quickened and became more popular in character and scale. The enormous expenditure it involved was offset by the profits from trade. The Crown took the initiative of founding fortified depôts like that of Mina, where the Portuguese bought gold from the Empire of Benin.

In 1483 Diogo Cao reached the river Zaïre and established friendly relations with the King of the Congo. In 1488 Bartolomeu Dias realized one of the ambitions of European sailors by passing the Cape of Good Hope on the southernmost tip of Africa. He thereby showed that the Atlantic and Indian oceans flowed into each other. From a scientific point of view this voyage was very important; however tenuously, it showed that the prevailing winds in the two hemispheres were symmetrical.

At about the same time King John received important information from one of his emissaries, Pero da Covilha, who in the guise of an Arab merchant had travelled in the East. There, he had obtained valuable data about the fabulous spice market and about sailing in the Indian Ocean. With this knowledge the Portuguese now held the key of the sea route to India.

Christopher Columbus: the Europeans discover America

Christopher Columbus was one of the key Europeans in the history of the world. Supposedly of Genoese origin, he had lived in England, where he had gained experience in deep-sea fishing. He had also lived in Portugal, where he had married a young woman from a seafaring family.

Unaware of the prowess of the Vikings, who had already reached North America in the 10th century, Christopher Columbus relied on ancient and medieval sources, on the *Imago mundi* by Pierre d'Ailly and the cosmography of the Florentine Toscanelli, in his hope of reaching Asia, Cipango (Japan), by an Atlantic route which he thought would be relatively short. Such an ambition was adjudged unrealistic by the Council of Portuguese Cosmographers, because it ignored the true dimensions of the planet. The Council rejected Columbus's plans: it already had the theoretical solution to the problem of reaching India by sea.

Christopher Columbus also had difficulty in getting his project approved in Spain. However, the favourable situation caused by the capture of

③ CHRISTOPHER COLUMBUS (1451–1506)
Several versions of his biography exist. The son of a Genoese weaver, he went to Portugal in 1476. There he married and studied cartography. He submitted his plans for finding a westward route to India to John II of Portugal and to the Kings of England and France, but without success. Then the Queen of Spain conferred the title of Admiral on him and gave him a fleet of three caravels. He left Palos on 3 August 1492. On 12 October he reached the Greater Antilles. Having returned, on 15 March 1493, he was appointed Viceroy and left again for the New World. He discovered Guadeloupe, Jamaica and Cuba.

Administrative blunders and harsh treatment of the natives led to his being stripped of his Viceroy's title. He died in poverty after a fourth voyage along the coast of Central America.

A WELCOME FROM THE NOBLE ④ SAVAGES

Théodore de Bry: *Les Grands voyages*, Vol. II (1528–98)
This engraving encapsulates the simplistic vision of distant lands. In the bay Columbus's three caravels have dropped anchor. The natives frolic like children while offering to Christopher Columbus presents whose exotic appearance is wholly European. Nor is religion forgotten: three 'sailors' are struggling to erect a cross.

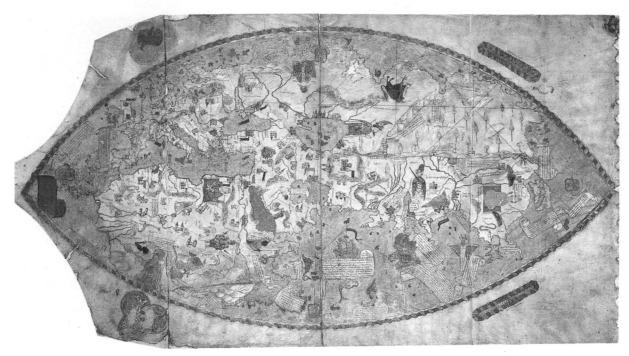

① TOSCANELLI'S PLANISPHERE
National Library, Florence

This planisphere was used by Christopher Columbus. But in view of its incomplete, indeed erroneous, view of the world, Columbus understandably insisted on taking with him astronomical and mathematical instruments.

② The Treaty of Tordesillas (1494)

Ferdinand and Isabella, by the Grace of God, King and Queen of Castile, of León, of Aragon, of Sicily, of Granada, of Toledo, of Valencia, of Galicia . . . . Thus his Highness the Most Serene King of Portugal, our wellbeloved brother, has sent us ambassadors and emissaries . . . to establish, to note and to agree with us . . . on what of the ocean that remains to be discovered belongs to one and to the other.

Their Highnesses desire . . . that there be traced and established on the said ocean a frontier or straight line from pole to pole, that is from the North Pole to the South Pole, which shall run from north to south . . . at three hundred and seventy leagues from the Cape Verde islands towards the west . . . . ; all that until now has been discovered or in the future shall be discovered by the King of Portugal and his ships, whether island or mainland, from that said line going eastwards . : . shall belong to the King of Portugal and his successors . . . . And thus all that has been discovered or shall be discovered, whether island or mainland, by the King and Queen of Castile and Aragon . . . from that said line going westwards . . . shall belong to the said King and Queen of Castile. . . .

In J. S. Silva Marques, *Descobrimentos Portugueses*, Vol. III

Granada in 1492, putting an end to eight centuries of Islamic rule in Spain, together with the need to stimulate the economy, persuaded Isabella the Catholic Queen to give Columbus the command of a small fleet of three caravels. Leaving the port of Palos in August 1492, he crossed the Atlantic with the help of the trade winds and approached the American continent. There, after 61 days at sea, he reached the island of Guanahani in the Bahamas archipelago, then put in at Cuba and Haiti. When he reached Cuba, he thought that he was in Cathay (China). After his return, he was enthusiastically welcomed in Spain and given other missions.

His second voyage took him to the Antilles. Between 1498 and 1504 he undertook two expeditions, during which he discovered the island of Trinidad and landed in Central America, in what is now the Republic of Honduras. Christopher Columbus had not discovered Asia, as he had thought, but – without realizing it – the great continent of America. It was owing to him that Latin America came into existence: the Spaniards and the Portuguese left in South America the indelible traces of their civilization.

Columbus's discoveries complicated relations between the two Iberian states. They became stable only after the Treaty of Tordesillas in 1494. This enshrined the principle of the *Mare clausum* and divided the world along a line of longitude at 370 leagues from the westernmost island in the Cape Verde archipelago. By this treaty, negotiated under Papal auspices, the true sea route to India remained within Portuguese waters. It was not until 1498, when Vasco da Gama discovered that route, that the Spanish authorities became aware of the geographical error committed by Toscanelli and taken up by Columbus.

Apart from its political significance, the Treaty of Tordesillas symbolized the victory of the experience, maritime knowledge and geographical understanding enjoyed by one of the protagonists, Duarte Pacheco, over the traditional book-learning on which the Spaniards relied.

Vasco da Gama and the sea route to India

Vasco da Gama achieved the great objective of Portuguese exploration: to reach the East by sea, thereby opening up a new spice route.

Leaving Lisbon on 8 July 1497 with a small squadron of three nefs and a supply ship, the expedition put in briefly at Cape Verde, then sailed broadly south in the Atlantic as far as the latitude of the Cape of Good Hope, profiting from the trade winds to sail past it. Vasco da Gama stopped on Mozambique, then at Malindi. From there, with the help of a Gujarati Moslem pilot, he crossed the Indian Ocean and dropped anchor at Calicut on 20 May 1498.

The Portuguese were impressed by the wealth of that city, set on the coast of Malabar, where trade was dominated by the Arabs. Vasco da Gama had difficulty in getting permission to trade from the Zamorin, the Hindu ruler of Calicut; but once he had obtained it he returned to Lisbon with a valuable cargo of spices.

The discovery of Brazil by Pedro Alvares Cabral was also linked to that of the sea route to India. King Manuel I entrusted to Alvares Cabral a powerful fleet of 13 ships, with the aim of imposing Portuguese influence in the East. The expedition left Lisbon in March 1500, following the same route as Vasco da Gama. But it went a little further towards the south-west, no doubt to avoid the Benguela Current, and it ended up, on 22 April, on the coast of South America, which Alvares Cabral named Terra da Vera Cruz and which later became known as Brazil.

Was this a discovery or a rediscovery? Was the fleet's long westward detour intentional? When King John II had negotiated the Treaty of Tordesillas, had he some information about the existence of this territory? Was it political secrecy, in which the King excelled, that had suppressed such information? To add to the mystery, maps dating from before 1500 seem to reveal the existence of land in this region of the South Atlantic.

After having explored a few miles of the Brazilian coast, Alvares Cabral set out for India, still the essential Portuguese objective.

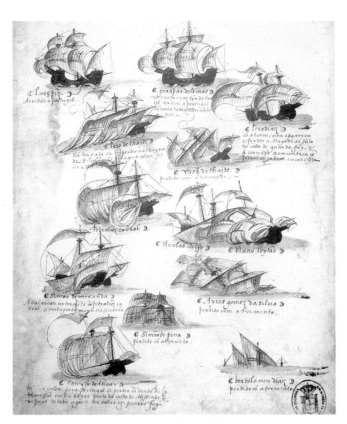

③ ALVARES CABRAL'S FLEET
Book of Fleets. Academy of Sciences, Lisbon
Alvares Cabral left in 1500 with a fleet of 13 ships to sail to India by rounding the Cape of Good Hope. After Cape Verde, he put out to sea boldly in a westerly direction, both to profit from the trade winds and to avoid having to sail against the Benguela Current further south. It was then that he discovered Brazil. Was it chance or a reconnaissance expedition?

④ BRAZIL IN THE 16TH CENTURY
Le Testu Atlas. Library of the National Defence Ministry, Paris

❶ AMERIGO VESPUCCI
Théodore de Bry, *Histoire de l'Amérique*, 16th century
Vespucci made four expeditions to the New World. It was Martin Waldseemüller, a German cartographer working at Saint-Dié in the Vosges who in 1507 used the term 'America' for the first time, thus ascribing to Vespucci the merit of having discovered the continent that now bears his name.

❷ MAGELLAN ENTERS THE PACIFIC OCEAN
Théodore de Bry. Bibliothèque Nationale, Paris
The astrolabe and the arbalest were the only instruments that Magellan had in this unknown ocean. He must have sailed there by dead reckoning. He succeeded, because he managed to find the South-West Passage, at the southern tip of the American continent.

Magellan: the first voyage round the world

Portuguese explorers did not remain on the coast of India, but pushed on to Java, Japan, China and the Moluccas, the famous Spice Islands. Other navigators sailed other waters, like the brothers Corte Real, who reached Newfoundland.

Spain, too, continued its expeditions to the American continent. In 1499, Ojeda and Juan de la Cosa, together with the Italian cosmographer Amerigo Vespucci, entered the Gulf of Maracaibo. In 1500, Rodrigo de Bastidas, La Cosa and Vasco Nunez de Balboa sailed along the coast of Colombia and reached Panama. Thanks to the natives, Balboa learned of a great ocean beyond the mountains. In 1513, he became the first European to gaze on the Pacific.

This confirmed the hypothesis already put forward in particular by Amerigo Vespucci, according to which the lands that had been discovered were not Asia but a 'New World'. By 1507 a cartographer in Lorraine had named them, in Vespucci's honour, 'America'.

To reach China by sailing west, then, it would be necessary to sail round the American continent – if such a thing could be done – and cross the Pacific. It was the Portuguese Ferdinand Magellan, in the service of Spain, who not only discovered a passage past America, but also achieved the most extraordinary exploit of that time: the circumnavigation of the globe. An experienced sailor, Magellan had served with the fleet that had been sent to ensure Portuguese domination of the Indian Ocean. Disagreements with the King of Portugal had led him to go to Spain, where he proposed a plan for reaching the Spice Islands without having to sail in Portuguese waters.

On 20 September 1519 he set out with a fleet of five ships on a veritable Odyssey. Before it was over, he had to face the violence of the waves, the stifling heat of the Doldrums, the cold and the cyclonic winds of the Southern Hemisphere, and even treachery on the part of his companions. After three months at sea he found the difficult and dangerous straits that bear his name, the passage between the Atlantic and the Pacific. The crossing of the Pacific was long and arduous: hunger and scurvy decimated the crew.

Magellan reached the Marianas Islands and then the Philippines, where in 1521 he was killed in a fight with the natives. The Spanish pilot Sebastian Del Cano completed the voyage. After crossing the Indian Ocean, he returned to Spain by the Cape route, with only one nef, almost three years after the expedition had set out.

It amounted to a double victory for Magellan, who had overcome every kind of natural and human challenge. As a result of his exploit, there was better understanding of the disposition of the oceans and the land-masses of the earth, while at the same time it was now possible to know more about its shape and size.

❸ THE GREAT 16TH-CENTURY MARITIME DISCOVERIES

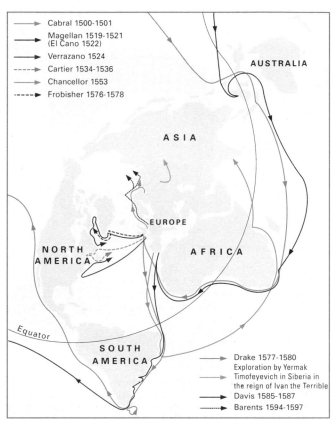

Cabral 1500-1501
Magellan 1519-1521 (El Cano 1522)
Verrazano 1524
Cartier 1534-1536
Chancellor 1553
Frobisher 1576-1578

Drake 1577-1580
Exploration by Yermak Timofeyevich in Siberia in the reign of Ivan the Terrible
Davis 1585-1587
Barents 1594-1597

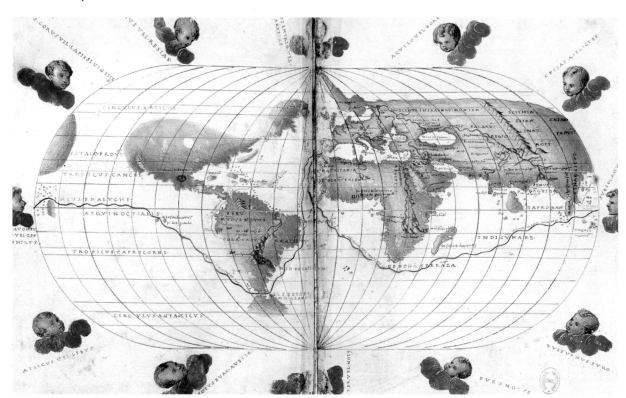

❹ AGNESE'S PLANISPHERE (1543) Bibliothèque Nationale, Paris
This map of the world shows the voyage undertaken by Magellan in 1519 and completed by Del Cano in 1522.

3 Exploration: Britain, France and the Netherlands (From the 15th to the 18th Century)

❶ SIR FRANCIS DRAKE

(1540–96)
English School,
16th century.
National Maritime
Museum,
Greenwich

He sailed round the world between 1577 and 1580, fighting and pillaging all the time. He brought back an immense amount of booty and Queen Elizabeth knighted him. In 1585, when hostilities with Spain had begun again, Drake destroyed the enemy fleet in the port of Cadiz and then led a squadron which faced the Invincible Armada in 1588. Greatly admired, Drake died of yellow fever during one of his expeditions to the Americas.

❷ THE PORT OF LONDON IN 1600

Cabinet des Estampes, Bibliothèque Nationale, Paris

In the late 16th century the port of London was at the centre of the world's new trade routes. The new Atlantic traffic gave it opportunities that were quickly exploited by ship-builders and 'merchant adventurers'. The Muscovy Company (1558), the Royal Exchange (1568), the East India Company (1600) and the Virginia Company (1606) helped to establish the first British Empire.

The expansion of Europe, begun by Spain and Portugal, had not left unconcerned other countries with a great sea-going tradition. The Genoese and the Venetians, despite their experience of navigation, preferred to send their people and their capital to the expanding markets of the world, in Seville, Lisbon, Antwerp and elsewhere.

But the English, the French and the Dutch tried to break the Spanish and Portuguese monopoly, before turning to the exploration of the Pacific.

Combating the Iberian monopoly (15th to 17th centuries)

Sailors from northern Europe then looked for a north-east passage to China to the north of the Old World as for a north-west passage to the north of the New.

From the late 15th century John Cabot and his son Sebastian, of Genoese origin, tried to find a north-west passage on behalf of England. All they achieved, however, was to reconnoitre the East Coast of America. In 1553, Richard Chancellor explored the coasts of the White Sea in search of a north-east passage. Between 1576 and 1578, Sir Martin Frobisher went on three voyages to the north-west, which contributed to the mapping of this part of the Arctic.

At about the same time Sir Francis Drake attacked Portuguese nefs laden with spices and Spanish galleons returning from America with gold and silver. Between 1577 and 1580, while trying to discover the mysterious Terra Australis Incognita, the Unknown Southern Land, he in fact made the second circumnavigation of the globe. After crossing the Atlantic and sailing

through the Magellan Straits, he went up the Pacific Coast of America and landed in California, which he named New Albion. He then headed for Asia and returned to England by the Cape route.

In 1585 John Davis discovered the strait that bears his name, linking Baffin's Bay to the Atlantic. Between 1586 and 1590, Thomas Cavendish achieved the third circumnavigation of the globe.

Breton and Norman fishermen had undoubtedly reached the Canary Islands as early as the 14th century and a century later had sailed to the coast of Guinea. In 1524 the Florentine Giovanni da Verrazzano looked for the north-west passage on behalf of France, but reached the coast of North Carolina and followed the shoreline north as far as Newfoundland. Jacques Cartier also looked for the north-west passage between 1534 and 1541. He reached Cape Breton and Anticosti Island, and sailed up the St Lawrence river as far as the Ile d'Orléans, outside what is now Quebec, thus discovering Canada.

The aims of exploration in the 17th century differed from those of earlier times. Economic interests were still predominant, but from now on scientific concerns played a larger part. Cultural change in Europe, the development of scientific academies, the more open attitude of certain universities and the spirit of inquiry among religious orders like the Jesuits or the Oratorians, all fed the desire to know more about the earth.

The United Provinces, led by an active bourgeoisie, became a great sea power, an important financial centre and a notable patron of the arts. The Dutch fleet was commanded by fearless 'sea pilots' who had mastered the latest technical devices, were skilled at reading the charts now produced by the renowned Dutch cartographers and had both an outstanding design of ship, the *fluyt* or flute, and exceptionally strong armaments. The powerful Dutch East India Company, established in 1602, and the West India Company, formed in 1621, gradually occupied areas over which the Spaniards and Portuguese had once had exclusive control and they traded in every kind of merchandise. Dutch exploration began to play a significant role from the end of the 16th century onwards. Willem Barents sailed in Arctic waters, while Cornelis and Frederik de Houtman, who knew the secrets of the Portuguese navigators, opened the way to the Far East by reaching Indonesia. In 1616 Dirck Hartogsz explored the western coast of Australia, while Abel Tasman reached New Zealand, Tonga, Fiji and the Solomon Islands, proving that Australia was not part of the Antarctic. From 1620 onwards Australia began to attract Dutch explorers.

③ THE GREAT 17TH-CENTURY MARITIME DISCOVERIES

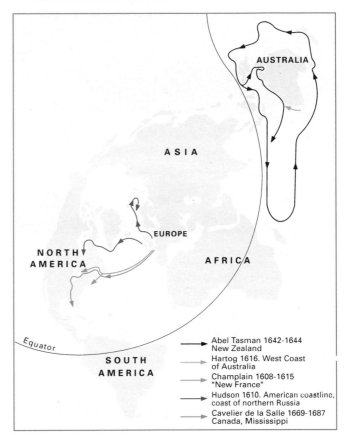

AUSTRALIA

ASIA

EUROPE

NORTH AMERICA

AFRICA

Equator

SOUTH AMERICA

→ Abel Tasman 1642-1644 New Zealand
→ Hartog 1616. West Coast of Australia
→ Champlain 1608-1615 "New France"
→ Hudson 1610. American coastline, coast of northern Russia
→ Cavelier de la Salle 1669-1687 Canada, Mississippi

④ A DUTCH FLUYT OR FLUTE
Maritime Museum, Amsterdam
This large supply vessel, with a flat, rounded hull and round stern, was used solely for cargo. It was broader below than above the waterline, because port dues were based on the breadth of the upper deck and ship-builders had found ways of making this as narrow as possible.

❶ QUEBEC

Anonymous engraving. Bibliothèque Nationale, Paris

Samuel de Champlain established 'a habitation' on the site of an Indian village. It was the birth of Quebec. Situated at the top of the St Lawrence estuary, it was continually attacked by the British. Besieged in 1629 and 1690, it fell to the invaders in 1759 and became British under the terms of the Treaty of Paris in 1763.

Henry Hudson, from England, undertook four expeditions in which he explored the northern coast of Russia, the shores of America and the bay that bears his name. The year 1600 saw the creation of the English East India Company, dealing in spices and other Oriental products.

Through Jacques Cartier, France became involved in the lucrative trade in Canadian furs, fish and timber. Jean Baptiste Colbert developed the French navy, offering premiums to ship-builders and making it easier to buy ships from abroad. Samuel de Champlain led several expeditions to North America, where he used great skill in making contact with the natives. He explored the St Lawrence river and the coast of New England; he established trading entrepôts and founded Quebec, opening the way to colonization in Canada. In 1682 René-Robert Cavelier de La Salle travelled through the Mississippi region and founded the colony of Louisiana. In the Caribbean the French occupied Guadeloupe, Martinique and Haiti, discovered by the Spaniards.

This period was also marked by piracy, a lucrative activity. Encouraged by the North American states, it aided the development of weapons and completely changed naval strategy.

Pacific exploration in the 18th century

The people of the 18th-century Enlightenment, devotees of rationalism based on empirical experience, wanted both to understand the universe and to spread culture and education to the whole of humanity. Exploration was no longer motivated only by economic interest: it was also inspired by science. As a result some ships gave the scientists who took part in these expeditions the resources they needed. Their research was concentrated mainly on the Pacific Ocean.

As the technical aspects of navigation advanced, it became possible to determine a vessel's speed. Optical instruments were improved: Robert Hooke was one of the first people to build a Gregorian reflecting telescope, while John Hadley invented his reflecting quadrant, which was in fact an octant: this made possible a more precise calculation of latitude. With the azimuth needle one could locate the heavenly bodies: the angle of dip gave the variations in the magnetic field, so that true North could be worked out. The chronometer gave the exact time at the home meridian and helped to establish longitude at sea.

These voyages were still considerable ordeals; but life on board had greatly improved. Scurvy could now be avoided by using lemons, celery and beer, all of which retained their vital properties for a long time.

❷ GREAT 18TH-CENTURY MARITIME VOYAGES

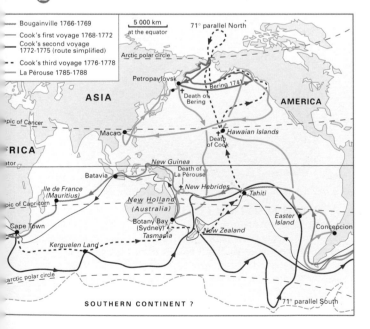

— Bougainville 1766-1769
— Cook's first voyage 1768-1772
— Cook's second voyage 1772-1775 (route simplified)
--- Cook's third voyage 1776-1778
— La Pérouse 1785-1788

5 000 km at the equator

71° parallel North
Arctic polar circle
Petropavlovsk
ASIA
Death of Bering — Bering 1741
AMERICA
Tropic of Cancer
Macao
Hawaian Islands
Death of Cook
AFRICA
New Guinea
Death of La Pérouse
Batavia
Ile de France (Mauritius)
New Hebrides
Tahiti
Tropic of Capricorn
New Holland (Australia)
Easter Island
Concepcion
Cape Town
Botany Bay (Sydney)
Tasmania
New Zealand
Kerguelen Land
Antarctic polar circle
SOUTHERN CONTINENT ?
71° parallel South

The great Danish navigator Vitus Bering undertook two expeditions for imperial Russia between 1725 and 1741, with the aim of exploring the northern coastline. Leaving the Siberian port of Okhotsk with a group of scientists, he sailed through the strait named after him, which divides America from Asia. The charts he made of Russia's Pacific Coast are very accurate.

The English explorer James Cook, following the route of his compatriot Samuel Wallis, tried to reach the great southern continent that was thought to lie south of the Tropic of Capricorn. Between 1769 and 1778 he sailed to New Zealand and to the east coast of Australia. He also discovered the Hawaiian Islands, which he called the Sandwich Islands, and the Antarctic polar circle. The scientists who went with him did very important work, especially in the field of botany.

Cook's voyages made it possible to draw an accurate map of New Zealand and of the Australian coast from the south-east as far as Cape York. On his last expedition, while looking for the north-west passage, he entered the Arctic via the Bering Strait. Blocked by ice, he returned to Hawaii, planning to try again the following summer. But in Hawaii he was killed by the natives, who had taken him to be a god.

Between 1766 and 1769 the French navigator Count Louis Antoine de Bougainville, with a group of scientists, made the first French circumnavigation of the globe. Louis xv had sent him to reconnoitre the great ocean between Asia and the American coast, and to find the legendary southern continent. He entered the Pacific through the Straits of Magellan, sighted Australia and sailed to the Moluccas. He left an important work on integral calculus, as well as an interesting *Voyage autour du monde* about his circumnavigation.

The expedition by Jean-Françoise Galoup, Count de La Pérouse, between 1785 and 1788, in which a number of scientists took part, was organized by the French Marine Academy. It consisted of two very well-equipped ships. La Pérouse sailed in the Pacific, putting in at Chile, Mexico, Alaska, China and Australia. The expedition vanished without trace in the New Hebrides, where some of its wreckage was not found until 1826: but its log had been sent from Kamchatka to Versailles before it disappeared.

By the end of the 18th century, then, geographical science had seen remarkable progress. There was better knowledge of the shape of the earth, slightly flattened at the poles; the form of the great land and ocean areas was now known, with the exception of Antarctica. But the interior of the continents, especially Africa, remained largely unmapped. To remedy that would be the task of 19th-century explorers.

❸ Hygiene, discipline and grumbles

Captain Cook used every means possible to avoid illness on board, imposing a minimum of hygiene on his crew and giving them a more sensible diet which included fruit. These methods, which he described in his journals, enabled him to save the crew's lives:

At first, the men refused to eat the sour-krout until I used a method which, to my knowledge, has never failed with seamen. I ordered some of them each day to dress so as to sit at the captain's table; I allowed all the officers without exception to partake of it and I asked them to leave their men the choice of eating their fill or not touching it. But the experiment lasted no longer than a week, for then a ration had to be given to all the people on board. In fact, the temperament and character of seamen are generally such that, whatever we give them that is out of the ordinary, although it be for their good, they will not have it, and nothing is heard but criticism of him who first invented it. But so soon as their superiors attribute qualities to it, then it becomes the best thing in the world and its inventor a very honourable man.

❹ LA PEROUSE ON EASTER ISLAND
Water-colour by Ovoje de Vancy
When the French arrived on Easter Island, the natives took them for their dead ancestors. The visitors took advantage of this to explore the island. Before sailing away, they left some presents unknown to the inhabitants: pigs, sheep and goats, among other things.

4 Building Colonial Empires

① LAS CASAS: DEFENDER OF THE INDIANS
Frontispiece of the first German edition (1669) of the *Brevísima relación de la destrucción de las Indias* by Bartolomé de Las Casas

Las Casas was a Spanish priest, born in Seville in 1474. Throughout his life he denounced the behaviour of the colonists and the company of the Indies. In this book he includes abuses by a German family to whom Charles V had ceded land in Venezuela.

---

② The colonies as markets for the mother country

The colonies having been established for the benefit of the mother country, it follows:

1 That they should be maintained as dependencies and protected by it

2 That trade must be reserved exclusively to the founders of these colonies

The colonies would not be useful if they could do without the mother country. It is a natural law, therefore, that the colonies' industry and agriculture should be restricted to specific products, according to the needs of the country that dominates them. If the colonies trade with foreign countries or consume foreign goods, the value of this trade is stolen from the mother country.

Article on 'Colonies' in Denis Diderot's *Encyclopédie* (1751)

The European states that explored the world by sea built vast land and maritime empires, not all of them on firm foundations. One reason for their weakness was the disproportion between their European and their native populations, the latter of which, especially in the east, were particularly numerous.

The Papacy, which aspired to international sovereignty as the spiritual guarantor of all humanity, had decided to intervene in the distribution of territory by means of the Bull *Inter Caetera* (1493), which divided the world between the Spaniards and the Portuguese. This division of the spoils, modified in 1494 by the Treaty of Tordesillas, convinced both Iberian peoples that their monopoly was something sacred. This is why they treated as pirates any foreign merchants and explorers who encroached on their territory. Francis I, invoking natural law, contested Papal authority by questioning its legal basis. In 1609 the Dutch jurist Hugo Grotius, author of the well-known treatise *De jure praedae*, wrote *Mare liberum*, in which he declared that the freedom of the sea and free trade, like the respect for treaties, were natural rights. In effect, this was a challenge to the theory of the *Mare clausum* on which the Iberian empires were based.

The role of Church and State in the Iberian peninsula

Spanish and Portuguese colonization took place essentially under the aegis of the state, although private initiative also played its part.

In Portugal Prince Henry the Navigator obtained the seignorial monopoly of exploiting the newly discovered lands. From 1474 onwards, under King John II, this became a wholly state monopoly and the government appointed overseas rulers. The senior representatives of the Crown were the viceroy in the East and the governor-general in Brazil. The Portuguese Empire was basically one long trade route along which goods were transported and whose nerve-centre was the *Casa da India* in Lisbon.

In Spain the Crown had absolute authority over the newly discovered lands and the natives were ruled according to Spanish law. The viceroys, supreme representatives of the Crown, had administrative and judicial functions. The *Casa de Contratación*, established in Seville in 1503, controlled all trade.

Spanish and Portuguese colonization in the 15th and 16th centuries was accompanied by marked economic growth. The demand for gold, silver, spices, wheat and slaves furthered the interests of the state, and vice versa. The colonizing urge was further strengthened by the aspirations of different social classes, and especially by rivalry between the bourgeoisie, eager to improve its position, and the nobility, anxious to consolidate and increase its privileges.

Colonization was inseparable from religion. The imposition of Christianity, often by brute force, led to the destruction of Indian civilizations and their 'idols'. But the Church and the missionaries did play an important role in aid and education. The colonists' determination to oblige the natives to do forced labour was opposed, often in vain, by a number of religious figures like Bartolomé de Las Casas and later the Jesuits. This attitude found a response among European intellectuals, from Montaigne to the 18th-century *philosophes*: thus there arose the myth of the 'noble savage', supposedly closer than Europeans to the state of nature. Spanish and Portuguese colonization was also marked by interaction in which the characteristics of European society, at first dominant owing to technological advantages, gradually mingled with local elements.

Portugal

Portugal turned its Atlantic islands into outlets for its population, adapting the methods of Mediterranean colonization. From the beginning, agriculture in Madeira and São Tomé was dominated by the production of sugar, a very profitable commodity much sought after in Europe. In Africa the Portuguese were more or less confined to coastal regions; in the richer areas of the Gulf of Guinea and on the east coast they established warehouses at staging-points for their fleets.

In the East, thanks to the action of several governors such as Alfonso de Albuquerque, they contested the Arabs' hegemony of trade, dominated the means of access to the Red Sea and the Persian Gulf, captured Malacca, controlled the Moluccas and, in the early 16th century, reached China and Japan. At Goa, which became the capital of Portugal's eastern domain, the town was planned on a Renaissance model and it was notable for the grandeur of its temples and palaces.

Brazil, divided into 'Captaincies', was eyed with greed by the French and the Dutch. To face this threat and give the colony a better administrative structure, the Portuguese set up a governor-generalship with the town of Bahia as its capital. Brazilian society was dominated by

❸ The Spanish conquest as seen by a Dominican friar

The Dominican Francisco de Vitoria attacked the methods used by the Spaniards in America, and even went so far as to defend the Indians' sovereignty over the land they lived on.

These demons devastated, destroyed and depopulated more than 400 leagues of ground where people were happy – great, admirable provinces, valleys 40 leagues long, pleasant regions, large villages rich in people and gold. They killed and totally massacred great diverse nations, leaving no survivors who spoke certain languages, save for a few who took refuge in caves and in the bowels of the earth, fleeing from so cruel and abominable a fate. In this way, using strange, diverse and new methods of cruel iniquity and impiety, they killed, destroyed and sent to Hell as many as (it seems to me) four or five million of these innocent peoples.

❹ PORTUGUESE LADY
Mogul miniature, 1750. Bibliothèque Nationale, Paris
Goa, capital of the Portuguese Empire, very soon became the centre of the new colonial bourgeoisie, notably owing to laws encouraging marriage between Portuguese and Hindus. In this way many low-caste women agreed to be converted to Christianity and marry Portuguese, thereby enjoying a more affluent life.

1 THE CONQUISTADORS

The arrival of Cortés as seen by a Mexican. Codex Axcatitlan.
Bibliothèque Nationale, Paris

For the Mexicans, Cortés and his men corresponded to a prophecy according to which the god Quetzalcoatl, who had gone to conquer new lands, would return with his descendants clad in golden armour. History soon showed how far Cortés managed to exploit this belief as a means of enslaving the Mexican people. By his side here stands his Indian interpreter Malintzin, nicknamed 'la Malindra'. She was also his mistress.

2 SPANISH CONQUESTS IN THE 16TH CENTURY

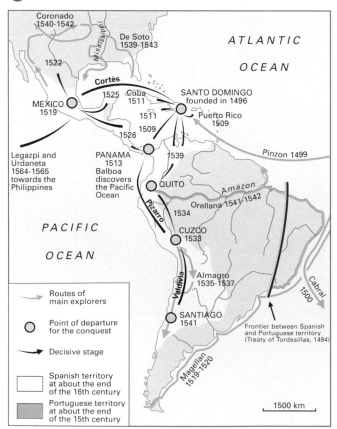

sugar-cane production, in which Brazil was pre-eminent in the world. It required a large number of slaves, who were imported from Africa.

Spain

With small but well-disciplined armies, and using canons and cavalry, which terrified the Indians, Spain managed to dominate three great empires in America. In 1519, with the help of some native tribes, Hernán Cortés defeated the powerful Aztec confederation and occupied its capital Tenochtitlan, a city of palaces, temples and gardens with a population of some 100,000 people. Francisco Pizarro conquered the Inca Empire, captured its capital Cuzco and took its fabulous treasures. Pedro Valdivia seized Chile, while in 1536 Pedro de Mendoza explored the region of Rio de la Plata and founded Buenos Aires. The conquistadors did not realize the greatness and mystery of the civilizations they encountered. Mistaking native idols for demoniac figures, they destroyed them and made off with their wealth.

The colonization of Spanish America, organized by the *Consejo de las Indias* and the *Casa de Contratación*, went through several phases. These included the exploitation of gold, silver and precious stones, and later the establishment of settlements which introduced European plants, animals and technology.

In the colonies the Spaniards applied the system known as that of the *Encomiendas*, whereby the Crown tried to attract colonists by offering them land and allowing them to make the Indians work for them, provided that they were also brought up in the Christian faith. *Reducciónes* ('reductions') were also set up: these were Indian reservations, in which the natives were confined and from which the colonists could recruit labour. Later, the Indians were replaced by black slaves. In these ways Spain not only brought wealth to Europe, but also created in Latin America a unique civilization, dominated by the Spanish language.

The role of the economy in northern Europe

In the second half of the 16th century, and more especially in the 17th, northern Europe, with greater economic and human resources, played an active part in expansion overseas. The English, the French and the Dutch profited from the political situation and from the weakness of the Iberian economies to build their own colonial empires. Seen in a mercantilist light, the colonies were regarded as a market supplying the raw materials needed for industrial growth and the products that the mother country either consumed or sold to other countries. The great trading companies, organized as joint-stock ventures and associations of merchants more or less linked to the state, controlled all overseas commerce and played a role that was decisive in the formation of their countries' colonial empires. This was the case with the Dutch and English East India companies. In France, the companies also played an important role, but the Crown intervened more, subsidizing their activities.

By that time the spreading of Christianity was no longer exclusively motivated by missionary zeal. Nevertheless, important missionary centres were established. In New France, for example, the Abenaki Indians of Canada not only became Christian but also allied themselves with the French, whom they regarded as brothers because they worshipped the same God.

Colonization by European countries shared a number of common features, especially as regards trade: the network of warehouses, the domination of strategic areas and the creation of settlements or plantations using slave labour. The colonies were an integral part of the realm and the legal system applied there was modelled on that of the mother country.

The Netherlands

Dutch colonization was closely linked with the mercantilist structure of the Dutch economy and the great companies that organized overseas trade. Batavia, on the island of Java, was founded in 1621: it became the transit centre for Persian silk, Indian cotton, Chinese porcelain, Japanese copper, Timor sandalwood and Moluccan spices.

The Dutch occupied vast areas in the East. On the eastern coasts of South America, they had warehouses in Guyana and the Antilles. Curaçao, off the northern coast of Venezuela, became the most densely populated and most highly developed of all the Dutch West Indian islands and the centre for contraband trade with Spanish America. At the mouth of the Hudson river, the Dutch founded New Amsterdam, which became New York when it fell into English hands. In Africa they controlled two strategic areas: southern Africa, where ships could put in on their way between the Atlantic and the Indian Ocean, and Guinea, one of the bases of the slave trade.

England

In England colonization was run by the great companies. The state confined itself to offering monopolies and charters, and laying down rules. Emigration offices were established to encourage

❸ The Bank of Amsterdam

It is in the City of Amsterdam that this bank is found, famous in all the world for its treasure and the greatest of all those that are known . . . . Observing this bank, one cannot fail to reflect that its treasure is great, owing to the great number of gold and silver ingots and the infinite number of bags that seem to be full of metal, silver and gold . . . .

Confidence in the Bank does not rest solely on gold and silver, but also on the credit which it grants to all the City and State of Amsterdam, whose capital is greater than that of many kingdoms. It is pledged indeed to reimburse all monies that are deposited there. Large payments between merchants are made by means of banknotes, and not only in the different towns of the province, but also in many other trading cities in the world. It can thus be said that this bank is truly a great coffer where everyone deposes his money, because he finds there greater security and greater ease of use than if he were to keep it in his own coffers.

William Temple, *Observations upon the United Provinces,* 1673

❹ THE DUTCH COLONIAL EMPIRE IN THE MID-17TH CENTURY

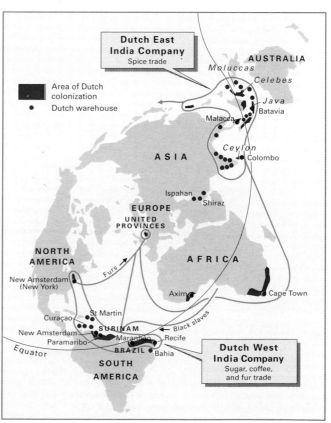

Dutch East India Company — Spice trade

Area of Dutch colonization
• Dutch warehouse

AUSTRALIA
Moluccas
Celebes
Java
Batavia
Malacca
Ceylon
Colombo
ASIA
Ispahan
Shiraz
EUROPE
UNITED PROVINCES
NORTH AMERICA
Furs
AFRICA
New Amsterdam (New York)
Axim
Cape Town
St Martin
Curaçao
Black slaves
New Amsterdam
Paramaribo
SURINAM
Maranhão
Recife
BRAZIL
Bahia
Equator
SOUTH AMERICA
Dutch West India Company — Sugar, coffee, and fur trade

❶ THE PURITANS

Puritans leaving the port of Delft to board the *Mayflower* on
the way to the coast of New England. Adam van Breen, 1620.
Terry Engel Gallery, London

*Persecuted for their non-conformist practices, 100 Puritans left
England on a ship chartered at Southampton, heading for America.
After 70 days at sea, they landed in what they called New England.*

❷ 'ENGLISH' CALCUTTA IN 1788

Engraving by Thomas Daniell

*This port in eastern India was founded by English merchants in
1690. It became the headquarters of the English East India
Company. Its position on a branch of the Ganges, where the Bengal
plains open out to the sea 150 kilometres downstream, made it a
very sheltered port for both merchant ships and junks.*

people to settle in the colonies, especially in the
New World.

In 1587 Walter Raleigh founded in America a
settler colony that he called Virginia, in homage
to Queen Elizabeth. But it was not until the 17th
century that colonization of the New World
began in earnest. It was marked by slow progress
westward, which continued throughout the 18th
century.

In 1620 a small group of emigrants, mostly
Puritans persecuted for their religion, landed in
America aboard the *Mayflower*. Europe's religious problems, the Thirty Years' War, the English Civil War and the rule of Oliver Cromwell,
persecution, the English Revolution and the custom of deporting criminals – all these fostered
large-scale migration to North America and the
growth of new colonies. Settler colonies were
established in the temperate zones, while plantations were formed in tropical regions. The great
sugar, rice and cotton plantations needed a large
labour force, so the colonists used slaves.

In the Indian Ocean, the English set up warehouses along the Malabar and Coromandel
coasts. They also occupied Madras and areas in
Bengal and, later, along the Ganges. British
domination in Asia was largely the work of the
East India Company, which took advantage of
the decline of rival colonial empires to occupy
more and more key regions.

France

French colonization began in the 16th century
with Jacques Cartier; but it was the great explorer
Samuel de Champlain who at the beginning of the
17th century founded New France. Cardinal
Richelieu tried to settle colonists in this vast area
with its inhospitable climate by setting up the
Company of 100 Associates and giving it a
monopoly of the lucrative fur trade. Under Jean-
Baptiste Colbert, French colonization took on a
new dimension, with the establishment of companies like those of the North (the Baltic), the
Levant, Sénégal and the East and West Indies. By
the second half of the 17th century France was the
world's third biggest maritime trader.

The French colonies were governed on the
institutional model of the mother country. In
New France there was a seignorial regime. The
French settled in Haiti, Martinique and Guadeloupe, developing there commerce with the
mother country, contraband dealings with the
Spanish colonies and trade in slaves. In Louisiana
they established plantations, mainly producing
sugar, tobacco and dye-plants.

In India, the city of Pondicherry became an
important centre, but passed under English con-

trol in 1761. France also spread its influence to Morocco and Black Africa, where it founded the colonies of St Louis in Sénégal and Fort-Dauphin (now Faradofay) in Madagascar.

Rivalry between the English and the Dutch in the 17th century was followed by a struggle for supremacy between the English, anxious to preserve their colonial empire, and the French, who were more keenly aware of conflicts in Europe.

Hostilities broke out in the French and English colonies in the New World. They spread to Asia and Africa; and France and Britain fought each other in the Seven Years' War, in which other European countries also took part. By the Treaty of Paris in 1763 France ceded Canada to England, as well as the vast stretches of land between the Mississippi and the Great Lakes, Sénégal and a large part of its possessions in India. England, Queen of the Seas, became the world's greatest colonial power.

The maritime states were not alone in undertaking exploration with expansionist overtones. In the 16th century, in the reign of Ivan the Terrible, the Cossack Ataman, Yermak, conquered western Siberia. By the mid-17th century, most of the country had been broadly mapped and explorers had reached the Sea of Okhotsk. Siberia supplied Russia with furs, which were exacted from the natives as a form of tribute (*yassak*). Serious exploitation of the country's resources did not take place until the 19th century.

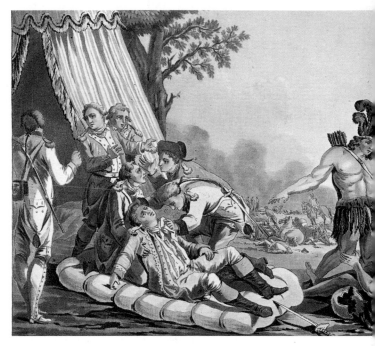

③ THE DEATH OF MONTCALM (1712–59)
History of North America, 18th century. Cabinet des Estampes, Bibliothèque Nationale, Paris
General Montcalm, commander of the French troops in New France (Canada) in 1756, was mortally wounded in the defence of Quebec, as was General James Wolfe, the commander of the British troops. The English capture of Quebec, and later of Montreal, led to the cession of New France to England.

④ COLONIAL EMPIRES AND TRIANGULAR TRADE PATTERNS, 1750 ONWARDS

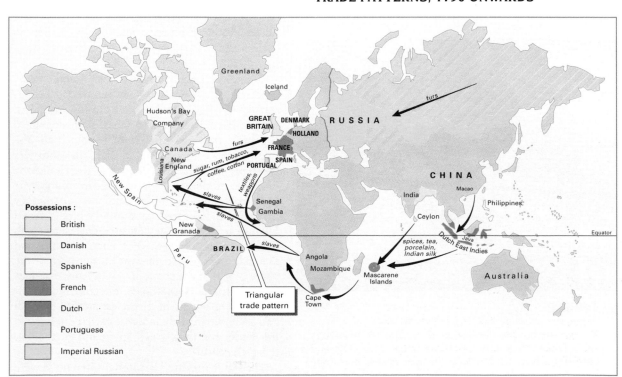

Possessions:
- British
- Danish
- Spanish
- French
- Dutch
- Portuguese
- Imperial Russian

5 A World-Scale Economy

❷ SEVILLE
Painting by Francisco Pacheco, 16th century. Madrid
At the crossroads of the Mediterranean and Atlantic trade routes, Seville became the most important commercial centre in Spain. The Casa de Contratación or House of Trade ensured its prosperity.

New economic horizons

Economic change on a world scale breathed new life into capitalism. The main economic focus shifted from the Mediterranean to the Atlantic and in the first half of the 16th century transatlantic trade grew apace, concentrating on the ports of Lisbon and Seville. These two towns supplied the market of Antwerp, which in turn supplied the great international trading companies. The main products, especially spices, African gold and American silver, were traded at Antwerp for manufactured goods which went to the markets of Spain and Portugal, and above all into overseas trade.

Between 1500 and 1620 the average level of prices in Europe rose by 300 to 400 per cent. This revolutionary price-rise was caused by the expansion of trade, the increase in the money supply owing to the influx of precious metals from overseas, the increase in demand for agricultural products which suppliers could not satisfy, the rise in the standard of living and the development of industry in northern Europe. Profits from trade and increased income led to greater investment, which in turn stimulated economic growth. Gold and silver, while contributing to international trade, encouraged Europe to live beyond its means and to spend more than it saved. This was why, given the growing demand for money, all the Antwerp banking institutions, leaders in their field in Europe, lent only at high rates of interest.

The 16th century seemed to be a golden age, especially for Spain, which received fabulous quantities of gold and silver from the Americas. More than Portugal, which had been unable to organize trading companies, Spain had the opportunity of becoming, in the 17th century, a great economic centre. It let slip the chance by failing to modernize its industry. The bourgeoisie preferred to buy land, while the aristocracy squandered its capital on luxury. As a result Spanish gold and silver were invested elsewhere in Europe, to the benefit of French, English and Dutch industries. North-west Europe became the nerve centre of the economy, with Amsterdam as its capital. The Netherlands, England and northern France, which had real economic, cultural and technological dynamism, suffered less from the depression that struck Spain and Portugal in the 17th century.

The staple products in international trade were

textiles and sugar, whose consumption continually grew. It was now that a triangular trade pattern began to emerge more clearly: European products were exchanged in Africa for slaves intended for the American plantations, and the ships that transported them brought back to Europe cargoes of sugar, tobacco and cotton.

The 18th century, during which London became the hub of world trade, saw a commercial revolution, dominated by trade with the colonies. Owing to this, French and English trade tripled between 1700 and 1770.

There was an increase, too, in shipments of precious metals – silver from Spanish America and gold from Brazil – and in the triangular trade in general. This tended to increase the numbers of slaves on the American plantations and the social and humanitarian problems involved. The world economy reflected the supremacy of Europe: it helped to increase the power of the United States and the bourgeoisie, and it revealed the decadence of the landed aristocracy and the weakness of the peasantry.

Innovation and trade in agriculture

The expansion of Europe also brought about great changes in the agricultural field. European techniques were introduced into the New World and plants and animals were exchanged between continents. This made a decisive contribution to surmounting or attenuating food crises.

Plants introduced and grown in Europe improved people's diet, curbed famine and helped increase the population. Particularly important in this respect were maize and potatoes, both from America. Beans, tomatoes and pumpkins also made for a more varied diet, as did imported products such as coffee, cocoa, vanilla, tea and spices.

At the same time the Europeans profoundly changed the American economy by introducing horses, sheep, cattle, cereals, vines, olives, sugar canes, coffee and rice.

In Africa the Europeans acclimatized wheat, cassava, beans, cashews, passion fruit, yams, rice and tea. In China they introduced American species such as groundnuts and maize. Large-scale production of maize, indeed, partly explains the growth of population there from the 16th century onwards.

③ THE SLAVE TRADE
18th century, anonymous
Traffic in slaves made the fortune of African kings, who skilfully used the competition among Europeans to push up prices. In ten years Guinea supplied some 50,000 slaves to the Spanish colonies in America.

④ SLAVES AND SUGAR CANE
18th-century engraving
Sugar cane developed rapidly owing to the enormous consumption of sweet things. It was one of the main products of Brazil, which to maximize profits employed slave labour. Some 70 per cent of the slaves brought from Africa ended up on Brazilian plantations.

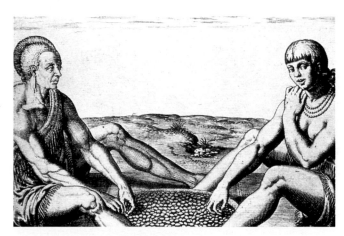

⑤ MAYAS SORTING COCOA
The cocoa tree is delicate: growing between four and ten metres tall, it requires a lot of heat, humidity and shade, and a soil rich in potash sheltered from the wind. Only the Mayas knew the quality of the 25 to 40 seeds contained in the large berries, known as pods. They agreed to initiate the Spaniards and Portuguese into the properties of cocoa, and the initiates kept the secret for a long time.

Civilizations Confront Each Other

① THE BELEM TOWER, LISBON
This is one of the most impressive examples of Portugal's golden age. Built on an island in the Tagus estuary, the façade of the fortress faces the water. It is a jewel of Romano-Gothic style, whose Moorish decoration was imported from Safi.

② BRAZILIAN BAROQUE
Cathedral do Pilar, 1704. Minas Geraïs
In this mining country, born of the gold and diamond rush, Baroque exuberance flourished as much in villas as in religious buildings. The Jesuits adopted the style with alacrity: nothing was too beautiful to thank God for His largesse.

When the meeting of civilizations did not destroy the peoples who were colonized, there could be a degree of interchange and mutual influence.

It was missionaries, colonists, officials and merchants who spread European culture, without always understanding local realities that were far removed from their own conceptions.

The world-wide use of certain European languages is one result of such culture-contact. Missionaries made important contributions to linguistic interchange, studying native languages, codifying their rules and vocabulary, and publishing grammars and dictionaries.

Science and technology

The superiority of European technology, and its spread among the native peoples, made obsolete some of the tools that had been evolved over the centuries by more vulnerable civilizations. But the Europeans could also learn from local technology. During his voyage to India Vasco da Gama exchanged maritime expertise with a Moslem pilot from Gujarat. Without his help, he would have found it harder to cross the Indian Ocean. In the same way the Portuguese would never have reached Canton so quickly if they had not been helped by local pilots – Arabs, Malays, Gujaratis and so on. And many explorers' expeditions were only possible with the help of native guides.

The expansion of Europe also contributed to scientific progress. Knowledge was revolutionized by the great spread of discoveries made in disciplines such as astronomy, mathematics, geography, botany and medicine, as well as by new thinking about slavery and colonization. In medicine, for example, a number of works informed their readers about the plants used by natives of Asia and America. The ideas of Copernicus and Galileo reached Japan through Chinese books printed in Peking by Jesuit missionaries.

The arts

In the arts, European and local sensibilities blended. The churches, fortresses and palaces that Europeans built overseas, in Renaissance, Mannerist, Baroque or neo-Baroque styles, reflected their own conceptions, but they also involved local elements.

Many of the buildings in Latin America and the East were designed in the style of colonial Baroque, whose extravagant ornament made it a powerful symbol of the state's authority. In the 18th century, in reaction against the Baroque, especially in North America, the Georgian style was favoured for its classical simplicity.

By making known European painting, engraving and sculpture, and training local artists, missionaries played an essential role in spreading the techniques and tastes of the 'Old World'. In this way themes treated by African, Asian and Native American artists were linked with Europe.

But the traffic was not all one way. Oriental artistic creations inspired, in Europe, the multicoloured decoration of porcelain and furniture, the building of Chinese pavilions and gardens.

Literature was enriched with new themes. Travel writers described distant lands and the customs of their inhabitants – as did William Dampier, author of *Voyage around the World*, written in 1697, who in the course of his voyages rescued Alexander Selkirk, who had been marooned for four years on Juan Fernandez Island and who inspired Daniel Defoe's famous novel *Robinson Crusoe* (translated into several languages). Count Louis Antoine de Bougainville, who combined his skill as a navigator with his training as a scientist, wrote an interesting *Voyage autour du monde*. In Italy in the 17th century a whole school of travel writing developed, much consulted by merchants. In Vienna, an academy was founded to study the curiosities of nature. Ships' logs also gave valuable information about their voyages and the cultural contact between civilizations. The epic *Os Lusíadas*, or *The Lusiads*, by the Portuguese poet Luis de Camões (1572), in which European culture is blended with Oriental experience, is a great poetic exploration of humanism.

A *universal dimension*

The voyages of discovery were one of humanity's great adventures. They revealed that the world was larger than had been imagined. Europeans had now met peoples little known to them, and in many cases not known at all.

The Europeans' arrival had been a shock from which some native societies, as in the Caribbean, never recovered. In other cases, as in the Amerindian empires, there was simply a change of rulers. The most ancient civilizations, in the Indies and in China, were better able to resist. But the slave trade decimated the peoples of Black Africa.

In the longer term, however, Europe's preponderance gradually gave way to reciprocal influence, and the confrontation of civilizations evolved in the direction of a better understanding of the human family as a whole.

③ CUZCO CATHEDRAL IN THE ANDES
Cuzco, which means the umbilicus of the world, was the centre of Inca civilization. It retained its importance in Spanish Peru, as witness the Spanish colonial architecture of its cathedral.

④ DUTCH ARCHITECTURE IN THE WEST INDIES
These houses, whose façades so obviously follow Dutch influence, were built on the fortunes made from the slave trade, of which the island of St Martin was one of the centres.

⑤ THE 'PORTUGUESE' SCREEN
Landing of the Jesuits in Japan, 16th century
The Jesuit Francis Xavier found in Japan an advanced civilization and an ancient religion. He went about converting the Japanese with endless patience. By the end of the 16th century the Japanese Church had 300,000 members.

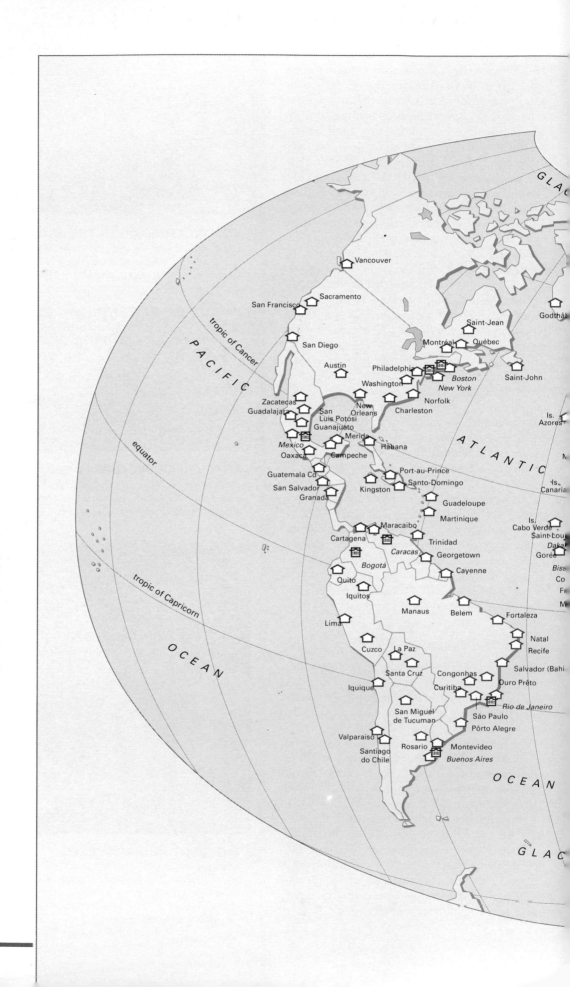

GLA...

Vancouver

Sacramento

San Francisco

San Diego

Saint-Jean

Montréal Québec

Godthå...

tropic of Cancer

PACIFIC

Austin

Philadelphia

Washington

Boston
New York

Saint-John

Zacatecas
Guadalajara

San
Luis Potosí
Guanajuato

New
Orleans

Norfolk

Charleston

Is.
Azores

Mexico

Oaxaca

Campeche

Merida

Habana

ATLANTIC

equator

Guatemala Cd

San Salvador
Granada

Kingston

Port-au-Prince

Santo-Domingo

Guadeloupe

Martinique

Is.
Canaria...

Cartagena

Maracaibo

Trinidad

Caracas

Georgetown

Is.
Cabo Verde
Saint-Lou...
Daka...
Gorée

Bogotá

Quito

Iquitos

Cayenne

Biss...
Co...
Fr...
M...

Lima

Manaus

Belem

Fortaleza

tropic of Capricorn

Cuzco

La Paz

Natal
Recife

OCEAN

Santa Cruz

Congonhas

Curitiba

Ouro Prêto

Salvador (Bahi...

Iquique

San Miguel
de Tucuman

Rio de Janeiro

São Paulo
Pôrto Alegre

Valparaiso

Rosario

Montevideo

Santiago
do Chile

Buenos Aires

OCEAN

GLAC...

The Past in the Present Day
EUROPE AND THE WIDER WORLD

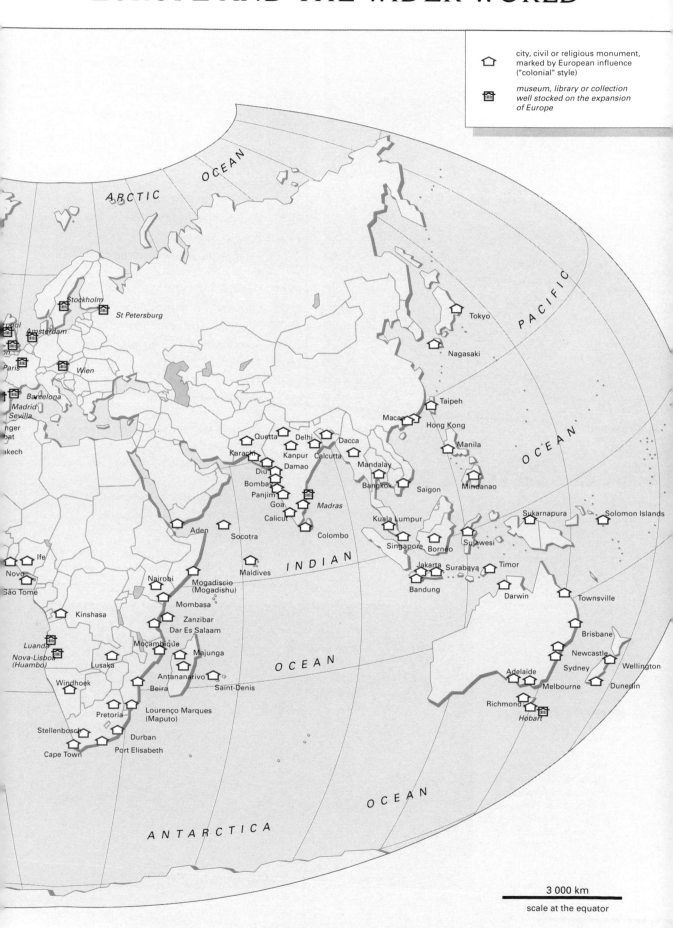

city, civil or religious monument, marked by European influence ("colonial" style)

museum, library or collection well stocked on the expansion of Europe

ARCTIC OCEAN

PACIFIC OCEAN

INDIAN OCEAN

OCEAN

ANTARCTICA

Stockholm
St Petersburg
Amsterdam
Paris
Wien
Barcelona
Madrid
Sevilla
nger
bat
akech

Tokyo
Nagasaki
Taipeh
Macao
Hong Kong
Manila
Mindanao

Quetta
Karachi
Delhi
Kanpur
Damao
Diu
Bombay
Panjim
Goa
Calicut
Dacca
Calcutta
Mandalay
Bangkok
Saïgon

Madras
Colombo
Kuala Lumpur
Singapore
Borneo
Sulawesi

Sukarnapura
Solomon Islands

Aden
Socotra
Maldives

Ife
Novo
São Tomé

Nairobi
Mogadiscie
(Mogadishu)
Mombasa
Zanzibar
Dar Es Salaam
Moçambique
Majunga
Antananarivo
Saint-Denis

Jakarta
Surabaya
Bandung
Timor
Darwin
Townsville

Kinshasa
Luanda
Nova-Lisboa
(Huambo)
Lusaka
Windhoek
Beira
Pretoria
Lourenço Marques
(Maputo)
Stellenbosch
Durban
Cape Town
Port Elisabeth

Brisbane
Newcastle
Sydney
Wellington
Adelaide
Melbourne
Dunedin
Richmond
Hobart

3 000 km
scale at the equator

① 'THE LAST JUDGMENT'
Fresco by Michelangelo, 1536–41. Sistine Chapel,
Vatican, Rome
*The rejection of proportion in favour of dramatic
effect and movement marked a break with
Renaissance Classicism.*

1511	Publication of Erasmus's The Praise of Folly
1513	Publication of The Prince by Machiavelli
1517	Luther puts up his theses against indulgences
1519	Charles V becomes Emperor. Luther breaks with Rome
1523	The Zurich Communal Council adopts Zwingli's reform programme
1524	Peasants' revolt in Germany
1529	Charles V halts the Turks outside Vienna
1531	The German Protestant Princes form the League of Schmalkalden
1534	Anglican schism
1536	Publication of John Calvin's Institution of the Christian Religion
1545	First meetings of the Council of Trent
1555	Peace of Augsburg
1566	Revolt of the Netherlands against Philip II of Spain
1571	Defeat of the Turks at Lepanto
1572	Massacre of St Bartholomew
1598	Edict of Nantes
1618	Beginning of the Thirty Years' War
1648	Treaties of Westphalia
1649	Execution of Charles I, King of England. Commonwealth headed by Oliver Cromwell, later to be appointed Lord Protector
1659	Treaty of the Pyrenees between France and Spain
1661	Beginning of personal rule by Louis XIV of France
1665	Louis XIV initiates his expansionist policy
1689	Declaration of Rights in England
1697	Treaty of Ryswick
1700	Death of Charles II of Spain: the cause of the War of Spanish Succession

② PROTESTANTISM
Engraving published by
Huyck Allardt
*'The Bible alone weighs
more than the Pope and
the monks.' To the right,
the Calvinist theologians;
to the left, the Pope, the
Cardinals, the Bishops
and monks and nuns at
prayer. This engraving,
a work of Protestant
propaganda, clearly
challenged the Church.*

REFORM-ATION EUROPE

THE 16TH AND 17TH CENTURIES

In the 16th century the Renaissance reached its apogee. It spread throughout Europe as economic expansion was spurred by the huge quantities of gold and silver imported from the Americas.

Humanism put humanity firmly at the centre of human preoccupations. The critical freedom that it demanded led to freedom of thought. In 1517 Martin Luther launched a profound religious reformation in Germany: its result was to put an end to the unity of Western Christianity.

The more radical work of other reformers like John Calvin, and the position adopted by the Council of Trent, explain the lengthy wars of religion that tore the West apart in the second half of the 16th century and until the beginning of the Thirty Years' War in 1618.

The revolution in thinking, together with religious, social and political strife, paved the way for absolutist monarchy in the mid-17th century – a concentration of power of which Louis xiv's reign in France was at this time the clearest example. The Netherlands and Britain, whose flourishing sea trade made them centres of wealth, enjoyed greater political freedom. The Declaration of Rights drawn up by the English Parliament in 1689 stipulated that the laws were above the power of monarchs.

The 17th century saw a worsening of social strife owing to the demographic crisis intensified by famine, war and disease. Nevertheless, it was also a time of great scientific progress and outstanding artistic achievement. It was now that Baroque taste broke with the symmetry of the Renaissance. It was Spain's 'Golden Century', a time of deep political debate in England and the heyday of classicism in France.

Frontier of the Holy Roman Empire	Aragonese possessions
Habsburg possessions within the Empire	Venetian possessions

1 Swiss Cantons
2 Duchy of Savoy
3 Duchy of Milan
4 Republic of Genoa
5 Modena
6 Tuscany

③ EUROPE AT THE END OF THE 15TH CENTURY

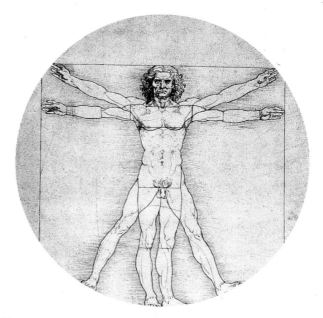

④ LEONARDO DA VINCI'S 'MAN'
Ink drawing, 34.3 by 24.5 cm, 1485–90. Accademia, Venice
Example of a technical drawing by Leonardo da Vinci, showing the ideal proportions of the human body. It was probably at this time that Leonardo wrote an anatomical treatise, now lost.

The Renaissance:
Europe Learns from Italy

❶ **THE DEVELOPMENT OF BANKING**
A money-changer and his wife, by Reymers Waele.
New Museums of El Escorial
Economic growth in Europe led to the development of a banking system, which included money-changing.

❷ **PRECIOUS METALS FROM THE AMERICAS AND CAPITALISM IN EUROPE**

The beginnings of capitalism

In the second half of the 15th century Europe began to recover from the grave economic problems of the century before. The recovery began in Germany and the Low Countries; and it developed into the prosperity of the Renaissance. A new form of commercial capitalism grew up.

Europe had now shaken off the plague epidemics of the Middle Ages and its population increased from 70 million in 1500 to more than 100 million in 1600. Although most people still lived in the countryside, towns were growing apace. Some of them, like Paris and London, had 200,000 inhabitants by the beginning of the 16th century. During that century, indeed, towns grew faster on average than the population itself.

At the same time as the population was increasing, the nobility and the prosperous bourgeoisie were buying more and more luxury articles at high prices. The textile industry, in particular, reacted to the pressure: Italian silks and Breton or German linen began to compete with material from Flanders.

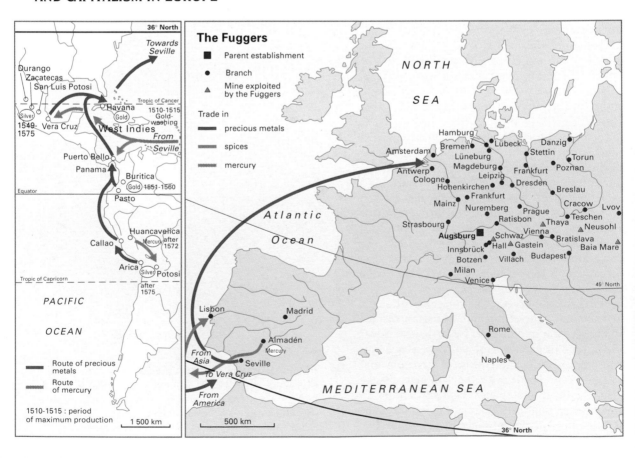

Industry also developed in England and central Europe. Progress in iron metallurgy was accompanied by advances in the use of charcoal.

But it was in trade that Europe's economic growth was most evident. The circulation of capital was at first dependent on the wealth of medieval merchants and on the output of the rich silver mines discovered in central Europe – in the Tyrol, Bohemia and Hungary. But the discovery of the New World by the Portuguese and Spaniards marked the birth of capitalism. Soon Europe was inundated by enormous quantities of precious metal from America and the circulation of wealth speeded up. From 1530 onwards silver from the mines of Peru and Mexico arrived by the shipload, causing an unprecedented price rise.

What was more, existing trade networks were abruptly displaced. Long-standing centres continued their activities around the North Sea, in the Alps and along the Rhône Valley. But the Atlantic was now the main focus of trade. Seville and Lisbon, the home ports for the new trade routes, were the first to benefit; and Antwerp, meanwhile, became a financial capital.

Trading associations, which brought together large sums of money, encouraged the development of the banking system; and the most influential firms set up branches in the major capital cities of Europe. At the same time, credit houses perfected their techniques and extended their scope. Capitalism was in its infancy: but it already had some effective instruments, such as double-entry book-keeping and letters of credit, while greater and more sophisticated use was being made of bills of exchange.

The beginnings of capitalism coincided with the emergence of modern states. Renaissance bankers made loans to kings and princes, who in turn intervened more and more in the running of the economy, often making it national by establishing customs tariffs, monopolies and various protectionist measures. The Fugger family was an early representative of infant capitalism.

Charles V and Europe

Italy, economically rich and politically divided, was greedily eyed by France and Spain, the most powerful monarchies in Europe. Their intervention on Italian soil was the beginning of a struggle that lasted a century and a half: it was typical of international relations at that time.

The first phase of the conflict (1494–1512) was a continuation of the medieval rivalry between the House of Anjou and the House of Aragon. The result was inconclusive. The Kingdom of Naples remained under Spanish domination and the French had to leave Italy. In 1515 the new

❸ THE PORT OF VENICE IN THE 16TH CENTURY
Jacopo Bassano. Prado Museum, Madrid
The 16th century was a period of triumph and ostentation at Europe's courts. Venice, though a republic, was no exception, especially when the Doge embarked at Piazza San Marco.

❹ MERCHANT OPULENCE: THE MEDICI
The Medici–Riccardi Palace begun by Michelozzo in Florence in 1444
Many of the merchants who built fortunes devoted part of their wealth to the arts, which made possible the efflorescence of the Quattrocento. Cosimo de'Medici was such a patron.

① FRANCIS I AND CHARLES V
F. Zuccari, fresco in the Villa Farnesina, Rome
*Charles V and Francis I enter Paris in 1540. They were
the leading characters and the two main rivals in the first half
of the 16th century.*

② Charles V, Burgundian Prince

*Master of an empire on which 'the sun never set', Charles V always remembered
that he was the great-grandson of Philip the Bold, Duke of Burgundy.*

*The County of Burgundy by itself, situated as it is at a great
distance from all my other States, is because of its position very
difficult and costly to defend in case of need. For that reason I
have taken great care, during the recent wars, to stipulate its
neutrality vis-à-vis France and to ensure that it enjoys the
advantages of the hereditary league formed between the House
of Austria and the Swiss. But one can have little trust in the
French, and little more in the Swiss, who while seeking only to
please France, would like at the same time to lay their hands on
that part of the Franche-Comté which is nearest to their
frontiers, and particularly the salt works. For this reason I have
given orders for Dole to be fortified: it is the chief city of that
country, and the aids that I have obtained will defray the
expense.*

Charles V, *Instructions to Prince Don Philip*, 18 January 1548, State
Papers of Cardinal de Granvelle, III

French King, Francis I, reconquered Milan after
the Battle of Marignano. Shortly afterwards,
however, the new Emperor, Charles V, threatened
France from every direction.

Charles had in fact inherited a 'universal'
empire. Born in Ghent in 1500, the son of Philip I
the Handsome and Joan the Mad, he was by birth
and education a Burgundian prince. From his
father he received the Burgundian territories (the
Franche-Comté and the Low Countries) and the
Archduchy of Austria, which in 1519 enabled
him to be elected German Emperor. From his
mother he inherited the kingdoms of Spain,
possessions in Africa and Italy (Sicily, Naples and
Sardinia), and immense colonies in America,
which continued to grow throughout his reign.

But the great threat to Europe came from the
Turks. Charles V worked to form a 'Universal
Concord' among Christian princes to stem the
Turkish advance, an idea also supported by the
humanists. Indeed, it was his idea of defending
Christianity on a basis of unity that gave Charles
V his European credentials. He took a number of
opportunities to proclaim his political aims and in
1521 he expounded them at the Imperial Diet of
Worms; seven years later, on the eve of his
coronation by Pope Clement VII, he outlined
them again to the Council of State in Spain; in
1536, in the famous speech that he made in
Spanish before Pope Paul III, he argued that
Christian sovereigns had a duty to make peace
among themselves in order to fight the Turkish
invaders; and in 1555 in Brussels he recalled his
incessant journeys through Europe in the defence
of Christendom. He had not attempted to establish a 'universal monarchy' as imagined by Dante,
but an organizing empire.

Against this *ordinatio totius mundi* had arisen
a host of individualist ideas. They seemed modern, and they finally prevailed. It was the triumph
of Protestantism and the national states. The
Emperor had faced a triple obstacle: constant
opposition from France, resistance from the German princes and the threat from the Turks.

By opposing Charles's plans, King Francis I
was in fact expressing the wishes of a modern,
nationalist France that felt threatened. The first
war broke out in 1521 and menaced all France's
frontiers. Defeated at Pavia in 1525, Francis I was
captured, forced to sign the Treaty of Madrid and
to surrender the duchies of Milan and Burgundy.

France's defeat led to a reversal of alliances.
The Italian states, led by Pope Clement VII, now
made common cause with France. There began a
war without any decisive battles, save for the sack
of Rome by imperial troops. It ended with the
Peace of Cambrai (1529), which recognized
Spanish supremacy in Italy and returned Burgun-

dy to France.

This balance of power was little changed by the two wars that followed. Francis I scandalized Christendom by seeking support from the Turkish Sultan Suleiman the Magnificent (1520–66) and occupied the Duchy of Savoy, the key to the Alpine frontier. The Peace of Crépy (1544) bore witness to the weariness of both belligerents and their concern at the rise of Protestantism in Germany and France.

The Emperor's call for a united effort by Christian Europe had echoes of medieval crusading, but it was in response to a real danger. Since the capture of Constantinople in 1453, the Ottoman Turks had made great strides. They had pushed forward into Thrace, Bulgaria, Serbia, Greece and Albania, as well as striking deep roots in Asia Minor. Its military power, moreover, was fired by religious fanaticism.

At Suleiman's command, the Turks took Belgrade in 1521 and defeated the Hungarians at the Battle of Mohacs in 1526. This breakthrough brought them to the gates of Vienna and made them a direct threat to the Empire. In the Mediterranean, meanwhile, they rallied Moslem troops in North Africa and threatened Spain.

Charles V checked the Turkish advance in Europe by defeating their siege of Vienna (1529). In the Mediterranean, he seized Tunis but was repulsed from Algiers. The Ottoman threat remained serious for much of the 16th century, until the Turkish defeat at Lepanto in 1571.

❸ THE TURKS BESIEGE VIENNA
Ottoman manuscript, 1588: Hunerrname, Vol. II. Topkapı, Istanbul
In his westward march, Suleiman the Magnificent (1490–1566) besieged Vienna in 1528. Charles V's troops succeeded in lifting the siege; but in 1536 an alliance between Francis I and Suleiman seriously threatened the Germanic Empire.

❹ THE MEDITERRANEAN, 16TH CENTURY

Personal possessions of Charles V

Venetian possessions

Frontier of the Holy Roman Empire

→ Turkish advance

1 'THE SCHOOL OF ATHENS' (c.1510)
Raphael. Stanza della Segnatura, Vatican, Rome
In the building depicted here, which to some recalls the Roman baths and to others Bramante's plans for St Peter's, Raphael brought together scholars, sages and philosophers from classical antiquity. In the centre, dominating the group, is Plato, holding his Timaeus in one hand and pointing upwards with the other, in conversation with Aristotle, who carries his Ethics and holds out one hand palm downwards. Each simple gesture indicates the essence of the philosopher's thought. Raphael could not resist the temptation of portraying some of his friends in the guise of the great men shown here. Thus, Leonardo da Vinci does duty for Plato and perhaps Diogenes, sprawled on the steps; while Michelangelo sits in a meditative, even Hermetic pose as the philosopher Heraclitus. The whole fresco, of which this illustration shows only a part, portrays the intellectual quest for truth.

2 ST PETER'S, ROME
This basilica (1506–1624), which synthesizes ancient and Christian art, is a late-Renaissance masterpiece. Many architects were involved in its creation. Michelangelo was responsible for the dome, 42 metres across and 123 metres tall. Carlo Maderna finished the façade in a Mannerist style.

The High and Late Renaissance

In the first third of the 16th century Rome became the new capital of Italian art, leaving Florence behind. Many artists settled in the Eternal City, tempted there by Popes Julius II and Leo X, who sought to revive the glories of its past.

St Peter's Basilica in Rome became the city's architectural masterpiece. Julius II commissioned it from Donato Bramante, a great admirer of Roman buildings, who drew up the initial plan of the new basilica, in the shape of a cross. This church, which was also a symbol of Christianity, was therefore seen as a synthesis between the Christian faith and Roman antiquity. In 1546 Michelangelo took over.

16th-century sculpture reached its height with Michelangelo, who was a typical example of the Renaissance man. Born in Florence in 1475, he learned his craft among the artists attendant on the Medici. Among other things, he carved the Pietà in St Peter's and the masterful David now in the Galleria dell'Accademia, Florence (that in the Piazza della Signoria being a copy). As a painter, Michelangelo brought the same powerful qualities to the frescoes in the Sistine Chapel in the Vatican, Rome – a further Papal commission.

Nevertheless, it was Raphael Sanzio who best used his talent to express Roman classicism, in perfect form and serene composition. Working in the Vatican from 1508 onwards, he painted vast murals showing Michelangelo's influence.

After the sack of Rome by imperial troops in 1527, the main centre of Italian art became Venice, whose rich patricians offered artists both patronage and protection. The architect Andrea Palladio published *Four Books of Architecture*, a work that had immense influence. Venice also left a remarkable heritage of paintings. The Venetian School was interested above all in light and colour, producing mainly portraits and landscapes: Titian excelled at pagan fables and nudes; Paolo Veronese, steeped in Mannerism, painted large groups with a pronounced taste for ostentation and luxury; Tintoretto, an admirer of Michelangelo and a further exponent of the same style, heightened its effects with chiaroscuro.

From the second half of the 15th century onwards the different artistic trends in Italy had found an echo in France. Although the Gothic tradition remained powerful, the artists patronized by Charles VIII and Louis XII were already imbued with the spirit of the Renaissance. The châteaux of Blois and Chambord, for example, combined borrowings from Italian models with the precepts of their French predecessors. From 1520 onwards Italian tastes began to predominate in France with the arrival of Francesco Primaticcio and his colleague Giovanni Battista di Jacopo Rosso, whom Francis I commissioned to decorate the Palace of Fontainebleau.

In the Low Countries the first signs of the Renaissance were the façades of the town halls of Antwerp and Leyden; but Gothic was not displaced altogether. In his famous peasant scenes the great master of the time Pieter Breughel the Elder remained faithful to national traditions.

The Renaissance also made only partial headway on German soil. Its arrival was delayed, in any case, by the religious dispute with Rome. The work of Albrecht Dürer certainly shows Italian influence, but it is also marked by Germanic traits. Lucas Cranach left portraits of the Protestant leaders; Hans Holbein the Younger worked at the court of King Henry VIII of England. A pioneer of the double portrait, he opened new horizons, which Van Dyck later explored.

The Renaissance was slower to reach England, through German and Flemish influence transmitted by Holbein and Antonio Moro. English architecture remained faithful to Perpendicular Gothic, although a number of architects were later influenced by Palladio.

③ 'BACCHANAL' BY TITIAN (1518–19)
Prado Museum, Madrid
Titian set this bacchanal on the island of Andros where, according to the Greek Sophist Philostrates, a spring flowed with pure wine, which kept the inhabitants in a permanent state of agreeable tipsiness. Titian, fully in touch with contemporary reality, portrayed the pleasures of an open-air feast where wine, dancing and flirtation whiled the hours away.

④ THE CHATEAU OF CHAMBORD
Built for Francis I, Chambord is the biggest of the Loire châteaux. The ground plan and the overall structure are still Gothic, but the decorations are Italian. Seen above is the main façade, facing north-west.

⑤ 'HAYMAKING'
Pieter Breughel the Elder (1525–69). Prague
A broad and peaceful landscape, a precise, anecdotal and sometimes ironical view of peasant life: such is the work of this painter.

❶ THE BURIAL OF COUNT ORGAZ

El Greco, 1586. Church of St Thomas, Toledo

This work, one of the finest galleries of portraits in the 16th century, expressed the ideology and beliefs then prevailing in Spain, where the sacred and the profane, religion and life, were closely intermingled.

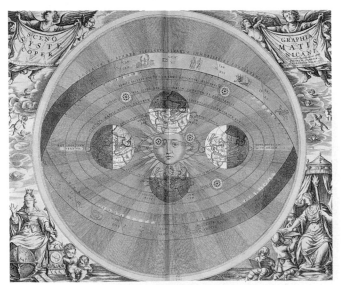

❷ THE HELIOCENTRIC SYSTEM OF COPERNICUS

In Copernicus's view, the sun was the centre of the universe. The earth and the planets revolved around it. The movement of the stars, he said, appeared to move because of the earth's rotation.

In Spain the decorative Plateresque style of architecture was inspired by Italy: it emerged at the beginning of the 16th century and gave rise to major buildings, such as the San Marcos monastery in León or the façade of the University of Salamanca. Spanish architecture found a more classical style with El Escorial, the monastery-palace built in the reign of Philip II.

El Greco (Domenico Theotocopulos) remains one of the leading figures in Spanish painting. A native of Crete, he blended Byzantine influence with Spanish mysticism and from Mannerism he borrowed the luminous colour it had inherited from the Venetian masters.

During the Middle Ages science in Europe had been subject to the rule of authority, which bowed to the doctrines of the great scholars of classical antiquity. This had discouraged direct observation of natural phenomena.

From the 15th century onwards a radical change took place. True, the translation of classical Greek and Latin works continued: physics was studied according to Archimedes, geography according to Ptolemy and medicine according to Hippocrates. But the humanists' curiosity and critical sense led them to look directly at the phenomena in nature. Gradually, personal experience began to displace the rule of authority and the way was open to modern experimental science. Leonardo da Vinci declared that appealing to information inherited from antiquity, without verifying it oneself, was to value 'memory more than intelligence'. Leonardo himself, a painter of genius, valued empirical observation, but with constant reference to mathematics.

The geographical discoveries made by the Spanish and Portuguese also enlarged the field of observation and revealed the existence of many phenomena hitherto unknown to Europeans.

Anatomical knowledge benefited from the work of Andreas Vesalius (Andries van Wesel), from Flanders, who studied at Louvain and Paris and became a professor at the University of Padua at the age of only 23. His theories, based on direct observation of dissected corpses, caused a scandal and exposed him to the wrath of the Inquisition. Using identical methods, the Spanish physician Michael Servetus (Miguel Serveto) was the first to describe the circulation of the blood in the lungs.

Knowledge of the universe was also transformed, when Nicolaus Copernicus propounded his 'heliocentric' theory of the solar system in 1543, refuting the old notion that the earth was the centre of the universe. He broke with the theories of Ptolemy and worked out a new system in which the earth and the other planets turned round the sun, which remained immobile. Copernicus did not dare publish the results of his research during his lifetime.

Renaissance political thought was enriched by humanist theorists with contrasting ethical principles and different notions of the state.

In *The Prince* (1513), dedicated to Lorenzo de' Medici, the Florentine Niccolò Machiavelli dealt with the exercise of political power, which he divorced entirely from moral considerations. In his view, power belonged to whomever was able to seize it. The Prince, guided by *virtù* – a blend of talent and cunning – must always take account of reality and allow no scruple to curb his ambitions. Ruling by fear, he would justify his actions by the success of his plans and would always be motivated by reasons of state.

In 1516 the English scholar Thomas More, a friend of Erasmus, invented the island of *Utopia*, where he imagined a happy world whose inhabitants renounced property, money and war. In the state he described nothing was lacking and tolerance had superseded religious disputes.

At the end of the 16th century the French political scientist Jean Bodin produced a genuine theory of absolutism, the type of government that prevailed in Europe in the following century. In *La République*, published in 1576, he introduced into political theory the doctrine of 'sovereignty' or supreme power, above the law and essential to the existence and unity of the state. In Bodin's view, three forms of government could guarantee sovereignty: monarchy, aristocracy and democracy. He opted for the first.

❸ Thomas More

Thomas More (1478–1535) studied at the University of Oxford, where he met Erasmus and became his friend. Chancellor of England under Henry VIII, he was executed for opposing the King's religious reforms.

Portrait by Jean Gossaert, known as Mabuse, c. 1470–1533. Musée Granet, Aix-en-Provence

All the Utopians work for all, no one having any thing of his own. The commonwealth ensures to every one abundance . . . and liberty for the free garnishing of the mind. That all things be set in good order in the commonwealth, they divide the day and assign but six hours to work, upon which they take meat in common. Every man is content thus, for the commonwealth assures to each a sufficiency. The laws, there being nothing that is private, or any man's own, are simple and few. The Magistrates need consider but few matters save overseeing work and the weal public . . . .

Believing that they possess in their commonwealth a felicity that no other can obtain, the Utopians never go to battle, but either in the defence of their own country, or to drive out enemies, or to deliver from the yoke of tyranny some people that be therewith oppressed.

Thomas More, *Utopia* (1516)

❹ EL ESCORIAL

This large and severe granite building was commissioned by Philip II in honour of St Lawrence. Its ground plan, a vast rectangle, was inspired by the grill on which the saint was martyred.

2 The Revolution: Religious Revolt

① POPE LEO X (1475–1521)
Raphael, 1483–1520. Capodimonte Museum, Naples
*The son of Lorenzo the Magnificent, Leo was Pope from 1513 to
1521. Like his predecessor Julius II, he proved incapable of
responding to the ideas for religious regeneration that were current
in Europe in his time.*

② Erasmus criticizes the temporal power of the Popes

Painting by Hans Holbein
the Younger. Private
Collection

*Erasmus of Rotterdam
(1469–1536), a Dutch
humanist and great traveller, wrote his Essay on Free Will during the
religious conflicts between Catholics and Protestants. His humanism was
moderate and wise: all his life he sought to reconcile the study of classical
antiquity with the teachings of the Gospels.*

*Lands, cities, taxes, imposts and sovereignties are all called
Peter's patrimony, despite the words in the gospel 'We have
forsaken all and followed thee'. Fired with zeal for Christ they
will fight to preserve them with fire and sword, and Christian
blood flows freely while they believe they are the defenders, in
the manner of the apostles, of the Church, the bride of Christ,
through having boldly routed those whom they call her foes.*

Erasmus, *Praise of Folly* (1511), translated by Betty Radice, Penguin
Books, London, 1971, p. 180

The revolution in religion begun by Martin
Luther in 1517 put an end to the unity of Catholic
Europe. But the origins of the crisis went back a
hundred years or more.

In the 15th century Europeans had suffered
deep religious uneasiness, linked with famine,
war and disease. The obsession with death and sin
had intensified religious fervour, often tinged
with superstition. There had been a growing cult
of the Virgin Mary and the Saints, while to save
their souls the faithful had resorted more and
more to relics and indulgences for the remission
of their sins.

The Church had failed to react effectively.
Indeed, the commotion produced by the Great
Schism in the West (1378–1417) had actually
encouraged new forms of dissent or heresy, as in
the case of John Wyclif and the Czech John Hus.

The general crisis of confidence was worsened
by indignation at the luxury – and frequent
scandal – of the Papal Curia. Friends and relatives
of the Pope with no other qualifications were
invited to fill the most senior posts in the Church,
which were sometimes even sold to them. In the
parishes and dioceses the clergy neglected
preaching and no longer attended the needs of the
faithful. Such unworthiness was thrown into
greater relief by the archaic formality of much
religious teaching.

The humanists called for reforms to put an end
to these abuses. At the same time new forms of
spiritual life emerged. The Dutch philosopher
Erasmus, who regarded all Europe as his homeland, pleaded for a more personal religion, a
sincere. dialogue between Man and God. He
preached tolerance and pressed for the use of
living languages so as to bring Christianity within
the grasp of ordinary people. Lefèvre d'Etaples, in
France, made similar proposals. In Germany
Nicholas of Cusa and other humanists also called
for reform; but senior Church dignitaries
opposed their efforts. In Italy the Oratorian
reform movement met fewer obstacles. In Spain,
meanwhile, a number of theologians supported
the similar efforts of Cardinal Cisneros.

Nevertheless, at the Fifth Lateran Council
called by Pope Julius II in 1512, conformism and
fear won the day, stifling any real initiative. The
Council ended in 1517, the very year Martin
Luther made public his revolt against the Church
of Rome.

The Lutheran Reformation

There were several reasons why Germany offered the most fertile soil for the revolution in religion. First, the Emperor's authority had been weakened by conflicts with the ambitious princes and cities that had elected him, while there was discontent among peasants and artisans. Secondly, German humanists led by Ulrich von Hutten had maintained national opposition to the Pope, whose unpopularity was increased by his having levied a tax. Thirdly, the German nobility, bourgeoisie and peasantry had all been antagonized by the life of luxury led by the bishops with too much land and income.

Against this background Martin Luther (1483–1546) took the initiative. A child of the lower middle classes, he studied law at the University of Erfurt and then entered an Augustinian monastery. With a doctorate in theology, he became a professor at the University of Wittenberg in 1512.

Tormented by scruples and agonizing for the salvation of his soul, he believed that only faith could make a person righteous and that good works alone could not wipe away sin and secure redemption. His break with the Church of Rome was provoked by a dispute over Indulgences. Pope Leo x decided to finance the building of St Peter's basilica by promoting the sale of Indulgences, which became a regular trade.

On 31 October 1517 Luther posted up in the University of Wittenberg 95 theses in which he contested the worth of Indulgences and described their sale as scandalous. The German nobility and the humanists supported his claims.

The Pope demanded that Luther retract his views: but he would not. In 1520 he was excommunicated, but he publicly burned the Papal bull containing the decree. In 1521, summoned to appear before the Imperial Diet or Assembly, called to meet at Worms by the Emperor Charles v, Luther held to his convictions and put himself under the protection of Frederick of Saxony.

As he pursued his debate with the Catholic theologians, Luther clarified his thought. His doctrine was made more explicit by his disciple Philipp Melanchthon in 1530 in the *Augsburg Confession*, the veritable Lutheran creed.

Its main teachings can be summarized as follows: only faith can make people righteous; Holy Scripture is the only source of faith; every believer can interpret them freely; the only sacraments worthy of retention are baptism and the Eucharist; the cult of the Virgin Mary and the saints should be abolished; purgatory does not exist; priests need not be celibate and the monastic and religious orders have no *raison d'être*.

❸ THE GERMAN MOSAIC AT THE BEGINNING OF THE 16TH CENTURY

❹ MARTIN LUTHER
(1483–1546)
German School after Lucas Cranach, 17th century. Library of Protestantism, Paris

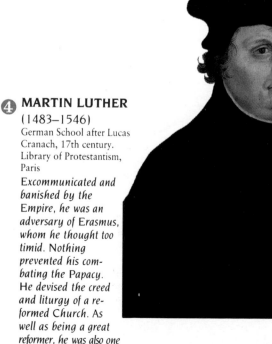

Excommunicated and banished by the Empire, he was an adversary of Erasmus, whom he thought too timid. Nothing prevented his combating the Papacy. He devised the creed and liturgy of a reformed Church. As well as being a great reformer, he was also one of the first writers in the German language.

❶ Luther: Justification by faith

So I was carried away by my troubled conscience and I always returned to knock at the same place in St Paul, burning to enter into its meaning. As I meditated night and day on those words (the Justice of God is revealed in Him, as it is written: 'The just live by faith'), God had mercy upon me. I understood that the Justice of God is that by which the just live, by the benefit of God, that is faith; and that the passage meant: the Gospel reveals the Justice of God, passive justice, by which God the merciful justifies us by faith.

Luther, Prologue to Volume I of the *Latin Works*, 1545

❷ CHARLES V
(1500–58)
Spanish School. Prado Museum, Madrid
Charles V's attempt to check the spread of Lutheranism in Germany had two results: a religious schism, contrary to his idea of Christian union; and a political split, since the Protestant princes wished to escape from imperial authority.

❸ The Emperor opposes Luther

It is clear that an isolated brother is in error when he contradicts the opinion of all Christendom, otherwise Christendom would have been in error for a thousand years or more. Thus I am resolved to commit my kingdoms, my possessions, my friends, my body, my blood, my life and my soul. For it would be shameful to you and to us, members of the noble German nation, if in our time and by our negligence, the mere appearance of heresy, a wrong done to the Christian religion, were to penetrate the hearts of men.

The Emperor's reply to Luther at Worms

Religious unrest in the Empire

In 1522 the knights of the Empire, poverty-stricken and hungry for land, declared themselves partisans of Luther and tried to seize the possessions of the Archbishop of Trier. Their attack, led by Franz von Sickingen, was thwarted in the following year by the combined efforts of Lutheran and Catholic princes. In 1524 the peasants rebelled with great ferocity against their lords, in the name of evangelical equality. Luther condemned the rebellion and supported the nobles when they crushed it in 1525.

It was the princes of the Empire who gained most from the Lutheran Reformation. Their interests rapidly converged with those of the Lutherans and a large number of them became converts in order to strengthen their position against the Emperor and to seize the property of the Catholic Church. Luther in fact maintained that religious authority should be attached to the civil power. The Prince Elector of Saxony and the Landgrave of Hesse quickly became Lutherans, followed by the Elector of Brandenburg and the Grand Master of the Order of Teutonic Knights, who created the Duchy of Prussia by taking over the Order's lands.

In 1529 Charles V held the Diet of Speyer in the hope of reaching a compromise: the Lutheran princes would be allowed to practise their religion within their own frontiers, but would be forbidden to proselytize. But the Lutheran princes and cities refused to agree and in 1531 they formed the League of Schmalkalden. So long as Charles V was preoccupied by the war with France, he paid little attention to the problem; but, once peace had been reached with France in 1544, he fought the Lutheran princes and defeated them at Mühlberg (1547). The League then secured the support of Henry II, King of France, in exchange for the bishoprics of Metz, Toul and Verdun, which hitherto had belonged to the Empire: and its troops surprised Charles V at Innsbruck.

By now Charles was weary. In 1555 he signed the Peace of Augsburg, then abdicated in favour of his son and his brother. The Lutheran princes, by virtue of the rule *cujus regio, ejus religio*, obtained the right to choose their religion and to impose it on their subjects. The peace lasted for 60 years. The German princes had managed to impose their will on the Emperor.

The doctrine of Zwingli

While Luther was launching the Reformation in Germany, the Swiss theologian Ulrich Zwingli (1484–1531) was preaching a similar doctrine. A priest and a learned humanist, Zwingli admired Plato and Erasmus. His essential teaching was that the Bible should be open to free interpretation and that the authority of the Church should be denied. He rejected the notion that Christ was really present in the eucharist and he argued that grace was arbitrary, granted by God only to those predestined to receive it.

In 1518 Zwingli began to preach in Zurich, where he convinced the most influential part of the bourgeoisie. In 1523 Zurich Council backed his reforms and they began to be taken up in Basle and Berne. But the religious dispute sharpened the rivalry that traditionally divided the Swiss towns. The five Catholic cantons, led by Lucerne, organized the Christian League and defeated the Protestants at the Battle of Kappel in 1531, where Zwingli was killed.

Calvinism

In the mid-16th century Calvinism gave shape to the Protestant Reformation by basing it on more radical logic.

The French theologian John Calvin (1509–64) seconded Luther's ideas. He had to leave France and for several years he travelled in Europe. His itinerary took him to Strasbourg, Basle and Fribourg, where he met Erasmus shortly before his death. In 1536 he settled in Geneva, at the

④ ULRICH ZWINGLI
(1484–1531)
19th-century miniature. University Library, Geneva
A preacher at Zurich Cathedral, Zwingli called for reform and was strongly supported by the independent and energetic city authorities.

⑤ THE LUTHERAN CHURCH AND THE PRINCES
Painting by Lucas Cranach, 16th century. Museum of Art, Toledo, Ohio
The Lutheran Church recognized the Bible as the sole authority, accepted two sacraments (baptism and the Eucharist) and called for a return to the early Church. It took root in northern and central Germany thanks to the support of the princes, such as the Elector of Saxony, here in the centre. At left is Luther.

❶ John Calvin: predestination

John Calvin (1509–64) stressed above all 'the honour of God' and defined predestination with a lawyer's rigour.

We declare then ... that God has decreed in His eternal and immutable wisdom those whom He would save and those whom he would send to perdition. We say that this decision, as to the chosen, is based on His mercy without any regard to human worth; and on the contrary that entry into life eternal is closed to all those whom He would send to damnation; and that this is done by His occult and incomprehensible judgment, although it be just and equitable .... I shall ignore here many dreams that people have formed to overthrow predestination .... For [many people] believe that God chose among people this one or that, according to what He foresaw would be the merits of each: that He adopts those whom He foresees will not be unworthy of His grace; and as for those whom He knows must be inclined to malice and impiety, them He leaves to their damnation.

Calvin, *Institution of the Christian Religion*

❷ RELIGION IN POST-REFORMATION EUROPE

Anglicans	Countries remaining Catholic
Calvinists	Catholic reconquests
Lutherans	Islam
Greek Orthodox Church	Charles V's Empire

invitation of Guillaume Farel, a promoter of religious reform. It was there that he published in Latin his *Institution of the Christian Religion*, his most crucial work.

Calvin's ideas were the product of a logical and rational mind, very different from Luther's. He believed:

- that the Bible, the source of faith, must be strictly observed
- that baptism and the Last Supper were the only valid sacraments, and Christ's presence in the Eucharist was only spiritual
- that worship should be limited to preaching, prayer and the singing of psalms
- in the doctrine of predestination, sketched by Luther but rigorously defined by Calvin. Faith justified any man on whom God had decided to confer it. Salvation depended on a timeless decision by God, who 'destined some to eternal life and others to eternal punishment'
- that, although human actions could not alter the divine decision, charity should be practised, allied to blind confidence in God

The Calvinist Church was ruled on democratic lines: its pastors were chosen by the faithful and hierarchy was abolished. The Church had very close relations with the state: both acted as vicars of God and interpreters of His will.

These decrees made Geneva 'the Rome of Calvinism'. The city became a theocratic society ruled by a church consistory by means of which Calvin imposed implacable intolerance. Worldly pleasures, regarded as the devil's work, were prohibited and strict morality was imposed. Calvin persecuted all those who opposed his orthodoxy, whether Catholic or Protestant: in 1553 the Spanish doctor Michael Servetus was sent to the stake.

Calvinism spread rapidly, through the efforts of pastors who received a thorough grounding at the academy in Genéva. The new doctrine was taken up in Switzerland and England, and important Calvinist centres emerged in Italy and Spain. In France and the Low Countries, Calvinism further inflamed the Wars of Religion. In Scotland, the Presbyterian Church, founded by John Knox, developed under Mary Queen of Scots in 1561, then reached northern Ireland at the beginning of the 17th century. Meanwhile, Calvinism spread to Hungary, Bohemia and Poland.

Calvin's doctrine enjoyed the support of the bourgeoisie and the nobility, who were jealous of the wealth of the Roman Catholic Church. Calvinism in fact gave its blessing to trade and profit, and thereby played a certain role in the development of capitalism.

The Reformation in England

In England, the initiative came from the King. Henry VIII (1509–47) had no male heir and he asked the Pope to declare the nullity of his marriage to Katherine of Aragon so that he could marry Ann Boleyn. When Rome refused his request, he opted for schism.

On the advice of Thomas Cranmer, a Protestant appointed as Archbishop of Canterbury, Henry VIII pronounced himself divorced and, by the Act of Supremacy of 1534, became head of the Church of England.

He severely suppressed opposition, whether from Protestants or from Catholics, as in the case of Sir Thomas More. He dissolved the monasteries and distributed their possessions among the nobility and the bourgeoisie, who declared themselves pleased with the new situation.

But Henry did not alter dogma: he confirmed Catholic orthodoxy, rejected the doctrine of justification by faith and recognized the value of charity. Calvinism was introduced in the reign of his son Edward VI (1547–53).

A bloodthirsty Catholic reaction set in with Mary Tudor (1553–8), daughter of Henry VIII and Katherine of Aragon, and wife of Philip II of Spain.

However, Elizabeth I, the daughter of Henry VIII and Ann Boleyn, succeeded Mary Tudor and re-established the Reformation, restoring to the Anglican Church all the prerogatives it had temporarily lost. Calvinism influenced the Thirty-nine Articles that now defined the Anglican faith.

Drawn up in 1563, this document recognized only two sacraments: baptism and the Eucharist. But the hierarchy and the Book of Common Prayer were maintained. Elizabeth drew her support from part of the nobility and of the bourgeoisie who had profited from the dissolution of the monasteries.

The reformed Church of England faced hostility from certain Catholics, from English Calvinists (Puritans) and from Scottish Presbyterians, who condemned its submission to royal authority and called for a simpler liturgy.

The Puritans were tolerated for a time, but later persecuted and imprisoned. Some emigrated to the United Provinces, then to America (1620). Dissidents under the first two Stuarts (1603–49), they took an active part in the Civil War and in Oliver Cromwell's Commonwealth (1649–60), until the restoration of the Stuarts re-established Anglicanism.

③ HENRY VIII (1509–47)
Portrait by Hans Holbein the Younger. Barberini Palace, Rome
Pride and obstinacy drove Henry to revolt against Rome. One can perhaps see in the King's enigmatic features the reflection of this crisis in moral and spiritual values, which was the drama of the Reformation century, but should not be identified with it.

④ ELIZABETH I OF ENGLAND
English School, Pitti Palace, Florence
A fierce defender of the Church of England, Elizabeth defied the Calvinists who contested the bishops' authority, and the Catholics for whom she remained 'the Bastard'. But her Church combined a theology tinged with Calvinism and a liturgy that remained Catholic.

3 The Counter-Reformation and Catholic Reform

① THE COUNCIL OF TRENT (1545–63)
Titian. Louvre Museum, Paris
This Nineteenth Ecumenical Council was convened by Pope Paul III at the request of the Emperor Charles V to tackle the Reformation. It restated Catholic doctrine and restored discipline.

② THE SOCIETY OF JESUS
17th-century painting. Gesù Church, Rome
Ignatius de Loyola hands to Pope Paul III the rules of the Society. It was the main vehicle of the Counter-Reformation, which altered the religious map of Europe, checked the spread of Protestantism and weakened it in Poland and central Europe.

In the face of the Protestant threat, the Catholic Church fought against the reformers' views but also profoundly redefined its own dogma, at the Council of Trent from 1545 to 1563.

The Council of Trent

Ever since the Protestant crisis had begun, there had been calls for an Ecumenical Council. In 1518 Luther himself had appealed for a council 'against an ill-informed Pope'. Catholic humanists, including Erasmus, Luis Vives and Pope Adrian VI, had also suggested a council, pointing out that it was in line with the traditions of the Church. In 1524 Charles V himself made the same proposal. But successive Popes, fearful for their own authority, used delaying tactics. Paul III, for example, tried to reform the Church by setting up a 'Council of Cardinals on Church Reform'. In 1542 Cardinal Carafa reorganized the Roman Inquisition, whose task was to suppress heresy. The following year saw the establishment of the Congregation of the Index, whose task was to censor written texts and to determine which books were forbidden by the Roman authorities. All these measures, however, proved inadequate. Faced with the necessity of reforming the Church, Pope Paul III finally decided to hold a Council at Trent (Trento), a strategic location since it was an imperial city on Italian territory, south of the Tyrol. The Council's discussions were remarkably free-ranging, although the Protestants shunned them.

Its conclusions defined modern Catholicism. They reaffirmed Catholic dogma, in particular on points rejected by the Protestants: tradition, as well as Holy Scripture, was a source of revelation and a criterion of faith. The Council condemned predestination and justification by faith; it reaffirmed the necessity of all seven sacraments and declared that Christ was really present in the Eucharist; it declared that the Latin Vulgate was the official version of the Bible. It fully endorsed the Church's hierarchy and the authority of the Pope; it maintained the celibacy of the priesthood and forbade the accumulation of wealth. Preaching and religious instruction, it declared, must be carried out under the strict authority of the bishops. Bishops and priests must reside in their respective dioceses and parishes, now reorganized; and the members of the clergy must be trained in diocesan seminaries.

The Society of Jesus

To counter Protestantism, new religious orders were established as part of the restoration of Catholicism as conceived by the Pope. In Spain there was a growth of mysticism, largely due to St John of the Cross and St Teresa of Avila. This spiritual revival also helped produce the Society of Jesus, an order founded in Paris by the Spaniard Ignatius de Loyola.

Born into an ancient noble family, Ignatius (1491–1556) saw combat as a soldier and was seriously wounded by the French at the siege of Pamplona in 1521. He withdrew to the monasteries of Monserrat and Manresa, where he began writing his *Spiritual Exercises*, then left on a pilgrimage to Rome and the Holy Land. Deciding to devote his life to God, he studied at Salamanca and settled at the College of Montaigu in Paris.

The Society of Jesus came into existence on 15 August 1534 in the little Montmartre church in Paris where Ignatius and six of his fellow-students met to make their vows. They then went to Rome, where in 1540 Pope Paul III recognized the new order as the armed champion of the faith. To the three traditional vows of poverty, chastity and obedience to the abbot it added a vow of absolute obedience to the Pope.

A difficult novitiate and extensive studies were required for admission to the order. With their strict discipline and intellectual training, the Jesuits became the essential corps of the Catholic Counter-Reformation. St Francis Xavier, a founder of the order in Paris, became a missionary in India and Japan. His work was the most characteristic of the apostolic role of the Society of Jesus, which rapidly spread throughout the world. By the time that Loyola died, in 1556, it already had more than 100 missions in the field.

Alongside the resurgence of the faith, the work of the Council of Trent was continued by three great reforming Popes. Pius V put the Council's decisions into practice; Gregory XIII promoted religious education; and Sixtus V reorganized the central administration of the Church. They drew up a Roman catechism, a breviary and a missal, which appeared between 1564 and 1570.

Catholicism was thus able to check the growth of Protestantism and recover much of the ground that it had lost. While the Company of Jesus had great success in Poland, Peter Canisius (also a Jesuit) gave further impetus to the restoration of Catholicism in Germany. France, Hungary and Bohemia remained under the tutelage of Rome.

So Lutheranism marked time and was limited to northern Germany and Scandinavia. Calvinism took root in Switzerland, Holland, Scotland, England and western Germany.

③ The Jesuits and education

Education was the main area of Jesuit activity.

More than the other remedies that may be used against the widespread evil that flourishes in Germany, it seems not only prudent but altogether necessary, and inspired by God, to seek that offered by the universities which, by the example of their religious life and the integrity of their doctrine, attract outsiders to virtue. May Providence ordain that this may be done, with the help of divine clemency, partly by the College of our Society that your Majesty is to establish in Vienna.

Letter from St Ignatius de Loyola to Charles V

④ THE INQUISITION
Execution scene by Pedro Berruguete. Prado Museum, Madrid
The Council of Verona (1183) laid the basis for the Inquisition when it ordered the Lombard Bishops to consign to justice those heretics who refused conversion. In 1223, to fight the spread of Albigensian heresy in Languedoc, Gregory IX organized a special tribunal run by the Dominicans. His practice gradually extended to the whole of Christendom. As the foremost weapon in the Counter-Reformation, the Inquisition was described by Pope Paul IV as 'the apple of his eye and the favourite of his heart'. He ordered it to pursue even the appearance of heresy and 'not resort ever to mildness'. The Inquisition was particularly forceful in Spain, where all suspects, 'remnants of Lutheranism' or 'henchmen of Erasmus', were condemned to the stake.

4 The Wars of Religion Divide Europe

① THE BATTLE OF LEPANTO
Paolo Veronese. Accademia, Venice

The Holy League of Spain, Venice and Rome (Pius V) defeated the Turks at the naval battle of Lepanto, at the entrance of the Gulf of Corinth, in October 1571. This put an end to the legend of Ottoman invincibility.

② Miguel Servia on the Battle of Lepanto

Seeing that his fleet was in difficulties, Uluj Ali tried to escape and fled with five galleys. The battle was very widespread, very fierce and very bloody . . . .

It took an hour and a half for the Christians to win, whereupon many Turks raced for the shore and some escaped with their lives, leaving their galleys behind. Two hundred and four ships were hit, in addition to those that sank or were burnt . . . .

The battle lasted from eleven in the morning to five in the afternoon . . . . Then the Turkish galleys and prisoners were shared out. Six thousand Turks had been captured and more than thirty thousand killed; and, since according to the rosters there had been fifty-six thousand all told, the rest must have escaped either by reaching the shore or by sailing away in the galleys that were still seaworthy. On our side, twelve thousand were wounded or killed.

Philip II defends the Catholic cause

Reacting against Protestant subversion, King Philip II of Spain (1556–98) lent his weight to the defence of the Catholic cause, which had been strengthened by the Council of Trent. He put at its disposal the immense resources of the Spanish Empire, which from 1558 onwards were further increased by the annexation of Portugal and its territories overseas.

On the abdication of his father Charles V, the old quarrel between Spain and France led Philip to declare war once again on the King of France, Henry II. Pope Paul IV, who opposed any Spanish presence on Italian soil, supported the French King. Under the terms of the Treaty of Cateau-Cambrésis (1559), France retained Metz, Toul and Verdun, and recovered Calais, but had to give up any claims to Savoy, Italy and the Low Countries. Spain thus obtained supremacy in the western part of the European mainland. In 1565 it liberated Malta from siege by the Turks. Henceforth, there could be no doubt about Philip's dominant position.

In 1568, however, the tables were turned. In the north, Calvinism took root in the Low Countries. In southern Spain, the Moors rebelled, while the Turks began a new offensive and captured Cyprus, hitherto held by Venice.

Philip II's first response was in the Mediterranean. In 1571 the Holy League formed by Spain, Venice and Rome destroyed the Turkish fleet at Lepanto.

With the Turkish threat out of the way, Philip tried to subdue the Low Countries, which enjoyed strong support from England and France. In view of the assistance given the Dutch rebels by Queen Elizabeth I of England, the attacks by English ships on Spanish possessions in America and the execution of the Catholic Mary Queen of Scots, Philip II tried to invade England.

The Invincible Armada, intended to escort Spanish troops, was attacked by the English and then destroyed by a storm in the Channel in 1588. This disaster weakened Philip in his struggle against France, where he was supporting the Catholic party against the Protestants.

At the end of his reign Philip signed a peace treaty with France and recognized its King, Henry IV, despite his Protestant past.

The Revolt of the Netherlands

Philip II intended to rule the Low Countries as an absolute monarch and he savagely suppressed Calvinism, which was spreading in the larger towns. In 1566 the Spanish measures sparked off a revolution. A complex of factors lay behind it.

The nobles were afraid of losing their power; the bourgeoisie thought taxes were too high; and Calvinism exacerbated religious disputes.

The rebellion began when the first centralizing measures were applied by the governor-general of the Netherlands, Margaret of Parma, and her principal adviser Cardinal Granvelle, Bishop of Arras. Under pressure from the Dutch states-general, Philip II dismissed Granvelle.

Encouraged by this first success, the nobles concluded the Compromise of Breda (1565) and demanded autonomy for the country and freedom of worship. Their example fired the religious fanaticism of ordinary people, who had suffered a great deal from the economic crisis and they destroyed a number of Catholic churches.

Philip II reacted energetically. He appointed the Duke of Alva as governor-general; and the Council of Troubles condemned to death, among many others, the rebel counts van Egmont and van Hoorne. These reprisals, coupled with a crippling tax system, led to a general revolt. Dutch Catholics and Protestants made common cause under the leadership of a convinced Calvinist, William of Nassau, Prince of Orange, Stadholder or Governor of Holland and Zeeland. The rebels, who called themselves Geuzen (*gueux*, 'beggars'), seized Brielle and Flushing in 1572. The Duke of Alva, despite his military successes, was replaced by Don Luis de Requesens, who pursued a policy of tolerance.

But, when Spanish soldiers, who had not been paid, sacked Antwerp, a general revolt broke out. The 17 provinces, Catholic and Protestant, united by the Pacification of Ghent in 1576, resumed their fight for freedom, this time against the Viceroy Don John of Austria, victor of Lepanto, who was unable to defeat the insurgents.

Philip II's new envoy, Alessandro Farnese, the son of Margaret of Parma, was an able negotiator. He succeeded in rallying the ten Catholic provinces of the south by promising them political liberty (the Union of Arras, 1579). The seven northern provinces riposted a few days later by forming the Union of Utrecht. The Low Countries were split in two. In 1588 the seven northern provinces established the United Provinces, loyal to Calvinism. With the support of France and England, they obtained their independence in 1609 and were recognized by Spain when the Treaties of Westphalia were signed in 1648.

③ PHILIP II, KING OF SPAIN (1527–98)
Alonso Sanchez Coello, *c.*1532–88. Prado Museum, Madrid
Philip II was the champion of the Catholic cause in the second half of the 16th century.

④ THE STRUGGLE IN FLANDERS
Painting by Baron H. Leys. Royal Museum, Belgium
The violence wrought by Spanish troops aroused the resistance of the people and contributed to the 'Black Legend' against Philip II.

① THE MASSACRE OF ST BARTHOLOMEW
François Dubois. Lausanne
Incited by his mother, Catherine de Médicis, Charles IX of France ordered Protestants to be massacred. More than 3000 Huguenots died in Paris on the night of 23–24 August 1572, after which similar persecution spread to a number of provincial towns. Was this Catholic fanaticism or political terrorism?

② HENRY IV OF FRANCE (1553–1610)
French school, 16th century. Château de Versailles
Although legitimate heir to the throne of France, Henry IV could not reign until he had renounced Protestantism.

The Wars of Religion in France

Under Henry II (1547–59), the son of Francis I, Calvinism won adherents in France despite the king's attempts to curb it. Known in France as 'Huguenots', the Calvinists were in effect a religious party led by the powerful Bourbon family. To bar their way, French Catholics gathered round another great princely family, the Guises.

While intolerance raged, the two parties fought each other for political control of the state. Wars of religion steeped France in blood from 1562 to 1589. On the Eve of St Bartholomew (23–24 August 1572) more than three thousand Huguenots were massacred in Paris.

Since Henry III had no children, a war of succession was now combined with the wars of religion. The Crown devolved upon the late king's nearest male relative, Henry of Bourbon, King of Navarre and leader of the Calvinists. French Catholics opposed him; and Philip II of Spain, who supported them, advanced the claims of his own daughter Isabella, whose mother had been the daughter of Henry II of France. The Calvinists, meanwhile, looked towards England.

In 1593 Henry of Bourbon renounced the Calvinism and ended the conflict: France accepted him and he became King Henry IV. By signing the Edict of Nantes in 1598, the new king brought new freedom to France. The Huguenots now had the right to public employment, to govern certain towns and – despite some restrictions – to practise their religion. After forty years of hostilities religious tolerance prevailed in France.

The Thirty Years' War

The Thirty Years' War, which dominated the first half of the 17th century, was in a sense a continuation of the religious wars and of the confrontation between France and the Habsburgs.

But the war originated both in conflicts between German Protestants and Catholics, and in a rebellion of German princes against imperial authority. When it became general, however, it finally turned into a competition for hegemony.

The rebellion of Bohemia against its king, who was also Emperor under the name of Ferdinand II, marked the beginning of hostilities. The Czechs, backed by German Protestants, deposed their sovereign and replaced him on the throne of Bohemia by the Elector Palatine Frederick V, a Calvinist and leader of the Evangelical Union. The Emperor, with the help of the King of Spain, managed to crush Bohemia; he also secured control of the Palatinate.

The Protestant states of northern Germany, feeling threatened by the Catholics, appealed to the King of Denmark, Christian IV. He, however, suffered a setback and was obliged to sign the Peace of Lübeck in 1629. The Emperor then forced the Protestant princes to return the Catholic Church's possessions.

France now became jealous of the authority the Emperor had regained and incited Gustavus Adolphus of Sweden (an ardent Lutheran) to declare war on him. After several brilliant victories, the King of Sweden died in battle at Lützen. France then plunged directly into war against the Habsburgs of Germany and Spain, securing some important victories and compelling the new Emperor, Ferdinand III, to make peace in 1648.

The negotiations took the form of a great European Congress and lasted four years. They took place at Münster and at Osnabrück in Westphalia, a province of Germany. France attained her ends: she dismantled the Spanish–German alliance and established a new balance of power in Europe.

The Emperor's authority was abolished, to the benefit of the German princes. Freedom of religion was reaffirmed everywhere. The balance of power established by the Treaty of Westphalia was thus tilted in favour of Louis XIV's France. Habsburg power was drastically curbed.

③ THE HORRORS OF THE THIRTY YEARS' WAR
(1618–48)

Engraving by Jacques Callot from his *Miseries of War* (1633). Bibliothèque Nationale, Paris

This political and religious conflict affected all Europe and fragmented Germany. Mercenary leaders and undisciplined troops made it particularly cruel and destructive.

④ EUROPE AFTER THE TREATIES OF WESTPHALIA

1 Duchy of Savoy
2 Duchy of Milan
3 Republic of Genoa
4 Modena
5 Tuscany
6 Parma
7 Lucca
8 Mantua

Habsburg possessions:
Spanish Habsburgs
Austrian Habsburgs

Treaties of Westphalia (1648)
Acquired by France
▲ Possessions of the Three Bishoprics confirmed as French
Acquired by Sweden
Recognized as independent
Frontiers of the Empire
☆ Acquired by France under the Treaty of the Pyrenees (1659)
🔥 Regions in revolt

5 The Europe of Absolutist Monarchs

① LOUIS XIV (1638–1715)
Portrait by Hyacinthe Rigaud. Louvre Museum, Paris
'It must be admitted that there was always in Louis's soul a certain loftiness that bore him on to great things.' Voltaire, Le Siècle de Louis XIV.

② THE CHATEAU OF VERSAILLES
Around Louis XIII's modest hunting lodge Louis XIV had built, by Le Vau and then by Jules Hardouin-Mansart, this vast palace surrounded by gardens designed by Le Nôtre. In 1682 he transferred his court and his ministers there.

The absolutism of Louis XIV

After the Treaty of the Pyrenees (1659) which followed that of Westphalia, France enjoyed unchallenged prestige: its main enemies, Spain and the Empire, had not only been defeated but seemed exhausted. With 18 million inhabitants, France was the most populous country in Europe: it was self-sufficient in agricultural products and had thriving industries. In the reign of Louis XIII (1610–43) Cardinal Richelieu had imposed obedience upon the Protestants and the nobility. While Louis XIV was still a minor, Mazarin defeated the Fronde, a rebellion against royal authority. With this behind them, the people wanted order and peace; rivalry between the nobility and the bourgeoisie made possible the emergence of a power which, in the hands of the king, now sought to level out society.

When Mazarin died in 1661, Louis XIV decided to govern alone. He was convinced that his power derived from God and that he himself incarnated the state. The strong position of France in Europe gave him the appropriate resources. His political ideas, set out in *Mémoires pour l'instruction du Dauphin* (Memorials for the training of the heir to the throne), in 1665, were completed by Jacques Bénigne Bossuet. The monarchy enjoyed divine right: 'Princes act as Ministers of God and are His lieutenants on Earth'. The king had absolute power and his person was sacred. But absolutism should not be confused with tyranny, because the king was responsible before God and must respect 'the fundamental laws of the realm'.

Louis XIV demanded obedience from everyone. The nobility was summoned to court to serve him and lost its power in the provinces. 'Levelled out' as the upper ranks of society now were, the nobility had the same rank as the bourgeoisie, which acquired the most important responsibilities. This new equilibrium in effect enhanced royal power. The communes, the *parlements* and the corporations all owed obedience to the sovereign.

In all circumstances Louis XIV reserved for himself the right of final decision: his closest collaborators, such as Jean-Baptiste Colbert and the Marquis de Louvois, advised him and carried out his orders. The comptroller-general of finances was in charge of the economy and of the country's internal affairs. The other responsibilities were entrusted to secretaries of state: war, the

Navy, foreign affairs, the royal household. The *Intendants* or provincial administrators were in charge of centralization: their task was to ensure that the king was obeyed in the provinces.

The principles of absolutism applied equally to the economy and were put into practice by Colbert. Convinced that the king's power depended on his wealth, he imposed great rigour on the economy and introduced mercantilism.

At that time the economic power of a country was measured by its wealth in bullion. The aim of policy was to attract gold and silver from other countries by means of a 'money war' that limited imports and increased sales abroad.

To encourage production Colbert set up royal manufactories, notably the Gobelins tapestry and furniture manufactory, which were subject to strict internal rules and rigorous inspection. The trading companies, also set up and controlled by the state, laid the bases for colonial expansion in India, the West Indies and Canada, which ensured regular supplies of raw materials.

King 'by the grace of God', Louis XIV also insisted on control of the Church in France. The Protestants, likewise, could not escape his authority. In 1685 he revoked the Edict of Nantes: this meant that Protestant pastors could no longer preach, while their schools and churches were closed. Despite royal interdict, some 200,000 Protestants went into exile abroad.

Absolutism also affected literature and the arts. The purpose of literary and artistic creation, now, was to celebrate the 'glories of the King'; and it was required to respect the canons of classicism as defined by the academies, which in turn were required to express the tastes of the king. The château of Versailles, the residence of the king and his court, was an excellent example of the precepts of this 'official' art.

The dawn of liberty: the United Provinces

While many European rulers moved towards absolutism, parliamentary regimes were established in Holland and Britain. These two countries were commercial powers whose great progress in sea trade enabled the bourgeoisie and the working aristocracy to amass enormous fortunes. As a group, they were large enough to play a political role and to demand certain 'guaranteed liberties'. It is no surprise that the great European political thinkers of the 17th century came from the United Provinces and Great Britain.

Hugo Grotius, from Holland, can be regarded as the founder of international law, in that he produced a synthesis of the mutual obligations that states ought to undertake. Thomas Hobbes,

③ JACQUES BÉNIQUE BOSSUET (1627–1704)
Portrait by Hyacinthe Rigaud. Louvre Museum, Paris
Bishop of Meaux and tutor of the king's son, Bossuet was a great orator of dramatic intensity and lyrical charm. He supported Louis XIV in his struggle against the Protestants.

④ Colbert (1619–83)

As 'agent' of the king, Jean-Baptiste Colbert was indefatigable: he had a hand in all areas of public administration. He assisted industry and trade, encouraged the establishment of state manufactories, reorganized the finances, the fleet and the law, and gave every stimulus to the India Company. It was an effort hard to sustain at a time of general economic crisis.

Claude Lefèbvre.
Château of Versailles

His plans for trade

Pleased that by his ability he had restored abundance to the King's coffers, Colbert embarked upon plans for trade, taking no account of reality but designing everything in his imagination. He believed that the Kingdom of France could be sufficient unto itself. He established all sorts of manufactures that cost more than they were worth. He set up an East India Company without the necessary funds, all unaware that the French, impatient by nature and in that respect very different from the Dutch, could never be constant enough to put money into a business for thirty years without drawing any profits.

Abbé de Choisy, *Mémoires*

❶ Grotius and the freedom of the seas

The Dutch lawyer and diplomat Hugo de Groot, known as Grotius (1585–1645), in his book Mare liberum, *championed the freedom of the seas against the claims of the Spaniards, the Portuguese and later the English, who sought to dominate and divide them.*

The debate between us and the Spaniards bears on the following points. Can the sea, which is immense and limitless, be the domain of a single kingdom and that not even the largest? Does a single nation have the right to forbid others to sell, trade and enter into relations with third parties? Can a nation give what it has never possessed or discover what already belongs to someone else? Does a flagrant injustice in the long run create a specific right?

Grotius, *Mare liberum*, 1609

JAN DE WIT.
Raet Pensionaris van Hollandt en Westvrieslant bewaerder van't grootsegel.
t'Amsterdam by Carel Allard op den dam inde warmoes...

❷ JAN DE WITT (1625–72)

Jan de Witt defended the interests of the commercial bourgeoisie against the warlike family of Orange. But he was taken unawares by the French invasion in 1672, for which he was partly responsible. He was killed by a lynch mob in a riot fomented by the Orangists.

from England, was a pessimist: in the state of nature, he held, the life of man is 'solitary, poore, nasty, brutish and short'. He believed that war was inherent in history and that to ensure peace it was essential to establish strong and despotic power. His compatriot John Locke, a generation younger, took a different line: in *Two Treatises of Civil Government* (1690) he condemned absolute monarchy. In his view, to defend their freedom men must unite in a 'civil society', in which the powers of government would be limited to those enjoyed by people in a state of nature. Locke had undoubted influence on European thinkers in the 18th century.

The proclamation of the Republic of the United Provinces did not mean that the seven provinces were totally unified. It was a confederation with common institutions such as the states-general or assemblies of delegates from the provinces.

The weakness of the confederal authorities soon became obvious. Every step they took had to be agreed on unanimously. There were in fact two opposing interests. The post of Stadhouder General, held by the powerful Nassau family, carried with it command of the army and navy; and the incumbent, who favoured centralized authority, was supported by the nobility, the peasants, the populace, the sailors and the most intransigent Calvinists. At the opposite pole was the 'Great Pensionary', who represented the merchant bourgeoisie and favoured peace and religious tolerance in a republic that left the provinces autonomous.

The tension between these two caused profound political crises. The authority of the Stadhouder tended to prevail in time of war and that of the Pensionary in times of peace.

In 1619 the Stadhouder Maurice of Nassau dismissed the Great Pensionary Johan van Oldenbarneveldt and dragged the country into war against Spain and into the Thirty Years' War. But the peace that was signed in 1648 favoured the bourgeoisie, supported by the government of the Great Pensionary Jan de Witt (1653–72). The United Provinces enjoyed a climate of freedom and tolerance that attracted thinkers looking for a country of refuge: the French philosopher René Descartes was just one. Economic prosperity went together with cultural development, represented by Spinoza and Rembrandt. It was well illustrated by Dutch painting, which concentrated on landscapes, still lifes and domestic scenes.

In 1672, when Louis XIV invaded the country, the partisans of the princes of Orange deposed Jan de Witt and power passed into the hands of the Stadhouder William III (1672–1702).

The English Civil War and the Glorious Revolution

In England in the 17th century two political revolutions with strong social and religious overtones secured constitutional monarchy against the absolutist ambitions of the Stuarts.

The first ended Charles I's absolute reign (1625–49): this was the 'tyranny' organized between 1629 and 1640 by the Earl of Strafford and Archbishop Laud. The latter was hated by the Puritans and Presbyterians. When he imposed the Anglican prayerbook on the Scots, they rebelled and invaded England. The king was then obliged to recall parliament in order to pay for his army; and parliament took the initiative from him. It condemned Laud and Strafford to death and addressed to the king the Grand Remonstrance of 1641, condemning his policy. An abortive *coup d'état* by the king led to the Civil War that had now become inevitable. Most of the parliament's troops, led by Oliver Cromwell, were Puritans. This 'Battalion of the Saints', which went into battle singing the Psalms, defeated the king's forces at Marston Moor (1644) and Naseby (1645). Cromwell became master of the situation and Charles I was condemned to death and executed in 1649. Parliament then proclaimed a republican Commonwealth, which during its eleven years of existence was dominated by Cromwell. Soon, indeed, under the title of Lord Protector, he established a dictatorship imbued with a Puritan spirit. When he died the English restored the Stuarts and crowned the son of the executed king, Charles II. During his reign, in 1679, the vital law of *Habeas corpus* was approved, guaranteeing individual freedom.

The second revolution – the Glorious Revolution – caused no bloodshed. The new King James II (1685–8) showed absolutist and Catholic tendencies, which led the English to offer the crown to the Dutch Stadhouder, William of Orange, son-in-law of James II and champion of the Protestant cause in continental Europe. William landed in England in November 1688 and marched on London, where the people had rioted to the cry of 'No Popery'. James II gave up his kingdom and took refuge in France. The parliament declared William and his wife Mary, James II's daughter, sovereigns of Great Britain after they had accepted a Bill of Rights in 1689. This document stipulated that 'the power of the laws is above the power of the King' and recognized the right of petition; it abrogated cruel sentences; and it required taxes to be approved by parliament. A few months later, the Toleration Act, although it made no mention of Catholics, established relative freedom of religion.

③ CHARLES I OF ENGLAND (1600–49)
Portrait by Van Dyck, 1635. 272 × 212 cm. Louvre Museum, Paris
A truly royal and highly distinguished portrait of the King who, despite his reputation as a patron of the arts, paid the painter only half the price he had asked.

④ A manifesto by the 'Levellers'
(January 1648)

The poverty and suffering caused by the Civil War gave the first English revolution a social content expressed by the 'Levellers', who preached a real class war and called for radical equality.

May the pressing needs of our stomachs reach Parliament and the City; may the tears of our unhappy starving babies be preserved; may the cries of their tender mothers begging for bread to feed them be graven in metal. Oh, may our dying bodies be seen by every pitying beholder. May it be known that to have bread we sell our beds and our clothing. Oh, our hearts are failing us and we are ready to faint at the end of every road.

① LOUIS XIV'S WARS

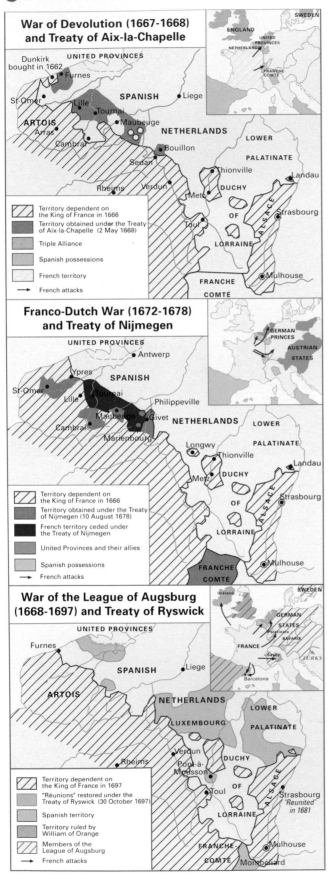

War of Devolution (1667-1668) and Treaty of Aix-la-Chapelle

Dunkirk bought in 1662
UNITED PROVINCES
Furnes
SPANISH
St-Omer
Lille
Tournai
Liege
ARTOIS
Maubeuge
Arras
NETHERLANDS
Cambrai
LOWER
Bouillon
Sedan
PALATINATE
Thionville
Landau
Rheims
Verdun
Metz
DUCHY
OF
Strasbourg
Toul
LORRAINE
FRANCHE
COMTÉ
Mulhouse
ALSACE

SWEDEN
ENGLAND
UNITED PROVINCES
NETHERLANDS
FRANCHE COMTÉ

▨ Territory dependent on the King of France in 1666
▨ Territory obtained under the Treaty of Aix-la-Chapelle (2 May 1668)
▨ Triple Alliance
▨ Spanish possessions
▨ French territory
→ French attacks

Franco-Dutch War (1672-1678) and Treaty of Nijmegen

UNITED PROVINCES
Antwerp
Ypres
SPANISH
St-Omer
Tournai
Lille
Philippeville
Maubeuge
Givet
NETHERLANDS
Cambrai
LOWER
Marienbourg
Longwy
PALATINATE
Thionville
Landau
Metz
DUCHY
OF
Strasbourg
LORRAINE
FRANCHE
COMTÉ
Mulhouse
ALSACE

GERMAN PRINCES
AUSTRIAN STATES

▨ Territory dependent on the King of France in 1666
▨ Territory obtained under the Treaty of Nijmegen (10 August 1678)
▨ French territory ceded under the Treaty of Nijmegen
▨ United Provinces and their allies
▨ Spanish possessions
→ French attacks

War of the League of Augsburg (1668-1697) and Treaty of Ryswick

UNITED PROVINCES
Furnes
Liege
SPANISH
ARTOIS
NETHERLANDS
LOWER
LUXEMBOURG
PALATINATE
Verdun
Rheims
Pont-à-Mousson
DUCHY
OF
Toul
Strasbourg "Reunited" in 1681
LORRAINE
FRANCHE-COMTÉ
Mulhouse
Montbéliard
ALSACE

Ireland
SWEDEN
GERMAN STATES
Palatinate
BAVARIA
FRANCE
Savoy
Barcelona
TURKS

▨ Territory dependent on the King of France in 1697
▨ "Réunions" restored under the Treaty of Ryswick (30 October 1697)
▨ Spanish territory
▨ Territory ruled by William of Orange
▨ Members of the League of Augsburg
→ French attacks

The Europe of Louis XIV: war and the balance of power

Louis XIV applied in Europe a policy of hegemony that led to a long series of wars. Like Richelieu and Mazarin, ministers to his father Louis XIII, Louis XIV wanted to prevent the Habsburgs dominating the continent. Linking his own taste for personal glory to the idea of the state's prestige, he aimed to become the arbiter of the political situation in Europe. What was more, the need to strengthen the country from attack in the north and the north-east encouraged him to try to extend the frontiers of France.

France's wealth and large population favoured its policy of prestige. To pursue that policy, the king raised taxes and recruited a standing army, organized by Le Tellier and Louvois. Its troops, the most effective and well-disciplined in Europe, were commanded by outstanding generals such as Condé, Turenne and Vauban.

The wars continued until 1684, while Louis XIV was still a young man. France revealed its expansionist aims by invading the Spanish Netherlands in 1665 and the United Provinces in 1672, and by annexing Montbéliard, Strasbourg and Colmar, and parts of the Saar and Luxembourg.

French power reached its height in about 1680. The Spanish Habsburgs were powerless to halt their countries' downfall, while the Austrian Habsburgs had been occupied since 1661 in fighting new Turkish attacks in Eastern Europe. In 1683 the Turks again besieged Vienna. It was saved by the King of Poland, Jan Sobieski; and at Mohacs in 1687 and Zenta in 1697 imperial troops defeated the Turks and liberated Hungary.

War began again in 1689 – and it coincided with the decline of absolutism in France. By this time the League of Augsburg had united the Catholics (Spain and the Empire) and the Protestants (England and Holland) against France. When the war ended, in 1697, the Treaty of Ryswick made a first attempt to achieve a balance of power in Europe. This was compromised as early as 1700 by a dispute over the succession to the crown of Spain, which was inherited by a Bourbon, Philip V, the grandson of Louis XIV. The long War of Spanish Succession ended in the Treaties of Utrecht (1713) and Rastadt (1714). France retained its supremacy; but Austria received the Spanish territories in the Netherlands and Italy, thereby counter-balancing French power in Europe. England strengthened its sea power: it won Minorca and Gibraltar, and by the *asiento* agreement could supply the Spanish American colonies with African slaves for 30 years.

Thus a union of the European powers had checked the hegemony of Louis XIV and France.

'Golden Century' or 'Century of Iron'?

By contrast with France, Europe's population as a whole remained static throughout the 17th century at about 100 million.

The reason for this was a disastrously high death-rate, which completely offset the growing number of live births. It resulted from a number of causes, notably war and devastation, and widespread famine due to poor harvests; but there was also an appalling series of epidemics – smallpox, typhus, cholera and above the plague – which ravaged the whole of Europe almost as badly as in the 14th century. The fear of death created a collective psychosis which sought relief in the exuberance of Baroque.

The 17th century was also a period of economic stagnation, from which Great Britain and the Netherlands were almost the only countries to be exempt. From 1630 onwards deliveries of gold to Spain began to decline; by the middle of the century they had virtually ceased. The development of capitalism slowed down to the point of recession, at its worst between 1660 and 1680.

Agricultural production also fell, owing to bad weather, the lack of technological progress, the population crisis and the fall in prices.

Only trade prospered; and its nerve-centre shifted from the Mediterranean to the ports of the Channel and the North Sea. Mercantilism had emerged as the concomitant to industrialization. The tendency now was to increase industrial production to earn gold and silver from abroad, and to develop trade, controlled by the state through great companies and protected against competition from neighbouring countries.

The Dutch, who had become the world's great shippers, dominated the Atlantic and Indian oceans, controlled the spice trade and founded a huge colonial empire. The great joint-stock companies stimulated this large overseas market: the Dutch East India Company, for example, which was formed in 1600, took over the very prosperous spice trade. Enriched by these operations, the Dutch dominated the capital market through the Bank of Amsterdam, founded in 1609, developed their industry and laid the bases for an 'agricultural revolution'.

Britain followed the example of the United Provinces, which in 1700 it overtook as the biggest international trader by sea. Its own East India Company, set up in 1601, was established in former Dutch territory in India. Across the Atlantic, Britain founded an empire, beginning with its 13 colonies along the east coast of North America, and its possessions in Canada and the West Indies. Between 1610 and 1640 British trade increased tenfold. The Bank of England,

② London and the East India Company

The East India Company was set up in London in 1600 to rival the Dutch for control of trade with the Orient. It was described thus in a letter from Diego Sarmiento to Philip III:

The East India Company increases its capital and its fleet a little every day, for its profits are said to be great, to such a point that one of my acquaintances, who had invested 2000 ducats in it two years ago and wanted to receive them back today, received from the hands of the Company itself 4000 ducats.

③ 'THE SYNDICS OF THE DRAPERS' GUILD'

Painting by Rembrandt, 1662. 191 × 279 cm. Rijksmuseum, Amsterdam
Officials of the wool industry whose duty was to verify the cloth and examine the colours of the samples. This group portrait of the members of the corporation was typical of the new bourgeois culture of the Low Countries in the 17th century.

④ Dutch trade

The main goods that the Dutch East India Company brings from India to Europe are spices, silks, cotton textiles, base and precious metals, and porcelain. Of all the spices, the most sought-after is cinnamon, of which there are two varieties, fine and coarse. The fine variety grows only on the island of Ceylon. The Dutch, who control it, prevent the propagation of cinnamon-trees, lest the value of the spice decrease.

Memorials on Dutch trade

① 'A PEASANT FAMILY'
Louis Le Nain. Paris

The peasant's house is where he takes his ease – often only one room, with an earthen floor. There is little furniture; a few sticks burn in the hearth. Sitting round it at night, they tell stories and drink rough wine. Their poverty in this case is illusory: the peasants in this picture are relatively well-to-do.

② 'DESCENT FROM THE CROSS'
Rubens, 1610. Central panel of the triptych in Antwerp Cathedral

This is one of the great Flemish master's first works in Antwerp. It has all the characteristics of Baroque painting: its fine sense of staging, its drama, its animation, expressed by its diagonal composition, and the lively expressions of the faces it portrays.

established in 1694, became the leading financial centre in the world and the pound sterling became Europe's strongest currency.

Elsewhere in Europe, owing to the critical state of the economy, social strife re-emerged throughout the century. Famine, with its devastating effect on the poorest in society, led to many revolts. At the same time, more and more members of the middle class were pauperized. The nobility, enriched by seignorial rents and taxes and subject to royal pressure, became courtiers, abandoning country estates to settle in sumptuous town houses. The sale of titles and public appointments, together with politic marriages, enabled bourgeois citizens to join the nobility. The old hereditary nobility detested what the Duc de Saint-Simon called this 'vile bourgeoisie', which threatened its political power.

The polarization of society was flagrant: there was a blatant contrast between the privileged minority and the downtrodden masses. Workers and employers clashed over wages and working hours, while rents and taxes ate into the meagre resources of smallholders. From 1620 onwards there were renewed conflicts between lords and vassals. And discontent in the countryside was echoed in the towns, where the poor were equally affected by the economic crisis.

In France absolute monarchy relied on the bourgeoisie to back its authority. But in Holland the capitalist bourgeoisie was able to impose its political will, while in England it contributed to the triumph of constitutional monarchy.

Baroque and classicism

The 17th century, midway between the Renaissance and the 18th-century Enlightenment, gave birth to a dazzling intellectual movement in spite of the unpromising context in which it emerged.

It was during this 'Baroque century' that the scientific revolution superseded the medieval view of the world. Now scientists were at odds with the universities and had to take refuge with princes and kings. The mathematician Johann Kepler entered the service of the Emperor; Galileo, a professor at the university of Pisa and Padua, placed himself under the protection of the Duke of Tuscany.

Kepler (1571–1630) followed Nicolaus Copernicus in exploring the universe; he determined that not only the earth but all the planets revolved round the sun. Galileo, from Italy, produced experimental proof of the theories of Copernicus and confirmed that movement obeyed mathematical laws. The problem of the vacuum was solved by Evangelista Torricelli and Blaise Pascal, who discovered atmospheric pressure.

This intense scientific activity reached its height in the work of Isaac Newton (1642–1727), who was a professor at Cambridge. He discovered the exact formula for the law of universal gravitation. Meanwhile, in medicine, his compatriot Sir William Harvey had worked out the principles of the circulation of the blood and the working of the heart.

Francis Bacon, also in England, demonstrated the validity of the experimental method, while the Frenchman René Descartes based his thinking on pure reason and in his *Discours de la méthode* (*Discourse on Method*) presented a rationalist view of the world that was a direct threat to absolutist regimes.

The end of the 17th century in Italy saw the rise of Baroque art. Its sensuousness was dramatic and expressive: Baroque artists rejected restraint and order and expressed their freedom with unexpected, grandiose and highly naturalistic, *trompe-l'oeil* effects. The work of Bernini (St Peter's Square in Rome) and Borromini (Sant'Agnese in Agone, in the Piazza Navona, Rome) were models for German, Austrian and Spanish architects. Baroque art was adopted as the art of the Catholic Counter-Reformation.

The enterprising painter Michelangelo de Caravaggio brought new ideas to an art that had remained derivative after the achievement of Raphael. In Spain painters pursued naturalism and chiaroscuro: the greatest of them was Velásquez. In Antwerp the dominant figures were Rubens and his disciple Van Dyck, who had a great influence on English painting. In the Netherlands, the great masters were Rembrandt and Vermeer.

17th-century Baroque also produced remarkable literature. In Spain this was the 'golden age'. In 1615 Miguel de Cervantes published *El Ingenioso Hidalgo Don Quixote de la Mancha* (*The Ingenious Knight Don Quixote de la Mancha*), which was at once Spanish and universal. Dramatists like Lope de Vega, Tirso de Molina and Pedro Calderòn de la Barca inspired many other Europeans. In England this was the age of Shakespeare and the Jacobean playwrights, while the Dutch read Pieter Corneliszoon Hooft's *De Nederlansche Historiën*, or *Dutch Chronicles*.

In France this was *le Grand Siècle*, the Great Century, marked by the classicism imposed by Louis XIV at Versailles. Nicholas Boileau's *L'Art poétique*, *The Art of Poetry*, laid down what rules it was considered writers must obey. Classical models from the ancient world inspired the comedies of Molière, the tragedies of Corneille and Racine, and the fables of La Fontaine. In the 18th century, classicism came to irradiate the whole of Europe.

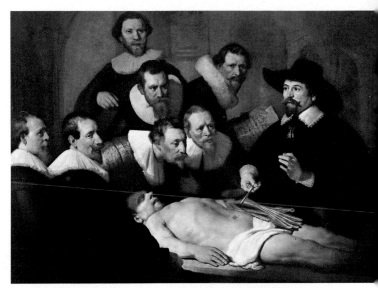

③ PROFESSOR TULP'S ANATOMY LESSON
Rembrandt, 1632. 169.5 × 216.5 cm. Mauritshuis, The Hague

④ THE ECSTASY OF ST TERESA
Marble sculpture by Bernini, *c.*1650, in the Cornaro Chapel of Santa Maria della Vittoria, Rome
Theatrical gestures, the effects of light, the expressive treatment of feelings here convey a dramatic quality. Bernini (1598–1680), a sculptor, architect, decorator, playwright and poet, was regarded as the master of Italian 17th-century Baroque.

Derry

Belfast

Galway

Bunratty

Drogheda

Dublin

Limerick

Blarney

Youghal

Kinsale

Edinburgh

Hardwick Hall

Wollaton Hall

Burghley House

Kirby Hall

Longleat
House

Oundle

Wilton
House

Montacute
House

London

Amsterdam

Haarlem

Ape

Den Haag

Rotterdam

Cleme

Brugge

Gent

Antwerpen

Liège

*Brussel
Bruxelles*

Douai

Charleville-
Mézières

Caen

Balleroy

Rennes

Chantilly

Écouen

Paris

Anet

Vaux-le-
Vicomte

Joinvi

Versailles

Fontainebleau

Blois

Chambord

Tanlay

Ancy-le-
Franc

Neufbri

Azay-le-
Rideau

Cheverny

Bussy-
Rabutin

Richelieu

Chenonceau

Valençay

Dijon

Neuchâtel

Gene

La Rochelle

Brouage

La Bastie
d'Urfé

Lyon

Biron

Santiago de
Compostela

León

Valladolid

Montauban

Braga

Porto

Viseu

Salamanca

Bayonne

Pau

Toulouse

Uzès

*Aix-en-
Provence*

Coimbra

Tomar

Zaragoza

Escorial

Madrid

Lisboa

Toledo

Aranjuez

Setubal

Valencia

Évora

Ubeda

Jaen

Sevilla

Murcia

Granada

The Past in the Present Day
REFORMATION EUROPE

Legend:

- civic building
- castle, palace or manor-house
- religious monument
- *museum, library or collection well stocked with items on this period*
- frontiers of 20th-century states

500 km

Map labels:

Stockholm
Riga
Kalmar
Vil'njus
København
Vallø
Gdansk
skov
Güstrow
burg
Schwerin
Poznan
Warszawa
Berlin
Celle
Braunschweig
Wittenberg
Kassel
Dresden
Zamość
Gotha
Praha
Lancut
kfurt
Bamberg
Litohyšl
Krakow
Würzburg
Nürnberg
Heidelberg
ttgart
Augsburg
Wien
Sucevița
München
Budapest
Moldovița
Salzburg
Voroneț
Innsbruck
Graz
Verona
Vicenza
Sibiu
no
Bucuresti
Venezia
Parma
Padova
Bologna
Firenze
Siena
Urbino
Perugia
Dubrovnik
Todi
Roma
Tivoli
Napoli
Lecce
Palermo
Catania

① LOUIS XV IN MAJESTY

Portrait by Louis Michel Van Loo. Château of Versailles

Succeeding to the throne at the age of five and nicknamed the Beloved, he gradually lost his popularity, but did not deserve the reputation for feebleness and frivolity that some historians have given him. At all events, his reign was marked by real national prosperity and the spread of French influence.

② PLANTING A TREE OF LIBERTY

Lesueur. Musée Carnavalet, Paris

'In their enthusiasm for the liberty they thought they had won, people had the idea of planting trees to perpetuate the memory of it .... The National Guards accompanied the mayor and fine music gave a fillip to the celebration.'

1700–21	Great Northern War
1701–13/14	War of Spanish Succession
1703	Foundation of St Petersburg
1740	Beginning of the reigns of Maria Theresa of Austria and Frederick II of Prussia
1756–63	Seven Years' War
1762	Beginning of the reign of Catherine II of Russia
1772	Completion of the Encyclopédie
July 1776	American Declaration of Independence
1780–4	The United Provinces at war with England
4 August 1789	French nobles' privileges abolished
23 August 1789	Declaration of the Rights of Man and of the Citizen
August 1791	Declaration of Pillnitz
21 January 1793	Execution of Louis XVI
1795	Partition of Poland
18 October 1797	Treaty of Campo Formio
9 November 1799	Coup d'état of 18 Brumaire
2 December 1804	Napoleon Emperor
2 December 1805	Austerlitz
1814/15	Congress of Vienna
1815	Creation of the German Confederation

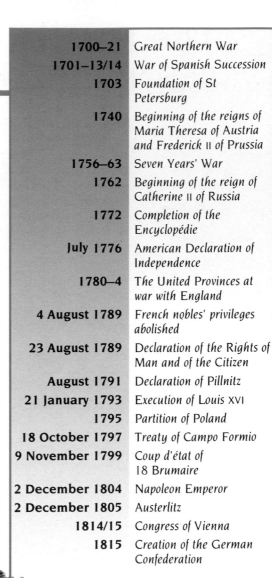

VIIII

THE ENLIGHTENMENT AND THE IDEA OF LIBERTY

FROM 1700 TO 1825

The period of relative calm that began with the Treaty of Utrecht in 1713 was particularly welcome. The Continent was once again open to travellers. Many young and less young people went on the Grand Tour and discovered the wonders of Europe in Amsterdam, Versailles, Florence and, above all, Rome.

The sovereigns and nobility of Europe shared a common culture: but sporadic conflicts revealed the tension and rivalry that continued to divide them. These were not 'people's wars', in which a whole nation took up arms to defend itself or attack the enemy. They were local confrontations caused by quarrels between dynasties that were often related by blood or marriage, and they involved armies of mercenaries in various different uniforms.

But changes were on the way. Since the 17th century science had made remarkable progress and people were beginning to pierce the mystery of the cosmos and its laws. Nature took an essential place in the writings of the Enlightenment. Its philosophers praised the natural way of life in recently discovered distant lands. They concluded that man should be subject only to 'natural' laws and they broadly criticized the political and religious establishment of European countries, which they thought infringed the liberty of the people.

The first to contest a European government of the *ancien régime* were the English colonies in North America, which rebelled against the British crown in 1776. Soon afterwards came the French Revolution. From that moment on France began to have a real citizens' army, which Napoleon Bonaparte led across most of Europe to spread revolutionary ideas and increase his own power.

Europe could no longer turn back. The ideas of 'liberty' and 'democracy' were henceforth implanted in people's minds.

❸ VERSAILLES: THE GALERIE DES GLACES

❹ EUROPE AFTER THE TREATY OF UTRECHT

——— Frontier of the Holy Roman Empire

▨ Possessions of the Austrian Habsburgs in 1715

255

1

The Grand Tour:
A European Education

① YOUNG ARISTOCRATS IN ROME
Painting by Nathaniel Dance and James Russell, 1750. British School,
London
*Rome was one of the favourite stopping-places for young aristocrats
looking for classical remains. Their tours were prepared long in
advance and guide-books were already in vogue.*

② 'IS THIS MY SON?'
Caricature by Grimm. British Museum, London
*The Grand Tour was not always seen as beneficial. It was often
feared that when they returned the young people would have
acquired eccentric behaviour and outlandish manners. This father is
clearly shocked by the Baroque appearance of his son.*

The cultural itinerary

Europe took a long time to recover from the
violence and destruction involved in the Thirty
Years' War (1618–48) and the wars of Louis XIV
(1667–1713). Yet, even if some parts of Germany
remained unsettled and dangerous for years to
come, life was returning to normal and at least
enough for travellers to go in search of adventure,
and particularly the young sons of good families
set out on the Grand Tour.

Usually accompanied by a servant and a tutor
to watch over their behaviour and their studies,
these young people from England, Ireland, Germany and elsewhere were sent abroad for a year
or two by their parents to learn languages,
encounter other ways of life and above all to
acquaint themselves with fine art and good manners. Because the Grand Tour was an essential
part of the education of young noblemen, all
Europe's aristocracy came to share the same
culture. Jean-Jacques Rousseau, speaking of the
need to put an end to international conflict,
declared: 'There are only Europeans; they all
have the same tastes, the same passions, the same
mode of life.' Whether French or German or of
whatever nationality, politicians and philosophers, scientists and artists were all conscious
of being European.

Dangerous roads, uncomfortable inns, strange
food and stranger diseases were what they met on
the way. But they had the services of numerous
guides and they often carried a medical kit in their
baggage. Their routes took them to Bruges,
Utrecht and other towns in the United Provinces
and the Austrian Netherlands, where they discovered the artistic wealth of what was then the
greatest trading region of Europe. At the end of
the 17th century, Amsterdam was the economic
capital of the world, just as France and the French
language were its cultural lodestone. A century
later, despite the French Revolution, Paris and
Versailles continued to have a large number of
visitors.

But Italy was the goal of the journey. The
Grand Tourists could be seen in Venice, Genoa,
Florence and above all in Rome, with their
sketchbooks, their note-tablets and their easels.
They bought paintings, sculptures and other
souvenirs of classical antiquity or the Renaissance, which they sent in crates to their family
mansions all over Europe, where these impressive

reminders of bygone travels can still be admired.

Russia and the countries of central and northern Europe were less traditional resorts for the Grand Tour, but they nevertheless attracted many visitors, who rediscovered the tastes and culture of the West at the Court of the Tsar or in the royal palaces of Denmark and Sweden.

On their journeys the travellers also discovered the treasures of Dresden, Potsdam, Prague and Budapest, as well as those of Vienna, where the Habsburgs had built the Schönbrunn Palace to rival Versailles. The kings of Poland, too, despite their precarious position, built grandiose palaces, as did their noble vassals.

Peter the Great of Russia enlisted an Italian architect and a French garden designer for his summer palace at Peterhof, 18 miles outside his new capital of St Petersburg (founded in 1703), while the superb Winter Palace in the capital was the work of an Italian trained mainly in France and Austria. The royal palace in Stockholm, although designed by a Swede, was largely inspired by the Louvre; and the Swedish court was a great centre of cosmopolitan culture. Paris also inspired the Danish architect responsible for the Kongens Nytorv or King's New Square in Copenhagen, a magnificent open space flanked by five palaces. Conversely, the fountains at Versailles were the work of a Dane, Ole Römer, and a family of Italian origin, the Francines.

❸SCHÖNBRUNN PALACE, VIENNA
The taste for grandiose palaces like that of Versailles went on spreading throughout the 18th century. Schönbrunn was no exception. The Habsburgs turned it from a modest hunting lodge to a summer residence with gardens in the French style, and a Galerie des glaces that reflected the wealth and taste of its owner.

❹THE KONGENS NYTORV, COPENHAGEN
Largely financed by the profits from trade and navigation, four palaces formed the octagonal Amalienborg Square. Built in 1760 for four members of the nobility, from 1794 onwards they were the official residence of the Danish sovereign.

① THE VILLA ROTONDA NEAR VICENZA
Andrea Palladio, the great Italian architect of the late 16th century, used ancient Rome as his model. His creations were widely acclaimed in Europe. The Villa Rotonda near Vicenza greatly influenced 17th- and 18th-century architecture: the Palladian style can be found throughout Europe.

② THE LAKE OF KILLARNEY IN IRELAND
J. Fisher. National Gallery, Dublin

A *common culture*

The Italian villas inspired by the architect Andrea Palladio are generally seen as typical of the aristocracy, just as the château of Versailles was a model for Europe's kings. Europe's noble mansions indeed borrowed elements from the architecture of the different countries that young gentlemen had observed during their Grand Tour. Often the great houses of England and Ireland looked like villas built in the Italian countryside. These imposing edifices might contain museums full of souvenirs brought back from Europe and elsewhere, as well as libraries of books on travel, science and architecture. Sometimes a zoological garden was established on the property, but as a rule the estate was set out on the rigorous geometrical lines of the great continental gardens such as those designed by Le Nôtre at Versailles.

During the 18th century, however, tastes evolved and soon the Romantic spirit, attached to nature in all its forms, preferred natural-seeming landscapes, carefully arranged, with hollows, lakes and woods tastefully disposed here and there, in the manner of the famous English garden and landscape designer 'Capability' Brown. Wild and majestic landscapes, like that of the lakes of Killarney in Ireland, aroused admiration and attracted tourists. Painters and poets echoed these tastes: one of them was William Wordsworth, who celebrated the beauty of the English Lake District.

A similar phenomenon appeared in music. European music-lovers discovered the works of the great composers, most of them German, whose patrons were the monarchs and aristocrats

③ THE CLASSICAL LANDSCAPE IN BRITAIN   *Crome Court*, painted by Richard Wilson (1713–88)
When he returned from Italy in 1750, impressed by the splendour of Roman monuments, Wilson transposed them into English landscapes, serene, simple and poetic.

of Europe. Thus Handel was welcomed by the Hanoverian court in London, while later, in Hungary, the Esterhazy family nurtured the talent of Haydn.

As the 18th century progressed, music became more and more Romantic, and works like Beethoven's Sixth Symphony, the 'Pastoral', celebrated the virtues of nature. Nor was music a pleasure reserved for the rich. Opera, which now became popular, attracted the crowds.

Emigration

While some went abroad to visit the cultural centres of Europe as they pleased or with permission from their parents, many men and women were driven into exile for political or religious reasons.

It was a general rule in Europe, in fact, that a monarch's subjects should practise that monarch's religion. It was unthinkable that another form of Christianity should be tolerated in the state, and still less another religion. In this respect, King Henry IV of France was ahead of his time when in 1598 he proclaimed the Edict of Nantes, putting an end to the War of Religion in France, and recognizing the Huguenots' or Protestants' freedom of worship and their full civic rights in certain parts of the kingdom.

When Louis XIV revoked the Edict of Nantes in 1685, this led to mass emigration by the Huguenots. Competent, hard-working and often ambitious, they were very well received by Protestant states in Switzerland, Brandenburg (which took more than 12,000), and the United Provinces, where some of them embarked for South Africa. William III and Mary II, the King and Queen of Britain and Ireland, as well as their successor Anne, realized the contribution that the Huguenots could make to Ireland, increasing the Protestant population and establishing a textile industry.

At that time the Irish Catholics were oppressed by the British crown, although they made up the majority of the Irish population. To practise their religion freely, to have the chance of an education and of entering the professions, some of them emigrated to Catholic countries. Despite the threats hanging over their families and themselves, many left Ireland to join the French or Spanish armies, to prepare for the priesthood in Irish seminaries in Spain, in the Spanish and later Austrian Netherlands, in France, Italy, or elsewhere, or to start up businesses which in many cases proved prosperous.

④ THE BEGGAR'S OPERA
Painting by William Hogarth. Tate Gallery, London
Hogarth, a passionate devotee of music and the theatre, illustrates here Act III, Scene 2, of The Beggar's Opera, presented in London in 1728. It was a parody of Italian opera and of the music of Handel. Opera was very popular in Europe, as much so in Britain as in Germany, where the Italian style developed. In France, after Lully, the creator of French opera, Rameau and Gluck in the 18th century made it their own.

⑤ THE EMIGRATION OF PROTESTANTS
Jan Luiken. Library of Protestantism, Paris
Despite a decree forbidding French Protestants to emigrate, many were so weary of persecution, intimidation and increasingly harsh legislation that they left. 173,000 fled to Holland and to Great Britain. 1450 less fortunate went to the galleys. All their possessions were confiscated and passed on to those who denounced them.

2 Dynasties and Wars

While the nobility in Europe shared a more or less uniform way of life, there remained considerable differences among national forms of government. Monarchy was certainly the general rule, but European monarchs exercised their authority in different ways.

'Absolutism' – a term much used at the time – was generally the model. An absolute monarch was responsible to nobody but God: he decided everything and the expression of his will had the force of law. Even if notions of 'individual freedom' and of a 'social contract' were beginning to emerge, they remained obscure to the great majority of people. It was more widely believed that the Emperor or the King was the embodiment of divine will and that he held his power by hereditary succession as part of a royal family or a dynasty chosen by God. The 'divine right of kings' meant that God the Father, the Creator, was the model for the head of state, as He was for the father, the head of the family. The Latin expression *Ex deo rex, ex rege lex* – The king comes from God and the law from the king – precisely expressed the sovereign's authority.

The United Provinces

In Europe the United Provinces were an exception. They formed a federation of seven provinces, each ruled by provincial estates. The Stadhouder, whom each province usually chose from among members of the Orange–Nassau family, was in principle at the service of the provincial estates, for whose military defence he was responsible. But the Orange family gradually turned towards a monarchical type of government and during the 18th century the office of Stadhouder became hereditary.

When William III of Orange became King of England in 1688, this brought the United Provinces politically close to their great economic competitor and from then on they could not resist England's sea power. The pro-British policy of Stadhouder William V (1751–95), which was against the interests of the Dutch upper bourgeoisie, led to opposition by the 'Patriots', who insisted on war with Britain (1780–4). This damaged trade and destabilized Dutch politics.

It was against this background that the armies of the young French Revolution came on the scene and were welcomed as liberators by the 'Patriots'.

❷ THE ROTTERDAM STOCK EXCHANGE
Engraving by Johannes de Vor. Maritime Museum, Rotterdam

Rotterdam was Holland's second largest trading town and its stock exchange was the country's largest. Maritime activity, and the development of trade and industry brought about prosperity.

England

The powers of the King of England were less than those of other contemporary monarchs, but for all that England was not a democracy in the modern sense of the term. The great aristocratic families, whose wealth and power came from their huge landed properties, steered the policy of the country, for it was they who dominated parliament; and parliament alone could vote the credits that enabled the king to govern and to maintain his army.

This state of affairs led enlightened circles on the continent to praise English institutions. Yet, this praise was based on illusions. The British sovereigns had never explicitly renounced their 'divine right', even after the 'Glorious Revolution' of 1688, which drove the Catholic Stuart James II from the throne to make way for his daughter Mary II and her Dutch husband William III of Orange, both Protestants.

For this reason some authors of radical pamphlets, including Thomas Paine, thought that the English monarchy was no better than its continental counterparts. And because Paine called for a significant reduction in the powers of the Crown and the Church of England, he was forced into exile under pain of prosecution and imprisonment. Even so, the kings of England were not despots, at a time when the best that could be said of the other monarchs in Europe was that they were 'benevolent despots'.

Russia

The Russians had been subject to the Mongols since 1240, but were freed from them in the late 15th century with the help of the Russian Orthodox Church, which for a long time had been separated from Byzantium. Those responsible for this reconquest were the Muscovite princes, who had developed serfdom to secure the loyalty of the minor nobility against the powerful boyars, and had extended their sovereignty towards the Baltic and the Black Sea. Westerners were for a long time unaware of these developments.

At the beginning of the 17th century Muscovite expansion towards the Baltic came up against the Poles and the Lithuanians, who counter-attacked and captured Moscow. In 1613 a popular uprising drove them out and put the Romanov family on the throne of the Tsars (from the Latin *caesar*). Peter I the Great, who came to power in 1689, hastened Russia's integration with the West. During his reign the country consolidated and extended its frontiers, establishing industry and improving the administration. He copied more advanced countries and encouraged foreign spe-

❸ THE HOUSE OF COMMONS, LONDON
1710. The Palace of Westminster, London
Elected by boroughs and counties, these 500 Members of Parliament had to satisfy the wishes of local groups, serve material interests and enhance the prestige of their families. Political life being dominated by trade, the great questions debated were those of loans, taxes and customs duties.

❹ PETER THE GREAT
Popular Russian woodcut, 17th century
The emperor visited Holland, England and Austria incognito to study the customs and technology of the West. When he returned to Russia, he imposed a number of reforms, some of them unpopular and rather superficial, such as the cutting-off of beards.

❶ THE PARTITIONING OF POLAND

300 km

Riga

Dvina

Danzig

EAST PRUSSIA

KINGDOM OF PRUSSIA

Niemen

Warsaw

Bug

R U S S I A

Desna

Oder

Vistula

Cracow

Dnieper

AUSTRIA

Danube

KINGDOM OF HUNGARY

Polish frontiers in 1772	1772 partition
Frontiers after the third partition in 1795	1793 partition
	1795 partition

❷ MEETING BETWEEN JOSEPH II AND CATHERINE OF RUSSIA

Historical Museum, Vienna

Two great representatives of 'enlightened despotism'. Aware of the changes that were coming about, they managed to introduce important reforms while taking care to preserve their own authority.

cialists to come to Russia. He went abroad to observe foreign ways. His new capital, St Petersburg, was based on Western models.

One of his most remarkable successors, Catherine II the Great (1762–96), took a lively interest in new ideas about politics and the art of government. She kept up a correspondence with Voltaire and even invited him to come to Russia to talk with her. She tried to rule as humanely as possible, but without calling into question the bases of an economy that relied largely on serfdom. Catherine was prepared to allow the Russian nobility certain rights over local administration. Yet she would never have dreamed of sharing her own authority. If she had done so, she would have thought it a dereliction of duty.

The example of Poland showed how difficult the situation could become when being sovereign no longer had any meaning. Because the Polish nobility elected the king, it thought it could also manipulate him; and this left the field wide open to conspiracies fomented at home or abroad. After suffering a series of attacks, the country saw its territory partitioned among its neighbours. Then, in 1795, Poland disappeared from the map for more than a hundred years.

The Habsburg Empire

More celebrated for its name and its titles than for its real power, the Habsburg dynasty ruled the last possessions of the Holy Roman Empire. Austria and about a hundred German-speaking states made up the German part of the Empire, which also embraced Hungary, Bohemia and a large part of Italy. When she was not fighting to protect her empire, the Empress Maria Theresa (1740–80) tried to improve her government and develop the economy. Her son Joseph II (1780–90) was no less autocratic, but he introduced religious toleration for the various Christian churches, while recognizing the supremacy of the Catholic Church. The abolition of serfdom, which he replaced with a system of paid labour, nevertheless led to serious social unrest.

Prussia, an important constituent of the empire, was opposed to the authority of Austria and in the following century it put an end to the Habsburg hegemony. Frederick II of Hohenzollern, who had developed the Kingdom of Prussia out of the Duchy of Brandenburg, allowed his subjects great religious freedom. Well aware of what the state could gain from the expansion of education, Frederick encouraged the establishment of schools. Like Catherine the Great, he took an interest in the writers of his day, who favoured effective and humane government. Although he was an absolute ruler, he used his power to modernize his country: he drained the Oder marshes and put them under crops; he set up new industries and established a better banking system; he improved the roads and he built canals.

Wars

The Emperor Charles VI feared that after his death the monarchs of Europe would contest his daughter Maria Theresa's succession to the throne of Austria. He therefore made them solemnly promise to do nothing against her interests. But, when the young empress succeeded to her father's throne, the temptation to profit from her inexperience proved too strong. Frederick II seized Silesia and threw Europe into turmoil. France allied with Prussia against its Austrian rival. Great Britain joined Maria Theresa to restrain France, which Britain feared would expand its colonies in North America and India.

After eight years of war Frederick II kept Silesia; and, despite the treaty signed in 1748, the Austrian empress went on seeking alliances in an attempt to recover her property. By dint of negotiation she achieved the unthinkable – an alliance with her perpetual enemy, France. And without too much difficulty she also obtained the support of Russia, which was worried by the devouring ambition of Prussia.

In view of these spectacular changes, Great Britain decided that it had every interest in forming an alliance with Prussia. This diplomatic revolution was known as 'the reversal of alliances'. The Seven Years' War that broke out in 1756 was by that time practically inevitable. Despite everything, it profited Maria Theresa not at all, since Prussia not only retained Silesia, but also became a more serious rival to Austria. France and Great Britain fought each other at sea and on land, in their colonial empires. By 1763 Britain had attained supremacy in India and North America.

Since 1721 the Scandinavian countries, and Sweden in particular, had no longer enjoyed the position they had had in Europe in the 17th century. Poland and Prussia had enlarged their Baltic coastline; Russia had opened a broad outlet on the Gulf of Finland. Denmark, which had once dominated all of Scandinavia, now held only Norway; while Sweden kept only Finland out of its Baltic empire.

When Charles XII (1682–1718) came to the throne of Sweden in 1697 at the age of 15, Sweden's enemies saw this as the moment to end its preponderance. Despite his military genius, Charles XII finally lost the Great Northern War (1700–21), ending the Swedish hegemony.

❸ A letter from Frederick II to Voltaire

. . . Germany today is as France was at the time of Francis I. The taste for literature is beginning to spread; we must wait for Nature to cause true geniuses to be born, as under the governments of Richelieu and Mazarin. The soil that produced one Leibniz can produce others.

I shall not live to see those fine days for my country, but I can foresee the possibility. You will tell me that this leaves you quite indifferent and that I can prophesy all too easily if I push my prediction as far into the future as I can. That is how I prophesy, and in full security, since no one can contradict me.

For myself, I am consoled by having lived in the century of Voltaire: that is enough for me. May he live, may he inwardly digest, may he be of good cheer and above all may he not forget the hermit of Sans-Souci. Vale.

24 July 1775

❹ CHARLES XII (1682–1718)
Painting by Huchtenburg. Gemälde Gallery, Brunswick
Throughout Charles's reign Sweden crossed swords with Frederick IV of Denmark, Peter the Great of Russia and Augustus III, King of Poland. In 1709 he took refuge with the Turks. His fortunes never recovered. While trying to restore them, he was mysteriously killed at the siege of Fredrikshald. He left Sweden exhausted, but he has gone down in history as a young and valiant military leader.

Social and Economic Life

1 A PEASANT'S LOT IS NOT A HAPPY ONE
George Morland. Tate Gallery, London

There were fewer famines in the 18th century, but peasants continued to live under the threat of a bad harvest which would reduce their purchasing power. So they sought industrial work that could be done at home – cottage industries – such as weaving, although it was badly paid. Life was still hard. The winter cold was mitigated by living with the cattle.

2 A PUBLIC HANGING

As a supreme example of cruelty, the spectacle of a public hanging was very popular. It was normal to take the children to the market-place where the scaffold had been put up. People even hired neighbouring windows to have a better view.

The life of the poor

Quite apart from war, the living conditions of much of Europe's population remained difficult in the 18th century. Towns were insalubrious, seldom paved, often ill-lit and unbearably evil-smelling. The absence of murderous conflicts like those of the 17th century led to a great increase in the population, with the result that the towns became more and more crowded. On a reasonable estimate, the population had grown by 50 per cent by the end of the century, although there were wide variations according to the decade and the area concerned. In England the number of inhabitants rose from 5.5 to 9 million and in France from 18 to 26 million.

People became aware of the need to improve the roads, refuse disposal, hygiene and safety of Europe's towns. Unhealthy and overcrowded districts were razed to the ground so as to create large open spaces like the Place Louis xv in Paris and its numerous imitations.

Even so, the great majority of people lived in the country and the land could not feed the many new mouths demanding nourishment. In the 19th century and long afterwards people condemned what William Blake called 'the dark Satanic mills' of the Industrial Revolution, contrasting their unhealthy working conditions with the open-air life of the peasants. Yet in the country the poor and their children endured long working hours, hunger and sickness, and lived in cottages that were dark and damp.

Life in the countryside began to change in the 18th century with the agricultural revolution, less famous than its industrial counterpart. The open-field system and common land gradually gave way to enclosures, especially in England.

But Europe was far from being able to absorb its growing population. So peasants began the emigration to the towns which increased in the centuries to come, swelling the ranks of the urban poor, who were often obliged to beg for a living. Painters have handed down pictures of these towns, where the dwellings of the rich coexisted with the blackest poverty and where the nobleman and the beggar rubbed shoulders in the crowd.

The rich and powerful were aware of the situation and fully realized the danger it involved. Although often motivated by Christian charity, philanthropy was also a means of protecting the interests of the better-off, who knew the threat that poverty represented for the security of the state.

Many efforts were made, therefore, to remedy the plight of the poor. Or, rather, that of the 'deserving' poor: there was no pity for the unworthy, even if finding work was almost impossible. They had to shift for themselves and often took to crime, which was harshly punished. Indeed, people had a particularly morbid taste for punishment of every kind. Long before the appearance of the guillotine, there was enthusiasm for the whip, for breaking on the wheel or – still more refined – for hanging.

The only haven of comfort for the poor was the Church. The sisters of St Vincent de Paul operated in a number of Catholic countries; other religious communities ran hospitals and organized works of charity. In the Protestant countries, notably in Scandinavia and England, there were taxes to help the poor. The Poor Law in England, for example, compelled every parish to raise money to finance aid. Nevertheless, none of these measures solved the problem and, even when assistance was possible, it carried a stigma.

The rate of infant mortality was extremely high. Whatever his or her social origin, a baby in arms was lucky to survive early childhood. The children of the poor were naturally the most vulnerable, especially in cases of unwanted births.

The problem of abandoned children was considerable, to judge by the number taken in by orphanages. Most of these institutions were sparing with the food they gave their inmates and ruled them with a rod of iron.

Those children that survived still had to overcome the hazards of life. However, the 18th century escaped the great killer epidemics like that of typhus in the 17th century or cholera in the 1830s.

Public health was still a serious problem; but it was improving. By the end of the 18th century hospitals were becoming numerous, sometimes thanks to Church funds, but often owing to the Christian charity of private citizens. Surgery was still rudimentary. The red and white emblem of the barbers was also that of the corporation of barber-surgeons. Anaesthesia was beginning to be used against pain, but it remained a perilous enterprise. Vaccination against smallpox, the disease that had disfigured and killed Queen Mary, the wife of William III, was another great discovery. Adopted by the English royal family in view of the results obtained among the poor, it spread very rapidly throughout the country.

③ THE DEBTORS' PRISON
William Hogarth. Sir John Soane Museum, London
'The world is a theatre', Hogarth seems to say. However, despite the rather theatrical nature of this painting, English prisons did receive a number of families whose only crime was debt.

④ Smallpox in the County of Devon

This account was given me by my correspondent in the County of Devon: 'A terrible fever is raging here.'

Exeter was affected at the first warm spell: robust men, until then in perfect health, died. Before the heatwave set in, their death-throes might last ten to fourteen days. Now, the sick resist for barely three or four days.

The appearance of the pocks is not systematic. If they erupt, the malady does not generally return. If not, the patient may relapse a first or even a second time and die when he thought himself cured.

The risks of contagion are such that only former patients are allowed to visit the sick.

Very often, the fever is accompanied by deafness, which even renders the patient insensible to the sound of a trumpet or a hunting horn. At first, people believed that this absence of reaction was a sign that the patient was dying. Unaware that it was a failure of hearing, and thinking that no more could be done, they expected death at any moment. Today, they contrive to communicate with the patient by showing him objects and thereby succeed in restoring his strength.

This fever is associated with a benign form of smallpox.

The ravages of smallpox and of an epidemic fever (probably influenza). Article dated 5 July 1695, extract from the Houghton archives

❶ A FLEMISH SCHOOL IN THE 17TH CENTURY
Adriaen van Ostade. Louvre Museum, Paris
A representative view of schools in Europe at that time. Note that the teacher deals with the children individually and not all at the same time.

❷ PUPILS OF A CHARITY SCHOOL
Plunket Museum, Dublin
The charity schools took on children and old people. Each institution was often distinguished by a colour which was also used in the pupils' uniforms.

Children and schools

Aware that poverty could breed revolt, the ruling classes saw in education a means of improving matters.

Irrespective of their social background, few children went to school. Those of good family generally had a tutor and sometimes continued their studies at a grammar school and then at a university – although these had a very poor reputation in most countries. The most fortunate, finally, embarked on the Grand Tour.

It was at home that the daughters of wealthy families learned to become ladies of quality. They were educated both by their mothers, who taught them needlework and the running of a house, and by masters of dancing and music.

The level of education of the people was usually very low, except in Prussia and Scotland. In Prussia, continuing the work of his father, Frederick II the Great made primary education compulsory long before other sovereigns did. Based on the idea of progression, the Prussian educational system took account of the interests and characteristics of every child. In Scotland universal education was organized by the Presbyterian Church and strongly influenced by Calvinist ideas about teaching.

In France the poor were educated by the Brothers of Christian Schools, a religious congregation founded at the end of the 17th century by Jean-Baptiste de la Salle.

At the beginning of the 19th century the Irish Christian Brothers undertook to educate the poor in much of Ireland. Later, their work spread to other countries.

In England, there was an increasing number of charity schools supported by local benefactors but financed by parish associations, which also laid down the curriculum.

Alongside these organized schools there were others established on the private initiative of men and women who set up a classroom in their own homes. These teachers were poorly paid, often daily, by the children who came to learn from them. But such infant schools enabled women, mostly widows, to earn a living.

Itinerant teachers travelled through Ireland, giving classes in hired halls or in improvised open-air shelters. In France similar open-air schools were known as 'country schools'.

It would be somewhat misleading to speak of classes within these schools, since the term presumes a separation of the children according to their level of education, i.e. roughly by age. But in the 18th century (and even in the 19th) the situation was very different: a single teacher, sometimes helped by the oldest pupils ('monitors') was in charge of all the children, giving them different texts according to the level they had reached. Since they did not always have books, the pupils sometimes had to be content with simple posters. The curriculum included reading, writing and elementary arithmetic. The textbooks that existed for each of these subjects were little used in children's schools. The pupils worked from whatever books, novels or religious tracts, their teachers managed to obtain.

Children's literature

But the situation evolved. People became aware that children were not just underdeveloped adults.

Until then, it had been thought that the overflowing energy, vivid imagination and insatiable curiosity so characteristic of childhood were puerile attitudes that should be repressed or at least curbed. Now, however, children came to be accepted as what they were and education had to take account of it. The impressive number of books written for young people amply reflected this new approach.

For example, Daniel Defoe's *Robinson Crusoe* and Jonathan Swift's *Gulliver's Travels*, originally written for adults, became favourite reading for children. Robinson Crusoe especially fascinated them, because his adventure carried them off into an extraordinary world. Parents and teachers appreciated the book all the more because it had a high moral tone, rewarding faith and virtue, and because it contained information about foreign countries and nature. Abridged and illustrated editions intended for children appeared in a number of languages. Jean-Jacques Rousseau himself made Defoe's novel one of the essential elements in the education of his imaginary pupil Emile.

Rousseau, and all practising teachers, created such a demand for children's literature that writers and publishers hastened to meet it. Many such books, especially those published in France, were translated into several languages and sold all over Europe.

❸ ROBINSON CRUSOE
Lyon, 1784

Daniel Defoe's book, published in 1719, was an immediate success. Translated into a number of languages, it was regarded as symbolizing salvation through work, triumph over solitude and recognition of the inequality of human relations. Rousseau called it 'the aptest treatise on natural education'.

❹ GULLIVER'S TRAVELS
Satirical novel by Jonathan Swift, 1726

Swift, a teacher to the core, preached a return to a healthy, ordered life, the democratization of employment and the deromanticization of marriage. Through the adventures of his hero Gulliver, a man of good sense, upright, inquisitive and practical, he denounced laws that were made to oppress people rather than defend them. During his fantastic journey, Gulliver met strange beings: Lilliputians six inches tall; in Brobdingnag, giants as tall as church steeples. He travelled to the flying island of Laputa, where scholars were befuddled with pedantry. This virulent satire, covering all fields of human thought, had immense success throughout Europe as soon as it was published.

Enlightenment Thinkers

❶ FOUR GREAT ENLIGHTENMENT FIGURES

Above, John Locke (1634–1704), English physician and philosopher, known as the defender of Liberalism. Top right, Mary Godwin (1759–97), one of the first British feminists. Right, Thomas Paine (1737–1809), American political thinker whose works greatly influenced American political awareness. Below, Jean-Jacques Rousseau (1712–88), author of The Social Contract *and* Emile. *His ideas had a profound influence on the French Revolutionary assemblies.*

Questioning society

New ideas were not confined to education. They also questioned numerous aspects of society. In France, some people railed against the influence that the aristocracy and the Church wielded over royal power, which itself too often seemed arbitrary. The term 'the Enlightenment', which refers particularly to the second half of the 18th century, derived from this outburst of critical thought.

The Enlightenment writers believed that the governments of England and Holland were the examples to follow. They particularly admired England and the writings of John Locke, whom they regarded as the mentor of his country's political regime. Locke, a philosopher of the 17th century, held that no government was possible without the consent of the people.

Yet England was in no way inspired by Locke's ideas, since neither the sovereign nor the ruling classes felt themselves to have been invested with power by the good grace of the governed. If there was government by consent, the consent had been given by a small and influential élite. Nor was the principle of 'consent by the governed' applied in the English colonies (as America was soon to realize) or in an adjacent kingdom such as Ireland.

For the thinkers and philosophers of the Enlightenment, government should above all be devoted to the well-being of the people, interfere as little as possible with individual liberty and respect freedom of worship.

The Church, which in some people's eyes was synonymous with intolerance and superstition, was subjected to fierce criticism. Because they regarded it as an obstacle to progress, writers like Voltaire became more and more anticlerical.

Through the ascendancy and even the control that they exerted over the Church, it was the sovereigns who gradually enforced tolerance, as did Joseph II in Austria. But tolerance in no way signified equality in civic rights.

Furthermore, while Rousseau was able to make atheism permissible, the freedom of worship later established by the *Declaration of the Rights of Man* was not extended to Judaism for many years. Nor did official government speeches prevent the Catholics and the Protestants from regarding each other as idolaters and heretics for generations to come.

The example of Nature

The Enlightenment thinkers believed that science was a better political guide than religion. It had made giant strides since the 17th century, thanks to the work of men like Francis Bacon and Isaac Newton. In his oratorio *The Creation*, inspired by the psalms, Joseph Haydn wrote: 'The skies reveal the glory of God.' Some believed that by following its own laws Nature would create a perfect world and that political and religious intervention by humanity should be as limited as possible. The human being was no more than a simple element in nature, and reason (often with a capital R to stress its importance) called upon man to blossom in liberty like 'the noble savage', the mythical inhabitant of recently discovered distant lands, of which ideal Robinson Crusoe and Man Friday were counterparts.

The high esteem in which Nature and Reason were held explains the success of the *Encyclopédie*, the French *Encyclopaedia or Descriptive Dictionary of the Arts, Sciences and Crafts*. Its editors, Denis Diderot and Jean Le Rond d'Alembert, had at first thought merely of translating the *Cyclopaedia* published in two volumes in 1728 by the Englishman Ephraim Chambers. Completed in 1772, the *Encyclopédie* comprised some thirty volumes, lavishly illustrated, and contributions by more than 200 authors.

②ANTOINE LAVOISIER (1743–94)
Painting by Jacques-Louis David. New York
Lavoisier, the father of modern chemistry, was appointed Controller of Powders and Saltpetre in Paris. He made its Arsenal one of the most highly regarded scientific centres in Europe.

❸ THE JARDIN DES PLANTES IN PARIS
Hilaire, 18th century. Bibliothèque Nationale, Paris
Originally the Royal Garden of Medicinal Herbs, it became a scientific centre when Georges-Louis Leclerc, assisted by Louis-Jean-Marie Daubenton, became its supervisor. The garden became the National Museum of Natural History in 1793.

① MADAME GEOFFRIN'S SALON
Gabriel Lemmonier. Rouen

In France as elsewhere there was great enthusiasm for the ideas of the Enlightenment. Gifted women often presided over these 'men's debates'. At Madame Geoffrin's they took place under the marble gaze of the 'destroyer of absolutism and the arbitrary', Voltaire.

② THE PATRIOTS' CAFÉ
Janinet. Carnavalet Museum, Paris

The cafés also formed a link between literary society in the Enlightenment and revolutionary circles. Newspapers were eagerly read: those from abroad, often written in French, were particularly prized.

The new ideas were debated everywhere, especially in France, where most of them originated. There were discussions in cafés and aristocratic salons. Enlightened members of the privileged classes recognized the need for reform, without always realizing that it might threaten their position. Sometimes, overvehement criticism of the monarchy sent writers like Voltaire to prison.

But their ideas continued to circulate. Rousseau, like Locke, thought that good government was not the monarch's only obligation. He claimed that government and the governed were bound by a 'social contract', and that if the former neglected its duties the latter could regard the contract as broken and therefore no longer requiring their loyalty or their obedience.

But it would have been hard to find a single monarch, even in England, who would be likely to accept such theories. From his native Scotland, where people were as excited by the Enlightenment as were the descendants of Calvinist Scots in Belfast and other parts of Northern Ireland, David Hume gave a more realistic description of the 'British model': 'We find everywhere princes who claim their subjects as their property and assert their independent right of sovereignty, from conquest or succession. We find also everywhere subjects who acknowledge this right in their prince and suppose themselves born under obligations of obedience to a certain sovereign, as much as under the ties of reverence and duty to certain parents.' ('Of the Original Contract', *Essays*, II, 12)

At all events, it is easy to see why monarchs who believed in the divine right of kings felt threatened by these ideas. Catherine II of Russia, Joseph II of Austria and Frederick II of Prussia took them seriously. But no ruler, however benevolent, would have accepted the idea of a 'social contract'. As Frederick VI of Denmark put it: 'Everything for the people, nothing by the people.' Paradoxically, it was the French rulers who seemed not to realize that times were changing, perhaps because the political influence of French philosophers was less great in France than elsewhere. Those who felt the need for a profound reform were accordingly frustrated.

ENCYCLOPÉDIE,
OU
DICTIONNAIRE RAISONNÉ
DES SCIENCES,
DES ARTS ET DES MÉTIERS,
PAR UNE SOCIÉTÉ DE GENS DE LETTRES.

Mis en ordre & publié par M. *DIDEROT*, de l'Académie Royale des Sciences & des Belles-Lettres de Prusse ; & quant à la Partie Mathématique, par M. *D'ALEMBERT*, de l'Académie Royale des Sciences de Paris, de celle de Prusse, & de la Société Royale de Londres.

Tantùm series juncturaque pollet,
Tantùm de medio sumptis accedit honoris ! HORAT.

TOME PREMIER.

A PARIS,
Chez {
BRIASSON, *rue Saint Jacques, à la Science.*
DAVID l'aîné, *rue Saint Jacques, à la Plume d'or.*
LE BRETON, Imprimeur ordinaire du Roy, *rue de la Harpe.*
DURAND, *rue Saint Landry, & au Griffon.*
}

M. DCC. LI.
AVEC APPROBATION ET PRIVILEGE DU ROY.

③ THE 'ENCYCLOPÉDIE'

This dictionary comprised 28 volumes, including 11 volumes of plates. Diderot and d'Alembert edited and partly wrote it, with the help of Voltaire, Montesquieu, Rousseau, Prades and many others. It took no less than 30 years to account for all the new ideas, all the criticisms of governments and all the scientific and technological knowledge of the time. Above, the title page of the 1751 edition. Opposite, fringe loom from the plate entitled 'Trimmings'. Below left, anatomical plate showing the arteries; below right, the best way of pressing silks.

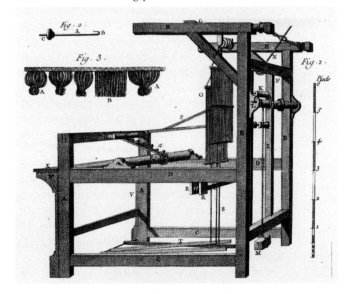

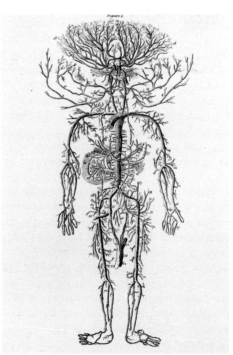

5 From the American Revolution to the French Revolution

① BRITAIN'S NORTH AMERICAN COLONIES

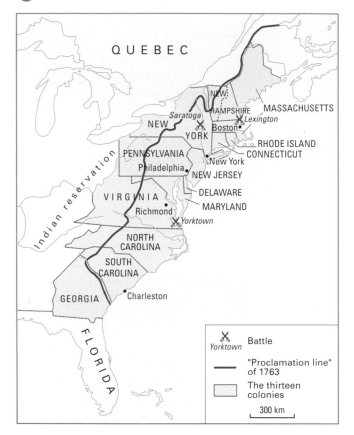

② THE BOSTON TEA PARTY

18th century. Bibliothèque Nationale, Paris

With the deterioration of relations between America and Britain, drinking tea became an unpatriotic act. The Tea Act of 1773, which imposed an import duty on it, aroused indignation. On 16 December 1773 a group of colonists disguised as Indians threw into Boston harbour 18,000 pounds of tea from the ships of the English East India Company.

America versus Britain

Between 1770 and 1780 all Europe was watching America. First, because the leaders of the American revolution claimed kinship with the ideas of Locke and the philosophers of the Enlightenment. Many saw in the young 'United States of America' a first application of Enlightenment theories. But secondly, political ideas did not flow only from East to West, from Europe to America. It was a two-way traffic: events across the Atlantic influenced those Europeans who sought to reform or even abolish their own monarchical regimes.

Great Britain had a large army in New England. But a deep disagreement arose between the colonies and the government in London concerning the amount of tax that the former should pay the latter for the army's upkeep.

For the colonists it was primarily a matter of principle. While the administration of the colonies was in the hands of locally elected 'assemblies', the colonists were not represented in the Westminster Parliament, which had decided on the new taxes. It had thereby violated the right of the colonists, who were still British citizens, to pay only those taxes to which their representatives had agreed.

In 1773, a cargo of tea from the East Indies was thrown into Boston harbour by a group of colonists. This 'Boston Tea Party' can be seen as the detonator of the American Revolution.

In May 1775, delegates from the thirteen colonies met in a continental congress at Philadelphia. It was not a gathering of extremists: most of the representatives were lawyers, physicians and merchants, who saw themselves as patriots and were not seeking war. But they appointed Colonel George Washington as Commander-in-Chief of the colonial army and decided to break the English monopoly of the tea trade.

In reprisal Great Britain stationed the Royal Navy along the American coast to prevent any import or export of goods. The gap between the two sides widened. In January 1776 the Congress declared: '. . . that these United Colonies are and of Right ought to be Free and Independent States; that they are Absolved from all Allegiance to the British Crown and that all political connection between them and the State of Great Britain is and ought to be totally dissolved.'

Six months later, on 4 July 1776, the Declaration of Independence was approved: 'We hold these truths to be self-evident, that all men are created equal, that they are endowed by their Creator with certain inalienable Rights, that among these are Life, Liberty and the pursuit of Happiness.'

These principles were fully in line with the ideas of the Enlightenment. But the critics of royal authority were not the only people in Europe to make common cause with the new American nation. The French and Spanish governments, Britain's two traditional enemies, gave military support to the new Republic, which in 1783 obliged Britain to recognize its independence.

France in 1789

France's participation in the American War of Independence had worsened the monarchy's long-standing financial problems. Instead of re-forming the financial system as they should have done, Louis XVI's governments took only timid steps, enabling their critics to blame the crisis on the Crown and the privileged orders.

The clergy and the nobility, in fact, as well as certain towns, were then exempt from most of the direct taxes that were paid by the artisans and the peasants, who were the poorest but also the most numerous. Indirect taxes, meanwhile, were oner-ous for those who paid them, but insufficient for the state's needs owing to the way they were levied.

As well as paying state taxes, the peasants also owed their lords what were known as feudal dues – in kind, in work or in money. Because they were so ancient, inflation had much reduced their real yield and time had erased any memory of their *raison d'être*. So when the nobility tried to increase its revenue by reviving these largely forgotten dues, their attitude seemed untimely, to say the least.

The French high aristocracy, unlike its British counterpart, was a closed caste that prevented the petty nobility or the rich bourgeoisie having any way of joining it.

The ills of French society did not begin in 1789, but two circumstances made that year a turning-point in history. While the wealth of the country had increased throughout the 18th century, dis-astrous harvests in 1787 and 1788 had caused serious supply problems, made worse by the precarious transport system. The price of wheat soared and the urban poor could barely buy bread.

This economic crisis was accompanied by a political crisis. Louis XVI, who – to put it mildly – was indecisive, had no idea how to tackle all these difficulties. He relied on one minister of finance

③ THE SIGNATURE OF THE AMERICAN DECLARATION OF INDEPENDENCE
Painting by John Trumbell
On 4 July 1776 the representatives of the 13 American colonies, meeting in Congress at Philadelphia, voted for the Declaration of Independence. Thomas Jefferson wrote this text, in which the Americans addressed the whole world.

④ LET'S HOPE THIS GAME WILL SOON BE OVER
18th-century engraving. Bibliothèque Nationale, Paris
This caricature of a peasant carrying a prelate and a nobleman alludes to the weight of taxes borne wholly by the people. The nobility and the clergy not only paid nothing, but received favours and pensions that in turn impoverished the state.

① IMAGE OF THE JACOBIN PATRIOT
Dutch caricature
Counter-revolutionary newspapers abroad showed the friend and defender of liberty and equality as an ass standing to attention and wearing thick spectacles.

② A list of complaints in 1789

The complaints of the inhabitants of Rossheim (extract):

. . . Rossheim also asks that pensions given to people who have done nothing for the town and which the town has to pay should be abolished, as well as unjustified pensions that give rise to wood being cut, causing the devastation of the forests and the ruin of the town's inhabitants . . . .
  They will ask that taxes on meat, bread and salt . . . and the 12 sous charged on each bag of fruit, should be abrogated
  that the press should be free
  that His Majesty be begged to allow communities of inhabitants pasture rights in the enclosable woods on his domains . . . .
  that the Gabelle or tax on salt should be abolished . . . .
  Everyone knows how odious this tax is and what a disastrous effect it has on cattle and on agriculture.

Extract from B. F. Hyslop, *A Guide to the General Cahiers of 1789*, New York, 1936

---

after another, each of whom proved incapable of solving the problems. When they envisaged increasing the number of taxpayers and moving towards equality before the fisc, there was an uproar from the privileged classes.

The Estates General

In an attempt to calm down passion, the King summoned to Versailles the Estates General, consisting of deputies of the three orders: the clergy, the nobility and the third estate (bourgeoisie and peasants). This body had not met since 1614: to convene it at all was a revolutionary step.

Every town and village in France prepared to elect its delegates and held long debates about the ills from which society was suffering. Everywhere lists of complaints were drawn up to present to the Estates General. While essentially they contained local grievances, they also expressed the need for a constitution to reform the government of France.

The nobility and the clergy asked that each order debate and vote in isolation, which would have given them together an almost automatic majority. The deputies of the third estate, knowing that they represented 93 per cent of the nation, and supported by the lower clergy, demanded that all the estates should debate together and that voting should be by person. Isolated in the Jeu de Paume at Versailles, they swore not to leave without obtaining satisfaction. Louis XVI gave in and the three orders met under the title of National Assembly.

But, when the most radical spirits like the Comte de Mirabeau called for reform, tempers ran high in the Assembly. The nobility, on the whole, showed no desire for change. In the towns, and especially in Paris, the anger and despair caused by unemployment, high prices and the threat of shortages and famine exploded in violence that reached its climax on 14 July 1789.

Seeing that royal troops were on the move in the capital, the population feared that the King and the nobility were mustering against reform. On 14 July 1789 the crowd attacked the royal prison, the Bastille, hoping to find a stock of weapons there. They were disappointed; but they did liberate the Bastille's prisoners – of whom there were very few. On the following day the king agreed to the tricolour flag, which united the colours of Paris (blue and red) with the monarchy's white.

Terrified by the rapid spread of unrest throughout France, the nobility emigrated *en masse*, mainly to Germany but also to Britain. The peasants, yielding to the 'Great Fear', panicked at

❸ THE JEU DE PAUME OATH

Jacques-Louis David. Carnavalet Museum, Paris

On 20 June 1789 the National Assembly took the oath in the Jeu de Paume (or real-tennis-court) at Versailles not to dissolve its meeting without drafting a Constitution. The revolutionary painter David, a friend of Robespierre and a member of the National Convention of 1792, immortalized the scene. 1200 people, depicted in the most lively attitudes, surround the President Sylvain Bailly, who is standing on a table.

rumours of a conspiracy fomented by the nobility: rumour had it that bands of brigands were ravaging the countryside. Groups of peasants took up arms to defend themselves and sometimes also to attack the châteaux, above all trying to destroy the land registers that listed the dues they owed to their lords.

The end of feudal society

It was against this background that on 4 August 1789 the Constituent Assembly voted to abolish the feudal society of the *ancien régime*. A solemn ceremony marked the abrogation of the nobility's privileges. Many of the grievances expressed in the lists submitted to the Estates General were thus met. Three weeks later the Assembly adopted the 'Declaration of the Rights of Man and of the Citizen'. It devoted the next two years to providing France with its first written constitution. The 1791 text made the king a constitutional monarch, no longer above the laws, but bound by them and required to enforce them. From now on, to the great advantage of the bourgeoisie, the Assembly's members would be elected by every man who could prove that he paid a minimum in taxes: property suffrage. As part of a policy of decentralization, departments, districts and communes were established and given powers over local administration. Everyone entitled to vote in elections for the Assembly could also elect the judges and jury members for local courts.

❹ EMIGRÉS CROSS THE RHINE

Caricature, 1792. Carnavalet Museum, Paris, Cabinet des Estampes

Nobles and bishops taking refuge from the Revolution leave France for exile in Holland, Germany or Britain. Here, the aristocrats and the clergy are preparing to attack the fortress of the Constitution. Would the Counter-Revolution be no more than a caricature?

❶ THE NIGHT OF 4 AUGUST 1789

Engraving by Helman. Bibliothèque Nationale, Paris

Following the example of Paris, the provinces rebelled: peasants took up arms against their lords, pillaging, stealing and burning. It was the summer of the Great Fear. To restore calm, the National Assembly abolished privileges on the night of 4 August. The clergy and the nobility mounted the tribune to ratify this decision.

The reorganization of the Church in France very much weakened the authority of the Pope. Monks and nuns were encouraged to break vows that they were no longer required to take. The possessions of the clergy were confiscated by the state and later sold at auction. Each diocese must henceforth coincide with a department; bishops and priests, locally elected, were paid by the state. The Pope condemned these new measures; and most of the priests and bishops who refused to swear allegiance to the nation were persecuted. All unawares, the Constituent Assembly had made the task of the Revolution more difficult, if it had not compromised it altogether.

The king finally ratified this 'Civil Constitution of the Clergy', although he could not in conscience approve it. It was largely for this reason that in June 1791 the royal family fled Paris, hoping to get to somewhere where it could find a loyal army and, if necessary, cross the frontier. Arrested at Varennes, near the eastern frontier, the royal family was forced to return to the capital. The patriots saw in this episode a proof of the king's treachery vis-à-vis the revolution. Men like Jean-Paul Marat and Maximilien de Robespierre, who wielded great influence through the political clubs, used the King's flight to discredit both his person and his throne.

The intervention of foreign powers

On the eve of fresh elections, however, the Constituent Assembly pretended to believe that the king's flight had been an abduction and it formally returned his powers to him in September 1791. But suspicion of the king grew greater when it became clear that a Counter-Revolution was threatened from abroad.

While Europe's sovereigns were disquieted by the example that the French were setting to their own subjects, they were nonetheless pleased to see France weakened on the international scene. They had no plans to make war on France, even if the Declaration of Pillnitz in August 1791 seemed to call for intervention: the Emperor and the King of Prussia had hemmed it in with conditions, making a declaration of non-intervention.

In fact, the war between Europe and the French Revolution was begun by France: the king saw it as a means of recovering his former prerogatives, the republicans as a way of unmasking the king's treachery and getting rid of him. War was declared on 20 April 1792. Who could have imagined that it would continue until 1815?

When hostilities began, France soon found itself at a disadvantage. The army was disorganized because many of its officers who were nobles had emigrated; and the Marquis de La

❷ THE SEPTEMBER MASSACRE, 1792

18th-century engraving. Bibliothèque Nationale, Paris

In an atmosphere of general over-excitement, the people's anger exploded. 1200 nobles, priests and prisoners were massacred. In the prison of the Abbey of Saint-Germain-des-Prés on 3 and 4 September, after a sham trial, 164 'suspects' were put to death.

Fayette lacked the authority to take it in hand.

Threatened by Prussia in Lorraine and then in the Champagne area, the Assembly proclaimed 'The country in danger' (10 July 1792). Volunteers flocked to the colours, identifying the defence of France with the defence of revolutionary ideas. These feelings especially inspired those who defied the royal veto and converged on Paris to defend the capital, to the strains of the *Marseillaise*, which long remained the battle hymn of all revolutions.

The pace quickened when a French nobleman who had taken refuge in Germany drew up the Brunswick Manifesto (25 July). This put Louis XVI in an awkward position, for it proclaimed the intention of Prussia and Austria to restore his full powers. All over France he was denounced for collusion with the enemies of the Nation. The revolution of 10 August 1792 put an end to the monarchy: the Parisian revolutionaries, helped by volunteers from Brest and Marseilles, captured the Tuileries and the legislative Assembly pronounced the king deposed.

The Republic under siege

The removal of the King invalidated the 1791 Constitution, so a National Convention was assembled, elected by male universal suffrage. When it met on 21 September 1792, its first act was to proclaim the Republic. On the previous day the army led by Charles Dumouriez had won the politically vital battle of Valmy in Champagne: the Prussians had withdrawn and the Revolution had been saved. This, incidentally, had been the aim of the uncontrolled crowds that between 2 and 9 September had massacred 'the enemy within' – more than a thousand aristocrats, priests and members of religious orders held in the prisons of Paris.

In the autumn of 1792 the fortunes of war began to favour the French. Thanks to promotion from within the ranks and the patriotism of its new recruits, the French army was in fine fettle. It took the offensive in the Austrian Netherlands and won the battle of Jemappes (in present-day Belgium). France began a revolutionary crusade, proclaiming self-determination by the people, which was incompatible with dynastic rights.

The trial, condemnation and execution of the former king, on 21 January 1793 served as a pretext for forming the First Coalition, in which almost all European states, disquieted by the Revolutionaries' zeal, declared war on France.

In the spring of 1793 the position of revolutionary France worsened. To face the Coalition, the National Convention decreed the conscription of 300,000 men. This led to the Vendée rebellion,

③ THE BATTLE OF VALMY
Jean-Baptiste Mauzaise, 19th century. Versailles
On 20 September 1792, around the Valmy windmill and in the face of the Austro–Prussians, the 'fifty thousand ragamuffins' of the revolutionary army, led by Charles Dumouriez and François Christophe de Kellerman, saved the nascent French Nation, opening what Goethe (who observed the battle) called 'a new epoch in the history of the world'. The next day the National Convention abolished royalty; on the 23rd it proclaimed the 'one and indivisible' Republic.

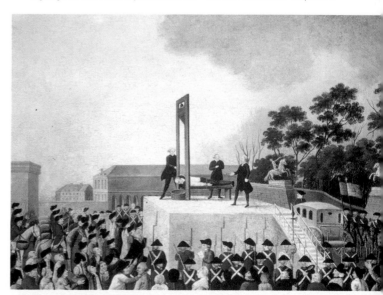

④ THE EXECUTION OF LOUIS XVI
Danish School, 18th century. Bibliothèque Nationale, Paris
'Louis Capet, the former Louis XVI, guilty of conspiracy against the liberty of the Nation and of crimes against the general security of the State', was brought to the Place de la Révolution at 10 o'clock on 21 January 1793. 'I am innocent!' he cried. The drums drowned his voice and the blade of the guillotine fell.

① ROBESPIERRE (1758–94)
Carnavalet Museum, Paris

The so-called 'Incorruptible' at the age of 35 when he set in motion the Terror. A great reader of Rousseau who wanted to establish the dictatorship of virtue, Robespierre was guillotined himself on 28 July 1794. Historians have been unable to decide whether idealism or fanaticism was his dominant motive.

② THE CULT OF THE SUPREME BEING
Pierre-Antoine de Machy. Carnavalet Museum, Paris

Against the cult of Reason, Robespierre established that of the Supreme Being to encourage good citizenship and Republican morality. He celebrated it spectacularly on 8 June 1794 in the Champs-de-Mars.

and an implacable civil war broke out in a country already at war. Faced with this crisis, the members of the National Convention divided into two camps. One group, followers of Jacques-Pierre Brissot de Warville and Pierre Vergniaud – the Brissotins or Girondins, since several came from Bordeaux – were anxious not to imperil the libertarian principles of 1789. The other group – known as the Montagnards because they sat in the higher tiers of the Assembly – thought it necessary to shelve them and organize a real dictatorship in the name of Public Safety. This was the view of Jean-Paul Marat, Georges Jacques Danton and Maximilien de Robespierre.

The Montagnards accused the Girondins of incompetence, a charge they soon changed to that of treason. Taking advantage of the revolution on 2 June 1793, they decided to arrest them. Most of the Girondins were executed after a sham trial.

The Terror

For a year, from June 1793 to July 1794, the Committee of Public Safety, set up some months before within the National Convention, was in the hands of the Montagnards. It established an emergency government, the Revolutionary Government, with exceptional methods – the *Terror*. It had to face foreign war on all the frontiers of France, a civil war in the Vendée, insurrections in the provincial towns – Bordeaux, Caen, Lyon, Marseille, etc. – that had not accepted the liquidation of the Girondins and finally economic problems that included the threat of famine.

Robespierre and his followers, however, now had the power to impose any draconian measures to save the Revolution and France.

Any person suspected of treason against the Republic was arrested. It became important to display one's support for the Republic by wearing such Revolutionary emblems as the Phrygian bonnet or the tricolour rosette. Mass executions of men and women were ordered by the Revolutionary Tribunal. Some 40,000 people were said to have been guillotined throughout France, although this figure is now very much questioned. Tens of thousands of others were arrested on very flimsy evidence or on none at all. Priests who refused the oath were persecuted more than ever.

Like Robespierre, most of the Montagnards acted from profound convictions. But there were many French people who supported the Terror for fear of losing their status or even their lives. Nobody felt safe.

Violence proved effective. By the end of 1793 internal order had been restored; and in the spring of 1794 the French resumed the offensive. To some people, however, the Terror seemed less necessary. For having said so, Danton became the first victim of these internal quarrels: he was executed on 5 April 1794. In July Robespierre was overthrown and decapitated in his turn.

Towards a military power

The fall of Robespierre (9–10 Thermidor of Year II in the revolutionary calendar) ended the Terror. This was the 'Thermidorean reaction'. The National Convention drew up a new Constitution, that of Year III. The Assembly was replaced by two Councils: that of the Elders, made up of married men aged at least 40, and that of the Five Hundred, composed of deputies over 30 years of age. The Five Hundred proposed laws: the Elders voted on them. Executive power rested with a Directorate of five members appointed by the Councils. There was no provision for conflicts between the Councils and the Directorate.

These new conditions helped the royalists to reappear. They won the election to the Councils in April 1797 and called for peace. As a result, the members of the Directorate decided to rely on General Napoleon Bonaparte to rid them of the royalists by force. Napoleon was winning his Italian campaign against the Austrians and his personal political interest was to impose a peace of his own on Austria. He sent a general to help the Directorate stage its *coup d'état* against the royalist Councils on 4 September 1797. From then on the army had more and more influence.

There remained Great Britain. Attempts were made to strike at it indirectly, by helping the Irish Republicans in 1798 or by landing in Egypt in 1799 to try to block the route to India. Neither had very great success.

Not without difficulty, revolutionary France had imposed itself on Europe. It had transformed the art of war, which now involved the whole nation, through conscription and promotion from the ranks. It had extended its territory by annexing the left bank of the Rhine and what is now Belgium, as well as Nice and Savoy.

The countries that France conquered were 'liberated' and turned into 'sister republics' on the French model: the Batavian Republic (Holland) in 1794, the Cisalpine Republic (Milan) and the Ligurian Republic (Genoa) in 1797, the Helvetic and Roman Republics in 1798, and the Parthenopian Republic (Naples) in 1799. Revolutionary principles spread at the expense of feudalism and the Church; but the presence of the French also involved requisitioning and the pillage of artistic treasures to be sent to Paris. As liberators, did the French not become oppressors?

❸ NAPOLEON BONAPARTE
Painting by David. Louvre Museum, Paris
Born in Ajaccio on 15 August 1769, Napoleon entered the Ecole de Brienne at the age of ten, followed by the Ecole Militaire in Paris. In 1789 he went to Corsica; but, under suspicion from General Paoli, he returned to France. In 1793 he recaptured Toulon from the British. At the age of 24 he was made a general. Suspected after Thermidor, he owed his safety to Vicomte Barras, who had him suppress the royalist uprising in 1795. After this success, Barras gave him command of the army in Italy, where he triumphed.

❹ THE BRIDGE AT ARCOLA
Painting by Bacler d'Albe. Château of Versailles
The speed of Napoleon's movements and the concentration of his attacks made possible victories like that of the bridge at Arcola, Italy, which he and Pierre-François-Charles Augereau crossed on 15 November 1796. Two days later the Austrians surrendered.

Napoleon's Empire and its Defeat

❶ THE EMPEROR NAPOLEON
Painting by Anne-Louis Girodet de Roucy Trioson. In the collection of
Comtesse de Caraman, Château de Courson, Essonne
*Arrayed like a Roman Emperor, Bonaparte became Napoleon I on
2 December 1804. He is here shown swearing to respect the 36
articles of the Civil Code, later known as the Napoleonic Code.*

**❷ A PUPIL OF THE
LYCEE NAPOLEON**
*Established in 1803, the
lycées replaced the
central schools. French
and mathematics were
taught there; the
organization was military
and all the pupils wore
uniform.*

Imperial France

'Caesar will come': these were Robespierre's
words to the legislative Assembly when it had
committed France to war. After the *coup d'état* of
the 18th and 19th Brumaire, Year VIII (9–10
November 1799), the prediction came true. The
Caesar in question was Napoleon Bonaparte.

The Constitution of Year VIII (1800) made him
First Consul for ten years; that of Year X (1802)
made him Consul for life; that of Year XII (1804)
created the Empire. On 2 December 1804 Bonaparte was crowned under the name of Napoleon
I, after a plebiscite had registered 3.5 million 'for'
and only 2580 'against'.

In reality, the essentials of the imperial regime
and its policies had been in place since Year VIII
(1800). After ten years of revolutionary upheaval,
the aim was to stabilize the country and absorb
the work of the Revolution into the continuity of
French life. Napoleon accepted reconciliation
with everyone, but around himself: this was the
Revolution wearing a crown.

The French wanted peace. It was achieved first
with Austria at Lunéville (1801), then with
Britain at Amiens (1802). It was fragile, but it
strengthened Napoleon's position at home. He
also put an end to the religious conflict with the
Pope: the Concordat of 1801 recognized Roman
Catholicism as 'the religion of the majority of the
French'. Priests were paid by the state and the
Church gave up any claim to its now nationalized
possessions. Similar agreements were reached with
the Protestants in 1802 and the Jews in 1808.

Administrative reforms continued, within
limits, the work of the Revolution. Laws were
standardized by the drafting of codes, notably the
Civil Code of 1804, which reaffirmed a number of
revolutionary principles, including the equality of
all citizens before the law. It strengthened the
authority of husbands over their wives and of
fathers over their children; but it abolished pri-
mogeniture. The departments remained the chief
administrative units, but each was now placed
under a Prefect appointed by Paris – a return to
centralization. Napoleon surrounded himself
with competent officials, and with the help of
censorship and the secret police he kept a firm
hand on the whole country.

He centralized French education long before
the establishment of the Imperial University in
1808. Primary education, which had been the

Church's responsibility, continued to be neglected, quite unlike the newly created *lycées*, whose purpose was to give basic training to future officials. This was based on classical literature and involved a wholly military discipline.

Energetic and successful efforts were made to restore the vigour of the French economy. The establishment of the Bank of France in February 1800 and of the *germinal* franc in 1803 inaugurated a period of monetary stability that lasted until the First World War. It benefited from the confidence that property-owners felt in the political security of the regime.

Renewed prosperity enabled Napoleon to be a Maecenas. He liked luxury, and his court mingled the splendour of Versailles with that of Imperial Rome. At his coronation he wore a laurel wreath like the Roman Emperors. But he also saw himself as the heir of the Revolution: the imperial eagle was backed by the tricolour flag. This double allegiance can be seen in the ornamentation of Empire-style furniture. Once again France was setting the fashionable tone, even among its enemies.

③ THE EMPEROR WITH HIS FAMILY

Jean-Baptiste Regnault, 1810. Historical Museum, Versailles

It is 22 August 1807 in the Tuileries. Jérôme Bonaparte has come to present to his brother his wife, the Princess of Württemberg. The whole family is there. On the left, Louis Bonaparte, Eugène de Beauharnais, Joseph and Elise Bonaparte, Hortense de Beauharnais, Pauline Bonaparte and Marie-Julie Clary. In the centre, the Emperor with Josephine on his right and Madame his mother on his left. On the right, Stéphanie Napoléon, the Princess Eugénie de Beauharnais, Camille, Prince Borghese, Madame Murat, the Grand Duke of Baden and Cardinal Fesch.

④ NAPOLEON'S CONQUESTS

France's 130 *départements*	French Empire	Vassal States of the French Empire	Allies of the French Empire	Napoleon's opponents

① REPRESSION IN MADRID
The *Tres de Mayo* by Francisco Goya, 1814. Prado Museum, Madrid
The Spanish people rejected Joseph Bonaparte as King. Madrid rebelled, staged ambushes and endlessly attacked isolated French troops. They, to repress the rebellion, shot en masse all the rebels they could capture.

② THE CONGRESS OF VIENNA
B. Wigand, Austrian School
The Congress lasted from September 1814 to June 1815. 15 kings, 200 princes and 126 European diplomats came to redraw the map of Europe. They worked in an atmosphere of continual celebration, as witness this sleigh party for the allied sovereigns on 22 January 1815. 'Congress dances' was the ironical comment.

The Napoleonic Empire

In May 1803 Britain resumed hostilities, blaming France for its imperialist policy in the West Indies, Italy and Switzerland. After defeating the French and Spanish fleet at Trafalgar in October 1805, the British were dominant at sea; but they had only small land forces and so were the brain rather than the arm of all the coalitions and their finance. In turn, Britain brought Austria, Prussia and Russia against France.

Napoleon crushed the armies of the *ancien régime* at Austerlitz (1805), Jena (1806), Friedland (1807) and Wagram (1809). But without naval power he could not defeat Britain, save by trying to throttle its economy by cutting off its outlets in Europe. He did this by means of the Continental Blockade, a form of economic warfare well ahead of its time; but although it had real impact it was not decisive.

The Napoleonic Empire seemed to be at its height in 1810 and 1811. France at that time had 130 departments: Rome, Brussels, Amsterdam and Hamburg were French prefectures. The Holy Roman Empire had been replaced in 1806 by the Confederation of the Rhine, practically a French protectorate. Members of his family ruled Spain, Naples and Westphalia; and most of the states on the mainland of Europe were his allies.

But in reality this edifice was maintained only by force. Nemesis was not far off. When Napoleon intervened in Spain in 1808, he confronted a whole people, backed by the British and the Portuguese; and the Grand Army of the French was gradually eroded by guerrilla warfare. In the Russian campaign of 1812 the armies of the Tsar were supported by the Russian people: they, and the rigour of the winter, turned the French retreat into a rout. In 1813 there was a national revolt in Germany and in 1814 France found itself invaded once again. Napoleon abdicated and the monarchy was restored under Louis XVIII, the brother of Louis XVI. Nationalism had been the strength of Revolutionary France: but now it had taken its revenge.

The Congress of Vienna

The victorious allies met in Vienna to remould Europe. The Austrian Metternich, the Englishman Castlereagh and the Frenchman Talleyrand all played leading roles, as did Tsar Alexander I. But the congress was interrupted by Napoleon's escape and temporary return to power: the 'Hundred Days' ended in defeat by the British and the Prussians at Waterloo on 18 June 1815.

The Final Act of the Congress stressed the principle of 'legitimacy'; but not all the sovereigns of the *ancien régime* were restored to their former authority. 39 German states now formed the German Confederation, instead of 300 in 1789, but without great power. The Confederation was the framework for growing antagonism between Berlin and Vienna; and it disappointed the national aspirations of the Germans, who had played a part in the defeat of Napoleon. France remained suspect: this was why the former Austrian Netherlands joined with the United Provinces to set up the Kingdom of the Netherlands as a better bulwark against France's northern frontier, which had always been unstable.

The impact of the French Revolution

The usurper Napoleon had been a product of the Revolution, lasting from 1789 to 1815. In France, by contrast, people preferred to emphasize that he had betrayed the revolutionary ideas of liberty – as others had done before him. Yet by bringing about long-term stability in France he had made permanent the essential core of the Revolution. Thanks to him, the restoration of the monarchy in 1814–15 was not a return to 1789.

The French Revolution had had great repercussions in Europe. Early on it had spread the new ideas of the time, which awakened echoes in the 'patriotic' movements in many countries. Thus, for example, the Irish republicans sang the *Marseillaise* when they attacked the British. With Napoleon there was an attempt to unite Europe by force – a French Europe very different from that of the Enlightenment philosophers.

The attempt was a failure because it aroused against it an upsurge of nationalism. Yet it had its successes. Its uniform system of weights and measures and its codification of the law in many cases survived. Political debates, too, now gave an important place to the notions of motherland, nation and individual liberty. Traditional social ties may have suffered, but their decline paved the way for capitalism and industrialization.

The invasion of the Iberian Peninsula even led, outside Europe, to some first steps in decolonization. The King of Portugal took refuge in Brazil, which in 1822 proclaimed its independence and was granted it in 1825. The Spanish colonies remained loyal to the Bourbons and refused to recognize Joseph Bonaparte. Their loyalty was hardly rewarded when Ferdinand VII returned in 1813. It took only three years for the colonies to revolt again and declare their independence.

North America, France, Latin America: all witnessed revolutions, on both sides of the Atlantic, which confirmed that history was now developing on a world scale.

3 14 JULY IN BELFAST
The Presbyterians in the North of Ireland saw the fall of the French ancien régime as a great event, and they even celebrated the 14th of July. In the rest of the country, without impugning loyalty to the crown, the Irish called for a reform of the government and demanded the right to trade freely with the rest of the Empire.

4 THE METRIC SYSTEM
A uniform system of weights and measures was one of the requests made in the lists of grievances submitted in 1789. It was based on studies that pre-dated that request. This was the metric system.

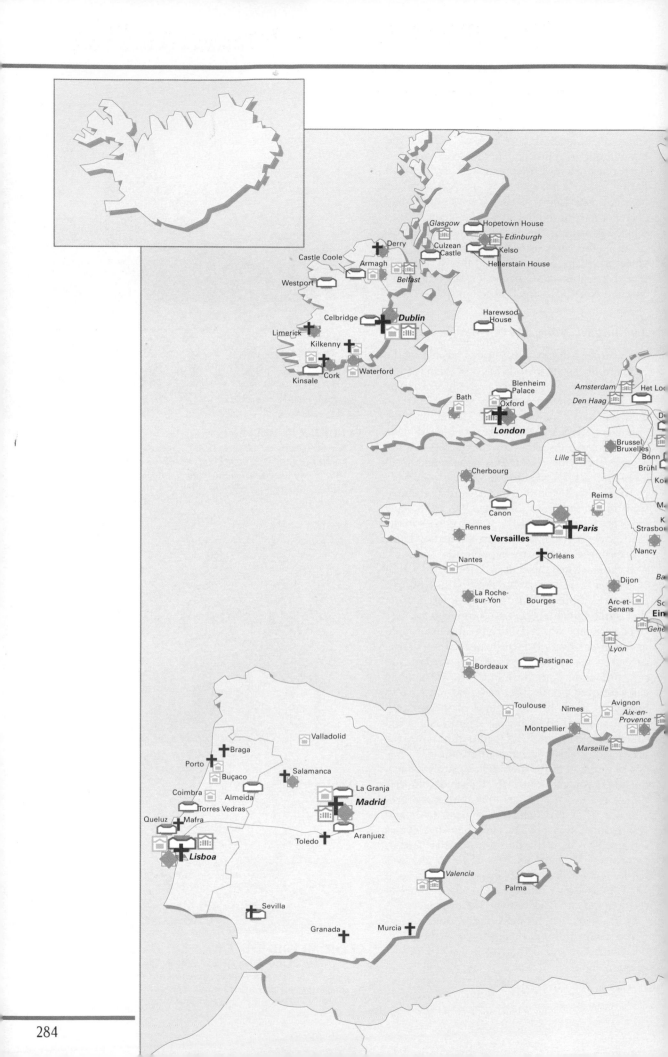

Glasgow
Hopetown House
Edinburgh
Culzean Castle
Kelso
Hellerstain House

Derry
Castle Coole
Armagh
Belfast
Westport
Celbridge
Dublin
Harewsod House
Limerick
Kilkenny
Cork
Waterford
Kinsale

Blenheim Palace
Bath
Oxford
London
Cherbourg
Canon
Rennes

Amsterdam
Het Loo
Den Haag
D
Brussel Bruxelles
Lille
Bonn
Brühl
Ko
Reims
M
K
Strasbo
Nancy

Versailles
Paris
Nantes
Orléans
La Roche-sur-Yon
Bourges
Dijon
Arc-et-Senans
Ba
Sc
Ein
Bordeaux
Rastignac
Gene
Lyon

Toulouse
Nimes
Avignon
Aix-en-Provence
Montpellier
Marseille

Valladolid
Braga
Porto
Buçaco
Salamanca
Coimbra
Almeida
La Granja
Torres Vedras
Madrid
Queluz
Mafra
Lisboa
Toledo
Aranjuez
Sevilla
Valencia
Palma
Granada
Murcia

The Past in the Present Day
THE ENLIGHTENMENT AND THE IDEA OF LIBERTY

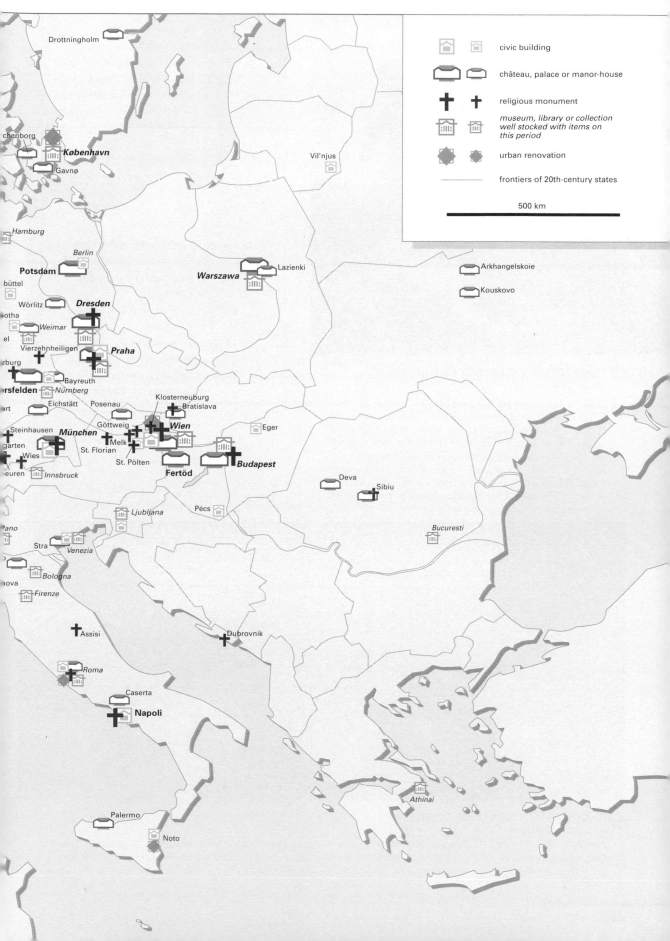

civic building

château, palace or manor-house

religious monument

museum, library or collection well stocked with items on this period

urban renovation

frontiers of 20th-century states

500 km

Drottningholm

chenborg

København

Gavnø

Vil'njus

Hamburg

Berlin

Potsdam

Warszawa

Lazienki

Arkhangelskoie

Kouskovo

büttel

Wörlitz

Dresden

otha

Weimar

el

Vierzehnheiligen

Praha

zburg

Bayreuth

rsfelden

Nürnberg

Klosterneuburg

Bratislava

Eichstätt

Posenau

Göttweig

Steinhausen

München

Wien

Eger

garten

Melk

St. Florian

Deva

Wies

St. Pölten

Sibiu

euren

Innsbruck

Fertöd

Budapest

ano

Ljubljana

Pécs

Bucuresti

Stra

Venezia

nova

Bologna

Firenze

Assisi

Dubrovnik

Roma

Caserta

Napoli

Athinai

Palermo

Noto

① 'THE SPIRIT OF LIBERTY GUIDING THE PEOPLE'
Eugène Delacroix. Louvre Museum, Paris
This allegorical representation of the 1830 Revolution was the first modern political painting. Delacroix left behind the inspiration of Classical antiquity to take part in contemporary life. He said of this work: 'I undertook a modern subject, a barricade . . . and, if I have not conquered for the motherland, I have at least painted for it.' He even showed himself in the picture as a member of the National Guard, wearing a top hat.

② PADDINGTON STATION, LONDON
W. P. Frith. Royal Holloway and Bedford New College, Surrey
Built by I. K. Brunel and M. D. Wyatt, this station very soon became, like its counterparts elsewhere, a popular rendezvous that much attracted the crowds. A beacon of capitalism and industrialization, such places were teeming emblems of the magic of departure for distant places, inspiring painters, poets, novelists and, later, film-makers.

THE MODERNIZATION OF EUROPE

THE 19TH CENTURY

At the beginning of the 19th century Europe was still mainly agricultural, but by the end of the century an agrarian society had become more industrialized.

With the population growing apace, many Europeans left the countryside to go to the towns, greatly increasing the population of the large urban centres. In the short term, for many people, the impact of industrialization and urbanization was disastrous. In the longer term these changes meant an improvement in living conditions and greater wealth for many classes of the population.

Great Britain was the first country to begin industrialization. It was followed by the rest of Western Europe and finally by the less developed countries of southern and Eastern Europe. A parallel revolution took place in transport and communications.

In politics Europe was greatly influenced by two concepts: nationalism and liberalism. New nation-states emerged, like Greece, Belgium and Romania; others, like Italy and Germany, achieved unity. The end of the 19th century saw the formation of political parties, the introduction of social reforms and an improvement in the status of women. At the same time the world of leisure, education and the arts was transformed by modernization.

The turn of the century marked the apogee of Europe's industrial and technological supremacy; and the great colonial empires founded by the European nations gave them all the influence of world powers.

QUEEN VICTORIA (1819–1901)
Victoria reviewing a regiment of the Grenadier Guards.
Coloured lithograph
Victoria's exceptionally long reign symbolized the apogee of Great Britain's world power. Queen of Great Britain and Ireland (1837–1901), she succeeded her uncle William IV. Her keen awareness of the role of the sovereign and her puritan austerity restored the slightly tarnished image of the British monarchy. She was the last British sovereign to leave a personal mark on political life.

Liberalism and Nationalism

① LUDDITE MACHINE-BREAKERS
Engraving by Hablot Browne. Mansell Collection, London
Mechanization led to rigorous and oppressive division of labour. Hunger and insecurity about the future weighed on these workmen, who at that time (1815–30) saw no solution except to destroy their great rivals, the machines.

② 'THE HEROES OF MANCHESTER'
English caricature

In the 19th century those who sought to transform Europe by revolution tried to promote the principles of nationalism and liberalism that had sprung from the French Revolution. The revolutionary tradition fomented national feelings in order to unite peoples and encourage them to throw off the yoke of foreign countries. Within the political structure of Europe's states, the liberals preached the new principles of democracy – a concept embracing the sovereignty of the people and representative government, as well as freedom of speech, religion and the press. The Romantics, meanwhile, exalted the heroic personality and the liberty of the individual above that of the nation.

Revolt and repression

Contrary to these ideals the 19th century was marked by political repression. Protest movements, riots and threats of revolution were firmly put down.

In many European countries, the Napoleonic Wars, the increase of the population, the growth of the towns and the movements for political reform, were followed by economic stagnation. The general discontent was expressed in various ways: riots as a result of famine, the destruction

Workmen did not want to be the victims of progress. In 1819 in Manchester, they gathered peacefully to demand reforms, but the local militia had to charge them and left eleven dead and hundreds wounded. This was known as the Peterloo Massacre.

of machines by workers fearing unemployment, clashes between students and the authorities, and petitions and meetings organized by the liberal bourgeoisie to seek political change.

There was unrest in England, where many called for a change of the electoral system. In 1819 a large meeting was held in St Peter's Fields, Manchester, but the authorities broke it up. Eleven people were killed and hundreds wounded. Known as the 'Peterloo Massacre,' this incident only led the government to promulgate stricter laws on the right to demonstrate.

In Germany the organized national movement was limited to a few isolated groups. Under the Carlsbad Decrees of 1819 the German states prohibited political meetings, censored the press and controlled the educational system.

In Spain the revolution led by Riego in 1820 attacked the brutal absolutism of King Ferdinand VII. In some Italian states revolutionary secret societies, the *Carbonari* (literally, charcoal-burners), called for an end to all foreign domination and the establishment of an Italian Republic. But the *Carbonari* were ill-organized and their uprisings (in Naples and Piedmont in 1820–1, and in the rest of the country in 1831) were too localized, sporadic and easily crushed.

Different forms of protest were met by different forms of law-enforcement. Thus in Ireland, a country under British rule but with strong impulses towards independence, members of the Royal Irish Constabulary (after 1867) were armed and lived in barracks, whereas in England the police force was unarmed.

Revolution and intervention

Europe's governmental systems varied greatly from one country to another. Great Britain refused to intervene in the internal affairs of other countries; but Prussia, Austria and, to a lesser degree, France were prepared to give military aid to governments or dynasties threatened by revolution. Austria supported the monarchical regimes of Naples and Piedmont; France enabled the King of Spain to recover all the powers he had partly lost to a liberal constitution. The Russian Empire survived a military conspiracy and a revolt in Poland.

Despite social unrest and difficulties in the towns, Great Britain had no revolution and managed to preserve its political institutions. The Reform Act of 1832, which increased the number of (male) voters to about 650,000, made possible a parliamentary system better suited to the needs of a country in the throes of modernization. The most important protest movement in Great Britain was the Chartism, which called for an

CARBONARI 1821

③ THE CARBONARI
Originally a guild of charcoal-burners, the Carbonari became in about 1808–11 a political secret society. It was very active in the Kingdom of the Two Sicilies, where its aim was to drive out the French occupying power, and later in northern Italy, where it prepared for the unification of the country by fighting the Austrian occupants. Many of its members who were arrested, like the four gentlemen pictured above, then imprisoned and/or expelled from Italy, took part in the continual uprisings in Europe between 1815 and 1835.

④ The Irish Question

Lord Macaulay (1800–59), English historian, essayist and statesman:

Many politicians of our time are in the habit of laying it down as a self-evident proposition that no people ought to be free till they are fit to use their freedom. The maxim is worthy of the fool in the old story who resolved not to go into the water till he had learnt to swim. If men are to wait for liberty till they become wise and good in slavery, they may indeed wait for ever.

Essay on Milton, *Edinburgh Review*, August 1825

The Rev. Sydney Smith (1771–1845), English wit and churchman:

The moment the very name of Ireland is mentioned, the English seem to bid adieu to common feelings, common prudence and common sense, and to act with the barbarity of tyrants and the fatuity of idiots.

The Letters of Peter Plymley, Letter II

Benjamin Disraeli (1804–81), British statesman and novelist:

Thus you have a starving population, an absentee aristocracy and an alien Church, and in addition the weakest executive in the world. That is the Irish question.

Speech in the House of Commons, 16 February 1844, Hansard, 3rd series, LXXII, 1016

❶ THE CHARTISTS
This British movement took its name from the People's Charter published in 1838. It used demonstrations, strikes and even riots to demand reform, including universal male suffrage, the secret ballot and payments of MPs.

❷ THE GREEK REVOLUTION
Eugène Delacroix. Musée des Beaux Arts, Bordeaux
This picture of a young woman in national costume, by a block of stone with the hand of a dead Greek rebel emerging from beneath it, was painted by Delacroix in memory of the Greek men, women and children who preferred to die by blowing up their town, on 23 April 1826, rather than surrender to the Turks.

increase in the representative power of the House of Commons.

Ireland was the only part of the British Isles that made the government fear revolution, because the 1800 Act of Union had brought the country more directly under British domination. The Irish demanded the law's repeal, and a nationalist movement developed. Daniel O'Connell, the leading Irish nationalist, nicknamed The Liberator, became a popular hero in the fight against the Act of Union.

The revolution in Greece

In 1821 the Greeks (Greek Orthodox subjects of the Ottoman Sultan) rose up against their Turkish rulers. The rebellion was organized by the *Philikí Etairéia* or Friendly Company, a secret society of Greek patriots founded by merchants and led by (among others) Prince Alexandros Ypsilantis, a Russian army officer who tried at first to foment an uprising in the Danube provinces.

Greece then plunged into a war of independence and became the inspiration of European liberals. The death of the English poet Byron at the siege of Missolonghi aroused pro-Greek feelings throughout Europe. Russia was encouraged to back the Greeks against the Turks not only by its national interests and its traditional policy of expansion towards the Mediterranean, but also by religious affinities. In 1827 intervention by Great Britain, France and Russia ended with the destruction of the Turkish fleet at Navarino. Greece became independent in 1830 and accepted as its sovereign a Bavarian prince, the son of Ludwig I of Bavaria. In 1843 the Greeks rebelled against the absolutist policies of their king and secured the establishment of parliamentary government with constitutional limits on the power of the monarchy.

The revolutions of 1830–31

Discontent with the political system was the main reason for the revolutions that broke out in several European countries in 1830 and 1831. In July 1830 in France, when the Bourbon monarchy tried to remove the constitutional limitations on the power of the king and his ministers, Parisians revolted and the king was overthrown. A new constitutional monarchy was established with Louis-Philippe as king. This French revolution of 1830 inspired other European liberals. The rulers of several German states were obliged to abdicate, and constitutions were set in place guaranteeing the rights of the individual and certain voting rights. In Italy uprisings took place in Modena, Parma and the Papal states, but were crushed by Austria. In Warsaw Russian soldiers were driven out by rebels who proclaimed a revolutionary government. Not until September 1831 did the Tsar of Russia put down the revolt.

Also in 1830 the Belgians rebelled against the union of their country with the Netherlands and their Dutch monarch, both imposed on them by the Treaty of Vienna in 1815, a landmark in Belgium's history. Austria, Russia and Prussia were unable to help the Dutch king on account of the uprising in the Russian area of Poland. After a revolt by Brussels in August and September 1830, Belgium achieved its independence in 1831. In 1839, after a further Belgo–Dutch war, the country's neutrality was guaranteed by the Treaty of London. The eastern part of Luxembourg, meanwhile, was made into an independent Grand Duchy, but within the Dutch kingdom. Its neutrality was declared by a further Treaty of London in 1867, and in 1890 it was finally detached from the Netherlands.

Young Europe

In 1831 the Italian nationalist and former *Carbonaro* Giuseppe Mazzini, then in political exile in Marseille, founded the Young Italy (*La Giovane Italia*) movement, whose aim was to arouse a popular revolt in order to establish a free and united Italian Republic.

The movement quickly gained recruits and inspired imitators throughout Europe, such as 'Young Germany' and 'Young Poland'. Mazzini brought them together in 'Young Europe' and promoted fraternity among the future republics, based on Christian brotherly love. 'Young Ireland', another revolutionary nationalist movement, was founded in 1840. Though none of these fraternities had much success, Mazzini became a source of inspiration for European nationalists and democrats.

③THE JULY REVOLUTION IN PARIS
Painting by Lecomte. Carnavalet Museum, Paris
In Paris, on 28 July 1830, students from the Ecole Polytechnique, former soldiers of the Empire and middle-class citizens joined the rebels marching on the Hôtel de Ville demanding a Republic. The royal troops of Charles X were unable to stop them.

④THE BRUSSELS REVOLT
Belgian print, late 19th century
Early in the morning of 23 September 1830 the army of William I, King of the Netherlands, marched into Brussels. To its astonishment, it met a fusillade of fire. 'Are these Brussels people defending themselves, then?' The Belgian nation was coming to birth.

⑤'THE MOST PERFECT ORDER PREVAILS IN WARSAW'
Caricature. Bibliothèque Nationale, Paris
Words of the French Foreign Minister, Horace François Bastien, on 16 September 1831. The order had been imposed by terror.

❶ THE GERMAN LIBERALS GIVE UP THEIR ARMS
Coloured engraving. Berlin

The economic revolution caused by the Zollverein or customs union of 1834, coupled with the rise of nationalist liberalism and the growth of Socialism, led to an uprising in Berlin in March 1848. But the new Frankfurt Parliament, elected in May by universal suffrage, was soon paralyzed by the confrontation between partisans of Greater Germany led by Austria and those of 'Little Germany' without Austria and led by Prussia. The defeated bourgeois liberals gave up their weapons to the Prussian soldiers.

❷ LAJOS KOSSUTH (1802–94)
Patriotic engraving, late 19th century. Private collection

Lawyer, deputy for Pest and a Hungarian patriot, Kossuth helped to draft the constitution at the time of the Revolution in March 1848. He was appointed Minister of Finance and President of the Defence Committee. After breaking with Vienna in October 1848, he raised a national army and became leader of Hungary. Posterity came to see him as an archetypal European popular hero.

The revolutions of 1848

The revolutions that took place in 1848 made far more impact than those of 1830. Now, discontent with political systems was reinforced by other factors, including economic and social problems that had begun as early as 1845: disastrous harvests, disease, a slump in trade, poverty and unemployment. The background to the revolutions differed from one country to another. But in general they were led by liberal intellectuals inspired by the ideals of 1789.

In February 1848 the Citizen King Louis-Philippe of France lost his battle against electoral reform and was obliged to abdicate. In March the Austrian Chancellor Prince Metternich had to flee Vienna. Constitutional governments were established in the Italian states and in all the capitals of central Europe hitherto dominated by Austria. In the German states, during the brief life of the Frankfurt Parliament from May 1848 to April 1849, there was repeated pressure for the establishment of representative government and for the unification of Germany.

These revolutions were short-lived: most were crushed in a few months. In France the landed proprietors put down the June riots in Paris and elected Louis-Napoléon Bonaparte, the future Napoleon III, as Prince President of the Second Republic. In England Chartism failed with the rejection of its Third Petition. Young Ireland proved unable to foment a peasant revolt. In Italy French soldiers overthrew the new Roman Republic championed by Giuseppe Garibaldi. In northern Italy the Austrians overturned the Venetian Republic and reimposed their authority on Lombardy; but Piedmont and Sardinia retained their liberal constitution with the accession of King Victor Emmanuel II.

The Hungarian nationalist Lajos Kossuth, who had led the revolt against the Habsburgs, had to flee the country when the Russians intervened to restore Austrian supremacy. In Germany the failure of the 1848 revolutions was due to the German liberals, who believed they needed the support of Prussia and were willing to accept its demands. But the Prussian King, encouraged by the success of the Austrian counter-revolution, dissolved the Prussian Assembly and promulgated a Constitution guaranteeing the maintenance of royal authority. The rulers of the German states followed suit and withdrew their own constitutional concessions. Significantly, however, the new Swiss democratic constitution remained unchallenged.

By the end of 1849 the political landscape of Europe looked very much as it had done two years earlier. But nationalist, liberal and democratic ideas had made headway. Absolutist monarchy was losing ground, and the power of aristocratic landowners was shrinking, while the peasantry in Europe was freeing itself completely from the yoke of feudalism. The time seemed ripe for the nationalist movements to succeed.

The new political map of Europe

For about forty years, thanks to the Treaty of Vienna (1815), European countries settled their disputes without any major war.

From about 1850 the states of Europe grew increasingly suspicious about Russian interests in the Balkans, where the power of the Turks was on the wane. Great Britain and France wanted to prevent Russia extending its influence towards the Mediterranean; and war broke out between Russia and a Franco–British–Turkish alliance.

The Crimean War (1854–6), which the allies won, put a brake for a time on Russian intimidation of Turkey: but the threat remained. The ancient lands dominated by the Turks nurtured powerful nationalist feelings, paving the way for a new Christian nation, Romania, established in 1862. The Crimean War revived the old rivalry

❸ THE CHARGE OF THE LIGHT BRIGADE
R. Caton Woodville, 1895
The Crimean campaign united the Turks, the French, the British and the Piedmontese against the Russian troops defending the port of Sebastopol. It included the battles of Alma, Inkerman, the Chernaya, Malakov and Balaclava, where the doomed heroism of the Light Brigade inspired the English poet Alfred Tennyson.

❹ EUROPE AFTER THE CONGRESS OF VIENNA (1815)

❶ THE IMPERIAL FAMILY EYED BY A NEW INVENTION: PHOTOGRAPHY

Napoleon III with the Empress Eugénie and Prince Louis-Napoleon, taking a rest from the worries caused him by, among others, Catholic opponents of his Italian policy. As he humoured the new fashion of photography, he gave an impression of bourgeois restraint that contrasted with the gilded luxury of the Second Empire in France.

❷ GARIBALDI ENTERS PALERMO
Engraving. Risorgimento Museum, Brescia

In the cause of Italian unity, Garibaldi (here in a red shirt with a sword in his hand) seized Palermo on 27 May 1860.

between Austria – which had kept out of it – and Russia over Eastern Europe and the Balkans.

In 1856, at the peace conference in Paris to end the Crimean War, Count Camillo Cavour, Prime Minister of Piedmont, whose soldiers had fought alongside the French and the British, raised the question of Italian unity. In 1858 Cavour and Napoleon III decided to liberate northern Italy from the Austrians; Napoleon asked for Nice and Savoy as the price for his help. In 1859 France and Piedmont drove the Austrians out of Lombardy. Cavour then joined Lombardy to Piedmont and, with the agreement of both, achieved by plebiscite, he enlarged the Kingdom of Piedmont–Sardinia by forming a union with other states in northern and central Italy. With Cavour's agreement, Giuseppe Garibaldi, the hero of the 1848 Roman Republic and a militant for Italy's *Risorgimento* or resurrection, left Piedmont with a thousand volunteers, the *Camicie Rosse* or Red Shirts, and overthrew the monarchy in Naples and Sicily. To prevent Garibaldi marching on Rome, which might have led to military intervention by France and Austria, both Catholic nations loyal to the Pope, Cavour bypassed Rome but united Sicily and southern Italy in the new Kingdom of Italy formed in 1861.

Unification was also on the way in Germany. In 1862 Otto von Bismarck, Prime Minister to the King of Prussia, brought together the German States. The Duchies of Schleswig and Holstein were ruled by the King of Denmark, but the majority of their inhabitants were German. In 1864, after a short war with Denmark, the two Duchies were ceded to the German States and put under Prussian and Austrian administration. In 1866 Prussia annexed them and defeated Austria, putting an end to more than a hundred years of rivalry. Driven out of Germany, the Habsburgs turned towards south-eastern Europe and the Balkans. In 1867 they ended their rivalry with the Magyars or Hungarians with the Dual Monarchy of Austria–Hungary. This, it was thought, would curb the aspirations of the Slavs in Austria and Hungary, whose nationalism had been kindled by the success of the Slavs in the Ottoman Empire – Serbs, Montenegrins, Albanians, Bulgarians, etc. – who were profiting from the Turkish decline to set up or develop their own states.

While the nationalist movement worked against the unity of the Austro–Hungarian or the Ottoman Empires, it was a factor for unity in Italy and Germany. Napoleon III, Emperor of the French since 1852, did not stint his support. But the growth of Prussian power after 1866 disquieted him, and in 1870 he fell into a trap laid by Bismarck, who needed a psychological shock to overcome the south German states' reluctance to accept the predominance of Prussia. The support Bismarck gave to a Hohenzollern prince, who was a candidate for the momentarily vacant throne of Spain, prompted France to declare war on Prussia, which rallied Germany to its cause.

French defeats (notably at Sedan on 1 September 1870) led to the fall of the Second Empire and to unification in Germany and Italy. On 20 September 1870 Italian troops entered Rome, where the Pope – hitherto protected by a French garrison – now considered himself a prisoner. After a plebiscite Rome was declared the capital of united Italy. On 18 January 1871, in the Galerie des Glaces at Versailles, King William I of Prussia was proclaimed German Emperor. When Germany annexed Alsace and Lorraine, a rift was caused between France and Germany that lasted for several generations.

The second half of the 19th century in Europe thus saw the general emergence of nation-states, often born of violence. But the inheritance from a sometimes distant past made it rare for state and nation to cover exactly the same territory, thus raising the problem of minorities. Europe was now living in an armed peace.

③ THE PROCLAMATION OF THE GERMAN EMPIRE
Anton von Werner. Bismarck Museum

On 18 January 1871, in the Galerie des Glaces at Versailles, William I was proclaimed Emperor. Here, he is flanked by the Crown Prince of Prussia and the Grand Duke of Baden. At the foot of the steps, in white, stands Prince Bismarck, the Prime Minister and main architect of German unity, together with Field Marshal von Moltke, who made the German army the most powerful of its time. The King of Bavaria, Ludwig II, sent his brother to represent him.

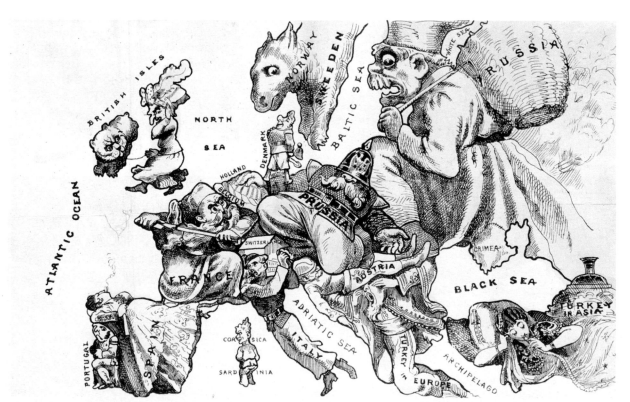

④ ARMED PEACE AT THE END OF THE 19TH CENTURY
A cartoon map of Europe

Britain holds untamable Ireland on a leash. Spain takes its rest on top of Portugal. France prepares to strike a sated Germany, which has a hand on Holland and a knee on Austria, and is quite indifferent to Italian threats of reprisals if it touches Corsica and Sardinia. Sweden is about to spring. Russia is starving. Only Turkey in Asia drowses in the fumes of the hookah.

2 Population and the Growth of Towns

❶ 'DON'T FORGET ME'
Caricature of an Irish landowner living a sybaritic life in Naples but haunted by the starving ghosts of Irish peasants.

❷ IRISH EMIGRANTS
The famine of 1845 drove 1,170,000 people out of Ireland – a seventh of the population. Many travelled steerage class to the United States, which took by far the greatest number.

The population explosion

During the 19th century Europe's economic superiority led to an increase in the population far greater than that in the rest of the world. The population of Europe including Russia rose from about 190 million in 1800 to about 420 million in 1900. The increase was not uniform throughout Europe: it varied by country and it fluctuated from year to year.

Such an unprecedented upturn attracted studies and theories as soon as it occurred. In 1798 the English churchman and economist Thomas Malthus published *An Essay on the Principles of Population*, arguing that, unless the growth of population (which was geometric) was checked by poverty, famine, disease, war or birth control, it would soon outstrip the growth of the means of subsistence (which was merely arithmetic). The merits or otherwise of Malthus's ideas were not tested in the 19th century. The growth of towns, and improvements in agriculture, industry and transport, made it possible to meet the needs of a growing population and even to raise the general standard of living. But in certain cases Malthus was proved right. In 1845–6 in Ireland, for example, a catastrophic potato harvest caused famine, followed by disease. Many people died of malnutrition. But everyone saw this as a tragic ecological accident, not a Malthusian crisis.

Various factors contributed to the growth of the population. In Western Europe the mortality rate decreased as a result of progress in public health. In England and Wales, for example, the average expectation of life rose from about 35 around 1780 to about 40 around 1840. In the less developed countries of Eastern Europe, on the other hand, mortality rates remained high. Meanwhile, the birthrate increased (it was 37 per cent in England and 42 per cent in Germany) because people were marrying earlier and using no new forms of birth control. France was exceptional: its birthrate was only 25 per cent around 1880. In general, however, the natural excess of births over deaths produced rapid population growth almost everywhere.

Migration also affected the growth of population. Immigrants, mostly from the countryside, were drawn to the towns and to industry by the chance of jobs and higher wages. Many Poles, for example, came to work in the mines of northern France or the Ruhr in Germany. A number of skilled workers left Scotland for England, while semi-skilled or unskilled Irish people crossed the sea to settle in English industrial towns and to work on building canals, railways and new roads. The highest rate of Irish emigration to the United States took place in the 1840s, when the potato famine ravaged Ireland. The Jews, meanwhile, who were persecuted in Russia, fled the pogroms by emigrating to Western Europe and the United States. In the 1830s there were some 100,000 European emigrants a year; by the end of the century there were about 1,500,000.

A growing number of Africans, West Indians and Chinese settled in Great Britain in the hope of enjoying better living conditions or, sometimes, to escape religious or political persecution.

The growth of towns

Even though agriculture remained fundamental in 19th-century Europe, the urban population greatly increased. By the end of the century British society was the most urban in the world: nine Britons out of ten lived in towns. Elsewhere the picture differed: in France, more than 70 per cent of the population lived in the countryside, and in Spain 80 per cent. But everywhere the urban population was growing apace. In 1800 London had 900,000 inhabitants, Paris 600,000 and Berlin 170,000. By 1900 London had 4.7 million, Paris 3.6 million and Berlin 2.7 million. Glasgow, Vienna, Moscow and St Petersburg also had more than a million inhabitants each, while sixteen other European cities each had more than 500,000.

The first industrialized regions, such as the

❸ INTERNATIONAL MIGRATION (1820–1910)

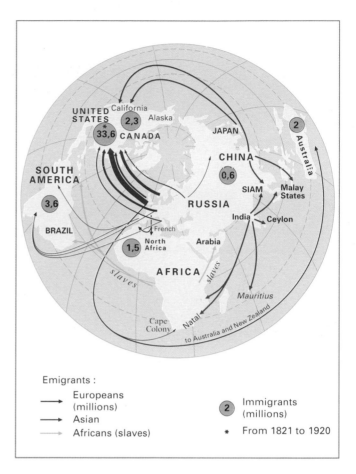

Emigrants:

→ Europeans (millions)
→ Asian
→ Africans (slaves)

② Immigrants (millions)

* From 1821 to 1920

❹ POVERTY IN LONDON
Gustave Doré, *c.* 1872. Bibliothèque Nationale, Paris
There was social segregation in the burgeoning towns. In London, then the biggest of them, the fashionable districts were in the west and the slums in the east. Here were crowded the new arrivals, who needed housing, food, health care, lighting and roads.

① THE KRUPP WORKS AT ESSEN

In the 19th century the name of Krupp became the symbol of steel and German munitions. At the beginning of the century the infant firm had ten workmen; by 1873 there were 7000. By exploiting the iron and coal mines of the Ruhr, Krupp was able to control the metal industry, as well as the Rhine shipyards.

② THE SLUMS OF BERLIN

For many people poverty was 'the inevitable price of progress'. Few employers built decent housing. Uprooted from their old homes in the countryside, the workers often lived in overcrowded, unhygienic cellars.

coalmining and steel areas of Britain, Belgium, France and Germany, were very highly urbanized. In Manchester, at the heart of the Lancashire cotton industry, the population increased more than tenfold between 1800 and 1900. Essen, in Germany's Ruhr region, the headquarters of the Krupp family, was a peaceful little village of some 4000 people in 1800. By 1900 it had some 300,000. The population of Marseille, then France's leading port, tripled between 1820 and 1870, rising from 100,000 to 300,000. In 1900 Odessa on the Black Sea, one of Russia's principal ports, had some 500,000 inhabitants. In 1800 it had had only 6000.

The growth of towns exacerbated social problems that had already existed before the onset of industry. Very often, rapidly expanding cities lacked basic services such as sanitation, water distribution and even street-cleaning. A vast population lived in poverty, crammed into overcrowded quarters, with a high risk of disease. In 1845 Friedrich Engels published *The Condition of the Working Class in England*, denouncing the appalling plight of the poor in Manchester. London's East End, in the 19th century, had the worst slums in Europe. In view of all this, some people saw the towns as synonyms for the destruction of traditional social behaviour and a threat to religion and the established order. They even believed that town life was a breeding-ground for revolution. The idea that some social classes were 'dangerous' now preoccupied a number of governments.

3 LOUIS PASTEUR IN HIS LABORATORY
Alfred Edelfeldt.
Versailles

Medicine and public health

Industrialization encouraged medical research. In 1796 the English physician Edward Jenner successfully used a vaccine against smallpox. Progress in other branches of medicine helped reduce cases of diphtheria, scarlet fever, whooping-cough and typhoid, all of which had previously caused a high rate of infant mortality. Louis Pasteur (1822–95) perfected the first effective vaccine against rabies. Joseph Lister, Professor of Surgery at the University of Glasgow, pioneered the use of antiseptics and James Simpson that of anaesthetics. Developing the work of Pasteur, the German Robert Koch showed that different diseases were caused by different bacteria and isolated the bacillus responsible for tuberculosis. Paul Ehrlich opened the way to chemotherapy. In 1895 the German physicist Wilhelm Röntgen discovered x-rays, making possible immense progress in diagnosis and surgery. Pierre and Marie Curie discovered radium and radioactivity.

Public health also benefited from 19th-century progress. Social reformers and engineers fought to achieve better public hygiene in towns: sanitary systems, sewers, water supply and drainage. These changes transformed many Europeans' lives. Between 1830 and 1850, especially, cholera had ravaged London and Paris. By 1900 it had been eradicated from the industrial towns.

Pasteur's work on fermentation enabled him to perfect a preservative technique that has ever since been known as 'pasteurization'. He discovered the vaccine against rabies and in 1888 established the institute that bears his name, where his pupils and successors continued his research on microbiology.

WILHELM RÖNTGEN 4
In 1895 this German physicist (1845–1923) discovered mysterious invisible rays that he called 'x-rays'. The way was clear for radiology.

5 JOSEPH LISTER (1827–1912)
Library of the former Faculty of Medicine, Paris
An operation being performed with the carbolic vapourizer invented by the British surgeon Joseph Lister, the creator of antiseptics, and used for surgery after 1875 to improve the operating conditions.

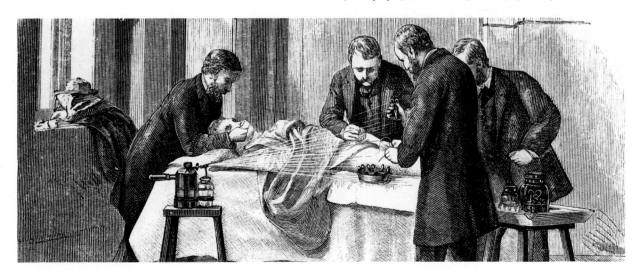

3 Agricultural Change

① A SHEEP MARKET

Thanks to feedgrains and chemical fertilizers, livestock was better nourished and grew in size and number. British stockbreeders pioneered the selection of species for different purposes. This was the beginning of genetic selection.

LES INSTRUMENTS DE TRAVAIL
84 sujets variés   La Batteuse à vapeur

② THE NEW MACHINES

Publicity material, late 19th century. Private collection

Farm tools and machinery changed. From the United States came the first reaping machines, steam-driven threshers, and mowers. Mechanization made work easier, but displaced many workers.

The food-producing revolution

During the 18th and 19th centuries agriculture developed rapidly. There was more effective rotation of the crops, a better yield from harvests, more mechanization and an improvement in animal breeding and farming techniques. The increase in the population and the growth of towns created a growing demand for food, which encouraged both more intensive farming and the use of more land. All this – much of it pioneered in Holland or Britain – is sometimes known as the 'agricultural revolution': but 'agricultural evolution' is a more appropriate term, since the pace of change was not as great in farming as in industry. In Britain the large open fields inherited from the Middle Ages were divided by hedgerows: this was known as the enclosure movement.

New machines appeared in the countryside, including the steam-driven thresher. In Britain the traditional peasantry disappeared and the land was now worked by farm labourers or smallholders. By the middle of the 19th century agriculture in Great Britain employed a much smaller proportion of the workforce than in other European countries at the same stage of development. In most other nations the great majority of country-dwellers often had a very stringent hold on the land as a result of communal laws and the excessive fragmentation of holdings. Some farmers even crossed the Channel to study new techniques, buy livestock or machinery, or ask the British for advice. So innovation spread throughout Europe. In France the rural world had not been as profoundly transformed as in Britain. In Germany, likewise, it was not until navigable waterways, roads and railways developed that the peasants' living conditions improved.

The 1848 revolutions, the growth of liberalism and the fear of popular rebellion greatly influenced the landowners of central Europe. In the west, by about 1850, feudalism had practically disappeared: the peasants were no longer bound to the soil and obliged to work for their lords. But the landed proprietors in Prussia and Poland retained their authority even after feudalism came to an end. In Russia serfdom was not abolished until 1861. But where all these changes had taken place, the peasants were freed from bondage to a particular piece of land and they now worked to meet their own needs. Wages were low, however, and often consisted of payment in kind.

Although the towns were the spearhead of the Industrial Revolution, Europe remained rural. In about 1900 the majority of its inhabitants still lived on the land.

The results of agricultural change

The improvement of farm yields and the development of transport meant that Europe's population was better fed. Periodic shortages of food became more and more infrequent. But progress was patchy: Ireland and Russia both continued to suffer from appalling famines.

Agricultural change was linked with industrialization. The surpluses created by new farming methods in turn supplied capital. Reinvested in transport and industry, this contributed to the spread of the new technology throughout Europe.

Now you little rascal, I'll give you your choice, either to stop by your handy work and be roasted, or come with me and be hanged a little bit.

THE SWING CATCHER GENERAL AT HIS AVOCATION

③ PEASANT REBELLIONS

In Britain in 1830 unemployment and extreme poverty led to revolts, often in the name of a mythical 'Captain Swing'. Setting fire to hayricks was one of the most common forms of protest, and one of the most effective ways of harming landowners' interests.

④ A MEETING OF RUSSIAN PEASANTS

On 3 March 1861 an Imperial Decree accorded freedom to Russian peasants, who had been serfs. They now enjoyed equality before the law, but the land belonged to the village or mir as a whole. Their new status was disappointing to many who left to swell the farm proletariat of the south, as here, or that of the industrial towns.

The Industrialization of Europe

❶ THE FIRST IRON BRIDGE, COALBROOKDALE
(1779)
William Williams. The Ironbridge, Shropshire. George Museum
This was one of the first landmarks in the British Industrial Revolution. Steel soon replaced cast iron, providing much greater strength. Plates and girders were mass-produced for bridges and viaducts, which spanned natural obstacles and were ideal and economical for railway trains. The iron bridge depicted here later had many counterparts throughout the world.

❷ THE MERSEY ESTUARY IN ENGLAND
T. A. Prior. Mansell Collection, London
Around Liverpool, factories and warehouses are shadowed by smoke-filled skies; sailing boats mingle with steamships. Industrialization certainly transformed both town and countryside with profits from industry and commerce.

Why Western Europe?

A number of elements are needed if a country is to become industrialized: larger units of production, greater division of labour and the replacement of people or animals by machines. The expression 'Industrial Revolution' was first used by a Frenchman at the beginning of the 19th century to describe the economic and social changes under way.

But why did modern industrialization first affect Western Europe? The principle of the steam engine had been known for a long time: but to make its development possible required economic structures and technological resources. Until the Middle Ages, countries such as China had been technologically ahead of Europe. Then, in the 18th century, Europe began to catch up and overtake them. By directing its trade overseas, it was able to enjoy greater resources, enlarge its markets, profit from its technological advantages and export capital. Rapidly expanding industry was easily able to absorb the growing number of workers leaving the land.

While industrialization shared common features throughout Europe, every country and especially every region developed in its own way. As iron-smelting technology progressed, industrialization tended to concentrate in areas rich in coal and iron ore, notably a belt stretching from Wales to the Donets basin and encompassing the Midlands and north of England, north-eastern France and Belgium, the Ruhr and Silesia. Steam soon became the key source of energy in the Industrial Revolution, even if water power still played a major role in many industries for much of the 19th century.

The spread of industrialization

So Great Britain, and more especially the Midlands, saw the birth of the Industrial Revolution. This incited British inventors to feats of ingenuity. The inventions of James Hargreaves, Richard Arkwright and Samuel Crompton led to the mechanization of the cotton industry. Factories used steam power provided by James Watt's rotary steam engine. By concentrating production in factories, manufacturers were able to economize on transport costs, apply new working methods, use more powerful machinery and impose discipline and punctuality. By about 1850 British steam engines were producing the equivalent of 1.2 million horsepower, more than half of Europe's total energy output, while 2.5 million tons of iron ore were being smelted in Britain, more than ten times the German figure. Nicknamed 'the workshop of the world', Great Britain enjoyed a period of exceptional economic growth and became the richest nation on earth: it accounted for half the world market of manufactured goods and about a third of the world's industrial production.

In the 19th century one of the characteristics of industrial development was the transfer of Britain's technological, commercial and financial expertise to the other countries of Europe.

Belgium was the first country in continental Europe to undergo the Industrial Revolution. Like Britain, it had natural reserves of coal and iron ore, a number of prosperous trading centres,

③ HOW THE BRITISH COALMINING LANDSCAPE CHANGED

In 1820 most working energy was supplied by people, animals and water-power. But with new forms of energy, work itself changed and the pithead was filled with specialized workshops.

④ THE LANARK SPINNING-MILLS IN SCOTLAND
I. Clark. Mansell Collection, London

Industrialization and the transport revolution brought astonishing development to once small places like Lanark. Buildings were of austere design, and workers used to their own surroundings were ruled by strict discipline.

❶ THE GRAND-HORNU, BELGIUM
The industrial buildings of the Grand-Hornu, in the Borinage district of Belgium, south-west of Mons, were put up by Henri de Gorge-Legrand between 1819 and 1840. They surround a central square containing a statue of their founder and comprise workplaces, shops and housing.

❷ THE MINE OF LE CREUSOT IN 1865
Bibliothèque Nationale, Paris
This mine was by no means the last to be modernized. Here, for instance, men in blue working clothes go down to the bowels of the earth in lifts, worked by a system of ropes with the help of horses. The neat and clean appearance of this illustration should not be allowed to disguise the danger and difficulty of the work.

such as the textile town of Ghent and a strategic geographical position between France and Germany. The ban on British exports to the continent during the Napoleonic Wars stimulated the cotton industry in Ghent. Further south the first blast furnace was built in the Liège coalmining area in 1823. It used coke for smelting local iron ore. Thanks to this innovation, the coal, iron, steel and chemical industries developed rapidly in the Sambre–Meuse basin. When Belgium became independent in 1831, its economic growth speeded up: between 1830 and 1850 its coal production grew from two to six million tonnes, and the number of steam engines used in Belgian industry rose from 354 to about 2300.

In France technological innovations first affected the large cities like Paris and Lyon, the coalmines of the north and the Massif Central, and the textile industries of the north-east. The linen industry flourished and silk production quadrupled in the first half of the 19th century. From the 1830s onwards cotton was processed in factories. French coal production rose, but imports were needed to meet the demands of expanding industry. French economic growth increased rapidly under the Second Empire (1852–70): the volume of imports and exports was multiplied by 400.

There were great changes, too, in banking and finance. The Pereire brothers dominated the French scene with the Crédit Mobilier, which for a large part funded the development of the railways. Other banking institutions, such as the Crédit Foncier and the Crédit Lyonnais, also contributed to the expansion of the manufacturing industries. Between 1850 and 1870 France's coal and steel production tripled, its energy production quintupled and its factories doubled the number of their employees. Financial crises in 1857 and 1863 slowed down the economy from 1865 onwards: but the mid-19th century remained a period of growing prosperity for most classes of French society.

In Germany, until 1870, political fragmentation greatly curbed industrialization, although the *Zollverein* or customs union of the German States helped to minimize the disadvantage. Until 1850 industrial development was limited to a small number of towns and regions: Hamburg and Bremen, as industrial ports; Bohemia, a province of the Austrian Habsburg Empire, as a producer of iron ore; Saxony, as an area of small cotton textile mills.

There were coalmines in Silesia and the Prussian part of the Rhineland; the Ruhr became famous for its reserves of high-quality coal; and industry developed first along the Rhine before rapidly spreading in the north. The valley of the river Wupper became a major German industrial centre. It was already famous at the beginning of the century for its textile exports and its cotton, coal and iron industries (in which an important change was from charcoal to coke for smelting). The regular growth of the industries in this region was stimulated by the ease of transport, the presence of labour and the wealth and energy of entrepreneurs. These factors played a similar role in the rest of Germany, notably in the Ruhr, where the firm of Krupp was founded at Essen in 1810.

Transport and communications

Industry and agriculture would have been unable to develop so rapidly if transport by land and sea had not undergone a similar revolution. In Great Britain, the appearance and maintenance of toll roads, the construction of canals and the later use of railways and steamships, made the transport of raw materials (especially coal), manufactures and passengers less onerous. By the mid-19th century Britain had 5000 miles of railways, even if their development depended on the goodwill of a plethora of often competing private firms. New industrial zones appeared along the railways and canals that could carry goods to distant markets, while ports expanded to deal with the increase in trade. In 1851, when the first Great Exhibition was held in London, half the world's railways were British, as were half the world's ocean-going ships.

In Belgium an ambitious railway network was built. Radiating out of Brussels, it served the main routes to France, Germany and Holland, and to the ports handling cross-Channel traffic to Britain. Once the state had established the basic structure of the system, private firms were encouraged to add new lines; but in 1870 the whole network returned to state control. Benefiting from the nearness of the Sambre–Meuse coal basin, the port of Antwerp prospered and the town became an important centre of international trade. A highly developed network of inland waterways supplemented the railways for the transport of heavy goods.

In France the first railways were built around 1830, partly by the state, partly by private companies. The design of the network, radiating out of Paris for political or administrative reasons, was more coherent than that of the railways in Britain. Yet by 1850 France still had only 2000 miles of track. Still, that was enough to help bring together the different regions of France. Under the Second Empire the state nationalized and then enlarged the network of canals. The electric telegraph was installed to link

3 THE FORGE
Painting by Adolph von Menzel, 1875. National Gallery, Berlin
Von Menzel made his name as a painter of historical and social subjects. This picture shows the toil and bustle of ironworks like those of Bohemia or Wuppertal, regions rich in iron ore, the raw material for one of the revolutionary products of the 19th century – steel.

4 OPENING THE STOCKTON TO DARLINGTON RAILWAY
Science Museum, London
This ceremony, on 27 September 1825, marked the beginning of a form of transport that never stopped, and never stopped developing. From 30 mph in 1829, its speed rose to more than 60 mph in 1835. When steel replaced iron rails in 1870, they became harder and stronger. Longer trains, more efficient boilers, compressed-air brakes and the use of a standardized gauge – all helped to make the railways the leading means of transport.

❶ THE GÖLTZSCHTALBRÜCKE VIADUCT
Near Gera, Germany, south of Leipzig.

❷ DIGGING THE MONT-CENIS TUNNEL
1875. Bibliothèque des Merveilles, Paris

❸ THE ROSSIO STATION, LISBON
The Franco–Swiss author Blaise Cendrars called railway stations 'the most beautiful churches in the world'. They were temples of technology, gathering all available material resources, and grandiose national shop-windows. The façade of the Lisbon station, in the neo-Manueline or Gothic Renaissance style, is no exception.

the major cities and by 1870 there were 12,000 miles of railway track. In the Alps, France and Italy were joined by the Mont-Cenis tunnel.

A certain number of German states, too, built and supervised a railway system. By 1850, indeed, the German network was twice that of France. To begin with, it deepened the divisions between different states, but in the longer term, when the unification of Germany began to be possible, it acted as a unifying force. The establishment of the *Zollverein* encouraged further developments. The resultant railway system gave Germany a strategic position in central Europe and it became a crossroads in European trade. The railways, in fact, not only helped to unite Germany, they also helped the German Empire develop as a nation-state.

The Spanish state financed the building of a railway network, centralized around Madrid; but by adopting a different gauge from that of France and the rest of Europe it hindered communications with the outside world.

By the end of the century the countries of Europe were already linked by telegraph; and in 1866 the first transatlantic cable came into service. In 1888 the first Orient Express ran between Paris and Constantinople and the Trans-Siberian railway was completed in 1904. Thanks to industrialization, maritime connections among European countries improved; and the building of the *Nieuwe Waterweg* in Rotterdam and the *Noordzee Kanaal* in Amsterdam made the Netherlands a major point of transit by inland waterway to the interior of Germany, at the expense of Antwerp, which had earlier benefited from the abolition of taxes on the Scheldt. The building of the Kiel Canal by Germany created a short cut between the Baltic and the North Sea. In Great Britain the Manchester Ship Canal enabled big ships to go into the heart of the industrial north.

An *age of progress*?

By 1870 Belgium, Germany, France and Switzerland had joined Great Britain as industrial powers. In Italy industrialization was limited to the north (Piedmont and the Genoa region), owing to fertile land and reserves of minerals. In Scandinavia, Sweden developed its metal and manufacturing industries, while Norway's textile industries benefited from British expertise. Portugal and Spain remained mainly agricultural. In Spain, nevertheless, the development of the railways and the new steel industry created a demand for coal which led to the growth of mining in the Asturias. In the Habsburg Empire, meanwhile, the economy did not begin to be modernized until the end of the 19th century, chiefly in Bohemia.

In the final years of the 19th century there was a shift in the balance of power among the industrial nations, whose rivalry had been increased by the establishment of customs barriers. The era of Britain's economic supremacy was coming to an end. True, Britain maintained its free trade policy and its lead over the other industrial nations; but by 1900 Germany was Europe's main producer of electrotechnical goods and the world's biggest producer of chemicals. The United States, benefiting from European technology, was also becoming a serious competitor.

By the end of the 19th century Europe and the European nations had shared among them most of the rest of the world, establishing or enlarging vast colonial empires. The industrialized nations used great universal exhibitions to display their economic power and colonial greatness. Yet, despite such benefits as better medical care, Europe's colonial expansion had tragic results for the natives of Africa, Asia and Australia, who were often exploited as pitilessly as the natural resources of their continents.

Considerable scientific and technological progress accompanied industrialization. Scientists like Alessandro Volta, André Marie Ampère, Georg Simon Ohm, Sir Humphry Davy, Joseph Henry and Michael Faraday pursued research on electricity and related subjects. From the 1830s their discoveries were in practical use. In 1866 Ernst von Siemens invented the dynamo. But electricity

**LONDON, 1851: ④
THE FIRST GREAT
EXHIBITION**
Painting by Henry Courtney. Victoria and Albert Museum, London
The Industrial Revolution in Britain was 50 years ahead of that on the Continent. Not surprisingly, the first Exhibition was held in London. On 1 May Queen Victoria inaugurated the pavilions of 'new techniques and new industries' in Hyde Park.

⑤ **THE UNIVERSAL EXHIBITION IN PARIS, 1889**
On the centenary of the French Revolution, Paris held the third Universal Exhibition since 1867. In the words of one critic, the Eiffel Tower was an 'odious shadow of a great lady'.

⑥ **EUROPEAN POSSESSIONS AT THE END OF THE 19TH CENTURY**

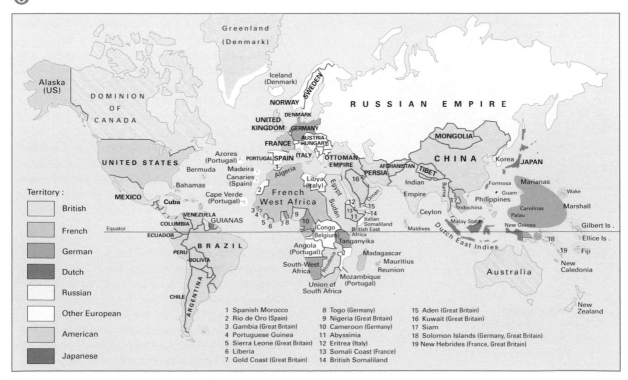

Territory:
British
French
German
Dutch
Russian
Other European
American
Japanese

1 Spanish Morocco
2 Rio de Oro (Spain)
3 Gambia (Great Britain)
4 Portuguese Guinea
5 Sierra Leone (Great Britain)
6 Liberia
7 Gold Coast (Great Britain)
8 Togo (Germany)
9 Nigeria (Great Britain)
10 Cameroon (Germany)
11 Abyssinia
12 Eritrea (Italy)
13 Somali Coast (France)
14 British Somaliland
15 Aden (Great Britain)
16 Kuwait (Great Britain)
17 Siam
18 Solomon Islands (Germany, Great Britain)
19 New Hebrides (France, Great Britain)

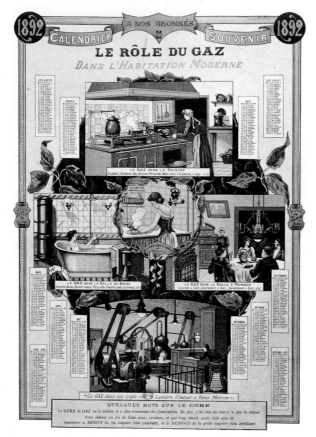

① THE ROLE OF GAS
Epinal print, 1892

Offering light, heat and motor power, gas was in household use by 1879, bringing a real improvement in standards of living.

② A MOTOR RACE
A drawing in *l'Illustration*, 8 July 1901

The first real automobile, the Daimler, appeared in Stuttgart in 1886. Fifteen years later the Paris–Berlin race drew a crowd.

was as yet little used for lighting and very rarely as a source of power for factories. During the 1890s the Italian Guglielmo Marconi showed the practicality of wireless telegraphy. In France the brothers Auguste and Louis Lumière pioneered the cinematograph; and the world's first cinema opened in Paris in 1896.

Progress was also achieved on the technology of the internal combustion engine. In 1860 the Belgian-born Etienne Lenoir used such an engine fixed to a road vehicle. In 1873 the Austrian Siegfried Markus showed an automobile at the Vienna Exhibition; but it was two Germans, Gottlieb Daimler and Karl Benz, the so-called 'fathers of the automobile', who built and perfected such cars. After 1880 numerous inventors worked on the internal combustion engine, including René Panhard and Emile Levassor from France.

Already, however, scientists were worrying about the effects that industrialization might have on the environment. In 1827 the French mathematician Joseph Fourier showed that carbon dioxide emissions threatened to heat the atmosphere. Later, the Swedish scientist Svante Arrhenius spoke of 'the greenhouse effect'. And at the beginning of the 20th century physicists foresaw the nuclear age with all its benefits and risks.

As living conditions improved, especially for the middle classes, organized leisure became more important and attracted commercial interests. Thanks to the railways, seaside resorts, spas and race-courses were now more accessible. Travel in Europe became fashionable. Thomas Cook, one of the first travel agents, organized his first Swiss tour in 1863. Later, he invented travellers' cheques.

Mountaineering became more popular and Alpine summits were successfully climbed – the Wetterhorn in 1854 and the Matterhorn in 1865. Skiing, which had been invented in Sweden five thousand years earlier, became a real sport after 1890. Swimming appealed to more and more people: in 1875 Captain Matthew Webb made the first cross-Channel swim. Bicycling became popular, thanks to technological progress and mass production: the first Tour de France took place in 1903. In 1894, meanwhile, motor racing had begun to arouse interest, with the first timed drive between Paris and Rouen, followed in 1895 by a run from Paris to Bordeaux.

Sport became more organized. The rules of football were standardized and the *Fédération Internationale de Football Association* (FIFA) was founded in 1904. In rugby an international championship between France and England was established in 1884. Tennis grew popular. In 1877 the Wimbledon Tennis Club became the

③ THE CYCLE CHALET IN THE BOIS DE BOULOGNE
Painting by Jean Béraud, *c.*1900. Musée de l'Ile de France, Sceaux

centre for international matches. In 1876 the first artificial skating-rink opened in London and in 1896 the first championships in artistic skating were held. By the beginning of the 20th century athletics federations already existed in Great Britain, Belgium, Sweden, Greece, Italy and Germany.

In 1896 a new version of the ancient Olympic Games was staged in Athens, on the initiative of Baron Pierre de Coubertin. He hoped that sport would reduce rivalry among nations. But very soon the Olympics began to be used politically to enhance national prestige.

The results of industrialization

Industrialization transformed human history as profoundly as the emergence of agriculture in Neolithic times, eight millennia earlier. Never had Europe undergone such sudden and intense change.

Between 1880 and 1914 Europe was swept by a wind of modernism with an optimistic tinge. Europeans believed in progress and had no fear of the future. European civilization at that time had unprecedented enterprise, adaptability and self-confidence. As a result its technology soon spread throughout the world. Indeed, industrialization created ideal conditions for overseas ventures. The European nations were able to increase their supremacy by commercial, cultural and diplomatic means. In the last quarter of the 19th century they incorporated new territory into their existing empires, either by conquest or by discovery, mainly in Africa.

④ 'LE DEJEUNER SUR L'HERBE'
Painting by Edouard Manet, 1863. Musée d'Orsay, Paris
With better working conditions, the French discovered the pleasures of bicycling, country cafés and picnics on the grass. This painting, typical of Manet's unconventionality, caused a great scandal when it was exhibited at the Salon des Refusés in 1863.

⑤THE REVIVAL OF THE OLYMPIC GAMES, 1896
'It is clear that the telegraph, the railways, the telephone, the eager quests of science, the congresses and the exhibitions, have done more for peace than all the treaties and all the diplomatic conventions. I have a hope that athletics will do even more.' Speech by Pierre de Coubertin, inaugurating the first modern Olympic Games in Athens.

Politics and Social Reform

❶ 'THE PROMISED LAND' OF MARXISM
Propaganda cartoon, end of 19th century
On a windswept shore, proletarians of all countries prepare to embark on the ships of their demands, guided by Karl Marx as Moses, with the Tablets of his Law under his arm.

❷ SOCIAL DEMOCRACY
Standard-bearer of Socialist ideology and the working-class, the German Social-Democrat Party was established in Gotha in 1875 at the instigation of August Bebel (centre). With its own schools and newspapers and its own discipline, it was a model for its sister parties, with which in 1889 it formed the Second International.

Political systems

By the end of the 19th century, partly as a result of nationalism, most Europeans were no longer ruled by absolutist sovereigns but by constitutional monarchs or republican presidents. In France, under the Third Republic, the ministerial Cabinet was answerable to the Senate and to the Chamber of Deputies, elected for four years by universal male suffrage. The members of the Chamber and the Senate elected a President for a term of seven years. In the Kingdom of Italy, only Piedmont had a parliamentary tradition and few Italians had the right to vote. Great Britain was a constitutional monarchy with a parliamentary system. In the German Empire, the Chancellor and his ministers were appointed and dismissed by the Kaiser or Emperor: they depended on him and not on the parliamentary institutions.

The scene was dominated by right-wing (Conservative) or centre (right or left-wing Liberal) political parties: but at the end of the century new parties appeared. In Germany it was a Catholic party, which later became the dominant partner in coalition with the Conservatives. In the United Kingdom the Irish Question was the politicians' stumbling-block: a movement for Irish independence emerged, calling for 'Home Rule' (Irish autonomy), the repeal of the Act of Union and the establishment of an Irish parliament.

Karl Marx, as a refugee in London, analyzed the economic machinery of British capitalism and based his analysis on a would-be scientific form of socialism that had considerable influence. With Friedrich Engels he drew up *The Manifesto of the Communist Party* in 1848, and in 1867 he published *Das Kapital*. The International Working Men's Association (the 'First International', 1864–72) was partly based on Marx's work.

Socialist parties were also emerging in Europe. In Germany the working men's party founded in 1869 by August Bebel led in 1875 to the Social-Democrat Party. From the 1880s Social-Democrat parties based on the German model were set up in Belgium, Austria, Hungary, Poland, the Netherlands and Russia. In Great Britain, in 1893, the Independent Labour Party was formed and in 1900 it linked with the trade unions to create the Labour Party. Social Democrats also became important in Scandinavia, where they worked closely with the trade unions. In Italy, despite the resistance they faced, the Socialists won more seats in parliament. In France

Socialism tried to recover from the crushing of the Paris Commune in 1871, which put an end to its utopian strain. Even so, French Socialism remained divided into a number of tendencies, which Jean Jaurès tried to bring together. He was a humanistic Socialist in the tradition of the 1789 Revolution and a champion of international peace.

Saving world peace was also the aim of the last congresses held by the Second International, founded in Paris in 1889 by the non-revolutionary Socialist parties, among which the German and Russian Social-Democrats were the most influential. At such gatherings all the problems of industrial society were discussed. 1 May was made International Labour Day. The workers' movement also increased their influence by European cooperation: in 1900 they established the International Labour Office in Brussels.

Despite strong opposition by employers, the trade unions were gradually recognized as the genuine representatives of the workforce. They acquired legal status between 1870 and 1900 (but not until 1906 in Russia). The first groups to organize were skilled workers. Trade union action was strengthened by large-scale strikes like that of the London dockers and the Ruhr miners, both in 1889. In Britain and Germany the unions mounted political pressure for building a Socialist society. In some countries, like Italy and Germany, Catholic workers sought to dissociate themselves from the Socialists and founded non-political unions. But everywhere, in Britain, France, Germany, the Netherlands and Sweden, the trade unions and the labour parties had acquired political weight and governments had to meet their calls for better working conditions.

Social reform

In the last years of the 19th century, attempts were made to eliminate the ill-effects of industrialization and in particular the exploitation of children in factories and workshops. All the countries of Europe, except Russia and in the Balkans, passed laws to deal with the length of the working day, working conditions and safety rules to protect employees. But child labour did not completely stop. Many workers still had to put up with unhealthy and often dangerous conditions, and in many cases the working day was more than ten hours long. Governments and reformers were equally concerned with the problems of housing and public health.

So it was that in the 1860s Baron Haussmann put into practice an ambitious plan of reform for the city of Paris, including among other things a system of sewers and water supply: whole dis-

③ THE SPRINGTIME OF SOCIALISM
In July 1889 two international workers' congresses decided to organize an annual demonstration on 1 May, in memory of 1 May 1886, when the American government had agreed to reduce the working day to eight hours.

④ 'THE MAKER OF THE NEW PARIS'
Painting by Yvon Adolphe. Carnavalet Museum, Paris
In 1859 Napoleon III hands to Baron Haussmann the decree annexing the peripheral communes of Auteuil, Grenelle, Vaugirard, Passy, Bercy, Charonne, Belleville, Batignolles, Chaillot, etc., needed to accommodate the factories and working population driven out by the demolition of Old Paris. This forced removal was much disliked by those who suffered it.

❶ THE PARISIAN WORLD ON FIVE FLOORS

Caricature by Lavielle, *c.* 1850. Private collection

Apartment houses appeared in the 19th century. They were microcosms of society. The first floor, with a balcony, belonged to the wealthy; the second, to well-off young couples with families; the third was often visited by cats and creditors; while no one, not even the concierge, ever went up to the fourth, under the eaves: that was reserved for maids, artists and the unemployed.

---

❷ The 'good fortune' of a factory girl

I had a recommendation to a famous factory. I had never been so well paid. My only wish was to have fine clothes. I wanted no one to know I was a factory girl when I went to church on Sunday, because I was ashamed of my position. When I was still an apprentice, I was always hearing people say that factory girls were loose-living and corrupt. They only talked about them scornfully. All I felt was that I was no longer poor. Our magnificent Sunday dinner seemed to me to be fit for a king. For 20 kreuzer we bought meat and when my salary went up we added a small glass of sweet wine.

A. Popp, *A Young Working Girl*, 1909

---

tricts were demolished and broad boulevards gave new grandeur to the city. This example was followed elsewhere, as for instance in Brussels. In Great Britain, France and Germany reformers called for landed property to be nationalized, for housing to be inspected by the state and for laws on town planning to be passed. In France a growing number of dwellings came to be provided by local authorities or cooperative societies. In some German cities such as Hamburg there were large-scale slum clearance schemes and a number of dwellings were built by cooperative societies or supplied by firms. In Great Britain philanthropic industrialists built 'model towns' for their workpeople. In 1887, in the East End of London, the Rothschild Buildings were filled mainly with Jewish immigrants, refugees from persecution in Eastern Europe. Dwellings in north-west Europe differed considerably from those in much of the rest of Europe: Great Britain, Belgium and Holland preferred small family houses, while the countries in the south preferred apartments. Even if some of the reforms were successful, not all the problems were solved. Many families suffered discomfort or overcrowding, and their meagre income often left too little for clothes and food.

In most European countries the state began to tackle the fight against poverty. Germany was the first to pass social legislation, after 1880, making old-age and sickness insurance compulsory, and establishing old-age pensions. In Great Britain a retirement scheme was established in 1909 and insurance against sickness and unemployment became compulsory in 1911. In most of the countries in Western Europe a growing number of people thought that governments should deal with social welfare, but the retirement pensions and health insurance actually provided gave only limited protection.

The changing status of women

As in previous centuries, men still dominated European society. Women's role was marriage, motherhood and child-rearing. They had few rights. Religion and convention discouraged them from pursuing professional careers or seeking equality with men. But at the end of the 19th century they began to enjoy a longer expectation of life and to devote fewer years to bearing and rearing children. Their legal status improved: in Great Britain married women now had property rights.

New jobs in offices (as secretaries or telephonists) and in department stores (as salesgirls) gave them the chance of employment. More and more women, too, obtained the qualifications needed for various professions. In the Netherlands the first woman physician began to practise in 1870; in France, the first woman lawyer in 1903. The most famous professional women included the educationist Maria Montessori, the physicist Marie Curie and the nurse Florence Nightingale.

There were new job prospects for women in education. In Great Britain, thanks to the Girls' Public Day School Trust, founded in 1871, more of the daughters of middle-class families could enjoy better teaching. In France the first *lycée* for girls was opened in 1884 in Montpellier. In Germany girls went to state schools from 1894 onwards. In 1867 the University of Zurich admit ted women students and its example was soon followed in Paris, Sweden and Finland.

In many European countries feminist movements arose, demanding the right to vote. Finland accepted female suffrage in 1906 and Norway in 1913. In Great Britain the Suffragists founded the National Union of Women's Suffrage Societies. French Socialists thought that the emancipation of the working classes was more urgent than that of women. The other parties ruled it out altogether.

③ LONDON SUFFRAGETTES
Le Petit Journal, September 1908

In England women campaigned for the right to vote, using every means in their power: speeches, writing on the pavement, door-to-door canvassing, wearing sandwich boards, demonstrating. Even imprisonment did not silence them. In 1918 women over 30 who (or whose husbands) occupied premises or lands to the annual value of £5 could vote. Not until 1928 was the age limit reduced to 21, like that of men.

④ A TELEPHONE EXCHANGE
Le Petit Journal, April 1904. Musée de la Poste, Paris

Alexander Graham Bell, a Scotsman who emigrated to the United States, invented the telephone in 1876, and two years later the first exchange had 21 subscribers. Not until 1890 did exchanges spread throughout the world, offering jobs for many young women.

6 Cultural Change in the 19th Century

① THE GERMAN MASTER OF ROMANTICISM
Caspar David Friedrich (1774–1840), *The Tree with Crows*.
Louvre Museum, Paris
The vivid movement in Friedrich's landscapes encouraged the use of bold, translucent colours. He was inured to solitude.

THE PRE-RAPHAELITES: D. G. ROSSETTI (1828–82) ②
The Bride.
Tate Gallery, London
Reacting against prosaic Victorian art, the Pre-Raphaelites painted a pristine, melancholy, romantic world in lively colours not unworthy of Botticelli and opposed to the murky patina of tradition.

③ VINCENT VAN GOGH (1853–90)
Van Gogh's *Room at Arles*, 1889. Musée d'Orsay, Paris
In his sanatorium the painter copied this canvas twice. It represented for him the comfort and security he had lost.

From the end of the 18th century onwards economic and social upheavals went hand in hand with revolutionary changes and new ideas in the creative and visual arts, as well as in the theatre. This effervescence of ideas was encouraged by the new insights of thinkers like Hegel, Schopenhauer, John Stuart Mill, Tocqueville, Marx and Kierkegaard. Similar progress was made in sociology by Auguste Comte and Emile Durkheim. At the same time the theory of natural selection developed by Charles Darwin called in question the literal interpretation of the Old Testament. A little later Herbert Spencer extended the theory of evolution to the whole of human knowledge. Progress in anthropology and archaeology, meanwhile, radically transformed the study of history, to which Henry Thomas Buckle and Leopold von Ranke attempted a more objective approach.

Romanticism and realism

The turn of the century was marked by two opposite and perhaps conflicting movements: neo-classicism and Romanticism. The Romantics valued the emotions and individual imagination more than society. The first products of the Romantic movement included the work of Goethe and Schiller in Germany and the lyric poetry of Keats and Wordsworth in Britain. In music the transition from the classical to the Romantic can be heard notably in the works of Beethoven, whose Ninth Symphony set to music Schiller's *Ode to Joy* and is today the European anthem.

Political movements for national independence inspired a number of Romantic poets and painters. In Italy, through his operas, the composer Verdi became a hero of the Risorgimento. Romanticism in many ways also influenced the novel, the dominant literary form of the 19th century. Examples include the Gothic novel *Frankenstein* by Mary Shelley and the works of Walter Scott, Alessandro Manzoni, Alfred de Vigny, Victor Hugo and George Sand. Similar influence can be found in historical writings, notably those of Jules Michelet and Thomas Carlyle.

While some artists felt at home in the new industrial age, others dreamed of returning to an idealized pre-industrial world. In Britain, for example, the painters and poets of the Pre-Raphaelite Brotherhood were inspired by the Italian artists who had preceded Raphael. In architecture the 19th century adopted the neo-Gothic style and its buildings in particular combined iron with stone and glass. Large buildings, prefabricated in British, French or German factories, were exported all over the world, especially to India, Indochina, Brazil and elsewhere.

Towards the end of the 1830s the conflict between neo-classicism and Romanticism began to give way to a debate about the social value of art. There was an urge to portray the world 'in its true colours'. These concerns were reflected in the 'reforming' novels of Charles Dickens and Benjamin Disraeli, in the social panoramas of Honoré de Balzac and in the objective realism of Gustave Flaubert. The painters of the Barbizon school in France depicted scenes from contemporary life. Realism in literature and art also coincided with the birth of modern photography, which was developed by Joseph N. Niepce, W. H. Fox Talbot and Louis Daguerre.

European theatre, too, saw the emergence of a new social and psychological realism in the works of Henrik Ibsen, Bjørnstjerne Bjørnson, August Strindberg and Anton Chekhov. The novel at this time was also marked by the psychological realism of Fyodor Dostoyevsky, as well as by Emile Zola's naturalism and symbolic realism.

Impressionism, Post-Impressionism, Futurism and Art Nouveau

The realistic painting of landscapes, the appearance of photography and the introduction into Europe of Japanese prints all contributed to the rise of Impressionism in France, which sought to express the immediate impression aroused by momentary scenes, visual surfaces and spaces, bathed in colour and light.

In the 1880s a number of artists in France reacted against Impressionism, experimenting with a return to shapes, compositions and less fleeting subjects: they included Paul Cézanne, Vincent Van Gogh and Paul Gauguin. Later, the Cubists explored form and space with fragmented sculptural arrangements of partly overlapping transparent surfaces. A separate movement, Art Nouveau, was notable for the use of exotic shapes: it found recruits in many parts of Europe and in all areas of art, including book illustrators, architects, sculptors and interior designers. In Italy the Futurists proclaimed the absence of tradition in art, poetry and the novel, glorifying the dynamism of the machine age.

❹ THE GLASS ROOF OF THE GRAND PALAIS, PARIS
Built between 1897 and 1900 by the architects Deglane, Thomas and Louvet
The Grand Palais was built on the occasion of the Universal Exhibition of 1900. It has a huge exhibition hall of metallic construction, whose enormous iron and glass roof is characteristic of Art Nouveau. The main hall is flanked by more traditional rooms.

❺ IMPRESSION, SUNRISE (1872)
Claude Monet (1840–1926). Paris, Marmottan Museum
'These patches of colour have been produced in the same way as daubing the base of a fountain. Slap! Slop! Flip! Flop! Get in there! It's outrageous, frightful!' So wrote the critic of the journal Charivari on looking at this canvas. As an insult he called Monet an 'Impressionist'.

❻ BARON HORTA
Staircase of the Hôtel Tassel, Brussels
Victor, Baron Horta (1861–1947), was a master of Art Nouveau whom his detractors called l'archisec (dry as dust). His architecture was all lightness, transparency and curves. He drew his inspiration from nature and animals; he used exotic wood (Congo mahogany, okoumé from Gabon); he experimented with the transparency of glass and the malleability of iron. To all that he added a form of functionalism that was unique at that time: 'It is necessary to clothe the purely useful, which is always repulsive and horrible.'

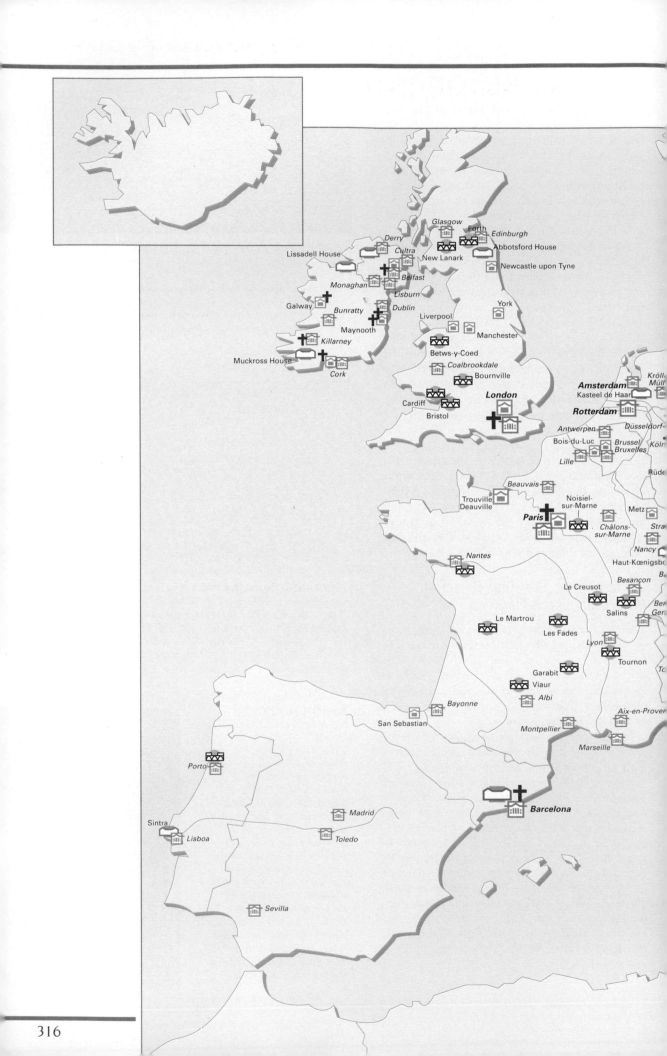

Glasgow
Forth
Edinburgh
Abbotsford House
Derry
Cultra
New Lanark
Newcastle upon Tyne
Lissadell House
Belfast
Monaghan
Lisburn
Galway
Bunratty
Dublin
York
Maynooth
Liverpool
Killarney
Manchester
Muckross House
Betws-y-Coed
Cork
Coalbrookdale
Bournville
Amsterdam
Kröll...
Müll...
Kasteel de Haar
Cardiff
London
Rotterdam
Bristol
Antwerpen
Düsseldorf
Bois-du-Luc
Brussel
Köln
Bruxelles
Lille
Rüde...
Beauvais
Trouville
Deauville
Noisiel-
sur-Marne
Metz
Paris
Châlons-
sur-Marne
Stra...
Nancy
Haut-Kœnigsbo...
Nantes
Besançon
Le Creusot
Ba...
Salins
Ber...
Le Martrou
Les Fades
Ger...
Lyon
Tournon
Garabit
Viaur
Albi
Aix-en-Prover...
Bayonne
San Sebastian
Montpellier
Marseille
Porto
Madrid
Sintra
Toledo
Lisboa
Sevilla
Barcelona

The Past in the Present Day
THE MODERNIZATION OF EUROPE

Legend:
- château, palace or manor-house
- religious monument
- civic monument
- museum, library or collection well stocked with items on this period
- industrial architecture
- frontiers of 20th-century states

500 km

Riga

Ordupgård
København

Hamburg Schwerin
Berlin
nover
Potsdam
Leipzig
Dresden
Marianske Karlovy Vary
Lazne
rankfurt Bayreuth
stadt Praha
heim
Nürnberg Regensburg
München
hwanstein Herrenchiemsee
erthur Linderhof Bad Ischl Graz
Wien

Warszawa

Wroclaw
Lublin

Krakow

Kiyev

Jassy

nola Ljubljana
o Trieste Zagreb
Padova Venezia
Piacenza
va
Bologna
Firenze

Budapest

Beograd

Bucuresti

Roma

Kercyra
(Corfu)

Palermo

Athinai
Nafplio (Nauplia)

❶ THE PALACE OF THE SLEEPING BEAUTY
Engraving. Carnavalet Museum, Paris

Europe inaugurated the 20th century with a universal exhibition in Paris. Its Palace of Electricity set the tone: modern and dazzling.

1900–14	Social tension and international crises	1923	Occupation of the Ruhr
1901	First Nobel Prize	1924	Stalin succeeds Lenin
1904	Entente Cordiale *between France and Britain*	1925	Locarno Treaties
		1923–9	International détente
1907	The Hague Convention on land warfare	1928	Briand–Kellogg Pact
1912–13	Conflicts in the Balkans	1929	Beginning of the great economic crisis
1914–18	First World War	1929–39	Rise of the dictators
1916	Battles of Verdun and the Somme	1933	Adolf Hitler becomes German Chancellor
1917	October Revolution in Russia	1936–9	Spanish Civil War
1918	President Woodrow Wilson's Fourteen Points	1938	Munich agreement
		1939–45	Second World War
1919	Versailles Treaty: League of Nations established	1942–3	Siege of Stalingrad
1922	Mussolini's March on Rome	1945	Defeat of Germany and Japan

❷ THE CRUEL MADNESS OF GUERNICA
Pablo Picasso

On 26 April 1937 the Basque town of Guernica was destroyed by the terrorist bombers of the Nazi Lûftwaffe. Picasso used this 'experimental' air raid as a symbol of the ultimate horror of war. His painting was shown at the Paris Exhibition in 1937.

IN DANGER OF SELF-DESTRUCTION

1900–45

I n less than half a century, Europe ceased to dominate the world.

Two wars, originally 'civil wars' within Europe, turned into world wars and led Europeans to the brink of ruin. Revolutions, including the October Revolution in Russia, swept away old institutions. Political regimes changed, empires collapsed, new states were created, new frontiers were drawn. Torn by countless conflicts, Europe was deeply affected and further weakened by the great economic crisis of the 1930s. The fate of the world gradually passed into the hands of other powers.

There were several reasons why Europe seemed bent on self-destruction. The great changes brought about by 19th-century progress had opened new and undreamt-of horizons, but they had also created powerful and dangerous tension. For a time aggressive nationalism managed to sublimate internal conflicts; but states and peoples were disinclined to settle international disputes by peaceful compromise and much more tempted to threaten and to use force. In the process Europe's shared interests were forgotten. Still more ominous was the rise of dictators who scorned all Europe's humanitarian traditions and sought only to enslave people under their respective ideologies. These totalitarian regimes set out to dominate Europe and the rest of the world.

Nevertheless, statesmen continued to seek a lasting peace acceptable to all Europeans, and a small but growing number began to look ahead to a united Europe in which states would be equal and people would be free.

❸ **FORWARD!**

At the 1937 Paris Exhibition the pavilions of Soviet Russia and Nazi Germany faced each other. The former was surmounted by two statues to the glory of people on the march – official art obeying the dictates of Socialist Realism.

❹ **STANDARD-BEARERS FOR NAZI GERMANY**
Hitler was a failed artist but a master of propaganda: he himself designed the standard of Nazi Germany. Delighted with his handiwork, he declared: 'In the red we see the movement's social ideal; in the white, the idea of nationalism; and in the swastika, our missionary struggle for the victory of the Aryan race.'

_1_ Europe in 1900

① CROSSING THE STRAITS OF DOVER BY AEROPLANE

On 25 July 1908 Louis Blériot made one of humanity's oldest dreams come true. At 4.41 he took off from Calais on board his monoplane Blériot XI. Thirty minutes later he landed on the cliffs of Dover. The air was conquered. Military men saw aircraft as a formidable weapon: they bought Blériot XI and commissioned from Blériot the first units of the future French air force. That was how he came to build the Spad for Georges-Marie Guynemer and the other French 'air aces' of the First World War.

② MIDDLE-CLASS AND WORKING-CLASS LIFE

The end of the 19th century saw the apogee of the successful bourgeoisie and the beginnings of militancy on the part of the working class. The bourgeoisie prized domesticity, but reserved the finest rooms (the dining-room and drawing-room) for receiving company. Their men dressed in sombre clothes, a sign of restraint and respectability; the women wore complicated, shimmering dresses that made clear their social status. Working people lived on the fringes of towns or in estates built for them. They had a minimum of comfort: a stove, electricity, a water supply on the landing. Conditions were improving, but it was hard to escape from their lot because of the widening gap between employers and employees.

The centre of the world

At the dawn of the 20th century Europeans could be proud of their success and look to the future with confidence. They had such a sense of superiority, moreover, that they thought their way of life the best in the world. London, Paris, Berlin, Vienna and St Petersburg were where everything was decided. The European states had vast colonial empires, acquired by dividing up almost all of Africa and a great part of Asia. Their weapons were the most powerful in the world and nowhere else produced so much merchandise or did so much trade. A tightly-knit system of roads, railways and canals ensured the rapid circulation of people and goods. Huge urban centres with millions of inhabitants had grown up in the great industrial areas. Among the most important were the region between Liège and Lille, the English Midlands, and the Ruhr.

Most scientific discoveries and technological innovations had been made in Europe, although some were now being made in the United States. Automobiles, aircraft, telephones, the cinema, certain medicines, artificial fertilizers and dye-stuffs – all these were European inventions. In about 1900 some key research heralded the beginning of the atomic age. The Franco–Polish physicist Marie Curie did important work on radioactivity, while Ernest Rutherford in England and Max Planck and Albert Einstein in Germany established the bases of nuclear physics. Some years later the Dane Niels Bohr synthesized these various pieces of research. Many people believed that nothing could halt human progress.

The 'Belle Epoque'

Away from the towns and industrial areas, however, vast stretches of Europe were still wholly devoted to agriculture. Most of Europe's 400 million people still lived in the countryside. There, time seemed to have stood still. The work was hard and leisure almost non-existent. The land could barely feed an ever-growing population. More and more country-dwellers went to the towns to find work. Many left Europe altogether to seek their fortune, generally in the United States.

The hope of a better future, however, helped many to put up with everyday privations. The situation of the miners, factory workers and domestic servants, as of all poorer people, was not as bad as it had been some decades before, but it was still difficult. Child labour had not been completely abolished. A working day of ten hours or more was still common. Not every employer observed the weekly day of rest. Insurance against sickness and old age was very limited and not always required by law. Working people's homes were often cramped and uncomfortable, and they had barely enough money to clothe and feed their families.

In the factories powerful organizations of workers challenged capitalism. In some countries – Britain, France, Germany, Sweden and the Netherlands – the trade unions and labour parties had become so influential that governments and employers could no longer ignore them. They demanded above all greater social security and better conditions of work. They also increased their strength by setting up an association at European level. In 1900 an International Socialist Bureau was established in Brussels; and the congresses of the Working Men's International in Paris (1900), Amsterdam (1904), Stuttgart (1907), Copenhagen (1910) and Basle (1912) were opportunities to assert the power of workers over employers.

But, if the proletariat was acquiring political power, it remained economically and socially weak. It was also overshadowed by those who had achieved prosperity and respectability, for the bourgeois way of life was everywhere regarded as a model. The culture of the bourgeoisie, its ethics, its energy, its tastes in decoration, architecture, dress and leisure were recognized and eagerly imitated almost everywhere in Europe. The French conception of the 'Belle Epoque' in the years between 1890 and 1914 became that of Europe as a whole.

Very few were able to see what was hidden behind the façade of this bourgeois Europe that seemed to be so triumphant. Only a few poets, philosophers and artists had any inkling that great changes might be on the way.

The Swedish dramatist August Strindberg expressed the unease and torment in which he himself lived. The threat of future catastrophe also haunted the plays of the Austrian Hugo von Hofmannsthal. And the Russian painter Vassily Kandinsky produced some of the first abstract pictures, whose colourful images arose from the artist's being and no longer sought to imitate the reality without.

Imperialism

In all European countries the population was divided by almost insurmountable barriers of

❸ INDUSTRIAL LANDSCAPE IN THE RUHR
Ludwig Heupel, 1906. Wistelisches Landesmuseum für Kunst und Kulturgeschichte

Western Europe became a constellation of huge industrial areas, often located near waterways for transporting goods. This process was accompanied by the formation of trusts and cartels. The workers, on their side, formed unions to improve their conditions of work. Europe was very soon divided, in effect, between the wealthy areas in the West – the Ruhr, the heavy industrial regions of Britain, the north of France and the east of Belgium – and the poorer nations in the south and east – Italy, Spain, Poland and Russia.

❹ The Congress of the Socialist International at Basle in 1912

The Congress notes the unanimous agreement of the Socialist International regarding its basic principles of foreign policy. It calls upon the workers of all countries to oppose capitalist imperialism with the strength of the international solidarity of the proletariat. It warns the ruling classes in all countries against warlike acts which would risk worsening the poverty of the majority caused by the capitalist mode of production. It insists that peace be maintained. The governments must not forget that, given the present situation in Europe and the state of mind of the working class, they cannot declare war without danger to themselves. Let them remember also that the war of 1870 resulted in the revolutionary movement of the Commune, that the Russo-Japanese war galvanized the revolutionary forces of the peoples in the Russian Empire and that the arms race by land and sea has led to an unprecedented aggravation of class conflicts in England and on the continent, with massive strikes. It would be sheer folly if governments did not realize that the mere thought of how monstrous a world war would be inevitably arouses the indignation and rebellion of the working class.

Lern- und Arbeitsbuch: Geschichte der deutschen Arbeiterbewegung

① THE FASHODA INCIDENT, 1898
Satirical drawing in the *Petit Journal*, 20 November 1898
Will the British wolf-disguised-as-a-grandmother devour or share the Fashoda girdle-cake that the French Little Red Riding-Hood is carrying? Franco–British colonial rivalry was such that this question was asked when British troops under General Kitchener met French troops under Captain Marchand. Kitchener, starting from the Sudan, was going up the Nile valley; Marchand was trying to link Sénégal with Djibouti. Their confrontation brought Europe close to the brink of war.

② THE AWAKENING OF NATIONALISM
H. Knackfuss, 1895
'Peoples of Europe, let us keep our sacred trust' says the angel to the helmeted goddesses of the nations. Almost everywhere in Europe's colonies nationalist movements were organizing resistance to imperialism. It was in Asia, and especially in China, that they seemed to loom like Buddha through the clouds. Europe was afraid of the 'yellow peril' after the Boxer Rebellion in 1900 and when Sun Yat-sen founded the Chinese people's national party.

wealth, education and power. For a century only one emotion was able to transcend all such differences: nationalism. There was increasing rivalry between European states, intensified by more and more fanatical national pride and a growing desire for superiority over one's neighbours. So great was this exacerbated nationalism that any sacrifice for the motherland seemed worthwhile. The reasons for this excess of national consciousness were many and they had their roots in the economic and social upheavals of the 19th century. The industrialized countries wanted to be sure of their raw material supplies and of the markets for their products. Acquiring colonies and dependencies seemed a form of insurance against future difficulties. What was more, the colonies distracted attention from conflicts within the mother country. Expansion overseas, it was hoped, would not only increase national power but also raise the standard of living and safeguard the established order at home. And rivalry became more bitter as there were fewer areas left to conquer and fewer new trading routes still to be found and mastered. In 1898 the French and the British confronted each other over Fashoda in the Sudan: Britain threatened to declare war and France backed down. The expansionist power politics of this period came to be called 'Imperialism'.

Rising nationalism did not, however, prevent a continuing sense of European solidarity, often based on a feeling of superiority over the rest of the world. Paradoxically, this feeling was intensified by the growing fear that Europe might one day be threatened by powers from overseas and particularly from Asia.

The fact that European nations were competing for influence and prestige, moreover, did not preclude their forming alliances in case war broke out. The most important of these were the Triple Alliance of 1882 linking Germany, Austria–Hungary and Italy, and the Triple Entente of 1907 signed by France, the United Kingdom and Russia. But if no one wanted war, very few were willing to make every effort to prevent it. War was regarded as a last but legitimate resort in foreign policy and military power seemed the best way to confront international competition. Armaments therefore became a priority. Germany formed a battle fleet, beginning a real arms race with Britain. Countless diplomatic incidents heightened the tension. In the Balkans, nicknamed 'the powder-keg of Europe' since the break-up of the Ottoman Empire at the end of the 19th century, rivalry between regional states, with intervention by the great powers, led to two Balkan Wars that reflected the general instability.

But not everyone called for war. The Working

Men's International campaigned for peace, as did various middle-class organizations. The Swedish industrialist Alfred Nobel, the inventor of dynamite, founded the Nobel Peace Prize. Its first recipient, in 1901, was the Swiss philanthropist Henri Dunant, who in 1864 had founded the International Red Cross. Initially intended to give first aid to war wounded, it soon became involved in a broad range of humanitarian work.

The cost of armaments was continually rising and Russia proposed an international conference to try to reduce the burden. In 1899, 26 states met in The Hague to discuss disarmament for peace. None of them really wanted to cut its military budget. They contented themselves with establishing a Permanent Court of Arbitration to settle international disputes and outlawing the most 'treacherous' weapons, such as bombs and poison gas. The second peace conference in The Hague, in 1907, laid down 'the most humane possible' rules of war. But, far from preventing war, these rules tended to confirm its legitimacy.

Virtually no one foresaw in these tensions the growing threat of a general war. War was seen rather as a cleansing storm that might clear the stifling atmosphere and at one stroke solve the most complicated problems.

❸ THE PALM TREE OF EUROPEAN PEACE
Cartoon in the German *Simplicissimus*, 27 March 1897. Bibliothèque Nationale, Paris
No one wanted war, but everyone was actively preparing for it. Despite this cartoon, Germany was pursuing its naval programme under the leadership of Admiral von Tirpitz, who made Germany the world's second biggest sea-power after Great Britain.

❹ EUROPE IN 1914

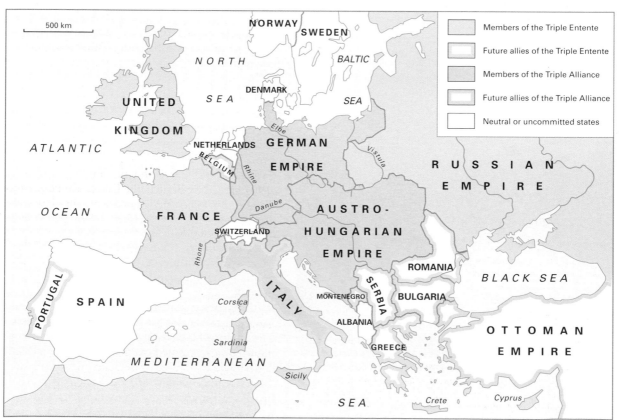

—2 The First World War

❶ MOBILIZATION IN GERMANY
*'Breakfast in Paris' – 'Every jab of the bayonet, one Frenchman'.
Graffiti like these covered the trucks taking German soldiers to the
capital. It was 4 August 1914, the barometer stood at Set Fair and
the morale of the troops was just as sunny. The government had
said, after all, that it would be a short war. . . .*

❷ MOBILIZATION IN FRANCE
*There were graffiti and smiles, looking forward to an excursion from
Paris to Berlin and back. Though the reality became quite different,
the new recruits left the Gare de L'Est 'with flowers in their rifles'.*

Why and how

On 28 June 1914, in a street in Sarajevo in
Bosnia–Herzegovina, then Austrian territory, a
Serb nationalist assassinated the Archduke Franz
Ferdinand and his wife, heirs to the throne of
Austro–Hungary. The government in Vienna saw
this as the outcome of a Serbian plot. Securing the
support of its German ally, it sent an ultimatum to
Serbia insisting that Austrian officials be allowed
to investigate on the spot without interference (23
July). When the Serbian reply proved evasive,
Austria mobilized and declared war (28 July).
Russia, which had already assured Serbia of its
support, now mobilized too, first against Austria
and then against Germany (29–30 July). Germany then demanded that Russia halt the mobilization. Receiving no reply, it in turn mobilized
and declared war, first on Russia (1 August) and
then on Russia's ally France (3 August). German
troops invaded Belgium, although it was neutral;
and this made Britain declare war on Germany (4
August). As a result, Europe became the theatre of
the most murderous war in its history to date.
Very few European states were able to preserve
their neutrality. The British Foreign Secretary Sir
Edward Grey declared: 'The lamps are going out
all over Europe. We shall not see them lit again in
our lifetime.'

The Sarajevo crisis was by no means the first
among the European Powers since 1900. The
others had been settled peacefully by diplomacy;
and in July 1914 the diplomats thought that they
could do the same again. But the German General
Staff, foreseeing a war on two fronts, feared that
Russia and France would strengthen each other
and thought that the military situation would
never be better than in the summer of 1914. All
attempts at a political solution having failed, war
became inevitable.

Responsibility for it is still a matter of controversy. Historians agree, however, that the
politicians and general staffs were ready to take
the risk.

All parties considered that they were fighting
for a just cause and for their legitimate interests.
The Austro–Hungarian monarchy, ruling many
nationalities, wanted to maintain its internal
cohesion and increase its influence in the Balkans.
Tsarist Russia was also anxious to defend internal
order against attacks by revolutionaries and also
had designs on the Balkans: the Russians had

special affinities with the Balkan peoples owing to their shared Slav origins (Pan-Slavism). Germany saw itself surrounded by hostile powers and wanted to break out of that encirclement and increase its own strength. France wanted to weaken its old rival and recover Alsace and Lorraine. Britain, finally, resented the German battle fleet, the embodiment of an expansionist policy that challenged British command of the seas.

On all sides, those mobilized were carried away, at first, by a sort of warlike delirium that stifled anxiety, doubts or gloomy forebodings. No one was fully aware of the horrors implicit in modern weapons of destruction. But it soon became clear to everyone that belief in a rapid victory with minimum casualties was a total error.

The new face of war

In August 1914 German troops crossed into Belgium, where King Albert I put up resistance around Ypres, and drove French defences back as far as the Marne (6 September). In the east the Germans encircled the Russian army at Tannenberg (30 August). But with no decisive victories, the war of movement then became a murderous static war. The main fronts were in the north and east of France and the west of Russia. Turkey and Bulgaria joined the Central Powers, in August 1914 and September 1916 respectively; but in April 1915 Italy broke the Triple Alliance and entered the war on the side of the Allies in the Entente. In 1917, when the United States declared war on the Central Powers, the European conflict became a world war.

As the fighting continued, weariness increased. There began to seem no point in going on. In the trenches soldiers suffered from heat in summer and cold in winter. They had to be ready at any moment to obey the order to attack or to resist an onslaught by the enemy, without ever reaching the decisive turning-point in the struggle.

Three things completely changed the face of war. The first was the use of weapons hitherto unknown: long-range artillery, machine-guns, hand-grenades, tanks, poison gas, fighter and bomber aircraft, and submarines. All these dramatically increased the number of killed and wounded. The gallantry of the soldiers now counted for less than the quantity of weapons and their fire-power. These changes led to appalling battles of fire and steel. During the fearful battles in 'the hell of Verdun' in 1916, thousands of field guns raked the ground with 20 tons of shells per acre. In a few months 700,000 French and German soldiers were killed. The town of Ypres

③ 1914–18: THE WESTERN FRONT

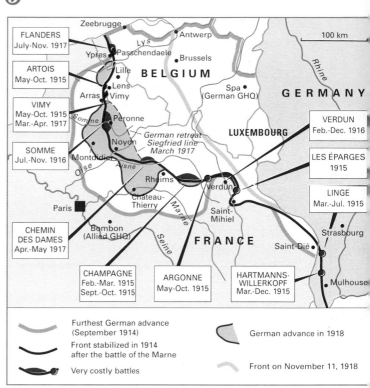

Furthest German advance (September 1914)

Front stabilized in 1914 after the battle of the Marne

Very costly battles

German advance in 1918

Front on November 11, 1918

④ TRENCH WARFARE

In 1915 and 1916 the war became bogged down. Here, German soldiers in grey-green uniforms and spiked helmets fire on the enemy through drainpipes covered with earth. This trench is barely 15 yards from its neighbour. But such rudimentary trenches soon became a defensive system that was difficult to destroy.

❶ The Battle of Verdun (1916)

21 FEBRUARY	*Beginning of German offensive*
24 FEBRUARY	*German troops in front of the north-west ramparts*
25 FEBRUARY	*The fort of Douaumont and the small fort of Hardaumont in German hands*
2 MARCH	*The village of Douaumont controlled by the Germans*
7 MARCH	*Point 304 largely controlled by the Germans*
22 MAY	*The French in front of the fort of Douaumont*
23 MAY	*Attack on the fort of Douaumont repulsed*
2 JUNE	*The Germans at Fort Vaux*
23 JUNE	*Attacks on the fortresses of Thiaumont and Fleury*
24 OCTOBER	*The French once more hold Thiaumont and Douaumont*
2 NOVEMBER	*The Germans evacuate the fort of Vaux and blow it up*
15–16 DECEMBER	*Victorious French offensive on the right bank of the Marne*

❷ WOMEN IN THE FACTORIES

Turning out shells in the munitions factories won some women the nickname of 'Munitionettes'. But work in the fields, factories, offices and on transport, opened the doors of employment for women.

in Belgium, the valleys of the Somme and the Marne, and the other fronts were the scenes of monstrous carnage.

The second great change took place behind the lines. Because victory could be won only if the whole nation made a concerted effort, the civilian population was involved as never before. For war industries to go on producing, women had to replace men in the factories and elsewhere. That did not prevent shortages, especially of food. People were often hungry. The Germans, moreover, tried to starve the British by all-out submarine warfare against merchant ships. In other words, war no longer concerned only the armed forces: it affected everybody. The age of conflicts limited to a few fields of battle was over. Total war had begun.

Finally, war propaganda burst on to the scene: posters, tracts and postcards on either side glorified the motherland and vilified the enemy. Every means was used to strengthen the will to win.

Signs of collapse

Growing disaffection and a tendency to mutiny revealed how wearisome the war had become. In many countries a hungry population protested against the difficulties of supply. In 1916 in Germany there were bitter large-scale strikes, which two years later became rebellions. In 1917 mass mutinies threatened the cohesion of French defences. In the following year strikes eroded the authority of the government in Paris.

War was also an opportunity for subject peoples to proclaim their will for national independence. At Easter 1916 the British put down the Irish rebellion in Dublin; and Ireland did not become independent until 1921, after a long period of insurrection and civil war. The new Irish state gradually threw off its ties with Britain, although Northern Ireland remained part of Great Britain. The Poles, meanwhile, tried to recover the national state that they had lost in the 18th century. The peoples within the Austro–Hungarian Empire – Czechs, Hungarians and Croats – intensified their demands for independence as the Central Powers' position seemed more and more precarious.

It was in Russia, however, that the most fateful events took place. In 1917, mutinies, demonstrations and strikes led to the February revolution. Tsar Nicholas II abdicated and the provisional government tried to set up a bourgeois republic. The country was still at war, but had no military successes. Conditions at home getting no better, those who promised both bread and peace became instantly popular.

In the same year, 1917, the Bolsheviks seized

power in the October Revolution. They were backed by councils of soldiers and workers, the Soviets, and led by a professional revolutionary, Vladimir Ilyich Ulianov, known as Lenin. In his long years of exile in various west European countries, he had carried further the thinking of Karl Marx and Friedrich Engels. He was convinced that the proletarian revolution would be possible only if it were stiffened by an organized and disciplined party. Applying this principle, Lenin and his comrades-in-arms sought to establish a Bolshevik dictatorship on the morrow of the Petrograd uprising (26 October 1917). They confiscated the estates of the great landowners and nationalized trade, banking and industry. At the cost of losing some considerable territory to the west, they made peace with the Central Powers in March 1918. For several years Russia was torn by a fearful civil war; but the Red Army and the Soviets finally won. In 1922 the Union of Soviet Socialist Republics was established. Moscow, the capital of the young USSR, was also the headquarters of an association of all the Communist Parties in a number of countries. This Communist International, the Comintern, aimed at world revolution to impose the dictatorship of the proletariat everywhere. As a result, Communism aroused throughout Europe enormous hope for some and panic for others.

While the Central Powers were dictating their peace terms to the enfeebled Russia of the Soviets, defeat was looming for them in the west. The United States' entry into the war in April 1917 tipped the scales decisively in favour of the Allies. While the Germans launched a further offensive in early 1918, the British counter-attack in August broke the front at Amiens and drove the German troops to retreat.

The Armistices

The defeat of the Central Powers was now inevitable. Bulgaria signed an armistice in September 1918, followed by Turkey in October. On 11 November, in the forest of Compiègne, the German representatives signed the final armistice. The guns were silent at last. The number of casualties was estimated to be eight million killed and twice that number wounded, many of them handicapped for life.

The First World War marked the end of an epoch. Everything that had seemed solid and unchangeable had been called in question or even destroyed. The European Powers had lost their supremacy. From now on the world's eyes turned towards Washington and Moscow.

The Hatred of the Huns

The Huns have taken our fishermen prisoner in the North Sea and thrown them into prison camps. On no proof at all they have accused them of minelaying and have condemned them without trial. Their punishment is to have one half of their head and face shaved. The Huns then paraded them through the streets to face the jeers of the German mob.

British sailors! Look! Read! And remember!

❸ PSYCHOLOGICAL WARFARE
Imperial War Museum, London
British propaganda poster during the First World War.

❹ THE SOVIETS IN POWER
Painting by Vladimir Serov. Lenin Museum, Prague
25 October 1917: Lenin and the Bolsheviks have seized power by joining the Central Committee and besieging Petrograd. In the hall of the assembly, the Duma, Lenin announces the first steps: nationalization of firms, land for the peasants, forming the Red Army and the Cheka or political police, forerunner of the KGB.

3 Making Peace between the Wars

① PEACE

Georges Clémenceau, Thomas Woodrow Wilson and David Lloyd George leaving the Château of Versailles after signing the Peace Treaty on 28 June 1919. Clémenceau was pleased: Great Britain and the United States had agreed to come to France's aid against any German aggression. But his satisfaction was short-lived. A year later the American Senate refused to ratify the treaty and hence to endorse such assistance.

---

② The Peace Treaties (1919–20)

1 Treaty of Versailles with Germany
- cession of all colonies
- limitation of armed forces to 100,000 men, with no heavy artillery, no tanks, no aircraft, no submarines or warships
- occupation of the left bank of the Rhine for 15 years
- demilitarized zone on the right bank of the Rhine
- cession of about one-seventh of German territory and one-tenth of the population
- reparations

2 Treaty of Saint-Germain-en-Laye with Austria
- separation of Hungary from Austria
- cession to Italy of the South Tyrol as far as the Brenner
- recognition of the independent states of Czechoslovakia, Poland, Hungary and Yugoslavia
- limitation of the armed forces to 30,000 men
- reparations

3 Treaty of Neuilly with Bulgaria
- cession to Greece of the coastal area of Thrace

4 Treaty of Trianon with Hungary
- cession of Slovakia to Czechoslovakia
- cession of Transylvania to Romania
- cession of Banat to Yugoslavia

5 Treaty of Sèvres with Turkey
- international control and administration of the Dardanelles
- limitation of the armed forces to 50,000 men
- cession of territory

A *peace imposed*

Germany, Austria–Hungary and their allies had been utterly defeated. The war was over: but what would be the basis for peace? The ideas of those who had won the war were very different and at times even contradictory. France's top priority was to be safe from its German neighbour: it therefore sought a dominant position in Europe. Great Britain, by contrast, wanted to maintain the balance of power, which meant not weakening Germany too much. What was more, solutions had to be found for all sorts of territorial, financial and legal problems in order to reach the goal that all parties envisaged: the establishment in Europe of a lasting peace.

Reality proved otherwise. The nationalist passions aroused in wartime did not die down. The victorious powers wanted to exploit their success; the vanquished could no longer defend themselves. None of the neutrals was big enough to act as moderator. Four years of cold war followed the four years of war itself.

On 18 January 1919 the representatives of the 27 victorious Allies met in the Galerie des Glaces at Versailles and the Peace Conference began. It was in this same room, at the end of the Franco–Prussian War of 1870, that the German Empire had been founded. Now the conditions for peace between that Empire and the Allies had to be settled and everyone wanted to impose his own solution. For France, Georges Clémenceau regarded the Rhine as his country's ideal frontier with Germany; but David Lloyd George, for Britain, categorically disagreed.

Great hopes were placed in the American President Thomas Woodrow Wilson. His proposals for a just peace settlement, put forward at the beginning of 1918, served as a basis for discussion. These 'Fourteen Points' included disarmament, rebuilding Europe in line with peoples' rights of self-determination and above all the establishment of a League of Nations to settle conflicts between states by peaceful means.

But the peace arrangements made by the treaties of 1919 and 1920 often caused bitter disappointment. They had been reached by the victorious Allies alone: the defeated Central Powers had had no hand in them and resented them as a *diktat* which they always refused as a basis for negotiation.

For the Germans the Treaty of Versailles was a

terrible shock. They saw its provisions as punitive and insulting, and were especially bitter at being officially blamed as solely responsible for the outbreak of war. With the other defeated powers, Germany deployed all its resources to try to get the treaty's provisions modified. But the victorious Allies saw them as their best guarantee of security and peace. They refused any changes.

Did the League of Nations guarantee peace?

On the basis of the nationality principle, new states were established and old states reshaped. This meant: the rebirth of Poland, the separation of Austria and Hungary, the enlargement of Romania, the creation of Yugoslavia and Czechoslovakia, the independence of the Baltic countries and autonomy for Finland. This re-drawing of the map reflected the desire of the victorious Allies to establish a counter-weight to Germany and a *cordon sanitaire* around Russia.

❸ 'HAPPY BIRTHDAY, YOUR MAJESTY'
(28 June 1919)
This German caricature shows the victors, Lloyd George, Clémenceau and Thomas Woodrow Wilson, in the Galerie des Glaces at Versailles. They are drinking a toast to the glory of Gavrilo Princip (who had assassinated the Austrian Archduke Franz Ferdinand in Sarajevo just five years earlier, on 28 June 1914), under the shadow of the Archduke: 'We are reaping today, noble Princip, what you sowed! Glory to you and thank you!'

❹ EUROPE AFTER 1918

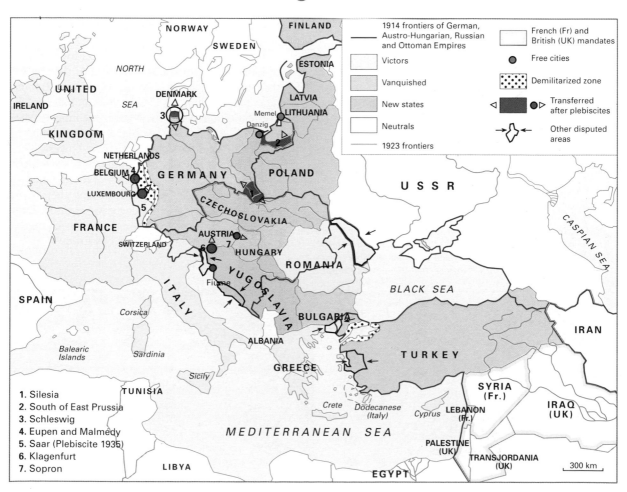

1. Silesia
2. South of East Prussia
3. Schleswig
4. Eupen and Malmedy
5. Saar (Plebiscite 1935)
6. Klagenfurt
7. Sopron

Map legend:
- 1914 frontiers of German, Austro-Hungarian, Russian and Ottoman Empires
- Victors
- Vanquished
- New states
- Neutrals
- 1923 frontiers
- French (Fr) and British (UK) mandates
- Free cities
- Demilitarized zone
- Transferred after plebiscites
- Other disputed areas

300 km

❶ The Covenant of the League of Nations

ARTICLE 8: *Reduction of national armaments to the minimum compatible with national security and international obligations.*

ARTICLE 11: *Any war or threat of war affecting a member is the concern of the League as a whole.*

ARTICLE 12: *Any dispute between members which represents a danger to peace should be submitted to an arbitration tribunal.*

ARTICLE 13: *Members agree to recognize and carry out the judgments handed down by this tribunal.*

ARTICLE 16: *If a member of the League resorts to war, contrary to its pledges, it is* ipso facto *considered as having committed an act of war against all other Members of the League. They pledge themselves to break off all commercial or financial relations with it, to prohibit all relations between their nationals and those of the state that is in breach of the Covenant and to halt all financial, commercial or personal communications between nationals of that state and those of any other state inside or outside the League. In such a case the Council has the duty to recommend to the various governments concerned the military, naval or air strength that the members of the League should each contribute to the armed forces required to ensure respect of the obligations of the League. Any member guilty of violating one of the duties incumbent upon it under the Covenant may be excluded from the League. Exclusion is decided by the vote of all the other Members of the League represented in the Council.*

❷ THE LEAGUE OF NATIONS: FROM DREAM TO REALITY

Caricature by Arpad Schmidhammer, 1920

Although this caricature is perhaps unduly pessimistic, it has to be admitted that, with the absence of the United States and Soviet Russia, the League's noble mission of guaranteeing the peace looked more like a dream than a reality. Very soon the wistful image of nations gathering under the wing of a guardian angel was replaced by that of a pack of hungry monsters ready to devour their frail protector.

But armed conflict did not end with the negotiation of the peace. The German Empire crumbled, William II abdicated and the Weimar Republic was proclaimed. Yet Germany had been in turmoil since the winter of 1918–19 and the years that followed saw repeated attempts to overthrow the republic. The frontiers of Poland were established only after a war with Soviet Russia, and without consulting the German-speaking peoples involved. Almost everywhere peace was accompanied by internal unrest and renewed hostilities. The new balance of power was precarious, mainly because nationalistic reflexes once more thwarted the quest for compromise. National egotism still prevailed in Europe. There was no disarmament. The self-determination principle was sometimes ignored.

The League of Nations proposed by Woodrow Wilson was established in Geneva in 1920. Its aim was to guarantee peace through rules that applied to all and through impartial arbitration. Representatives of its member states met regularly in a General Assembly. The Council comprised permanent members: France, Britain, Italy and Japan, joined by Germany from 1926 to 1933 and the USSR from 1934 to 1940. Other member states took part in the Council on a temporary basis. Current business was dealt with by the Secretary General.

The League was the first organization seeking to bind European states and those of the rest of the world in a system of collective security. But its influence was limited. Despite the fact that the US President had been involved in creating it, the United States did not become a member; nor, to begin with, did the defeated Central Powers. The Soviet Union did not join until 1934, by which time the League was rather a spent force. Finally, Britain and France used it only to serve their own interests. So, while the League of Nations laid down some new international rules, it changed nothing in the political reality of Europe.

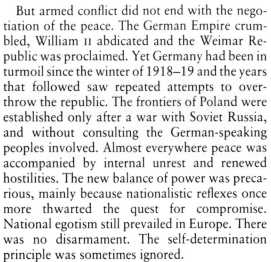

Unsolved problems

After the Bolshevik revolution in Russia, the fall of the monarchy in Germany and the dismemberment of the Austro–Hungarian Empire, an important question remained unanswered: what kind of political regimes would be adopted in European countries old or new? At first, democracy seemed to be the answer: but its comparative lack of roots in central and Eastern Europe very quickly changed the course of events.

During the war many peoples in Europe had shown their desire for independence. Each of them would have liked its own nation-state; but Woodrow Wilson's idealistic vision of self-determination ran into insoluble frontier problems wherever different nationalities shared the same limited area. Czechoslovakia, for example, was a smaller version of what the Austro–Hungarian Empire had been on the grand scale – a state with many nationalities, including not only Czechs and Slovaks, but also Germans, Hungarians, Ukrainians and Poles. Yugoslavia, likewise, contained Slovenians, Bosnians, Croats, Serbs, Italians and Albanians. Many Ukrainians and Russians lived in eastern Poland. Finally, ethnic minorities were scattered through many parts of central Europe. Often at a disadvantage, they were a cause of permanent tension, of latent conflict that an incident or a misunderstanding was enough to revive.

There were also economic and financial problems. The war had been very costly and the economy had to be reconverted to peacetime. The new frontiers had fragmented old economic entities; and the victorious Allies obliged the defeated Central Powers to pay reparations. Postwar hopes sooner or later proved false. The economy had trouble recovering: unemployment and inflation took their toll. The United States, to whom their European allies were in debt, demanded repayment, and endless bargaining followed. Yet the countries of Europe made no attempt to solve these massive problems by common accord.

The peace settlement was threatened even before it was complete. One example was the relationship between France and Germany. As a victorious power, France was eager to safeguard itself against Germany; so it concluded a series of alliances with various new states in central Europe and insisted on the strict application of the Treaty of Versailles. The Weimar Government of Germany, meanwhile, tried to escape from its diplomatic isolation. It made overtures to Soviet Russia, although its links with Western Europe remained vital. In 1923, when Germany fell into arrears with reparations, French and Belgian troops occupied the Ruhr, arousing indignation among its German inhabitants.

Slavs

☐	Russians, Ukrainians, Byelorussians
■	Poles
☐	Czechs
☐	Slovaks
☐	"Yugoslavs" (Slovenes, Bosnians, Croats, Serbs)
☐	Bulgars

Non-Slavs

☐	Germans
☐	Scandinavians
☐	Finns (Finnish and Estonian)
■	Hungarians
☐	Turks
☐	Italians
☐	Romanians
■	Greeks
☐	Albanians
⋰	Letts
⁄⁄	Lithuanians

300 km

❸ EUROPEAN NATIONALITIES FROM THE BALTIC TO THE AEGEAN

When the 1919/20 peace treaties redrew Europe's frontiers, two things were clear: the desire to create nation-states in Eastern Europe and the virtual impossibility of doing it. The nationalities concerned were inextricably intermingled. Problems of German or Hungarian minorities arose in Czechoslovakia, Romania, Poland, Yugoslavia and elsewhere. Nationalities linked by language but divided by religion, culture and economics were flung together in single states. In Yugoslavia Orthodox Serbs were uneasy with Catholic Croats and Slovenians, as well as with Moslem Bosnians and Albanians. The removal of the common enemy, Turkish or Austrian, allowed the strong to oppress the weak.

❶ PROTECT OUR FAMILIES!
Poster by Steinlen, 1922

The 1918 peace seemed precarious and German reparations were problematical. Between France and Britain, by 1922, the entente was no longer cordiale or (if cordial) no longer an entente. In 1923 French and Belgian troops occupied the Ruhr to oversee deliveries of reparations. In such a climate the peace movements feared that politicians might drag people and their families into a further war, supposedly to uphold international treaties. Posters, like this from the Dutch Socialist party, covered walls all over Europe.

❷ Aristide Briand's plan for European union

The task of uniting Europe is so urgently and vitally necessary that really constructive work must be done to achieve it so that no one may ever stand in its way. Indeed, the task must be undertaken in an atmosphere of absolute confidence and friendship and even, on many occasions, in collaboration with other states that have a sincere enough interest in organizing world peace to recognize the importance of building a united Europe.

Plans for Europe

Although nationalism still prevailed, the champions of peace were more numerous than before the war. Unfortunately, they could not agree on how to achieve a peaceful Europe. Some thought that peace should be based on the existing treaties; others believed that only their abolition would enable Europe's nations to live in harmony. These deep divergences prevented pacifist organizations having any real political influence. But the peoples of Europe still desperately longed for peace.

War had also given fresh impetus to champions of a united Europe. Their aim was not only to make war impossible: they also had economic motives. Customs barriers, they pointed out, greatly hampered the movement of goods, thereby limiting mass production, which was otherwise rapidly expanding. Many drew attention to Europe's common roots in ancient Greece, the Roman Empire and early Christianity. They emphasized similarities in the later history of European countries, which repeated readjustment of frontiers could not efface. This 'Euro-enthusiasm' actually produced practical plans. A book by the Danish author Heerfordt, called *A New Europe*, had a certain success; and the Pan-Europa movement founded by the writer and political activist Count Richard Coudenhove-Kalergi, born of an Austro–Hungarian diplomat father and a Japanese mother, brought up in Bohemia and educated in Vienna, won a significant number of adherents. But opinions differed – on how to achieve a united Europe, on the countries and peoples it would comprise, and on the political regime it should adopt. Everyone in the movement realized the need for a united Europe. But the reality of sovereign states was ever more inescapable.

In the mid-1920s Europe's political situation changed, under pressure from the United States. The Americans were worried by unrest in Europe, where their economic and financial interests were by now quite extensive. In 1924 the banker Charles G. Dawes headed a committee that proposed reducing the reparations still to be paid by Germany, in line with its real economic resources. The result was a marked improvement in relations between European countries. After the evacuation of the Ruhr in 1925, reconciliation culminated in the Locarno Treaties of 5–16 October 1925, signed by Germany, Belgium, France, Britain, Italy, Poland and Czechoslovakia. Belgium, France and Germany recognized their common frontiers; the Rhineland remained a demilitarized zone; and the signatories agreed to settle any disputes by peaceful means. In the following year Germany was admitted to the League of Nations, while the French Foreign Minister Aristide Briand and his German counterpart Gustav Stresemann jointly received the 1926 Nobel Peace Prize. In 1928, with Briand's support, the US Secretary of State Frank B. Kellogg proposed a pact outlawing war. It was signed by 54 countries. In the same year the Young Plan replaced the Dawes Plan. The reparations required of Germany were once more reduced; and in 1932 it unilaterally decided to cease all payments.

It was during this period of rapprochement that Briand put forward the plan that bears his name. In 1930 he proposed a European federal union: representatives of all European countries except the Soviet Union and Turkey should meet to extend the international guarantees undertaken at Locarno and to establish a 'common market'. Hesitations on the part of various governments caused the project to fail. Nationalism was back in force.

Yet, despite national antagonism, both political and ideological, voices had been raised to appeal for cooperation and unity in the rebuilding of Europe. They may have lacked concrete ideas; they certainly lacked lasting support from Europe's peoples and governments. But their ideals and their vision survived them, to be taken up again after 1945.

❸ THE MEN OF DETENTE

Aristide Briand, in the centre, and Gustav Stresemann on the right, photographed here in Geneva, frequently met to try to obtain a revision of the Versailles Treaty and Germany's admission to the League of Nations. While this rapprochement aroused controversy in France, the world saluted the two men's idealism when in 1926 they received the Nobel Peace Prize.

❹ A CERTAIN IDEA OF EUROPE

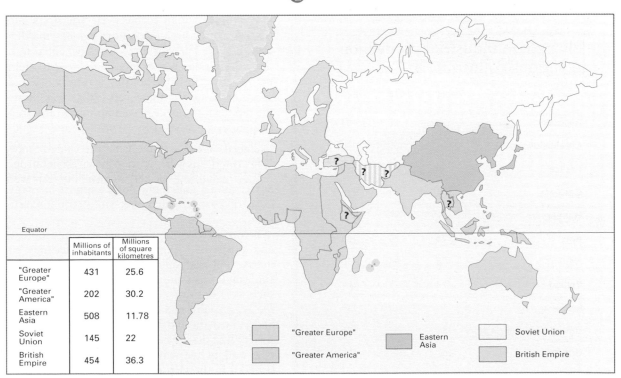

	Millions of inhabitants	Millions of square kilometres
"Greater Europe"	431	25.6
"Greater America"	202	30.2
Eastern Asia	508	11.78
Soviet Union	145	22
British Empire	454	36.3

"Greater Europe"   Eastern Asia   Soviet Union

"Greater America"   British Empire

This map illustrates the ideas expressed by the Pan-Europa movement led by Count Richard Coudenhove-Kalergi in the 1930s.

4 From Recovery to Crisis

1 MODERN TIMES
*After the war the world of work had a single watchword: produce.
The machines were there: they simply had to be exploited. The
assembly line was invented in the United States and the automobile
industry was one of the first to adopt it, reducing from 12½ to 1½
hours the time it took to make a car. This 'scientific organization of
work', as it was called, made it possible to lower costs and raise
wages, making workers the prime consumers of industrial products.*

2 Changes in industrial production in various countries (1929 level = 100)

	1931	1934	1937
Austria	70	70	103
Czechoslovakia	81	67	96
France	89	78	83
Germany	72	83	116
Hungary	87	99	130
Italy	78	80	100
Norway	78	98	130
Poland	77	77	109
Sweden	96	110	149
United Kingdom	84	99	124
USSR	161	238	424

Precarious prosperity

The political détente of the mid-1920s was
accompanied by a degree of economic recovery.
Inflation and unemployment were curbed. The
mass production assembly-lines turned out more
goods at lower prices. More and more people
could afford cars. Gramophones, radios, re-
frigerators, vacuum cleaners, electric irons and
central heating began to feature in many middle-
class homes. The working classes benefited too:
the working day was gradually reduced to eight
hours, new affordable housing was provided and
social security was improved. What was more,
the labour movement played an important political role, since moderate socialist and social-
democrat parties in certain countries held or
shared power. The communists remained devoted to the idea of proletarian revolution on the
Soviet model and found little support in many
areas of Europe which were still predominantly
rural.

Before 1914 a number of artists, philosophers
and poets had expressed general feelings of
unease and foreboding. Many saw the war as a
confirmation of the sombre views expressed in
such works as Oswald Spengler's *The Decline of
the West*, published in 1918. They thought war
had ruined the old Europe and that bourgeois
society had destroyed itself. People had to find a
new and better way of living together. Some
believed in the victory of the proletariat; others
hypnotized the crowds with nationalism, promis-

ing equality, security and prosperity to all the members of the same people or race.

After the privations of war and its immediate aftermath the people of Europe were eager for entertainment and leisure. The cities, in particular, met these needs. There were controversial new plays and films, such as *All Quiet on the Western Front*, based on the novel by Erich Maria Remarque; there were night clubs, cabarets, dance halls and exhibitions; there were new and varied goods in the department stores; there were sporting events of all kinds to draw the crowds – football and boxing matches, bicycle races and so on.

In the 1920s Europeans discovered for the first time the American way of life. Many adopted it as a model, rejecting traditional differences of class, custom and taste. They delighted in everything transatlantic, especially a kind of music that had emerged around 1900 in New Orleans: jazz.

This was 'the jazz age'. In all the arts novelty reigned. Artists produced work that many found strange, arousing enthusiasm or indignation with Cubism, Dada and Surrealism. Some women defied convention by refusing to be simply wives and mothers. The press, the radio and the cinema newsreels kept up a barrage of sensation. Leisure and recreation were no longer a minority privilege, but part of ordinary life for growing numbers of people. Economic recovery led many Europeans to look to the future with hope.

❸ THE JAZZ AGE
Poster by Paul Colin for the *Revue Nègre* at the Music-hall des Champs-Elysées, 1925

Insouciance – pleasure – luxury – excess: the image of the jazz age was reality for only a few. But France and Europe in general were certainly looking for entertainment after the privations of war and the drudgery of work. America came to the rescue with the new pleasures of revues nègres, *jazz, and stars like Josephine Baker.*

❹ THE MUSIC ROOM AT THE BAUHAUS SCHOOL
The Bauhaus (literally 'the building house') was set up in 1919 by the German architect Walter Gropius. Its teaching aimed to reconcile art, craftsmanship and industry; it used new materials and paid special attention to the aesthetic design of everyday objects that could be mass-produced. Although it imposed no formal rules, it tended towards geometric abstract art and functionalism, as the furniture and décor here show. The victory of Nazism led to the school's being closed in 1933; but it had already greatly influenced contemporary designers and architects, especially in the United States, where many members fled.

❶ THE MARCH ON ROME
30 October 1922

The Fascists, who had destroyed labour exchanges and violently overthrown Socialist and trade union bastions in northern Italy, seized Milan with the tacit complicity of its municipal authorities and leading citizens. Mussolini, in fact, reassured the bourgeoisie while his Blackshirts mounted a reign of terror in the streets. The Fascist Congress in Naples decided to march on Rome if it was not invited to form a government. King Victor-Emmanuel III caved in and invited Il Duce (The Leader), as Mussolini was called, to name his cabinet. But to put on a show, 126,000 more or less armed men staged their march on Rome and Mussolini joined them.

❷ POLITICAL REGIMES IN EUROPE, 1937

—— Frontiers of dictatorships or authoritarian regimes	▢ Parliamentary democracies
▨ Nazi and Fascist dictatorships	▨ Popular Front parliamentary democracies
▨ Authoritarian regimes	♛ Monarchies
▢ Marxist dictatorship	

The rise of the dictators

Behind the promising façade, however, social and political conflict continued. In Italy fear of Communism and dissatisfaction with the peace treaties – which had not met all the country's territorial demands – caused many industrialists, business-men, landowners and officers to join the ranks of the extremist party known as the Fascists (from the Latin *fasces*, the bundle of rods and an axe with which criminals were scourged and beheaded in ancient Rome). The party even had some sympathizers inside the Catholic Church. In 1922 its leader Benito Mussolini seized power after his 'March on Rome'. Fascism was opposed not only to Communism, but also to parliamentary democracy, which was working only moderately well in some of the countries where it was in force. The Fascists preached order and discipline, and systematically silenced their critics. Many Italians were fired by this nationalistic propaganda. Job creation programmes and other social measures won Mussolini widespread public support. Italian Fascism was a model for similar movements in other European countries.

'The economy', as a German politician once said, 'determines our fate.' In other words, a modern and efficient economy should make it possible to overcome any social or political problems – whereas on the contrary an ailing economy could put the population in serious danger. By the 1920s Europe's economic future was more than ever bound up with the state of the world economy, because since the war Europe had lost its economic supremacy. In 1913 it had accounted for 52.6 per cent of the world's total exports; but by 1928 its share was only 45.5 per cent. Heavy industry, which had done well during the war, suffered from over-capacity after 1918. At the same time trade among European countries was slowing down. More and more the feeling grew that every country should seek economic independence and close itself off from the rest. A crisis was becoming inevitable.

In October 1929, for reasons exclusive to the United States, prices on the New York Stock Exchange (Wall Street) collapsed. Owing to the close economic and financial links between America and many other parts of the world, the crisis had wide repercussions, notably in Europe, where recovery in the 1920s soon proved precarious. The results of the world economic crisis weighed very heavily on millions of Europeans.

The after-effects of the Wall Street crash were especially harmful in Germany. American banks called in their loans, depriving the German economy of support that it desperately needed. By 1932 six million Germans were out of work.

Profiting from this general economic disaster, but also ably exploiting the nostalgia and resentment felt by many Germans, Adolf Hitler and his National Socialist or Nazi party won more and more votes in elections. Calling himself *Der Führer* (the Leader), Hitler promised work and food. Those responsible for Germany's plight, he claimed, were the Jews, the Communists and the Treaty of Versailles. He reviled the parliamentary regime, accusing its representatives of weakness and corruption. He alone, he declared, could restore Germany's energy and power. Although the Nazis had never had a majority in free elections and had even lost many votes in the election of November 1932, President Paul von Hindenburg appointed Hitler Chancellor of the Reich in January 1933. The other parties were divided and unable to prevent dictatorship. The Weimar Republic crumbled and the Third Reich took its place. The Nazis believed that they were reviving the great traditions of the two previous German imperial regimes, the first in the Middle Ages, the second in 1871. Meanwhile, other authoritarian regimes were established – in Bulgaria, Yugoslavia, Austria, Poland, Portugal, Romania and Hungary. In Spain in 1936, General Francisco Franco led a military revolt against the republican government. For three years there was a fearful civil war: it cost half a million lives. With help from Fascist Italy and Nazi Germany, Franco's nationalists won. During the fighting the Nazi air force destroyed among other things the small Basque town of Guernica. Volunteers from many countries fought alongside the Spanish republicans in the International Brigades, backed by arms from the Soviet Union and France.

Of all the dictatorships, that of the Nazis was the most fateful. With a population of 80 million people, some of them living abroad, Germany dominated central Europe. Its aggressive foreign policy threatened the whole continent. And Germany was modernizing: its industries, its roads and other means of communication, and its public services were soon the most advanced in Europe. This up-to-date infrastructure made it easy for the Nazis to strengthen their totalitarian regime and use all its resources to carry out their criminal plans.

The democracies, and especially France and Britain, seemed unable to combat the irresistible rise of dictatorship. Even there Fascist movements developed and fought with the Communists. Democrats were now trapped between two extremes. Nevertheless, in both France and Britain they prevailed at the polls – the Conservatives in Britain in 1931, and in 1936 in France the Popular Front, which introduced such social reforms as holidays with pay.

❸ 'OUR LAST HOPE: HITLER'
Poster by M. Jölnir, 1932

In 1930 Germany had 6 million unemployed; many farmers, shopkeepers and small businessmen were ruined. Following on the imposed peace of Versailles and the bankruptcy of 1923, this traumatized German public opinion. Many saw the extremist parties as the only hope. The Nazis capitalized on that. In seven years the number of their deputies in parliament rose from 12 to 107. In 1932, in the last free elections, their leader Adolf Hitler won nearly 40 per cent of the votes. On 30 January 1933 he became Chancellor of the Third Reich.

❹ THE SPANISH CIVIL WAR (1936–9)
On 18 July 1936 General Francisco Franco organized a revolt against the Popular Front Government in Spain. From then on the country was torn by civil war. The mass of the people and the International Brigades of foreign volunteers were helped mainly by the Soviet Union, while Mussolini and Hitler sent Franco experts in new methods of warfare, including heavy weapons. In 1939 Franco won – at the cost of 500,000 dead, a third of them in battle.

5 Preparing for War

① From a speech by Hitler in 1928

In the first place, our people must be freed from the hopeless chaos of internationalism and deliberately, systematically trained to be fanatically nationalist . . . . In the second place, we shall tear our people away from the absurdity of parliamentarianism by teaching it to fight the folly of democracy and recognize the need for authority and command. Thirdly, we shall free the people from pathetic faith in external aid, faith in the reconciliation of peoples, in world peace, in the League of Nations and in international solidarity; and thereby we shall destroy those ideas. There is only one right in this world and that is might . . . .

Walther Hofer et al., *Der Nationalsozialismus*, Dokumente 1933–45, Frankfurt, 1957, p. 37

② NAZI POSTCARD, 1936
Book by Elvira Bauer, Stürmer, Nuremberg
The caption reads: 'All will go well in this school now that the Jews are leaving.' For the Nazis, the Master Race was tall, blond and blue-eyed. . . . But their leader was short, brown-haired and dark-eyed!

Germany under the Nazis

From 1933 onwards Germany was a threat to peace, for Hitler and the Nazi party had no intention of limiting their dictatorship to German territory. They believed that the Germans, confined in an area they regarded as too small, had every right to demand more living space or *Lebensraum*. Regarding people as divided into races, they placed the Germans, the 'Master Race', at the top and the Jews, 'subhuman' at the bottom. Hitler had expounded his views and purposes in 1924 in his book *Mein Kampf (My Struggle)*, but they had attracted little attention.

As soon as they came to power, the Nazis began securing their position by means of intimidation and terror. They crushed all resistance with violence and imprisonment. They tortured and assassinated their opponents in the first concentration camps, opened in 1933. They quickly imposed dictatorship. No people, young or old, had ever been so thoroughly drilled. Private life was controlled. The press, radio and cinema were no longer free. Human rights were systematically violated. The Third Reich revealed its true identity as a totalitarian regime.

But Nazi barbarity was not always recognized at first, for German daily life changed only very gradually. Some Nazi misdeeds were even enthusiastically welcomed. To begin with, indeed, Hitler's policies impressed many people both in Germany and abroad: the country seemed to have recovered its strength and dignity under its *Führer*. These reactions blinded people to the total suppression of basic freedom.

From 1933 onwards the Jews became the scapegoats for Germany's ills. German Jews were banned from public office; thousands, like Albert Einstein, sought refuge in emigration. On 1 April the Nazis launched a boycott of Jewish shops. In 1935 the 'Nuremberg Laws' forbade marriage between Jews and Gentiles. On the night of 9 to 10 November 1938, known as *Kristallnacht* (Crystal Night), violent pogroms were carried out all over Germany: synagogues were burned, cemeteries desecrated, windows smashed and Jews molested.

Yet many Germans willingly supported Hitler, with no regard for the fate of his opponents or the segregation of their Jewish fellow-citizens. Germany, they thought, was making progress again and that was what really mattered. Munitions industries and major public works like motor-ways had quickly mopped up unemployment. All Germans were urged to buy Volkswagens or 'people's cars'. Skilful propaganda gave everyone the impression that they were living in heroic times. Until 1939 Hitler never ceased declaring his passionate love of peace and everyone blindly followed him. At the Berlin Olympic Games in 1936 the Führer seemed like a popular and moderate statesman.

Hitler's foreign policy

In reality Hitler never lost sight of his essential aim – expansion, if need be by war. Despite his obligations under the Treaty of Versailles, he set about re-arming Germany, at first in secret, then quite openly. Propaganda accustomed the German people to the idea of war and 'festivals of defence arts' prepared them for fighting. Huge parades celebrated the masses against the individual and the whole of public life took on a military air. Boys of 15 to 18 received military training in the 'Hitler Youth'.

In the early years of the Nazi regime Germany was too weak to make war. So Hitler began by avoiding any action that might lead the European Powers to intervene. His first agreements with the Vatican, Poland and Great Britain made him quite acceptable in the eyes of the European chancelleries. He made countless soothing speeches to disarm mistrust and fear. Playing on the fact that the Allies of 1918 had a bad conscience about the Treaty of Versailles, he called for Germany now to have the equal treatment it had been deprived of then.

A series of successes, with no apparent threat to peace, made Hitler still more popular at home. In October 1933 Germany left the League of Nations, which still refused it equality on military matters. In January 1935, 90 per cent of the inhabitants of the Saar voted to be part of the Reich. Two months later Hitler reimposed military conscription, thus violating the Treaty of Versailles. In March 1936 he denounced the Locarno Treaties and sent his troops to occupy the Rhineland, which had been a demilitarized zone since 1918. Two years later, early in 1938, he invoked the right of self-determination to decide on the *Anschluss* – the annexation of Austria by the Third Reich.

Despite these ominous moves, the Allies were not united in their attitude to Hitler. France was embroiled in domestic problems, with scandals and extremists threatening the parliamentary regime: on 6 February 1934, 15 people were killed in a riot outside the Chamber of Deputies. Great Britain, hard hit by the world economic

❸ 'THE PEOPLE'S CAR'

German poster, 1939

'If you save 5 marks a week –
You'll have a car and that's unique!'
This promise from the Führer could not be kept, because of the war. It was much later that the 'Beetle' from the Wolfsburg factory became a popular car. But it had made possible the development of an industry capable of switching to war production; and it had given work to the unemployed.

❹ 'THE GODS OF THE STADIUM' (1936)

At the Berlin Olympic Games the Germans won 89 medals, more than the United States, proof to Hitler of their superiority.

❶ Hitler's speech to the Reichstag, 21 May 1935

The blood spilled for three centuries on the continent of Europe is out of all proportion with the impact that the events concerned have had on Europe's peoples. In the end, France has remained France, Germany Germany, Poland Poland, Italy Italy, etc. The apparently profound political changes obtained, at such a cost in lives, by dynastic egoism, political passion and patriotic blindness, have always had superficial repercussions on the peoples from a national point of view, but without their frontiers being greatly modified. If the states concerned had devoted even a fraction of their victims to more judicious ends, the results would undoubtedly have been more spectacular and longer-lived . . . .

Nazi Germany's desire for peace is based on solid ideological convictions. Germany wishes to see peace endure and this on the basis of a simple and elementary realization: that no war could make it possible to put an end to the poverty that afflicts us all in Europe; on the contrary, any war would only increase it.

Hofer, *op. cit.*, p. 178

crisis, thought a strong Germany would maintain the European balance of power. Fascist Italy, engaged in a colonial war against Ethiopia, was drawing closer to Hitler. Even so, it joined Britain and France in 1935 at Stresa to form a 'united front' against German re-armament. It had no effect. Great Britain embarked on the 'appeasement' of Germany to avoid war; Italy formed a 'Rome–Berlin axis' in October 1936, together with Japan and then, in 1939, with Franco's Spain; France tried to escape from the economic crisis by forming a 'Popular Front' government, in May 1936, backed by the parties of the Left.

Few European statesmen realized at the time that Hitler's aim was not just to overthrow the Treaty of Versailles but to dominate the whole of Europe. Most of them believed that he merely wanted to restore Germany's great-power status: they compared him with Kaiser Wilhelm II. Finally, and perhaps most crucially, a number of people saw the Third Reich as a useful bulwark against Communism. For all these reasons, when Hitler broke the peace treaties, there were only scattered protests and vague complaints. Governments hoped to preserve peace by a policy of appeasement, giving in to Nazi Germany's demands.

In September 1938 Europe was once again on the brink of war. Hitler had just launched his plan to dismember Czechoslovakia. German troops were already mustered on the Czechoslovak frontier. Britain and Italy proposed a last attempt at mediation: it managed to check the momentum of events. On the night of 29–30 September Hitler and Mussolini met Neville Chamberlain and Georges Daladier, the British and French Prime Ministers. 'The Four' concluded an agreement obliging Czechoslovakia to cede to Germany the border areas known as the Sudetenland, where there were sizeable German populations. Hitler

❷ PEACE AT MUNICH?

On 30 September 1938, at 3 am., the Treaty and its seven appendices, in four languages, was signed by Neville Chamberlain, Edouard Daladier, Adolf Hitler and Benito Mussolini, accompanied by Count Galeazzo Ciano. It authorized the Führer to annex those Czechoslovak territories where the Germans were in a majority. On his return to London Chamberlain told the crowd: 'It is peace for our time.' He was unaware that on the evening before Hitler had said to Mussolini: 'The day will come when we shall have to strike both England and France together. It is important that it should happen while we are both still leading our countries.'

claimed that these were his last territorial demands. Chamberlain declared that the peace had been saved, to the huge and joyful relief of a majority of Europeans.

Six months later, on 15 March 1939, German troops entered Prague. For the first time since Hitler had come to power, the German army was invading a country that included no appreciable German community. The European powers at last realized that Hitler's ambitions could never be appeased and they made ready for war.

Dictatorship against democracy

The idea of Europe as a community of interdependent states with equal rights had now completely vanished. Two implacable totalitarian ideologies confronted each other: Soviet Communism, which supported the Communist parties in the west, and Fascism, which took different forms in Italy, Germany, Spain, Portugal and a few other countries. The energy of the dictatorships faced only feebleness on the part of the democracies, not least Britain and France. In 1939 it seemed as if the future belonged to those political systems that regimented people in every aspect of their lives, scorning all the old European values. The parliamentary regimes, preaching individual liberty, freedom of opinion and equality before the law, seemed out of date, weak or corrupt. The dictators, after all, had been better at solving the problems of the day. In their countries there were no strikes, unemployment had been overcome and there seemed to be great internal stability, impeccable organization and unconquerable power. To many Europeans the price that had been paid for these results did not seem very important.

Hitler had wanted war and it was he who set the train in motion. The next stage of his plan was to crush Poland: many Germans even contested that country's right to exist when it was recreated after 1918.

❸Hitler's statement to journalists and editors, 10 November 1938

For decades, circumstances have forced me to speak almost exclusively about peace. Only by constantly reaffirming Germany's peaceful desires and plans have I been able step by step to recover freedom for the German people and give it the armament that seems more and more the necessary condition for the next stage . . . .

Only under constraint and against my will have I spoken of peace all these years. Then, it was necessary gradually to change the psychology of the German people, to make it understand, little by little, that there are things which, if they cannot be obtained by peaceful means, have to be taken by force.

Günther van Norden, *Das Dritte Reich im Unterricht*, Frankfurt, 1970, p. 39

❹GERMAN FRONTIERS IN 1939

	Germany in 1937	Annexations	
▨	Rhineland remilitarized, March 1936		German
	Czechoslovakia, 1937		Hungarian
	New state		Polish
—	Frontiers in August 1939		Italian
▬		Frontiers of Germany, 31 August 1939	

6 The Second World War

① POLAND OVERRUN, SEPTEMBER 1939

Was the German army trying to remove this barrier in Danzig so as to avoid damaging its tanks? In four weeks the Wehrmacht occupied the whole of Poland. Hitler had launched his favourite tactic – the Blitzkrieg or lightning war.

② THE STUKAS

The Wehrmacht had two favourite weapons: tanks assembled in armoured divisions, the famous Panzer divisions, and aircraft (the Luftwaffe), including the Messerschmitt 109 and the Stuka. This last, a dive-bomber, terrorized not only land-based troops but also civilians fleeing from the enemy advance.

In April 1939 Hitler ordered the Wehrmacht to prepare itself for an attack on Poland. He denounced the non-aggression pact that Poland and Germany had signed five years earlier, and Nazi propaganda claimed that life for the German minority in Poland was intolerable. But this time the governments in Paris and London would accept no compromise and they officially guaranteed Polish independence.

The Nazi–Soviet Pact

The big question now was what attitude the USSR would take. Since the death of Lenin in 1924 Stalin had gradually turned the regime into a personal dictatorship, replacing the aim of world revolution by that of 'Socialism in a single country'. In 1917 the Soviet Union had been essentially agricultural. Stalin had launched a campaign of headlong industrialization. The all-powerful secret police kept the population in a state of constant terror. Millions of people were deported to labour camps. Others were the victims of show trials in which they had to confess their 'guilt'. The successive waves of liquidation spared neither senior officials of the Communist Party nor generals in the Red Army. Stalin cared little whether this weakened the country: what counted for him was imposing his own power and winning a place for the USSR on the international scene.

On 23 August 1939, although their ideologies were at opposite poles, Nazi Germany and the Soviet Union signed a non-aggression pact. Stalin had preferred Hitler's terms to those of France and Britain, mainly because they included a secret protocol giving him a free hand in Poland and other parts of Eastern Europe if frontiers were being 'redrawn'. In this way the Soviet dictator avoided having to wage war in central Europe, while the Nazi dictator avoided having to fight on two fronts at once. Even so, the USSR remained Hitler's main ideological opponent.

The Blitzkrieg

German troops entered Poland on 1 September 1939. Hitler's pretext was the allegation that Polish soldiers had attacked a German radio transmitter on the frontier between the two countries. The 'Polish soldiers' were in fact German prisoners, brought from the concentration camps and dressed up in Polish uniforms: their bodies had been left in the transmitting station. But, contrary to Hitler's expectations, Britain and France kept their word and declared war on Germany, on 3 September 1939, without, however, making an attack.

After a few weeks of Blitzkrieg, with aircraft and ground armour acting as a team, Poland was beaten. The Red Army occupied the eastern part of the country, as agreed in the Nazi–Soviet non-aggression pact. The western part was swallowed up by the Reich. What remained of the country was placed under a governor-general whose tyranny knew no limits. Expulsions, persecutions and executions continued without a pause. The Nazis claimed that the Poles were 'an inferior race' to justify the massacres.

On 30 November 1939 the Soviets attacked Finland. In March 1940, despite fierce resistance, it had to submit to its territory being truncated.

Paris and London turned deaf ears on the peace proposals that Hitler made after his victory in Poland. Applying the same military strategy, he then had further success. In April 1940 German troops occupied Denmark and Norway, both neutral countries, in order to ensure access to Swedish iron ore. By this move Hitler pre-empted a Franco–British plan to land in Scandinavia. His Blitzkrieg tactics were also successful in the west. On 10 May, ignoring the neutrality of Belgium, the Netherlands and Luxembourg, the Wehrmacht broke through French defence lines, again thanks to its aircraft and tanks. On 17 June, the French government asked for an armistice. Italy, meanwhile, had entered the war as Germany's ally.

By the summer of 1940 Hitler was victorious almost everywhere and seemed on the point of dominating Europe completely. He was already dreaming of conquering the world. But Great Britain was not yet beaten. Systematic bombing of British towns and cities, from the summer of 1940 onwards, failed to break the people's determination to resist. The Prime Minister, Winston Churchill, categorically refused the idea of making peace with the Nazis. Hitler finally had to give up his plans to invade British soil. Only the Channel islands, off the coast of France, fell into his hands.

Mussolini, meanwhile, wanted to show his independence of Hitler; and on 28 October 1940 he used his occupation of Albania to launch an attack on Greece. The air Battle of Britain in the summer of 1940, followed by the Greek counter-attack in October, were the first setbacks suffered by the Axis powers. In April 1941 Hitler attacked Yugoslavia and Greece: resistance in Crete delayed his attack on the USSR.

③ WAR, 1939–42

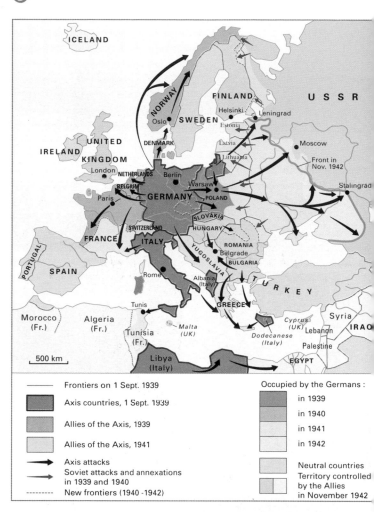

——— Frontiers on 1 Sept. 1939	Occupied by the Germans:
▨ Axis countries, 1 Sept. 1939	in 1939
▨ Allies of the Axis, 1939	in 1940
▨ Allies of the Axis, 1941	in 1941
→ Axis attacks	in 1942
→ Soviet attacks and annexations in 1939 and 1940	Neutral countries
----- New frontiers (1940 -1942)	Territory controlled by the Allies in November 1942

④ CHURCHILL'S BRITAIN
Although the British were pounded by the Luftwaffe, they would not give in. Liverpool and Coventry were in flames. In the autumn of 1940 London was bombed every night. With patriotism and cool courage people accepted the blood, toil, tears and sweat called for by the Prime Minister, Winston Churchill.

① THE V2
*These long-range rockets were used
against London and Antwerp after the
summer of 1944. With the rocket-launcher
and the pilotless plane, the V2 was one of
the Third Reich's technological triumphs.*

② STALINGRAD
*On 11 June 1941, 3 million German soldiers invaded Russia,
backed up by 5000 aircraft and 3500 tanks. It was a massive
attack; but the weather worked against it: badly equipped, the
Wehrmacht was bogged down by snow. In the summer of 1942
Hitler gave orders to attack Stalingrad, thinking that its capture
would have symbolic force. The Russians fought furiously to defend
it, street by street, cellar by cellar. Nine-tenths destroyed, the city
became a symbol of indomitable resistance. The German army of
200,000 men found itself doomed. Between 30 January and 2
February 1943, hope changed sides.*

In March 1941 US President Franklin D.
Roosevelt in effect abandoned his neutral stance
by authorizing the delivery of war supplies to
Great Britain. In August of that year he and
Churchill signed the Atlantic Charter setting out
the democratic principles that would have to be
the basis for any future peace.

The Wehrmacht attacks the Soviet Union

On 22 June 1941 Hitler attacked the USSR –
without any declaration of war. He may have
done so partly on account of Britain's continued
resistance, which denied him a decisive victory in
the west. But he broke the non-aggression pact
also because he saw Communism as the enemy to
be destroyed and was determined to secure in the
east the 'living space' (*Lebensraum*) that he
thought Germany needed. The Wehrmacht advanced rapidly, but was not able to wage a
'lightning war' or Blitzkrieg like its campaigns in
Poland and France. In the winter of 1941–2
German troops were halted outside Moscow and
Leningrad. Stalin had proclaimed the 'Great
Patriotic War' and managed to redouble the
Russian people's will to resist.

Save for the neutral countries (Ireland, Portugal, Spain, Sweden and Switzerland), all Europe
was now involved in the war. During the autumn
of 1942 German troops reached the Volga and
prepared to attack Stalingrad. But the Red Army
put up a fierce resistance and in February 1943
the Wehrmacht was forced to capitulate. This
great defeat was a major turning-point in the war,
but hostilities continued for two more years,
mainly through obstinacy on the part of Hitler
and the Nazis. Ubiquitous propaganda tried to
maintain optimism among the people of the

Reich; and, despite growing doubts, most were still convinced of their military superiority.

By the time that the Germans were defeated at Stalingrad the European war had already become a world war. The Japanese, who wanted to build an empire in the Pacific, had provoked America's entry into the war, against both Japan and Nazi Germany. Japan's surprise attack on Pearl Harbor, Hawaii, on 7 December 1941, was followed by a year of American defeats; but after that the United States' superiority became very clear.

In many respects, the Second World War was an escalation of the First, notably in the firepower of the artillery and of automatic weapons. More and faster tanks were used in large numbers, organized as autonomous units. Command of the air was essential to victory. At sea, convoys of Allied merchant ships paid a heavy toll to German submarines in the Battle of the Atlantic. And for the first time combat was not limited to the fronts. Civilians were also involved, in the Resistance, as deportees and hostages, and as victims of air-raids: bombers destroyed roads and railways, and reduced whole towns to ruins and ashes. In the United States scientists and technologists worked feverishly to produce a bomb of unprecedented power. It was not yet ready when the war ended in Europe. So the first atomic bombs were dropped on Hiroshima and Nagasaki in August 1945.

The demand for war materials (weapons, munitions, vehicles, uniforms, etc.) was so great that the whole economy had to be devoted to their production. Access to raw materials was therefore vital for the countries concerned. To reduce this state of dependency, efforts were made to find substitutes. In Germany, for example, the chemical industries made gasoline from coal.

Those vestiges of Europe's old social system that had survived the First World War disappeared almost completely. Millions of people were forcibly exiled or fled before the enemy advance. Once again women had to do the work of men called to the colours and to take on their responsibilities. Women's new independence later helped the growth of feminist movements.

War crimes

In the countries occupied by the Nazis, the people were oppressed and exploited. Millions were compelled to work for the Nazi war machine. All resistance was savagely suppressed: a mere breath of suspicion could mean death. Hostages were systematically executed. It was in the east that Nazi occupation was the most ruthless: here, people not only had to acknowledge German supremacy: Bolshevism had to be stamped out

❸ ALLIED LANDINGS

	Extent of the Axis in November 1942
	Frontiers of the Reich

Allied attacks :
→ In the east
→ In the west
⫸ Allied landings

Territory liberated by the Allies :
Between Nov. 1942 and the end of 1943
In 1944
Axis territory unliberated at the end of 1944
Territory occupied by Germany at the end of 1944
Neutral countries

❹ PERSECUTING THE YUGOSLAV RESISTANCE

German troops defeated the Yugoslav army in 1941. Many of the population resisted fiercely and were subjected to imprisonment, deportation or summary execution. Croatia, however, became largely subservient to the orders of the Reich, which relied on the Fascist 'Uštaše' movement led by Ante Pavelić.

① THE DEATH CAMPS
To reach the quarry at Mauthausen, the inmates had to climb the 'staircase of death' (186 steps). Anyone who failed to bare his head to the Master Race was signing his death-warrant. 120,000 deportees died at this camp.

② DE GAULLE'S CALL TO RESISTANCE
'I, General de Gaulle, at present in London, call upon those French officers and soldiers who are on British soil or can reach it, with or without their weapons, to make contact with me. I call upon those defence engineers and specialist workmen who are on British soil or can reach it to do the same. Whatever happens, the flame of the French Resistance must not go out. It will not go out.'
(18 June 1940)

and 'Slav subhumans' had to become slaves of the Master Race.

During the war Hitler and the most fanatical racists in his entourage decided to apply what they called 'the final solution to the Jewish problem'. From 1933 onwards Jews had increasingly been humiliated and deprived of their rights. Many had left Germany before it was too late. Now, Jews in the occupied countries were under the threat of death. Throughout Europe they were hunted down for extermination. In the death camps in Poland five or six million perished in the gas chambers. Two million were murdered in Auschwitz alone.

Collaboration and resistance

Trying to win over the people of the occupied countries, the Nazis presented their struggle against the Soviet Union as a defence of European culture against Bolshevik barbarism. Partly as a result, some volunteers from Belgium, Denmark, France and a few other countries fought alongside the soldiers of the Wehrmacht. A certain number of inhabitants and governments, notably the Vichy regime of Marshal Philippe Pétain, assumed a German victory and were ready to collaborate with the occupying power. Most people, however, preferred to wait and not take risks. But, as the war went on, Resistance movements came into being. These underground organizations, often politically divided, used strikes, sabotage, assassination, espionage and every other device calculated to thwart the enemy. In London, from the summer of 1940 onwards, General Charles de Gaulle led the Free French movement and eventually took the Resistance under his wing. In Eastern Europe the partisans waged a merciless campaign against their occupiers. Even in Germany many people were revolted by the crimes being committed in their name. These men and women came from all walks of life; but the totalitarian regime made any action they took against Nazi madness very difficult and especially dangerous. In July 1944 a number of Wehrmacht officers organized an attempt on Hitler's life. It only narrowly failed, and all the countries' resistance movements worked out political plans for after the war.

The defeat of Nazi Germany

From 1943 onwards the war turned more and more to Allied advantage. The Americans and British bombed German cities, some of which were completely demolished. The number of killed and wounded, on all sides, reached monstrous proportions. There were millions of prisoners of war. In July 1943 Allied troops landed in Sicily and gradually liberated all of Italy. Only Nazi support enabled Mussolini to cling to power. In 1944 the Allies landed in France – in Normandy on 6 June and on the Mediterranean coast on 15 August. On the Eastern Front the Red Army advanced, though with heavy losses. It reached the German frontier at the end of 1944 and Soviet soldiers took their revenge on civilians who had not fled in time. Hitler's 'Fortress Europe' was crumbling. At the same time Allied troops entered Germany from the west. But not until Hitler committed suicide and the Soviets captured Berlin did Germany surrender on 8 May 1945. Japan did likewise on 31 August.

Preparations had been made for after the war. Having met at the Casablanca and Teheran Conferences in 1943, the Allies met again in February 1945 at Yalta in the Crimea. Their agreements provided for Germany to be divided into occupation zones and the frontiers of Poland to be moved about 100 miles westwards, reducing German territory and increasing that of the USSR. Before Germany's unconditional surrender, the ideological differences that divided Stalin from Roosevelt and Churchill were not made public. Very few could foresee, at that time, the future division of Europe into two mutually hostile blocs.

Much more than the Great War of 1914–18, this had been a total war. The First World War had been about redistributing power in Europe. The Second, in 1939–45, had been ideological. It had begun as a confrontation between dictatorship and democracy. The German attack on the Soviet Union had been the beginning of a fight to the death between Fascism and Communism.

The Allies put what they thought were the finishing touches to their victory in the summer of 1945, at Potsdam, near Berlin, the former residence of the Kings of Prussia. The fourth Ally, France, had not been represented at Yalta and was not represented here. The Potsdam agreements drew the boundaries of the German occupation zones and determined the attitude to be adopted vis-à-vis Germany on political and economic affairs. This was the last document drawn up jointly by the Allies before they were divided by the 'Cold War'.

No previous conflict in history had claimed so many victims, dead or missing. At a conservative estimate there were 50 or 60 million, of whom many were civilians. But figures cannot express the amount of suffering that war had caused, in Germany, which had started it, as well as elsewhere. In 1945 the old continent was exhausted, while the United States and the Soviet Union had definitely become world powers.

3 AN ANGEL SURVEYS THE RUINS OF DRESDEN
In the night of 13–14 February 1945 a single Allied air-raid reduced Dresden, 'the Florence of the Elbe', to ashes. It killed 250,000 people, three times as many as at Hiroshima a few months later.

4 EUROPE, 1944–5

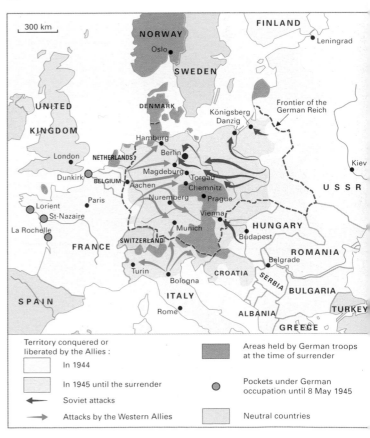

Territory conquered or liberated by the Allies:
- In 1944
- In 1945 until the surrender
- ← Soviet attacks
- → Attacks by the Western Allies

Areas held by German troops at the time of surrender

Pockets under German occupation until 8 May 1945

Neutral countries

Glasgow

Cultra

Belfast

Bunratty Dublin

Glencree

Liverpool

Coventry

Cambridge

Cardiff

London

Amsterdam
Utrecht

Esterw

Vugh

Den Haag

Ov

Rotterdam

Düsseldorf

Ypres
(Ieper)

Brussel
Bruxelles

Cherbourg

Le Havre

Compiègne

Cotentin

Caen

Verdun

Saint-Marcel

Paris

Natzwei
Strut

Chateaubriant

Besançon

Ber

Ger

Oradour-sur-
Glane

Lyon

Les Gliè

Le Vercors

To

Sa

Guernica

Porto

Coimbra

Valle de
los Caidos

Fatima

Madrid

Barcelona

Lisboa

Cartagena

The Past in the Present Day
MEMORIES OF WAR

Legend:

- main concentration or death camps
- place of remembrance
- religious monument
- museum, library or collection well stocked with items on this period
- public building
- frontiers of 20th-century states

500 km

Map labels:

Riga
Humlebaek
København
Gdansk · Stutthof · Ketrzyn
nburg · Neuengamme · Ravensbrück · Sachsenhausen · Treblinka · Khatyn
Bergen-Belsen · Chelmno · Warszawa
Potsdam · Berlin · Sobibor · Kiyev
over · Dessau · Majdanek
Halle · Gross-Rosen · Belzec · Rava-Russkaia
Dresden · Terecin (Theresienstadt)
Buchenwald · Lidice
adt · Oswiecim (Auchwitz)
Flössenbürg
Nürnberg
gart · Jassy
Dachau · Mauthausen · Wien
hur · München · Budapest
Ljubljana · Bucuresti
o · Zagreb
Venezia · Beograd
Faenza
ogna
a · Roma · Sabaudia
Athinai
Maleme

① BUILDING THE BERLIN WALL

Between 1945 and 1961 three million East Germans fled to the West. This was intolerable to the Communist authorities. In August 1961, under the protection of the 'Vopos' (Volkspolizei – the East German armed police), builders laid the first courses of a wall 27 miles long.

② THE TREATY OF ROME

To prevent any risk of further conflict with Germany, statesmen envisaged a united Europe. On 25 March 1957 the Treaty of Rome, signed by Belgium, France, the Federal Republic of Germany, Italy, Luxembourg and the Netherlands, established the European Economic Community (EEC), often known as the Common Market.

8 May 1945	German army capitulates
1946–9	Civil war in Greece
June 1947	Marshall Aid offered to all European countries that were victims of the Second World War
October 1947	Establishment of the Cominform
25 Feb 1948	'Prague Coup'
4 April 1949	Establishment of NATO
May & Oct 1949	Establishment of the two Germanies (FRG & GDR)
5 May 1949	Council of Europe established
18 April 1951	Treaty of Paris establishing the European Coal and Steel Community (ECSC)
5 March 1953	Death of Stalin
14 May 1955	Establishment of the Warsaw Pact
February 1956	20th Congress of the Soviet Community Party
Oct & Nov 1956	Risings in Warsaw and Budapest
25 March 1957	Treaty of Rome establishes the European Economic Community and Euratom
August 1961	Berlin Wall built
20 August 1968	'Prague Spring' crushed
15/16 April 1974	'Revolution of the Flowers' in Portugal
23 July 1974	Fall of the Colonels in Greece
20 Nov 1975	Death of General Franco
1 August 1975	Helsinki Act signed by members of the Conference on Security and Cooperation in Europe (CSCE)
7 & 10 June 1979	First election of the European Parliament by direct universal suffrage
17 Dec 1985	The 12 member states of the European Community sign the Single European Act
9 Nov 1989	Fall of the Berlin Wall

③ THE COMMUNIST WORLD GATHERS ON STALIN'S BIRTHDAY, 21 DECEMBER 1949

From left to right: Palmiro Togliatti (Italy), Alexei Kosygin, Lazar Kaganovich, Mao Tse-tung (China), Nikolai Bulganin, Stalin, Walter Ulbricht (East Germany), Tsedenbal (Mongolia), Nikita Khrushchev, Klopenig, Dolores Ibarruri (the Spanish Pasionaria), Gheorghe Gheorghiu-Dej (Romania), Mikhail Suslov, Nikolay Shvernik, Konstantin Chernenko, Georgy Malenkov, Viliam Siroky (Czechoslovakia), Lavrenti Beria, Kliment Voroshilov, Vyacheslav Molotov, Anastas Mikoyan, Mátyás Rákosi (Hungary).

CHAPTER

THE END OF DIVIDED EUROPE?

1945–1990

From the end of the Second World War to the end of the 1980s events in Europe were dominated by two contrasting themes.

One was the rise of the two super-powers, the United States and the Soviet Union. Their competition for world hegemony, each trying to attract into its orbit as many countries as possible, in the one case as allies and in the other as puppets, destroyed the old order of the world, in which Europe had had a major role. Now Europe was devastated and impoverished, economically and politically dependent. But it reacted against being dwarfed by the 'Big Two'.

The other factor affecting Europe, both East and West, was the need for economic, political and cultural integration. At times this aroused resistance, especially when it was too rapid or – as in Eastern Europe – imposed by force. But since 1945 Western Europe (and hopefully now Eastern Europe) has been carrying out a unique experiment for the sake of peace, freedom and the well-being of its citizens. Nation states have been trying to achieve this union by the consensus of the people, rather than by force of arms.

In less than twenty years after Europe had been devastated by the Second World War, it also gave up its colonial empires. But this loss of influence did not prevent Western Europe from making an economic and social recovery that came to full fruition in the 1960s.

In 1973 the sharp rise in the price of oil showed how vulnerable prosperity was in Western Europe, while the Communist systems imposed by the USSR were choking to death. To overcome the economic crisis, Western Europe speeded up its own integration, while the Soviet Union itself helped to dismantle the Eastern bloc.

④ JEAN MONNET
(1888–1979)
French economist and financier Jean Monnet had an extraordinary career before becoming Deputy Secretary General of the League of Nations (1919–23). At the Liberation of France he proposed and headed the first plan to modernize the economy. He later devised what became the Schuman Plan for the European Coal and Steel Community, of which he became the first president. History has called him 'the Father of a United Europe'.

⑤ GORBACHEV: 'GLASNOST' AND 'PERESTROIKA'
Speaking of 'openness' and 'reform', Mikhail Gorbachev denounced Stalin's crimes and rehabilitated the victims of the show trials and the intellectuals who had been exiled. Originally an engineer and agronomist, he became Secretary-General of the Soviet Communist Party in 1985. His vision of a new Soviet Union transformed Eastern Europe, unchanged since the late 1940s.

1 Destroyed, Divided, Dominated: Europe from 1945 to 1962

① EUROPE PARTITIONED

┈┈┈┈ 1937 frontiers	Territory annexed:
──── Postwar frontiers	by the USSR
▨ Neutral countries	by Poland
	by Bulgaria
	by Yugoslavia
☐ Countries under military occupation	
── Frontiers of occupation zones	
⊕ Four-power occupation	

300 km

② 'THE MAN STRUCK BY LIGHTNING'

Statue by Ossip Zadkine, 1951. *The Second World War left Europe's cities in ruins. This statue by Ossip Zadkine, a French sculptor of Russian origin, is dedicated to Rotterdam.*

Fifty million victims

The war that ended in August 1945 had been a total war and a turning-point in the history of the world. Europe was traumatized by the violence it had itself provoked and then suffered. The emergence of two super-powers of continental size, the United States and the USSR, was matched by the decline of European countries that had dominated the world for more than two hundred years.

Never had a single war claimed so many victims: more than 50 million. The USSR had lost 20 million, 7 million of them civilians. The next worst affected on the Allied side were Poland, which had lost 6 million or 20 per cent of its population, and Yugoslavia, with 1.7 million. Germany, with 6 million dead, paid a heavy price for the genocidal madness of its leaders, although its capitulation may have saved Europe from an atomic holocaust. France, divided during the war, lost 600,000 people, 150,000 of them service personnel. Death had not spared civilians – quite the reverse. They had suffered from bombing, deportation and hunger. Human disaster on that scale affected society as a whole: some age-groups were greatly reduced in numbers; there were more women than men survivors; and the average age of the population rose. Whole generations suffered from deprivation, not only economically and physically, but psychologically too.

Large-scale air-raids had devastated many cities, some of them more or less totally. The victims included Warsaw, Coventry, London, Berlin, Hamburg, Dresden, Rotterdam and Caen. In France one house in twenty had been destroyed. Soviet territory had been laid waste, notably in fertile areas like the Ukraine, where some of the fiercest fighting had taken place. War had also reduced Europe's economic potential by at least 50 per cent. The monetary system was in disarray and currencies were devalued; there was a shortage of gold reserves to back them up. To make matters worse, trade had been disrupted.

These material losses were made worse by emotional trauma – deep shock at the appalling reversion to barbarism revealed in war crimes and crimes against humanity. Atrocities included the Soviet massacre, at Katyn Wood near Smolensk, of several thousand Polish officers captured in 1939, as well as the deliberate Nazi massacre of civilians at Oradour-sur-Glane in France or Lidice in Czechoslovakia, to say nothing of the torture and assassination of anti-Nazi Resistance fighters. Crimes against humanity – 'the Holocaust' – left even deeper scars on Europe. In the name of a spurious ideology 10 million human beings perished in the death camps: 6 million of them were Jews, hunted down all over Europe and systematically exterminated.

To all this was added the postwar plight of millions of 'displaced persons', whether deportees, refugees from Hitler or Stalin, or victims of the new frontiers imposed in 1945.

So far, the terrible shock of the Second World War and the growing sense that a European identity exists over and above purely national feelings have been powerful enough to prevent another European civil war.

The two blocs

Immediately after the war Europe's former great industrial powers (Germany, France, Italy and Britain) proved incapable of vigorous or rapid recovery. Britain, although it took part in the Yalta and Potsdam Conferences, was now no more than a brilliant adjutant to the United States. The USA and the USSR, in fact, were the two powers that counted. The former, with its territory intact and its industry powerfully stimulated by the war effort and the liberation of Western Europe, played the leading role in the peace. President Roosevelt wanted to build a new world order based on cooperation between the United States and the Soviet Union. The USSR, although exhausted by war, still had an army renowned for liberating Eastern Europe – most of which the Soviets still occupied.

In 1947 the Soviet Union increased its pressure on East European governments by setting up the Cominform. In France, Belgium and Italy the Communists left the coalition governments, some thought under American pressure. The USSR and its satellites refused the American offer of Marshall Aid. With that, 1947 saw the birth of a bipolar world, confirming Churchill's statement at Fulton, Missouri, on 5 March of the year before, that an 'iron curtain' had descended on the continent. But this *de facto* and then *de jure* partition of Europe was not accepted without protest. There was resistance, notably in Czechoslovakia and Greece.

In the free Czechoslovak election of 1946 the Communists and their allies had won 51 per cent of the vote. The resultant coalition government was inclined to accept the Marshall Plan – until Stalin put his foot down. The trial of strength between the Communists and their opponents ended in a Communist coup on 25 February 1948. After five days of crisis President Edvard

❸ Churchill in Moscow, 9 October 1944

The moment was apt for business, so I said: 'Let us settle about our affairs in the Balkans. Your armies are in Romania and Bulgaria. We have interests, missions, and agents there. Don't let us get at cross-purposes in small ways. So far as Britain and Russia are concerned, how would it do for you to have ninety per cent predominance in Romania, for us to have ninety per cent of the say in Greece, and go fifty-fifty about Yugoslavia?'. . . .

I pushed this [the paper on which he had written the proposal] across to Stalin, who had by then heard the translation. There was a slight pause. Then he took his blue pencil and made a large tick upon it, and passed it back to us.

Winston S. Churchill, *The Second World War*, Cassell paperback edition, Vol. XI, pp. 187–8

❹ Soviet deportations

The secret clause at Yalta included the commitment to 'repatriate', willingly or by force – and therefore forcibly – persons arbitrarily classified as Soviet subjects, of very diverse categories, who were outside their native lands. No one in the West was aware of this appalling action by Roosevelt and Churchill, who were ignorant of the subject and thought they must refuse Stalin nothing. They thereby handed over to the myrmidons and executioners of the GPU more than two million people, men, women and children. Many of these poor creatures preferred suicide, many others gave in only after the cruellest violence and most perished amid the horrors of the Gulag, whose name was not then infamous throughout the world, although self-respecting Heads of State, or their advisers, had no right not to know it.

Boris Souvarine, *Staline*, Gérard Lebovici, 1985

❺ THE USSR AND THE 'PEOPLE'S DEMOCRACIES' IN EUROPE

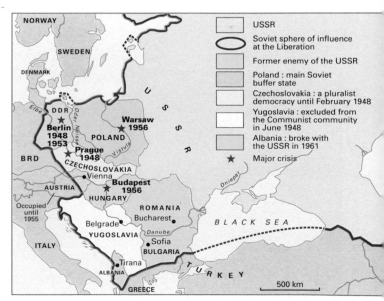

① CIVIL WAR IN GREECE (1946–9)
*The Greek Communist 'National People's Army of Liberation'
(ELAS), which had harassed the occupation armies and taken over
two-thirds of the country, was opposed to EDES, the Greek National
Democratic Army. Soon, a virtual civil war broke out. The British
intervened and managed to disarm ELAS after a month of bitter
fighting (December 1944), in which the Communist army defended
every inch of ground. An atmosphere of anarchy and terror
developed, and at the end of 1946 a full civil war broke out. It took
the government troops three years before the Communist forces were
defeated in September 1949.*

Beneš accepted the new government headed by
the Communist leader Klement Gottwald. All its
members were Communists. The western frontier
was closed. The 'Prague Coup' had succeeded.

In Greece the Communists had played a large
part in the liberation of the country. Under the
former guerrilla commander Markos Vafiades,
they made an unsuccessful bid to seize power. The
result was a civil war that lasted from 1946 to
1949. The government troops led by Marshal
Alexander Papagos, assisted by the American
military mission, finally forced the Communist
partisans to take refuge in Bulgaria and Albania.
The partition of Europe between East and West
was not completed without a struggle on either
side.

A further question was dividing Europe. It lay
at the heart of the Cold War: the question of
Germany. It involved at least three problems:
denazification, the eastern frontiers and war
reparations. A meeting of the powers in Moscow
in spring 1947 ended in deadlock. Nor was any
progress made at the London conference in
November and December 1947. The German
question became the bone of contention among
the former Allies; and its most controversial
aspect was the status of Berlin. A trial of strength
began after a further conference in London in
June 1948, when the three Western powers united
their three occupation zones and decided to
establish a common currency, the *deutsche Mark*.
This angered the Soviets, who riposted by block-
ading Berlin. For a year the Americans and their
allies supplied 95 per cent of the city's needs by
means of an airlift. In May 1949 the Soviet Union
stopped the blockade. In April of that year the
Washington Agreements created the Federal Re-

**② THE BLOCKADE OF
BERLIN**
*On 12 June 1948 the
Soviets closed the land
routes to Berlin and on 23
June they cut off its
electricity. The Americans,
French and British supplied
the Berliners from the west
by air. 380 aircraft carried
in 1,500,000 tonnes of
goods between 28 June
1948 and 12 May 1949.*

public of Germany, with elections to be held in August. The Soviets countered on 7 October by setting up the German Democratic Republic in what had been the Soviet occupation zone.

But the German question still divided the Western Allies. The fear of war in Europe led the Americans to suggest, in September 1950, that Germany be re-armed. France categorically refused, creating great embarrassment to NATO, the Western defensive alliance established in April 1949. On a proposal from Jean Monnet, put forward by the French Prime Minister René Pleven, it was decided to form a European army by integrating units from the national armies of Belgium, France, Italy, Luxembourg and the Netherlands, together with units from Germany. This would enable Germany to contribute to European defence by supplying soldiers, but without having to form a German national army.

The treaty to establish this European Defence Community (EDC) was signed on 27 May 1952. But it failed to come into force – on account of the country that had proposed it, France. In 1954, after many nationalist polemics and much American pressure, the French National Assembly refused to ratify the treaty, although it had been passed by four of its partners, while Italy still waited on France. Ironically, EDC was replaced, under the Paris agreements of 20 December 1954, by the Western European Union (WEU), comprising the EDC Six plus Britain – and in WEU Germany had its own national army. It now enjoyed full sovereignty and in May 1955 became the fifteenth member of NATO. It was not long before the Soviet Union riposted: on 14 May it established the Warsaw Pact. In the same year the Treaty of Vienna made Austria a neutral power.

The end of empire

In 1955, 29 Asian and African countries met in Bandung, Indonesia, and made clear their desire for decolonization, marking a turning point in world history. Shortly afterwards the US and the USSR decided to no longer limit the admission of new members to the United Nations, thus encouraging the liberation of colonial peoples.

The Second World War had greatly changed relations between the European countries and their colonies. It had shown the fragility of empires undermined by nationalist excitement. Ideologically, the Soviet Union favoured decolonization as a means of weakening Western capitalist countries. In principle, the United States also backed the efforts of colonial peoples to win their freedom, but they did not adopt official attitudes to avoid embarrassing their allies. Between 1945 and 1962 decolonization took place

3 NATO
British poster for the tenth anniversary
The North Atlantic Treaty, signed on 4 April 1949 in Washington, aimed 'to promote stability and well-being in the North Atlantic area'. Ten years later it had fifteen members: Belgium, Britain, Canada, Denmark, France, Germany, Greece, Iceland, Italy, Luxembourg, the Netherlands, Portugal, Turkey, the United Kingdom and the United States.

4 THE BELGRADE CONFERENCE
The policy of non-alignment was adopted by 25 countries in Belgrade in 1961. Its promoters were (left to right, above) Gamal Abdel Nasser, Jawaharlal Nehru and Josef Tito. They belonged to neither bloc and thought the blocs should be dissolved for world peace.

① THE BIRTH OF PAKISTAN, 1947

The Indian Empire was divided. To reach the new state of Pakistan, hundreds of thousands of Moslems took the Delhi–Lahore railway.

② DECOLONIZATION

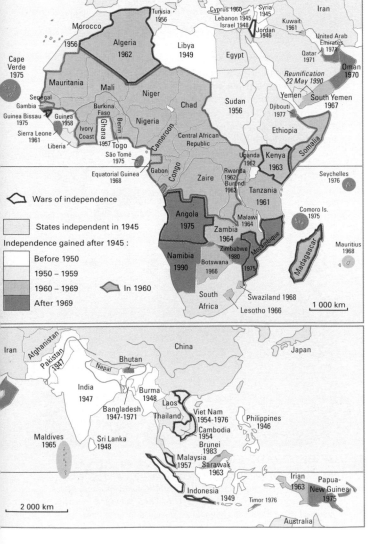

Wars of independence

States independent in 1945

Independence gained after 1945 :
- Before 1950
- 1950 – 1959
- 1960 – 1969
- After 1969

In 1960

1 000 km

2 000 km

Map labels (Africa): Morocco; Tunisia 1956; Cyprus 1960; Lebanon 1945; Israel 1948; Syria 1945; Jordan 1946; Kuwait 1961; Iran; United Arab Emirates 1971; Qatar 1971; Oman 1970; Algeria 1962; Libya 1949; Egypt; Reunification 22 May 1990; Yemen; South Yemen 1967; 1956; Mauritania; Mali; Niger; Chad; Sudan 1956; Djibouti 1977; Cape Verde 1975; Senegal; Gambia; Guinea Bissau 1975; Guinea 1958; Burkina Faso; Benin; Nigeria; Ethiopia; Sierra Leone 1961; Liberia; Ivory Coast; Ghana 1957; Togo; São Tomé 1975; Cameroon; Central African Republic; Somalia; Uganda 1962; Kenya 1963; Equatorial Guinea 1968; Gabon; Congo; Zaire; Rwanda 1962; Burundi 1962; Tanzania 1961; Seychelles 1976; Angola 1975; Zambia 1964; Malawi 1964; Comoro Is. 1975; Zimbabwe 1980; Mozambique 1975; Mauritius 1968; Namibia 1990; Botswana 1966; Madagascar; South Africa; Swaziland 1968; Lesotho 1966

Map labels (Asia): Iran; Afghanistan; Pakistan 1947; Nepal; Bhutan; China; Japan; India 1947; Burma 1948; Bangladesh 1947-1971; Laos; Thailand; Viet Nam 1954-1976; Cambodia 1954; Philippines 1946; Brunei 1983; Maldives 1965; Sri Lanka 1948; Malaysia 1957; Sarawak 1963; Indonesia 1949; Timor 1976; Irian 1963; Papua-New Guinea 1975; Australia

---

in two stages. The first concerned mainly the Near and Middle East and south-east Asia; the second, beginning in 1955, mainly Africa.

Although the colonial powers were once more going through a shared experience, it affected them in different ways.

The United Kingdom, under a Labour government, tackled the problem gradually. On the initiative of Prime Minister Clement Attlee, honouring pledges made by Churchill during the war, Britain granted India independence in 1947. Lord Louis Mountbatten, the last Viceroy of India, carried through the process and became the first Governor-General in August 1947. It was under his authority that the old Indian Empire was split into two countries, India and Pakistan, whose birth was marred by inter-ethnic massacres. Both states became members of the Commonwealth, defined in 1949 as a multi-ethnic and polyglot association whose head was the Queen, though with no effective power and only a symbolic role. At present it includes 48 countries.

The Netherlands were tempted to fight decolonization, but became resigned to it. In December 1949 they granted Indonesia full independence.

The fate of the Italian colonies was initially the subject of an agreement in the spring of 1949 between Count Carlo Sforza, the Italian Foreign Minister, and his British counterpart Ernest Bevin; but this was rejected by the United Nations, which decided on independence for Libya and Somalia. The Belgian Congo, which became independent in 1960, was one scene of superpower confrontation in the Third World; but when almost a dozen British colonies in Africa won their freedom, especially after 1960, it was clear that European colonization was coming to an end. The Portuguese, who had been the first Europeans to set foot in Africa, were among the last to leave. They tried to hold on to Angola and Mozambique; but after a lengthy war of independence they were obliged to quit in 1975.

France was rather different. It regarded its empire as a means of recovering its status as a great power; but it failed to opt clearly between a policy of association and one of assimilation and became embroiled in two long wars. The first was in Indo-China (1946–54), where the Communist revolutionary Ho Chi Minh, who had fought the Japanese occupying powers, proclaimed a Democratic Republic of Vietnam in September 1945. The conflict culminated in the defeat of the French army at Dien Bien Phu on 7 May 1954, while peace negotiations were under way in Geneva. An armistice was finally signed on 20 July 1954, dividing Indo-China along the 17th parallel. The Geneva Agreements marked both the victory of a revolutionary movement over a

European power and the loss of French influence in south-east Asia – soon replaced by that of America, China and the Soviet Union.

No sooner was the war in Indochina settled than France had to confront what was then known as 'the Algerian problem', exacerbated because about a million Europeans were living there. The conflict had two phases. In the first, from 1954 to 1958, France sought to restore order, but that proved unsuccessful. In the second phase, from 1958 to 1962, the war was internationalized. Every year, France came under attack in the UN General Assembly, and had to manoeuvre to avoid being condemned by an Afro–Asian resolution. When General de Gaulle returned to power in 1958, France was in a crisis. After long negotiations, De Gaulle signed the Evian Agreements on 18 March 1962. With the double aim of avoiding a further colonial defeat and ridding himself of the Algerian millstone, he had given himself a free hand to pursue a new foreign policy. In 1969 the Yaoundé Convention provided the framework for special relations between the then six-nation European Community and its members' former colonies.

But one of the major results of decolonization was that now the world was helping to determine Europe's future, rather than the other way round, as in the past. This was a real turning-point.

The Suez crisis, 1956

The Suez crisis, which broke out during the Algerian war, was an illustration of that fact. On 20 July 1956 the Egyptian leader Gamal Abdel Nasser nationalized the Suez Canal. Faced with this challenge, France, Britain and Israel launched a joint operation, in which the Franco–British forces were supposedly to 'separate' the Egyptians and the Israelis. At first, Egyptian troops lost control of the Sinai Desert and most of the Canal. But on 5 November the USSR threatened France and Britain with nuclear rockets, and the United States disavowed its allies, making no move to support sterling, for example, until £100 million had gone abroad. In the UN General Assembly, Britain and France were condemned, and they evacuated their bridgehead in December. The most obvious result of the affair was to curtail their influence in the region. Gunboat diplomacy had failed; middle-sized powers were no longer free to act as they thought fit. They had been let down by their ally and protector, leading to a crisis within NATO. Nasser, meanwhile, had become the champion of nationalism and decolonization; and the USSR could pose as a defender of small powers against imperialism. The European powers were already overshadowed in Europe.

❸ EXPATRIATES FROM ALGERIA ARRIVE IN MARSEILLE

The Evian Agreements of 18 March 1962 and the recognition of the Algerian Republic on 3 July were not accepted calmly by Europeans living in Algeria. Fearing a bloodbath, more than 800,000 of them headed for France. To carry them, special ferry services were laid on. Here, the Ville de Marseille steamer brings back 1541 people, including 105 children aged less than three. Their suitcases contained all they had.

❹ THE FRENCH AND BRITISH LEAVE PORT SAID

The refusal of Anglo–American credit to finance the Aswan Dam led Nasser to nationalize the Suez Canal in July 1956. France, Britain and Israel responded with military intervention, which was unsuccessful due to pressure from the USA and the USSR.

357

2 Reconstruction (1947–1960)

① COMMUNISM IS NO FAIRY-TALE
Dutch cartoon, 1947

The establishment of Communist regimes in Eastern Europe was achieved in record time (1945–8) because the USSR was afraid of American 'imperialism' and needed its satellites' resources for its own reconstruction. It was not surprising, therefore, that some waspish cartoons appeared in the West. For the Dutch the Soviet Union had all the menace of a bear from the steppes of central Asia. The East German Little Red Riding Hood would soon be dancing to the same tune as the other 'People's Democracies'.

---

② Tito answers Soviet accusations

The Soviet people and above all their leaders must believe that the new Yugoslavia under her present leadership is moving irresistibly to socialism . . . .

We consider that small people's democracies like Yugoslavia and others, which are treading new paths to socialism, must in every case, both for internal and external reasons, remain completely independent and sovereign at the present stage, though firmly bound to each other and to the Soviet Union by treaties . . . .

The experiences of successful revolutionary development in every people's democracy should be considered a continuation and addition to the experiences of the great October Revolution, as something new in revolutionary practice . . . .

The role of the Soviet Union should consist in extending the full and comprehensive support of her authority to the new democracies, making special use in propaganda of the successes achieved in these new democracies in the realization of socialism.

Letter sent by Tito to the USSR, 12 April 1948, in Vladimir Dedijer, *Tito Speaks*, Weidenfeld & Nicolson, 1953, pp. 346–7

After 1947/48, Europe was divided into two opposing halves: Western Europe, under American influence, and Eastern Europe, under Soviet control. Both undertook economic reconstruction, but in diametrically opposite ways, each with a logic of its own. This was also the period of the Cold War. After 1949, when the USSR had its own atomic bomb, the threat of nuclear war led to the so-called 'balance of terror'. The French philosopher Raymond Aron summed up the situation: 'War unlikely, peace impossible'.

The Soviet model

The Soviet Union's concern to extend its influence throughout Eastern Europe was a facet of its foreign policy, dominated by its obsession with security. Moscow was convinced that the capitalist world was fundamentally hostile and that America might well launch an atomic attack. It therefore turned the Red Army from an army of liberation into an occupying force. East Germany, Poland, Czechoslovakia, Romania, Bulgaria, Hungary and Albania signed treaties of alliance with the Soviet Union and with each other. These political alliances were backed by military measures, such as making the Soviet Marshal Konstantin Rokossovsky War Minister of Poland (7 November 1949), and above all by installing Communist governments in the so-called 'People's Democracies'.

Political integration began with the liquidation of non-Marxist parties in Romania, Bulgaria, Poland and Hungary. It continued in September 1947 with a meeting in Szklarska-Poreba, Poland, where representatives of the Communist parties from nine European countries, including France and Italy, set up an information bureau, the Cominform, to act as a link among the Communist countries. Under Andrei Zhdanov it became the spokesman of Communist orthodoxy, denouncing American 'imperialism' and 'warmongering', extolling the 'genius' of Stalin and denouncing the 'duplicity' of Tito.

From 1945 onwards, in fact, Tito had used his undoubted authority in Yugoslavia to treat the USSR as an equal. His desire for independence irritated Stalin, who in March 1948 recalled his advisers from Yugoslavia, bringing 'the Tito crisis' to a head. It was a danger for Soviet policy, because Tito's 'deviationism' might have encouraged other Communist leaders to revert to national versions of socialism. Moscow also purged the Communist parties in other 'People's Democracies', where leaders regarded as too 'nationalist' were hounded from office and in some cases executed. They included Wladyslaw Gomulka in Poland (dismissed in 1948), Laszlo Rajk in Hungary (hanged in 1949) and Rudolf Slansky in Czechoslovakia (accused of Zionism and hanged in 1952). Finland also had to accept Soviet tutelage.

Integration into the Soviet system was economic as well as political. This was achieved by the establishment of COMECON, the Council for Mutual Economic Assistance, in 1949. Its aim was to develop trade and promote economic cooperation between the Soviet Union and its satellites, who thereby lost their economic independence. The 'People's Democracies' socialized their economies and adopted planning systems taken over wholesale from the Soviet model. From the end of the 1940s, they began agrarian reform, collectivizing land everywhere – except in Poland, where unusually fierce resistance by the peasants enabled them to keep their holidays. Industry and services, meanwhile, were expropriated and became state property.

Equally, the USSR sought to impose its own culture, both to spread propaganda and to ensure conformity. It had a triple purpose: to control thought, to glorify Communist achievements and to denounce 'deviationism'. A strict watch was kept on the press. Education was used to promote the Russian language. Soviet universities trained the future Communist élite, the 'Nomenklatura'. Art, literature and science were forced to deal with approved subjects and follow set rules. Painting had to espouse 'Socialist realism', officially defined as 'the concrete, truthful and historical representation of reality in its revolutionary development'. It must, the definition continued, 'contribute in particular to the ideological transformation of workers' education in the spirit of Socialism'. Those who ignored or impugned this prescription were threatened with imprisonment in forced labour camps. The Church, which soon clashed with such attempts at indoctrination, was seriously disturbed. In December 1948 Cardinal József Mindszenty, the Primate of Hungary, was arrested and condemned to penal servitude for life, later commuted to house detention. In 1949 a similar fate befell Cardinal Josef Beran, the Primate of Czechoslovakia.

Two events, however, enabled criticism to be voiced. The first was the death of Stalin; the second was the 20th Congress of the Soviet Communist Party, from 14 to 25 February 1956. Stalin died in 1953 and from then on writers and

❸'THE CONFESSION' ('L'AVEU')
This film, by the Greek director Costa-Gavras, was based on the book by Artur London, former Czech Foreign Minister, about his experiences as a victim of the Communist purge. Released in 1970, the film was shown all over Europe, as this Italian poster suggests; it also had an audience in the wider world. The actor playing London, Yves Montand, had earlier been a Communist fellow-traveller but had soon been disillusioned by Communist practice.

❹'THE TRACTOR-DRIVER'
Soviet painting, 1957
As a piece of Socialist realism, this picture obeys Stalin's rules, transforming nature and portraying a young athletic man, a future member of the Party, ready to toil for the USSR.

① SOVIET TANKS IN BUDAPEST

In October 1956 Hungary tried to throw off Stalinism. Imre Nagy, an anti-Stalinist Communist, came to power and obtained concessions from Moscow: but the USSR refused to allow Hungary to leave the Warsaw Pact. On 14 November Soviet troops went on the offensive in the capital, Budapest, violently crushing the rebellion. But the country had passed an important landmark. Although it returned to the Soviet ranks, Hungary remained one of the Communist countries most open to the West.

---

② Robert Schuman talks to US Secretary of State Dean Acheson

On 9 May 1950, at the instigation of Jean Monnet, the French Foreign Minister Robert Schuman proposed to establish the European Coal and Steel Community, with a 'common market' in coal, coke, steel, iron ore and scrap. The plan was enthusiastically welcomed by the Americans. Here Secretary of State Dean Acheson gives his personal impression of Schuman:

After a few words of greeting and appreciation of my coming to Paris, Schuman began to expound what later became known as the 'Schuman Plan', so breathtaking a step towards the unification of Western Europe that at first I did not grasp it. The whole French–German production of coal and steel would be placed under a joint high authority, with an organization open to the participation of other European nations . . . .

As he talked, we caught his enthusiasm and the breadth of his thought, the rebirth of Europe, which, as an entity, had been in eclipse since the Reformation.

Dean Acheson, *Sketches from Life*, New York, 1961, pp. 36–7

---

students began to criticize certain aspects of his regime. In Hungary the Prime Minister Imre Nagy denounced the abuses committed by the police and those involved in collectivizing the land. On 14 April 1955 he was expelled from office and excluded from the Party. The 20th Congress of the Soviet Communist Party, chaired by the new Secretary General Nikita Khrushchev, had on its agenda de-Stalinization and the abolition of the Cominform (17 April 1956). It opened the way to seeking national routes to Socialism.

In Poland in 1956 there was a revolt against economic and social hardships: in strikes and rioting at Poznań at the end of June 53 workers were killed. To defuse the crisis, Stalinist leaders were dismissed, and Wladyslaw Gomulka, accused of nationalism in 1948, was made First Secretary of the Party. Having himself been a victim of Stalinism, he was acceptable to Polish patriots, who mistakenly believed in the promise of policies that would be more national and more liberal towards the Catholic Church.

In that same year insurrection in Hungary came to a far more dramatic end. Encouraged by the Polish example, a number of opposition groups re-surfaced and they pressed the new government, headed by Imre Nagy, to go further than Moscow would tolerate. Faced with plans to restore private property, reinstate the Catholic Church, leave the Warsaw Pact and become neutral, Moscow reacted. On 4 November 1956 the Soviet army went into Budapest and crushed all resistance, arresting Nagy and replacing him with János Kádár. Kádár restored the Communist Party to supreme power; Hungary returned to the Warsaw Pact and the *status quo* was resumed. Thus the Soviet Union staked out the limits of the autonomy it allowed its satellites, calling a halt to the search for national routes to Socialism. There was reconstruction in the East, undoubtedly, but only on Soviet terms.

On 13 August 1961, when the East German government decided to stem the tide of refugees to the West by building a wall between East and West Berlin, it gave literally concrete form to the tragic division of Europe.

Towards a 'common market' in the West

On 5 June 1947 the US Secretary of State General George Marshall had proposed collective aid to the Europeans for four years, on condition that they agree on how to share it out. The Bretton Woods agreements of 1944 had already established the US dollar as an international reserve currency and the free-market economy as a model. The authors of the Marshall Plan saw it as a way of assisting Europe's economic recovery, encouraging Europeans to act together and strengthening their resistance to Communism. There were important choices to be made: one was that of part of Europe to opt for the plan. As a result, Western Europe was reconstructed on lines very different from that followed in the East.

By establishing the Organization for European Economic Cooperation (OEEC), the body for distributing Marshall Aid, on 16 April 1948, the Europeans committed themselves to cooperation. From 1948 to 1952 the aid amounted to more than $13,000 million, with $3176 million for the United Kingdom and its dependencies, $2706 million for France, $1474 million for Italy and $1389 million for Germany. The OEEC ensured commercial and monetary cooperation among its 16 members; and from 1950, with the European Payments Union set up in that year, its policy of liberalization moved rapidly ahead. In 1960 the OEEC became the OECD, the Organization for Economic Cooperation and Development.

Closer links among Europeans were being forged elsewhere. A number of movements in favour of European unity sponsored a Congress of Europe in the Hague in May 1948, which called for political and economic union in Europe, a European Assembly and a European Court of Human Rights. Despite Anglo–French disagreements about sovereignty and supranationality, this led to the Council of Europe, set up in 1949, in which ten European countries agreed to work together on the basis of the cultural roots they shared, their vision of humanity and their devotion to democracy. Established in Strasbourg, the Council of Europe developed into a forum for consultation and cooperation on political, social and cultural affairs. On 4 November 1950 it produced the European Convention for the Protection of Human Rights, a document that was both a pledge for the future and the basis for practical work by the Court and Commission of Human Rights in Strasbourg.

A number of efforts had been made to overcome Franco–German antagonism by working towards a united Western Europe. The most important was the plan proposed on 9 May 1950 by the French Foreign Minister Robert Schuman, at the suggestion of Jean Monnet, to pool Franco–German coal and steel production in an organization open to the other democratic countries of Europe. By accepting it, the German Chancellor Konrad Adenauer anchored Germany to the West without giving up hopes of reunification and he began turning European cooperation into real integration. Belgium, France, Germany, Italy, Luxembourg and the Netherlands established the European Coal and Steel Community by the Treaty of Paris (18 April 1951), which gave

3 THE MARSHALL PLAN, 1947
Swedish poster
The Marshall Plan proposed aid over four years to all European countries that wanted it. It covered goods as well as capital; and its distribution was to be determined together by the recipients. Voted in March 1948 by the US Congress, the Plan involved annual credits until 1952. But it inadvertently confirmed the partition of Europe, because the Soviet Union refused American capital as early as 1947 and obliged its satellites to do the same.

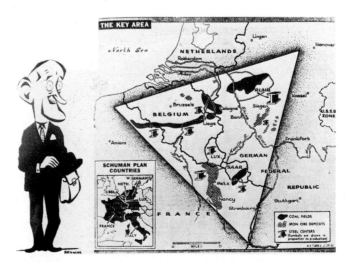

4 THE 'GOLDEN TRIANGLE' OF THE ECSC
Cartoon and map from *The New York Times*, 1951
Robert Schuman's and Jean Monnet's European Coal and Steel Community (ECSC) had a 'golden triangle' comprising the coal and steel areas of Belgium, the Saar, the Ruhr, Luxembourg and Lorraine. But Italy and the Netherlands also benefited from its 'common market'. Only Britain, of its own free will, remained outside.

❶ Preamble to the Treaty of Rome, 1957

Determined to lay the foundations of an ever closer union among the peoples of Europe,

Resolved to ensure the economic and social progress of their countries by common action to eliminate the barriers which divide Europe,

Affirming as the essential objective of their efforts the constant improvement of the living and working conditions of their peoples,

Recognizing that the removal of existing obstacles calls for concerted action in order to guarantee steady expansion, balanced trade and fair competition,

Anxious to strengthen the unity of their economies and to ensure their harmonious development by reducing the differences existing between the various regions and the backwardness of the less favoured regions,

Desiring to contribute, by means of a common commercial policy, to the progressive abolition of restrictions on international trade,

Intending to confirm the solidarity which binds Europe and the overseas countries and desiring to ensure the development of their prosperity, in accordance with the principles of the Charter of the United Nations,

Resolved by thus pooling their resources to preserve and strengthen peace and liberty, and calling upon the other peoples of Europe who share their ideal to join in their efforts,

Have decided to create a European Economic Community.

❷ BRITAIN BRINGS ITS FRIENDS AND RELATIONS
Dutch cartoon, 1962
The British seemed at one time to want to join the EEC with 'their Commonwealth family'. Britain did not join the EEC until 1973, this time adopting its common outer tariff vis-à-vis the Commonwealth as well as the rest of the world.

limited supranational power to an independent nine-member High Authority. There was initial opposition from the German Socialists, the French Communists and various employers' organizations; but in 1953 the ECSC opened a European common market in coal and steel. Benelux – an economic union of Belgium, the Netherlands and Luxembourg initiated in 1943 – played an important role in building the ECSC. For Konrad Adenauer, the German Chancellor, it was an opportunity not to be missed, since it enabled Germany to end its diplomatic isolation. The United Kingdom remained aloof from the new Community to preserve its national sovereignty and its economic links with the Commonwealth.

The question of the Saar, however, continued to divide Germany and France. In October 1955 the people of the Saar voted in a referendum to become part of Germany. In October 1956 their choice was confirmed by treaty and in 1960 France definitively gave up its tutelage. The creation of the ECSC had eased the problem, since, although the Saar's coal and steel industries now became German again, this took place in a European context, making them a European and not simply a German resource.

The European Economic Community

In June 1955 representatives of the six ECSC countries met in Messina to relaunch the uniting of Europe after the failure of the European Defence Community in 1954. Experts meeting in Brussels under the chairmanship of Paul-Henri Spaak, the Belgian Foreign Minister, then worked out the detailed plans for the European Economic Community (the EEC or 'Common Market') and the European Atomic Energy Community (Euratom). The treaties establishing them were signed on 25 March 1957 in Rome. The EEC was based on a customs union, in which the member states were to reduce to zero the customs tariffs among themselves and adopt a common tariff vis-à-vis the rest of the world. At the same time they were gradually to remove the barriers to the free movement of people and capital. Euratom, meanwhile, was to promote the safe and peaceful uses of atomic energy on a European basis and give Europe greater independence both in atomic matters and in energy supplies. In effect, the two Rome Treaties established an economic entity limited for the time being to the six continental European member states.

The United Kingdom, which declined to join this Community, tried to establish a huge free trade area encompassing all the member states of OEEC and including the European Community. France finally rejected the plan, and Britain established, with Austria, Denmark, Norway, Portugal, Sweden and Switzerland, the European Free Trade Association (EFTA), whose founding treaty was signed in Stockholm on 20 November 1959.

The European Economic Community or 'Common Market' came into force on 1 January 1958 and, despite competition from EFTA, soon acquired a decisive role. Among other things, it began to work out a common agricultural policy and lay the bases for economic and eventually monetary union. So successful was the EEC that in the summer of 1961 the British Prime Minister Harold Macmillan decided to open negotiations for possible membership. The British had to exercise patience for more than ten years. Twice, in 1963 and 1967, the French President, General Charles de Gaulle, vetoed Britain's candidature. In his view the United Kingdom was still a Trojan Horse for American influence and sought to join the Community simply to destroy it.

Economic reconstruction in the West, although given an American blessing, was the work of the Europeans themselves. But other aspects of European society were more open to transatlantic influence, which affected many facets of everyday life. In the 1950s such phenomena as American cigarettes, chewing-gum, Coca-Cola, Westerns, jazz and rock 'n' roll were all examples of 'Americanization'. This was not imposed on Europeans: they actually sought it out, if only for novelty's sake. How otherwise can one explain the belated success of Roger Vadim's film *Et Dieu créa la femme*? This appeared in France in 1956 amid widespread indifference; but then, put on the Index by the Vatican, it went to the United States, where it aroused both polemics and enthusiasm. Back in Europe, flaunting its American success, it became a cult film. America also became the scene of most of the architectural and artistic avant-garde.

This was not true of all the arts, where there were also powerful European traditions. In Italy, Roberto Rossellini (with *Roma città aperta*, *Rome Open City*, 1945) and Vittorio De Sica (with *Ladri di biciclette*, *Bicycle Thieves*, 1948) consolidated neo-realist cinema. Later, in France, the 'New Wave' of Jean-Luc Godard, François Truffaut and others revolutionized the art of filmmaking. Novels and plays were influenced by the existentialist philosophy of Jean-Paul Sartre (*L'Etre et le Néant*, 1943), which came to imply a way of life as well as a way of thinking. Drama was revitalized by the avant-garde theatre of Samuel Beckett, Eugène Ionesco and Jean Genet; and painting, through the work of the Cobra group and the English artist Francis Bacon, among others, found new languages and forms.

❸ 'ROME, OPEN CITY'
This film by Roberto Rossellini dealt with the secret struggle to liberate the Italian capital: its sharp immediacy made it one of the early landmarks in cinematic neo-realism.

❹ IONESCO AND AVANT-GARDE THEATRE
Dora Doll and Roger Hanin in *The Lesson*, staged in 1951
Son of a Romanian father and a French mother, a teacher of French in Bucharest and a member of the French Academy, Eugène Ionesco skilfully blended parody, logic and psychological truth. His first play, The Bald Prima-Donna (1950), was a failure. But with The Lesson he won a reputation as a sensational and even scandalous playwright, so much so that avant-garde directors were eager to put on his work.

Stagnation in the East, Prosperity in the West (1960–1974)

❶ THE PRAGUE SPRING (1968)
Once again it was a matter of reforms aiming to democratize one of the Communist satellite countries – this time Czechoslovakia. The USSR was worried; Poland and Eastern Germany feared that the unrest would spread to them. In August 1968 troops from the Warsaw Pact countries invaded the Czechoslovak Republic. Tanks were on the streets of Prague. 'Socialism with a human face' was crushed.

❷ The Brezhnev Doctrine

The Communist Party of the Soviet Union has always laboured to enable each Socialist country to determine for itself the concrete forms of its evolution on the way to Socialism, taking into account its specific national conditions . . . . And when internal and external forces hostile to Socialism seek to steer the evolution of a Socialist country and to press for the restoration of the capitalist state of affairs, when in other words there is a serious threat to the cause of Socialism in that country, a danger for the security of the whole Communist community – then that becomes not only a problem for the people of that country, but also a common problem, a matter of concern for all the Socialist countries.

Extract from the speech made by Leonid Brezhnev to the 5th Congress of the Polish Communist Party, 12 October 1968

The Brezhnev Doctrine

In Eastern Europe the 1960s saw both a slow-down in economic growth and a tightening of Soviet control.

Nikita Khrushchev's promise to raise the Soviet standard of living to that of the West proved illusory. The plan for a Socialist version of the international division of labour, put into practice in 1962, provided for specialization among the East European economies, closer cooperation in science and technology, and joint investment projects. But this not only failed to produce the desired results: it also caused sullen resentment.

The dismissal of Khrushchev and his replacement by Leonid Brezhnev in 1964 was a victory for those who refused to liberalize the life of the Soviets and their European allies. The disciplining of the Soviet intelligentsia and the prosecution of the writer Yuri Daniel in 1966 signalled the beginning of the 'Brezhnev Doctrine'. Yet at the same time, among the European 'People's Democracies', there were aspirations that Moscow interpreted as resistance to Russification.

In Czechoslovakia social and economic disillusionment among the people, and a desire for freedom on the part of the intellectuals, resulted in the 'Prague Spring' of 1968. It was accompanied by a resurgence of ancient tensions between the Czechs and the Slovaks. Antonín Novotný, the Czechoslovak Communist Party's Stalinist leader, lost control of the situation. Gustav Husák and Alexander Dubček, veterans of the Communist purges in the 1950s, came to the fore again. Manoeuvring between Moscow and the people, they tried to establish 'Socialism with a human face'; but their promises – to liberalize the mass media, to free the Church and to hold free elections – came too late. The *Two-Thousand Words Manifesto* published by a number of intellectuals called for even more radical reform. For Moscow it was the last straw. On 21 August 1968 tanks from members of the Warsaw Pact, save for Romania, entered the capital and the 'Prague Spring' was brutally crushed.

In Poland Wladyslaw Gomulka, who had been in power since the 1956 revolts, crushed rioting in Gdansk on 14–15 December 1970; but spreading unrest led to his replacement as First Secretary by Edward Gierek, a Moscow nominee. During the 1970s, in fact, the Soviet Union continued to rule its satellites with a rod of iron.

Consumer society in the West

In Western Europe the situation was very different. Unprecedented economic growth (on average 5 per cent a year) seemed to have come to stay. It was a time of economic miracles, of growing consumer affluence, of welfare states and liberal reforms.

Never before had Europe experienced such economic progress, surpassing even the peak years of the 19th century and seeming to have overcome cyclical crises. The rapid spread of technological innovations, the growth of electronics and biological discoveries that contributed to medical advance and the prolongation of life – all were part of the same optimistic picture.

To which has to be added the rapid growth of European and world trade. More and more motorways and motor vehicles boosted road transport. Jet aircraft, container ships and supertankers gave a fresh stimulus to overseas commerce, liberalized by tariffs and other measures adopted under GATT, the General Agreement on Tariffs and Trade established in 1948. In 1973 the proportion of the world's total production going for export was 15 per cent; that of France's was 20 per cent, that of Germany's 28 per cent, that of Japan's 13 per cent and that of the United States's 7 per cent. Thanks to sustained growth, the West Europeans enjoyed a spectacular improvement in their standard of living and their creature comforts.

Greater productivity made possible a substantial increase in wages and salaries: purchasing power in Western Europe actually doubled in the space of ten years. This brought a change in household spending. Expenditure on food increased: but the really big rise was in spending on manufactures – consumer durables. Many households acquired a whole outfit of goods, usually including an automobile, a washing machine, a refrigerator and other household 'white goods', a television set, a telephone, a hi-fi system and so on. At the same time more people were able to own their own homes, partly because of easier credit – whose real cost was reduced by inflation – and partly as a result of the building boom.

With greater affluence the demand for services increased. Leisure and vacations created a new market for holiday firms, travel agents and other vendors of escape. With cars, more and more Europeans migrated south in the summer, to the sun-drenched coasts of Italy, Greece, the Côte d'Azur or the Costa Brava. Ever more tempting advertisements increased the consumer urge. Not everyone, however, enjoyed the same advantages. Economic growth affected the structure of society and especially favoured the middle classes.

❸ THE AFFLUENT SOCIETY

Publicity and consumer credit profoundly changed domestic life. People no longer hesitated to buy household electrical goods. There was no more question of 'doing without'. Europeans bought European and foreign goods, many more than could be squeezed into this refrigerator. For many households in Europe that too was a novelty: in France 51 per cent of families bought one in 1954 alone.

❹ TOURISM AND TAX HAVENS

As a social phenomenon, vacations meant large-scale migration in search of the sun, sight-seeing, getting a tan – and picking up bargains. As here, in this Land of Cockaigne between Spain and France: Andorra. Because of its low customs duties and its lack of luxury taxes, lines of cars several miles long waited at the frontier between June and September. To save a little money, people came to Andorra to buy tax-free goods and fill their fuel tanks: in 1960 they could do so at about 15 pence a litre.

❶ THE BUREAUCRATIC LABYRINTH
Playtime, 1957
In his film Playtime *Jacques Tati made fun of the bloodless, labyrinthine honeycomb of modern offices in the expanding services sector, full of executives and bureaucrats in three-piece suits and sober tailor-made dresses.*

❷ The Beveridge Plan proposes the British social security system (1942)

The aim of the Plan for Social Security, concluded Sir William Beveridge, is to abolish want by guaranteeing at all time, to every citizen who is prepared to work according to his ability, an income sufficient for him to meet his responsibilities . . . . The answer to the question whether the total abolition of want should be regarded as a post-war aim capable of securing rapid results is affirmative, on four conditions. These conditions are as follows. First, that the post-war world be a world in which nations make the effort to work together peacefully for production and not plot mutual destruction by means of open or latent warfare; secondly, that the political and economic structure of the United Kingdom be reformed to meet the needs of the new post-war conditions so that productive employment may be maintained; thirdly, that a Plan of Social Security, that is for the maintenance of income, be adopted, free from unnecessary administrative costs and other waste of resources; fourthly, that decisions about the nature of the Plan, that is regarding the organization of social insurance and related services, be taken during the war . . . .

Broadly speaking, growth altered the balance among the three sectors of the economy – agriculture, industry and services. In France, for example, the proportion of the active population employed in agriculture fell from 36 per cent in 1946 to 10 per cent in 1975, while that in industry remained constant around 38 per cent and that in services rose from 32.5 per cent to 50.8 per cent. This change, which was more marked still in northern Europe, swelled the ranks of the middle classes, mostly executives and salaried employees. Wages being higher in the service sector, the beneficiaries there profited more than others from the return to prosperity. The middle classes set a social norm, and working-class life tended towards it: 'blue-collar' workers began to share 'middle-class' ways. There were still great contrasts of wealth and income, but they were now less visible. Real poverty seemed limited to particular deprived groups, such as immigrants, the elderly, the physically disadvantaged and the unskilled. Many called for the state to ensure a fairer distribution of the fruits of growth.

The Welfare State

The period of 1945–73, nicknamed by the French sociologist Jean Fourastié 'the Thirty Glorious Years', saw states in Western Europe intervening decisively in various sectors of society to create what German and Austrian economists called 'a social market economy'. Such intervention was more marked in northern Europe than in the Mediterranean countries or in Portugal and Spain. These two countries, moreover, were dictatorships, Portugal since 1926 and Spain since 1939. In April 1967 Greece suffered the same unhappy fate.

In the rest of Western Europe the state had played a key role in regulating growth since the end of the Second World War. In doing so, it had followed the doctrine of the British economist John Maynard Keynes, intervening in the economy to maintain prosperity and full employment. By damping down the business cycle, it hoped to avoid 'overheating' or excessive growth that would generate inflation and a commercial deficit. The Welfare State, meanwhile, was inspired by the report published in Britain by Sir William Beveridge in 1942. These ideas came gradually to influence the economic policies of all the capitalist countries in Western Europe; and they were never totally called in question as a result of changes of government. Admittedly, there were differences of nuance between the policies pursued by different states. But the system of social security, in particular, became general throughout Western Europe, making provision against all the major risks – sickness, accident, unemployment, old age. In addition there were family allowances, regional aid, tax concessions and cash benefits for the very poor, housing policies, huge increases in expenditure on education and training, etc. Pupils stayed at school longer, often by law. New universities were founded. As well as creating a more skilled workforce, one aim of the system, whether avowed or not, was to maintain a high level of demand so as not to hamper economic growth.

But ironing out inequalities was not enough to provide a lasting solution to the problems of demand management; so state intervention in all sectors of the economy increased. It became a guiding force in most of the key sectors, often as an active participant. From 1946 onwards nationalization became a tool of economic policy. By controlling electrical and nuclear energy, rail and air transport, and credit via the banks, the state was able to orchestrate the economy on a national basis; and inter-state cooperation partly extended such public responsibilities to the European scene.

Admittedly, in Western Europe the state's role varied from one country to another. But it was never negligible. It was especially important, at that time, in electronics and aeronautics, which were responsible among other things for the building of a European supersonic aircraft, the Concorde, a joint venture by Great Britain and France. In 1973 Europe decided to build a powerful satellite launcher; and on 24 December 1979, from Guyana, it successfully put in orbit *Ariane 1*. Within ten years this had been followed by more than fifty other satellites.

The state's position in the economy gave it a preponderant role in the market for jobs. Basically, the level of employment or unemployment depended on the state's influence on the major private industries and on those jobs it directly or indirectly controlled. As a leading 'employer', through the civil service and the nationalized industries, it found itself in the front line as a regulator of unemployment.

So the Welfare State of the 'Thirty Glorious Years' was at once a stimulant of growth, an economic regulator and a distributor of growth's rewards. But, if in theory it was egalitarian, in practice it still produced frustration and discontent.

③ SOME TRAVEL: OTHERS CANNOT

The poster's promise of carefree vacations in the sun contrasts with the reality below it. The 'Thirty Glorious Years' of economic growth in Western Europe risked creating a two-speed society in which the élite left the remainder of the workforce in subordinate, unskilled roles, threatened by unemployment and ultimately abject poverty.

④ 'ARIANE', SYMBOL OF EUROPE

In December 1979 France launched the satellite Ariane 1. In March 1980 the man responsible for the project, Frédéric d'Allest, set up Arianespace, which within ten years became the leading launcher of commercial satellites. Its other shareholders were all European; and its order book had 34 launchings planned.

① MAY 1968 IN PARIS

The movement began at Nanterre on 22 March 1968, then spread to the Sorbonne, the provinces and the secondary schools. In the night of 10–11 May there were violent clashes between students and police in the Latin Quarter of Paris, notably in the rue Gay Lussac, where cars were set on fire. The student revolt was followed on 13 May by a huge demonstration against President de Gaulle and then by the longest strike in French history. It ended in an election – which the government won with a large majority.

Rebellion

The affluent consumer society had its drawbacks. It encouraged individualism at the expense of more traditional solidarity. Comfort scarcely bred conviviality: on the contrary, it tended to coop people up in their own homes, where the television screens replaced social evenings with friends and neighbours.

Towards the end of the 1960s young people in Europe began more or less violently attacking the affluent society, which seemed to be eroding human ideals and values for purely material ends.

Their rebellion was often triggered by strictly national and seemingly trivial causes: opposition to the future Queen of the Netherlands' marriage to a German, the Shah of Iran's visit to Berlin, rivalry in Belgium between Walloons and Flemings, or – as in France and Italy – the need for university reform. Slogans like 'It is forbidden to forbid', 'Vote for imagination', 'No one falls in love with the growth rate' or 'Small is beautiful' were protests against a soullessly technical society and appeals for more democracy and justice. The rebels were supported by politically committed singers, 'alternative' publications and provocative stunts.

② 'WOODSTOCK': ALTERNATIVE VALUES

Young people looked for alternative values in the counter-culture. 'Make love not war' chanted the hippies, champions of liberty and non-violence. Great open-air concerts like that at Woodstock in the U.S. from 15 to 18 August 1969, with 400,000 people and 40 musical groups, were communal celebrations of a different way of life.

This all gave a number of groups in society the chance to make their voices heard – the young, the handicapped, the disadvantaged of all kinds. The May 1968 crisis in France and elsewhere revealed not only social anachronisms but also a generation gap.

One particular and very large group in society benefited, quite rightly, from the questioning of traditional habits. This was what Simone de Beauvoir memorably called 'the second sex'. Women's long fight for greater equality, which early in the century had involved the suffragette movement, now turned to seeking freedom from every kind of tutelage, including that of the husband as 'head of a family', a concept very dear to Roman law.

As more and more women now went out to work, they demanded equal rights: as citizens (in most European countries they now had the right to vote), in workplaces and also in private life. Feminist movements campaigned in favour of free love, divorce and abortion. The sexual revolution was aided, among other things, by the growing use of the contraceptive pill.

If traditional sexual morality was being defied or ignored, what would become of religion? The Catholic Church tried to meet the challenge of change at the Second Vatican Council (Vatican II, 1962–5), convened by Pope John XXIII and completed under Paul VI. Its agenda included: relations with the modern world and dialogue with other religions; the unity and universality of the Church; the collegiate status of bishops and the role of the laity; and priestly celibacy. One practical decision was that Latin was no longer obligatory in the liturgy. But the results of the Council fell short of the hopes it had aroused: it failed to stem the tide of secularism that was rising throughout Europe – and even to prevent an anti-Vatican II movement within the Church itself. Traditional religious ethics seemed all too vulnerable in an affluent world.

This being so, debates took place at a European and also a world level to try to measure and correct the excesses of the consumer society. The reports of the Club of Rome (1971) upheld the notion 'Small is beautiful', setting economic growth in a broader ecological and demographic context. The ecology movement drew attention to the need for urban renewal, the threat to landscape and the forests, the role for local action and local radio, the urgency of improving life in the inner cities and the general necessity to treat the environment more carefully. But already there were growing signs that the period of rapid growth might be coming to an end. In fact, the West's economic growth was greatly dependent on the rest of the world.

③ THE SECOND SEX
Feminist movements were active throughout Europe. The polemics concentrated on matters like birth control, but history will surely record that this was a time when a majority of women and some men realized how much had to be changed if women were to have an equal place in society.

④ VATICAN II MEETS IN ST PETER'S, ROME
Vatican II began in October 1962, with 2500 participants from all over the world. It was initiated by Pope John XXIII, who was unhappy about the dispersion of the Church. Among its objectives were to relate to the modern world and to begin an ecumenical dialogue.

⑤ THE 'GREENS'
Every country in Europe began to embrace ecology. In the German Federal Republic the movement was particularly strong. On 25 September 1977 the Greens demonstrated peacefully against nuclear power stations, but in the summer of 1981 some extremists began using bombs to make themselves heard.

4 Crisis and Response (1974–1985)

① THE OIL TRADE

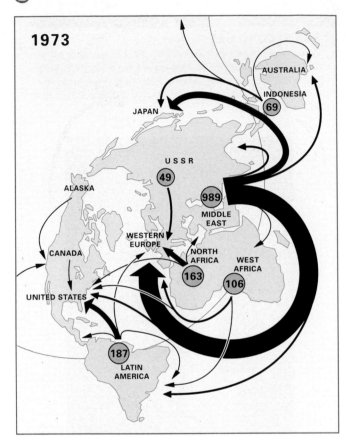

1973

AUSTRALIA

INDONESIA
69

JAPAN

U.S.S.R
49

989
MIDDLE
EAST

ALASKA

WESTERN
EUROPE

CANADA

NORTH
AFRICA
163

WEST
AFRICA
106

UNITED STATES

187
LATIN
AMERICA

② INFLATION AND UNEMPLOYMENT FROM 1970 TO 1990 IN THE EUROPEAN COMMUNITY

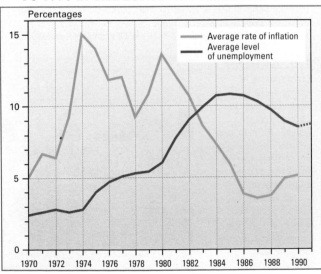

Percentages

15

Average rate of inflation
Average level
of unemployment

10

5

0

1970 1972 1974 1976 1978 1980 1982 1984 1986 1988 1990

The economic crisis that began in 1974 halted economic growth. The end of cheap energy revealed the weaknesses of the European economies and Europe saw its share of the world market shrink, while more was sold by the newly industrialized countries, mainly in south-east Asia. What were the European Community's responses to this new challenge?

In Eastern Europe nothing appeared to change, even though the origins of the popular democracies' collapse at the end of the 1980s were already very present in the 1970s.

Stagflation

Two things may be said to have been responsible for the economic crisis of 1974. One was the dismantling of the international monetary system established at Bretton Woods in 1944. The other was the oil price shock of 1973, followed by another in 1979. On 15 August 1971 the US dollar, which since 1944 had been the standard currency for Western economies, was devalued, losing its parity with gold. This destabilized world trade. The main currencies now floated: the system invented at Bretton Woods was dead. The first oil price shock, coming as it did at the height of this monetary disorder, cast a damper on hopes of recovery. At the end of 1973 the Arab member countries of OPEC, reacting to a fresh war with Israel, quadrupled the price of oil in three months. They also nationalized the Western oil companies' installations. They followed this first shock with a second in 1979–80. The reduction in supplies pushed prices to more than $30 a barrel. The oil price increase triggered off the crisis, which revealed that many of Europe's basic industries were in need of updating – mainly steel, shipbuilding and industrial chemicals. Long sheltered by cheap energy, important sectors of industry in Western Europe were revealed as uncompetitive on a world scale.

An inflationary spiral followed, with price rises greater than 10 per cent a year. Soaring prices inevitably caused a trade deficit. Activities directly linked with oil, like car manufacture and air transport, went into recession. Inflation worsened. From 1973 onwards Western Europe suffered a period of stagflation – limited recession with a degree of inflation. Bankruptcies became more frequent; the industries of the first Industrial Revolution – natural fibre textiles and steel –

were the first victims of the crisis.

Unemployment, hitherto very limited, now reappeared. What was new was that it was selective. It particularly affected the young, women, immigrant workers and employees in traditional industries. In 1983 there were more than 12 million unemployed in the European Community, 10 per cent of the active population. For all these misfortunes many people found a scapegoat: immigrant workers, who had been broadly welcomed in the 1960s, were now marginalized and excluded. The battle against unemployment, together with immigration, became leading subjects in political polemics. Steps to limit immigration were taken in various European countries. Even so, xenophobic movements gained influence in public opinion and extreme right-wing parties were reborn.

Many of the parties previously in power had to yield to their opponents. In Britain, the Labour Party was replaced by the Conservatives, led by Margaret Thatcher. In the Federal Republic of Germany, Helmut Kohl's Christian Democrat party, the CDU, won the election, defeating the Social Democrats. In France, by contrast, François Mitterrand, First Secretary and founder of the new Socialist Party, was elected President, but with limited room to manoeuvre.

④ NUCLEAR POWER STATIONS

③ THE OIL TRADE

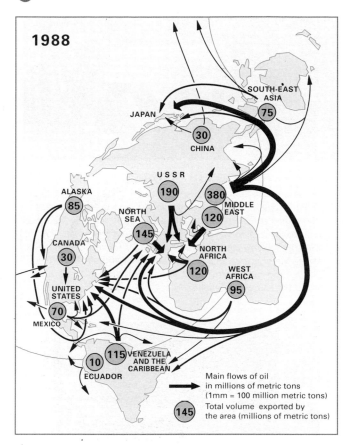

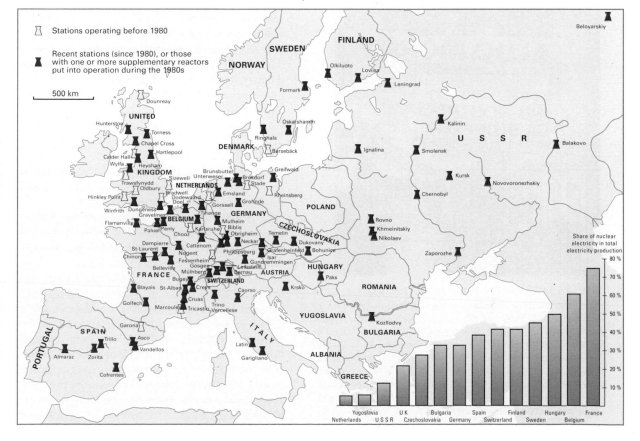

THE END OF DIVIDED EUROPE?

① THE REVOLUTION OF FLOWERS

In Portugal, in April 1974, the 'Armed Forces Movement' staged a military coup 'to save the nation from the Government'. In this 'Revolution of Flowers', people and soldiers fraternized in the streets of Lisbon. Freedom was re-established. During 1975 and 1976 the left-wing military government made way for the moderate Socialist leader Mario Soares. In 1979 the Liberal Right won the election; but in 1983 Soares returned to power. On 1 June 1986 Portugal joined the European Community.

② THE ASSASSINATION OF ALDO MORO

'Aldo Moro has been assassinated. May his faith in liberty live on in our hearts.' Aldo Moro was kidnapped by the Italian Red Brigades on 16 March 1978. His body was found in Rome on 9 May. The murder of the President of the Christian Democrat Party horrified the Italians, more and more under threat from terrorism. The Red Brigades, set up in September 1970, had links with other terrorist movements such as the IRA. In 1977 the Italian police estimated that the Brigades' 'turnover' from kidnapping that year was well over a quarter of a million dollars.

European integration – and the prospect of Community membership – may well have helped democracy take root in place of the last dictatorships in Western Europe: in Spain, after the death of Franco in November 1975; in Greece, after the fall of the Colonels in July 1974; and in Portugal, after the 'Revolution of Flowers' had put an end to the dictatorial regime that had survived the death of Antonio Salazar in 1970. Here, it also helped the moderates defeat the extremists in Portugal's first free election for 50 years, held in 1976.

Nevertheless, the economic crisis only increased some people's hatred of capitalism. A wave of political radicalism arose in Europe, invoking such names as Mao Tse-tung, Fidel Castro or Che Guevara. Some of its devotees resorted to violence. The Red Army Faction in Germany and the Red Brigades in Italy went on until the 1980s, attacking representatives of 'bourgeois' society – statesmen, judges and industrialists. Their exploits included hostage-taking and assassination, such as the kidnapping and murder of Aldo Moro, President of the Italian Christian Democrat Party, in March to May 1978.

Opposition to capitalism was not the only pretext for violence. There were also minorities in revolt against the state. In Northern Ireland the Irish Republican Army (the IRA) continued its terrorist campaign against British rule. Politico–religious differences underlay the basic dispute about the province's future between 'Loyalist' and Nationalist politicians, neither of whom backed the terrorists. In the Spanish Basque country, meanwhile, the separatist organization ETA continued its terrorist activities against the authorities in Madrid.

From Six to Twelve

In this climate of economic, social and political crisis, with everyone calling for change, how did the European Community respond?

In 1965, to defend 'Europe of the States' against European integration, General de Gaulle had provoked a serious crisis: for six months France stayed away from all but minor meetings of the Community's Council, practising 'the policy of the empty chair'. The new relationship between France and Germany – and de Gaulle's failure to win outright in the first round of the 1966 French Presidential election – helped to end the crisis. Soon afterwards the institutions of the ECSC, the EEC and Euratom were merged to form a single Council and a single Commission: they had always had a single Assembly and a single Court. In 1968 the Community completed its customs union, two years ahead of schedule. The worst had been avoided: pragmatism had won.

But in 1973 the Community seemed to risk reliving the earlier crisis. Three new countries – Britain, Denmark and Ireland – had just joined it, on 1 January 1973, making it larger but not necessarily more cohesive. Would the 1973 oil shock destroy the Europe of the Nine? When in difficulties, the Community all too often failed to act as one. Its lack of a joint response to the oil crisis undermined Community rules and morale. Italy and Denmark applied protectionist measures. In 1974, after a change of government, the United Kingdom also asked to renegotiate its terms of membership; in the following year a two-thirds majority of British voters decided by referendum to stay in the Community.

In an atmosphere none the less uncertain, priority was given to completing the single market, originally due in 1980. It faced two obstacles: the need to maintain and reform the Common Agricultural Policy (CAP), and the fluctuation of national exchange rates. Satisfactory solutions to the CAP's problems were hard to find – as witness consumers' complaints at high prices, overseas objections to protectionism and farmers' discontent at low incomes. But the European Monetary System (EMS) established on 13 March 1979, without Britain as a full member, did for some years help stabilize exchange rates against a common unit of account, the ECU or European Currency Unit. Even so the EEC's failure to adopt a common energy policy, or a joint strategy against unemployment and inflation, led to a further crisis in 1984. What was more, the British Prime Minister Margaret Thatcher demanded and finally obtained compensation for a Community budget contribution she thought too high. Thus at odds economically, would Europe be able to achieve a show of unity in the political field?

On 9 December 1974, on the initiative of the French President Valéry Giscard d'Estaing and the German Chancellor Helmut Schmidt, the Community's Heads of State and Government decided to turn their regular meetings into a new Community institution, the European Council. It soon won its spurs. In July 1976 it decided that the Community's Assembly, the European Parliament, should be elected by direct universal suffrage. In June 1979 Simone Veil from France became the parliament's first woman President.

The Community then began to accept new member states from southern Europe – a new challenge, since their economies were less advanced and risked causing disequilibrium, as well as needing help. Greece joined in 1981. Agreement with Spain and Portugal was harder to reach, partly owing to French fears of competi-

Dates of joining the European Economic Community:
- 25 March 1957 (Treaty of Rome)
- 1 January 1973
- 1 January 1981
- 1 January 1986
- 3 October 1990 (Reunification of Germany)

❸ BUILDING EUROPE

Before the European Community began, with the aim of 'ever closer union', Europe had two organizations based on cooperation among separate states. One was the Council of Europe, set up in May 1949. The other was the Organization for European Economic Cooperation (OEEC), established in April 1948, complemented in September 1950 by the European Payments Union (EPU) and replaced in September 1961 by the Organization for Economic Cooperation and Development (OECD). The move from international cooperation to integration in a 'supranational' Community came on 9 May 1950, when at Jean Monnet's instigation Robert Schuman proposed the European Coal and Steel Community (ECSC), one of the first steps on the road to a federal Europe. On 25 March 1957, on the basis of work by experts chaired by Paul-Henri Spaak, the ECSC governments established a European Economic Community (EEC) and a European Atomic Energy Community (Euratom). All three organizations merged to form the European Community (EC).

❹ Jacques Delors, President of the Commission of the EEC

For my part, I have often had recourse to federalism as a method, including the principle of subsidiarity. I see in it a means of reconciling what many people think irreconcilable: unity in Europe and loyalty to the nation; the need for a European authority proportionate to the problems of our time, and the vital necessity of maintaining the nations and regions in which we have our roots; with a decentralization of responsibilities so that no task is entrusted to a larger entity if it can be performed by a smaller. That is precisely what 'subsidiarity' means.

Speech at the College of Europe in Bruges on 17 October 1989

THE END OF DIVIDED EUROPE?

① THREE COMPETITORS

Drawing by Bruno Congar,
'Debout l'Europe', in *L'Expansion*,
November 1986

In 1986, the world economy was dominated by Uncle Sam (with his triumphant eagle), the growing weight of Japan and the Community of the Twelve. The figures give the ratio of purchasing power. In 1970 they had been 157 for the United States, 100 for the EEC and 94 for Japan.

② THE ACP COUNTRIES

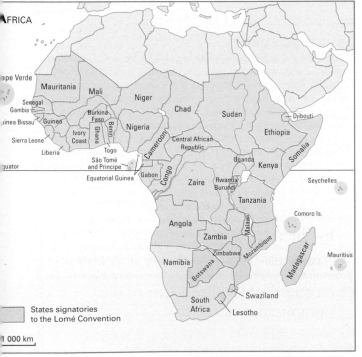

States signatories
to the Lomé Convention

1 000 km

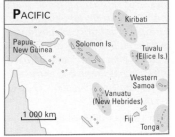

tion from their wine. But they finally joined on 1 January 1986. The Community now had 315 million inhabitants.

Crises had not prevented political progress. But they had slowed down economic integration. The lack of a common economic policy handicapped Europe in a free-trading world where competition reigned supreme.

New international competition

At the request of the European Council, the Belgian Minister Léo Tindemans produced a report on Europe's economic situation. He concluded that it faced a climatic change, not a temporary storm: the days of easy access to abundant cheap raw materials were gone for good. Adjustment was necessary – and very difficult, because Europe rejected excessive protectionism and therefore had to compete in conditions of free trade. And since 1973 world competition had become extremely fierce.

This was because the old European industrial countries were now challenged by newly industrialized countries in Asia, such as South Korea and Taiwan. Their disciplined and lower-paid workforce greatly helped their exports by producing at lower cost.

The United States, meanwhile, accused the EEC of unfair competition, claiming that it subsidized not only its cereal exports but also its aeronautical and military equipment sales.

Europe in turn was disturbed by the growing economic challenge from Japan, and accused the Japanese of protecting their home market. Indeed, Japan was flooding the world with its automobiles and its photographic and electronic goods, putting out of business whole sectors of the European consumer durables industry.

Europe's response was often to set up firms in the developing countries, where production costs were lower. One example was Volkswagen in Brazil. Only the most sophisticated products were still made in Europe in the headquarters plants. And competition in production went together with competition for market outlets. In 1975 the EEC signed the Lomé Agreements, opening its frontiers to products from 46 (and 69 by 1991) countries in Africa, the Caribbean and the Pacific (the ACP countries). The counterpart of their trade advantage in Europe was that their export earnings enabled them to buy European goods.

The economic crisis and its aftermath made very clear how deeply the national situation was affected by pressures from outside. This meant that every economy had to adapt to the laws of the market, curbing inflation, eliminating uncompetitive industries, redeploying productive resources and accepting the international division of labour. During this period, the German Federal Republic did everything that was needed and became the spearhead of Europe, economically, in the world. It could also undertake a major diplomatic effort vis-à-vis the Eastern bloc.

Opening to the East

In the East, at the beginning of the 1970s, the Brezhnev Doctrine still weighed heavily on Soviet society and on the East European states. But if resistance to change was the watchword for internal policy, there was nevertheless an increase in exchanges between East and West. The new openness involved beginning to deal with two of its elements: the nuclear balance of terror and the coexistence of two German states.

The *Ostpolitik* or Eastern Policy pursued by the Federal German Chancellor Willy Brandt made it possible to reconcile the Federal Republic with Eastern Europe. To this end the Chancellor recognized German responsibility for the Second World War and its outcome, including the establishment of the German–Polish frontier on the Oder–Neisse line. In this atmosphere of détente the four wartime Allies (the USA, the USSR, the United Kingdom and France) signed an agreement on 3 September 1971 to facilitate contacts between East and West Berlin. In further pursuit of recognition for the two Germanies Willy Brandt secured the ratification, on 21 December 1972, of a basic treaty, one of whose results was that many Western states now recognized the German Democratic Republic (East Germany), while in 1973 both Germanies were admitted to the United Nations. More generally, Willy Brandt's *Ostpolitik* also made possible the East–West Conference on Security and Cooperation in Europe (CSCE), which was held in Helsinki.

On 1 August 1975 the Helsinki Conference reached a broad agreement on European security. The United States, Canada, the USSR and all the European countries except Albania recognized Europe's frontiers as laid down at the end of the Second World War. The agreements made a concession to Brezhnev: they recognized that Europe was divided in two. But they also enshrined some important principles: equality among states, non-interference in another state's internal affairs, the right of self-determination, the inviolability of Europe's frontiers and the renunciation of force as a means of settling disputes. They provided for cooperation on economic, scientific and technological subjects; and finally they guaranteed respect for human rights.

❸ WILLY BRANDT'S PILGRIMAGE

Elected Federal Chancellor in 1969, the Social-Democrat Willy Brandt helped to open up to the East. The Federal Republic recognized the Oder–Neisse frontier imposed by the victorious Allies between Germany and Poland. On his visit to Warsaw in 1970, he stood in silence before the monument to the victims of the ghetto.

❹ The Helsinki Agreements (1 August 1975)

The participating states recognize the territorial integrity of each of the other participating states . . . . In the same way the participating states each abstain from making the territory of any of them the subject of military occupation or of other measures involving a direct or indirect recourse to force contrary to international law, or the threat of such measures. No occupation or acquisition of this kind shall be recognized as legal. The participating states respect human rights and fundamental freedoms, including freedom of thought, conscience, religion or conviction for everyone without distinction of race, sex, language or religion.

Declaration signed by the 35 participating states: all of Europe except Albania, plus the United States and Canada

❺ New institutions set up by the CSCE

The intensification of our consultations at all levels is of primordial importance to give shape to our future relations. To this end we decide as follows:

We, the Heads of State or Government, will hold our next meeting in Helsinki on the occasion of the follow-up meeting of the CSCE which will be held in 1992. Thereafter, we shall meet on the occasion of the further follow-up meetings.

Our Ministers of Foreign Affairs will meet regularly in Council at least once a year. These meetings will constitute the central core of political consultations within the framework of the CSCE process. The Council will examine those questions that arise from the Conference on Security and Cooperation in Europe and take the appropriate decisions.

The first meeting of the Council will be held in Berlin.

5 Contesting Yalta (1985–1990)

① SOLIDARNOŚĆ

Legend has it that the founder of Poland was a peasant named Lech. Was it pure chance that the founder-president of Solidarność bore the same name? At 37, Lech Wałęsa, an electrical engineer, became the symbol of Polish working people. 'Without faith,' he said, 'I should not have been able to hold out or to do what we have done.'

② MISSILES

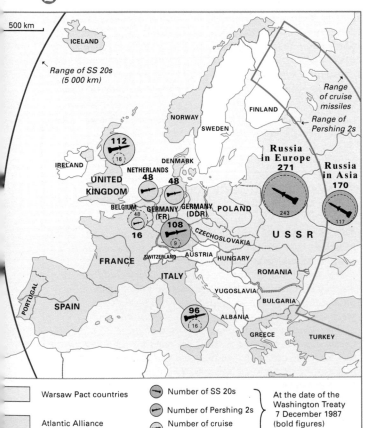

500 km

ICELAND

Range of SS 20s
(5 000 km)

Range of cruise missiles
Range of Pershing 2s

FINLAND
NORWAY
SWEDEN

112
16

IRELAND
DENMARK
NETHERLANDS
48 **48**
UNITED KINGDOM

BELGIUM
48
GERMANY (FR) GERMANY (DDR)
108
16
9
CZECHOSLOVAKIA
POLAND

Russia in Europe 271
243

Russia in Asia 170
117

U S S R

FRANCE
SWITZERLAND AUSTRIA HUNGARY
ITALY
ROMANIA
YUGOSLAVIA
BULGARIA
96
16
ALBANIA
PORTUGAL SPAIN
GREECE TURKEY

Warsaw Pact countries	⊙ Number of SS 20s	At the date of the Washington Treaty 7 December 1987 (bold figures)
Atlantic Alliance	⊙ Number of Pershing 2s	
	⊙ Number of cruise missiles	
Neutral or non-aligned countries	⊙ Number of missiles in November 1983 (non-bold figures)	

The policy of Mikhail Gorbachev

Despite having signed the Helsinki Agreements requiring respect for human rights, Moscow had no intention of ceasing to persecute movements of resistance against Communist society, either inside the Soviet Union or in its satellite states. Those movements were all the more active in that they now invoked the spirit of Helsinki.

In Czechoslovakia the protest movement was limited to an intellectual élite, the signatories of 'Charter 77'. In Poland the economic crisis caused the revolt of the intellectuals to spread to the majority of industrial workers and peasants. It was encouraged by powerful national feelings and by the support of the Catholic Church. The Polish Church's influence was strengthened by the election of the Archbishop of Cracow, Carol Woytila as Pope John Paul II on 19 October 1978, and also by his visit to Warsaw in June 1979. With this stimulus Poland rebelled once again, in February 1980. The movement began in Gdansk, where Lech Wałęsa founded the free trade union *Solidarność* (Solidarity), denouncing the social and economic situation, the lack of liberty and the official attacks on the Church. By 1981 *Solidarność* had nearly ten million members. In the face of this threat the Polish authorities arrested its leaders and banned the union. The Church remained the refuge and symbol of resistance. The 'victory' of the Communist Party, led by General Wojciech Jaruzelski, who imposed a state of siege in November 1981, was merely provisional.

After the death of Leonid Brezhnev in 1982, the Soviet Union went through a governmental crisis. Rivalry for the succession caused tension within the Party. The deaths of two elderly First Secretaries, Yuri Andropov and Konstantin Chernenko, in quick succession, did nothing to restore stability. Then, on 11 March 1985, Mikhail Gorbachev was elected Secretary General. His election led to a return of Socialist legality and the liberation of the dissidents best known in the West, such as Andrei Sakharov, who returned from six years' exile in Gorky in 1986.

The year 1985 was a decisive turning-point: the paralysis of Brezhnev's rule was over. Presenting himself as a reformer, Gorbachev sought to revivify Socialism. He committed the country to *glasnost* (openness) and *perestroika* (restructuring), seeking to revolutionize people's minds, their administrative system and their economic organization, as well as to democratize society. The new policy had nevertheless still to cope with the many weaknesses of the Soviet system, including the still unsolved nationalities problem and the people's democracies' desire for autonomy. So, although there was satisfaction in Western Europe at Soviet and American progress towards disarmament (notably the INF Treaty signed in Washington in 1987), West Europeans still remained alert. They too were deeply involved in change – integrating their economies.

The Single European Act

Following an initiative from the Italian activist Altiero Spinelli, the governments of the ten European Community's member states took a decisive step forward: on 17 December 1985 they signed the Single European Act, modifying the Rome Treaty and providing for a single, frontier-free market by 31 December 1992. Henceforward, Community policies would include the protection of the environment, external policy, technological cooperation and regional aid. To this end the Council and the European Parliament would jointly wield legislative power, while the Council would take decisions concerning the single market by qualified majority and no longer by unanimous vote.

This new step aroused anxiety and some resistance among the ten member states (who became twelve with the entry of Spain and Portugal on 1 January 1986). Research showed that achieving the single market would pose problems of adaptation. In some sectors, especially services, mergers would mean fewer jobs; and mergers, like takeovers, were inevitable. In 1987, for instance, the Italian De Benedetti group made a bid to take over the Belgian *Société Générale*; and in this case, as in others, the Commission had to lay down rules to prevent unfairness and hardship.

Even after that there was continued concern about the single market's likely social effects. Some feared that disparities between the wages and social security systems in different member countries would lead to 'social dumping' – the tendency of firms to shift production to wherever such costs were least. The trade unions therefore insisted that a Social Charter be drawn up to set minimum standards and protect existing rights.

In practice, a single market implied a move towards Economic and Monetary Union (EMU). Unless the growth rates, inflation rates, national debts and unemployment levels in the member states evolved along similar lines, the single market would face serious problems. In the long run, the solution would have to be a single currency. True, the ECU existed already as a unit

③ CHERNOBYL: HUMANITY AT RISK

On 26 April 1986 reactor No 4 at the Soviet nuclear power station of Chernobyl exploded. Officially, the casualties were 31 dead: Moscow News put the figure at 250, while Ukrainian ecological groups said it was 7000. Hundreds of thousands of people were evacuated, in what state is not known. Overtaken by the horror, the Kremlin came out of the disaster badly destabilized, while the world looked on aghast. The region around Chernobyl will remain radioactive for thousands of years.

④ 'Europe 1992'

The cost of 'non-Europe' – the absence of a European economy – would be high. It can be summarized as follows:

- *administrative expenses to comply with different national regulations*
- *long and costly customs formalities, increasing transport costs*
- *expense resulting from divergent national standards that limit production runs*
- *duplication of effort in research and product design*
- *expenditure resulting from different procedures for public tender*

According to a recent report, a 'non-common' market would cost some 200,000 million ECUs [£164,000 million or $240,000 million]. European consumers should save 6–7.5 per cent on prices as a result of the single market.

From *1992: Le Marché unique européen, un défi pour la Belgique*, published by the Belgian Ministry of Foreign Affairs

❶ A FRENCH VERSION OF THE ECU

This is the unit of account of the European Monetary System. But this 15 ECU coin, worth 100 French francs, is totally unknown to the public, since the ECU is not yet a currency. The figure on the ECU side of the coin is that of Charlemagne.

❷ EUROTUNNEL

Some 94 miles of tunnels, 320 feet deep in the soil beneath the Channel, now link Great Britain with the continent. This will mean uninterrupted three-hour train journeys between London and Paris.

❸ 'ROMANIANS ARISE'

Bucharest,
23 December 1989

The army, fraternizing with the people, tried to root out members of the Securitate secret police, still loyal to Nicolae Ceauşescu, although he had fled. He seemed to have forgotten his prophecy: 'Romania will change when the Transylvania poplars produce pears.'

of account, but much more had to be done if eventually there was to be a single European currency issued by a European Central Bank. And many problems remained to be solved before that could happen, including the harmonization of taxes and the stabilization of exchange rates. The pound sterling joined the European Exchange Rate Mechanism (ERM) only in 1990 and was forced to leave it again in 1992. In Germany the *Bundesbank* and business circles were wary of undue haste; and the monetary turmoil of late 1992 only confirmed their caution. Full economic and monetary union would involve far greater merging of national sovereignty than ever before. In February 1992 the Community governments signed the Maastricht Treaty on European Union with this in view. Although it confirmed the principle of subsidiarity (decisions to be taken at the lowest level possible), its critics feared greater centralization. Many others, however, thought political union had now become indispensable.

Clearly, then, the building of Europe was possible only if its citizens felt a shared loyalty to its spirit and its way of life. Hence the Community's ERASMUS programme, established in 1987 to help students in higher education to pursue part of their studies in another member state. Other programmes with similar aims include LINGUA, for languages, and TEMPUS, to extend teaching to Poland and Hungary.

As the European Community prepared for the 21st century, despite doubts and problems, it had won recognition as an economic and political power in the world. One proof was the growing number of applications to join it, from Austria, Norway, Sweden, Switzerland and Turkey. At the same time, however, the disintegration of the Eastern bloc and the reunification of Germany suddenly faced it with new challenges and tasks.

The Berlin Wall comes down

Since 1985, very obviously, the ideological bonds between Moscow and its satellites had been relaxed. When Gorbachev visited East European countries, he was warmly welcomed, except perhaps by those of their leaders still hostile to *glasnost* and *perestroika*. The hardliners' fears were understandable. After Poland and Hungary had peacefully rid themselves of Communist domination early in 1989, the other countries of the Eastern bloc – the German Democratic Republic, Czechoslovakia, Bulgaria and Romania – overthrew their Communist leaders that autumn. In early 1990 the new regimes were confirmed by free elections, the first for more than forty years. The Yalta agreement was dying or dead.

The division of Germany, so long a bone of

contention, also came to a happy but surprising end. On 9 November 1989 the government of the German Democratic Republic allowed partial breaches in the frontier between the two Germanies and in the Berlin Wall. The crumbling of the Wall destroyed the most eloquent symbol of the Cold War and the division of Germany. German reunification was back on the agenda. The West German Chancellor Helmut Kohl, who favoured rapid reunification, won the election of 18 March 1990, to the delight of many East Germans. In January and July 1990 Moscow recognized that a united Germany was inevitable. On 3 October 1990 it was achieved.

So many great changes in so short a time perplexed the world and its rulers. How should they respond? After forty years of stalemate they had to grope for a new equilibrium. That was only one of the dilemmas left by the disintegration of the Eastern bloc. Should Mikhail Gorbachev's idea of 'a European home from the Urals to the Atlantic' – shades of De Gaulle – become a reality? Could it? And if so, how?

The European Community, like its partners, faced many such questions. But its minor role in the prelude to the Gulf War in 1990 and its impotence in the Yugoslavian tragedy showed how far it had to go before its political weight matched its economic strength, its cultural wealth and its human potential.

④ **EAST EUROPEAN DEBTS, 1989**

THE BERLIN WALL IS BREACHED

④ **THE BERLIN WALL IS BREACHED**

⑤ **THE BERLIN WALL IS BREACHED**
In the summer of 1989 thousands of East Germans had fled to the West by every conceivable means. On the night of 9–10 November the Berlin Wall was breached; and on 22 December the Brandenburg Gate was opened. This also opened the question of German reunification, which was accomplished on 3 October 1990. With that, a new phase of Europe's history had begun.

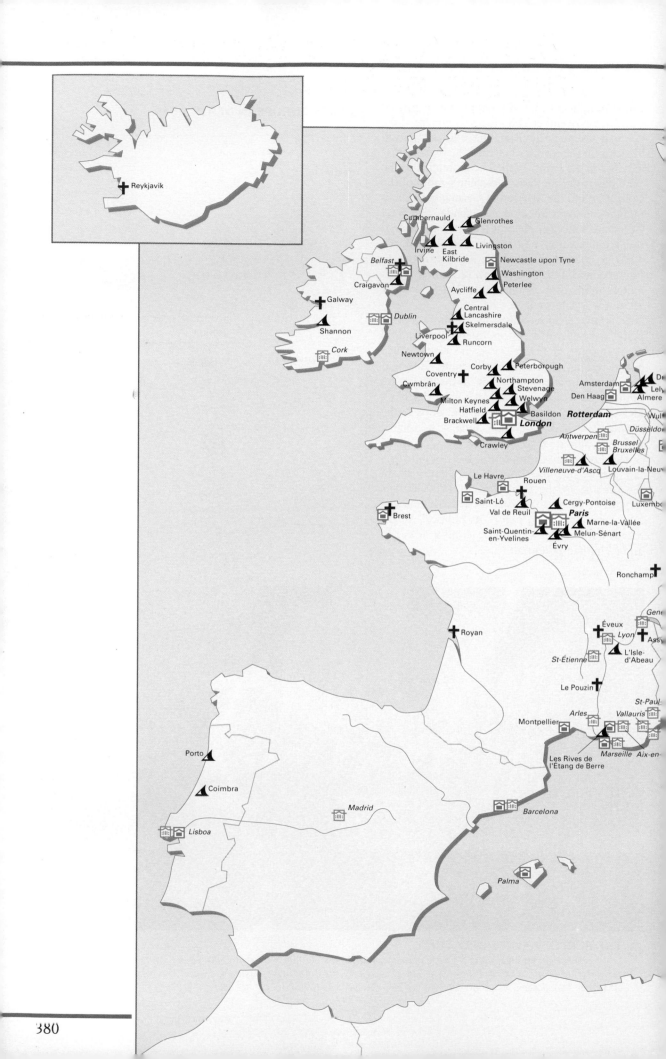

Reykjavik

Cumbernauld
Glenrothes
Irvine
Livingston
East Kilbride
Belfast
Newcastle upon Tyne
Craigavon
Washington
Aycliffe
Peterlee
Galway
Central Lancashire
Skelmersdale
Dublin
Liverpool
Shannon
Runcorn
Cork
Newtown
Corby
Peterborough
Coventry
Northampton
Amsterdam
Lely
Cwmbrân
Stevenage
Almere
Milton Keynes
Welwyn
Den Haag
Hatfield
Basildon
Rotterdam
Wulf
Brackwell
London
Düsseldo
Crawley
Antwerpen
Brussel
Bruxelles
Le Havre
Rouen
Villeneuve-d'Ascq
Louvain-la-Neu
Saint-Lô
Cergy-Pontoise
Luxemb
Brest
Val de Reuil
Paris
Marne-la-Vallée
Saint-Quentin-
en-Yvelines
Melun-Sénart
Évry
Ronchamp
Royan
Gene
Éveux
Lyon
Assy
St-Étienne
L'Isle-
d'Abeau
Le Pouzin
St-Paul
Porto
Arles
Vallauris
Montpellier
Coimbra
Les Rives de
l'Étang de Berre
Marseille
Aix-en-
Madrid
Barcelona
Lisboa
Palma

The Past in the Present Day
THE END OF A DIVIDED EUROPE?

Legend:

- new town
- public building
- religious monument
- museum, library or collection rich in items from this period
- frontiers of 20th-century states

500 km

Vällingby

Ålborg
Ikeborg
Fredensborg
Humlebaek

Rostock
Hamburg
Berlin — Berlin-Marzahn
sburg — Magdeburg
Halle Neustadt
Leipzig — Dresden
Jena
Chemnitz
ankfurt
mstadt — Praha

Plock
Warszawa

Kiyev

Nowa Huta

gart
München
Wien
Tatabanya — Budapest
Szaszhalombatta
Dunaujvaros

Gheorghiu-Dej

Ljubljana — Pécs
lano
Venezia — Zagreb
Bologna
Beograd — Bucuresti

Bregovo

Roma

Athinai

INDEX